D0454243

El Gran Pueblo
A History of Greater Mexico

Third Edition

Colin M. MacLachlan
Tulane University

William H. Beezley
University of Arizona

PEARSON
Prentice
Hall

Prentice Hall, Upper Saddle River, New Jersey 07458

Library of Congress Cataloging-in-Publication Data

MacLachlan, Colin M.
   El Gran Pueblo: a history of greater Mexico/Colin M.
   MacLachlan, William H. Beezley.—3rd ed.
      p. cm.
   Includes bibliographical references and index.
   ISBN 0-13-184114-9
   1. Mexico—History—1810   2. Mexican-American Border Region—
   History.   I. Beezley, William H.   II. Title.

F1231.5.M32 2004
972—dc21   2003049898

Senior Acquisitions Editor: Charles Cavaliere
Editorial Director: Charlyce Jones Owen
Associate Editor: Emsal Hasan
Editorial Assistant: Shannon Corliss
Director of Marketing: Beth Mejia
Executive Marketing Manager: Heather Shelstad
Senior Marketing Assistant: Jennifer Bryant
Managing Editor (Production): Joanne Riker
Production Liaison: Marianne Peters Riordan
Manufacturing Buyer: Tricia Kenny
Cover Design: Kiwi Design
Composition/Full-Service Project Management: Lithokraft/Marty Sopher
Mgr. Prod/Formatting & Art: Guy Ruggiero
Printer/Binder: R. R. Donnelley and Sons Company
Cover Printer: Phoenix Color Corp.

Credits and acknowledgments borrowed from other sources and reproduced, with permission, in this textbook appear on appropriate page within text.

Copyright © 2004, 1999, 1994 by Pearson Education, Inc., Upper Saddle River, New Jersey 07458
Pearson Prentice Hall. All rights reserved. Printed in the United States of America. This publication is protected by Copyright and permission should be obtained from the publisher prior to any prohibited reproduction, storage in a retrieval system, or transmission in any form or by any means, electronic, mechanical, photocopying, recording, or likewise. For information regarding permission(s), write to: Rights and Permissions Department.

Pearson Prentice Hall™ is a trademark of Pearson Education, Inc.
Pearson® is a registered trademark of Pearson plc
Prentice Hall® is a registered trademark of Pearson Education, Inc.

Pearson Education LTD.
Pearson Education Singapore, Pte. Ltd
Pearson Education, Canada, Ltd
Pearson Education–Japan
Pearson Education Australia PTY, Limited

Pearson Education North Asia Ltd
Pearson Educación de Mexico, S.A. de C.V.
Pearson Education Malaysia, Pte. Ltd
Pearson Education, Upper Saddle River,
   New Jersey

10 9 8 7 6 5 4 3 2 1
ISBN 0-13-184114-9

To Blue

Contents

6   Prelude to Revolution   184

7   Making a Revolution: The Borderlands Emerge, 1905–1917   211

8   Making a Revolution Work: Part I, 1917–1927   247

9   Making a Revolution Work: Part II, 1927–1937   294

10   The Revolution Becomes the Miracle, 1937–1946   338

Converging Cultures: New Century, New President   482

Preface to the Third Edition

Mexicans, in some ways, have remade their national administration by electing an opposition president for the first time in a century. Vicente Fox, after winning the office in 2000, has made some headway against the national challenges of political corruption, economic stagnation, and drug associated crime. This new president and new enthusiasm notwithstanding, Mexicans, find themselves in the early twenty-first century faced with many old difficulties and stagnant institutions. The struggle against corruption, if it is ever is to escape its Sisyphusian legacy, must become a struggle against corrupt public officials and the campaign to revitalize institutional inertia requires inspired individuals eager to invigorate such disregarded units as the national congress and the Mexico City police. Both of these latter examples are currently beginning to show new life, the deputies in the preparation of an independent national budget and the police with a new cadre of responsible officers determined to reduce crime. Nevertheless, indigenous demands, migrant issues, and national poverty demand immediate attention at the same time that Fox nurtures his rather fragile regime.

As in the second edition, we recognize the assistance of numerous colleagues. Again, we received considerate help in interpreting recent events in Mexico from Rod Camp, the Philip M. McKenna Professor at Claremont McKenna College, and David Lorey, senior fellow at the William and Flora Hewlett Foundation. We have been challenged to rethink the history of Mexico since independence by our recent graduate students, especially James Garza at TCU, Dina Berger, Monica Rankin, Glenn Avent, and Rachel Kram Villarreal at the University of Arizona, and Bill Connell, Christoph Rosemüller, and Lisa Edwards at Tulane University. Moreover, the faculty, distinguished lecturers, and the Fellows of the Oaxaca Summer Institute

(I-V) have had an indelible imprint on our interpretations. In particular, John Hart, Gil Joseph, and Alan Knight have challenged our earlier views. We express our gratitude to friends, who are also our professional colleagues in Mexico City, especially Carmen Nava, Guillermo Palacios, Javier Garciadiego, Josefina Vázquez, and Norma Mereles de Ogarrio. We also acknowledge the Oaxaca team of Francisco José Ruiz C. (Paco Pepe), Anselmo Arellanes, Carlos Sánchez Silva, Víctor Raul Martinez, and Daniela Traffano and reviewers Ben W. Fallaw of Eastern Illinois University and Barbara M. Corbett of Amherst College. We hope those who have discussed this textbook with us will recognize the ways we have appropriated their advice.

Colin M. MacLachlan
New Orleans

William H. Beezley
Tucson

Acknowledgments

We embarked upon the daunting task of writing the history of Greater Mexico with absolute confidence that we could rely upon our friends, colleagues, and fellow teachers at universities, colleges, and community colleges to assist us. Their thoughtful comments have guided our research and writing. Moreover, a sizeable number of individuals in Mexico, the United States, Canada, Australia, and Europe in journalism, business, government, and diplomatic service helped broaden our understanding of Mexico's history. We also became aware of the debt we owe to generations of talented scholars in the field of Mexican studies. It is their efforts that have made our work possible.

Jaime Rodríguez O. offered advice and critically read drafts of the work. His many conferences, seminars, and publications about Mexico since its independence collectively advanced our appreciation of its history. Michael C. Meyer inspired and assisted us in ways too numerous to list. Rod Camp provided unpublished materials and discussed our analysis of modern Mexico, offering us critical suggestions. John M. Hart and Mark Wasserman read the entire manuscript and contributed several helpful comments. Paul Vanderwood read several versions. Bill French made extensive critical notes on the manuscript. David LaFrance spent considerable time and effort to clarify our argument. Stuart F. Voss offered stimulating suggestions on Porfirian Sonora and the revolutionary 1920s. Paul Ganster directed us to numerous useful sources on the border region. Chris Archer shared his often amusing and perceptive insights with us. Alan Knight contributed in many ways to our reconsideration of the Mexican past. Mary Kay Vaughan gave us an insightful commentary. Judy Ewell, Susan Deeds, Brad Burns, Barbara Tenenbaum, Oscar Martínez, Jim Wilkie, David Walker, David Weber, David Lorey, Karen Harris, Ward Albro, Francis Chassen-López, Tony Morgan, William K.

Meyers, Scott Whiteford, Steve Niblo, and John Lynch provided unpublished material, or assisted us in other ways.

Over the years, usually in a casual, relaxed setting, we have enjoyed many informal discussions that have shaped our approach to writing history. In this pleasant yet greatly appreciated and important category, we thank Ken Andrien, Joe Arbena, Linda Arnold, Silva Arrom, Kendall Brown, Pat Seed, Lyle Brown, Mark Burkholder, Franklin Knight, Evelyn Hu-deHart, Larry Clayton, Barry Carr, Bob Claxton, Helen Delpar, Michael Gonzales, Donna Guy, Harold Hines, Gil Joseph, Brian Hamnett, John Kicza, Allan Kuethe, Peggy Liss, Cheryl Martin, Vic Niemeyer, Ray Sadler, Jim Sandos, Pedro Santoni, Susan Schroeder, Fritz Schwaller, Tom Wright, Charles Harris, Carlos Larrolde, Tom Benjamin, Dirk Raat, Don Stevens, Eric Langer, Alex Saragoza, Guy Thomson, Hernán Horna, Rosalie Schwartz, Magnus Mörner, Dawn Raby, François Guerra, Will Pansters, Ramón Ruíz, Allen Wells, Bill Sherman, Mario García, Erroll Jones, Manny Machado, Lyman Johnson, Eric Van Young, Mark Gilderhus, Margorie Becker, Doug Richmond, Samuel Schmidt, Elinor Melville, and Daniel Masterson.

In Mexico, José Mariano Calderón Salazar, drawing on over twenty-five years' experience as a high government official, provided guidance often over an instructive dinner at his Mexico City home or at the Club "R" in Culiacán, Sinaloa. Ernesto Navarro Calderón, a transnational banker, focused our attention on the importance of the borderlands. His father, Miguel Navarro Franco, who ran his extensive business enterprises from the busy comfort of Chic's Coffee Shop in Culiacán, Sinaloa, provided an unparalleled description of the Mexican Revolution as he knew it firsthand, as well as an example of modern entrepreneurship. Alicia Romero de Milla, who served with ex-president Miguel Alemán when he created the modern tourist boom following his presidency, shared her perceptions and experiences with us. José "Pepé" Trejo and his wife Eva both gave us an enlightening view of Mexican politics. Alfonso Iriate provided a fund of historical information. Roberto de Castro, yet another transnational person, offered us a glimpse of how state politics functioned, as did Luis Enrique Calderón, at the time a local level Partido Revolucionario Institucional (PRI) official. Josefina Z. Vázquez, Virginia Guedea, Anne Staples, Elsie Rockwell, Sergio R. Nuñez-Reynoso, Elle Bartra, and Xavier Noguez offered their professional insight, in addition to printed works, some of which appear in our bibliography.

Several recent Ph.D.s and Ph.D. candidates, through their insightful dissertation research, influenced our interpretation of Greater Mexico. We recognize particularly the work of Adrian Bantjes, Rob Buffington, Ellen M. Litwicki, William Schell Jr., Mary Angeline Watrous, Victor Story, Robin King, Friedrich Schuler, Jeff Pilcher, Anne Rubenstein, and Eric Zolov.

At our home institutions many individuals offered valuable assistance. At Tulane, Ralph Lee Woodward read the entire manuscript and made suggestions. Paul Lewis and Bill Canek offered insightful comments. Michael Boardman, Jerry Snare, and Sam Ramer made organizational suggestions based on their classroom experience. Bill Nañez, director of the Tulane Latin American Library, demonstrated why a librarian is the scholar's best friend.

John Crocetti went back and forth to the library to locate sources. Bill Cooper, a scientist turned reluctant humanist, provided institutional support and encouragement.

At Texas Christian University (TCU), Don Coerver generously gave us copies of his work. Don Worcester, a legend among Latin American historians, provided both organizational and interpretative insights over several enjoyable lunches. Jorge Hernández, Carlos Cuéllar, and Wendy Waters served as helpful assistants. The Penrose Endowment and a TCU faculty award allowed time and travel for research. The project received encouragement (at times unknowingly) from Spencer Tucker, Michael McCracken, Larry Adams William Koehler, and William Tucker.

We received extraordinary assistance in locating photographs. John Mraz provided guidance. At the Harry Ranson Humanities Research Center, University of Texas, curator Roy Flukinger directed us to several previously unused collections in the Center's rich holdings. On the same campus, John Slate, the photographic archivist at the Barker Texas History Center, guided us efficiently through the extensive collection of visual materials. Helen M. Plummer of the Photography Collection offered the assistance that makes the Amon Carter Museum one of the most pleasant places to do research in the United States. Wayne Daniel made the highly regarded photographic collection at the El Paso Public Library available to us. Danny Turner of Dallas, Texas permitted us to use the photograph that he took of Super Barrio that appeared in American Way magazine, September 1, 1992. The extensive holdings of the Latin American Library, Tulane University, were placed at our disposal by director Bill Nañez. Arizona ranger Greg Welden of the Jerome State Park assisted us in our search for photos of Mexican and Mexican-American workers in Greater Mexico. Photographer Lisa M. Murillo of The Prospector, the campus newspaper at the University of Texas, El Paso, took the picture of the Virgin of Guadalupe Mural in El Paso. Harold E. Hinds Jr., the leading authority on Kaliman, provided the photograph of this comic book hero and assisted in obtaining permission for its use from Modesto Vázquez Gonzáles of Promotora K. The use of Fernando Valenzuela's photograph was arranged by Los Angeles Dodgers' general counsel, Santiago Fernández. The maps and charts are the work of Chase Langford, cartographer at the University of California at Los Angeles (UCLA).

Introduction

It has become increasingly obvious that a continuous process of fusion characterizes the history of the world. The roots of this phenomenon reach back beyond recorded time. Barbaric invaders brought separate worlds into collision to be forever altered. Merchants, traders, and philosophers added their contributions, as did Mongol armies, Roman legions, Viking raiders, administrators, jurists, and Berber armies intent on the expansion of the Muslim world. Ancient languages and religions gave way to the new or joined in a fresh linguistic or spiritual synthesis. China, India, Africa, and Europe changed other distant cultures, and in turn modified their own. In the New World the process of fusion operated in a similar fashion, but in isolation from the broader world until that fateful moment in 1492, when Europe and the Western hemisphere came into contact.

The Industrial Revolution in more recent times accelerated cultural amalgamation. The search for resources and markets led to organized conquests, colonization, colonialism, and increasingly disastrous and bloody conflict between the dominant modernizing powers. It forced previously provincial people to confront other cultures and make adjustments, often painful and sometimes negative, or risk disappearing from the world stage. The transformation of peasants into workers eventually spread to all parts of the world, and in the course of the metamorphosis they altered perceptions forcing economic, political, and social change. Literacy needed for modern tasks provided access to knowledge, modified previous configurations, and challenged old and narrow elites. Transportation and communication technology encouraged the ever-accelerating movement of people, goods, and capital around the globe. Modernization in both its positive and negative guises pressed states to at least direct the process even as they understood it could not be controlled. In short, to choose not to modernize was not a viable option—a harsh realization that jolted Japan into furious action following Commodore Matthew C. Perry's unwanted intrusion (1854) into the previously closed islands. China chose to resist modernization and barely escaped being dismembered by modern powers.

The Mexican elite understood, virtually at the very moment Mexico became independent, that the country had to be modernized or face extinction. Thus, the history of Mexico after independence in 1821 is one of conscious movement toward the projected ideal of a fully developed country able to assume a place of reasonable equality with Europe and the United States. The road to modernity provided a rocky one, involving war, civil war, loss of territory, and foreign intervention. Cultural destruction and economic exploitation accompanied the often brutal transformation of the country. Understandably, the governing elite became vulnerable to a series of panaceas, including foreign immigration and political models drawn from Europe and the United States. European philosophical systems appeared to promise a mental schema that could indicate the sure path toward progress.

Attracting foreign capital by providing investment opportunities with the promise of handsome returns became a central objective in the nineteenth century. Commercialization of land, labor, and indeed all resources seemed necessary. With an expansionist United States to the north, disorder might well supply the pretext for progressive annexation and perhaps the total absorption of Mexico within the perceived to be more dynamic Anglo-Saxon nation. The question that haunted both liberals and conservatives was how much would have to be sacrificed in order to survive. Moreover, if one became too much like the United States in terms of political organization and culture, did an independent existence make any sense? Could a line be drawn that could preserve some essence of Mexican identity while the country fashioned itself into a modern nation? Pretending to be more in control of Mexico's destiny than was in reality possible constituted a defense against foreign intervention or destructive meddling. Thus, the Porfiriato desperately used smoke and mirrors to project a stable, prosperous image both to entice foreign capital and to buy time to strengthen the republic's grasp on modernity. The relationship between Mexico and the United States became, and remains, crucial.

Failure to expand political participation and distribute the economic and social fruits of the new economy in a timely manner, coupled with institutional weaknesses, led to revolutionary violence. Starting as a "great rebellion," it soon required revolutionary changes in order to sufficiently incorporate those elements created, and those left behind, by the process of modernization. A new sociopolitical consensus would be negotiated in part on the battlefield. It was not accidental that the storm began in the north. Díaz's involuntary resignation after the seizure of Ciudad Juárez by rebels and the fall of Torreón broke the sociopolitical paralysis that had gripped the regime since 1892. A determined middle class allied with the lower class demanded political inclusion, access to resources, and respect. Widespread reaction to change, and the destruction of culture that it entailed, engendered the formation of an emotional, nostalgic, and partly xenophobic nationalism. Thus, northerners, who swept the country into the Mexican Revolution and who themselves had only weak ties to Indian Mexico, became avid proponents of the republic's aboriginal cultural uniqueness. While the Porfiriato used the pre-Columbian past to establish Mexico's historic greatness, northern revolutionaries sought to establish national uniqueness by drawing upon what they saw as surviving Mexican virtues. Their desire to locate a source of historical continuity constituted a reaction to the sense of detachment that came with headlong development. It also facilitated the incorporation of previously targeted groups, particularly Indians, within a new Mexican ethos. It allowed the country to move backward in order to reintegrate those elements left behind during the Porfiriato. The Mexican Revolution represented a redistributive stage of the modernization process. New sociopolitical and economic configurations brought class relationships into a more acceptable balance. The nature and composition of the elite at both the regional and national levels underwent drastic modification. A more complex structure emerged, which permitted the development of distinct groups that were anxious to forge new alliances in order to confront the competition for resources and power.

The Mexican diaspora, created and encouraged by development, became an obvious reality by the turn of the century, and continues into the present. Recognition of Mexican Americans or Chicanos eventually extended to an understanding of their influence on the general culture far beyond the border regions of both republics. In the 1990s, the phenomenon of Anglos stopping at a donut shop in the Mexican-American barrio of East Los Angeles to hire mariachis for a bar mitzvah celebration captures the everyday impact of cultural hybridization resulting from modernization. The continuous process of refinement or transculturization is demonstrated by the opening of a Taco Bell restaurant in Mexico City (June 1992), whose success has already led to the expansion of outlets in the capital. Taco Bell, the leading American fast Mexican food chain, originally took its inspiration from the popularity of Mexican food in the United States. It is now in turn influencing culinary tastes in Mexico. Hispanic Business noted that pozole (hominy and pork broth) served in the Taco Bell in Mexico City probably would not be introduced in the United States, however, one can expect some new products to emerge from the experience. Modernization creates a ping-pong effect of continuous modification back and forth across all borders. The interdependency of Mexico and the United States has now arrived at the point that the formal creation of the North American Free Trade Zone constituted more of an act of recognition than one of radical change.

The celebratory aspects of historical fusion need not blind us to the many difficulties encountered along the way. Violence, discrimination, and exploitation all are reflected in the history of the Mexican experience. No doubt they will form a part of the future. We have chosen to acknowledge the dramatic and at times painful struggle by borrowing the title El Gran Pueblo (the great people) from Francisco Madero, who himself played a role in the process until his violent death in 1913. Where the constant hybridization required by the worldwide sweep of modernization will take Mexico is a matter of speculation. It is clear, however, that it will continue.

Readers of this work will note that we refer to citizens of the United States in general as Americans, ignoring the attempts by some scholars to insist on the term North American to make the obvious point that all inhabitants of the Western Hemisphere are Americans. Most Mexicans use the term Americano, or the less polite term gringo, to refer to individuals from the United States. We also employ the admittedly imprecise term Anglo to refer to persons other than Mexicans, Mexican Americans or Chicanos, usually in the context of the United States. To present a complex reality with as much clarity as possible, we rely upon subheadings. This facilitates quick reference to select parts of the work that may be of particular interest.

We make a number of original contributions based on our own research and study of the Mexican Republic, its history, and its people. As classroom teachers, researchers, and directors of graduate students, we have been actively engaged in the process of rediscovering the past. In our own way, we are part of the melding of culture we examine in this work with family, friends, and colleagues on both sides of the border and scattered throughout Greater Mexico. Our study is the first to integrate the Mexican experience in the United States as an integral part of Mexican history. To accomplish this, we laid aside the traditional approach that presents Mexico's history by dealing with one presidential term after another, and instead sought to identify underlying patterns and historical trends. In the process, we have reevaluated the contributions of many, including Porfirio Díaz and Lázaro Cárdenas, and emphasized the remarkable continuity that characterized the country from the early nineteenth century to the present. We break from previous studies of the Mexican economy to emphasize the crucial importance of the Dublán Convention, the Lill Report, and the Keynesian policies of Eduardo Suárez. The drawing together of Mexico and the United States, a well-established trend, required us to focus long overdue attention on the crucial role of the transnational borderlands. This represents a major historiographical shift, with an important consequence for how Mexico's history is interpreted. Another development previously overlooked is the rise of popular culture and its impact on Mexican politics. Comic books, the influence of the massive rock-and-roll event that took place at Avándaro, referred to as a Mexican Woodstock, and the rise of caped crusaders such as Super Barrio appear to have blurred that political line between fantasy and reality. Finally, we believe that the history of the Mexican people in the modern era cannot be understood apart from events in the United States, just as the history of the American people must include the Mexican experience.

Chapter 1

COLLAPSE AND SURVIVAL

THE COLONIAL LEGACY

Mexico's historical experience, from pre-Hispanic times through the colonial period, the nineteenth century, and into the twentieth, continues to influence the present in ways both obvious and subtle. The forging of a mestizo nation commenced after the Spanish conquest, creating a unique Mexican culture that struggled to bridge the aboriginal Indian cultures and new Western culture introduced by Spain. A shared sense of philosophical and psychological legitimacy provided the necessary confidence to construct a reasonably acceptable, productive society. Nevertheless, philosophical, economic, and social strains began to erode the colonial compact in the latter half of the eighteenth century, and independence all but destroyed it. Independence from Spain in 1821 required a traumatic civil war, and less than 100 years later Mexico plunged into revolution.[1] In between, the new nation experienced episodic violence, regional conflicts, attempted and actual secession, war, the loss of fifty percent of its national territory, foreign intervention, and rapid modernization. Mexico's leaders found themselves desperately reacting to events, unable to develop calmly a popular consensus concerning the desired nature of the new republic.

In the eighteenth century, the Spanish monarchy, under the influence of enlightened ideas, attempted to centralize and depoliticize its empire, an aggressive reform program aimed at administrative uniformity with discipline and order rather than political control.

1

Collapse and Survival

Colonial Legacy

1519	Fernando Cortés arrives in Mexico
1521	Conquest of Tenochtitlan, the Aztec capital
1521–1703	Hapsburg Kingdom of New Spain
1531	Alleged appearance of the Virgin of Guadalupe
1551	National university founded
1558	Valencia mine begins operations
1703–1821	Bourbon Kingdom of New Spain
	Bourbon administrative reforms
1767	Jesuits expelled

Civil War and Independence

1808	Napoleon dethrones the Spanish king
1810–1821	Independence movement
September 16, 1810	Miguel Hidalgo ignites struggle for independence
1810–1811	Hidalgo phase of independence movement
1811–1815	José María Morelos leads independence movement
1812	Spanish Cortes and Constitution
1814	Fernando VII restored to Spanish throne
1820–1821	Agustín Iturbide leads independence struggle
1821	Plan of Iguala (Plan of Three Guarantees) drafted
1822–1823	First Empire and Emperor Agustín I
1824–1828	Presidency of Guadalupe Victoria
1824–1830	Early Republic
1828–1830	Presidency of Vicente Guerrero
1830	Revolt of Anastasio Bustamante
1832	Revolt of Santa Anna

Era of Antonio López de Santa Anna, 1833–1855

1794	Born
1821	Switches from Spanish to Iturbide's side
1823	Under Plan de Casa Mata leads revolt against Emperor
1829	Commands Mexican troops who defeat Spanish invaders at Tampico
1832	Revolts against Bustamante dictatorship

1833	Elected president as Liberal. Vice President Valentín Gómez Farías, as interim president, enacts Liberal program.
1836–1846	Santa Anna leads revolt against his vice president; establishes new constitution that centralizes authority.
	States revolt against centralized authority; most disastrous, the Texas rebellion.

Enlightened reformers developed a disdainful view of colonial society. Their efforts to modify what they viewed as undesirable behavior extended to issuing regulations governing personal conduct during holidays that altered the civic, religious, and popular fiestas celebrating Corpus Christi, Day of the Dead, and Carnival.[2] In spite of the energy of enlightened reformers, Mexico's inhabitants clung to the old system and traditional ways and eventually forced a repolitization of the country that permitted them to control their own internal destiny to a reasonable extent. The eighteenth-century battle with the centralizing reformers in fact accelerated the movement toward a commonwealth structure.

Napoleonic pressure on Spain and the subsequent invasion of the Iberian peninsula (1808) caused a political crisis. French occupation and the imprisonment of King Fernando VII led to the establishment of juntas, as sovereignty reverted back to the people. In Mexico, the municipal council in the viceregal capital of Mexico City insisted upon assuming sovereignty as the institutional representative of the people. Unfortunately, a coup by the elite, designed to maintain the status quo, further unbalanced the institutional structure, damaging legitimacy. Those illegally deprived of a political role resorted to conspiracies, hoping to effect a countercoup of their own. Among those who schemed was the parish priest of Dolores, Miguel Hidalgo. Fear of premature discovery of the conspiracy led to a hasty mobilization of the lower classes with consequent unforeseen circumstances.

The revolt of September 16, 1810, officially recognized as the beginning of the independence movement, began as a political struggle and ended as a rural uprising with aspects of a social revolt. Two areas of the country had been hard hit by an economic reorientation from local and regional marketing to production for the growing urban centers of the country. The Bajío, a region northwest of Mexico City in the Lerma River valley, and the area of Jalisco around the city of

Guadalajara, experienced drastic changes. Large estates began to concentrate on wheat, fruit, and vegetable production demanded by urban consumers. Production of corn and beans, the rural staples, declined, and livestock raising moved northward. This combination raised food prices beyond the means of many rural workers. In addition to the desperate rural situation, the largest and most important manufacturing sector went into decline. Textile manufacturing suffered from competition from cheap Catalán and British imports.[3] Moreover, mining activity, while still profitable, struggled with increased costs. Declining wages and the closing of marginal mines and textile factories resulted.

The level of desperation in these two agricultural regions and the difficult adjustments forced on the textile and mining sectors provided abundant justification for social violence. Yet, in many parts of the country, people remained reasonably prosperous. The checkered pattern of desperation and prosperity provided plenty of recruits for insurrection, but also many defenders who were anxious to preserve existing advantages. The upheavals of the independence period coincided with changing economic conditions and a severe drought in 1808 and 1809 that again reduced many to starvation and threatened areas of the country with famine. Some traumatized people sought refuge in millenarian beliefs, hoping for a savior to lead them away from their present suffering. After 1800, several Indian messiahs unsuccessfully attempted to fill that powerful psychological need. Father Hidalgo, a respected and popular criollo parish priest, in the end offered them both salvation and destruction.[4]

CIVIL WAR AND INDEPENDENCE

Father Hidalgo called upon a desperate people to join him in a political adventure. Not surprisingly, Hidalgo's followers seized the opportunity to vent their desperation in looting and burning without much thought to more complex political notions. The sack of the city of Guanajuato shocked the country. Many now feared the development of a race and class war, like that in Haiti in the 1790s. Alarmed Indians and small landholders saw in the poor, hungry, and landless followers of Hidalgo a threat to their own existence. Even some of Hidalgo's fellow conspirators became apprehensive.[5] Miguel Allende, one of the principal leaders of the movement, considered poisoning Hidalgo to bring an end to the violence. Allende ignored the fact that Hidalgo could not control his followers. Hidalgo's army of eight thousand, after hovering on the outskirts of Mexico City, turned away, providing sufficient time for viceregal forces to regroup. It proved to be a fatal error. General Félix Calleja drove the insurgent force northward. Hidalgo, now a virtual prisoner of his own disillusioned inner circle, fell into viceregal hands in March 1811. Hidalgo and the other top leaders were executed. The banner of insurgency now fell to José María Morelos, a mestizo priest, who developed a skillful guerrilla campaign. Morelos evoked the images of preconquest Mexico to separate those of mixed and Indian ancestry from Europeans and their New World descendants. At the Congress of Chilpancingo, Morelos laid out a new scheme for an independent Mexican nation, and at Apatzingán he issued a constitution. Viceregal forces captured Morelos in the autumn of 1815, and he suffered the same fate as Hidalgo. Violence, now largely undirected, continued to sweep across New Spain. Between 1811 and 1815, almost 15,000 Spanish soldiers arrived in Mexico seeming to add to the violence as the revolutionary movement fragmented into innumerable small groups that waged a destructive guerrilla war that could not be extinguished.[6]

In Spain the political confusion caused by the French invasion cleared as one central junta emerged. Spanish liberals supported the notion of a constitutional monarchy and vastly expanded political participation throughout the Spanish empire. In early 1809, the junta requested that the various parts of the New World empire, including New Spain (Mexico), send delegates to a Cortes (parliament) in Spain. Subsequently, the Spanish Constitution of 1812 attempted to bring all parts of the Spanish world into a new constitutional configuration. Power, responsibility, and authority went to the regional level, as voters, including Indians, throughout Mexico voted for electors to choose deputies to the Spanish Cortes. The ideal of political equality of the parts floundered on Spain's unwillingness to relinquish its dominant role. The return of the king in 1814 and the suppression of the liberal constitution, the subsequent revolt of 1820, and the reestablishment of the Constitution of 1812 caused concern and uncertainty in Mexico. Spanish instability and the reluctance of Spanish liberals to make necessary accommodations weakened the internal bonds of the empire.

Banditry, destruction, terror, and counterterror led to a breakdown of class relationships, eroded the credibility of the government, and destroyed its legitimacy. Unable to reach an agreement with Spain for autonomy that would preserve Hispanic legitimacy while permitting needed accommodations, the elite, along with small landholders, urban professionals, petty merchants, and elements of the army, determined that the break with Spain should be accomplished as quickly as possible and a new, yet to be agreed upon structure put into place. The Plan of Iguala, pulled together by the elite to end the impasse, called for an independent Mexico to be ruled by the Spanish king or another prince and acceptance of the Constitution of 1812, but with military and clerical rights intact. All ethnic distinctions were to end, and the new nation would recognize virtue and merit. If a royal ruler could not be recruited, Mexico would choose its own monarch. The Plan of Iguala, a purely political document, promised something to everybody. It proclaimed three principal guarantees: political independence, religion (i.e., recognition of the Catholic Church and protection of clerical privileges), and equality. The soon to be victorious red, white, and green flag of the "Three Guarantees" rallied a population anxious for peace. As a result, it created a consensus for action on the issue of independence, but little else.

On September 28, 1821, a declaration of independence cut away the dead body of the old colonial system. Agustín de Iturbide, military leader of the plan's "Army of the Three Guarantees," believed that he represented the national will as expressed on the field of battle. Unfortunately, without sword in hand, Iturbide proved a poor politician. Conflict over the nature of the new government began almost immediately. Mexican legislators, following the pattern and theory behind the Spanish Cortes and the Constitution of 1812, believed that Congress should be supreme because it represented the people, while Iturbide thought in terms of executive authority. A compromise could have been worked out were it not for Iturbide's intransigence. His momentary popularity following the victory of the Army of the Three Guarantees misled him into believing that he had a constituency willing to back his own political notions. Rather than working out an acceptable arrangement with legislators, he went ahead and crowned himself emperor (May 19, 1822), jailed his opponents, dissolved Congress, and established the Junta Nacional Instituyente as a captive political body. Iturbide, along with many others, failed to understand the critical condition of the country he now attempted to rule. Eleven years of war had left the new nation exhausted. Class distrust and uncertainty led to a general withdrawal from civic responsibility as individuals sought to assure their own survival. Without broad support, surrounded by untried advisors, unable to raise taxes or even to regenerate old revenues, the regime of Iturbide quickly became ineffectual.

Appointing military men to political positions in the provinces failed to give Iturbide the firm grip on the nation he had hoped for and instead fueled unrest. Opposition to the emperor stemmed from a desire for more regional autonomy, although virtually all agreed on the need for a national government. Antonio López de Santa Anna pushed their discontent into action. Other army officers joined in the insurrection under the banner of the Plan of Casa Mata, which called for the election of a new Congress. Significantly, their plan did not demand the establishment of a republic, nor the removal of Iturbide, but focused on the ideal of congressional superiority and reasonable provincial home rule. The emperor's continued refusal to compromise forced the provinces to contemplate a new political structure. Iturbide, now faced with widespread opposition, in large part his own making, reconvened the first Congress and abdicated the Mexican throne (March 19, 1823). With the end of the empire, Central America broke away from the political union of which it had so reluctantly formed a part to become the United Provinces of Central America, which eventually also splintered. Only Chiapas elected to remain within the Mexican Republic. After Emperor Iturbide, a constitutional monarchy, along the lines of the Spanish Constitution of 1812, no longer appeared to be a feasible option. Thus, in a negative fashion, Agustín de Iturbide, a would-be emperor, became the father of the reluctant republic.[7]

ECONOMIC AFTERMATH OF CIVIL WAR

Rebuilding the shattered economy proved difficult. Domestic savings had been lost and little internal credit remained. During the destructive phase, the silver mines, the engines of prosperity, had been flooded and the machinery destroyed and neglected. The flooding of the Valencia, the world's greatest mine, left the city of Guanajuato without an economic base. Joel Poinsett, the first American representative to Mexico, noted that "scarcely a house was entire." Another traveler reported that ranchos (middle-sized farms) lay in ruins, "houses roofless and the walls blacked by fire, and the surrounding fields still bearing the faint traces of previous plowing now lay deserted."[8] Domestic trade and commerce declined precipitately and international trade only slowly recovered. Economic recovery began slowly in the 1820s, and several regions had regained a measure of prosperity by the 1830s. Real estate prices in some areas returned to pre-1810 levels, while agricultural rents jumped substantially between 1835 and 1839, indicating the return of agricultural profitability. By the middle of the century, surplus capital enabled a number of entrepreneurs to import foreign technology and machinery, with mixed results. Puebla's textile industry experienced growth in the 1840s as a result of returning internal demand. In a similar fashion, mining recovered in a checkered pattern of continued decline in some areas and boom times in others. Guanajuato experienced the return of good times thanks to the rich silver strike at La Luz.[9] Regional economic recovery, however, did not benefit the national government, which remained too weak to enforce tax collection outside of its immediate location. As a consequence, Mexico, at the national level, presented an image of an impoverished, bankrupt nation, while recovery and even a degree of prosperity characterized various regions. The desire to hold on to the fragile threads of a rebounding economy made provincial elites deeply suspicious of the intentions and political ability of Mexico City's national politicians.

While regional internal markets sought to regain equilibrium, foreign trade began to make a modest recovery. Trade contacts with the United States gradually began to gain importance, although in the early part of the century Britain remained the major trading partner and source of desperately needed foreign loans.[10] While the port of Veracruz provided access to the weakened Spanish market, trade between the United States and northern Mexico began to expand. By the 1820s, American businessmen penetrated the border states. As a result, the United States Congress authorized the opening of a consular office in Chihuahua in 1825. American merchants used the Santa Fe Trail from St. Louis to Santa Fe, and then the Camino Real from New Mexico into Chihuahua. El Paso del Norte (today Ciudad Juárez) emerged as an important link between Santa Fe's Missouri trade and Chihuahua. In 1846, some 750 men with 363 wagons brought a million dollars worth of goods to Santa Fe, then to El Paso, and eventually sold the bulk of their stock in Chihuahua and nearby settlements. Earlier, in 1835, the Mexican government established a customshouse in El Paso. In addition to goods imported from the United States, trade in horses and mules, often stolen in Chihuahua by Indians and sold to unsuspecting or unconcerned individuals in New Mexico, formed a lively part of regional commerce. A few Americans, such as Kentucky-born James Magoffin, engaged in several different activities, including copper mining. Hugh Stephenson, also originally from Kentucky, married the daughter of a wealthy paseño and participated in the family's mining and commercial activities. A number of American merchants became Mexican citizens, including Magoffin, who had at one time served as U.S. consul in Saltillo (1825–1831). Consul Magoffin married a Mexican woman, subsequently served on the municipal council of Chihuahua (1841–1842), and appears to have moved back and forth between Missouri and Chihuahua. These men, and others like them of both nationalities, became the prototype of the emerging borderlander who operated with equal facility and comfort in both cultures. On the eve of the Mexican–American War, trade was worth well in excess of a million dollars, and tied frontier businessmen together in a profitable relationship. In contrast to growing commerce in the north, the economic potential of Mexico's heartland remained burdened with lingering effects of the independent wars.[11]

An all-but-bankrupt treasury depended upon custom revenues and what could be squeezed out of its citizens in the immediate vicinity of the national capital—barely enough to keep the government intact, but not sufficient to meet other needs, no matter how urgent. In an attempt to pull together scarce capital, the government established the Banco de Avío in 1830. Funded by tariffs on imported textiles, the bank theoretically could extend long-term loans. Unfortunately, it never succeeded and limped along until it disappeared in 1842.[12] Recovery, as it occurred, relied upon individual regional efforts, not on the national government.

PHILOSOPHICAL DISTORTION: REACTION TO INDEPENDENCE

The most distressing casualty of revolutionary destruction was the social consensus that had emerged from the country's long colonial experience. The Mexican elite, frightened and distrustful, now assumed a hostile and repressive attitude toward the lower classes. Those groups viewed as responsible for the random violence and destruction forfeited political consideration and became objects to be controlled, not accommodated. The elite ignored the fact that many Indian communities and small landholders had been devastated. Both liberals and conservatives shared a negative view of the nature of the Mexican lower classes. They agreed that the essence of nationality lay with criollos, those individuals oriented toward European culture, regardless of actual racial origins. Thus the elite viewed Indian culture as a national problem. Both liberals and conservatives supported European immigration and subsequent intermarriage with the aboriginal population as a means of absorbing Indians into the criollo population, as well as filling up the vast empty regions in the northern reaches of the country.[13]

In the opinion of the elite, Mexico's Indian population appeared culturally unable to participate in the grand task of constructing a modern republic. The liberals blamed Spanish colonial paternalism for overprotecting the Indians, leading to their infantilization in the course of the colonial centuries—an explanation rejected by the conservatives. The newspaper *El Monitor* observed in 1848 that only two possibilities existed: extermination or civilizing the Indians by miscegenation. The liberal approach devalued the contemporary Indians, while glorifying the pre-Cortesian indigenous civilizations to demonstrate how far they had fallen under colonial rule. Glorification in the abstract served to protect the liberals against anti-indigenous charges, while not affecting the actual treatment of the contemporary Indian. *El Universal,* arguing the conservative view, agreed that intelligence lay with the Spanish race, meaning the criollos. Nevertheless, the Indians constituted an "auxiliary mass," invaluable if properly directed—but directed it must be; it could not be left to its own devices.[14] Elite characterization of the Indians as a negative force and a major problem helped form an unfavorable international perception of Mexico as a nation struggling to deal with an irredeemably backward population.

Attracting a new population to rescue the country became an enduring panacea. Foreign immigration appeared to offer a way to advance the creolization of the Indian and also to preserve national sovereignty. Iturbide charged the Junta Nacional Instituyente with elaborating a colonization law to encourage settlement of unpopulated areas of the newly independent country. The need for prompt action was underscored by the 1822 mission of Stephen F. Austin to press the government to ratify a colonization concession granted to his father by the authorities in Nuevo León. Another consortium sought permission to settle 10,000 Catholic families from Ireland and the Canary Islands in Texas. Schemes to direct immigrants to other parts of the nation also existed. Finally, the law of January 4, 1823, set the basic terms, including a Catholic religious requirement and permission for the introduction of slave property, while prohibiting sale or transfer and providing for the freeing of slave children at age fourteen. Iturbide's Mexican empire hoped to entice Mexicans along with Europeans to settle in the dangerously underpopulated northern borderlands.[15] After the collapse of the empire, successor regimes modified colonization regulations but held on to the fantasy.

POLITICS OF THE EARLY REPUBLIC

Reestablishing a political consensus and reaching agreement on the nature of the new nation proved difficult. The development of conspiratorial politics dating back to the secret societies, such as the Guadalupes, who clandestinely functioned on the eve of the collapse of Spanish power, made it difficult to engage in frank and open political debate. A secret agenda, shared by a small inner circle, made public discourse a manipulative tool rather than a means to achieve openly political objectives. In a new nation without identifiable poles of power, a bold public stance could have unpredictable consequences. Prudence, coupled with secrecy, made it difficult to establish common ground or determine actual objectives. Consequently, behind-the-scenes deals, rumors, and a great deal of paranoia characterized the politics of early independent Mexico. Under the circumstances, the national elite in Mexico City understandably misjudged the intentions of the provinces and the degree of autonomy they would accept. Mexico City feared that Guadalajara might become a rival capital ringed by its own provinces. Overreaction or underreaction both served to delay the needed political solution. The possibility of armed violence, even civil war, endured until the establishment of a federal republic under the Constitution of 1824. While acceptance of the constitution guaranteed the territorial integrity of the nation, it gave an excessive amount of power to the federal states. The inability of the national elite to respond rationally to reasonable demands for power sharing in the end had driven the ex-provinces to insist on more and more freedom from a center that seemed unable to overcome its reactionary paranoia. During the course of the struggle, provincial elites associated Mexico City with a grasping desire to absorb all the authority of various regions in opposition to actual needs of the people. The states viewed themselves as the heirs of Spanish liberalism besieged by a reactionary center.[16] Federalism and liberalism became synonymous, as did centralism and conservatism. Only the bitter experience of the first half of the nineteenth century would blur such absolutes. The political turmoil of the early nineteenth century caused by elite fragmentation nevertheless excluded lower class political involvement. Fanny Calderón de la Barca, a Scottish-born former Staten Island boarding house proprietress who became the wife of the Spanish ambassador, noted that these political debates and contests never involved the broader society itself. The lower classes supplied the armies, not the ideas. They functioned as pawns in a game directed by others.[17]

In the struggle for control, the regional elites almost completely triumphed over the national elite. Thus Mexico's first constitution (1824) provided for a president and vice president elected by the state legislatures. Under the Constitution of 1824, a series of weak and ineffectual presidents occupied the national palace. Emperor Iturbide's intransigence had made it impossible to counterbalance the philosophical influence of the Spanish Constitution of 1812 and the actual institutional changes it had brought about. Vast numbers of new constituents had been empowered and insisted on a political role. The 1812 document had provided for an expansion of the number of municipal councils in New Spain, endowed them with more independent sovereignty, and created a number of elected provincial deputations to represent regional needs. The dispersal of authority ushered in by Spanish liberalism in the last decade of colonial rule now could not be gathered in or easily curtailed by a national government. Nevertheless, the federal states agreed on the need for a *centro de unión*. In short, they accepted the idea of a Mexican nation that extended beyond their own limited regions, but saw themselves as the true depository of the people's sovereignty. Because of the difficulty of elaborating a set of workable as well as acceptable principles for a national government, and the absence of political parties that could develop a consensus, national politics remained an ad hoc opportunistic affair.[18] In order to lend at least some coherence and structure, the various

Political Divisions of the Republic of Mexico
Federal Constitution of 1824

Figure 1.1 Political divisions of the Republic of Mexico Federal Constitution of 1824.

factions attached themselves to Masonic lodges. As semisecret mystical bodies, they fit in with the conspiratorial politics of the age. The two branches of the movement, the York Rite and Scottish Rite Masons, served as surrogate political parties with the more radical federalists associated with the York Rite (Yorquinos), and those that favored more centralism gathered around the Scottish Rite (Escoceses).

In spite of major difficulties, the first president, Guadalupe Victoria, survived, but the second election witnessed the loser contesting the results and forcing his way into office. Politics became a dangerous activity. Both Iturbide and Vicente Guerrero eventually died in front of firing squads. Violence emerged as a political instrument. Unpredictable violence sprang from a political climate lacking sufficient philosophical grounding and thus unable to produce a consensus. As a

result, the presidential palace became easy prey for personal oppor-
tunism. A vulnerable Mexico fell easily into the hands of Antonio
López de Santa Anna. A soldier able to claim heroic efforts on behalf of
his country, he seemed a plausible savior.

Born in the last decade of the eighteenth century, Santa Anna
served Spain and briefly Iturbide. He defended the first president
against an attempted coup by the vice president and defeated a Spanish invasion in 1829.[19] While few understood Santa Anna's politics,
to a tired and exhausted nation he seemed the only hope. In fact,
Santa Anna was a political creation pushed forward by events and
made into an attractive political figurehead by an opposition group
with its own long-range interests in mind. This would be only one of
many attempts to use Santa Anna to carry out a political program
designed by others. Opposition to then president Anastasio Bustamante's increasingly dictatorial regime was coordinated by a semisecret group that engineered antigovernment activities, both in the
capital and in the various states. The press rallied popular opinion
against Bustamante and his ministers. The crucial alliance with military commanders did not emerge until the national government
moved in a heavy-handed fashion to reorganize Veracruz's military
command structure, leading to a revolt. Santa Anna, invited to head
the insurrection, would be made into a brilliant symbol of Mexican
virtue by the Mexico City conspirators. Heedless of the danger that
their manufactured hero might believe the propaganda along with the
masses, with total confidence in their ability to manipulate the general, politicians created a useful, but only partially controllable, popular figure. General Santa Anna easily won the presidential election
along with Valentín Gómez Farías as vice president.[20]

Unlike the general-president, liberal Gómez Farías had well-
developed views on the need for reform in order to establish a prosperous and progressive republic. He believed that only a strong
national government able to work with regional elites could end the
paralysis that gripped the nation. The army and the Church posed
major obstacles. Armed respectively with physical and moral force,
both institutions distrusted change and feared the loss of their privileges. The army devoured funds that the impoverished nation could
not afford, while the Church held resources that a financially starved
government could not tap. Without fiscal muscle, the national government had little hope of bringing regional factions under control.
Breaking up stagnant corporate bodies in order to free resources became and remained a major liberal objective, right through the Mexican Revolution of 1910.

In the struggle for control, the Church proved the most difficult to deal with effectively. While the army's strength relied upon

weapons, the Church advanced disinterested functional claims to its social position and so-called privileges. Entwined in Mexico's Catholic culture and with spiritual claims on the mentality of virtually every Mexican, the Church appeared to be overwhelmingly powerful. Church assets represented immobilized wealth to the liberals, while to the clergy they constituted a sacred trust. Income from pious endowments supported Church activities, orphanages, and hospitals, as well as perpetual prayer for some deceased donor's troubled soul. Church funds also served as a source for reasonable loans and mortgages. The Church demonstrated its active involvement in all aspects of secular life through extensive and virtually constant ceremonial activities. Processions, perhaps capped with a mass, marked religious and civic occasions. From small villages to large cities, public celebrations required a prominent clerical presence. For example, Guadalajara's fiesta patronal featured four trumpeters in the lead, the city's patron saint carried by eight young girls flanked by candle-bearing women, followed by thousands of the common folk, including Indians along with more musicians, a statue of the Virgin borne by twelve girls in white with the priest walking behind. The entire glorious processing ended with several brass bands. The liberals who legislated restrictions on clerical ceremonial activities during the Reforma understood that it was politically too dangerous to permit the Church to monopolize public ceremonies.[21] From a religiocultural standpoint, clerics functioned at the center of the nation's ceremonial life.

The early republic continued to respond to long-established Catholic rhythms. Pedestrians bowed to images of the saints that occupied niches of buildings and often joined in daily morning prayer, as well as afternoon and evening devotions. They knelt whenever a priest in vestments rushed by with the holy oils to perform last rites. Their spiritual and material life seemed entwined beyond separation. Priests did not perceive of any activity as being beyond benefiting from clerical influence, if not direct participation. Clerical involvement in the secular life of the nation naturally included a lively interest in politics. The Church called upon old loyalties and cultural claims to justify its participation. Thus an understandable cultural ambivalence characterized the efforts to displace the Church from its position. As an institution, the Church represented a formidable enemy or a powerful friend.

The Church made some limited concessions to changing times. Prelates moved holy images inside buildings, ostensibly so they would receive better care and avoid the irreverence of foreign heretics, and curtailed bell ringing. The cannonade of bells that marked Corpus Christi, which had numbed the eardrums of foreign travelers, would become a thing of the past. While seemingly slight, such concessions indicated a willingness to compromise. Liberals, however, believed that the pace of change did not proceed at a rapid enough clip.[22] Thus frustration characterized the relationship between the liberals and churchmen, with spasmodic intervals of cooperation viewed as major by the Church and minor by its opponents. Religious holidays posed some difficulties in the early years of independence, as government officials attempted to promote industry and thrift in an effort to bring about recovery from the economic disruptions that attended the wars of independence. Hard work and holidays collided in the numerous religious celebrations, the holy days of obligation that mandated attending Mass and refraining from manual labor. As part of an effort at reconciliation between the Mexican government and the Holy See, Pope Gregory XVI in 1839 issued a directive to the Mexican bishops that reduced the number of religious holidays that should be honored as holy days. Churchmen and the Pope believed this an important concession.[23]

Political conflict between the Church and the new state began almost immediately. In 1824, fearing that provisions of Jalisco's state constitution represented the opening wedge of government control, the cathedral chapter of Guadalajara declined to swear allegiance to the constitution. Clerics all over Mexico rallied to the cause. Puebla's bishop declared that the constitution represented a veiled attempt to seize assets as well as authority away from the Church hierarchy. After considerable tension had built, the national government arranged a face-saving settlement—the basic problem, however, remained. The states of Zacatecas and Durango called upon the national government to exercise control over the Church without waiting for an agreement with Rome. For their part, priests urged the faithful to resist the "godless." The Church increasingly saw itself under financial, political, and moral siege. While the liberals threatened expropriation, the conservatives, professing to support the Church, demanded loans that appeared unlikely to be repaid. Moreover, "heretical philosophies" abounded along with a "horrifying progress." An alarmed reactionary Church saw little hope of reaching an accommodation. In the end, the inability to establish an acceptable balance between church and state contributed to the disorder that plagued Mexico in the early nineteenth century.[24]

Liberal theoreticians had to develop an acceptable argument to justify their attitude toward the Church. José María Luis Mora, a man of impressive intellectual talents, suggested that the Church, before the conversion of Emperor Constantine to Christianity, functioned as a spiritual association without property or a clerical hierarchy. Property and other temporal concerns came with the transformation of the Church into a state religious entity. In an 1831 essay, Mora asserted that the Church had a right to hold property, but it had to be regulated in the same fashion as all other property holders under civil law. Property remained a physical asset, not a spiritual one, even when it passed into clerical control. Moreover, while the state could not restrict the right of an individual to acquire property, it could do so in the case of communities or "moral bodies." He concluded by urging the Church to return to Caesar what belonged to Caesar and to acknowledge that the heavenly kingdom existed only as a purely spiritual one, "not of this world." Clerics angrily rejected the notion.[25]

The conservative opposition, on the other hand, believed that the Church provided an important element of social stability, particularly among the lower classes, where there remained a high degree of attachment to religion. In Lucas Alamán's opinion, the Church provided the only remaining bond shared by all Mexicans, regardless of class or caste. Supposedly, the independence period with its violence had destroyed every other common tie.[26] Thus conservatives believed that in the struggle to control the country the Church could be an effective ally, and therefore it should not be weakened or indiscriminately deprived of its resources. Liberal politician and jurist Mariano Otero represented the middle ground between Mora and Alamán. Otero suggested that the Church's position would weaken inevitably as civilization progressed. Therefore, attempts to circumvent or speed up the historical process caused unnecessary social unrest. Time and patience, however, did not provide immediate revenues, nor accelerate the restructuring of property ownership that constituted an important element of the liberal agenda.[27]

The struggle over resources constituted a major problem, but not the only one. Mexico's lack of religious toleration appeared to many liberals as an embarrassing symbol of the nation's cultural backwardness. Moreover, modernization of clerical relations seemed necessary if the country hoped to attract foreign immigrants. As previously noted, as early as 1821 criollo emperor Agustín de Iturbide urged his countrymen to encourage immigrants to fill up the underpopulated reaches of the nation and develop its resources. Nevertheless, the Republican Constitution of 1824, with its prohibition of religious toleration, discouraged non-Catholic immigrants.

Sole recognition of the Roman Catholic faith complicated everyday life for foreign Protestants. While non-Catholics could be married legally by a consular representative or by a captain aboard a ship, mixed marriages as well as the services of an ordained minister required subterfuge, and the result might be illegal. Juan de Dios Canedo, an advocate of religious toleration, raised the issue of Protestant burial rights. He observed that inevitably foreigners would die in Mexico leaving the country with the option of burning, burying, eating, or exporting the corpses. Reality forced the issue—non-Catholics could be buried in an appropriate cemetery. Vicente Rocafuerte, then the Mexican representative in London, urged full religious freedom to attract Protestant immigrants. He associated religious toleration with material progress. Rocafuerte believed that northern European Protestants made such superior immigrants that Mexico could not afford to exclude them.

In 1831, Rocafuerte's *Essay on Religious Toleration* caused a furor. He argued for a complete separation of church and state based on their different functions. Moreover, he warned that the religious monopoly conceded the Roman Catholic religion could only lead to spiritual tyranny. As if to prove the point, the Press Board, charged with protecting freedom of expression, nevertheless caved in to clerical pressure and charged Rocafuerte with sedition. His essay allegedly violated the article of the Constitution of 1824 that established the Catholic faith as Mexico's official and only religion. With Rocafuerte arrested and held, the case became a cause célèbre. After a tumultuous trial, during which clerical stubbornness and inquisitional intolerance appalled all but the Church's most ardent apologists, Rocafuerte went free. The proceedings caused many to reexamine the wisdom of church–state ties. The episode pushed moderates over to the liberal position. Even those moderates who did not favor religious toleration condemned clerical oppression, ironically one of the major points made in the Rocafuerte essay.[28]

Conservatives, on the other hand, wondered whether non-Catholics could be integrated into Mexican culture if the country adopted religious toleration. A newspaper article in *El Sol* suggested that it might be necessary to strengthen the criminal code if Protestants flooded into the country.

While de facto religious toleration developed, foreigners could not publicly conduct religious services, and all of the legal complications remained—a situation that endured until Benito Juárez decreed religious freedom on December 4, 1860. Meanwhile, the issue lingered on, poisoning clerical–state relations. The Church insisted that advocates of toleration supported heresy.[29]

THE CONSERVATIVE REACTION

Gómez Farías, left in charge of the nation by an impulsively energetic Santa Anna, reduced the size of the army, abolished its special privileges, and moved to reduce clerical influence in education by closing the University of Mexico, then dominated by a clerical faculty. The government assumed control of the clerical appointment process, pushing aside the authority of Rome. In an effort to weaken the

Church fiscally, the tithe, formerly a mandatory tax, became optional. New government regulations permitted priests and nuns to renounce their vows. As a prelude to bolder moves to come, the Franciscan missions in California became state property. Gómez Farías believed that an anticlerical attack in distant California would not provoke much reaction. Nevertheless, he moved too rapidly. His opponents understood that he intended to expand his campaign to the more important regions of the country unless stopped.

The Church and the army, supported by alarmed conservatives, prevailed on Santa Anna to head a movement against his own former vice president. Because of this event, Santa Anna is often portrayed as a loose cannon on the deck of the ship of state. It should be kept in mind, however, that the real issue remained effective control of the country. Both liberals and conservatives and the various factions within those groups agreed on the goal, but disagreed on the methods to bring it about. General Santa Anna, more concerned about attacks on the army than the Church, toppled the liberal government.

Santa Anna viewed the Church as a ready source of funds, either in "loans" or, if necessary, through confiscation of clerical assets. In an attempt to make his government financially effective, he seized clerical property and sold it off, abolished the Colegio Mayor de Santos and absorbed its endowment, and on occasion sent troops to withdraw funds from Church coffers. Assets of the confiscated California missions were transferred to direct army control. Santa Anna saw the Church with a nonideological pragmatism that usually ended up costing the institution dearly. Nor in clerical matters unrelated to finances did he jump automatically to the Church's defense.[30] Like many others, he was a predator on the one obvious source of funds. Consequently, not all of the anticlerical liberal legislation would be undone. The law ending civil action to enforce collection of the tithe remained in effect. Even the law that permitted clerics to renounce their vows remained in force until the latter half of 1854. Clearly, society was divided on how to regulate church–state relations.[31]

Meanwhile, the reactionary new regime ushered in by Santa Anna moved to alter the balance between the national government and the states. An order to reduce the size of state militias provided the most ominous indication of impending change. Zacatecas officials refused, and Santa Anna led 4,000 troops into the state, sacked the city of Zacatecas, and returned to the capital confident that he had intimidated the opposition.[32] A new constitution of 1836 now provided for regional political bosses selected by the president. States lost most of their independent authority, much to the anger of the regional elites. Instead of continuing Gómez Farías's tactic of centralizing control in the capital, while manipulating the federal system as needed, the new constitution attempted to institutionalize centralized authority abruptly. Between 1837 and 1841, revolts in favor of federalism swept the nation, including seven such movements in Jalisco, eight in the newly designated (formerly state) department of México, and five in Puebla, in addition to other areas of the south-center of the country and in the north.[33] Regional elites on the periphery of the nation had a better chance of success. Yucatán, more closely tied with Havana and even New Orleans than with Mexico City, remained independent from 1840 to 1846. The most disastrous and fateful revolt occurred in Texas.

NOTES

1. For a concise treatment of the violence that accompanied the collapse of the empire, see Colin M. MacLachlan and Jaime E. Rodríguez O., *The Forging of the Cosmic Race: A Reinterpretation of Colonial Mexico,* expanded edition (Berkeley: University of California Press, 1990), pp. 294–342; Christon I. Archer, "'La Causa Buena': The Counterinsurgency Army of New Spain and the Ten Years' War," in Jaime E. Rodríguez O., ed., *The Independence of Mexico and the Creation of the New Nation* (Los Angeles: UCLA Latin American Center Publications, 1989), pp. 85–108; Brian R. Hamnett, *Roots of Insurgency: Mexican Regions, 1750–1824* (Cambridge: Cambridge University Press, 1986).
2. William H. Beezley, Cheryl E. Martin, and William E. French, eds., *Rituals of Rule, Rituals of Resistance: Public Celebrations and Popular Culture in Mexico* (Wilmington, forthcoming, 1993); Juan Pedro Viqueira Albán, *¿Relajados o reprimidos? Diversiones públicas y vida social en la ciudad de México durante el Siglo de las Luces* (Mexico: Fondo de Cultura Económica, 1987).
3. Richard J. Salvucci, *Textiles and Capitalism in Mexico: An Economic History of the Obrajes, 1539–1840* (Princeton: Princeton University Press, 1987), pp. 157–58.
4. Eric Van Young, "Quetzalcóatl, King Ferdinand, and Ignacio Allende Go to the Seashore; or Messianism and Mystical Kingship in Mexico, 1800–1821," in Rodríguez O., ed., *The Independence of Mexico,* pp. 109–27.
5. Eric Van Young, "Agustín Marroquín, The Sociopath as Rebel," in Judith Ewell and William H. Beezley, eds., *The Human Tradition in Latin America: The Nineteenth Century* (Wilmington: SR Books, 1989), pp. 17–38.
6. Brigadier and later Viceroy Félix Calleja, in charge of the military effort, described it as "a hydra reborn as fast as one cuts off its heads." Archer, "'La Causa Buena,'" p. 86.
7. Ralph Lee Woodward Jr., *Central America: A Nation Divided* (New York: Oxford University Press, 1976), p. 91; Jaime E. Rodríguez O., "The Struggle for the Nation: The First Centralist–Federalist Conflict in Mexico," *The Americas* (July 1992), pp. 1–22; Timothy E. Anna, *The Mexican Empire of Iturbide* (Lincoln: University of Nebraska Press, 1990), pp. 217–26; José Barragán Barragán, *Introducción al federalismo* (Mexico: Universidad Nacional Autónoma de México, 1978), pp. 11–20.
8. Joel R. Poinsett, *Notes on Mexico* (Philadelphia: H. C. Carey and I. Lea, 1824), pp. 178–79; G. F. Lyon, *Journal of a Residence and Tour in the Republic of Mexico in 1826,* 2 vols. (London: J. Murray, 1828), vol. 1, pp. 192–93.

9. An assessment of the regional recovery is provided in Margaret Chowning, "The Contours of the Post–1810 Depression in Mexico: A Reappraisal from a Regional Perspective," *Latin American Research Review* 27: 2 (1992), pp. 119–50. For the textile industry, see Guy P. C. Thompson, *Puebla de los Angeles: Industry and Society in a Mexican City, 1700–1850* (Boulder: Westview, 1989).

10. Jaime E. Rodríguez O., "Mexico's First Foreign Loans," in Rodríguez O., ed., *The Independence of Mexico*, pp. 215–35.

11. Mark Wasserman, *Capitalists, Caciques, and Revolution: The Native Elite and Foreign Enterprise in Chihuahua, Mexico, 1854–1911* (Chapel Hill: University of North Carolina Press, 1984), p. 74; Inés Herrera Canales, *El comercio exterior de Mexico, 1821–1875* (México: Colegio de México, 1977); W. H. Timmons, *El Paso: A Borderlands History* (El Paso: Texas Western Press, University of Texas at El Paso, 1990), pp. 82–83.

12. For a grim view of public revenues, see Barbara Tenenbaum, *The Politics of Penury: Debts and Taxes in Mexico, 1821–1856* (Albuquerque: University of New Mexico Press, 1986), and by the same author, "Taxation and Tyranny: Public Finance during the Iturbide Regime, 1821–1823," in Rodríguez O., ed., *The Independence of Mexico*, pp. 201–13. For the Banco de Avío, see Robert A. Potash, *The Mexican Government and Industrial Development in the Early Republic: The Banco de Avío* (Amherst: University of Massachusetts Press, 1983).

13. Nettie Lee Benson, "Territorial Integrity in Mexican Politics, 1821–1833," in Rodríguez O., ed., *The Independence of Mexico*, pp. 275–307.

14. Charles A. Hale, *Mexican Liberalism in the Age of Mora, 1821–1853* (New Haven: Yale University Press, 1968), pp. 243–44.

15. Anna, *The Mexican Empire*, pp. 137–38; Benson, "Territorial Integrity," p. 279.

16. Virginia Guedea, *En busca de un gobierno alterno: Los Guadalupes de México* (México, Universidad Nacional Autónoma de México, 1992); Rodríguez O., "The Struggle for the Nation," pp. 30–31; Both liberals and conservatives engaged in conspiratorial politics. See, for example, Miguel Soto, *La Conspiración Monarquía en Mexico, 1845–1846* (México: Editorial Offset, 1988); Donald Fithian Stevens, *Origins of Instability in Early Republican Mexico* (Durham: Duke University Press, 1991), p. 83.

17. Fanny Calderón de la Barca, *Life in Mexico* (Garden City: Doubleday & Co., 1970), p. 497.

18. An interesting view of the struggle between the regional and national elites is presented in Jaime E. Rodríguez O., "From Royal Subject to Republican Citizen: The Role of the Autonomist in the Independence of Mexico," in Rodríguez O., ed., *The Independence of Mexico*, pp. 19–43.

19. Christon I. Archer, "The Young Antonio López de Santa Anna: Veracruz Counterinsurgent and Incipient Caudillo," in Ewell and Beezley, eds., *The Human Tradition*, pp. 3–16.

20. Oakah L. Jones Jr., *Santa Anna* (New York: Twayne Publishers, 1968), p. 56; Jaime E. Rodríguez O., "The Origins of the 1832 Rebellion," in Jaime E. Rodríguez O., ed., *Patterns of Contention in Mexican History* (Wilmington: SR Books, 1992), pp. 145–62. Others, including Michael P. Costeloe, *La primera república federal de México, 1824–1835* (México: Fondo de Cultura Económica, 1975), pp. 327–28, give Santa Anna credit as the direct engineer of the 1832 rebellion. We have drawn our interpretation from Rodríguez's recent archival research.

21. Guy P. C. Thompson, "The Ceremonial and Political Role of Village Bands in Mexico, 1846–1968," in Beezley, Martin, and French, eds., *Rituals of Rule*, p. 7.

22. Anne Staples, "Policía y buen gobierno: Nineteenth-Century Efforts to Regulate Public Behavior," in Beezley, Martin, and French, eds., *Rituals of Rule*, pp. 115–126.

23. Pope Gregory XVI, "Breve Pontificio sobre diminución de días festivas en la República Mexicana," May 16, 1839, published as decree number 104, September 14, 1839, by the Mexican government in parallel Latin and Spanish. Rare Book Collection, Latin American Library, Tulane University, New Orleans.

24. Jaime E. Rodríguez O., "The Conflict between Church and State in Early Republican Mexico," *New World: A Journal of Latin American Studies* (1987), pp. 93–112.

25. Hale, *Mexican Liberalism*, pp. 133–34.

26. Stevens, *Origins of Instability*, p. 36.

27. Charles A. Hale, *The Transformation of Liberalism in Late Nineteenth-Century Mexico* (Princeton: Princeton University Press, 1989), p. 6.

28. Vicente Rocafuerte, *Ensayo sobre la tolerancia religiosa* (México: Imprenta de Rivera, 1831), p. 63; Jaime E. Rodríguez O., *The Emergence of Spanish America: Vicente Rocafuerte and Spanish Americanism, 1808–1832* (Berkeley: University of California Press, 1975), pp. 204–07.

29. Dieter Berninger, "Immigration and Religious Toleration: A Mexican Dilemma, 1821–1860," *The Americas* (April 1976), pp. 553–54, 562–63.

30. Stevens, *Origins of Instability*, p. 35.

31. Jesús Reyes Heroles, *El liberalismo Mexicano: La integración de las ideas* (México: Universidad Nacional Autónoma de México, 1961), vol. 3, pp. 149–50.

32. Conservatives interested in a military career usually entered the national army rather than regional militias. Stevens, *Origins of Instability*, p. 57; Pedro Santoni, "Los federales radicales y la guerra del '47" (Ph.D. diss., El Colegio de México, 1987).

33. Cecilia Noriega Elió, *El constituyente de 1842* (México: Universidad Nacional Autónoma de México, 1986), p. 18.

Chapter 2

CENTRIFUGAL FORCES

REVOLT IN THE NORTH

Texas, an underpopulated and distant province, constituted a marginal region of the republic. Immigrants from the United States outnumbered Tejanos by a large majority, although the entire population numbered only 40,000. Politically, Texas reluctantly functioned as part of the state of Coahuila. As an immigrant province tied weakly to Mexico both politically and culturally, Texas naturally preferred the looser federal system to the aggressive central government provided for by the Constitution of 1836. Immigrants from the United States, overwhelmingly Protestant, tended to be disdainful of any political connection with Mexico or its Catholic culture. Mexico City, meanwhile, worried that Protestantism, an important part of the culture of the new settlers, posed a problem of political loyalty and an obstacle to social integration. Liberals who supported religious toleration of a foreign minority in the center of the nation reacted uneasily to the existence of a Protestant majority on the fringes of the republic bordering on Protestant United States. Conservatives in general opposed accommodating non-Catholics, maintaining that the danger to Mexican culture was too extreme to entertain, whether in Texas or in the heart of the nation.[1] Mexican politicians had been concerned about the future of the province for some time. Various incidents and jarring statements made it obvious that elements in the United States coveted Texas as well as the vast stretch in between, all the way to California on the Pacific coast. The colonization law of 1830 had prohibited further immigration from the United States and called for an increased Mexican presence on the northern border. Nevertheless, the heavy-handed dismantling of the federal system outraged both American expansionists and Tejanos.

The political reaction in Texas was complex and confusing. Many individuals driven to the same end had wildly conflicting motivations. Tejanos and Anglo-Americans reacted to many of the same grievances, including the region's political amalgamation with Coahuila, unrealistic tariffs, unnecessary and disruptive demands from Mexico City, and the general attitudes of hostility toward the frontier population; yet, on some major issues, including slavery and ties with the United States, they differed totally. Nevertheless, the abrupt end of the

Centrifugal Forces

1836–1846	States revolt against centralized authority; most disastrous, the Texas rebellion

Texas Episode

1821	Moses Austin receives grant to settle Texas; grant confirmed to Stephen F. Austin
1829	Emancipation decree directed at slaves in Texas
1830	Immigration law prohibits migration from United States
1835	Texas Declaration of Independence
1836	Battles of the Alamo, Golidad, and San Jacinto
1836–1845	Lone Star Republic

U.S.–Mexican War, 1846–1848

1845	Annexation of Texas
1846	U.S. declaration of war
	Battle of Buena Vista
1847	Battle of Cerro Gordo
	Battle of Chapultepec
1848	Treaty of Guadalupe Hidalgo

Postwar Mexico

1853	Santa Anna returns to Mexico to establish a unity regime. Gadsden Purchase of Mesilla Valley from Santa Anna
1854–1855	Revolution of Ayutla against Santa Anna
1860	Juárez declares religious toleration.

Constitution of 1824 and the increasingly arbitrary approach of the central government forced an unnatural alliance into existence. Thus, Lorenzo de Zavala, a liberal leader and former Mexican minister to France, became vice president, while David Burnet, veteran of an ill-starred effort to liberate Venezuela before coming to Texas, served as president of an independent Lone Star Republic. Tejanos joined Anglo-Texans in spite of well-founded suspicions about the issue of annexation. Tejanos numbering 160, including Colonel Juan Nepomuceno Seguín and Plácido Benavides, took part in the siege of Mexican troops at San Antonio in late 1835, and subsequently José Antonio Navarro and Francisco Ruiz signed the declaration of Texas independence. The alliance between the two groups lasted long enough to be fatal to the Mexican cause in Texas. What many members of the elite long feared appeared to be coming true—Mexico hovered on the verge of disintegration.

An alarmed Santa Anna refused to preside over the dismemberment of the nation. Taking to the field at the head of an avenging army, he arrived in San Antonio, Texas, in early March of 1836. The first violent clash set the tone for the entire military campaign. The storming of the old Franciscan mission of the Alamo resulted in the death of all of its defenders, including prisoners. The subsequent execution of 365 prisoners taken in another engagement, at Goliad, under the direct orders of General Santa Anna, made any political compromise impossible. Eventually the Texans, reinforced and supplied from the United States, defeated the Mexicans and captured Santa Anna himself. In his capacity as president, Santa Anna signed an agreement providing for the independence of the province. While an outraged country rejected and repudiated Santa Anna's actions, events had moved beyond return.

Rebellion spread across Mexico's northern tier of provinces. Antigovernment violence broke out in 1837 in New Mexico and Sonora. General José Urrea, the military commander in the northwest, demanded the reestablishment of a federal system. An ambitious individual born into a military family at the fort of Tucson, Urrea had served Santa Anna and expected to be rewarded with the governorship of Sonora. Disappointment motivated his actions, but nevertheless he attracted support from the federalists in that state. Unfortunately for his ambitions, Manuel María Gandara, appointed governor of Sonora by the national government, conquered the state after a bloody six-month civil war. Farther north in New Mexico the revolt took on unique characteristics. In New Mexico a strong sense of regionalism already had psychologically detached that province from the republic and made it vulnerable to separatist movements. When in 1837 a centralist governor, Albino Pérez, a non-New Mexican, assumed control of the province, he faced resentment and open hostility. Lower class inhabitants, including both acculturated and Pueblo Indians, reacted to social and economic grievances that had been smoldering for years. Excessive taxes, militia service, and the wide gap between the well to do (*los ricos*) and the ragged marginals at the bottom caused much resentment and weakened the social fabric. The sudden political changes damaged the sense of stability and legitimacy of New Mexico's government, providing the opportune moment for a social revolt. While professing loyalty to federalism, Nuevomexicanos had their own immediate and local agenda. The lower classes wanted municipal autonomy, in effect a return to the village-centered structure of pre-Hispanic days. However, to place it in the context of the times, it was called a "canton government." In the struggle to put down the rebellion that began north of Santa Fe, the governor lost his life, as did some prominent ricos.[2] José González, an illiterate *genizaro* (racially mixed person) from Taos, became interim governor. Rebel leaders convoked a *junta popular* to open up and broaden access to political power. Mexican forces with the aid of a frightened elite crushed the revolt in January 1838, but continued to ignore the social and economic issues that underlay the violence. The nation's grasp on the region remained tenuous. A Mexico City newspaper advised the government in 1842 to give frontier inhabitants greater freedom because in practice an imposed centralization weakened the nation's hold on the periphery.

Farther west, upper California functioned in virtual isolation from both central Mexico and the frontier provinces to the east. Early economic activity revolved around the mission system until 1781, when forty-four settlers and four soldiers founded Los Angeles. Ten years later, Los Angeles had become one of the most prosperous settlements in California, although the nearby mission of San Gabriel still produced more agricultural wealth. By 1800, its 139 inhabitants made the settlement a major outpost. On the eve of American occupation, Los Angeles, then the provincial capital, had an impressive population of 2,550. Political change in central Mexico only weakly influenced events. Even after the secularization of the missions, the distant government in Mexico City made only sporadic and ineffectual attempts to impose its will.

Local politics, sometimes violent, determined who became governor, and the national authorities usually accepted the arrangement. With the end of federalism, California declared itself provisionally independent, pending restoration of the Constitution of 1824. Concerned that regional adjustments made to facilitate foreign trade and provide access to political offices might be endangered by uninformed meddling from Mexico City, the province reacted with hostility when

Mariano Chico arrived at Santa Barbara as the new centralist governor. Within months Chico had fled, leaving the remaining Mexican force to meet defeat shortly thereafter. Juan Bautista Alvarado emerged as governor, receiving support from his uncle Mariano Guadalupe Vallejo, military commander in the north. From the then capital of Monterey, the new regime urged Sonora to revolt and called on the support of Southern California. The province, however, divided along regional lines, as indeed the state still is inclined to do. Santa Barbara northward supported Alvarado; Southern California did not, in spite of a brief occupation by northern forces.

Ironically, Governor Alvarado became a convert to the Constitution of 1836 and under it united the entire province. Clearly, the major issue was native rule rather than a government by an outsider sent from Mexico City. Consequently, when General Manual Micheltorena arrived in 1842 the Californios again rejected a non-native. The fact that convicts, along with women companions, came with the Mexican governor became an additional issue. An apprehensive Micheltorena requested more troops and suggested that if the national government could not afford to defend its interest then it should consider ceding the province to British creditors before the Californios declared themselves independent. Indeed many Californios believed that with British or French protection they could defend themselves against both Mexico and a possible seizure by the Americans.

Micheltorena and the convicts fled California with the revolt of 1844; subsequently, Mexican forces met defeat at Cahuenga pass, just north of Los Angeles. Pio Pico, with his capital in Los Angeles, became governor. California might have declared itself independent at that moment except for the failure to arrange with a European power for protection. The American threat appeared too great to take the risk. Under the circumstances, California reluctantly and theoretically remained in the Mexican republic. With the war between the United States and Mexico, the Californios made an effort to resist the American invaders. Governor Pio Pico attempted to rally a defense and had some limited success. After the war, the treaty transferring the region to American sovereignty caused great bitterness. As one Californio put it, a feeling of "revulsion. . .toward Mexico" swept the dismayed population who felt they "had been sold. . . ."[3]

Mexico at War

In the United States, the movement toward annexation of Texas gained rapid support. Many politicians openly proclaimed annexation of Texas as the first step toward the acquisition of Mexico's entire northern region. Negative stereotypes suggested that a rich but squandered region peopled by an indolent and unworthy population awaited rescue. Richard Henry Dana, in his classic *Two Years Before the Mast* (1846), wrote of "California Fever," allegedly a laziness so pervasive that it constituted an endemic disease. He evoked an apocryphal gravestone that read, "Here lies Juan Espinosa. Never did he do anything else." Dana implied that unlocking the untold riches of Mexico's northern territories awaited the Yankee touch.[4] In 1844, James K. Polk, a solid advocate of expansion, won the presidency of the United States. War became inevitable—it remained only for Polk to find a suitable pretext. In May 1846, news arrived at the White House that a skirmish had occurred with Mexican forces in what is now the state of Texas—the war was on.

In Mexico, politics could not be laid aside, even in the face of an impending national disaster. General Mariano Paredes, ordered to the border to defend the nation, instead installed himself as president, only to be overthrown by the army. Santa Anna again was called back to save the republic. To unite the country, he declared the restoration of the Federal Constitution of 1824. Meanwhile, Mexico's underpopulated northern provinces fell into American hands without much struggle. The war itself shed little glory on either side. American general and subsequently president, Zachary Taylor, known as "Old Rough and Ready," was rough, but seldom ready. Doubt remains about whether he won the battle of Buena Vista that made him a household name. As luck would have it, his opponent, General Santa Anna, captured a few American battle standards, concluded he had won, and left for Mexico City to receive the public's acclaim. Taylor, now alone on the field of battle, leapt to the most agreeable conclusion, that he had gloriously defeated the Mexican forces. The battle of Buena Vista (1846) became a question of interpretation by two opposing egos. In contrast, as the theater of battle shifted to central Mexico, General Winfield Scott provided competent leadership. He planned and executed the amphibious landing by combining army and marine troops at Veracruz, handed Santa Anna another defeat at Cerro Gordo, and used engineers (including Robert E. Lee) to open the route to the Mexican capital.[5] Scott, also a man of tremendous egotism, hoped to become president, but lost out to Taylor in the race for glory.

The final battle for Mexico City required a series of pitched battles and considerable loss of life. At Chapultepec Castle, the Mexican defenders, including military cadets, would become an enduring and partly mythical symbol of patriotic valor and self-sacrifice. The war with Mexico proved to be one of the deadliest for American soldiers, with a mortality rate of 153.5 per 1,000 compared to 98 per 1,000 subsequently experienced by the Union during the Civil War. Disease, poor equipment, inadequate supplies, mismanagement, and the enemy extracted a terrible toll. The war could have as easily been lost as won. Many victories seemed more like narrow escapes.[6]

Both sides sought to subvert the other with limited success. When war broke out, the Mexican government appealed to foreign immigrants in the United States to assist Catholic Mexico in its struggle with the Protestant United States. In case such a cynical appeal fell on unsympathetic ears, the government also offered free land and other possible rewards. While few responded, the Mexican army organized several companies composed of foreign residents in Mexico and deserters from the American army into units collectively known as the San Patricios (St. Patricks). John Riley, a deserter from the 5th United States Infantry, probably suggested the name. The invocation of St. Patrick and the number of Irishmen who served in the unit led to the erroneous notion that Catholic soldiers in the United States Army were prone to join their coreligionists on the other side. In fact, Protestants deserted just as readily, nor did one have to be a deserter to join the San Patricios. Scotsmen such as James Humphrey and Lachlan McLachlen served Mexico in the unit as did Germans and other nationalities. With the American victory most of the deserters who had joined the San Patricios were executed, while the others became simple prisoners of war.

In a similar fashion, the United States attempted to recruit Mexican irregulars to harass and control troublesome guerrilla bands, as well as to function as scouts. Manuel Domínguez, a suspected bandit with some 200 men, served with the American army. Ulysses S. Grant, then a junior supply officer, relied upon Domínguez's Raiders to indicate resupply routes. After the war, Colonel Domínguez moved to Texas and eventually ended up in New Orleans, all but forgotten by the American army.

An almost predictable consequence of the war and its aftermath was banditry. Deserters and a number of soldiers from both armies took to robbing Mexicans and Americans with greedy impartiality. Ten Americans stormed the house of a well-to-do Puebla woman, stripped the place, and threatened to rape the victim. Another gang allegedly consisting of an American army officer and two enlisted men robbed an American merchant of $3,000. Similarly, Mexican deserters and soldiers roamed the countryside terrorizing the luckless population. The line between war and banditry blurred easily. In the end, however, stories of valor and patriotic sacrifice by both sides pushed the mixed reality of war into the more acceptable realm of heroic mythology. In 1974, the Mexican government erected a monument in San Angel in honor of the San Patricios, thereby securing their place in history and myth.[7]

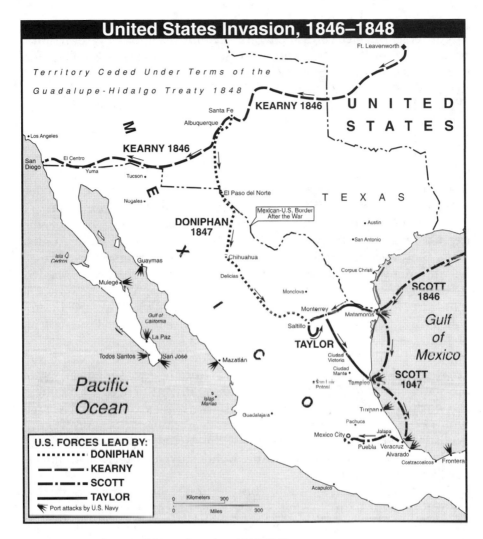

Figure 2.1 United States Invasion, 1846–1848.

Forced to endure an occupation army, and without much choice, Mexico signed the treaty of Guadalupe Hidalgo that ceded half of the national territory, a region encompassing present-day California, Nevada, Utah, Arizona, New Mexico, Texas (technically outside the treaty because it became independent in 1836), most of Colorado, and parts of Wyoming, Kansas, and Oklahoma. Not all of the territorial ambitions of the United States would be satisfied by the treaty. California, considered one territorial entity by the defeated republic, would be divided into two parts with Baja (lower) California and its vital land bridge to Sonora remaining in Mexican hands. American naval forces in fact controlled Baja California and only reluctantly withdrew after the treaty went into effect. Acquisition of Baja California and access to the Sea of Cortés by the inland territories of what are now the states of Arizona and New Mexico remained an objective. While Mexico regained its sovereignty with the Treaty of Guadalupe Hidalgo, the threat remained.[8]

THE NORTH UNDER AMERICAN RULE

Mexicans in the former northern provinces, approximately 50,000 across the region, remained under a guarantee of civil protection. In parts of the newly acquired lands, Americans assumed control and capitals were transferred to areas of high concentrations of Anglos. Thus San Antonio lost out to Austin, Sacramento replaced Los Angeles and Monterey, California, while Phoenix in western New Mexico, made a separate territory in 1863, became Arizona's seat of government. In New Mexico, designated a territory in 1850, American officials appointed Nuevomexicanos to public office because of the paucity of American settlers and accepted Santa Fe as the region's capital. Nuevomexicano Miguel Antonio Otero served as New Mexico's congressional delegate from 1855 to 1861. Otero had attended college in Missouri and New York and was undoubtedly influenced by business ties with Missouri merchants involved in the Mexican trade through Santa Fe. Subsequently, he married into a prominent Southern family, eventually becoming vice president of the Atchison Topeka and Santa Fe Railroad. His son with the same name served as territorial governor from 1897 to 1906.

At least as late as 1859, the territorial legislature conducted all of its business in Spanish. After New Mexico became a state in 1912, the legislature made New Mexico into a bilingual state for all official purposes. The continued foreign aspect of the territory annoyed many Americans. Chicago's major newspaper, the *Chicago Tribune,* complained (1889) that the region's population was not American but "greaser." It is obvious that Nuevomexicanos became adept at American-style politics at both the local and national levels.[9]

The Otero family strongly supported statehood for New Mexico apart from Arizona, which was dominated by Anglos. Governor Otero, a friend of President McKinley, energetically backed the Spanish–American war effort. Spanish-speaking Nuevomexicanos formed an important part of Teddy Roosevelt's Rough Riders. Nuevomexicanos managed to hold onto substantial political power, in part because the region did not experience the unsettling economic boom that hit Texas and California. Consequently, Americanization proceeded at a slower rate than in other parts of the formerly Mexican territory. Nevertheless, violent conflicts occurred, particularly when Anglo cattlemen pushed west confronting the territory's sheepherders. The Lincoln County War (1876–1878) combined economic and racial tensions. In some sections of New Mexico, Anglos attempted to annex themselves to Texas or Arizona to escape what they viewed as political domination by Nuevomexicanos.[10] Many small settlements, remote from the cultural center of Mexico City as well as from American cities, remained isolated. They retained their own unique local culture at the expense of isolation and remained unconcerned with full economic and political participation in the new society.

In a manner evocative of Spain's evangelization effort in the aftermath of the conquest of Indian Mexico in the sixteenth century, American culture entered New Mexico along with missionaries. The Catholic hierarchy in the United States viewed New Mexico as a mission field and continued to do so into the twentieth century. Jean Baptiste Lamy became Vicar Apostolic of New Mexico in 1850, and three years later, Bishop of Santa Fe, under the Archbishop of St. Louis. Lamy brought in clerics and over time succeeded in revitalizing the Church in the territory. The Jesuits established schools in Albuquerque and elsewhere, and the Christian Brothers organized St. Michaels College (1859) for boys in Santa Fe. Schools for girls opened under the supervision of the Sisters of Charity and the Sisters of Lorreto.

American culture entered many isolated areas with earnest Protestant missionaries intent on redeeming the people from what they viewed as their priest-ridden ignorance. Early accounts of Protestant preachers indicate that they had little understanding or respect for what they perceived to be a "benighted" population huddled together in physical squalor, poverty, and illiteracy. Bringing a message of individual self-help, Protestant evangelists underestimated the overriding importance of the community on the frontier in a harsh and ungiving land. The sharp differences between nineteenth-century American culture, with its emphasis on individual advancement, if necessary, even at the expense of family and community, and the survival-oriented regional culture could not easily be accommodated. Subsequent missionaries learned to respect the attachment to the community as they became more familiar with New Mexican culture. Protestant missionaries established the first schools in many remote pueblos, hoping that education eventually would lead the enlightened into their churches—they experienced a bitter disappointment. Nuevomexicanos took grateful advantage of the schools, but did not rush to abandon their spiritual beliefs, so deeply grounded in the region's unique culture.[11]

Even when California and the territory of New Mexico began to attract a new wave of immigrants from Mexico, the old provincial inhabitants often preferred to see themselves as unique. Later Mexican immigrants arrived in a much different context with other interests, drawn into the region by economic objectives. An estimated 90,000 Mexicans entered the region between 1850 and 1900. The California gold rush of 1849 represented the first of what would soon be a series of pull factors for Mexican workers into the United States. San Francisco witnessed the arrival of some 8,000 Mexicans in 1849. Immigrants, attracted by gold fever, overwhelmed the Californios, who numbered only 15,000 in 1850. While many Mexicans returned home for various reasons, including ethnic violence in the gold fields, and the xenophobic Foreign Miners Tax (1850) aimed at Mexicans in particular, the newcomers abruptly changed the demographic and cultural character of California.[12]

In the state of Texas, the Tejano population not only retained significant influence, but continued to flourish. They constituted a cultural, political, and economic bridge between Mexico and the United States, despite racism and the narrow ethnicity of the new settlers flooding in from other regions of the northern republic. Tejanos held on to a sense of place without a psychological retreat into isolation. Texas, because it served as the main contact point between the two republics, encouraged them to be Mexicans as well as Americans—a reality that made them interested in the politics and economic possibilities of both countries. Tejanos developed a usable understanding of American culture. Even before the war, José María Sánchez, a Mexican official, reported in 1828 that the inhabitants of Texas had "accustomed themselves to north Americans."[13] Clearly, the process of biculturation antedated incorporation.

In the latter half of the century, Tejanos continued to support and reinforce their culture through benevolent societies such as the Sociedad México-Tejano, Sociedad Benito Juárez, and others. Many organizations functioned under constitutions written in both English and Spanish. Newspapers in Spanish thrived among the Tejano population and reflected their interest in both cultures. A notable example of biculturalism is provided by José Antonio Navarro. A signer of the Texas Declaration of Independence in 1836, Navarro's son Angel attended Harvard University in the 1840s, and several sons subsequently fought for the Confederacy. While fully involved in the broader society, José Antonio Navarro remained a Tejano.

South Texas provided a cultural and economic base for Tejanos. Hipólito García Randado's 80,000-acre ranch sold cattle to buyers as distant as Indian territory (Oklahoma). The village of Randado, with a population of 300, had a post office and a school that required fluency in both languages. Ramón Guerra and José Salinas traded in $20,000 worth of horses imported from Mexico each season. In the Laredo area, Darío Sánchez imported cattle, dogs, and chickens from Kentucky to sell in Mexico. Judge José María Rodríguez shipped cattle north to Chicago. Rodríguez (1828–1912), a well-educated individual fluent in French, English, and Spanish, attended school in New Orleans. He served also as a Webb County judge for thirty-five years. Judge Rodríguez's influence touched every aspect of life on the border. Manuel Guerra became one of the most successful border merchants, establishing stores throughout the region and traveling as far away as New York for merchandise. In a similar fashion, Francisco Tovar of San Diego (Duval County) bought stock in Galveston and New Orleans.[14]

Tejanos also maintained a vigorous presence in the professions, from physicians to teachers. Public school teacher Luis Puebla of San Diego prepared for his chosen profession at Georgetown University in Washington, D.C. Benavides Francisco Carrillo, a graduate of the Mexican military school and subsequently a veteran of fighting against Porfirio Díaz, instructed Tejano pupils. Along the border, many Tejanos enforced the law. Sheriff Santiago Breto of Cameron County became a regional hero, universally admired for his sense of justice as well as for his efficiency. Tejano Protestant preachers played a role in blurring the religious divisions between the population's Catholic culture and the beliefs of many of the Anglo-Texans. The reverends Arturo Castro and J. J. Mercado served as evangelical leaders in the latter part of the century. In Bandera, the Mexican Methodist Church featured sermons by clergymen in Spanish and English. While most Tejanos and Mexicans along the border remained Catholics, Spanish-speaking preachers made the point that religion did not present an impenetrable barrier between the two cultures.

Nevertheless, Catholic priests warned their parishioners that Protestant missionaries threatened both their religion and Mexican culture. Resistance to Protestant missionary activities took the form of avoiding contact and on occasion, violence. A Methodist preacher who addressed an outdoor meeting (1893) struggled to ignore stones and clods of dirt tossed into the crowd. Protestant groups understood that the charge that their beliefs undermined Mexican culture had some validity and could only be countered by recruiting Mexican preachers. The Reverend Dr. Ward at the Northwest Mexican Conference of the Southern Methodist Church meeting in El Paso in 1906 observed that Protestant nations represented the highest level of civilized prosperity; thus Protestant redemptive activities had an important economic and social component capable of elevating the individual Mexican out of poverty and social misery. The antielitism and social leveling message of Protestant preachers, combined with useful social services and self-help, gave them an influence that extended beyond their own immediate converts. While Dr. Ward noted that Mexico needed a Martin Luther, he emphasized that he "must be a Mexican."[15]

Celebrations and folktales reflected biculturalism as well as a healthy pride in Texas. Attachment to place is evident in a Tejano adaption of the folktale of Pedro de Urdemales. As a man of worldly excesses, Pedro arrived in hell. Full of the glories of his state, he soon convinced the devil to see for himself. A series of unfortunate and painful encounters with chili peppers, cactus, and an aggressive cow sent the devil back to his kingdom, where he angrily expelled Pedro, who returned to resume his old ways.[16]

Civic celebrations revolved around social clubs that provided the organizational structure and planning. Clubs such as the upper class Casino Club of Río Grande included non-Tejano members as did Laredo's Hidalgo-Washington Club (1887). Less exalted groups, for example Los Mexicanos Tejanos, proudly did not include Anglo-Texans. Texans observed the national holidays of both nations. Mexican independence day demonstrated the level of cultural fusion. American and Mexican flags followed by colorful bands and floats moved through enthusiastic crowds. Marchers included labor, political and social groups, and schoolchildren, with music provided by the United States Cavalry. At the appropriate hour, an official shouted the "grito" of Hidalgo and read the Mexican Declaration of Independence. While the crowd shouted "¡Viva México!" a battery of United States Army artillery fired a twenty-one-gun salute. Speeches in Spanish and English ended the formal observation of the holiday.

The music that independence day revelers listened to or danced to reflected biculturalism. Corridos addressed subjects and events drawn from both sides of the border, including one that recorded the exploits of General Ulysses S. Grant.[17] Tejano musicians incorporated the accordion, introduced by European immigrants, to form the distinctive *conjunto,* while also performing mariachi music, another synthesis, in this case, traditional central Mexican forms along with French-valved trumpet music. Mariachi bands combined strings with modern brass instruments. European band masters during the French intervention encouraged experimentation that mixed Mexican and European forms and techniques. Mexican musicians created the most pleasing synthesis. The new valved wind instruments gave the music its distinctive sound. Mariachi and conjunto music developed contemporaneously, each strongly associated with a particular regional culture. Because of the political importance of the south-center, mariachi music has come to symbolize the spirit of Mexico. To northerners it represents a tie with the nation. Nevertheless, the soul of the northern borderlander responds to the conjunto. Conjunto music provided an important element of social cohesion among Tejanos, as it continues to do so in south Texas today.

The city of San Antonio emerged as the informal Tejano capital, although Anglo-Texans constituted the majority. Mexican visitors favored the city, and it became a convenient and relatively comfortable place for political exiles to regroup before returning to the struggle. The Tejano ambiance of San Antonio remains one of its charms. Aptly named chili queens, who presided over popular chili stands, became a notable feature of the city in the last half of the nineteenth century. Set up in the evening after the regular markets had closed, with huge pots of steaming chili con carne, the stands offered a generous meal that included beans and tortillas, all for ten cents. Wandering musicians provided entertainment. Over the years, adjustments accommodated the tastes of the many Anglo-Texans, resulting in what is referred to today as Tex-Mex food.[18]

While Tejanos preserved and demonstrated their cultural vitality, they often did so in the face of racism, hostility, and, on more than a number of occasions, violence. The new settlers arriving from other parts of the United States had little to guide them in establishing relationships with the Tejanos, other than negative stereotypes and cultural myths. Referred to as greasers or dismissed as only semi-acculturated Indians, the Tejanos labored within a society that saw progress as an activity only of the English-speaking majority. Anglo-Texans not only governed the state, but also wrote its history. Predictably, their own heroic virtues benefitted greatly from a comparison with the alleged vicious depravity of vice-ridden Mexicans. Texas hispanophobia, with its poisonous anti-Mexican core, remained destructively, even dangerously, violent well into the latter half of the twentieth century.[19]

In the face of a hostile ignorance, the Tejanos took what they needed, contributed to the broad community, and refused to retreat from the new society. Texans of all origins blended cultures in a unique and positive manner in spite of themselves or socioeconomic obstacles. The importance of Texas as a bridge between the two republics became evident well before the turn of the century, and it remains important today. As an observer noted in the late 1860s, the Río Grande represented only a political boundary; the actual melding of cultures began farther north in San Antonio's central plaza. Almost half a century later, writer Neven O. Winter, traveling by rail in 1906 to gather material for his book on Porfirian progress, perceptively observed that Mexico began in Texas long before one crossed the actual border. He reported that San Antonio appeared to be "a Spanish city modernized." Tejano ties with Mexico had not been severed, but continued to flourish in the new hybrid environment of the state of Texas.[20]

POSTWAR MEXICO

For Mexico the military occupation and the massive loss of territory, even if underpopulated and only weakly incorporated into the republic, were traumatic. The central issue for thoughtful Mexicans was whether a weak, disorganized, and prostrate nation could survive as an independent sovereign entity. The loss of the republic's northern expanse physically and psychologically stripped away the buffer zone that previously separated the nation from its northern neighbor. The international border had advanced dramatically to within striking distance of the Mexican heartland. Few assumed the new border to be permanent. Having moved once, could it not do so again and again, eventually extinguishing the country's sovereignty? Establishment of a permanent boundary might well require the transfer of additional territory to another party, not necessarily the United States. Much as the legendary Siberian sled driver cutting off one horse at a time to keep the ravenous wolves from overtaking him, Mexico prepared to preserve its essence. The grim reality resulted in contingency acceptance of the possible need to sell or deal off additional parts of the northern region to preserve the real Mexico. Northerners, as will be noted shortly, did not appreciate such an attitude.

Both liberals and conservatives reluctantly concluded that Mexico must seek some sort of protective arrangement, possibly with France, Britain, Spain, or the United States. Liberal antipathy to the notion of a monarchy forced them to consider how best to manipulate an arrangement with the United States, without being annexed. Pragmatic liberals attempted to pull survival as well as progress from the cannon's mouth. Even before the end of the American military occupation, liberals, with the backing of the occupation authorities, used the municipal council of Mexico City to launch local reforms. Miguel Lerdo de Tejada and other liberals came very close to crossing the line between self-interested cooperation and collaboration. They viewed the country's plight with a grim analytical intensity that avoided the emotional trap of a reactionary anti-Americanism. Their clinical attitude is exemplified by José María Mata, who became the principal framer of the liberal Constitution of 1857. Captured at the battle of Cerro Gordo in 1847, he refused a conditional parole, choosing instead to go to New Orleans as a prisoner of war. He returned to his native country deeply impressed with the United States.[21] A deep pessimism in the nation's ability to survive without a radical restructuring of its institutions at every level underlay the attitude of postwar liberals and conservatives. Pessimism motivated the search for a suitable model. In effect, the liberals decided to ride on the back of the American tiger.

In contrast, the conservatives believed that only an alliance with a European monarchy would provide the necessary protection from an expansionist United States. To entice a suitor, Mexico's economic potential could be dangled before appropriate candidates. Economic concessions and promises constituted Mexico's one card to play if it were to survive. Santa Anna's return to power from exile in 1853, meanwhile, would rally the country and provide a breathing spell in which to deal with the grim reality. One of the most powerful and intelligent conservatives, Lucas Alamán, hoped to direct the government from behind the scenes, while liberal theorist Miguel Lerdo de Tejada drew up an economic strategy for the new regime.

Lerdo saw the urgent task of *regeneración* as one of economics more than politics. The lower classes, unable to comprehend the problem, could not provide a solution, so the task fell to an enlightened elite. He posited the notion that political instability and revolts resulted from the frustrating inability of the working classes to obtain material advantages through productive work. They had to be given the means and skills to do so if the country was to continue to exist. On Lerdo's recommendation, a new Ministry of Development (Fomento) was established in 1853, which constituted both a political and an economic act. A major part of Lerdo's economic strategy as a high officer in Fomento involved the colonization of underpopulated stretches of the country with European immigrants. Foreign immigration appeared to be an urgent necessity. The widespread belief that a nation exercised power in direct proportion to the size of its population seemed evident after the country's military defeat by the United States. Adding to a sense of urgency was the notion that Mexico possessed fabulous but untapped wealth that could not be defended or exploited by its inadequate population. The Directorate of Colonization asserted that the country had only a tenth of the population it needed and could support. Thus, Mexico's population of an estimated seven million around 1850 had to grow to seventy million to become economically effective. Observers noted that while New York received some 500,000 immigrants a year, only a relative handful arrived in Mexico, allegedly accounting for the prosperity of the United States and the backwardness of Mexico. Antiforeign sentiment in the United States in the 1850s seemed like an opportunity for Mexico, and Mexican agents in Europe and the United States did their best to lure immigrants. Attempts to divert the flow of European immigrants from the United States to Mexico never succeeded. In 1852, an estimated

5,412 foreigners resided in the republic, most of them in the capital.[22] In spite of obvious problems, the goal of attracting an influx of productive foreigners as a panacea persisted into the 1890s.

During Santa Anna's national unity regime the world seemed a nightmarish one filled with vicious foreign predators. Recovery from the disastrous defeat and subsequent American occupation posed psychological obstacles, including acceptance, regaining confidence, and managing an understandable apprehension that yet another disaster might engulf the nation. Santa Anna instinctively understood the political utility of patriotic ritual. In an inspired attempt to rally the Mexican people, he invited Catalán composer Jaime Nuño to come to Mexico as the Inspector General of Military Bands. Santa Anna had encountered the powerful emotional impact of modern band music at a concert given by Nuño in Havana. In Mexico, Nuño composed the Mexican national anthem, organized some 230 military bands throughout the republic, and in general helped restore the battered spirit of the country. Liberal generals such as Porfirio Díaz quickly organized and equipped their own military musicians with valved wind instruments. Brass bands soon became a standard feature of political rallies. Villages throughout Mexico organized bands to instill a sense of command, pride, and social cohesion.[23] President Santa Anna, although often ridiculed for his love of ceremony, in fact understood the power of ritual and ceremony in providing a surge of emotional energy during difficult times. General Santa Anna realized also that loud, stirring music alone was not enough. Consequently, President Santa Anna requested the Prussian representative Baron Von Richthofen to arrange for five or six thousand Prussian soldiers to help train the Mexican Army. Prussia declined the request.

France, on the other hand, indicated some interest. Unfortunately, France saw its possible role in Mexico as that of a predator rather than a protector. With the tacit approval of the French government, adventurer Count Gaston Roausset de Bourbon, along with some 200 Frenchmen recruited in San Francisco, embarked on a filibuster expedition to Sonora, only to be defeated by Mexican forces at Guaymas in July 1854. Another French expedition, under Jean Napoleon Zerman, sailed from San Francisco in October 1855 and ended up imprisoned in La Paz at the tip of Baja California. Some 1,400 Frenchmen lived in Mexico, and as a result Paris understood the economic possibilities of some sort of association with the besieged republic.[24]

United States expansionist pressure posed the immediate threat. President Franklin Pierce faced a crisis over the actual border between the New Mexico territory and the Mexican state of Chihuahua. Imprecise language in the treaty of Guadalupe Hidalgo left ownership of the Mesilla Valley uncertain. Officials constantly clashed over the area, especially as American settlers moved into the valley. As a further complication, railroad interests claimed that the peace treaty had left the route for a southern railway line to the west coast on the wrong side of the border. Supposedly the best route for a railway from New Orleans to California lay in Mexican territory. The future of American trade with Asia seemed at risk, at least for the American South.

In a similar fashion, access and control over the Isthmus of Tehauntepec engaged the fancy of American interests. New Orlean's *De Bow's Commercial Review* asserted that a Tehuantepec railway constituted a major part of a comprehensive program to make the port of New Orleans a leader in international trade. Southern interests intent on reducing the dominance of northern economic power in the region saw Mexico and Latin America as their best hope. Southern railroad promoter James Gadsden thought in grand terms. He envisioned a plan in which Florida, fortified by the acquisition of Cuba and Yucatán, would provide a base to drive the British out of the West Indies, turning the Gulf of Mexico into an American lake and placing the Caribbean trade in Southern hands. Reducing British commercial advantages in the hemisphere appealed to both the North and the South. Senator Robert Toombs of Georgia and Senator Henry Wilson of Massachusetts agreed that "our India is south of us in this continent." President Pierce found it difficult to keep ahead of such expansionist pressure. The filibustering activities of William Walker in Baja California (1853–1854) added further complications.

Given the South's preoccupation with Mexico, American sectional politics invariably had an impact on Mexico. Because the Southern wing of the democratic party needed to be placated, Jefferson Davis became a cabinet member and James Gadsden of South Carolina became United States representative to Mexico. Gadsden had opposed the acquisition of the entire country after the war, on the grounds that Mexico's population could not be culturally or socially absorbed. Thus he appeared to be at least committed to the existence of an independent Mexico of some undetermined size. The underpopulated expanses of northern Mexico were a different matter. Gadsden arrived in Mexico City in August 1853. After Santa Anna agreed to consider a new boundary treaty to settle the Mesilla Valley issue, the actual amount of territory to be acquired in the north became subject to negotiation. The United States saw a natural boundary that took in all of Baja California, most of Coahuila and Nuevo León, half of Tamaulipas, Chihuahua, and Sonora, and a small section of Durango, an arrangement that gave the United States a major port on the Gulf of California.[25]

Santa Anna moved to shore up Mexico's bargaining position by proposing an alliance with Spain and authorizing his agents to identify sources of mercenary soldiers. He also advised the British that the United States threatened war unless the country agreed to sell territory. It was pointed out that if Mexico was annexed, British economic interest could not be sustained. Both Spain and Britain could not be drawn into the desperate game. Fortunately for Mexico, the proposed treaty would be defeated in the clash of interests in the U.S. Senate. The Gadsden Purchase as ratified included the disputed valley that now forms southern Arizona and New Mexico. In return, Mexico received ten million dollars. Santa Anna later maintained that by selling the area he had forestalled the United States from seizing all of the northern states. The image of a beleaguered Mexico throwing a hunk of meat to the wolf is unescapable.

Some important economic developments occurred during the Santa Anna regime (1853–1855). Miguel Lerdo as the *official mayor* of the Ministry of Development arranged a number of railway concessions. The Mexican government granted railway contracts to construct a line from Veracruz through Mexico City to the Pacific coast. Other grants tied in Tampico, Puebla, Manzanillo, and Guaymas. In the capital, a planned tramway linking the Villa de Guadalupe with the city began actual operations on July 4, 1857. Hungarian American promoter Gabor Naphegyi constructed a gas lighting system for the port city of Veracruz. While little rail construction occurred during the Santa Anna regime, the basic terms and objectives of the government in granting concessions would be worked out. Companies accepting contracts had to agree to be subject to Mexican law as national entities. Any attempt to claim foreign protection nullified the concession. Duty-free importing of material and other exemptions were granted. In some cases the government shared earnings, and at the end of an agreed-upon period, the lines and their assets reverted to the nation. Lerdo subsequently urged the government to grant generous subsidies and free land to harness the "greediness of speculators" in the national interest.[26] During this period, the Pacific ports of Mazatlán, Guaymas, San Blas, La Paz, and Manzanillo developed close ties with the San Francisco market as a result of demands created by the gold rush in the decade of the 1850s. Mazatlán became a major port as well as a stopover point for vessels bound from Panama to San Francisco. Food, clothing, and mining supplies of all kinds passed through the ports on the way to the gold fields. The future pattern of economic reliance on the American market first became evident along the Pacific Coast and its northern interior.[27]

Cooperation between some prominent liberals and conservatives within the framework of Santa Anna's national unity regime resulted

The Expansion of the United States, 1790–1853

Treaty Line of 1846

Red River Basin Ceded by Britain 1818

Oregon Country 1846

Spanish Treaty Line of 1819

Mexican Cession 1848

Louisiana Purchase 1803

Extent of United States 1790

Gadsden Purchase La Mesilla Treaty 1853

Texas Annexation

Republic of Texas 1836–1845

Florida Cession from Spain 1819

Miss. Terr. 1798

Spanish Treaty Line of 1819

Originally Held by Spain and/or Mexico

Figure 2.2 The Expansion of the United States, 1790–1853.

in setting important developmental goals that would not bear evident fruit immediately. To outside observers, Mexico City remained a provincial place, exotic to be sure, but linked to the past. Visitors found it interesting, if uncomfortably primitive. Robbers, pickpockets, and those given to undesirable behavior appeared to abound. The police force seemed constantly involved in rounding up drunken citizens and dealing with a "plague of 6,048 dogs." *Leperos,* marginally employed or vagrant, filled the plazas. Foreigners with refined tastes complained about the lack of suitable dining establishments, not to mention the table manners of the clientele. A frustrated gourmet reported that after a meal diners drank a mug of water, crossed themselves, intoned "God be praised," and then allowed their "stomachic gas to explode."[28]

Sundays and holidays provided the occasion for bullfights, often attended by Santa Anna and other officials. The old eighteenth-century San Pablo ring had earlier presented the young impressionable Santa Anna with the formative experience of observing the ring littered with seventeen horses and one picador dead in the sand. A new ring, the Plaza del Paseo, built in 1851, included 272 luxury boxes as well as more modest seating. Clowns, acrobats, and jugglers entertained street crowds. Cockfights attracted avid fans, including the president. Santa Anna, who relished public ceremonies and showy events, moved in tune with the times and general social expectations. Even his often bizarre sense of ceremony did not appear to be totally outrageous, except to foreigners. Underneath it all, the modernization process, still in its nascent stage, was overlooked.

POSTWAR CONTEMPLATION IN THE UNITED STATES

In the United States, the war and its aftermath proved equally important, although tinged with euphoria rather than trauma. It brought both countries face to face for the first time. James Fenimore Cooper, one of the century's most popular American novelists, believed that Mexico would eventually rejoice in the war because, "If the crust which has so long encircled the nation [Mexico], enclosing it in bigotry and ignorance, shall now be irretrievably broken letting in the light," disaster could become its salvation. Bigotry and ignorance of course lay on both sides of that imaginary crust. Both nations had a lot to learn about each other, although Mexicans may have had a better understanding of their neighbor than Americans had of Mexico. United States observers, military, consular, and private, dispatched reports on all aspects of Mexican life and economic activity. Specimens of plants, animals, and birds arrived at the newly established Smithsonian Institution. The American Ethnological Society, also recently founded, published an important series of articles on Mexico's ancient civilizations. Ephraim G. Squier, a leading ethnoarchaeologist, noted that the war indirectly had contributed to "enlighten us." Squier subsequently investigated the connection between Mesoamerica's ancient inhabitants and those of the now–American Southwest using linguistic and archaeological techniques, suggesting a prehistoric and historic unity of the transborder region.

National confidence in the still young and insecure United States received an invigorating jolt. The Mexican war represented the first American war fought on foreign soil. The fact that the United States had defeated a supposedly well-disciplined and trained army with a motley assortment of backwoods volunteers led to many overblown statements regarding the amazing inner strength of American democracy. To the country's delight, even foreigners professed respect and wonderment. An aged Baron Alexander von Humboldt, who had long before predicted a brilliant future for preindependent Mexico, remarked to an American visitor to Potsdam that all Prussia could talk of little else besides Taylor and his victorious army. American pride evident in innumerable books and pamphlets spilled over into advertising of every conceivable item. Port and Lemon's Manhattan Fresh

Milled Effulgent Horse-Radish Sauce sported a new label complete with "old glory" and the motto "Rough and Ready . . . Our Country, Horse-Radish and Liberty." Those less commercial and more pessimistic wondered whether the deal was advantageous after all. Perhaps the United States had senselessly paid fifteen million dollars for California's "impenetrable mountains and dry narrow valleys" and "utterly uninhabitable" New Mexico—a land fit for savages and desperados to be maintained only at great expense to the national treasury.[29] The more reflective pondered whether the acquisition of Mexican territory would exacerbate sectional differences between slave and free states. The Gadsden Purchase transferred yet another group of Mexicans to the United States, as well as territory. It also changed the nature of the western part of the territory of New Mexico (Arizona) that up to that time did not have much of a Mexican population. The same process of transculturalization that had occurred earlier in south Texas began in what is now southern Arizona. As in Texas, the struggle would be difficult, but eventually Tucson and its variation of border culture became a prized element of Arizona's heritage. Americans viewed themselves as superior. In 1858, Phocion R. Way described Tucson to his sister as a place where Anglos monopolized business and politics and where the women fancied Americans while "a greaser stands no chance with a white man." Phoenicians dismissed Tucson as just a "little Mexican town" until the railroad changed that view in 1880. Prior to the coming of the railroad, intermarriage blurred cultural differences. After 1880, the newcomers tended to remain apart from the Tucsonenses.[30] In Tucson, people of Mexican heritage took pride in their origins. When Mexico's development became obvious in the latter decades of the century, they pointedly emphasized the progress of their people. Leaders such as Carlos Velasco, through the Spanish-language press, urged those of Mexican origin to immigrate to Mexico and to participate in the construction of the "new" Mexico.

During the 1890s, Tucson's emergent Mexican-American middle class forced an end to the secular fiestas of San Agustín that featured gambling and drinking bouts in honor of Tucson's patron saint and focused celebratory attention on Mexico's Independence Day. By doing so, they reaffirmed their ethnic heritage while demonstrating also that they possessed the same moral values as their Anglo compatriots. Independence festivities included the reenactment of Hidalgo's *grito,* a twenty-one-gun salute, fireworks, and the most popular event, a parade that featured a triumphal float carrying thirty young women, who represented Mexico's twenty-seven states, "America," "Liberty," and "Justice." Tucson's annual Mexican Independence Day event emphasized standard middle-class values and binational patriotism and confirmed then-current social roles, with women assuming primarily decorative roles on floats and preparing fiesta foods.

The cultural struggle for acceptance and respect had overcome the threat earlier posed in 1885 when Tucson's representative to the territorial legislature proposed a statue abolishing all Mexican fiestas in Arizona. The bill, hotly debated, eventually lost. Mexican Americans in the region demonstrated their belief that Mexican culture, as a result of the achievements of Hidalgo, Juàrez, and Díaz, possessed the same liberal, republican, and moral value as that of the United States. Independence Day celebrations also reassured them that they could combine their ethnic heritage with American culture. They convinced Anglos that an acceptable accommodation between the cultures could be achieved without destroying Mexican traditions. Tucsonenses successfully rallied their intellectual, cultural, and political forces to protect themselves. Some forty-six prominent Hispanics founded the Alianza Hispano-Americana in Tucson on January 14, 1894, an important forerunner of the more militant Mexican-American organizations established after World War II. Early protective and fraternal organizations included the Liga Protectora Latina, the Club Unión, and others. These organizations insisted upon the right of Hispanics to be treated with respect. Their success represented yet another triumph for the malleable, resilient border culture.[31] The Gadsden Purchase added the connecting link that socially and geographically united the border as a distinct region from the Gulf of Mexico to the Pacific Ocean. This development could not have been foreseen by Santa Anna and a desperate nation at the time of the transaction, nor by those in distant Washington. A buffer zone

Figure 2.3 Delivering water around 1910 to a border home. *Printed with permission, Photography Collection, Harry Ransom, Humanities Research Center, University of Texas at Austin.*

with its own internal dynamics began to emerge, marking the high tide of American territorial expansion and creating a hybrid culture that occupied the attention of and, on many occasions, aggravated both republics. The almost 2,000-mile border that now divided the United States and Mexico soon evolved into a distant economic and social region sandwiched between the two republics.

NOTES

1. Evelia Trejo, "Consideraciones sobre el factor religioso en la pérdida del territorio de Texas, 1821–1835," *Estudios de historia moderna y contemporánea de México* (no. 13, 1990), pp. 47–60.

2. David J. Weber, *The Mexican Frontier, 1821–1846: The American Southwest Under Mexico* (Albuquerque: University of New Mexico Press, 1982), p. 265.

3. Ibid.

4. Quoted in David J. Weber, *Myth and the History of the Hispanic Southwest* (Albuquerque: University of New Mexico Press, 1988), p. 162.

5. Josefina Vázquez de Knauth, *Mexicanos y norteamericanos ante la Guerra del 47* (México: Secretaría de Educación Pública, 1972); John S. D. Eisenhower, *So Far from God: The U.S. War with Mexico, 1846–1848* (New York: Random House, 1989).

6. Douglas Richmond, ed., *Essays on the Mexican War* (College Station: Texas A&M University Press, 1986), p. 35.

7. Dennis J. Wynn, *The San Patricio Soldiers: Mexico's Foreign Legion* (El Paso: Texas Western Press, University of Texas at El Paso, 1984), pp. 3, 33, 37, 45.

8. Marcela Terrazas, "Hacia una nueva frontera: Baja California en los proyectos expansionistas norteamericanos, 1846–1865," *Estudios de historia moderna y contemporánea de México* (no. 13, 1990), pp. 105–10.

9. David J. Weber, ed., *Foreigners in Their Native Land: Historical Roots of the Mexican Americans* (Albuquerque: University of New Mexico Press, 1973), pp. 215–16.

10. John R. Chávez, *The Lost Land: The Chicano Image of the Southwest* (Albuquerque: University of New Mexico Press, 1984), pp. 57–58, 74.

11. Randi Jones Walker, *Protestantism in the Sangre de Cristos, 1850–1920* (Albuquerque: University of New Mexico Press, 1991), pp. 10–11, 14–16; Nancie L. González, *The Spanish Americans of New Mexico: A Heritage of Pride* (Albuquerque: University of New Mexico Press, 1967), pp. 33–46. For the initial cultural conflict between aboriginal beliefs and those introduced by Spain, see Ramón A. Gutiérrez, *When Jesus Came the Corn Mothers Went Away* (Stanford: Stanford University Press, 1991).

12. Richard Griswold del Castillo, *The Los Angeles Barrio, 1850–1890: A Social History* (Berkeley: University of California Press, 1979), pp. 38–39; James E. Officer, *Hispanic Arizona, 1536–1856* (Tucson: University of Arizona Press, 1987), p. 246.

13. Arnoldo de León, *The Tejano Community, 1836–1900* (Albuquerque: University of New Mexico Press, 1982), p. xii; Moisés González Navarro, *Anatomía del poder en México (1848–1853)* (México: Colegio de México, 1977), pp. 75–76.

14. Ibid, pp. xvi, 80, 96; Jerry D. Thompson, *Warm Weather and Bad Whiskey: The 1886 Laredo Election Riot* (El Paso: Texas Western Press, University of Texas at El Paso, 1991), p. 15.

15. Mario T. García, *Desert Immigrants: The Mexicans of El Paso, 1880–1920* (New Haven: Yale University Press, 1981), pp. 98–101, 220.
16. Ibid, p. 168. Pedro de Urdemales, sometimes referred to as Juan, a wicked traitor and bandit, always returned evil for good. Urdemales implies evil wrapped in evil. Pedro symbolized the evil in all men. Most stories concerning Pedro involve a trick. The Tejano version is more amusing. Frances Toor, *The Treasury of Mexican Folkways* (New York: Crown Publishers, 1947), pp. 529–31. See Riley Aiken, *Mexican Folktales from the Borderland* (Dallas: Southern Methodist University Press, 1980), pp. 55–61 for other adventures of Pedro Urdemales.
17. León, *The Tejano Community,* p. 158.
18. Ibid., p. 95.
19. David J. Weber, "The Spanish Legacy in North America and the Historical Imagination," *Western Historical Quarterly* (February 1992), pp. 9–10.
20. David Montejano, *Anglos and Mexicans in the Making of Texas* (Austin: University of Texas Press, 1987), p. 36; Nevin O. Winter, *Mexico and Her People of Today: An Account of the Customs, Characteristics, Amusements, History and Advancement of the Mexicans, and the Development and Resources of Their Country* (Boston: L. C. Page Co., 1907), p. 22.
21. Donalthon C. Olliff, *Reforma Mexico and the United States: A Search for Alternatives to Annexation, 1854–1861* (University AL: University of Alabama Press, 1981), p. 12.
22. González Navarro, *Anatomía del poder,* pp. 81–96.
23. J. D. Thompson, *Warm Weather,* pp. 10–11; Geronimo Baqueiro Foster, *Historia de la música en México* (México: Secretaria de Educación Pública, 1964), vol. 3, pp. 565–68.
24. Ibid., pp. 16–18, 38, 53; Eugene K. Chamberlin "Baja California after Walker: The Zerman Enterprise," *Hispanic American Historical Review (1954),* pp. 175–89; Olliff, Reforma Mexico, pp. 58, 19–20.
25. Ibid., pp. 27–28, 39–41.
26. Miguel Lerdo de Tejada, *El comercio exterior de México desde la conquista hasta hoy* (México: R. Rafael, 1853); John G. Chapman, *La construcción del ferrocarril mexicano* (México: Secretaria de Educación Pública, 1975), pp. 44–45.
27. Inés Herrera, "Comercio y comerciantes de la costa del Pacífico mexicano a mediados del siglo XIX," *Historias* (April-September 1988), pp. 129–53.
28. Ruth R. Olivera and Liliane Crete, *Life in Mexico Under Santa Anna, 1822–1855* (Norman: University of Oklahoma Press, 1991), pp. 56, 128.
29. Robert W. Johannsen, *A New Era for the United States: Americans and the War with Mexico* (Urbana: University Lecture Series, 1975), pp. 16–32.
30. Quoted in Officer, *Hispanic Arizona,* pp. 310–13.
31. Ellen M. Litwicki, "From Patron to Patria: Fiestas and Mexicano Identity in Late Nineteenth-Century Tucson," paper presented at the 1992 meeting of the Organization of American Historians.

Chapter 3

LIBERALISM DEFINED

The 1855 Revolution of Ayutla, which removed Santa Anna permanently from politics, indicated a move toward a liberalism that accepted the primacy of economics over all other considerations. While the new generation of Mexican thinkers still looked for ideas that could explain as well as correct the Mexican reality, they now believed that they had succeeded in getting a sufficiently useful mix of ideas. Ideological leaders, such as Melchor Ocampo and Benito Juárez, set the tone and agenda of Mexican liberalism that still survives in modified form today. Ocampo, much taken with French thought, translated the work of Pierre Proudhon into Spanish. In 1840 and 1850 he served as governor of the state of Michoacán, as well as in the national legislature. A lawyer, amateur naturalist, and student of Indian languages, Ocampo had one of the finest libraries in the country. Benito Juárez, a Zapotec Indian educated by a Franciscan lay brother who came to symbolize the historical era as well as the ideas of nineteenth-century Mexican liberalism, also became a lawyer and governor of his home state of Oaxaca. Santa Anna ordered his imprisonment, but he fled into exile in New Orleans. In Louisiana he worked out his ideas with other liberal refugees from Santa Anna, including Melchor Ocampo and José María Mata. The exiled liberals denounced Santa Anna's failure to maintain the territorial integrity of the republic with the implication that only a liberal government under their direction could do so.[1] The New Orleans group joined the revolt of Juan Alvarez, then based in the state of Guerrero. From exile, Juárez arranged for shipment of arms

Liberalism Defined

1854–1855	Revolution of Ayutla
1855	Santa Anna goes into exile until 1876.
1856	Juárez and Lerdo laws
1857	Iglesias law
	Montes–Forsyth treaties fail in U.S. Senate.
	Constitution of 1857
	Pope Pius IX condemns Constitution of 1857.
1858	Benito Juárez assumes presidency.
1858–1861	War of the Reform
1861	Rurales established as constabulary.
1862	French, Spanish, and English ships blockade Veracruz
1862	May 5 (Cinco de Mayo): Mexican troops defeat the French at the Battle of Puebla.
1862–1867	French intervention
1863	French troops occupy Puebla and Mexico City.
1864	Maximilian and Carlota arrive in Mexico.
1867	Maximilian executed in Querétaro
	Juárez reclaims Mexico City.
	National Preparatory School founded
1872	Díaz's unsuccessful La Noria revolt
	July 18: Juárez dies in office.
	Sebastián Lerdo de Tejada assumes presidency.
1876	Revolution of Tuxtepec
	Díaz installed as president

and supplies and then went to Acapulco to join the active movement. The Revolution of Ayutla swept the country, sending Santa Anna into his last exile. He died in 1876, destitute and forgotten.

Gadsden, who had adopted a proliberal stance, became the first foreign diplomat to recognize the Alvarez government. Amid all the confusion of creating a new government, rumors of a protectorate circulated. Mexico City's French-language newspaper published drafts of two treaties that allegedly had been signed, or would be shortly, between the liberals and Gadsden. In the treaties, the United States would guarantee the territorial integrity of the nation, along with economic development loans, in exchange for shared control over the workings of the Mexican economy, such as tariffs and international customs duties. Foreign minister Valentín Gómez Farías evinced cautious interest. He noted that the suggested protectorate maintained political sovereignty and guaranteed territorial integrity. Moreover, it held out the lure of a development fund, modern transporation facilities, and a flood of European immigrants. It seemed evident that some such plan or plans had been discussed in liberal circles, but the premature exposé made it politically impossible. Lerdo, identified as a major supporter, found it necessary to deny loudly any involvement, and President Alvarez denounced it as a conservative plot to discredit his government. Even Gadsden denied the existence of such a plan. The private reaction of many liberals indicated their continued obsession with the need to make a deal with the United States. It also indicated their willingness to concede advantages in exchange for economic development. Protection and economic assistance had the same fascination to Mexicans as a flame to a moth. Not surprisingly, the only institution of the deposed Santa Anna regime to remain in place was the Ministry of Development. Lerdo, who had served that government, retained his liberal standing and influence.

Liberals saw the Revolution of Ayutla as an opportunity to rearrange forcefully the basic features of the nation and open the way to progress, as they defined it. To engage in political persuasion, compromise, and the slow creation of a national consensus only delayed the cure. Thus the new regime ushered in a reform period that radically changed the nature of the country. La Reforma is considered one of the crucial points in Mexico's modern history. The first major law, the Ley Juárez, struck at the military and clerical court system by restricting their privileges and permitting only routine and professional jurisdictional authority over their members, reserving actual civil and criminal authority to the state.

Another major reform involved a direct attack on corporate property and the economic logjam it represented to liberals. The Spanish Constitution of 1812, which remained in effect until superseded by Mexican enactments, abolished all distinctions based on race. Indians became citizens with the same rights as all other inhabitants of the empire. The constitution ended the special status of Indian communal land by endowing all citizens with the right to hold, acquire, or sell land. Although not abolished, communal land was no longer immutable. While extending unrestricted property rights to Indians did not force communal property on the market, it opened up the option to transfer property to any other citizen, Indian or non-Indian, through legal sales. How much property would be offered for sale as a result of this important modification is not clear, but it appears to have been limited. The Pecos Pueblo in the province of New Mexico demonstrated the possibilities. Authorities upheld the Pueblo's right to hold on to legal ownership of its land in spite of a small and shrinking population. Non-Indian settlers had demanded free distribution of unused and surplus Pecos Pueblo land. The Indians of Pecos indeed sold land, probably to individual squatters, and exercised their right to hold on to their legal property.[2] The slow transformation of Indian land into private holdings in the end gave rise to attempts to force them to do so. The move to abolish communal property began at the state level. Chihuahua, Jalisco, and Zacatecas abolished communal ownership of land in 1825; Chiapas and Veracruz the following year; Puebla and Occidente (Sinaloa and Sonora) in 1828; and the newly created state of Mexico in 1833. Complete implementation of such laws was not possible, and many states developed an ad hoc, case-by-case approach to land reform.

Church property also came under pressure. In 1833 the State of Mexico's legislature provided for the seizure of land belonging to the Philippine missions.[3] It remained to develop a comprehensive policy. The assault on clerical property rested on the claim that it represented static assets—an ideological position that brushed aside reality. As the provincial of Carmen observed in 1834, the Church could sell real estate and often did so. Indeed, the Church came to the conclusion that investments, mortgages, and loans, rather than easily confiscated real estate, offered the best return as well as protection against confiscation. A series of government decrees attempted to stop property sales by requiring official permission before the Church could sell property.[4] Clearly, liberals coveted clerical wealth and intended to end Church economic power and hence reduce drastically its political and social influence. For public consumption, however, they preferred to picture clerical property as an immobile economic mass that required the government to break it up forcefully if the country was to prosper. With the Ley Lerdo, the attack on corporate holdings became national policy. The Ley Lerdo, framed by Miguel Lerdo de Tejada, now the most influential economic theorist and secretary of the treasury, forced the divestment of property not directly related to Church functions. Millions of pesos of Church property sold to the highest bidder and taxed by the government fattened the national treasury. It also provided for the breaking up of Indian communal land dividing it up into private holdings. As José María Lafragua advised the Ministry of Foreign Affairs in 1847, the breakup of communal holdings would provide the foundations for a new yeoman farmer nation, a process that could be speeded up with foreign immigration.[5]

At the regional level, officials did not necessarily reject the need to create new communal land but saw it as a transitional stage. Landless Indians posed a danger to social stability and perhaps could be recruited by those seeking a reactionary return to the old colonial system. Thus, Lorenzo de Zavala, as governor of the state of Mexico, expropriated vast private holdings in the valley of Toluca and distributed them among forty Indian villages. He also seized the property of Fernando Cortés's heirs to finance public schools. In Zacatecas, the state purchased land and divided it into small private holdings. Valparaíso, a former hacienda, became a town, and its owners pledged to pay off the hacienda's creditors. Some of Valparaíso's land became private and the rest became communal property. A proposal to create a land bank to buy large holdings and resell small lots constituted a limited agrarian reform program.[6] To the liberals the key to a new and prosperous society lay with the wealth currently locked within a relatively static land system that had to be made more fluid. Ironically, the land policy as it evolved led to the concentration of ownership and became a factor in pushing agrarian elements to revolt in 1910. It also led to the subsequent establishment of the *ejido* (communal land) after the Mexican Revolution—a system that evoked the former colonial land pattern. Mexican liberalism encompassed a romantic vision of a nation of sturdy property owners upon which a great, prosperous, and politically stable republic would rise, similar to that of Thomas Jefferson for the then–underpopulated United States.

The bulk of the Church's assets consisted of urban property, while Indian corporations held agricultural or rural properties. In the race to acquire property, those who had cash had the advantage. Many liberal leaders themselves purchased Church assets, including the author of the law, who acquired Mexico City property worth over 30,000 pesos ($30,000). Benito Juárez purchased a 3,200-peso ($3,200) house in Oaxaca. Merchants, tradesmen, and professionals rushed to buy attractive property. Less desirable assets, however, found few bidders. By the end of 1857, the Ley Lerdo created approximately 9,000 new proprietors—few of whom could be remotely conceived of as yeoman farmers.[7] Freeing the assets of the country for profitable accumulation by the industrious ignored the uneven cultural development that characterized nineteenth-century Mexico. Many groups only weakly grasped the notion of private property. Moreover, liberalism did not anticipate the rapid growth of capital resulting from international demands for primary products that placed great financial and competitive advantages in the hands of the elite.

Individuals able to conceptualize the new political and economic reality soon amassed fortunes. By the latter part of the century, their power could not be denied. The liberal ideal placed no limit on what an industrious individual could accumulate. They assumed that a rough economic equality would emerge naturally, as if Mexico functioned in idyllic isolation apart from the world economy, and that all of its citizens were prepared to engage in the grand project of building a perfect nation. It had the effect of throwing many Indians into the competitive economy with noncompetitive small plots or depriving them of

land entirely. As a consequence, many holdings ended up in the hands
of large landholders.

The impact of the Ley Lerdo varied, depending on the region and
the circumstances. In central Oaxaca, where many inhabitants understood the notion of private property, disentailment would not be resisted. New ranchos carved out of newly privatized land, or in recently
cleared areas, produced citrus fruit, coffee, cotton, and tobacco, among
other crops. These new property owners, including a number of
women, understood the advantages of individual ownership of land
and the profit to be made in new crops. A similar reaction occurred in
some districts of Guerrero. Villages such as Huetzuco and Huixtac formally requested the division of property in the 1870s. In Taxco, when
division of land finally occurred in the 1880s, outsiders established
footholds from which they illegally occupied adjacent land.[8] Fraud
and corruption could easily enter the process. In many areas the government did not press for disentailment. Some Indian groups understood that although the law had stripped their historical property
structure of legal standing, they could reconstitute themselves as condominium associations in which the participants became owners. An
administrative committee, headed by a president or legal representative, ostensibly ran what legally constituted a land company. In a
number of cases, non-Indians and Indians participated in the same organization. The hacienda of San Felipe (Hidalgo) eventually had 250
associates. In a similar fashion, the association of San Antonio, controlling 9,300 hectares of land in 1871, purchased more property to expand its commercial agricultural production. In effect, some Indian
groups conserved both their land and village adminstrative structure
intact by recasting the form to preserve the substance.[9] At the outbreak of the Mexican Revolution of 1910, a considerable amount of
communal land remained in mountainous, isolated regions or was
protected through legal devices. In accessible and agriculturally valuable parts of the republic, division of communal property proceeded at
a more urgent pace. Sugarcane, aguardiente, cotton, indigo, coffee,
rice, peanuts, and cattle raising slowly transformed Chiapas. Expansion into former communal lands grew, along with a developing economy and the expanding rail network. By 1910, Indian communities
had lost substantial amounts of land in various regions where economic pressures were greatest. In central Mexico, including the states
of Mexico, Morelos, and Hidalgo, the pattern was mixed. The Ley
Lerdo constituted a disaster for some, while others retained their
land. Nevertheless, the threat as well as the reality assured that the
subject of communal land would become a major issue in the Revolution of 1910.

The liberal ideological objective of forming a group of small property owners floundered. Inevitably, corporate assets fell into the hands of those able to afford the required down payment of 20 percent of the fixed value of the property. German-born Bernardo Wiener, for example, purchased slightly over one-third of Church property sold in the State of Mexico between 1861 and 1866, including urban dwellings, ranchos, and haciendas. Another five individuals accounted for approximately another third, while thirty-one investors bought around thirty percent. The same amount remaining, less than six percent of former clerical property, went to eighty-two new owners.[10] The same pattern characterized the distribution of assets in other states. Small property holders, and those who wanted to be, could not compete for the best property, nor were they likely to hold on to small plots if they were lucky enough to acquire them. Liberalism failed to create an instant yeoman class.

The other objective of freeing assets to form a more fluid and dynamic market in land-based capital succeeded. Liberal land reform thus established the foundations upon which commercial agriculture subsequently flourished during the Porfiriato. With the combination of internal peace, railways, and new markets, land became a valuable asset that had to be used in a productive manner. Rapid economic progress beginning in the 1880s overshadowed the social failure. Eventually, economic development created a middle class, but a dependent one rather than the sturdy yeoman class liberalism had intended.

Liberals had greater success recasting municipal life. Municipal reforms envisioned clean water (prohibiting animals from using town fountains, for example); public sanitation (ordering the construction of indoor toilets or privies as a way to halt the dismay of passersby); and personal hygiene (making it a misdemeanor to answer the call of nature in public streets, squares, or cemeteries). Town thoroughfares received attention with prohibitions against grazing animals, especially pigs, and restrictions on religious processions. Ordinances reserved sidewalks for "decent" people and required that anyone carrying anything on his or her back walk in the street—both restrictions aimed at keeping Indians off the sidewalks. Other reforms established street names and building numbers, posted lists of merchandise and prices, and created written business signs to replace hanging symbols, whose shape indicated the enterprise. These practices, implying a need for literacy, created some hardship for the common people.[11]

The lower classes bore the brunt of liberal reforms in both a direct and indirect fashion. Loss of land either through disentailment or the sale of small holdings pushed many into the transient labor market, or onto haciendas as debt peons, and the reduction of clerical assets had an impact on hospitals, schools, orphanages, and other social services previously financed by the Church. While the liberals gave lip service to establishing schools, little money was available for social services. Mexico in 1843 had 1,310 primary schools; fourteen years later, in the year of the Constitution of 1857, another 114 had opened—an expansion of roughly eight per year. Few Mexicans expected to attend a school at any level—a harsh realization that held true into the next century. Although the government decreed primary education free and obligatory and mandated that all towns with over 500 inhabitants must establish one school for males and another for females, little could be done without money. State governments and municipalities rarely met their obligation to fund primary schools. School attendance depended upon both the existence of schools as well as sufficient family earnings to free children from the necessity of work. Inhabitants of urban centers had more opportunity and a disproportionate number of existing schools. Mexico City had 246 schools in 1867, with 7,492 students—3 percent of the capital's population.[12] Understandably, the establishment of rural schools became one of the objectives of the Mexican Revolution of 1910.

Meanwhile, the government sought to gain control over assets, stimulate the economy through structural reforms, change attitudes, loosen philosophical ties with what it believed to be archaic institutions, and strengthen the national government. In short, liberal reformers took but had very little to give. They believed their reform program would in time benefit the lower class and elevate all Mexicans.

Many reforms seemed so manifestly beneficial that little was done to explain the advantages to those most directly affected. On occasion, making ideological points appeared more important than the actual reality. For example, the law that regulated fees for clerical services, as well as provided free religious services for the poor, cost the government nothing, but made the point that clerics exploited their own believers. Yet, as a practical matter, few had anything to do with the official Church. Overwhelmingly rural throughout the nineteenth century, most Mexicans rarely encountered a priest. In San Luis Potosí, individuals as old as forty had never attended a mass. Many remained unbaptized and a Church marriage seemed an impossible fantasy. To be relieved of clerical fees meant little without actual access to Catholic services. In 1850, only 4,350 clerics attempted to deal with a population that required the attention of an estimated 20,000 priests.[13] Religious instruction became cultural lore as cults filled the vacuum. Thus, in the countryside, liberal attacks on the Church appeared to be some sort of inexplicable assault on rural culture. The politics as well as economics of anticlericalism could not be fathomed by rural Mexicans. In the cities, where the clerical presence could be observed and spiritual as well as charity services utilized, the lower classes stood to lose much more than they could gain from liberal clerical reforms.

A DEAL IS STRUCK

Liberal attempts to work out some sort of protective arrangement with the United States floundered on Gadsden's antagonistic personality. The new American representative, John Forsyth, a politically well-connected newspaper editor in Alabama who had served in Mexico during the war, provided yet another opportunity to reach a useful arrangement. He became a close friend of Miguel Lerdo, and they put together a new proposal. The actual extent of Lerdo's influence is subject to debate, although it seems clear that the proposal had the backing of Lerdo and other important liberals. The central problem appeared to be the extent of Mexico's debt. Mexico owed some 120 million pesos, while its annual income barely reached 10 million pesos. Meeting interest payments and operating expenses kept the nation in a perpetual fiscal crisis. The solution suggested required that the United States buy the European debt, thereby protecting Mexico's sovereignty from action by the holder of the debt; in return Mexico would concede a dominant economic position to its northern neighbor. A series of four treaties comprised the package, which included stimulating trade on the northern border. The proposal seemed to offer advantages for all sections of the United States. Such an arrangement assured Mexico's territorial existence and economic development. Forsyth anticipated that bilateral trade would jump from 4.5 million to 40 million pesos a year and force European trade through American trade channels as well. Proximity and close economic ties would keep Mexico from disintegration, Americanize the population, and in the future could lead to a voluntary union. The Mexicans envisioned a slightly different outcome. They thought in terms of using American capital to achieve an equality of development. By following what they believed to be a successful model, in both the political and economic spheres, they hoped to enter a similar period of rapid development. Economic growth in turn would stimulate a flood of European immigrants, as it had in the United States, and give them the population base needed to sustain their claim to an independent sovereignty. At the end of such a process Mexico would take its place as an equal member of the world's modern nations with a status on par with the economic and politically developed countries of Britain, France, and the United States. Lerdo still believed that the greed of speculators could be employed, even manipulated, to the ultimate advantage of the Mexican republic. Meanwhile, an economic protectorate would provide space (territorial integrity) and time to achieve the desired goal. In short, the dream encompassed a gambler's scheme. The agreement went to Washington for the senate's ratification only eight days before the end of Pierce's administration. The incoming administration of James Buchanan declined to take the proposal seriously. The rejection of the Montes–Forsyth treaties stunned liberal politicians and threw the issue of assistance from the United States back into the grasping realm of territory for money.[14]

MEXICO UNDER THE CONSTITUTION OF 1857

Mexico, on the eve of the Constitution of 1857, existed as a series of regions within a national structure increasingly irrelevant to its erstwhile citizens. Regional elites and politicians manipulated the concept of a broader nation only when it offered some immediate advantage. They expected little from Mexico City, rejected any proffered advice, and received no significant financial benefits from the national government. Moreover, state politicians in the north suspected the motives of the federal government, particularly its apparent disquieting readiness to mortgage the country's resources and even sell territory. Northern insecurity and suspicion of the central government's motives had a historical foundation. In colonial times, the northern reaches, called the *Provincias Internas*, functioned as a distinct region apart from the settled regions of the Viceroyalty of New Spain. When Mexicans contemplated the creation of an independent sovereign nation they did not automatically include the far north in their mental construct. At the Congress of Chilpancingo (1813) on the eve of actual independence, the delegates excluded the Provincias Internas from what they envisioned would be the boundaries of an independent Mexico. At the time, the north consumed revenues, had a scant population, and showed little promise of contributing to the anticipated well-being of a new nation. Nevertheless, an independent Mexico inherited the Provincias Internas as an appendage of the actual nation of the south center. It formed a buffer zone that could offer some protection. As a fringe area, it faced a potentially hostile neighbor that might well succeed in slicing it off from the Mexican republic. The territorial integrity of the nation remained uncertain throughout much of the nineteenth century. Northerners who feared their parent might abandon them reacted to rumors with an alacrity born out of their fears.[15] When a story circulated that President Comonfort planned to sell Sonora, the state informed Mexico City that the Sonoran people would resist. Subsequently, when newspapers in the United States began to call for prompt annexation, the newspaper *La Voz de Sonora* defiantly proclaimed, "We don't want to be Americans."[16] From the vantage point of the north, one could not trust neither an aggressive United States nor a desperate Mexico City. The federal government, in fact, avoided selling national territory in spite of extreme pressure. National politicians played a high stakes game with the United States and won. The north, in spite of its distrust of Mexico City, clearly insisted upon being part of the Mexican republic. Their allegiance, perhaps designed more to preserve their essentially independent existence, nevertheless constituted a strong barrier to the further encroachment of the United States on Mexican territory.

Thrown back on their own resources, many states functioned as all-but-independent entities within the fragmented republic. Men such as Santiago Vidaurri, who united Coahuila and Nuevo León, ran things as they pleased, as did Luis Terrazas in Chihuahua and Ignacio Pesqueira of Sonora. Some parts of the country operated at an acceptable socioeconomic level while essentially isolated from the rest of the nation. Other areas suffered greatly from national weakness. In northern Mexico, the termination of subsidies to the Apaches coupled with the withdrawal of troops led to a resurgence of destructive raiding and pillaging. Large landowners could survive long enough to learn from experience. Indian attacks, market cycles of boom and bust, and wildly jumping variations in the amount of rainfall made life nearly impossible for small landowners along the frontier. They lived day to day, and hard experience appeared to mean little. The institutional and socioeconomic adaptation to this insecurity was the *hacienda*. These great estates, owned by powerful families such as the Sánchez Navarros in Coahuila, marshaled enough workers to withstand most Indian raids, expanded and contracted commercial efforts to match available markets, and relied on diversified crops and herds as a hedge against inclement weather and other disasters. Combining commercial production and food self-sufficiency, the great haciendas endured in a region where the small holder had no chance.[17] These self-reliant estate owners saw little that the central government could provide. To their minds, the *municipio libre*, the independent local government, was the essential administration. Depredation by Apache raiding parties resulted in depopulation, as isolated villages withdrew into more secure areas abandoning mines, property, and homes. The proximity of the international border provided Indian raiders with a useful sanctuary from pursuing forces. As a result, the Mexican population withdrew from the border. Those on the United States side viewed the abandonment of territory as an opportunity for expansion, perhaps even providing the Southwest access to the Sea of Cortés. National weakness made northern Mexico vulnerable. It was a lesson northerners have never forgotten nor forgiven.

The elaboration of a constitutional structure able to reassure the various states of the republic and provide for a reasonably effective national government had been called for in the Plan of Ayutla. The United States served as the intellectual foil for the discussants who sought to establish a direct connection between consitutional forms and material progress. July 4, 1856, the day set to consider the document, indicated the extent the American constitution influenced deliberations. Conservatives derisively charged that it demonstrated liberal subservience to the United States, but it actually indicated the feverish desire to find the same magic formula that had transformed New England farmers and Western backwoodsmen into the collective colossus of the north. Mexican liberals may have been political alchemists, but not sycophants. Their new constitution provided for a federal republic, but one with a stronger central government. The document included a bill of rights protecting free speech, assembly, press, and other privileges of Mexican citizenship.[18]

The framers of the constitution believed their document had lifted the dead hand of the past from the prostrate nation, making rapid economic development possible. Virtually every clause of the new constitution could be related to material modernization. Liberals viewed politics and economic development as indivisible; thus they established commissions to study and advise the government on agriculture, mining, railroads, and a host of other promising activities, enlisting the support of a wide range of individuals. The Railway Commission, the most prestigious, served not only as an advisory group, but bore responsibility for overseeing completion of contracts and promoting others. It also received federal revenues and disbursed funds as appropriate. Utilization of such commissions, as well as the Ministry of Development, to focus concessions on selected projects became more refined under Porfirio Díaz, but the liberals of the Reforma set the pattern.[19]

Proclerical elements reacted hysterically to the new constitution. An enraged Pope Pius IX issued a statement condemning the document and the Mexican hierarchy threatened excommunication. The still shaky leadership of the liberal regime could barely withstand the pressure. President Ignacio Comonfort, who had assumed office after the less than one month provisional presidency of Juan Alvarez, provided weak leadership. Benito Juárez, who became the chief justice of the Supreme Court, and thus next in line for the presidency, pushed for complete implementation and defense of the constitution, while the conservatives demanded major modifications. The constitution had been elaborated without regard to contrary opinion, and in an effort to make it secure, the regime ordered the clergy and all government officials and employees to swear allegiance or face dismissal.

Heavy-handed coercion alienated many individuals who might have accepted at least part of the liberal program and outraged others. Support outside of Mexico City was more illusory than real. As Francisco Bulnes noted, regional political bosses, the great caciques, provided only a supporting façade. In reality they were not reformers but federalists. They associated conservative control of the national government with centralism and therefore often supported the liberals. Regional bosses went along with liberalism, provided it did not limit their actual political control. Pragmatism, not philosophy, governed their actions. Their allegiances followed their interest and hence could change in an instance. In short, a proliberal consensus sufficiently strong to support radical measures did not exist.[20]

A weak president could not restrain his radical associates, nor bargain or negotiate with the opposition. Comonfort appeared to be a hapless cork bobbing in an ideological sea. Radical intransigence polarized the country, making a civil war unavoidable in 1858. The conservatives now announced their Plan of Tacubaya. General Félix Zuloaga, while permitting President Comonfort to remain in office, dissolved Congress and arrested Juárez. Comonfort resigned after briefly attempting to hold the impossible together, but not before releasing Juárez, who assumed the legal and constitutional presidency and fled the capital. A bitterly divided Mexico dissolved into three years of civil violence, called the War of the Reform (1858–1861), characterized by arbitrary executions on both sides, an indication of the uncompromising frustration and anger experienced by conservatives and liberals alike.

LIBERALISM UNDER SIEGE

With difficulty the liberals established a provisional capital in Veracruz and slowly reversed the tide of battle. Both sides, starved for cash, entertained even the most unreasonable revenue proposals. Interest rates fluctuated daily, reaching incredible heights. The most notorious contract, the Jecker Loan, provided the conservatives with needed operating funds in exchange for a staggering debt of fifteen million pesos. During this desperate time, the United States pressed the Juárez regime to sell Lower California and make other concessions in return for sorely needed funds. The liberals reluctantly negotiated the McLane–Ocampo Treaty (1859), which conceded to the United States the right of transit across the Isthmus of Tehuantepec and along the northern border from the Gulf of Mexico to the Sea of Cortes.[21] Fortunately for the liberals, Washington did not ratify the treaty. Benito Juárez entertained other concessions and appeared willing to sell territory if necessary; however, in the end, he avoided selling off bits and pieces of the nation. President Buchanan, although interested in crude territorial expansion, failed to override sectional problems and political opposition in the United States and could not sustain consistent pressure on the liberals. Mexico's territorial integrity had been saved by external politics.[22] Finally, a liberal army retook Mexico City on New Year's Day 1861, ending the War of the Reform.

Once again the country had been subjected to fruitless violence and destruction. A depleted treasury could not meet internal needs nor foreign debt payments quite apart from demands for indemnifications made by foreigners for damages suffered during the civil war. Federal government revenues depended on taxes collected within the capital itself. Collections from customhouses, the traditional source of funds, had been pledged long ago. Eighty-five percent of Veracruz's receipts went to foreign debt payments, while those of smaller ports on both the Atlantic and Pacific coasts carried similar burdens. Other sources of income had been taken over by the hard-pressed states, leaving only a few minor crumbs for Mexico City. To raise taxes on the inhabitants of the capital could be counterproductive and might jeopardize the existing collection of revenues. The only hope for the nation's finances appeared to be the anticipated effects of the reforms—a long-range prospect at best. Financial weakness, as Minister of the Treasury Guillermo Prieto reminded state governors, "can make a farce out of our national independence."[23] While the governors at least offered understanding, unsympathetic foreign creditors turned to their governments for collection assistance.

On the Eve of Disaster

In early 1861 both Mexico and the United States hovered on the edge of disaster. Abraham Lincoln, elected in November 1860, made ready to assume the presidency, while a recalcitrant South talked of secession. Force threatened to rend the political and social fabric of the United States. Mexico, a year later, faced a French intervention that threw liberalism's fate into doubt. In uncertain times, Matías Romero traveled to Springfield, Illinois, to deliver a message from President Juárez to the president-elect. The Mexican liberals believed that the republican electoral victory brought both countries into close philosophical harmony. The democrats, the party of expansionism and slavery, had been defeated—surely a good sign for Mexico. Romero reported that Lincoln, while uninformed, was well disposed toward the Mexican republic.

When the Civil War erupted in the United States, Mexico momentarily had a favorable bargaining position between the Confederacy and the Union—a situation that could change rapidly if European creditors failed to be reasonable. Lincoln's appointment of Thomas Corwin to represent the United States in Mexico indicated the importance assigned to the neighboring republic. Corwin, a former congressman, senator, governor of Ohio, and secretary of the treasury, had opposed the Mexican war. His appointment promised to usher in a new era of mutual respect. Mexico City's expectations soon became more realistic, as Corwin appeared to support the validity of the French–Jecker loan, which subsequently provided the pretext for France's assault on Mexican sovereignty. Liberal politicians demonstrated their willingness to accommodate the Union by agreeing to Secretary of State Seward's request for permission to land troops at Guaymas and transport them across Mexican territory into Arizona. Mexican willingness to assist the Union stemmed from the belief, as noted by José María Mata, that if Lincoln lost the Civil War, the country would have to fight the South to preserve its territory and stop the expansion of slavery across the Río Grande. Indeed, John T. Pickett, representing the Confederacy in Mexico City, believed that the North intended to block future Southern expansion; thus Mexico had become a battleground between two competing systems—the Confederacy, allied with Mexican conservatives, and the Church, with an economy based on slavery and peonage, against the Union, liberals, and free labor.

Both sides attempted to entice Mexico into cooperation. Pickett, laboring under the disadvantage of his own personality and without formal recognition of the South, suggested that a grateful Confederacy might agree to return a portion of the territory conceded under the terms of the Treaty of Guadalupe—not a credible ploy given Southern expansionism. The Union in turn offered a series of treaties and loans as a possibility. An extradition treaty of 1862 aimed at controlling transborder violence, as well as a postal convention the same year, indicated a more cooperative stance. Corwin negotiated two loan treaties (1861, 1862), which provided direct U.S. loans to the Mexican government. Washington also offered to buy Baja California to avoid any threat to the hoped-for Pacific trade. Both treaties secured by land would have resulted in territorial loss if Mexico defaulted. The U.S. Senate rejected the treaties in spite of worries that European creditors might press Mexico for debt payment.

To demonstrate military concerns, Secretary of State Seward advised President Lincoln to dispatch General Winfield Scott to Mexico. Scott's age and infirmities caused the nomination to be withdrawn, but the point had been made. Mexico, anxious for loans, implied that if the United States did not approve them it would lead to the Europeanization of the country rather than its Americanization. Moreover, the idea of settling freed black slaves in southern Mexico, talked about in Washington at the time, would be impossible. The development of a grand diplomatic strategy by the Union, the Confederacy, or the Mexican government could not be done given the chaotic reality that faced them all. By the time the Union's military situation stabilized, France had already placed Maximilian on the Mexican throne.[24]

FRANCE IN MEXICO

Under pressure from creditors, Britain, Spain, and France jointly seized the customhouse in Veracruz to ensure collection of outstanding debts. It soon became evident that France had a larger design in mind. French troops stayed on after the departure of their fellow debt collection allies. French interest in Mexico may be traced to several factors. Emperor Napoleon III, intent on adding to the grandeur of his empire, had established a protectorate over Indochina and founded colonies elsewhere. His interest in Latin America dated back to his early years in political limbo. After an attempt to convince the French army to return the Bonapartes to the throne failed, the young man spent months at sea until finally being allowed to disembark in New York. A perceptive observer, he studied conditions in the United States for almost three months. Subsequently, imprisoned in France for yet another try for power, he spent his time studying world affairs. In the process, he developed an intense interest in the possibility of an interoceanic canal while poring over information supplied by the Nicaraguan government. After his escape to England (1846), he published a pamphlet on the Central American canal project. In 1848, he came to power as the elected president of France and five years later overthrew the Second French Republic to become Napoleon III, Emperor of France. The emperor's interest in the Americas had roots that extended beyond economics or mere academic pursuits. Napoleon III developed a psychocultural attachment to the New World. His grandmother had been born in Haiti and his own mother spent three years of her youth on the sugar island. One of his aunts, Elizabeth Patterson of Baltimore, whose grandson subsequently served as Theodore Roosevelt's secretary of the navy, provided a direct connection with the United States, as did his first cousin, Achille Murat. Murat, Crown Prince of Naples, emigrated to the United States and became a convinced democrat and an American citizen. Murat married a great-grandniece of George Washington, became a planter and lawyer in Florida, and eventually served as a county judge near Tallahassee. Joseph Bonaparte, Napoleon I's brother, and briefly the imposed King of Spain, suffered exile in New Jersey. Napoleon III's extensive family ties in the New World provided a strong emotional connection with a transatlantic world.

In Emperor Napoleon's view, the crass vitality and expansionism of the United States, coupled with the vast resources of the Western Hemisphere, posed a potential threat to Europeans, particularly Latin European civilization. Convinced that American political, economic, and cultural imperialism threatened both "Latin" America as well as European hegemony, the French emperor hoped to at least counterbalance the United States. Unless stopped, he feared the creation of some sort of horrendous democratic superpower able economically, even militarily, to dictate to European states. The emperor subscribed to the notions of François Guizot, who had earlier warned that the Anglo-Saxon United States hovered on the verge of destroying the hemisphere's "Latin" people. Clearly, Napoleon III's grand, if vague, scheme to contain the emerging colossus had developed an emotional life of its own. It encompassed a rescue effort, civilized noble ideals, and a moral crusade against a democratic Anglo-Saxon demon. In contrast to this well-developed emotional invention, little was done to investigate the actual reality. Emotional affirmation romaticized everything—a sure recipe for disaster. Napoleon III assumed that the Brazilian empire of Pedro II in South America could be relied upon to join a monarchial alliance to turn back the democratic Anglo-Saxon assault. After all, had not France and England recently tripped the expansionist Russian bear in the victorious Crimean War? It is obvious that the French episode in Mexico went far beyond a mere adventure.[25]

Mexico provided an interesting economic and political opportunity and the natural place to draw a line between monarchial civilization and democratic barbarism. The United States, its hands full with its own bloody civil war, could hardly block an intervention. Moreover, many Mexican conservatives, unconvinced by the political logic of the Revolution of Ayutla and the subsequent liberal victory in 1861, believed that the establishment of a European monarchy backed by France offered the only hope for stability, independent sovereignty, and economic progress. With monarchial paternalism uniting all classes, including those at the bottom, together with the support of the army and the Church, a workable national consensus could be established. A socially and politically united Mexican empire could resist American expansionism. Not all conservatives favored blatant foreign intervention, but many could be induced to support a monarchy, at least passively. With everything seemingly in place, Napoleon III reinforced the French troops already in Veracruz.

For the French the first taste of reality proved bitter. Under the illusion that the clergy and the conservatives, with a bit of help from their French friends, would soon topple the liberal regime, military preparations were minimal. Puebla, a city known to be proclerical and conservative, appeared to be a good place to start. The unexpected defeat of French forces stunned Emperor Napoleon III. The Mexican hero of the moment, General Ignacio Zaragoza, along with Brigadier General Porfirio Díaz, helped repulse the enemy attack on May 5, 1862.

Although the victory at Puebla did not halt the intervention, it subsequently came to symbolize the country's will to survive. *Cinco de Mayo* has become a major holiday, even today celebrated with more pride and enthusiasm than the anniversary of Mexico's independence. In the meantime, the victory provided only a brief respite. Napoleon dispatched another 30,000 troops at this time ordered careful preparation. A bitter two-month siege ended in the capture of the city of Puebla and opened the way to the national capital. Benito Juárez still hoped for a reasonable settlement. Mexican politicians, accustomed to temporarily abandoning the capital or being pushed out of Veracruz and elsewhere, viewed territorial loss or gain as a matter of tactics. Civil wars, revolts, exile, and other forms of political violence had engendered a resilient stamina as well as a sense of stoic coolness in the midst of what to an outsider might appear to be an utter disaster. After all, the French commander talked of respecting the will of the people. Once France had retrieved its honor by seizing the Mexican capital, Juárez believed something could be arranged. The United States representative in Mexico shared this view. Indeed, it might have been rationally resolved had it not been for Napoleon III's non-rational grand scheme. Meanwhile, welcome support for the liberal cause came from the Peruvian representative, Manuel N. Corpancho, who urged Juárez to join a proposed American union already endorsed by Chile and Ecuador. An appreciative Mexico signed the Corpancho treaty designed at least rhetorically to defend the independence and philosophical unity of the American republics. Unfortunately, rhetoric would not be enough.[26] Juárez, along with his cabinet, withdrew to the north.

Austrian Archduke Ferdinand Maximilian agreed to become emperor, provided a national plebiscite indicated support, and in a burst of reality, if French troops remained. After the occupation forces arranged for the proper results, Mexico's new emperor and Carlota the empress arrived in May 1864. Mexico, in the year of his arrival, appeared extremely primitive. At that very moment the city of Veracruz experienced one of its periodic outbreaks of yellow fever, making for a sparse and subdued welcome for the imperial party. Countless Paula Kolonitz, who accompanied the royal couple, recorded her vivid impressions. After enduring the trip to Mexico City, she toured parts of the countryside for almost six months. Her comments, sometimes harsh but balanced, pictured a world that lay beyond the imagination and comprehension of a European aristocrat. She noted the beauty, ugliness, and dirt, as well as the charming aspects of what she viewed as an endlessly interesting country.[27] She also was aware that the new emperor faced a daunting challenge. Nevertheless, few of those who surrounded Maximilian doubted that Mexico had great potential.

Even before Maximilian set foot on Mexican soil, Napoleon III requested his general to submit a report on Sonora's mineral wealth, as well as whether the region could be pacified. At least part of the country's northern expanse stretching from Baja California and Sonora to Chihuahua would make a suitable addition to France's empire and provide a buffer zone between Mexico and the United States. Maximilian, while open to French investment, refused to cede territory. Differences over economic issues cast doubts upon the long-term duration of their political alliance.[28] Ironically, a liberal Maximilian did not view his role as that of a reactionary savior of the Church or the conservatives. He refused to undo the liberal reform laws, hoping to draw the liberals into an alliance. In the end, he failed to attract sufficient liberal support and alienated the conservatives. His conciliatory approach, along with attempts to soften the impact of the Ley Lerdo on the Indian community, would have been admirable if he had not been a foreign prince imposed on the country. Even those who recognized Maximilian's sincerity could not overlook that one fact.

Physical control of Mexico depended almost entirely on the well-trained and disciplined French troops, who easily swept weak Juarista resistance before them.[29] Benito Juárez, without reliable generals, trained troops, and sufficient resources, could not offer much more than token military opposition as he struggled to maintain a semblance of national authority. Dissidents within his own cabinet and muted demands that he step down as president weakened his personal authority—virtually the only governing tool that remained. By the beginning of 1865, only Chiapas, Chihuahua, Guerrero, Sonora, and part of Michoacán—in effect the fringes of the republic—remained outside of the new imperial structure. French troops appeared unstoppable. By October 1863, under the impression that the country had been pacified, the emperor sought to end the residual violence by issuing a decree that all Juaristas captured with arms in hand would receive the death penalty with no possibility of appeal. It seemed just a question of a little more effort before Maximilian could enjoy his new empire in peace. The situation looked bleak for the liberals and their embattled leader.

Washington continued to recognize the Juárez regime, but with the American Civil War raging could not offer much assistance. The United States made its position clear to Napoleon III, but hesitated to do more until the successful conclusion of its own civil war. Lincoln's diplomacy sought to head off recognition of the Confederacy by major

Figure 3.1 Carte-de-viste showing Maximilian and Carlota kneeling before the Virgin of Guadalupe, used by the royal couple in an effort to increase their identification with Mexican culture. *Courtesy of Amon Carter Museum, Fort Worth, Texas*

European powers, as well as war with France; therefore, pressure on Napoleon could not go beyond polite pressure. For his part, Juárez rejected overtures from Confederate agents for supply depots and access to Mexican ports. Regional bosses on the northern border, such as Ignacio Pesqueira in Sonora, favored the Union in the belief that a victory for the Confederacy could only lead to expansionist pressure as it sought to add more slave states. Santiago Vidaurri, the *caudillo* of Nuevo León and Coahuila, on the other hand, cooperated fully with the Confederacy. Matamoros became the major gap in the Union blockade as an endless procession of ships arrived with arms, ammunition, and other necessities for the hard-pressed Confederates and left with cargoes of cotton. An estimated 7,000 bales of cotton a month passed through the port, providing Vidaurri with 50,000 pesos in custom duties. By 1865, Matamoros had become a major port city of 30,000 people, and the capital generated provided the region with the resources that fueled the economic development that began in the 1870s and continued through the years of the Porfiriato. Vidaurri, in the end, made the fatal error of siding with the French. As a consequence, he subsequently died before a liberal firing squad, commanded by Porfirio Díaz.[30]

The border region had its own Civil War sideshow in addition to Confederate supply activities. Some 3,000 Tejanos joined the Confederate army. The Thirty-Third Texas Cavalry (Confederate States of

America) under Colonel Santos Benavides valiantly protected Texas. In Zapata County (south Texas), Antonio Ochoa, a ranchero, and forty armed followers revolted in support of the Union, causing general panic along the international line. Those who joined the Union often reflected anti-Texan attitudes more than pro-Union sentiments. Washington hoped to recruit a sufficient number of soldiers to tie down Confederate troops in Texas. Union recruiters offered bounties and promises to entice enlistments. Union Tejano soldiers seized cotton, harassed Confederate outposts and supply wagons, and drove stolen cattle to Brownsville for use by federal forces. Tejanos formed the Second Regiment of Texas Union Cavalry (USA). Of the several thousand who served the United States, most had been born in Mexico. Eventually, the Union Tejanos served in Louisiana. Among the many colorful Civil War participants, perhaps the most interesting was Adrián J. Vidal, who served the Confederacy, then the Union, before deserting and joining the Juaristas, only to be executed by Maximilian's troops. Few Union Tejano veterans benefitted from military service. An exception would appear to be Ignacio Borrego who, as late as 1898, had the American consul deliver his six-dollar-a-month pension to his prison cell in Nuevo Laredo. In spite of desertions and isolation from the main elements of the Union Army, Tejano soldiers in fact succeeded in tying down Confederate forces that could have been deployed in the east.[31]

Avoidably, the American Civil War and the French intervention in Mexico became pieces of the same complex diplomatic puzzle with deadly implications for both the liberals and the Union. Even before Maximilian left Europe he expressed the desire for a Confederate victory to General James Williams of Tennessee. Subsequently, his agent identified the cause of an imperial Mexico with that of the American South.[32] Secretary of State William Seward maneuvered to head off French recognition of the Confederacy, as well as hostilities with France. Involvement in a war with France might have resulted in the survival of the Confederacy and the permanent division of the former United States. Fear of such a disastrous wider conflict made Lincoln and his secretary of state extremely cautious. Napoleon's offer to mediate between the Confederacy and the Union left little doubt that France favored a divided United States. As for Mexico, a successful French–Confederate alliance would be the end of liberalism. Napoleon understood the possibilities. In discussions with University of Virginia professor Sichele de Vere, the emperor indicated that France would require a "Gibraltar" on the Florida coast to protect anticipated Gulf trade and perhaps a location in Louisiana. Clearly, Lincoln and Juárez stood to lose in any deal between Richmond and Paris.

A fearful United States adopted a neutral stance that worked against the liberals in their attempt to obtain military supplies, while the French purchased what they needed in New York, New Orleans, and San Francisco. Matías Romero, Mexico's representative in Washington, constantly railed against Seward and Lincoln for their timidity. In the process he went beyond normal diplomatic practice to become involved in antigovernment intrigue aimed at the American president and his secretary of state.

Even before the French intervention, Matías Romero understood the utility of lobbying American officials, as well as manipulating public opinion. In 1861 he proposed that Edward E. Dunbar be retained at two hundred dollars a month to plant favorable stories in American newspapers. The Mexican government declined the suggestion. Romero relied on carefully cultivated friends to slip articles into important journals and newspapers. *The New York Tribune* as well as the Associated Press representative in Washington provided a useful outlet for propaganda. After successfully pressing his government for sufficient funds, Romero, foreshadowing twentieth-century lobbyists, embarked on a major campaign to influence American political opinion. After a careful search he found just the right residence, furnished it well, trained an attentive staff, and began a series of elaborate dinner parties. His guest list included cabinet ministers, congressmen, members of the executive branch, and opposition politicians. Fine food in pleasant surroundings, good wine, and strong drink earned the Mexican representative a reputation as a genial, even brilliant host, well connected with interesting political views. He carefully cultivated Charles Sumner of the Senate Foreign Relations Committee and forged a close friendship with Postmaster Montgomery Blair, who passed on cabinet gossip to the eager diplomat.[33] Matías Romero's objective, to acquire influential political friends, succeeded.

In New York City, Herman Sturm, commissioned a general in the Mexican Army, performed the same task, along with the important duty of buying equipment and signing up volunteers. He proved good at both sending some two million dollars worth of supplies and hundreds of volunteers to the liberal army, in spite of political obstacles. On the Pacific coast, Mexican agents established Mexican clubs for Spanish-speaking supporters and the Monroe League for American sympathizers. Both groups agitated for full implementation of the Monroe Doctrine to drive the French out of Mexico. The dangers of such heavy reliance on the United States did not go unappreciated. Mexico appeared to have no choice. As Matías Romero noted, Mexico previously had only one enemy—the United States—which posed a "constant menace." Now the American Civil War promised to render Washington powerless—a pleasurable prospect for its neighbor. With the French intervention, however, the republic faced the "hard alternative of sacrificing our territory and our nationality" to the United States or "our liberty and independence to the despotic thrones of Europe." Romero grimly observed that the latter threat appeared more immediate.[34]

As the American Civil War moved toward its conclusion, the situation changed in an unpredictable manner. The continued presence of the French in Mexico raised the possibility of drawing a soon-to-be victorious Union and a faltering Confederacy together to restore the sanctity of the Monroe Doctrine. To unite in a common cause would end the Civil War, speedily drive out the French, and heal many of the wounds of a restored United States. Francis P. Blair, father of Lincoln's postmaster-general, Montgomery Blair, and personal friend of Matías Romero, elaborated the scheme. With a safe-conduct pass from President Lincoln he met with Confederate President Jefferson Davis in early January 1865. The plan called for the appointment of the Confederate leader as a temporary dictator by Juárez, sending a joint Confederate Union Mexican military force against the French and demonstrating to the rest of the world that the Monroe Doctrine had returned to life. As Blair observed, the South had historically supported the Monroe Doctrine. Moreover, Napoleon's public pronouncements that he intended to strengthen "Latin America" against the "Anglo-Saxon" United States implied an attempt to block American commercial as well as territorial expansion, another historic goal of the South. Meanwhile, Matías Romero drafted an agreement to permit two army corps composed of Union and Confederate veterans under American command to enter Mexico. Blair suggested that Jefferson Davis be placed in supreme command with Robert E. Lee and Ulysses S. Grant as his commanders. Final authorization by the Juárez regime arrived too late—the Confederacy had already collapsed.

While it is evident that Mexico took the plan seriously, it is not clear to what extent Washington did so. Lincoln's encouragement of Blair's mission may have stemmed from his desperate search to find the appropriate means of reconciling the South. The notion of uniting the country in a common moral task, enforcing the Monroe Doctrine, and avoiding the need to designate a victor and a vanquished had an obvious appeal. It would have also laid to rest General Grant's great fear that ex-Confederate forces united with those of Maximilian would prolong sectional violence requiring the sacrifice of more lives to defeat. Besides Blair's plan, other schemes along the same lines existed. Eventual realization that the South had been utterly exhausted by the Civil War made all such plans look fanciful in retrospect.[35]

Benito Juárez, chased around the northern reaches of the country by French troops, finally found a haven in El Paso del Norte (now

Ciudad Juárez) on the border only a few steps away from exile in the United States. Juárez operated from El Paso del Norte from August 15, 1865, to June 17, 1866. The hard-pressed Mexican president drew safety, comfort, and strength from his border haven. Balls, receptions, and entertainment relieved some of the stress of the grim struggle for survival as the liberals attempted to rally their meager resources. Transborder solidarity motivated the United States Army to invite President Juárez to a reception in his honor in Franklin (now El Paso, Texas). The Mexican president declined to leave Mexican soil while the invaders remained, so the affair was moved to El Paso del Norte. Border social events, whether hosted by Mexican officials or their American counterparts, drew in the most influential people of Franklin, Las Cruces, San Elizario, and from Mexican towns and villages across the international line.[36]

Even before the end of the Civil War the American government allowed weapons to slip across the border, and with the Union victory diplomatic pressure on the French to withdraw their troops intensified, as did arms shipments. W. W. Mills, in charge of the El Paso, Texas, customhouse, a stone's throw away from Juárez's refuge in El Paso del Norte, also quietly furnished weapons to the Mexican government. The United States–Mexico border became the major source of supplies for Juárez's forces.[37] General Phil H. Sheridan noted that the Union army supplied arms and ammunition to the liberals, including some 30,000 muskets from the Baton Rouge, Louisiana, armory. The fear that fleeing Confederate soldiers allied with Maximilian's forces could still threaten the Union militarized the border. Under the circumstances, concentrating federal troops in south Texas seemed prudent. Consequently, the Fourth Army Corps established encampments at Victoria and San Antonio, while the Twenty-Fifth Corps occupied Brownsville.[38]

In Europe, the alarming rise of Prussia under Bismarck's iron rule further complicated French policy. Deployment of troops and resources in a distant campaign seemed unwise to a suddenly prudent Napoleon III. Consequently, in the fall of 1865, a limited withdrawal occurred as French troops retired to the center of the country. Ironically, they had been on the verge of consolidating control over Mexico. Distant political considerations saved the Juárez government, although the beleaguered Mexicans believed that whatever happened, the United States eventually would rescue them. The *Periódico Oficial* constantly reminded the American government of the intent of the Monroe Doctrine.[39] Maximilian had relied almost entirely on French troops, and as a result had not expended sufficient funds or effort in building his own effective force. The military balance swung against him as the Juaristas began the drive to recapture the nation.

Napoleon III soon withdrew his troops, and the empire collapsed, leaving an abandoned Emperor Maximilian to face a firing squad. Near Querétaro, a victorious Benito Juárez extracted his revenge—it appeared long overdue. Fortunately, Empress Carlota had returned to Europe in a vain attempt to raise support for her husband, and thus did not witness the collapse of Napoleon III's now abandoned fantasy. She retreated into madness. On July 15, 1867, a triumphant Juárez arrived in Mexico City on the heels of General Porfirio Díaz, commanding the liberal troops that retook the city.

LIBERAL RECONSTRUCTION

Benito Juárez, the *benemérito* of his country, understood that a weakened and discredited conservatism, associated with foreign intervention, had lost its credibility. Juárez now sought a national consensus, but one dominated by the liberals. Concentration on the common objective shared by both the liberals and conservatives of economic development, rather than emphasis on philosophical differences, had been suggested by Miguel Lerdo during the War of the Reform. Ever the economic man, Lerdo had sought to avoid destroying the capital's productive resources as well as the potential material contribution of the opposition. At that time Juárez rejected any compromise, but now a chastened conservatism and a bedraggled, relieved liberalism

Figure 3.2 Maximilian's shirt worn for his execution. *Courtesy of Amon Carter Museum, Fort Worth, Texas.*

attempted to find common ground. Juárez adopted a conciliatory approach to those who had collaborated with the French, releasing prisoners and softening war-time decrees. Once back in the capital he issued a long-delayed *convocatoria* (proclamation) calling for national elections. Contained within the document was a reform program to be adopted by public referendum. It proposed to permit the clergy to vote, to allow federal employees to serve in congress, to end all residency requirements for deputies, and to establish a senate. In addition, the government could respond to congress in writing, and the legislative body's ability to call special sessions would be curtailed. A new succession order in case of a presidential vacancy would also be arranged. If the referendum succeeded, all of the states would incorporate identical changes in their constitutions. The convocatoria's defenders pointed out that many of these elements appeared in the old Constitution of 1824 and in the Constitution of the United States. In fact, the convocatoria represented a move to the right justified by the need for a stronger executive to maintain order. The proposed referendum appealed more to conservatives than to liberals. As a result of opposition, President Juárez withdrew the proposal and urged passage of appropriate legislation to implement the changes. His successors subsequently succeeded in pushing through the suggested modifications to the Constitution of 1857. On the local level, liberal tenets had become widely accepted in municipal politics. The experience of wars and the deprivation of economic decline combined to forge local insistence on the rights of community autonomy that meant control of town commons, local taxes, and village militia. Caciques, most often veterans of the war against the French, arose, who acted as brokers between the national and state administrators and town residents to preserve these local rights. Francisco Lucas in the sierra of Puebla state became the archetype of the liberal cacique determined to protect community control of land, taxes, and militia service.

As for the Juárez program, ironically the convocatoria's move to the right sparked revolts that themselves reinforced the belief that more centralized and effective control should be put in place. Outbreaks occurred in Puebla and Tamaulipas in February 1869 and in the following month in Nuevo León and Sinaloa. Chronic violence characterized Guerrero and Jalisco and other states. Most of these disturbances did not threaten the national government's existence, although the revolt in San Luis Potosí at the end of the year caused grave concern. Unrest in the army also contributed to the tension, as Juárez moved to reduce the armed forces to 16,000 men. To many, endemic revolts appeared to be a continuation of the old cycle that had led to the disaster of territorial loss and foreign intervention. Juárez's inept move to the right and its consequences influenced the political strategy of his heirs—particularly Porfirio Díaz.[40]

MEXICAN POSITIVISM

Justifying a more authoritarian regime as well as cementing the emerging alliance with the conservatives, Mexican liberals turned to a new European philosophy—the positivism of Auguste Comte. Comte, born in France the year of the French Revolution (1789), grew up in its turbulent aftermath. As a result, he sought order above all else, an impulse that compelled him to study engineering—in essence, a constructive order. Comte elaborated a philosophy that linked order with progress as well as divided history into evolutionary stages. In the final stage, a society governed by scientific laws could look forward to perfection. At that point a technocratic, not a political, elite would regulate the nation under the benevolent guidance of a director. Before this stage could be reached, however, order had to be achieved. Comte's philosophy not only fused order and progress, but required a high degree of control by a directive elite. Such a philosophy appealed to both liberals and conservatives. It justified a certain type of state, with the promise of achieving progress.

Pedro Contreras Elizalde, an individual with European and Mexican roots, appears to have been the first Mexican positivist. He studied medicine in France, personally knew Comte, and participated as a charter member of the Société Positiviste in 1848. Returning to Mexico in 1855, he married one of President Juárez's daughters and subsequently served in the government. The person destined to be the leading popularizer of Comtean notions, Gabino Barreda, probably came into contact with positivist ideas through Contreras. Barreda also studied medicine in Paris and attended Comte's lectures. Drawing upon the basic elements of positivism, Barreda developed a useful interpretation of Mexican history. He portrayed the violence and disruption of the nineteenth century as a heroic and an epic struggle between the forces of darkness pitted against those of enlightenment and progress. By bracketing the disorder as a stage that occurred between 1810 and 1867, Barreda suggested that another era had begun. Moreover, he grandly proclaimed that Mexico's triumph represented a victory for all humanity. While Europe had failed to vanquish archaic forces, Mexico had struggled through into the new age. In doing so, the Mexican republic had saved the United States from contamination from reactionary French imperialism. Barreda's approach to Mexico's history gave value to the difficult past, while envisioning a progressive future. It provided a philosophy of development as well as psychological reassurance that the trauma of the nineteenth century had not been in vain.[41]

Barreda's view of the broader implications of the struggle against the French mirrored that of many Americans. The *Chicago Tribune* editorialized in 1867 that the "Southern rebellion" and the French adventure in Mexico constituted part of a seamless movement to reverse the tide of republicanism in the hemisphere. Former Secretary of State Seward, invited to visit Mexico by President Juárez in 1869, spoke repeatedly of the failed attempt of a reactionary European form of government to reestablish its grip upon the New World. The decisive moment allegedly came with the American Civil War and the French seizure of Mexico. The triumph of Juárez liberals and the American Union assured the survival of a republican continent that would soon regain its strength and demonstrate its ability to provide prosperity and happiness for its citizens.[42] Barreda, Juárez, and other reflective Mexicans agreed. Republican order, no longer threatened by monarchial imperialism, only needed to identify the path best able to facilitate material progress. Gabino Barreda offered a modified positivism as the philosophical structure able to focus the nation's energy on material progress. It remained to educate the people to appreciate positivism. The opportunity came when President Juárez appointed Barreda chairman of a commission to reorganize the country's educational system. The Barreda commission included all of the early Comteam disciples. Predictably, the commission recommended a more scientific organization of the educational structure—positivism's roots had been planted.

Gabino Barreda subsequently organized (1867) the Escuela Nacional Preparatoria (National Preparatory School), which opened in 1868 with 900 students. A whole generation of Mexican positivists soon emerged from its classrooms. José Yves Limantour, destined to be Porfirio Díaz's powerful secretary of the treasury and development from 1893 to 1911, and a major architect of the Porfiriato, enrolled in the school in 1869. Ironically, Ricardo Flores Magón and his brother Enrique, who posed a radical challenge to Porfirio Díaz from 1892 to the collapse of the regime in 1911, also attended the same school. In 1877, positivist students formed the Asociación Metodófila Gabino Barreda and proselytized the new faith through speeches, formal sessions, and articles published in the Anales of the association, as well as in the journal *Revista Positiva*. To Barreda and his earnest disciples, Mexico, having arrived at a critical juncture in its historical development, now had the obligation to move toward the Comtean ideal.[43]

The final struggle between progressive and retrograde elements appeared to have concluded within the Mexican arena. The decisive defeat of the monarchists and their natural allies, the Church and the conservatives, opened the way to the final stage of human development. The confusion, disorder, bickering, and fratricide that had characterized the country since independence had terminated in the victory of the progressive and rationally civilized elements over the forces of the past. To the positivists, the establishment of a disciplined order, coupled with acceptance of Comtean doctrines, assured a brilliant future. The fusion of Mexican liberalism and positivism provided the core intellectual underpinning of the Porfiriato that would soon take the liberalism of Juárez to its logical climax. Positivist influence on the Juárez regime itself was minimal, but the *benemérito* helped it take root, to flower under his successors. Meanwhile, Barreda picked through the ideas of Comte to assure a close fit between philosophical notions and what he perceived to be the actual circumstances of Mexico at that moment in its history. Following Juárez's general instructions, he brought Mexican liberalism and positivism together by skillfully adjusting both to meet the needs of the country as he saw them. The religion of humanity suggested by Comte was rejected in favor of the emphasis on rational logic. The Comtean motto of "Love, Order and Progress" in its Mexican metamorphosis became "Liberty, Order, and Progress," symbolizing the fusion of liberalism with an orderly scientific progress.[44]

Mexican positivism, while responding to a basic Comtean core of ideas, also absorbed elements drawn from Herbert Spencer, Charles Darwin, Edouard Laboulaye, and others. Translation into French of Spencer's *The Study of Sociology* made him known to the literate public. Darwin's *Descent of Man* (1871) caused a splash in Mexico because of its impact on religious beliefs, probably more so than his *Origin of the Species* (1859). Social Darwinism, a simple formulation drawn from Darwin's complex ideas, nevertheless entered into popular philosophy.[45] Less trendy but important ideas drawn from the historical and comparative school came through the works of the French philosopher Edouard Laboulaye. The historical school closely linked law and social development, thus the scientific use of law could construct the preferred society. Mexican positivism constituted a philosophical compound, an amalgam of ideas, all of which suggested the possibility of scientific control and the positive ability to move toward the desired republic. Nevertheless, with notable scholarly exceptions, most individuals acted on a "philosophical perception" rather than a detailed understanding or reading of the literature. While it is impossible to determine how many people actually read Spencer, Darwin, Laboulaye, or even Comte, as distinct from purchasing their works, one can assume that most received the "perception" from journals, newspapers, and short pieces written by people such as Gabino Barreda, Francisco Bulnes, and Justo Sierra. This made it possible to adjust fundamentally conflicting philosophical points, such as Spencer's individualism and Comte's emphasis on harmony, and integrate them into a popular philosophical mindset.[46]

The developmental thrust of positivism appealed to those Mexicans intent on upward movement into the professional class. Comtean notions posited a wide and respected role for a professional techno-cratic elite. As a result, the majority of professional school students, along with their professors, supported the modernization process. Even in the law schools, where antipositivist notions subsequently be-came popular, most individuals supported the expansion of economic opportunities for the rising middle class. Moreover, the emphasis on education inherent in both traditional Mexican liberalism and posi-tivism disposed the government to favor higher education. While bud-getary limitations made it impossible to adequately fund primary education, professional schools required much less, and their gradu-ates immediately contributed to the new economy. As a consequence of the economic reality, a mutually supportive relationship emerged among the government, the middle-class professionals, and students. Student political pressure, including demonstrations, was felt but re-flected their self-interest. For example, medical students in 1875 vio-lently protested the functioning of the School of Medicine, and in 1884 students protested what they believed to be government corruption under the presidency of Manual González that threatened to derail the modernization process. President Porfirio Díaz, on the other hand, as the philosophical heir of Juárez, usually could count on student ap-proval. Such support faltered in 1892 over whether Díaz should con-tinue into a fourth term, although many students joined the Club Porfirista de la Juventud, a pro-regime organization. Significantly, after 1910, when it became obvious that change was in the offing, middle-class professionals and students switched their support to Francisco I. Madero, the most conservative of the opponents of the old regime.[47] The economic promise of Mexican liberalism, infused with Comtean ideas, constituted a powerful influence on the professional class. The lower classes would not fare as well.

MOLDING THE NATION

The semimythical Benito Juárez often is portrayed as a friend of the humble classes. In reality, the picture is not quite so clear. Nineteenth-century liberalism, with its ideological emphasis on individual initia-tive, tended to assign only negative value to groups. While liberals did not believe in gratuitous cruelty, nevertheless they viewed the lower social elements as collective obstacles to development. Liberals did not want to befriend the lower classes; they wanted to transform them for their own good and the well-being of the country. This attitude led to all sorts of individually harsh acts, as peasants became unwilling instruments of development. As a consequence, people beginning to be displaced by philosophical and economic forces reacted with violence. Agrarian unrest during the period 1868–1870 touched most of central

Mexico, extending south into the Isthmus of Tehuantepec and east into Campeche and Tabasco. The lower classes, faced by an unsympathetic and often hostile political system, identified as a retrograde element to be transformed or pushed aside, resorted to reactionary violence, including banditry.

Unraveling the component parts of rural violence in the 1860s is difficult and perhaps unnecessary. A volatile combination of perceived political betrayal, disputes over land, exploitative wages, and abusive treatment created a socially explosive situation that could be set off by an event that in another time would be ignored. For example, political manipulation by the federal government of state politics provided the pretext for a three-day occupation of the state capital of Puebla. The complex frustration that fueled the seizure needed only the slightest provocation to burst out into action. Toluca, the capital of the State of Mexico, barely withstood a campesino blockade as armed peasants closed roads to press their demands. In the Sierra Gordo of Querétaro conflict over land continued from the 1840s into the 1880s. Otomí Indians claimed land held by the Augustinian monastery near Dehedo. Troops had to be sent to control the situation. In Puebla the state government attempted to defuse the land situation by negotiating an amnesty and dividing up a hacienda among several villages. These proto-rebellions kept the regime busy, but did not threaten its existence nor force a change in Juarista policy.[48]

Another serious threat to the government's legitimacy came from its inability to control criminal elements in the countryside. Enclaves of law and order in the cities contrasted sharply with conditions in rural areas. An acceptable degree of formal justice and an official presence needed to be maintained throughout the republic. Whether this could be done by the individual states or the federal government remained in doubt. In the 1860s a group of bandits called *plateados* emerged; these "elegant bandits" adorned their clothing and saddles with silver. They functioned as a group of booty capitalists, seizing a share of the wealth and publicly proclaiming their newly acquired socioeconomic stature by possession of fine horses, expensive firearms, and silver-encrusted clothing. They often moved into politics on one side or another, or pursued their own political objectives in an era characterized by civic strife and, on occasion, civil war. They responded to order imposed by themselves, as well as economic incentives, and had socially moved, if by illegal or criminal means, beyond their former position of rural workers.

Ignacio M. Altamirano captured the sociopolitical ambivalence of the plateados in his book *El Zarco* (written in the 1880s, but published in 1901). The mixed sociopolitical impulse of the plateados is evident in the case of Manuel Villa, originally from the small village of

Tecomatlán. His group, known by the regional designation as the *plateados de tierra caliente* (a reference to the more tropical lowlands), sacked villages, talked of the "tyranny of Juárez," warned local officials to watch their step, and in general presented themselves as defenders of campesinos. One could buy safety by cooperating with the bandits, or, in the case of merchants, by paying them to "protect" their goods.[49] The plateados provided a warning to the liberals that the lower classes should not be deprived of the ability to influence their own destiny—a message repeated by Emiliano Zapata and Francisco Villa in the twentieth century.

Some forms of banditry caused the government greater embarrassment than others. In the early 1870s the Mexican railway (Veracruz to Mexico City) experienced attacks on its trains and property. Railway officials threatened to end construction unless the government took action against the bandits. As is often the case, such activity had political overtones. Fernando F. Migoni, self-designated Colonel in Chief of the Popular Army of *tierra caliente*, mixed politics and banditry in a fashion reminiscent of the insurgency that accompanied the independence movement. The government placed guards on trains, which caused further problems. In a notable incident, the head guard ordered the locomotive engineer to return to the station to retrieve his forgotten hat, brushing aside explanations that backing up a train entailed a major and time-consuming procedure not to be undertaken lightly. Fortunately, the train arrived at another station before bloodshed ended the argument. Company officials had scant confidence in the government's ability to control banditry or offer any other assistance and as a result resisted pressure to hold their freight charges down, claiming they needed the revenue. A weak government, barely able to restrain banditry, had correspondingly feeble regulatory influence.[50]

President Benito Juárez skillfully co-opted upwardly mobile bandits into a rural police force (1861). These official plateados (*rurales*) would be invested with the virtues of loyalty, bravery, and perseverance in order to justify their absorption into the structure of the state. The line between simple virtues and unacceptable behavior blurred out of necessity. At least the government had some claim to legitimacy in rural Mexico and could pretend to be in more control than in fact was possible. Rurales wore the same type of clothing as the plateados, although standardized to provide an institutional identification. During the Porfiriato, corpsmen wore light gray bolero jackets, suede leather tight-fitting trousers, braided and decorated with silver buttons and topped with a heavy felt sombrero. By the end of 1861, four units operated in and around Mexico City. Rurales often moved from law enforcement to banditry and back.

The trick remained to make it more profitable to enforce the law than to break it. Rafael Cuéllar, who started his career as the head of a private security gang that patrolled the highway from Mexico City to Veracruz under contract and who became the inspector-general of the rurales in the 1880s, indulged in various profitable lines of corruption, including selling government arms for his own account. Profitable corruption kept him in government service, although he could just as comfortably function on the other side of the law. On a number of occasions, entire units looted and robbed the area they supposedly were assigned to protect. Nevertheless, the rural police force represented a step forward in extending law and order into the countryside.[51]

Juárez could be brutal when faced by a direct physical or ideological challenge. The president tolerated little social opposition from those who did not share his vision of Mexican liberalism. Popular radicalism, an ideological reaction to the elitism of Mexican liberalism, could not be ignored by Juárez. One of the most significant challenges occurred in Chalco in the person of Julio Chávez López. An Indian educated in the "School of Enlightenment and Socialism," founded by European radicals, Chávez López developed a vision different from that held by the liberals. His ideology identified the problem and indicated the solution. Well grounded in anarchist theory, he called for a violent struggle against the state, associating the abolition of government with the end of exploitation. A movement, not a mere revolt, it represented a major advance beyond the 1849 agrarian revolt of Eleaterio Quiroz that had offered no broad ideological critique of liberalism. Chávez López recruited a ragtag army, issued a manifesto, and began seizing haciendas. No match for the national government, Chávez López died on September 1, 1869, in front of a wall on the order of Benito Juárez. Reportedly, his last words were "Long live socialism."[52]

Juárez's decision in 1872 to run for a fourth term split his followers. Moreover, physical restructuring of the republic also created uncertainty. The carving of two new states, Hidalgo (January 15) and Morelos (April 17, 1869), from the expanse of the old state of Mexico suggested a new alignment of regional power blocks. In addition, the national government's use of the army in the elections in San Luis Potosí, Puebla, and Jalisco, coupled with rigged elections in the capital and jailings of opposition members, indicated an ominous change in the regime's approach. Those who moved in hostile opposition included Sebastián Lerdo de Tejada, who had served in Juárez's cabinet, and General Porfirio Díaz. The general public, aware of its inability to influence events because of indirect elections, resented the violence and wrangling while the nation teetered on the verge of some as yet unknown disaster. Díaz's call for effective suffrage and no reelection spoke directly to those outsiders. As a result, General Díaz enjoyed wide popularity.

Uncritical and reactionary support gave rise to unrealistic expectations among the diverse groups that rallied to the Porfirista cause—in the end, most would have to settle for order and progress. Meanwhile, liberal control over congress enabled Juárez to arrange another presidential term. Díaz, who had opposed Juárez in the election along with Lerdo, now took to the field in revolt. Díaz announced the Plan of La Noria, claiming that constant reelection violated liberal principles, as well as the spirit of the Constitution of 1857. Juárez received extraordinary dictatorial powers to deal with Díaz. Although the revolt failed, the notion of no reelection entered into the consciousness of the nation.

THE REVOLUTION OF TUXTEPEC

The lingering armed remnants of the La Noria revolt ended their activities when Juárez died in office (July 19, 1872). A new election, in which Díaz again ran, gave the presidency to Sebastián Lerdo de Tejada, brother of Miguel Lerdo. The country, as well as Porfirio Díaz, accepted the results although Díaz clearly enjoyed more popular support, while Lerdo had manipulated the system to his own advantage. President Lerdo preferred a strong centralized government to maintain order in the states. A captive congress allowed Lerdo to act as he believed most useful. The opposition claimed that only the czar came close to matching the president's power. Ironically, Díaz in turn would be compared to the Russian ruler. Indeed, although Lerdo acted forcibly he seldom lost all restraint. The newspaper *El Ahuizote* (the lash), with a malicious tongue in cheek, reported that Lerdo intended to extend political rights to women so that he could select a congress composed entirely of pretty young girls—the paper observed that the "women of today are more independent than the men and will oppose seduction . . . with greater resistance." Under President Lerdo, the Laws of Reform became part of the constitution (1873), much to the Church's displeasure. The following year an enabling act prohibited religious instruction in schools, the wearing of clerical garb in public, and other restrictions on open displays of religion. The Church suspected, probably rightly so, that Lerdo favored Protestants. When a mob in Jalisco murdered an American missionary he moved rapidly to punish the guilty. Among other things he hoped to avoid any American claim that his government failed to protect U.S. citizens. Beyond immediate political consideration, Lerdo may well have shared Juárez's desire, as expressed to Justo Sierra, to encourage a religion that would make Indians read and would not force them to spend their money on "candles for the saints."[53] It seems probable that the Church's active hostility made President Lerdo appreciate a religious group that caused little trouble; as he observed, Protestant preachers had distinguished themselves as citizens "who obey the law."

Lerdo also pushed through a constitutional amendment establishing a senate as proposed in the convocatoria of 1867. Following a modified American model, it provided for two senators from each state for a four-year term. The senate, a hand-picked group, helped balance the sometimes troublesome lower house. Even more useful, the amendment provided a legal basis for the national government to intervene in the states. The senate could declare an absence of state power and authorize the president to appoint a provisional governor to organize new elections. In case of conflict between a governor and the state legislature, the senate also could request the federal government to intervene. Under these provisions the national government exercised a moderating power over potentially disruptive state politics. While Lerdo, driven from office, never had a chance to use these devices, his successor Porfirio Díaz found the mechanism politically useful.

With Lerdo, the nation's modernization seemed assured. Railway construction contracts, many with foreigners, began to bring the nation together. Lerdo, intent on avoiding past difficulties, sought to make sure that railway projects responded to Mexican law. By 1876, Mexico had only 416 miles of track, but the groundwork for a more extensive system had been laid. Legal, financial, and political issues no longer slowed the process. Nevertheless, even by the end of Díaz's first term in office, only another 258 miles had been added to the network. Telegraph lines spread across the land, making it increasingly possible to govern the country from the center. An understandably confident President Lerdo sought reelection in 1876. Díaz again protested accusing the president of abusing regional politicians, selling out the nation's interest to foreign speculators, and other highly exaggerated indictments. Porfirio Díaz's Plan of Tuxtepec struck a responsive chord, particularly among state politicians, again calling for effective suffrage and no reelection. In short order, the Revolution of Tuxtepec succeeded in forcing Lerdo to flee into exile in the United States.[54]

Liberalism's convulsion, while politically important, did not draw in the great mass of people. Most of them still struggled to come to accommodation with the profound structural changes brought about during the Juárez era. They could not foresee the impact of the mature liberalism that the nation experienced under Porfirio Díaz. In the borderlands, northerners, isolated from Mexico City, continued to develop their own transborder culture. Hardy entrepreneurs, Indian traders and fighters, and cattlemen from both sides of the border created a hybrid culture. Politics and economics blended with intermarriage as borderlands searched for security and prosperity. The process would not be without violence, but for the most part borderlanders became functionally bilingual, understood each other's cultural practices, enjoyed each other's culinary delights, and modified their own culture accordingly.

NOTES

1. Olliff, *Reforma Mexico*, p. 44.
2. G. Emlen Hall and David J. Weber, "Mexican Liberals and the Pueblo Indians, 1821–1829," *New Mexican Historical Review* 59: 1 (1984), pp. 5–32.
3. Stevens, *Origins of Instability*, p. 40.
4. Michael P. Costeloe, *Church Wealth in Mexico: A Study of the Juzgado de Capellanías in the Archbishopric of Mexico, 1800–1856* (Cambridge: Cambridge University Press, 1967), pp. 99, 124.
5. Richard N. Sinkin, *The Mexican Reform, 1855–1876: A Study in Liberal Nation-Building* (Austin: University of Texas Press, 1979), p. 169.
6. Stevens, *Origins of Instability*, p. 39.
7. Jan Bazant, *Alienation of Church Wealth in Mexico: Social and Economic Aspects of Liberal Revolution, 1856–1875* (Cambridge: Cambridge University Press, 1971), pp. 287–90.
8. Ian Jacobs, *Ranchero Revolt: The Mexican Revolution in Guerrero* (Austin: University of Texas Press, 1982), pp. 48–49; Heather Fowler Salamini and Mary Kay Vaughan, eds. *Women of the Mexican Countryside, 1850–1990: Creating Spaces, Shaping Transitions* (Tucson: University of Arizona Press, 1994), p. 11.
9. Charles R. Berry, *The Reform in Oaxaca, 1856–76: A Microhistory of the Liberal Revolution* (Lincoln: University of Nebraska Press, 1981), pp. 138–91; Antonio Escobar Ohmstede and Frans J. Schryer, "Las sociedades agrarias en el norte de Hidalgo, 1856–1900," *Mexican Studies / Estudios Mexicanos* (winter 1992), pp. 1–21.
10. Milada Bazant, "La desamortización de los bienes de la iglesia en Toluca durante la Reforma," in María Teresa Jarquín O., ed., *Temas de historia mexiquense* (Toluca: Colegio Mexiquense—H. Ajuntamiento de Toluca, 1988), pp. 237–39.
11. Staples, "Policía y buen gobierno", *Rituals of Rule*, pp. 115–126; Antonio Barbosa Heldt, *Cien años en la educación de México* (México: Pax-Mexico, 1972), p. 88.
12. Josefina Vázquez de Knauth, *Nacionalismo y Educación en México* (México: Colegio de México, 1970). Describes the psychological significance of rural schools as well as the gap between theory and practice that helps account for their importance following the collapse of the Porfiriato.
13. González Navarro, *Anatomía del poder*, pp. 88–90; Francisco López Camara, *La estructura económica y social de México en la época de la Reforma* (México: Siglo Veintiuno, 1967), p. 196.
14. Olliff, *Reforma Mexico*, pp. 60–76.
15. Barbara A. Tenenbaum, "The Making of a Fait Accompli: The Mexican State, 1821–1857," in Rodríguez O., ed., *Patterns of Contention*.
16. Rodolfo F. Acuña, *Sonoran Strongman: Ignacio Pesqueira and His Times* (Tucson: University of Arizona Press, 1974), p. 42.

17. The process of survival and adaptation is discussed in full in Charles H. Harris, *A Mexican Family Empire: The Latifundio of the Sánchez Navarro Family, 1765–1867* (Austin: University of Texas Press, 1975).
18. Olliff, *Reforma Mexico*, p. 61.
19. Ibid., p. 64; Daniel Cosío Villegas, *La Constitución de 1857 y sus críticos* (México: Editorial Hermes, 1973).
20. Francisco Bulnes, *Juárez y las revoluciones de Ayutla y de Reforma* (México: Antigua Imprenta de Murguia, 1905), p. 536.
21. Ramón Eduardo Ruiz, *Triumphs and Tragedy: A History of the Mexican People* (New York: W. W. Norton & Company, 1992), p. 239.
22. Walter V. Scholes, *Mexican Politics During the Juárez Regime, 1855–1872* (Columbia: University of Missouri Press, 1957), p. 36; Olliff, *Reforma Mexico*, pp. 115–16.
23. Scholes, *Mexican Politics*, p. 63.
24. Thomas D. Schoonover, *Dollars Over Dominion: The Triumph of Liberalism in Mexican–United States Relations, 1861–1867* (Baton Rouge: Louisiana State University Press, 1978), pp. 19, 26, 48–77.
25. Alfred J. Hanna and Kathryn A. Hanna, *Napoleon III and Mexico* (Chapel Hill: University of North Carolina Press, 1971), pp. 5–7.
26. Hanna and Hanna, *Napoleon III*, p. 85; Emilia Romero de Valle, *Corpancho: Un amigo de México* (México: Junta Mexicana de Investigaciones Históricas, 1949).
27. Condesa Paula Kolonitz, *Un viaje a México en 1864* (Mexico: Secretaria de Educación Pública, 1976).
28. Acuña, *Sonoran Strongman*, p. 82.
29. Jack A. Dabbs, *The French Army in Mexico, 1861–1867* (The Hague: Mouton, 1962).
30. Curtis R. Tyler, "Santiago Vidaurri and the Confederacy," *The Americas (1969)*, pp. 66–76; Alex M. Saragoza, *The Monterrey Elite and the Mexican State, 1880–1940* (Austin: University of Texas Press, 1988), pp. 22–23. Because Confederate cotton often was exchanged in Matamoros directly for military supplies, rather than sold for cash, a certain amount ended up in New England mills. How much remains a question. Thomas Schoonover, "Mexican Cotton and the American Civil War," *The Americas* (April 1974), p. 447.
31. Jerry D. Thompson, *Mexican Texans in the Union Army* (El Paso: Texas Western Press, University of Texas at El Paso, 1986), pp. 8, 22, 38, 42.
32. Hanna and Hanna, *Napoleon III*, p. 119.
33. Robert W. Frazer, "Matías Romero and the French Intervention in Mexico" (Ph.D. diss., University of California, 1941).
34. Hanna and Hanna, *Napoleon III*, p. 56.
35. Schoonover, *Dollars Over Dominion*, pp. 90, 115, 129, 132–37, 160.
36. Armando B. Chávez, *Historia de Ciudad Juárez, Chihuahua* (México: Editorial Pax 1991), p. 263; Nancy Hamilton, *Ben Dowell: El Paso's First Mayor* (El Paso: Texas Western Press, University of Texas at El Paso, 1976), pp. 41–42.
37. W. W. Mills, *Forty Years at El Paso*, 1858–1898 (El Paso: By Author, 1901).
38. P. H. Sheridan, *Personal Memoirs*, 2 vols. (New York: C. L. Webster, 1888), vol. 2, pp. 224–26, 213.
39. Scholes, *Mexican Politics*, p. 110.
40. Brian Hamnett, *Juárez* (London: Longman, 1994); Guy P .C. Thomson with David G. LaFrance, *Patriotism, Politics and Popular Liberalism in Nineteenth-century Mexico: Juan Francisco Lucas and the Puebla Sierra* (Wilmington, DE: SR Books, 1998).
41. Hale, *The Transformation*, p. 141.

42. Schoonover, *Dollars Over Dominion*, pp. 279–83. For Seward's speeches in Mexico, see Albert S. Evans, *Our Sister Republics: A Gala Trip Through Tropical Mexico in 1869–70* (Hartford: Columbian Book Co., 1870).

43. Barreda (1818–1881) studied law as well as medicine. He fought in the war with the United States, then studied in France and spent the Maximilian period practicing medicine in Guanajuato. Leopoldo Zea, *Positivism in Mexico* (Austin: University of Texas Press, 1974), pp. 36–46; Lourdes Alvardo, "Asociación Metodófila Gabino Barreda: Dos ensayos representativos," *Estudios de historia moderna y contemporánea de México* (México: Universidad Nacional Autonoma de México, 1989), pp. 211–45.

44. Vázquez de Knauth, *Nacionalismo y educación*, p. 49.

45. See the introduction in Roberto Moreno, *La polémica del Darwinismo en México: Siglo XIX (Testimonios)* (México: Universidad Nacional Autónoma de México, 1984), pp. 17–42.

46. Hale, *The Transformation*, pp. 205–18.

47. Javier Garciadiego Dantan, "Movimientos estudiantiles durante la Revolución Mexicana," in Jaime E. Rodríguez O., ed., *The Revolutionary Process in Mexico: Essays on Political and Social Change, 1880–1940* (Los Angeles: UCLA Latin America Center Publications, 1990), pp. 115–60.

48. John M. Hart, *Revolutionary Mexico: The Coming and Process of the Mexican Revolution* (Berkeley: University of California Press, 1987), p. 40; Ana Ma. D. Huerta Jaramillo, "Insurrecciones campesinas en el estado de Puebla, 1868–1870," in Andrea Sánchez Quintanar and Juan Manuel de la Serna H., eds., *Movimientos populares en la historia de México y América Latina* (México: Universidad Nacional Autónoma de México, 1987), p. 225.

49. María Dolores Illescas, "Agitación social y bandidaje en el estado de Morelos durante el siglo XIX," *Estudios* (fall 1988), pp. 79–84; Huerta Jaramillo, "Insurrecciones campesinas," pp. 224–27.

50. Arthur Paul Schmidt Jr., "The Social and Economic Effects of the Railroad in Puebla and Veracruz, Mexico, 1867–1911," (Ph.D. diss., Indiana University, 1974), pp. 174–75.

51. Vanderwood, *Disorder and Progress*, pp. 54–59.

52. John M. Hart, "Agrarian Precursors of the Mexican Revolution: The Development of an Ideology," *The Americas* (1972), pp. 131–50.

53. Justo Sierra, *The Political Evolution of the Mexican People* (Austin: University of Texas Press, 1969), p. 348.

54. Frank A. Knapp, *The Life of Sebastián Lerdo de Tejada, 1823–1889: A Study in Influence and Obscurity* (Austin: University of Texas Press, 1951), pp. 186–91, 213, 217

Chapter 4

PORFIRIO DÍAZ TRIUMPHANT

Porfirio Díaz as president followed the governing pattern so well established by Juárez and Lerdo. The authoritarian tendency of Mexican liberalism, now a strong admixture of liberalism and positivism, became obvious under Díaz as the national government began to use modern communication and transportation technology to its political advantage. Nevertheless, he understood the needs of the regional elites and their fear of excessive control from Mexico City. Díaz would be careful not to make the same mistake as Lerdo. Like his distinguished predecessors, he had strong liberal credentials and his military service added an important patriotic luster, as his frequent appearance in military uniform emphasized. In fact, Díaz identified intensely with the Mexican republic, perceiving himself as much a patriot as a national savior. He viewed his personal esteem, dating back to the heroic moment on the Cinco de Mayo, as inseparably entwined with the nation. Subsequently, he manipulated his daughter's birthday to fall on the anniversary of the French defeat at Puebla. Appropriately named Luz Aurora Victoria Díaz, she was registered on May 5, 1875. He moved the date of Hidalgo's grito of independence to coincide with his own birthday celebration. These were not mere sentimental gestures, but part of a process of bonding with the country and his national mission.[1] As a result, General Díaz commanded a strong loyalty from his supporters and a respect that facilitated his dealing with regional elites, whom he perceived to be constructively involved in establishing stability and progress.

Porfirio Díaz Triumphant

1876–1911	The Porfiriato, the regime of Porfirio Díaz
1878	Ley del Pueblo, radical program for agrarian reform
1880–1884	Manuel González interregnum
1882	Banco Nacional de México founded
1883	Land survey law
1884	Mining code revised to permit ownership of subterranean rights
1884–1911	Díaz reelected president
1888	Dublán Convention
1892	Tomochic Rebellion
1897	General Law of Credit Institutions allows for orderly expansion of banking system.
1904	Monetary Reform Act

Díaz deliberately projected a statesmanlike concern for the national interest, placing himself above narrow personalistic or partisan concerns. While more than willing to reward devoted followers, he also appointed individuals to office on the basis of the country's needs, regardless of whether they had supported him in the past. Thus Matías Romero, who had served Juárez so ably and backed Lerdo, and Felipe Berriozábal, a leading political general who had supported another presidential contender, both received high ministerial appointments. He even sought to draw in José Hipólito Ramírez, a former conservative supporter of Maximilian. Although a public outcry blocked Ramírez's appointment, Díaz nonetheless succeeded in constructing a national unity regime that helped legitimize his own unconstitutional rise to power, as well as compensate for his lack of an actual electoral mandate.[2]

While sympathetic to regional elites, his attitude toward those who disrupted order could be harsh, regardless of whether the motivation was political or economic. Nonideological pragmatism governed the president's actions and determined the response. Ironically, the peasants who had rallied to the Plan of Tuxtepec believed Díaz supported agrarian objectives as they defined them. They were wrong. Hopes for municipal autonomy quickly faded as Díaz failed to act on the issue. Agrarian reform returned as an objective with a vengeance after 1911 during the Mexican Revolution. Its explosive appeal could not have been anticipated. Indeed, during the revolt against Lerdo, vague promises had been made to virtually every group—industrialists, foreign investors, elite landholders, peasants, Río Grande Valley ranchmen in Texas, urban labor, and others—to secure the broadest possible transnational support and financial assistance.

The new president could not respond to the multitude of claims. Feeling disappointed and betrayed, campesinos resorted to endemic violence that lasted from 1878 to 1883 in northern and central Mexico. Urban radicals provided an ideological framework for rural discontent, drawing up the Ley del Pueblo (1878), the most elaborate agrarian program up to that time. They demanded absolute spiritual and economic equality for the peasantry, municipal ownership and assignment of hacienda land, as well as low interest agricultural loans. The Ley del Pueblo represented a philosophical link among urban workers, radicals, and campesinos.[3] The army, reinforced by the revitalized rurales, struggled to suppress the wave of rural disorder. Along the border with the United States, Díaz acted quickly and forcefully to suppress banditry, thereby demonstrating his intention to control border violence. Washington had to be convinced that Mexico could be brought under firm control.

General Porfirio Díaz employed personal skills as well as his national prestige to persuade the nation and the United States to trust his intentions. After a long series of dashed expectations, many hoped the country had at last found an individual able to maintain order and usher the nation into the modern age. During his first term, Díaz concentrated on clearing away political and diplomatic obstacles to foreign investment and on projecting a stable image. While he had little money to invest in modernization, he managed to at least create the feeling of political stability.

Díaz accepted the evident reality that Mexico's economic future depended almost completely on the United States. Few alternatives remained in the face of a British retreat, the fiasco of the French intervention, and the growing economic power of Mexico's northern neighbor. British commercial power in the country had lasted only a brief forty years. As early as 1859 the British legation in Mexico City lamented the noticeable drop in the number of English merchant houses, as did the French consul in the port of Tampico. Only three British import firms remained in the capital in 1863. German traders picked up most of the business as British firms pulled out. British goods still dominated the market, even as that country's merchant-traders physically withdrew from Mexico; nevertheless, the writing was on the wall. In the year of Tuxtepec, Britain supplied 35 percent of Mexico's imports compared with 25.8 percent from the United States. Four years later, the United States had pulled ahead, and by 1905, American producers supplied 50 percent of all imports. The same trend could be observed in Mexican exports.[4] Mexico and the United States had become inseparable trading partners. Díaz understood that it was no longer simply a question of his nation modeling its institutions and economic development along American lines. That notion belonged to a more naïve era. It remained to deal pragmatically with an economic reality dominated by the United States. Nevertheless, Díaz did what he could to encourage European, Canadian, and other investors to compete with American capital. The old dream of reaching economic and political equality with the United States, however, appeared to be even more distant.

Díaz had to deal with an aggressively petulant administration in Washington, D.C. President Rutherford B. Hayes had little respect for the Mexican government. While American troops often crossed into Mexico in pursuit of Indian raiding parties, they did so unofficially. However, in 1877, the American Commander, E.O.C. Ord, received instructions to inform the Mexican government that it would now be official policy to do so. Unilateral action challenged Mexican sovereignty. Armed incursions along the border could not be ignored without damaging, perhaps fatally, the government's legitimacy. Moreover, the possibility of a bloody confrontation between Mexican and American troops heightened the danger of war between the two republics. Hayes also pressed Mexico to abolish the free zone in the north and settle other matters before receiving U.S. recognition. Díaz coldly pointed out that his government had met all of the requirements for diplomatic recognition laid down in international law. Finally, in early 1878, the United States extended recognition. Typically, Díaz threw a banquet to honor the occasion and toasted the American representative in appropriately flattering terms. Díaz subsequently managed to have the Ord frontier crossing instruction rescinded. A combination of principled firmness and reasonableness forced the United States to accommodate the Díaz regime.[5]

Díaz's early efforts set the basic conditions for subsequent rapid development. Díaz astutely instructed European agents to buy up the Mexican debt on the open market at an average price of four cents on the dollar. While the American representative in Mexico, John W. Foster, viewed it as morally outrageous that a country would sell bonds, default, then buy them back cheaply, the government nevertheless began clearing away its outstanding debts. The Mexican government negotiated a comprehensive border claims settlement with the United States, paid the first installment, and hoped that American investors, as well as the United States government, would look at Mexico with new eyes. In addition, the opening of consulates along the border emphasized the Mexican government's political control over the border and facilitated transnational economic activity. Faced with a severe financial crisis to the extent of establishing an order in which government employees received their pay depending on how much money remained, Díaz desperately sought to stabilize falling revenues. He moved aggressively against smugglers in the hope of increasing customs revenues. When he left office the treasury remained empty, but he had persuaded both Mexico and the United States that his formula for progress was the correct one—it merely had to be consistently followed into a more stable and prosperous future.[6]

As Díaz's term drew to a close many of his political associates urged him to continue in office. Although tempted, the president felt trapped by his own political rhetoric. In the end, the principle of no reelection that lay at the core of the Plan of Tuxtepec forced him to relinquish the presidency. While many admired Díaz's attachment to principle, few believed that one successful term in office could reverse the nation's drift toward some as yet unforeseen disaster. Rigid adherence to the ideal of no reelection, or excessive concern for constitutional government, should not be allowed to jeopardize Tuxtepec's elaboration of an effective political system that had elicited a workable degree of elite cooperation. The fear that it would all collapse after Díaz left office haunted the country. Thus, a regrettable ambivalence swept Mexico as President Díaz prepared to step down.[7] As his immediate successor, he endorsed Manuel González, his secretary of war and a fellow general. González, often viewed as a mere Díaz puppet, in fact functioned independently. Nevertheless, he remained a loyal and close friend of don Porfirio and strongly supported his return to office sometime in the future. Few personal, philosophical, or operational differences divided them.

INTERREGNUM

The friendship and trust between the two men had been forged on the field of battle and they shared a sense of camaraderie developed in the close proximity of camp life. During the War of Reform, General González backed the conservative cause and actually fought against troops commanded by Díaz. With the French intervention, González switched sides and eventually served as Díaz's chief of staff. González symbolized the ideological fusion of conservatives and liberals that resulted from the modification of liberalism under the impact of Comtean ideas, as well as the nationalist reaction to foreign intervention. He supported his friend and political mentor during the aborted La Noria revolt against Juárez, as well as the victorious Revolution of Tuxtepec that brought Porfirio Díaz to power. General González subsequently served as governor of Michoacán and as secretary of war. As a military man he knew how to be the faithful subordinate, but also understood the role and responsibility of supreme command. An active Díaz accepted the new president's appointment as secretary of development. Later, Díaz served as governor of his home state of Oaxaca. While Díaz's advice was sought, it is clear he did not function as a political puppet master.

During the González presidency a number of important structural changes occurred. Mining was assigned the leading role in the drive for economic expansion. Although silver had served as the engine of colonial Mexico, the new plan called for the comprehensive exploitation of all mineral resources, including coal. A mining society established in 1882, subsidized by the government and chaired by the minister of development, encouraged new technology and expanded awareness of the possibilities in the industry for both Mexican investors and foreigners. For its part the federal government moved to rationalize the tax structure and develop a simplified and uniform approach to mineral development. As a major step in this direction the constitution, which allowed states to regulate mines, was amended to give the national government authority to enact a uniform code that went into effect in 1884. It provided for private ownership of subsoil rights as long as the mines remained active. An idle mine could be denounced and purchased by an individual or company interested in working it. The 1884 code thus adjusted the traditional vesting of subsoil rights in the state inherited by the republic from the colonial regime. Under Spanish rule, individuals effectively owned the concession or right to mine, but not the mineral deposit itself. Denunciation of unworked mines also had been provided under the Spanish code. The 1884 modification had a major psychological impact on foreign investors, who could exercise direct ownership as well as dispose of their property. The change also facilitated mortgaging, enabling individuals to raise working capital. In reality, however, the code conveyed only a conditional ownership. The state reserved the right to revoke proprietorship in the event the holder failed to exploit continuously the mineral resource. In effect, the government retained its directive role and exercised it throughout the nation.

In a similar fashion, the land law of 1883 represented an attempt by the government to force resources to develop. It drew upon a previous enactment by the Juárez regime, also with colonial antecedents, that permitted individuals to denounce and acquire vacant land, as well as a law of 1875 that called for the surveying of vacant land by companies that in return received one-third of the land surveyed. Such land then could be colonized by productive immigrants or sold to agricultural interests. The 1883 law went further in that current occupants had to prove legal title. Small landholders unable to produce documentation or unable to afford the legal defense of their property had no hope of retaining possession. As a consequence, surveying companies acquired large tracts of land. Vast expanses of territory could be switched from use by marginal agriculturalists, usually Indians, into the hands of those deemed more productive and modern. In effect, the law made land available for speculation as well as for large-scale agricultural activities. While the government's economic objective had been met, the more complex notion of strengthening the country's socioeconomic structure through the introduction of immigrants solidly based on moderate landholding floundered. By 1900, the total failure of the colonization aspects of land reform had become evident, while land ownership became more concentrated. Capital-intensive agriculture reinforced the trend toward large holdings.

A chronically depleted treasury impelled the president to gamble on projects that promised a rapid return. González's willingness to make quick and risky economic decisions and support problematic ventures made him vulnerable to promoters and their exaggerated claims. Many ill-considered projects failed, making the regime look incompetent and giving rise to a public suspicion that excessive corruption and fraud were involved. A weak fiscal structure continually tottered on the verge of bankruptcy.

By the 1880s the ministry of development became the first government agency in Mexico's history to have a larger share of the budget than the war department, exemplifying the emphasis on economic development over all other state objectives. President González, in an effort to stimulate the confidence of foreign investors as well as facilitate access to European money markets, took the bold and highly unpopular step of recognizing the long-outstanding British debt, including some questionable obligations of doubtful legality. Many, in particular, students, saw the government's acquiescence as a shameful caving in to European pressure.[8] The González government hoped that its acceptance of responsibility would clear the way for normal financial relations with foreign capital markets. President González's action, coming at the end of his term in office, relieved the incoming Díaz administration of making a necessary if disagreeable accommodation with British creditors. The González interregnum provided a general housecleaning period during which difficult and sometimes unpopular decisions were made that smoothed the way for his successor.

While he had a circle of supporters, González did not enjoy anything close to the popularity of Porfirio Díaz. He realized that he could not hope to rival, even had he wished to do so, the stature of his friend and predecessor. President González paid scant attention to his personal reputation. He hoped to be an effective president, but entertained no ambitions beyond one term, and thus spent little time burnishing his image. In contrast, Díaz understood the importance of a favorable public persona and did what appeared necessary to achieve that goal.

The antigovernment press could be relied upon to cultivate a hostile view of the administration. While President González sought to control the level of criticism by subsidizing newspapers, bribing editors, even threatening legal action, the opposition press nevertheless succeeded in tarnishing his image. Díaz, an avid student of reality, drew valuable lessons from the fiscal and economic blunders of the González regime, as well as his inept managing of public relations. Consequently, press policy during the Porfiriato, while embodying the same techniques with force held in ultimate reserve, became much more effective in controlling the level of criticism than during the González presidency.[9]

Not surprisingly, demand mounted for Díaz's return to office. A de facto alliance between liberals and conservatives made him the only choice. Subsequently, Díaz made the issue of political indispensability one of his enduring political weapons—only he could govern the country effectively. General Díaz also developed a smoother social exterior, thanks to the efforts of his second wife, Carmen Romero Rubio, an eighteen-year-old from a well-to-do and refined family, who polished the then fifty-one-year-old rough soldier into a more cosmopolitan gentleman. The couple married in November 1881, a little less than a year and seven months after the death of his first wife, Delfina. President Manuel González served as one of the civil witnesses.[10] Díaz and Carmen met at one of the American diplomatic representative's Tuesday night receptions in the legation. Minister John W. Foster's wife introduced them. Carmen represented the modern Mexican woman—young, fresh, urbane, and optimistic—an important symbol of the projected "new Mexico" in an era that depended heavily on perception in the absence of substance. She charmed international financiers in fluent English, gently reassured the socially inept, mingled easily with the elite, and expressed appropriate concern for working women. Ironically, as a childless second wife, Carmen never enjoyed the full acceptance of Díaz's family, a reality that forced her on to a broader stage. To foreigners she presented a startling contrast of an apparently wholly modern woman in a country where many of her sisters remained caught in another time. A Victorian woman in the presidential palace suggested that Mexico hovered on the edge of nineteenth-century progress. Porfirio Díaz and Carmen Romero Rubio de Díaz projected an achievable goal of order and progress, in short, the Porfirian persuasion. Americans, who viewed Mexico as a politically immature country without much individual or collective discipline, believed Mexico finally had found the strong hand it needed.

THE DÍAZ REVOLUTION

With national and international support, Porfirio Díaz won reelection as expected. The Porfiristas believed that the rise to power of General Díaz constituted a revolution. The so-called Revolution of Tuxtepec perhaps began as a revolt, but had broadened into something much more in response to the country's pressing concerns. To many the central issue and objective had to be political stability. Unless a governing system could be elaborated that was able to maintain order and establish socioeconomic and political cooperation, the country appeared doomed. The continuous disasters of the nineteenth century had to be stopped and decline reversed. The rallying cry of the Plan of Tuxtepec, effective suffrage and no reelection, remained an ideal objective, but one that on the national level should await the moment the nation appeared ready to shoulder the heavy responsibility of stable governance. Meanwhile, effective suffrage implied that the legitimate interests of regional elites, who had the task of assuring a viable degree of order in their own states, would be respected. The national government itself would be only one of a number of political players in any region. Effective suffrage also suggested that the authorities in Mexico City supported necessary and flexible accommodations as shifts in regional power blocks occurred. The Mexican president exercised a moderating influence by tipping the balance toward one regional group or another. Díaz thus represented the one element of continuity in the process of constant adjustment and realignment in state politics. Consequently, to regional elites the notion of no reelection at the national level did not seem a pressing issue. To them, stability and the return of confidence represented the crowning achievements of the Revolution of Tuxtepec. Mexico in 1884 seemed poised on the edge of history a new era in which the earlier promise of the Mexican nation could be realized. To many relieved Mexicans, Díaz symbolized that new age. The Porfirian persuasion eventually crystallized into the Porfiriato, which radically transformed Mexico into the next century.

Matías Romero, who represented Juárez in Washington during the French intervention and the American Civil War, served as Díaz's first minister of development. Convinced, as Miguel Lerdo before him, that the energy and financial resources of the United States must be harnessed to help develop Mexico, Romero sought to interest leading capitalists in investing in the country. He identified and encouraged potential investors during his official residence in the United States. Dinner with Matías Romero at Delmonico's, then New York's most fashionable restaurant, became a sought-after invitation for railwaymen and financiers. An ever-impatient Matías Romero could not resist chiding Americans about letting the earlier invitation of Miguel Lerdo to join in the material feast go unheeded.[11] Romero had become a close friend of then General Ulysses S. Grant, visiting him and his Army of the Potomac during the siege of Petersburg. Grant, a taciturn man, somewhat provincial, and usually highly suspicious of foreigners, nevertheless liked the more urbane Mexican representative. In General Grant, the liberals finally found their ideal American political figure—an individual strongly and publicly committed to upholding Mexican territorial sovereignty, while willing to support the investments needed to assure the country's rapid economic development. As Romero commented to President Juárez in 1865, "The favors which Grant does us exceed our expectations, he would hardly be able to do more if he were Mexican."[12] The Romero–Grant friendship had important consequences for Mexican development.

General Grant's connection with Mexico dated back to his service as a lieutenant with General Winfield Scott's 1847 invading force. He had always publicly regarded the war as being totally unjustified and a source of national shame. In the closing months of the American Civil War, he predicted that the Union Army would move to confront the French in Mexico. With the surrender of Confederate forces, he ordered General Phil Sheridan to the Mexican border, hoping for a French provocation. Grant also instructed Sheridan to collect Confederate equipment and leave it where the Mexican liberals could find it.

As president of the United States (1869–1877), Grant took a strong stand against forceful annexation of Mexican territory. Several border incidents that could have supplied a pretext were not exploited, although the lawlessness along the border, along with the public perception that smugglers in the free zone had a damaging impact on customs revenues, caused concern. Mexican Presidents Juárez and Lerdo both approved of their friendly counterpart in Washington, D.C. The country's most influential newspaper, *El Siglo Diez y Nueve*, called Grant a "simple republican at heart, and generous in character" as well as a dependable friend of Mexico. General Grant's prestige and status, as both a president and victorious national hero, lent currency to his opinions and attitudes in the United States that reassured Mexico.

Mexicans believed that a sharp and, many hoped, permanent change in the American mindset toward Mexico and possible annexation had occurred. While the covertness of its northern neighbor had not been extinguished, the tide appeared to have turned. They understood that long-courted American investments would make the issue of annexation unimportant as investors found that an independent Mexico welcomed their presence. Moreover, economic development itself would strengthen the country's sovereignty. Mexican observers proved to be correct in their assessment. While the United States would not hesitate to put political and economic pressure on its neighbor, the days of crude territorial expansion had ended. Increasingly, the United States viewed its relationship with Mexico as being a mutually beneficial one, defined in American economic and political terms to be sure, but one in which all parties stood to gain. A new respect for Mexico emerged from that country's republican victory over European imperialism.

Americans acknowledged that Juárez and his generals had accomplished the task with little actual assistance from Washington. Public opinion in the United States elevated President Juárez to the same semidivine position as Abraham Lincoln. Both leaders had persevered in war and reacted magnanimously in victory. The American Union and the Mexican Republic both had in their own admirable fashion turned back the forces of disintegration. Now together they would show the world the social, political, and economic benefits of independent republics. Thus reflecting American public sentiment, Gorham D. Abbot, writing at the time of Grant's election to the presidency, flatly stated that the "two republics have a common cause, mutual relations, and identical interests." Abbot's concluding sentence quoted the alleged words of President Lincoln, "The Republic of Mexico must rise again."[13] Significantly, the work included only two steel engraved portraits: one of President Juárez and the other of Matías Romero, the former representing republican political virtue and the latter entrepreneurial economic development.

Wall Street appeared more than ready to be seduced by tales of fabulous wealth awaiting the industrious, and Mexico City was ready to take the political risk. The Romero–Grant friendship provided an important element of psychological reassurance if not total trust between the important leaders of the two countries.[14] Without such well-publicized goodwill, the cooperation between foreign investors and Mexican interests politically would have been much more difficult to initiate. Undoubtedly, Mexico and its future dominated after-dinner discussions when Grant entertained Porfirio Díaz in New York in 1883, just a year before Díaz's second term and two years before General Grant died.[15] Díaz and his ministers succeeded in gaining some conditional respect and cooperation from foreign governments, at least sufficient to reassure the all-important international investor. In retrospect, it appeared relatively easy to do so, but at the time seemed almost miraculous.

To rally internal support, Díaz relied upon an emotional, nonxenophobic nationalism. He submerged himself in a semimythical liberalism employing the largely fabricated historical charisma of Benito Juárez. The fact that he had revolted against Juárez shortly before the benemérito died could be dismissed as a reasonable break with a hero in decline. Porfirio Díaz's service to the country, his military success against the French, and his support for a beleaguered Juárez during the dark days of the retreat to El Paso del Norte made the Noria revolt appear to be a mere political disagreement. Díaz participated in the dedication of Juárez's tomb in 1880 and backed the naming of Avenida Juárez in the late president's honor in 1887. One of President Díaz's last official acts was the dedication of the grand monument to Juárez, the *hemiciclo*, in September 1910. Originally authorized in 1873, it consisted of twelve doric columns of marble, with a representation of Juárez the law giver, surrounded by two allegorical figures. Glory, in white marble, places a Roman wreath on his head, while the Republic rests her sword on the ground to signify eternal victory. The centennial of Juárez's birth in 1906 became a cult celebration that swept the entire country. The Porfiriato fashioned the Juárez myth to provide an emotional mantle for the pragmatic adjustments of liberal principle undertaken by the government. In essence, the myth suggested that while Benito Juárez provided the dream, Porfirio Díaz made it work. The danger of straying too far away from the dream, even if mythical, was not understood until the end of the regime. The government sought to portray liberalism as a virtually seamless historical process, with Benito Juárez as a civic paragon and Porfirio Díaz as his worthy successor. As with all propaganda, its very success made the contradictions between myth and reality even more evident. The regime's opponents inevitably found their own uses for the Juárez myth.[16]

La Frontera: The Border as a Distinct Region

Sporadic outbursts of lawlessness and violence characterized the border and on a regular basis captured public attention. To outsiders the rather homogeneous community that straddled the international boundary seemed disposed to disruptive behavior. Both governments failed to appreciate the fact that borderlanders functioned within their own region. The diplomatic niceties of an international border seemed irrelevant to their well-being or even survival. Their hold on existence depended on adapting to a reality that ignored national boundaries. Flexibility did not guarantee survival, but without it life became next to impossible. Frontier conditions gave rise to a self-motivated, self-interested, independent-minded population that depended upon itself. Flexibility led to the establishment of Nuevo Laredo on the Mexican side of the Río Grande. When Laredo's inhabitants were informed in 1848 that "Mexico has lost Laredo forever," most stayed in place, while Andrés Martínez, the alcalde of Laredo, led a group across the river to establish a twin settlement. Technically divided by nationality and a demarcated border, the population of both Laredos continued to act as a regional entity, even voting in elections on both sides of the river.[17]

Typical of the border region was the life experience of Ramón Ortiz. A priest, landholder, and miller, Ortiz arrived in El Paso del Norte in 1837. He resisted the American invasion of 1846 and as a national congressman voted against the Treaty of Guadalupe Hidalgo in 1848. Nevertheless, he adjusted to reality and became a major transborder personality known for his generosity and grasp of border culture. Much of El Paso's social life revolved around Father Ramón's activities. By the time he died in 1896, El Paso del Norte had become the busy commercial center of Ciudad Juárez. Mariano Samaniego, his grandnephew, arrived from Sonora as a child and subsequently earned a medical degree from the University of Paris, where he studied under Louis Pasteur. Like most *paseños* he saw himself as a self-made borderlander who owed little to anyone. Such people embraced survival over other considerations. While they wished the best for both countries, they understood that they lived within their own region with its peculiar imperatives, including a high level of lawlessness.

Business, family, and vengeance spilled across the border regardless of the wishes of Mexico City or Washington. Innumerable incidents kept diplomats busy exchanging excuses as well as protests. For example, the murder of A. M. Conklin, editor of the *Socorro Sun* (New Mexico), by two Mexicans after Christmas services resulted in the usual dead-or-alive reward. Judge José Baca of El Paso county, an uncle of the two wanted men, did his best to protect them. Texas Ranger Jim Gillett, upon receiving information that Enofre Baca had been seen in Zaragoza, Mexico, four miles from Ysleta and a scant mile from the border, apprehended Baca at gunpoint and spirited him across into American jurisdiction. In spite of Gillett's protests, a Socorro mob hanged Baca from the gate beam of a corral. While both governments exchanged notes over the incident, to the borderlanders it represented merely a regional, albeit violent, adaptation to reality.[18]

During the 1870s and 1880s, hostile Indians and bandits raided both sides of the border, resulting in deaths and destruction of property. The general insecurity caused by these depredations flared into ethnic conflicts, including the "Mission Camp Affair," an 1870 theft that ended in a shoot-out along the Sonora–Arizona border, leaving four Anglos and two Mexicans dead; the "Mesilla Riots," an 1871 New Mexico political outburst that saw nine supporters of Colonel J. Francisco Chávez killed and forty to fifty more men wounded; and the "Corpus Christi Raids," an 1875 Texas affair in which bandit activity provoked Anglo attacks on local Mexican settlers, resulting in many deaths. These troubles climaxed in the 1877 El Paso "Salt War," in which Tejanos from San Elizario, Texas, supported by some 200 Mexicans from south of the Río Grande, took up arms to protect their access to the salt deposits claimed by an Anglo businessman. For 100 years or more, the inhabitants of San Elizario, Ysleta, and other small villages along the upper Río Grande had free access to salt deposits. Local merchants distributed salt throughout northern Mexico. In the late 1870s, the new settlers sought to commercialize the West's resources, including land, water, and mineral wealth, in the words of Judge Charles Howard, to make the salt beds into "a money making proposition."[19] The Salt War and other similar conflicts represented the deadly clash between differing approaches to resources. Murder, violence, and destruction accompanied the process of nineteenth-century commercialization. The arrival of Texas Rangers resulted in several clashes in which three Anglos and three Tejanos were shot to death.[20] The residents of the border, on both sides and of both nationalities, in the last two decades of the century faced increasing pressures on communities from outside men of enterprise. Those moving into the American Southwest understood that some would employ force, legal or extralegal, to protect or extend their interests. The struggle over the resources of a new land could be brutal. Nevertheless, the attractions outweighed the negatives and drew people into the borderlands in increasing numbers. For Mexicans, an understandable ambivalence, best captured in a *corrido*, characterized their attitude as they moved into the borderlands:

> Goodbye! Beloved country,
> ....
> And so I take my leave
> of my country Mexico
> I have reached Ciudad Juárez
> Oh, Virgin of Guadalupe![21]

While violence and insecurity remained a reality of life on the border, the well-being of communities on both sides of the line inevitably rested upon socioeconomic cooperation. A border distant from the more settled parts of both republics shared a common destiny, regardless of the occasional violent clash of cultures. As a region apart, it had its own internal boundaries. On the American side, an informal sense of its territorial extension existed, while in the Mexican part, an economic free zone running the entire length of the international line from Matamoros to Tijuana, twelve and a half miles into the interior, provided a formal demarcation of the distinct region.

Maintaining a sufficient population presence along the border to ensure sovereignty could only be accomplished by allowing border towns to prosper. After the peace treaty with the United States that established the new boundary, the Mexican population had been drawn into Texas because of lower prices and the availability of food and everyday items. To halt depopulation, in 1849 the Mexican government lowered tariffs on certain items used on the border. The governor of Tamaulipas took the next logical step and decreed a free trade zone in 1858. The zone's acceptance by the national government in 1861 constituted recognition of a transborder regional economy. In 1885, the zone was extended the entire length of the border. Mexico City only reluctantly tolerated the zone and constantly attempted to restrict its privileges. In 1896, an 18.5 percent tariff on all goods was imposed, with additional fees levied if goods entered the interior. Smuggling and other methods of tax avoidance constantly angered the government. Goods manufactured in the free zone caused further problems. Officials suspected that manufacturing on the border merely provided a means to avoid customs fees. Acting on this belief, in 1891 the Mexican government decreed that all products manufactured in the zone, regardless of the origin of the raw materials, must pay an import duty when entering Mexico proper. New regulations in 1896 softened restrictions by allowing border zone products to circulate freely but only after complex, burdensome paperwork was filed.[22]

With the American Civil War, the Mexican side went through its first boom. Confederate cotton poured out to the rest of the world through Mexican border ports. Matamoros, across from Brownsville, Texas, became a major port, with dozens of vessels anchored offshore to be loaded or unloaded. Bagdad, an instant city at the mouth of the river, suddenly had 12,000 inhabitants. River towns from Brownsville to Laredo and their twin settlements on the Mexican side engaged in the Confederate trade. Mexican merchants shipped freight up the river as far as San Ygnacio in Zapata County. Many members of the Tejano elite supported the Confederacy, combining loyalty with profit. Colonel Santos Benavides and fellow Confederate officer Antancio Vidaurri profited both financially and politically by serving as mayors of Laredo. Benavides became the acknowledged "merchant prince of the Río Grande." Mexican–Tejano families with branches on both sides of the river enjoyed a thriving legal as well as illegal trade on the border.[23] In the post–Civil War period, Texas border towns declined, losing both population and business. Three times as many people lived across the line in Mexico. American politicians blamed the decline on Mexico. Consequently, the United States government pressed Mexico to abolish the zone, claiming it provided criminal elements a base from which to bring illegal goods, particularly European products, into the country.

By the 1870s, the American side began to recover. John W. Foster, the U.S. representative to Mexico, an opponent of the zone, toured the border region in 1876, reporting that the American side supplied most of the items entered into trade. He concluded that, if anything, Mexico lost more than the United States from smuggling. Matías Romero, representing Mexico in Washington, D.C., characterized the zone as a free market for American products. In fact, he noted that the only real complaint could be that it did not extend throughout the Mexican republic. Warner P. Sutton, a U.S. consul on the border, reported that American merchants supplied groceries, dry goods, furniture, wheat, flour, corn, bacon, lard, and virtually every other commonplace item used by Mexicans. On the Mexican side, because of restricted drinking laws in the United States, bars flourished. Sutton observed that while uninformed people in the United States agitated against the zone, Mexican inhabitants in the interior did the same. The border region responded to its own rhythm, however, in spite of rejection by its two parents. Consul Sutton asserted that politics distorted reality, damaging the commerce of both republics. As he put it

> Mexico needs our products and has always been disposed to meet us halfway. Too much protection buncombe by one party and too much free trade theorizing by the other has prevented our doing five to ten million dollars worth of commerce with Mexico every year to the benefit of both countries . . . why not have complete free trade with Mexico as our next neighbor?[24]

Finally, in 1905, Díaz abolished the free zone, commenting that the development of railways and general tax reform made it unnecessary. Moreover, he noted that without the zone, local industries would be forced into existence to meet the region's needs. Border industrialization in turn would attract a larger population, making the border much more a part of the Mexican republic. The official end of the free zone did not suppress smuggling, nor did it end the unified perception of the region shared by border residents of both nationalities.[25]

THE DUBLÁN CONVENTION AND PORFIRIAN PROGRESS

At the beginning of his second term, Díaz recognized the need for completing the country's infrastructure, especially its transportation system, and, encouraged by Matías Romero, planned to finance these projects through the sale of government bonds to foreign investors. Before this could be done, however, government officials had to improve the nation's reputation as a dreadful credit risk by dealing with outstanding bonds left dangling from the early republic through the U.S.–Mexican War, the Reform era, and Juárez's 1867 suspension of all debt payments, to, only two years after resuming payments on the English debt, Díaz's own default in 1886.

Manuel Dublán, another Oaxaca native prominent in liberal politics, became the secretary of treasury at the beginning of Díaz's 1884 term. For the next four years, Dublán carried on intense negotiations with creditors and finally succeeded in restructuring the total foreign debt using new railroad construction bonds.

The Dublán Convention of 1888 arranged with British and German bondholders to consolidate past debts in a new issue of bonds worth £10,500,000 at 6 percent for thirty-five years. German investors bought the majority of bonds at about 70 percent of their face value. The Convention represented the triumph of Matías Romero's nearly ten-year struggle to resolve the nation's debt crisis. This agreement enabled Díaz's government to attract additional foreign investment and overcome its bad credit reputation. The debt had to be refinanced in 1899 and again in 1911, but the old debts no longer prevented the Díaz government from obtaining foreign capital. According to the Convention, most of the debt did not become payable until after the turn of the century. Thus, Porfirio Díaz mortgaged the future, gambling that profits from industrial growth would provide the national income to meet the payments. His strategy rested on an unrealistic plan for the retirement of the nation's indebtedness. When Díaz departed in 1911, the debt was more than that of any other Latin American country and three times his government's annual income. President Díaz bought time and respectability. In the end it remained uncertain who owned whom. Bankers and purchasers of Mexican bonds had to believe in Mexico's future, and Díaz willingly assured them that the future would be bright as well as solvent.[26]

As a consequence, in the last twelve years of the nineteenth century, resting securely on the Dublán Convention, the modernization process picked up momentum and literally transformed both the countryside and urban centers. Foreign investors, avidly courted by the government, saw Mexico as a stable country open to secure and profitable investments. Even more important, a sense of confidence, opportunity, and hope swept the Mexican elite, who reorganized their own resources to maximize profits. The conquest of space and distance not only linked the country to the dynamic American market to the north but also changed the perspective of the elite. The fact that foreigners could be enticed to speculate caused a flurry of developmental excitement.

Tax or land concessions appeared to be a rapid, inexpensive way to build a transportation infrastructure. In the whirl of exciting activity, reality occasionally lost out to fantasy. It appeared as though everyone had his own railway project. Even old schemes, such as that of prominent Californio Mariano Vallejo, who became an American citizen by treaty and went to Mexico City in 1877 to promote a railway between the Mexican capital and California, now appeared less fanciful.[27] Many of the projected lines never moved beyond the planning stage. Indeed, some railroad concessions contained only a vague plan of what route might be followed. The Railway Company of Tucson, Arizona, and the Gulf of California, for example, received permission to construct a line from Tucson into Sonora and eventually back to some unspecified point on the border. Out of the flurry of concessions a few lines actually materialized. The Atchison, Topeka, and Santa Fe constructed the Sonora Railway that linked the Pacific Coast port of Guaymas with Nogales, Arizona. American capital built the Mexican Central Railroad, which linked Mexico City with El Paso, Texas, while another line, financed by French and English investors, tied the capital with Laredo, Texas.

Rail links created a national and international market, breaking down regional economies in the process. The rail network helped reorient trade over land, although maritime traffic remained important. Traditionally, Europe, particularly Britain, absorbed most of Mexico's exports, but by the last decade of the nineteenth century, the United States purchased over 70 percent of the country's foreign sales.[28] Mexico also entertained the hope that a rail network across its territory linking Atlantic and Pacific trade routes would make it the crossroads of the world. The Tehuantepec railway project promised to cut time and miles off the more traditional routes to the Orient. The Isthmus of Tehuantepec lay only 810 miles away from the mouth of the Mississippi River. It seemed reasonable to envision linking manufacturing centers on the North American river network with the Tehuantepec railway. The dream ended after the opening of the Panama Canal in 1914.[29] The Díaz government, convinced of the vital importance of railways, bought controlling stock in the principal lines but permitted them to function as private companies. The weak return on railway securities facilitated the Mexicanization of railways. Eventually, in 1909, the government formed a unified rail network, Ferrocarriles Nacionales de México. By 1910, Mexico had some 15,000 miles of track.

THE BOOM IN THE EXTRACTIVE INDUSTRY

Closely related to the expansion of a rail network was the development of extractive industries. These two economic activities absorbed slightly over 83 percent of American investments in Mexico by 1911. A combination of rail access, high demand, and new technology made even low grade ore profitable. The Mexican rail system began to carry increasing quantities of copper ore north to border towns like El Paso,

Eagle Pass, and Laredo, Texas, to be shipped farther north to the Globe smelter in Denver and its rivals. These shipments began in 1884, and by the early 1890s, they had become so important that Dennis Sheedy, who owned the Globe smelting enterprise, hired Henry Raup Wagner (a Yale graduate trying to avoid family pressures to pursue a career in law) to coordinate the firm's multifarious operations in Mexico. Wagner advanced through the corporate ranks and later became an important figure in the industry, before he turned to books.[30] Mexican ores became a crucial source for the smelting industry. Silver, gold, zinc, and copper fueled the mining boom. The development of electricity made copper mining into a highly profitable enterprise, both in Mexico and adjacent regions of the American Southwest. Electrification of the United States and Europe created a gigantic market for copper wire and the electrification of the mines themselves increased their productivity. In Mexico, the introduction of electricity in urban centers depended upon European capital more than on American investments.

The open investment climate attracted entrepreneurs such as Colonel William Greene. Colonel Greene, with an option on a Sonora copper mine, raised funds on Wall Street, established the Cananea Consolidated Copper Company, and soon employed some 3,500 workers. American interest in Mexican petroleum became evident as early as 1865, when New York entrepreneur Wedworth Clarke attempted to get as large a drilling concession as possible. Veracruz, Tabasco, Campeche, and the Isthmus of Tehuantepec appeared to be the most promising areas. In 1866, the newspaper *El Mexicano* reported a major find in the Isthmus of Tehuantepec. Political uncertainty, however, delayed active exploration and investment in the nascent industry.[31] American petroleum interests eventually drilled the first commercially feasible oil well. Edward L. Doheny, along with British capitalist Sir Weetman Pearson, dominated the Mexican petroleum industry. Mexico became an important oil producer, just at the time the world was in transition from coal to petroleum energy.

PORFIRIAN CITIES: MONUMENTS TO PROGRESS

A newly beautified Mexico City became the symbol of modernization, in both physical and psychological senses. The population of the federal district increased from 327,000 in 1877 to 720,753 in 1910, creating an atmosphere of big city hustle and excitement.[32] The Calzada de la Emperatriz, built to connect the capital's center with the royal castle at Chapultepec during the Maximilian period, became the Paseo de la Reforma—a scenic tree-lined monument to liberalism. More than a boulevard, it physically and visually represented the fusion of Juárez and Porfirian progressive liberalism. Resplendent with grand circles (*glorietas*) studded with impressive civic statuary, the *paseo* evoked the image of Paris much to the satisfaction of a proud elite. As a symbol of modernity the Paseo de la Reforma became the national ceremonial avenue—a site for civic events and a route for parading soldiers or mounted rurales. Its role today remains the same.[33]

To police the ceremonial city, the government organized a modern police force along the lines of the French model. Called the *gendarmería*, they sported blue uniforms topped with kepis. Relatively well paid, the force grew to some 3,000 men, a ratio of one policeman to every 153 inhabitants. The gendarmería concentrated its efforts in the better neighborhoods of the city and in areas frequented by foreigners. As a consequence, Mexico City appeared to be one of the safest cities in the world. Behind the façade, unpoliced poor areas fended off crime as best they could. When they came into contact with the police, the relationship often involved corruption, extortion, bribes, and brutality—a reality out of sight of foreigners and the elite, who viewed the modern force as yet more evidence of the country's civilized progress.[34]

Carefully attended parks and gardens added a touch of peaceful elegance in sharp contrast to the quickening tempo of the modern capital. The Alameda, situated close to the city's center, provided a beautiful setting for the fashionable to stroll down flower-lined paths to the muted strains of a military band. The *zócalo* in front of the presidential palace, today a vast paved square suitable for massive political rallies, then had trees and benches, a precious oasis in the city's old colonial heart. Chapultepec Park's gracefully contoured lake accommodated enthusiastic boaters attired in the most stylish costumes. In the early morning, riders outfitted in the English manner cantered their exquisitely groomed horses through the park politely saluting fellow equestrians. To foreigners, the beauty and elegance on one level and the crude backwardness on the other seemed surreal.[35]

Electricity transformed the city. Carlos Pacheco, the minister of government, in 1882 switched on the first electric-powered domestic lighting, and by 1900, it extended to 30,000 houses in the capital. This new power source transformed domestic and public life, including mobility. In 1898, the Guadalupe–San Angel line was electrified for twenty-six miles to provide a rapid-transit spine running north–south directly through the city. The sight of the first brightly lit streetcar lurching through the night streets symbolized the changing speed of Mexico City life.

Similar changes swept other cities into the modern age. Between 1902 and 1906, the Yucatecan capital of Mérida underwent extensive

Figure 4.1 A foreign diplomat posing in front of his residence in a well-to-do section of Mexico City around 1900. *Printed with permission, Photography Collection, Harry Ransom, Humanities Research Center, University of Texas at Austin.*

renovation and improvement. Now a clean and sparkling city of macadam streets, electric lighting, streetcars, and policemen in trim uniforms, it never ceased to amaze visitors. The new and aptly named port of Progreso established in 1870 in a swampy coastal area soon became the site of trading companies, modern warehouses, and even waterfront homes for the Yucatecan elite. Soon, only the port of Veracruz handled a larger volume of trade.[36]

In the north, the city of Monterrey began its rise to industrial prominence—promotional brochures touted it as the Mexican Chicago. After recovering from the devastation of a long, smothering American occupation during the war, Monterrey regained its control of the interior trade that entered the country through the ports of Tampico and Matamoros. A redrawn border advantageously placed the city in a commercially useful proximity to the United States. By 1869, the telegraph linked Monterrey and the state of Nuevo León with the wider world, as did the road network that spidered out from the city in all directions. A large part of the credit for facilitating the city's rise to regional dominance went to General Bernardo Reyes, who assumed the governorship in 1884. Reyes, a dedicated Porfirista, supported public works, education, and key investments in industry and commercial agriculture. Civic-minded entrepreneurs paved the streets, built department stores, donated property for parks, and

Figure 4.2 The lushly landscaped Zócalo in Mexico City, bordered on one side by the cathedral, provided a pleasant haven in the heart of the city. *Printed with permission, Photography Collection, Harry Ransom, Humanities Research Center, University of Texas at Austin.*

renamed a street and erected a statue to honor Benito Juárez. The newly built (1906) state palace represented Porfirian monumental art, a secular shrine to both national and Nuevo León heroes. Six stained glass windows contained life-sized figures of Miguel Hidalgo, Benito Juárez, and four local champions, while inside the building, historical relics—including three rifles used by local soldiers in the firing squad that executed Maximilian—were displayed in the governor's reception area and public rooms.[37]

THE JUGGERNAUT OF PROSPERITY

In Monterrey, local capital started Mexico's first completely modern brewery, the Cervecería Cuauhtémoc (1892). Governor Bernardo Reyes in 1890 granted the standard seven-year tax exemption to a group of local investors. Joseph Schnaider, an experienced brewmaster in St. Louis, Missouri, joined the group. In its first year of operations, the brewery produced 60,000 barrels and 4,000 bottles of beer. To further promote the industry, the government imposed a 75 percent tariff on bottled beer and artificially raised the price of imported barrel beer to 25 dollars per unit over its St. Louis price of eight dollars. Beer imports dropped 600 percent within a year (1889 to 1890). The Cervecería Cuauhtémoc captured most of the newly created domestic market. Carta Blanca, its premium product, won a prize at the 1893 Chicago World's Fair. In 1899, the brewery began experimenting with bottle production, and with the introduction of Owen's automatic bottle process, the Vidriera Monterrey (1909) supplied all of the brewery's needs. Other subsidiary companies furnished caps and cardboard products. In early 1900, construction began on an iron and steel plant, the Fundidora de Hierro y Acero de Monterrey. To meet the iron and steel plant's energy needs, local interests formed the Compañía Carbonífera de Monterrey to mine coal. Regional capitalists linked one industry to another in a highly effective developmental chain. Significantly, although they utilized foreign financing as well as their own resources, Mexicans not only dominated the process of industrialization in the city of Monterrey but also determined the nature of the city's development.[38]

The textile industry in the state of Puebla restored the colonial city of Puebla to a modern version of its old glory. New technology

Figure 4.3 Traditional transportation in Mexico City at the turn of the century. In contrast, note the overhead electric lines, street lighting, and tram lines. *Printed with permission, Photography Collection, Harry Ransom, Humanities Research Center, University of Texas at Austin.*

brought about an almost total transformation of the mills now able to use electricity. In Puebla, unlike the modernization process in Monterrey, foreign capital played a major role. French capital channeled through the Sociedad Financiera para la Industria de México, founded in Paris in 1890, financed a modern textile industry. The Compañía Industrial de Orizaba (CIDOSA) established the Río Blanco factory in 1892, which became the largest and most modern in the country. Río Blanco utilized some 1,650 looms and 43,000 spindles. The industrial transformation of the textile industry reached a high point with the establishment of the Santa Rosa factory in 1899, also with French capital. Santa Rosa had 1,400 looms, 40,183 spindles, and 4 textile printers, requiring a work force of 1,800.[39] The rail system made it possible to distribute inexpensive textiles throughout the country. In 1877, it cost $61 a ton to ship cotton products from Mexico City to Querétaro, some 130 miles away; by 1910, the cost had declined to $3 a ton. Domestic textile production dramatically cut imports from 32 percent of the market in 1889 to 3 percent by 1911.[40]

Outside the cities, agriculture adopted modern organizational structures to meet the demand for primary products. Haciendas, a term almost lost in the stereotype of a grand semifeudal estate and lavish lifestyle, in fact functioned as farm factories—known today as agribusiness. Vast expanses of land, often with their own mini-rail system, processing and warehouse buildings, a store for employees, and medical dispensaries, made them impressive enterprises. In Yucatán, corn and cattle raising gave way to new henequen (sisal used to make binder twine) plantations. Demand for sisal by American cordage manufacturers resulted in the expansion of production from 41,864 bales in 1876 to 680,000 by 1911. The insatiable need for sisal twine created by the development of the mechanical knotting device for the McCormick reaper–binder in 1878 promised endless prosperity for those who controlled the industry. By 1890, Yucatán had the most extensive rail network in the republic, with some 600 kilometers of private track that tied henequen plantations to the 800-kilometer main line. Another 1,000 kilometers of movable tram tracks crisscrossed individual plantations. Easy access to the new port of Progreso, coupled with telegraph and telephone lines, enabled producers to monitor market conditions and arrange shipment of fiber to the external market. Return on investment never fell below 50 percent between 1900 and 1910 and at times soared to 400 to 600 percent. Even during periods of slack demand the larger henequen planters still managed to turn a profit.[41]

The state of Sonora, formerly a sleepy marginal area of the republic lying between the United States and the more populated parts of the country, became an economically important component of the "new" Mexico. After the 1886 pacification of the Apaches and the subsequent opening of the rail link from Guaymas to the Arizona border, the entire region boomed. By 1911, American investors had poured in some $45 million, one-third of which went into mining. Copper transformed Cananea, a settlement of a scant 100 people in 1891, into a city of 14,841 by the end of the Porfiriato. Cananea functioned as a self-contained company city, with an aqueduct, electric plant, rail system, bank, hospital, houses, restaurants, and stores owned and operated by the company. In Nacozari, the Moctezuma Copper Company drilled a deep well, built the Nacozari railroad, opened a public library, and operated a school and a modern hospital. In 1910, the company owned all of the real estate in the town of 4,000 people. The Mexican government encouraged large mining companies to operate public facilities such as schools and hospitals, which the state itself could not afford to build or staff. While a mutually beneficial arrangement, the mining companies exercised social, economic, and political control over their worker-inhabitants.[42] Large-scale mining operations constituted economic development settlements laid out around the productive mineral core. Modern Sonora grew out of commercial agriculture and exploration of a variety of minerals. It became one of the most important states in the Mexican republic—all in a mere quarter of a century.

Coffee production intruded into remote areas that previously had been outside the national economy. The production in 1877 of 8,161

Figure 4.4 Port of Tampico in the last decade of the nineteenth century. *Printed with permission, Photography Collection, Harry Ransom, Humanities Research Center, University of Texas at Austin.*

tons rose to 28,041 tons by 1910. Mexican coffee enjoyed an excellent reputation for smoothness. As a premium coffee, it competed with the best Brazilian grade for at least a modest share of the international market. The United States absorbed most of the country's coffee exports. In 1880, the state of Veracruz accounted for two-thirds of Mexico's coffee production, followed by Chiapas, Guerrero, Michoacán, Morelos, Oaxaca, and Tabasco. Many states hoped that coffee would replace products that had lost their market, such as cochineal and indigo, and also make use of previously unused or marginal hillside land that could not be used for more standard crops. Oaxaca distributed some three million coffee plants in an effort to stimulate the industry. After 1892, with rail services to Mexico City and subsequently at the end of the century to Veracruz, the state enjoyed some success. Colima offered prizes, tax benefits, and much rhetorical inducement to interest landholders in coffee cultivation. In some areas, coffee plantations completely altered the lifestyle and economic base of the population. Soconusco (Chiapas), a backward region in all respects, became a major producer of coffee by 1890. In twenty years, Soconusco's character changed dramatically. A skillful coffee plantation manager could squeeze a 24 percent return on invested capital, although prices could rise or fall with little warning. In some parts of the republic, it proved to be an unsuccessful fad. Misguided efforts to introduce its cultivation in Puebla, where soil conditions were unfavorable, failed. Coffee also exhausted nutrients and the industry often left behind a trail of eroded and damaged land.[43]

New products and fresh opportunities flourished on the peripheries of the nation. Even the Lacandón jungle experienced an economic transformation, as lumber companies harvested tropical hardwoods and rubber plantings filled newly cleared land.[44] The sugar industry in Morelos, although its roots went back to the sixteenth century, took over much of the state, isolating Indian villages and absorbing communal land to meet demand. In Chihuahua, the cattle industry expanded along with the railways, shipping thousands of head of cattle to the American market. The shift from peasant subsistence agriculture and small-scale activities to commercial production occurred with unsettling speed. The rush to extract profit from previously neglected resources spared neither the land nor the native population. Rubber, while not as important as some other export products, nevertheless exemplified the speculative nature of Porfirian commercial agriculture development. Latex could be obtained from a variety of plants that grew naturally in various parts of the country. In the 1870s, only a small amount entered the market, but as demand rose the national government encouraged the commercialization of the industry. The demand for latex created by the bicycle craze and later the automobile seemed boundless. Developmental fever with the promise of quick and plentiful revenues swept both the state and national government. The ministry of development signed an agreement in 1889 for the planting of 15 million rubber trees on the coast of Oaxaca in return for a subsidy and tax concessions. Production increased 56 percent a year between 1896 and 1899. Large tracts of land were purchased, many by foreigners, based on the speculation that latex prices would continue to climb. By 1907, a ton of raw rubber sold for 953 pesos; three years later, a ton returned 2,840 pesos, while the actual cost of production remained at 80 to 100 pesos a ton under normal conditions.[45] Unfortunately, the rubber boom came crashing down shortly thereafter, as British Malaya began to flood the market with plantation-produced latex.

Agriculture appeared to have achieved an almost magical commercial transformation. Agribusiness in Mexico accounted for 70 percent of all landholdings by 1910. Medium to small farms (*ranchos*), while not capitalized to the same extent, also shifted production to export crops. In areas of large-scale expansion, ranchos were bought out by the new agricultural enterprises. Export agriculture grew at an annual rate of 6.29 percent between 1877 and 1810. The rate of growth, however, did not rise in a steady and orderly fashion, but frequently in boom or bust cycles that encouraged speculative expansion followed by a contraction with unexpected negative economic and social consequences.

A MEXICAN MIRACLE: THE LAGUNA SHOWCASE

The Laguna region of north-central Mexico became an important northern showcase of Porfirian Mexico. "The Miracle of Laguna" transformed the barren region into a major agricultural zone, mining area, manufacturing center, railhead, and location of the country's fastest-growing city. The region, virtually a desert without an indigenous population nor significant settlements, developed rapidly after 1880, the year it surpassed Veracruz in cotton production, and for the next thirty years became a booming economic frontier. In the decade after 1880, cotton production increased fivefold, and in the next decade, it doubled again. The rural population grew from 20,000 to 200,000, augmented each year during the harvest by 40,000 cotton pickers. The coming of the railroads led to urbanization, with the founding of Torreón (1883), an American-style city, and Gómez Palacio (1884). Without a traditional landed elite, the new oligarchy developed varied interests in land, mines, industry, finance, and commerce. With no traditional peasantry, migrants flocked to the region to find work on cotton plantations, railroads, and mines, or as seasonal cotton pickers, drawn by the highest wages in Mexico. Regional industries developed rapidly, especially textiles, cotton processing, ore smelting, and rubber refining, making Laguna one of Mexico's most important industrial zones. By 1910, Laguna had the largest number of foreigners in Mexico outside of the capital city, and the United States, Great Britain, France, Belgium, and China all had consulates.

Torreón, Mexico's fastest-growing city, became the industrial and commercial center of Laguna, with ten branch banks, telephone and telegraph connections to Mexico City and world markets, and factories for cotton processing, soap, textiles, and flour. The town, a modern showcase with pavement, sewers, telephones, streetcars, schools, hospitals, theaters, a bull ring, and social clubs, seemed to represent the miracle of civilized progress.

The elite reflected the pioneer spirit of self-reliance, a willingness to take risks and work hard, and pride in having built a booming zone out of a barren expanse. They expected to be recognized and rewarded for what they had achieved. Here opportunities abounded. Nevertheless, much of the land, production, and profits went into the hands of Spanish property owners, British agriculturists, German miners, French textile companies, and U.S. railroad and smelter magnates. The Madero family was one of the few Mexican families able to participate fully in the boom. Large numbers of foreign managers and technicians arrived in Laguna, where they joined the foreign doctors, dentists, and pharmacists. Each nationality soon had its own club for social activities; they also tended to marry only within their national group. Foreigners, especially the Chinese, dominated the small, neighborhood shops. These shopkeepers earned the animosity of workers, since the companies generally would not provide credit (even plantations would only rarely offer yearly credit, which had to be settled after the harvest). Workers resented the high interest and higher prices charged by the Chinese and a few Spanish merchants.[46] Foreigners who visited Laguna or its capital Torreón could only marvel at the great opportunity that had been created by the Porfirian regime. Because of the obvious and ubiquitous presence of foreigners in the region, Mexicans wondered whether their government served them or merely facilitated the enrichment of a bewildering array of other nationalities. In the long run, the Mexican elite would have supplanted the foreign entrepreneurs, or joined them as partners, after the early boom period because of their ability to use politics as a competitive tool. Time, however, ran out for the region before that more mature stage of development occurred.

FISCAL MODERNIZATION AND STRUCTURAL WEAKNESS

Mexico's modernization required the mobilization of capital. A primitive banking system seriously retarded development. Private money lenders functioned in a highly personalized fashion to channel resources, including those of the Church, and constituted an informal financial network. The Monte de Piedad (National Pawnshop) performed a number of basic banking services, including issuing bank notes, discounting, and receiving deposits. Together with some very minor regional banks, the Monte de Piedad provided the formal financial structure. A British institution, the London Bank of Mexico and South America, established in 1864 with capital of one million pounds, offered links to the European market. The first modern commercial bank to operate in Mexico City, it soon became one of the British bank's most successful branches. French interests had attempted unsuccessfully to block its establishment, hoping to use their influence with Emperor Maximilian to form a National Bank of Mexico. In spite of opposition, the Bank of Mexico and South America soon issued its own bank notes and shipped silver to England.[47]

Expansion of the banking system became imperative by the 1880s. Consequently, the Banco Nacional Mexicano, a branch of the Franco-Egyptian Bank, received a charter with permission to issue notes equivalent to three times its capital as well as represent the government's fiscal interests. The bank opened in early 1882. A network of branches and agencies soon followed, the first of which was established in the major port city of Veracruz. A group of Spanish merchants formed the Banco Mercantil Mexicano virtually at the same time. Subsequently, these banks merged to become the Banco Nacional de México, with exclusive emission authority. A commercial code promulgated in 1884 shored up the system, but orderly expansion of the financial system came only with the General Law of Credit Institutions in 1897.[48] Bank assets soared from under three million to thirty million pesos. While the banking structure remained inadequate throughout the Porfiriato, this restructuring represented a major accomplishment. The newly created banking system gave Mexico City limited control over the regions through manipulation of the financial system. In 1897, the government, using a combination of foreign investments and loans, restructured the credit establishments. The law created three categories: banks of issue, mortgage banks, and investment banks. By 1904, twenty-eight banks serving as the primary credit institutions existed in the first division, but there were only two in each of the other two classifications. The law included regulatory restrictions on bank activities, but lacked adequate provisions for enforcement. Nevertheless, these measures improved the fiscal structure.[49] As a result, foreign investment could be absorbed and redirected in a reasonably effective manner. Existing assets, newly mobilized Mexican capital, and foreign investments provided sufficient resources to fund modernization.[50] Regional banks often controlled by small family groups complemented the national system. Family controlled banks, however, tended to lend money to themselves on extremely favorable terms. As a consequence, regional institutions often controlled local development and directed the fruits of modernization into their own hands. Those outside of the family circle struggled to establish useful connections, perhaps acquiring a partner who could gain access to capital. The ratio of assets to liabilities typically remained dangerously out of balance. Moreover, the regional nature of these banks made it difficult to geographically spread the risk. A localized economic downturn, adverse weather conditions, or a dip in the market demand for a principal product could deplete the resources of these institutions with alarming speed.

Unanticipated credit needs could not be met by a fragile and as yet incomplete banking system. Mining and commercial agriculture fueled the modernization process under normal circumstances, but were themselves subject to sharp contractions. While mining operations often had access to American capital, commercial agriculture frequently experienced severe credit shortages. Land, processing machinery, transport, and unharvested crops could not be converted into fluid assets nor easily used to secure short-term credit. Money needed to bridge temporarily unfavorable market conditions or solve cash flow problems often could not be found. Operations that only required time to return a handsome profit faced disaster without credit. Their only hope for survival depended on rapidly cutting back costs, particularly labor costs.

In 1905, exports fell from 27.1 million in British pounds sterling to 23.5 in 1908, a 20 percent drop, while imports fell during the same period by 34 percent, resulting in a sharp contraction and massive unemployment. A recession in the United States had, in effect, thrown the Mexican economy into crisis beyond the ability of the country's banking system to adequately cope. Secretary of the Treasury José Yves Limantour, aware of the root of the problem, moved skillfully to bolster the banking system. A decree of June 17, 1908, authorized the government to invest 25 million pesos in agriculture and the law of June 19, 1908, moved to protect the overextended banking network. The government organized an agriculture bank, the Caja de Préstamos para Obras de Irrigación y Fomento de la Agricultura, in cooperation with four private banks. Initially capitalized at a 10 million pesos, its resources grew to 50 million as a result of bonds floated on the New York market. Limantour's actions constituted an important step forward in providing for the future financial health of the agricultural sector. Meanwhile, the credit crisis during the period 1907–1908 demonstrated that banks lacked the liquidity necessary to meet their obligations, a realization that shook the political foundations of the Porfiriato.[51]

Another serious difficulty resulted from the limited tax resources of the federal treasury. The government's frantic desire to attract foreign investment stemmed in large part from its traditional fiscal weakness. Taxes on new enterprises offered the only hope of breaking the national government's destructive dependency on customs revenues. Tariffs, while justified on the basis of protecting Mexican producers, in fact also served to generate desperately needed revenue. Taxes amounting to 500 to 600 percent had a negative impact on trade and commerce, held down consumption, and raised prices. Frequent changes in levies, arbitrary extractions, and fines inevitably led to corruption and illegal smuggling. The free zone created along the northern border, established in recognition that the frontier region could not be serviced from central Mexico, served as a convenient base of operations for contrabandists. Internal tariffs imposed on interstate commerce by individual states created yet another barrier to the free flow of goods. The combination of corruption and smuggling reduced actual revenues; however, tax evasion moderated consumer costs. Clearly, the legal tariff system itself acted as an economic barrier that had to be circumvented. Lowering tariffs and diverting trade back into legal channels, while rational, could be accomplished only with difficulty and over an extended period of time. Creation of a new tax base eventually would make it possible, but meanwhile the existing revenue system itself constituted a drag on the economy. Moreover, a silver-backed peso failed to provide sufficient currency stability. Silver prices fluctuated and new processing methods constantly cheapened silver, leading to a downward drift of the peso relative to the American dollar and European currencies. Prices of imported food, manufactured products, and machinery increased consistently, even sharply on occasion. Mexico's current accounts deficit undermined confidence in the country's ability to pay for imports.

Tax collection posed a major problem. The federal treasury slowly convinced the populace of the need for national taxes collected throughout the republic. Internal federal taxes placed on manufactured goods gained support from domestic producers, mainly because the amount levied on foreign manufactured goods was higher, giving them a decided price advantage and protecting their market, while the consumer bore the cost. Other national internal taxes had to be slowly and carefully introduced. Regional elites continued to hold

Figure 4.5 Porfirio Díaz Tunnel, an aptly named symbol of a Porfirian infrastructure investment. *Printed with permission, Photography Collection, Harry Ransom, Humanities Research Center, University of Texas at Austin*

on to fiscal control of revenue in the belief that tax resources should be directed toward their own particular regional needs. They resisted more than a limited transfer of resources to the national level. While internal taxes as a percentage of federal income increased from 14 percent during the period 1875–1876 to 30.3 percent during the period 1910–1911, actual control of potential tax sources remained in the hands of regional elites.[52]

The government's industrial policy also had unforeseen fiscal consequences. A fragile market, with only a limited number of people able to consume modern products, encouraged industrialists to protect their market through monopoly practices, tax advantages, and political deals. A noncompetitive pattern emerged during the Porfiriato that continued to characterize Mexico industry into the 1990s. The well-being of industry depended on the close cooperation between capital and the government. Industrial entrepreneurs saw market controls as vital. Fortunately for them, because the government viewed the construction of an industrial base as being crucial to the transformation of Mexico into a fully developed nation on a par with the United States, Britain, and France, officials seldom refused requests for tariff protection or other types of state assistance. A sense of making a national contribution justified requests for government help. The founders of the Monterrey brewery selected the name Cuauhtémoc, the last Aztec emperor, as the company name in a conscious act of nationalism.[53] Their patriotism challenged the state to match their dedication with tax subsidies and tariff protection. They would not be disappointed. Direct as well as indirect subsidies to industry came at the expense of investments in more mundane areas such as road construction or education.

The belief of investors in an immensely profitable future activated them to develop an industrial base that the country would have to grow into as modernization progressed. Meanwhile, return on investment remained modest, with some exceptions. The latest machinery had a capacity that exceeded the ability of the market to absorb. As a consequence, factories ran far below capacity, adding significantly to the unit cost of their production. The Fundidora Monterrey provided Mexico with a modern steel industry it could not support, returning only losses to investors throughout the Porfiriato. In a similar fashion, the glass bottle factory had enough capacity to bottle virtually every last drop of liquid in the country. The same situation prevailed in cement and other industries.

Exporting surplus production proved almost impossible. In 1902, prominent merchants and industrialists traveled to South America to investigate the possibility of opening new markets for Mexican products. Even getting there became an adventure. To reach Brazil, they had to pass through New York, then England, before booking passage to South America. Without steamship connections, intra-American trade could not be contemplated. Moreover, most modernizing Latin American nations faced the same problem as Mexican manufacturers. In short, the only market remained the internal one. Complicating structural problems was the contradiction between holding wages down while stimulating consumption. Real wages for unskilled workers fell behind prices by some 25 percent between 1898 and 1910. Skilled workers did better, but expansion of modern consumption remained dependent on the extremely slow growth of the middle class, including government workers, managers, and technicians who could purchase modern products. High prices excluded the lower classes from the market; they barely could afford food.[54] As many contemporary observers, such as Francisco Bulnes, warned, the majority of the Mexican people faced "death by starvation."[55] Under the circumstances, the development of a mass market could not take place.

Mexico's price and monetary instability, owing to its insistence on maintaining a bimetallic (gold and silver) system, concerned both national leaders and foreign investors. American businessmen, interested in Mexico and several other countries without a gold standard, pressured the government to create the "United States Commission on International Exchange" within the Bureau of Insular Affairs. The Commission's director, Edwin Kemmerer, later known as the "Money Doctor" for his activities as a financial wizard and consultant throughout Latin America, blamed the unreliable silver standard for a host of monetary problems, including Mexico's declining ability to purchase machinery and other imports from the United States, and he pre-scribed conversion to the gold standard as the cure for these difficul-ties. His recommendation formed part of the Commission's *Report on the Introduction of the Gold-Exchange Standard into China, the Philippine Islands, Panama, and Other Silver-Using Countries (1904).* This report provided enough support for Limantour to persuade Díaz, and the result was the Monetary Reform Act of 1904.[56]

This law allowed the government to set the gold exchange rate and peg the value of silver to it. Placing Mexico on the gold exchange standard stimulated international trade and investment by creating new confidence in the economy. When the law went into effect, it de-valued the currency, with the silver peso dropping to fifty cents, equal to .75 grams of gold. Foreign investors benefitted; importers and con-sumers suffered—marking the beginning of their disaffection with Díaz. The government netted a short-term profit through the mone-tary reform of eight million pesos, but the benefits did not compensate for sacrificing internal Mexican business to exporters and foreigners. Moreover, any decline in foreign investment would encourage the flight of capital and destabilization of financial institutions.[57] Adop-tion of the gold standard provided some export price stability but damaged the internal economy. The depression during the period 1907–1908, along with poor harvests and labor trouble, both in Mex-ico and the United States, aggravated the suffering. Subsidized food provided welcome but only short-term relief. Exchange rate reforms aggravated the underlying structural weakness in the agricultural and industrial sectors.

MOBILIZATION OF LABOR

Rapidly accelerating demand for primary products created a labor shortage that put pressure on various groups, particularly Indians, that had not fully entered the labor market. More attuned to an iso-lated and subsistence lifestyle, they could not be attracted by wages alone. Given the already exploitative view of the lower classes inher-ent in Mexican liberalism, coupled with resistance to routine labor, the move to coercion was predictable. Wages, viewed as an ineffectual method of holding labor, had to be reinforced by the more binding ties of debt. Through the device of advancing cash needed for marriage, death, or other major events, as well as liberal credit at the hacienda store, an individual could be indebted to an employer. In some regions, employers engaged professional labor contractors to recruit labor. In the early period of agribusiness, expansion contractors used coercion, but as the number of landless individuals grew, they drew upon a larger pool and used more refined recruiting methods. In Chiapas economic realities forced many families to relocate from highland villages to lowland plantations. Crop harvesters included a high percentage of women and children, a characteristic of cotton and coffee cultivation in particular. Transformation of villagers into agricultural workers and the redefinition of economic roles for men, women, and children could be a brutal process, not yet fully understood.

Wages relative to recruiting and credit costs were low. Frustrated employers, always short of workers, blamed the inherent nature of the labor force for their problems. Constant complaints were recorded that if the employer paid more, the laborers worked less and spent more on alcohol. Even when workers adjusted to wage labor, employers maintained a negative attitude toward their labor force. In reality, control over labor lay at the heart of the matter. Rather than shifting resources from recruiting, credit, or debt costs to wages, employers preferred expenses that provided a permanent labor force. Reliance on wages alone would have stimulated competition for workers because of the relatively small labor pool. The methods used denied labor the ability to use demand or market forces to their advantage and enabled employers to sustain a high level of return on their investment. Only along the border could workers insist upon better compensation because of competing wage levels across the line in the United States. Not surprisingly, these areas attracted labor from other parts of the republic.

Schemes to import hard-working Chinese, Japanese, and Korean workers provided some additional labor. Ironically, many of the Chinese who entered the country preferred to become small shopkeepers. A few Chinese immigrants became manufacturers and large-scale wholesale dealers. Yet Asian labor remained a dream.[58] In Soconusco, an even more exotic scheme hoped to attract Polynesians from the Gilbert Islands. An initial group of 300 arrived only to fall victim to smallpox—one alone escaped the disease. In Yucatán, where henequen (sisal) can be harvested year-round, desperate landholders used every device imaginable to hold on to labor. Work on henequen plantations involved strenuous labor under poor conditions in a hostile tropical climate. Many workers fled in spite of their debts, hoping to avoid the bounty hunters who tracked them down. Newspaper advertisements alerted the public to watch out for the fugitives.

Sisal plantations depended heavily on foreign capital. It required seven years to bring in the first harvest and an average-sized operation consumed some $130,000 before it reached that point. In a market dominated by International Harvester in close and secret collaboration with Olegario Molina, the most powerful *henequenero*, producers struggled to meet semimonopolistic pricing demands and maintained profitability by relentlessly squeezing labor. In the rest of

Mexico, henequen planters earned a reputation for being only slightly removed from slaveholders. Yucatán agribusiness plantations functioned as all but hermetic workers' villages, with an average population of 100 to 150 residents. Some larger estates numbered from 600 to well over 1,000 workers. By 1910, three-fourths of all Yucatán's inhabitants resided on henequen plantations. An estimated 96.4 families were landless, and as a result, independent Mayan village culture collapsed throughout the henequen zone.[59]

In some of the northern areas where a sparse population made for an impossible labor situation, wages were above the national norm. In Sonora, higher wages attracted an influx of migrant labor to tend the cotton fields. The wage structure, however, could suddenly collapse, depending on demand for cotton and the weather. Weak demand and bad weather could be a disaster for workers. Massive unemployment and near starvation created a sense of panicky anger at forces beyond their control. Those who retained jobs did so only after deep wage reductions. Northern economic cycles went through periods of boom and bust. By 1910, the most economically dynamic areas of the north able to pay acceptable wages attracted a flow of immigrants.

In a rapidly industrializing Monterrey (Nuevo León), companies offered shorter hours, free housing, schools, medical attention, and recreational facilities. The Cuauhtémoc brewery also added day care and primary schools, while the Monterrey Brick Company touted its free enclosed housing and the Fundidora steel works provided a hospital as well as housing. Worker response never quite met the expectations of management. Bitter complaints about the workforce failed to take into account the extremely difficult process of adjustment to factory work that could not be obviated even by the most paternalistic or desirable incentives. Mexican workers followed a pattern similar to that evident in Europe during the transformation of peasants into workers in the early period of the Industrial Revolution.

The textile industry, the first to experience rapid expansion and modernization, played an important role in the transformation of peasants into a working class. New plants located along recently constructed rail lines drew labor from other parts of the republic. Workers often remained on the job for a matter of weeks before returning to their subsistence agricultural pursuits, perhaps to return several months later or to sample yet another new occupation. The best location for a modern plant might be in areas without a substantial population base or interest in factory work. The selection of Orizaba as the site of a major factory rested on its location on the rail line with connection to the port of Veracruz in one direction and the federal district in the other, abundant water, and a more humid climate suitable for manufacturing fine cloth. The one problem was labor. Orizaba drew its force from Puebla, a historical center of the textile industry since the colonial era, and many other areas of the country that could funnel labor into the factories via rail lines. When the Mexicano del Sur line began functioning in 1892, workers came from previously isolated Oaxaca. The inability to hold on to labor for a reasonable period forced the industry to constantly train a new group of peasants in the art of being a worker. Labor from Puebla, with its experienced textile background, made it possible to function; however, the needs for labor exceeded the supply of trained textile workers. Modern textile plants employed large numbers of workers. For example, in Atlixco (state of Puebla) demand for labor in textile factories grew by almost 12 percent between 1902 and 1908, drawing in labor from many other localities and different regions. Factories supplied modest housing to hold on to employees; nevertheless, as factory records indicate, they lost 60 percent of the force within two years and suffered a complete turnover of their workforce in five years.[60] Textile migrants averaged between eighteen and thirty years of age. Adolescents composed one-fourth of textile workers. The combination of skilled Puebla workers and children eventually resulted in the development of a working class occupationally lined to the textile industry—a process similar to the experience of England and elsewhere in Europe. The problems of nineteenth-century development came from the imposition of modern industries, based on the latest technological innovation, upon an agriculturally oriented labor force, in some cases, a largely subsistence agricultural culture. What made sense in terms of modern rational economic criteria often encountered the reality of preindustrial labor.[61]

Resistance to routinized labor by peasant workers, whether in factories, mines, or commercial agriculture, took the form of tardiness, absenteeism, an unwillingness to accept direction, and wildcat work stoppages. For example, San Antonio Abad textile workers walked off the job when the manager attempted to end the practice of drinking pulque with lunch. Leaving work without permission to attend some celebration occurred frequently. Once reasonably accustomed to routine work, employees refused to tolerate any innovations. Even when high-speed automatic machines made it possible for one person to tend many more machines than before, workers often declined to do so. As a consequence, the Mexican textile industry required twice as many workers as British mills and two and one-half times the number employed in American factories.[62]

As workers understood, modern machines eliminated the need for a skilled trained work force and reduced the number of employees needed. Management could ride out strikes by increasing production at other plants or by hiring replacements. Moreover, new machines often created a problem of overproduction, further weakening the power of labor to force concessions. In 1889, for example, a new cigarette machine tended by unskilled workers could turn out 150,000 uniform units a day, the equivalent of approximately fifty skilled women workers. A tobacco processor could choose to compete with technology by various means, including lowering wages or bowing to progress and installing the new equipment. In either event, the impact on the worker was adverse. Technology threatened wage levels, devalued skills, and pushed workers even further away from the apparent benefits of modernization that appeared to be transforming the nation and enriching others.

Paradoxically, while the demand for labor remained strong, the quality of the workforce, and hence its rewards, progressively deteriorated as machines reduced the need for skilled and experienced workers. Declining demand for skills made it easier to move labor from one activity to another. The unskilled labor pool constituted a rootless, floating element without any attachment to a particular line of work and unable to demand more than marginal compensation. At the same time, as more and more daily necessities were produced in factories the need for money in the form of wages in order to survive grew, forcing workers to move to regions that offered higher wages, particularly the north. Self-sufficiency, more characteristic of artisanal production than modern industrial manufacturing, declined dramatically.[63]

In Chihuahua, the Terrazas family, the state's largest and most important employer, could be generous, but refused to be pressured by labor. Thus when workers at one of their textile factories pressed for higher wages, they closed the plant. Yet, at another location the family constructed houses for employees, subsidized schooling, and made donations for various community improvements. It is important to note that such voluntary expenditures, while admirable and no doubt greatly appreciated, had no effect on the actual cost of production. Moreover, wage differentials between regions provided only illusionary competition. Higher wages tended to be offset by equally elevated living costs. Improvements, marginal at best, fell far short of expectations. Unskilled laborers who migrated to a new area had to survive at a level lower than the regional norm to accumulate savings. This economic reality also applied to workers who entered the United States, attracted by higher wages. Mexican labor in the American Southwest often lived in temporary makeshift camps in the style of employed hoboes until they returned home with a horde of dollars. The working poor struggled to produce a surplus over their already minimal expenses. Workers left family members and spouses at home when they embarked on such uncertain economic adventures. In contrast, some skilled workers could use wage competition to their advantage. For example, cowboys on the Terrazas estate received good wages because of the lure of high demand across the border and the difficulty of devising a means to replace labor with machines in the cattle industry. Wages for *vaqueros* doubled between 1902 and 1913. Some 8,500 people worked on Terrazas haciendas, and 40 percent of the state's industrial workforce depended on the family. As a consequence, Terrazas enterprises set the prevailing wage and working conditions standard in Chihuahua.[64]

Labor demands and technology had a negative impact on family life and the traditional productive unit composed of the parents and their children working together on a particular portion of land. The male, because of cultural factors, could be more easily detached from the peasant unit. Nevertheless, women would be drawn into wage labor at an increasing rate. The transformation of rural women into workers did not result in a corresponding adjustment in their traditional family role as the preparers and providers of food. The most energy- and time-consuming domestic task involved the grinding of corn into *masa* (dough) and shaping and cooking tortillas. The *metate* (grind stone) occupied much of a woman's time, regardless of her other activities, including wage labor. In effect, women continued to deal with the hard remnants of the traditional peasant life to a greater extent than their children or an adult male, while drawn into wage labor at rates lower than those of men. Modernization of women's roles and status lagged far behind the general transformation of the Mexican economy. Women comprised 20 percent of the wage labor force by 1910.[65]

Workers followed the rails, completely transforming the north. The states of Coahuila, Durango, Nuevo León, Tamaulipas, Sonora, Nayarit, and Veracruz had a population in 1910, composed of 70 percent non-natives, as did the cities of Mexico City and Puebla. Outside of these two cities the central part of the country lost population. Mostly young and without families, 62 percent of the migrants fell into the eighteen-to-thirty age group.[66]

TECHNOLOGY AND FOREIGN TECHNICIANS

Coupled with the problem of the labor supply was the difficulty of providing for the utilization as well as transfer of technology. New techniques in mining, railway construction, agriculture and processing, and textiles and petroleum engineering underpinned the modernization process. Machines compensated for problems of employing preindustrial labor and made it possible to use unskilled workers at lower wages. Electrification and telegraphs required a small, but skilled group of technicians. Ever since the days of Benito Juárez the national government had wrestled with the problem of providing trained professionals able to employ effectively the latest technology. Chronic financial weakness made it impossible to spend vast amounts of money to strengthen public technical education. The search for a quick and inexpensive solution led inevitably to the old and as yet unrealized dream of European immigrants. Attracting a sufficiently large number of skilled European colonists who could meet immediate needs, help train Mexican workers, and contribute to the nation's development proved much more difficult than liberal theoreticians imagined. With the failure to attract high-quality immigrants, the modernization effort depended on foreign technicians who had no intention of becoming Mexican citizens, nor of making a permanent contribution to the country. To meet their urgent needs for a small technologically trained workforce, employers recruited foreign workers and professionals.

Rapid expansion of mining required attracting and quickly training a technical staff. Full utilization of the mines required a large labor force directed by a core of skilled foreign miners. Agricultural workers who could be enticed into the mines during certain seasons could be effective only with the use of machines under the direction of a technician. As a result, a pattern of constant movement of labor between the two sectors developed. At harvest times, landowners enticed workers, usually with previous experience on the land, to leave the mines for the fields. Most then returned to the mines after the harvest. The employment of unskilled labor resulted in frequent accidents and lower productivity. The $2^{1}/_{4}$-inch drill handled by one skilled miner required two novices. Even the removal of ore depended on a larger workforce than was customary.[67] The copper works at Cananea, which enjoyed close and easy access to the American railway system, and hence more competition, paid much higher wages than elsewhere in an effort to hold on to as many workers as needed. Smaller companies in more inaccessible locations justified lower wages because of the quality and productivity of their workforce. Marginal mines unable to afford advanced technology that required a technical engineering staff survived only because of low wage scales. If foreign technicians had to be employed, the higher salaries and preferential treatment demanded was offset by holding down other expenses—a solution sure to be resented by common laborers.

When the mining company of Real del Monte y Pachuca suffered a severe decline in profitability between 1872 and 1875, with losses in excess of one million pesos, it predictably sought to regain financial stability by forcing wages down and increasing work loads. Arbitrary wage reductions at most levels in fact succeeded in saving the company, but not without massive labor troubles. Common laborers, previously paid fifty centavos a day, suffered a cut of half their day's wages. Skilled and semiskilled workers faced a 50 to 60 percent cut. Foreign technicians at Real del Monte threatened to abandon their duties and let the mines flood, forcing management to back down. At the Pachuca works foreign technicians did not succeed in such a thorough fashion, but did manage to defend their wage level. After months of labor unrest the bulk of the workforce accepted the harsh reality of lower wages.[68] The absence of solidarity within the workforce made it possible for an employer to achieve a great deal of control over the wage level and conditions of work. Worker morale appears to have been of little concern, probably because of the high turnover, characteristic of the workforce in general.

After 1880, the industry progressively became capital rather than labor intensive. American smelters imported Mexican lead content ore until the McKinley tariff of 1890 forced the construction of Mexican smelters. High demand provided the capital to modernize and transform mining. New technology such as pneumatic drills, air compressors, generating plants, dynamite, and the safety fuse increased productivity and dramatically reduced reliance on skills. With electrical energy, mines could be sunk to new depths without concern for flooding. At the Candelaria mine (Chihuahua), heavy machinery lowered into the mine itself made it possible to construct the reputedly largest underground pumping system then in use. After 1900, the cyanide process made it feasible to extract gold and silver from previously marginal ores at lower costs. Cheap silver put small operations out of business. Without vast amounts of capital, one could neither enter the industry nor succeed. The number of workers constantly shrank before the onslaught of technology. An increasingly larger proportion of miners were unskilled laborers. Job and pay insecurity became a constant preoccupation of a technologically threatened workforce.[69] Management skills, technological expertise, and close attention to the bottom line, introduced by foreigners, constituted the keys to profitable operations.

In nonmining activities, employers in need of foreign experts also paid higher wages and provided them with better working conditions than those offered to Mexican workers. Even when Mexican workers acquired new skills, the general pattern of preferential treatment lingered on. Mine and railway laborers perceived themselves as victims of a double standard, a perception that resulted in an extreme amount of resentment and hostility. They bitterly resented the foreign workers who trained or supervised them. In areas where large concentrations of foreign workers existed, hostility created a constant undercurrent of tension. The copper mining center of Cananea, with its substantial population of foreign technicians, would soon come to be known as one of Mexico's many "Cradles of the Mexican Revolution." Nevertheless, both foreign and Mexican skilled and semiskilled labor faced obsolescence with the introduction of new machines. In the long run, the higher wages paid to foreign technicians provided employers with an incentive to dispense with them and Mexicanize the labor force as in fact occurred in the railway system and the Cervecería Cuauhtémoc brewery.

The brewery in Monterrey initially depended upon foreign expertise, from design engineers to skilled mechanics, to install equipment. Americans occupied the top technical positions within the company. Brewmaster Joseph Schnaider, followed closely by a Spanish language translator, supervised the start-up and production process. By 1894, technology transfer enabled the company to nationalize its technical staff. Unlike most other operations, the brewery paid Mexican technicians at the same rate as foreigners. When Schnaider left the company in 1900 the expert staff had been completely Mexicanized. To meet its needs the company opened its own school in 1912 (Escuela Politécnica de Cuauhtémoc), with classes in chemistry, physics, fermentation, and other useful subjects. Selected individuals received grants to study in the United States and Germany. Out of this modest educational structure emerged the Monterrey Technical Institute, modeled after the Massachusetts Institute of Technology, the alma mater of important second-generation family members. Today, Monterrey Tech has branches throughout the republic. The Cuauhtémoc brewery soon developed and exported technology, acquiring some 100 U.S. patents. The brewery and its network of companies demonstrated a remarkable, enlightened self-interest that went far beyond simple paternalism.[70]

Most Mexican companies purchased technology; they did not develop it themselves. In contrast, marketing, in an effort to overcome relatively high prices, attracted major imaginative efforts as industrialization proceeded. Promotion remained extremely limited before the turn of the century, when the owners of rival cigarette companies, El Buen Tono and La Cigarrera Mexicana, began trying to upstage each other. Buen Tono's Ernesto Pugibet launched an aggressive foreign campaign exhibiting working machines in Paris and New York. The rival company, La Cigarrera Mexicana, countered the public attention given to Pugibet's international initiative by sending girls to distribute packets of its new brand "Electra" to men and flowers to their ladies attending a performance of Electra at the Abreu Theater. The marketing efforts then escalated: Pugibet showed free films at his factory and in the Alameda to working-class audiences, and La Tabacalera Mexicana offered free admission on Independence Day to circus and opera performances for its factory groups and to the Orrin Circus for smokers of its Flor de Canela brand. Buen Tono came back with film advertisements (probably the first in Mexico), topped by La Taba-calera's use of prize coupons worth 100 pesos in its packets. Contests and sample giveaways quickly became the focus of advertising: comely cigarette girls distributed free samples at the bullfights, and monthly lotteries offered prizes such as a crocodile, 12,500 pesos in cash, a French automobile, and a new house. Advertising signs, usually painted in vivid colors, created a new lifestyle model, spreading from the cities to adorn the adobe walls of rural Mexico.[71]

FOREIGN ENTERPRISES IN THE SOCIAL CONTEXT

Apart from the issue of foreign technicians, reaction to foreigners was mixed, depending on the location and the activity. Many foreign com-panies paid better wages than those offered by Mexican firms. Ameri-can and European managers unfamiliar with Mexican cultural and political methods of coercing workers, with a different experience with wage labor, relied mainly upon monetary incentives to attract and hold their workforce. Foreign tobacco planters in San Andrés Tuxla, for example, developed an incentive system designed to keep quality and production high, while Mexican planters maintained a fixed price system that controlled costs, but without such incentives. Mexican employers viewed the higher wages offered by foreign concerns as an attempt to lure away their workers. Labor, of course, saw things dif-ferently. The proximity of the international border, conveniently linked to all parts of Mexico by rail lines, made it possible for workers to pursue the higher wages offered in the United States. Northern mi-gration accustomed workers to foreign employers and altered their perception of the value of their labor. While they might well be ex-ploited by employers in the United States, often living in miserable circumstances with few provisions for sanitation, water, or other facil-ities in an effort to avoid the higher cost of living, better wages consti-tuted an irresistible attraction. Many Mexican states prohibited labor contractors from recruiting within their boundaries in a futile effort to retain their workforce. Between 1902 and 1907, an estimated 60,000 Mexican workers a year crossed into El Paso, Texas. Other border towns experienced a similar outflow of workers into the American labor market.[72]

When the violent stage of the revolution broke out, many foreign enterprises were subjected to the demands of revolutionary forces, but continued to enjoy the support of the local population. When threat-ened by revolutionaries, the manager of the Cedral Mine in Tamauli-pas escaped harm, thanks to a group of local women who insisted he had been the town's benefactor. In Sinaloa, the United Sugar Com-pany established amicable relations with its Mayo Indian workers, who viewed the company as a generous employer. Fair treatment avoided both labor problems and antiforeign sentiment.[73]

Not all foreign managers and enterprises, however, acted in a sensitive or socially responsible fashion and became the focal point of hostilities and violence. Foreigners purchased what they viewed as cheap land. From their legalistic viewpoint they had bought the land legally, complete with a valid title, paid their taxes, and expected to enjoy full and peaceful use of the land whether they hoped to speculate, exploit its resources, or merely hold it for pleasure. They perceived the Indian population as nomadic peoples without a legal right to any particular piece of property and without any claim to a territorial sovereignty that overrode state or national property legislation. Cultural insensitivity, reinforced by the attitude of the Mexican government itself, led to violent clashes. In the Yaqui River valley, the historic homeland of the Yaqui Indians, the Richardson Construction Company of Los Angeles acquired 993,650 acres from a Mexican who had taken title to the land as a result of the surveying law of 1883. The Phoenix-based Wheeler Land Company purchased an adjacent 1,450,000 acres. Other more modest holdings legally belonged to other interests, both foreign and Mexican. The Yaqui, with rights based on historical occupation and use, reacted violently to such land transfers, and as a consequence, the Mexican Army conducted endless campaigns against the Yaqui in the interests of the new proprietors. Yaqui men, women, and children were transported forcibly to Yucatán. Many fled across the border into southern Arizona. In the Tomochic region of southwestern Chihuahua, a mestizo area, foreign lumbermen leased timber-cutting concessions from José Limantour, secretary of the treasury, who personally held title to the land. The result was the Tomochic Rebellion (1892) that required the dispatching of troops and resulted in the massacre of some 300 villagers.[74] In northern Mexico, large tracts of foreign-owned land stretched from the United States border deep into Mexico. While foreigners acquired property throughout the republic, land purchases in the north were the most resented. Population displacement, apparently not a concern to the Mexican government nor to the various state administrations, did not disturb the new landowners.

William Benton provided an interesting example, as well as a notion of the dangers involved. Benton, an Englishman, bought a hacienda in 1908, evicted the tenants, and switched from agricultural production to cattle ranching. He then proceeded to encroach on land belonging to the village of Santa María de las Cuevas. Surrounded by a personal bodyguard of twenty short-tempered henchmen, and with a detachment of rurales at his disposal, he acted without restraint. Pancho Villa had him shot in 1914, allegedly for attempting to assassinate him.[75] Few mourned his passing. Economic callousness in the end proved fatal, at least to some foreign interests.

THE SOCIAL CONTEXT OF DEVELOPMENT

Legal and illegal encroachment on rural villages and commercial land by Mexican interests far exceeded that of foreigners. Unlike American, British, Canadian, German, French, and other foreign entrepreneurs, Mexicans could not claim cultural or historical ignorance. They understood the value of land and water and calculated the reaction and strength of the local population before deciding on a course of action. Imbued with Mexican liberalism, they possessed an unshakable confidence that their economic activities, while personally profitable, also responded to higher civilized goals that eventually would transform the country and its population into a modern nation. Thus, aggressive commercial sugar growers in Morelos felt little compunction about moving to seize village land. The owners of El Hospital Hacienda, for example, illegally incorporated adjacent property belonging to the villages of Yautepec, Ayala, and Anenecuilco. Armed retainers guarded their illegal seizure. A delegation that included Emiliano Zapata met with President Díaz in 1892 to protest. In response, the government sentenced the delegation's leader to penal servitude in Yucatán and conscripted Zapata into the army. The village of Anenecuilco, and Emiliano Zapata, had to wait some eighteen years before taking revenge.[76]

In their zeal to bring land under commercial cultivation, landholders did not hesitate to drastically alter the ecology. The village of Naranja (Michoacán), which had thrived by the shore of a productive marshy lake since pre-Cortesian days, found itself suddenly dispossessed and its old ways irrevocably destroyed. The soil of the Zacapa marsh, a rich mixture of volcanic ash and organic deposits, had been noted in 1881. Several years later, the Spanish-born Noriega brothers acquired legal title and in 1886 formed a commercial company to drain the marshlands. Twelve thousand hectares of reclaimed land fell into the hands of large-scale agriculturalists, while a scant four hundred hectares remained for the villages affected by the drainage project. The Noriega brothers called their new enterprise "Cantabria," after their native Spanish province. A family-financed railway carried their agricultural production to Pátzcuaro and on to major markets throughout the country. The Noriegas pointed with pride to the creation of such a fertile hacienda and noted that the elimination of marshes had reduced the problem of mosquito-borne disease. In sharp contrast, the impact on several Indian villages that had used the marshes was severe and negative. A reduction in fish and other water-dependent creatures caused a disastrous decline in food stocks and a drop in the local dietary standard. Reed weaving of mats, hats, and other items, previously an important village indus- try, dependent on the aquatic environment, withered away. Survival depended on becoming migrant laborers.[77] Not surprisingly, one of the village's native sons, Primo Tapia, became a leading agrarian ac- tivist in the 1920s after serving as an apprentice in Los Angeles with Ricardo Flores Magón as a member of the anarchist Partido Liberal Mexicano (PLM) and subsequently as an organizer for the Industrial Workers of the World (IWW) in the United States before returning to Mexico.[78]

The commercialization of agriculture and modernization changed the relationship between the classes. Larger and depersonalized units of production segregated the worker from those who owned the enter- prises. The intimate contact of artisan shops formerly had mitigated some of the negative aspects of life at the bottom. In contrast, modern organizations appeared impersonal and uncaring. Control of costs, in- cluding wages, became vital to employers in order to preserve their markets and maintain profitability—the harsh reality of the market fell heavily on the lower classes. Real wages relative to purchasing power declined approximately 20 percent between 1876 and 1910. Many foreigners had been convinced to start various enterprises by the almost incessant propaganda of slick promoters and the govern- ment itself said cheap labor would give them a valuable cost advan- tage. As Matías Romero succinctly put it

> The investor doubles his capital when he brings it to Mexico. He gets the advantage of cheap and docile labor for silver, and sells his exported product for gold.[79]

The expectation of inexpensive labor, coupled with the destruc- tive disdain for the lower classes that permeated the thinking of the more favored, held down wages and discouraged active wage competi- tion except in certain regions and activities, particularly in the north- ern transborder region. Low wage levels benefitted primarily product exporters, but had a damaging effect on the development of industries dependent on an internal market as well as the standard of living of the lower classes. A population that could barely afford to buy manu- factured goods or a train ticket acted as a brake on national develop- ment. University of California Professor Bernard Moses, one of the early academic pioneers of Latin American history in the United States, observed Indians carrying heavy clay jars from Toluca to the Mexico City market along a road that ran parallel to the Mexican National Railway. Moses noted that the "Indian and his donkey are the persistent rivals of the railways and the Indians without donkeys are carriers with whom it is hard to compete."[80] In reality, the low prices received for such goods made rail transportation impossible for a large segment of small-scale village producers. Even modern manufacturing found itself hobbled by high transportation costs. It was cheaper to import English cement from Liverpool to meet the needs of the port of Tampico than to bring it by rail from a Mexican plant several hundred miles away. Because of freight rates Mexican cement became prohibitively expensive beyond a 250-kilometer radius. Consequently, the country's cement facilities operated below capacity and were unable to achieve the economy of scale customary for a bulk product.[81] Low productivity, in spite of the most advanced equipment, could be partially compensated for by controlling expenses, including holding wages at the lowest level possible.

Matías Romero, aware that Mexican labor had few of the benefits of its counterpart in Europe and the United States, understood that ill-paid workers could not become modern consumers. He asserted that the country's historical experience explained attitudes held by both workers and employers as well as the conditions of work. Romero linked productivity to wages—both were low. He estimated that Mexican labor at best accomplished only 25 percent of the production of American workers, noting an example offered by Enrique Creel that a Mexican bricklayer laid 520 bricks a day compared to 5,000 a day by a worker in the United States. The difference more than justified the three dollars a day paid in the United States and the fifty cents paid in Mexico. Low productivity needed to be addressed and corrected through education and technical training for wages to rise. As the country developed, the standard of living would be elevated for all, including labor. Matías Romero, well acquainted with conditions in the United States, believed Mexico would follow the same pattern established in the advanced countries. Any changes in labor's situation north of the border eventually would have a Mexican reflection. Railways already had broken down some of the isolation of workers and facilitated their movement around the republic. As a developmentalist, Romero pinned everything on the future. Meanwhile, he could not resist slipping in the observation that many individuals wondered whether in fact Mexicans led a happier life because they were not so burdened with materialism—backward, poor, but happy.[82]

NOTES

1. Alberto Marí Carreno, ed., *Archivo del General Porfirio Díaz: Memorias y documentos*, vol. 1 (México: Editorial "Elete," 1947), p. 192.
2. Hale, *Transformation*, p. 58.
3. Hart, *Revolutionary Mexico*, p. 42, and "Agrarian Precursors," p. 145.
4. Hilarie J. Heath, "Los primeros escarceos del imperialismo en México: Las casas comerciales británicas, 1821–1867," *Historias* (April–September 1989), pp. 87–88.
5. Daniel Cosio Villegas, *Estados Unidos contra Porfirio Díaz* (Mexico: Editorial Hermes, 1956), pp. 227–52; Samuel E. Bell and James M. Smallwood, *The Zona Libre, 1858–1905: A Problem in American Diplomacy* (El Paso: Texas Western Press, University of Texas at El Paso, 1982), pp. 36–39.
6. John H. Seward, "The Veracruz Massacre of 1879," *The Americas* (April 1976), pp. 588, 590.
7. Justo Sierra believed that "constitutional order" was more important than the constitution itself. Hale, *Transformation*, pp. 55, 61.
8. Hale, *Transformation*, p. 195.
9. Donald M. Coerver, *The Porfirian Interregnum: The Presidency of Manuel González of Mexico, 1880–1884* (Fort Worth: Texas Christian University Press, 1979), pp. 215, 230.
10. William Schell Jr., "Integral Outsiders: The Role of Mexico City's American Colony in the Making of Porfirian Mexico," (Ph.D. diss., University of North Carolina, 1992), p. 27. See "Acta de matrimonio del General Porfirio Díaz con la señora doña Carmen Romero y Castello. 5 de noviembre de 1881," in Carreno, ed., *Archivo del General Porfirio Díaz*, vol. 1, pp. 197–98. His first wife died on April 8, 1880, at the age of thirty-two of metroperitonitis puerperal after the birth of their daughter Victoria Francisca Díaz, on April 2, 1880. Ibid., pp. 194–96.
11. Olliff, *Reforma Mexico; Matías Romero, Mexico and the United States: A Study of Subjects Affecting Their Political, Commercial and Social Relations Made with a View of Their Promotion* (New York and London: G. P. Putnam's Sons, 1898), p. 68.
12. Schoonover, *Dollars Over Dominion*, p. 138.
13. Gorham D. Abbot, *Mexico and the United States, Their Mutual Relations and Common Interests* (New York: G. P. Putnam & Son, 1869), pp. 390–91. The copy of Abbot's book used for this study originally came from the personal library of John W. Foster, U.S. representative in Mexico in the 1870s. It is now held in the Latin American Library, Tulane University, New Orleans.
14. Francisco Bulnes, demonstrating a talent for capturing the essence of an individual, described Matías Romero as a person who had adopted a puritan style after many years in the United States and consequently dressed like a Methodist preacher. In a upright honest style he went to work on horseback rather than in a coach. Francisco Bulnes, *El verdadero Díaz y la Revolución* (Mexico: Editorial Nacional, 1920), p. 198. Justo Sierra admiringly described Matías Romero as a veritable dynamo constantly at work whose reports became opúsculos, whose works became books, and his memorias libraries. Justo Sierra, *Viajes en tierra Yankee, en la Europa latina* (Mexico, 1948), pp. 115–16.
15. Pletcher, *Rails, Mines and Progress*, p. 154.
16. Charles A. Weeks, *The Juárez Myth in Mexico* (University: University of Alabama Press, 1987), pp. 26–42.

17. For an informative view of border politics, see J. D. Thompson, *Warm Weather*. Quote is from Thompson, p. 5.

18. Frank Louis Hall Jr., "El Paso, Texas, and Juárez, Mexico: A Study of a Bi-Ethnic Community, 1846–1881" (Ph.D. diss., University of Texas, 1978), pp. 53–56, 73–74; James B. Gillett, *Six Years with the Texas Rangers, 1875–1881* (Lincoln: University of Nebraska Press, 1976), pp. 211–22. "Cooperative Understanding" along the border is evident in a 1992 incident. Fred Lawrence, Customs Service Director in Nogales, Arizona, reported that Mexican Federal Judicial Police chased a van into Douglas, Arizona. A Mexican policeman ordered the two occupants out at gunpoint and took them back across the border. Director Lawrence excused the incident on the basis of the "adrenaline" of "hot pursuit" and stated that American officials on the scene had been outgunned by the Mexicans (*The New York Times*, June 19, 1992, p. 9).

19. David Montejano, *Anglos and Mexicans*, p. 33.

20. Oscar J. Martínez, *Troublesome Border* (Tucson: University of Arizona Press, 1988), pp. 83–86, 155.

21. John R. Chávez, *The Lost Land*, p. 84.

22. Romero, *Mexico and the United States*, vol. 1, pp. 431–79; Oscar J. Martinez, *Border Boom Town: Ciudad Juárez since 1848* (Austin: University of Texas Press, 1975), pp. 14–17.

23. Montejano, *Anglos and Mexicans*, pp. 47–48.

24. New York Evening Post, May 19, 1894, reprinted in Romero, *Mexico and the United States*, pp. 492–94.

25. Bell and Smallwood, *The Zona Libre*, pp. 58–59.

26. Mary Angeline Watrous, "Fiscal Policy and Financial Administration in Mexico, 1890–1940" (Ph.D. diss., Washington State University, 1991), pp. 16, 17, 24, 96, 99.

27. John R. Chávez, *The Lost Land*, p. 50.

28. Daniel Casío Villegas, ed., *Historia moderna de México*, 8 vols. (México: Editorial Hermes, 1974), vol. 7, pp. 658–85.

29. Matías Romero, *El ferrocarril de Tehuantepec* (Mexico: Secretaria de Fomento, 1894), p. 29.

30. James E. Fell, Jr., *Ores to Metals: The Rocky Mountain Smelting Industry* (Lincoln: University of Nebraska Press, 1979), p. 153. On Henry Raup Wagner, see his *Bullion to Books* (Los Angeles: Zamorano Club, 1942).

31. Schoonover, *Dollars Over Dominion*, pp. 268–69.

32. Moisés González Navarro, *Estadísticas sociales del Porfiriato, 1877–1910* (México, 1956), table 1.

33. William H. Beezley, "The Porfirian Smart Set Anticipates Thorstein Veblen in Guadalajara," Anthony Morgan, "Proletarians, Políticos and Patriarchs: The Use and Abuse of Cultural Customs in the Early Industrialization of Mexico City (1880–1910)," and Barbara A. Tennenbaum, "Streetwise History—the Paseo de la Reforma and the Porfirian State 1876–1910." in Beezley, Martin, and French, eds., *Rituals of Rule*.

34. Lawrence John Rohlfes, "Police and Penal Correction in Mexico City, 1876–1911: A Study of Order and Progress in Porfirian Mexico" (Ph.D. diss., Tulane University, 1983), pp. 77–78.

35. Winter, *Mexico and Her People*, p. 60.

36. Gilbert M. Joseph, *Revolution from Without: Yucatán, Mexico, and the United States, 1880–1924* (Durham: Duke University Press, 1980), p. 36.

37. Steven B. Bunker, "Making the Good Old Days: Invented Tradition and Civic Ritual in Northern Mexico, 1880–1910" (Honors Thesis, University of British Columbia, 1992).

38. Saragoza, *The Monterrey Elite*, pp. 52–63; Barbara Hibino, "Cervecería Cuauhté-moc: A Case Study of Technological and Industrial Development in Mexico," *Mexican Studies / Estudios Mexicanos* (winter 1992), p. 27.

39. Cosío Villegas, *Historia Moderna*, vol. 7, p. 456.

40. Roger D. Hansen, *The Politics of Mexican Development* (Baltimore: Johns Hopkins Press, 1971), pp. 19–20.

41. Joseph, *Revolution from Without*, pp. 34, 37.

42. Héctor Aguilar Camín, *La frontera nómada: Sonora y la revolución Mexicana* (Mexico: Siglo Veintiuno Editores, 1977), pp. 110–13.

43. Cosío Villegas, *Historia Moderna*, vol. 7, pt. 1, p. 101; Daniela Spenser, "Soconusco: The Formation of a Coffee Economy in Chiapas," in Thomas Benjamin and William McNellie, eds., *Other Mexicos: Essays on Regional Mexican History, 1876–1911* (Albuquerque: University of New Mexico Press, 1984), pp. 123–43.

44. Robert Wasserstrom, *Class and Society in Central Chiapas* (Berkeley: University of California Press, 1983), p. 115.

45. Cosío Villegas, *Historia Moderna*, vol. 7, pp. 100–10.

46. William K. Meyers, *Forge of Progress, Crucible of Revolt: The Origins of the Mexican Revolution in La Comarca Lagunera, 1880–1911* (Albuquerque: University of New Mexico Press, 1994), pp. 8, 46–51, 111–42, 166.

47. David Joslin, *A Century of Banking in Latin America* (London: Oxford University Press, 1963), p. 88.

48. Leonor Ludlow, "La construcción de un banco: El Banco Nacional de México (1881–1884)," in Leonor Ludlow and Carlos Marichal, eds., *Banco y poder en México, 1800–1925* (Mexico: Grijalbo, 1986), pp. 299–346.

49. Watrous, "Fiscal Policy," pp. 29–31.

50. Joslin, *A Century of Banking*, p. 88; Coerver, *The Porfirian Interregnum*, p. 228.

51. Abdiel Oñate, "Banco y agricultura en México: La crisis de 1907–1908 y la fundación del primer banco agrícola," in Ludlow and Marichal, eds., *Banco y poder en México*, pp. 347–73.

52. Marcello Carmagnani, "El liberalismo, los impuestos internos y el estado federal mexicano, 1857–1911," *Historia Mexicana* (January-March 1989), pp. 471–96.

53. Hibino, "Cervecería Cuauhtémoc," p. 29.

54. The Fundidora Monterrey seldom operated at more than one-third capacity, and the Vidriera Monterrey bottle works with its monopoly use of the Owens automated methods of manufacturing could produce some twelve billion bottles annually. Stephen H. Haber, *Industry and Underdevelopment: The Industrialization of Mexico, 1890–1940* (Stanford: Stanford University Press, 1989), pp. 39, 85, 90. On profit, see Haber, *Industry and Underdevelopment* pp. 103–21; Hansen, *Politics of Mexican Development*, p. 23.

55. Bolnes, *El Verdadero Diáz*, p. 195.

56. For a discussion of these financial programs throughout Latin America, see Paul W. Drake, ed., *Money Doctors and Foreign Debts in Latin America* (Wilmington: SR Books, 1993), and for Kemmerer's South American activities, Drake's *The Money Doctor in the Andes* (Durham: Duke University Press, 1989). Also see Edwin Walter Kemmerer, *Modern Currency Reforms: A History and Discussion of Recent Currency Reforms in India, Puerto Rico, Philippine Islands, Straits, Settlements and Mexico* (New York: MacMillan Co., 1916); Emily S. Rosenberg, "Foundations of United States International Financial Power: Gold Standard Diplomacy, 1900–1905," *Business History Review* (summer 1985), pp. 176–89.

57. Watrous, "Fiscal Policy," pp. 44–45, 50, 53.

58. Victor Dahl, "Alien Labor on the Gulf Coast of Mexico, 1880–1900," *The Americas* (July 1960), pp. 21–35.

59. Joseph, *Revolution from Without*, p. 24.
60. Leticia Gamboa Ojeda, "Dos aspectos de la clase obrera textil de Atlixco a fines del Porfiriato," *Historias* (October 1989-March 1990), pp. 68, 72.
61. Bernardo García Díaz, "La clase obrera textil del Valle de Orizaba, en México: Migraciones y origen," *Siglo XIX* (July-December 1988), pp. 77–108. For an account of the struggle of turning peasants into miners see William E. French, *A Peaceful and Working People: Manners, Morals, and Class Formation in Northern Mexico* (Albuquerque: University of New Mexico Press, 1996).
62. Saragoza, *The Monterrey Elite*, p. 90; Haber, *Industry and Underdevelopment*, pp. 35–36.
63. Carmen Ramos, "Mujeres trabajadoras en el Porfiriato," *Historias* (October 1988–March 1989), pp. 113–21; Rodney D. Anderson, *Outcasts in Their Own Land: Mexican Industrial Workers, 1906–1911* (DeKalb: Northern Illinois University Press, 1976), p. 303.
64. Wasserman, *Capitalists, Caciques, and Revolution*, pp. 47, 52, 67.
65. Salamini and Vaughan, eds., *Women of the Mexican Countryside*, pp. 7–8.
66. This may have indicated the existence of a transitional generation detaching itself from village roots, at least for considerable periods of time. Early movement into the United States probably was similar in age and composition. This basically rootless, restless, and exploited population in part explains why the Mexican Revolution swept down from the border region to engulf the country. David Piñera Ramírez, "La frontera norte: De la independencia a nuestros días," *Estudios de historia moderna y contemporañea de México* (México: Universidad Nacional Autónoma de México, 1989), pp. 36–38 states that the changes in the north explain why the northern border area played the decisive role in the Mexican Revolution.
67. *Engineering and Mining Journal* contained administrative advice that reflected a negative opinion of labor and how to deal with it.
68. Eduardo Flores Clair, "Mecanismos de resistencia en Real del Monte y Pachuca," *Historias* (October 1989–March 1990), pp. 39–53.
69. Cosío Villegas, *Historia Moderna*, vol. 6, p. 248; Marvin D. Bernstein, *The Mexican Mining Industry, 1890–1950: A Study of the Interaction of Politics, Economics, and Technology* (Albany: State University of New York Press, 1965), pp. 40–41; William E. French, "'Progreso Forzado': Workers and the Inculcation of the Capitalist Work Ethic in the Parral Mining District," in Beezley, Martin, and French, eds., *Rituals of Rule*.
70. Saragoza, *The Monterrey Elite*, p. 91; Hibino, "Cervecería Cuauhtémoc," pp. 27–28.
71. Morgan, "Proletarians, Políticos and Patriarchs," in Beezley, Martin, and French, eds., *Rituals of Rule*.
72. Wasserman, *Capitalists, Caciques, and Revolution*, p. 122.
73. Alan Knight, "The United States and the Mexican Peasantry c. 1880–1940," in Daniel Nugent, ed., *Rural Revolt in Mexico and U.S. Intervention* (San Diego: Center for U.S.-Mexican Studies Publications, 1988), p. 45.
74. Hart, *Revolutionary Mexico*, p. 45.
75. Charles C. Cumberland, *Mexican Revolution: The Constitutionalist Years* (Austin: University of Texas Press, 1972), pp. 282–87.
76. Hart, *Revolutionary Mexico*, p. 43.
77. Paul Friedrich, *Agrarian Revolt in a Mexican Village* (Englewood Cliffs: Prentice Hall, 1970), pp. 43–46.
78. Ibid., pp. 66–70.
79. Romero, *Mexico and the United States*, vol. 1, p. 571.

80. Bernard Moses, *The Railway Revolution in Mexico* (San Francisco: The Berkeley Press, 1895), p. 78; Pletcher, *Rails, Mines, and Progress*, p. 305; Schmidt, "The Social and Economic Effects of the Railroad," p. 260; Arturo Grunstein, "Railroads and Sovereignty: Policymaking in Porfirian Mexico" (Ph.D. Dissertation, UCLA, 1994).

81. Haber, *Industry and Underdevelopment*, p. 40. Approximately 100 years later (in 1991), newspaper publisher Alejandro Junco (*El Norte*) observed that it cost more to ship goods from Monterrey to Tampico, a distance of 200 miles, than from Amsterdam to the Port of Tampico (4,000 miles). The earlier pattern continues to hinder internal commerce. "The Case for an Internal Mexican Free-Trade Agreement," *Wall Street Journal* (March 22, 1891), quoted in James W. Wilkie, "The Political Agenda in Opening Mexico's Economy: Salinas Versus the Caciques," *Mexico Policy News* (PROFMEX, San Diego, spring 1991), pp. 11–13.

82. Romero wrote for an American audience, as much if not more than for Mexicans. His writings conveyed the liberal position with a clarity and directness very much appreciated in the United States. Romero, *Mexico and the United States*, vol. 1, pp. 506–7, 521–22.

Chapter 5

THE PORFIRIATO

THE PORFIRIAN SOCIAL STRUCTURE

The structure of Mexican society during the Porfiriato consisted of a number of levels that must be noted in order to understand the social dynamics of the era. Large holders of commercialized agricultural land constituted the top of the pyramid. Land provided the economic core as well as social status. From this base large landholders diversified into manufacturing, mining, or other profitable activities. An elite group allied with national and regional political groups, with business or personal connections to foreign capitalists and investors, formed an interlocking socioeconomic and political directorate. They used their political, economic, and social influence to reinforce their position. Economic concessions, contracts, and other forms of political patronage fell to this group. They negotiated among themselves for a share of the political power and economic fruits of modernization. Between 1896 and 1910, Mexican entrepreneurs invested 87 million pesos in manufacturing alone, compared to some 131 million pesos poured into Mexico by international investors during the Porfiriato. Foreign investors often took on Mexican partners for political and management reasons. Energetic individuals could rapidly augment their wealth through these alliances. Olegario Molina in Yucatán formed just such a partnership with the International Harvester Company and established an informal empire. It is clear that Molina, rather than the company, set the pace, although he had to be responsive to the company's economic agenda.

The Porfiriato

1876–1911	The Porfiriato, the regime of Porfirio Díaz
1877–1878	Military administrative reorganization
1891	Papal proclamation Rerum Novarum promotes labor and social reform
	Plan Revolucionario of Catarino Garza
1892	National Liberal Convention
1895	Crowning of the Virgin of Guadalupe
1899	Mexico–United States Extradition Treaty
1903	Second National Liberal Convention
1905	Saga of Gregorio Cortez

The lifestyle of these individuals, no more than 2 percent of the population, could only be envied. They purchased foreign-made luxury goods, imported linens, grand pianos, European wines and liquors, and all the bric-a-brac of European civilization. Their mansions appeared to some as magical transplants from Paris, complete with ubiquitous servants who attended to their every need. They sent their sons and daughters abroad to French convent schools, private academies, and major universities around the world. The elite monitored European fashions and adjusted their taste to conform to the latest dictates of London and Paris. French cuisine became the current trend, while a preference for traditional Mexican food marked an individual as being rather gauche and perhaps even suggested evidence of a rustic background. The city's most elegant restaurants did not dare open their doors without a French chef. Socially prominent individuals such as Ignacio de la Torre y Mier did their utmost to retain a European cook. When don Ignacio managed to convince the celebrated French chef Sylvain Daumont to perform gastronomical miracles in his personal kitchen, he became the envy of the fashionable. He graciously allowed don Porfirio to borrow Chef Daumont for special occasions. Eventually, Daumont opened his own establishment, which instantly became the fashionable place for the rich, elegant, and refined. In addition, the Maison Dorée and the Fonda de Recamier offered a tasteful change of pace. Menus, all in French, separated the truly sophisticated from the mere neo-chic pretenders.[1]

Olive Percival, an American observer, at the turn of the century noted that even at a country home the furnishings and entertainment had a European flavor. Wine and French cakes followed by an hour or so of Schumann, Grieg, and Chopin, played by a daughter recently returned from a finishing school in Germany kept the guests amused.[2]

Figure 5.1 A view of Chapultepec castle then in use by President Porfirio Díaz. Notice the elegant strollers and the waiter on the corner attired in the French fashion. *Printed with permission, Photography Collection, Harry Ransom, Humanities Research Center, University of Texas at Austin.*

High culture entered the country through French books and magazines. The important nineteenth-century works of Herbert Spencer, Charles Darwin, and other British thinkers filtered into the Mexican consciousness in French translation. The Parisian *Revue des Deux Mondes*, a biweekly review of politics, philosophy, and letters, enabled the elite to feel connected at least spiritually with the broader intellectual world. Mexican literary magazines such as *La República Literaria*, published in Guadalajara, printed poems in French as well as translations from German works. European literary trends and fashions found a receptive audience. Even the wave of romantic suicides that removed a number of emotionally overheated European literary personalities from life's active stage had a reflection in the death of Mexican poet Manuel Acuña (1849–1873), who wrote the amorous *Nocturno* just before he took his life.[3] Spanish books, periodicals, and styles also enjoyed some attention; for the Porfirians, however, French remained the language of haute couture. More vulgar pursuits also had a continental flair. In Mexico City the gaming tables of the prestigious Jockey Club had a decided look of Monte Carlo about them as the swirling press of the fashionably rich, politically powerful, and famous placed their bets. On a given evening one might see Ricky Creel, Pepe Limantour, or even don Porfirio and his charming wife Carmen make a grand appearance at the Jockey Club. Visitors from the provinces avidly looked forward to an invitation to the club and a chance to mingle with the movers and shakers of Mexican society and national politics.

Elite acceptance of European cultural superiority inevitably placed Mexico's culture in an inferior and a subordinate position. They believed the lower classes and some of the provincial elites who failed to comprehend the value of a refined, but also progressive, European model remained caught in the web of a stalled culture that impeded modernization. The Porfirians sought to graft on a European shoot that could invigorate and redirect the country's cultural resources toward the goal of creating a modern nation. Just as they believed the world moved toward a common industrial future, in a matrix formed by telegraph wire and rail links, they foresaw the emergence of a modern universal culture. The Mexican elite lived in fear that the universal culture would be dominated by the United States.[4] While they admired the economic vitality of the colossus of the north, they viewed elements of American culture as inferior, even crass, with an irresistible tendency to pull society down to the lowest common level. It remains a concern of Mexico today. They pondered whether, if Mexican culture became Americanized, there would be any hope, or even point, in retaining their independent sovereignty. Thus, the elite geographically and

Figure 5.2 Mexico City's country club provided relaxation and a place to practice modern sports. Note the small boys engaged in retrieving tennis balls. *Printed with permission, Photography Collection, Harry Ransom, Humanities Research Center, University of Texas at Austin.*

psychologically leapfrogged toward what they believed was a more desirable cultural fate. While the activities, posturing, and exaggerations encouraged by this attitude can be seen as an amusing caricature of European models, the underlying motivation must be recognized as an important defense of a projected cultural idea.

On an emotional and intellectual level the Mexican elite accepted the pan-Latinism of François Gurzot and Napoleon III while rejecting the imperial political structure. Mexican culture would be directed toward a "Latin" American future as distinct from an "Anglo" one. An important part of this strategy required an assessment of the republic's cultural resources. The government actively supported the writing of history, commissioning research in European archives and within the country. Historians Fernando Paso y Troncoso and Ignacio B. del Castillo received financial help, as did Nicolás León for a bibliographical study of the eighteenth century. José María Vigil wrote a guide to Mexican literature while receiving a government stipend. The blending of Mexican culture into the protective framework of Latin civilization required sacrificial adjustments. Yet many believed that adoption of European models had gone too far. Author Julio Guerrero decried the uncritical acceptance of French models; nevertheless, he excluded much of Mexico's cultural experience as being incompatible with the objectives of a new age. Achieving an acceptable balance that offered some hope of fending off the cultural danger posed by United States while preserving the core of Mexico's culture continues to be a problem in our own time.[5]

Regional elites did their best to keep up with the Mexico City lifestyle. Nuevo León's Monterrey elite, flush with industrial wealth and success, came close to matching the social splendor of the capital. Membership in the Casino Monterrey Club affirmed a family's high social standing and provided an ideal matchmaking environment for their sons and daughters. The younger set also gathered at the Monterrey Athletic Club and the Terpsecore club, or for drinks at the Teatro Progreso bar. Local newspapers carried avidly anticipated photo spreads of high society activities. Monterrey's clubs organized civic ceremonial events and parades. In 1910 the Cervecería Cuauhtémoc float, loaded with young members of the elite, won first prize. Parades always included automobiles carrying distinguished citizens and their families who delighted in waving to the crowd. Every Sunday the city's elite went to church in the finest of imported carriages complete with servants clad in the "English style" with red coats, white gloves, black boots, and tricornered hats. Foreign dignitaries and important visitors from Mexico City, often treated to lavish banquets by the still insecure Monterrey elite, could only profess astonishment and admiration. The luxuriant lifestyle of the national and regional elite suggested that the fruits of modernization indeed could be sweet.[6]

Even sports became Europeanized. The traditional amusements of cockfights, bullfights, and the rustic *charreada* became associated with the lower classes, while horse racing, formal equestrian events, a stylized *charrería*, polo, and bicycles indicated one's attachment to modernity. The Jockey Club purchased land for a racetrack and the initial opening (1882) was the social event of the year, attracting then-president Manuel González, his cabinet, the entire diplomatic corps, and anyone of note in Mexico City society. The area set aside for the common folk was filled up by crowds of people who rode the streetcar from the downtown *zócalo* to the track. Polo matches were first played in the Hipódromo Francés in the 1880s, and in 1888 devotees established a polo club.[7]

Some new sports activities became general fads, enthralling all classes. Roller skating swept the capital in the 1870s. In December 1875 a rink opened at the Tivoli de Ferrocarril where patrons could skate to the music of an orchestra on the very latest wooden-wheeled skates. Rinks opened throughout the republic and attracted all classes.

Bicycles arrived in Mexico City in 1869 but did not become a widespread fad until the 1890s, when the Columbia Bicycle Agency opened a store downtown. By then the bicycle consisted of equal-sized wheels and pneumatic tires. Newspapers predicted the bicycle would become the most important means of transportation in the country. Cycling clubs, races, and rallies provided opportunities to practice the sport that all equated with progress.

Baseball's popularity coincided with the growing influence of Americans in Mexico. American workers played the first games in the early 1880s. Railway workers in particular exposed Mexicans to the attractions of the game. Northern Mexicans, and those who customarily crossed the international border, picked up the game and it slowly made its way to the capital. Baseball clubs gradually appeared in Mexico City. On the eve of the Mexican Revolution, baseball had been Mexicanized.[8]

Foreign sports were promoted as being more healthy, requiring better skills, and therefore useful in the modernization process. Traditional Mexican amusements were viewed as having a deleterious effect on morals, public conduct, and work habits. Díaz, during his first term in office, prohibited bullfights in the capital, as did several of the more advanced states responding to the charge made by foreigners that it represented a barbaric primitive sport. Díaz's successor, President González, appears to have permitted the sport. Nevertheless, unpleasant incidents, such as a disgusted General Ulysses S. Grant

Figure 5.3 A flower parade of bicycles in Mexico City in the 1890s. *Printed with permission, Photography Collection, Harry Ransom, Humanities Research Center, University of Texas at Austin.*

fleeing the bullring, embarrassed the Mexican elite. Perhaps it represented one slaughter too many for the general with vivid memories of Civil War battlefields.[9] If the country could be encouraged to take up the new salubrious athletic activities, alcoholism, gambling, and general laziness could be mitigated if not totally eliminated.

Part of this healthy program sponsored by the elite and the still small-but-growing modernizing middle class, as well as the government, involved an antialcohol campaign. Drunkenness reduced productivity as well as weakened discipline among the workers. Observance of San Lunes (Saint Monday) by hung over workers following a weekend of heavy drinking had a direct impact on factory operations. Employers and society in general perceived the lower classes as being uniquely susceptible to alcoholism if left to their own idle wishes. Fermented maguey pulque fortified with special roots provided a cheap drink readily available in all parts of the republic; it could be purchased on the streets from vendors, from women dispensing glasses from small huts, or in more colorful cantinas. *Pulquerías*, cantinas or saloons that sold only pulque, had a distinct smell that could be recognized 500 yards away. Often painted in bright colors, perhaps with a wall mural, they provided momentary relief for the lower classes but seemed an affront to more civilized ways. Because of its food value, pulque became part of the subsistence diet of the lower classes. Old women drank fresh pulque (nonfermented) to maintain their stamina. To the more favored classes, pulque, a preconquest drink clearly linked to the past, had no virtues—only vices. Around the turn of the century Mexico City's approximately 1,600 pulquerías were required by law to close promptly at six o'clock in the evening. In spite of government and social pressure against the use of pulque, it remained an important part of life at the bottom. Even the names of pulquerías reflected a certain class defiance. "The Retreat of the Holy Virgin," "The Hang-Out of John the Baptist," "A Night of Delight," "The Fountain of Angels," and "The Land of the Lotus" promised at least a momentary haven from the demands of a modernizing society.[10]

Alleged lower class weakness for strong drink provided justification for withholding wages forced consumption of approved products through the use of script at company stores or other controlled outlets, and additional redemptive efforts to save them from themselves. Getting them out of the pulquería and onto bicycles would not be easy. The rejection of traditional amusements, including alleged vices and the demands for their replacement by modern activities, constituted a broad cultural attack by the elite and part of the modernization process as they defined it. The elite set the tone of the Porfiriato and provided the general framework within which all other classes and groups lived, worked, and even played.

The middle class joined with the elite to bring about the regeneration of the lower classes through moral reforms. By doing so they demonstrated their social superiority and participation in modernizing Mexico. Local officials hoped to replace gambling, drunkenness, and prostitution with the values of thrift, sobriety, and hygiene. In their efforts to carry out reforms and control public space, they developed what could be called a moralizing discourse.[11] Their effort resulted in regulation of closing times for cantinas and restriction of brothels to zones away from the center of towns.

Reformers established the national direction of public welfare, when Díaz removed it from local jurisdiction to federal authority (eventually placing it under the supervision of the Ministry of Interior (Gobernación)). Encouraged by the national government, these reformers, using scientific-sounding rationales, devised programs for bringing "modern" management to public health, welfare, hospitals, asylums, orphanages, and prisons. All of these betterment campaigns, worked out in new, specially constructed buildings, attempted to discipline behavior, intrude into family relationships, and define gender and class roles, especially of poorer Mexicans.[12]

In response to imposed modern mores, workers continued to purchase liquor, ignored tavern closing laws (abetted by owners competing with illegal sales), frequented unregistered prostitutes, and continued to gamble with impunity. Moreover, they shed work clothes in their free time and dressed up in social status with factory-made clothing and shoes, violating the "hierarchy of appearances." Nevertheless, rural and urban workers maintained their folk culture along with its virtues and vices. For example, to demonstrate their cultural independence, underground cult chapels (Corralitos, Chihuahua, has a typical one) continued to celebrate unapproved festivals such as the May 3 observance in honor of Santa Cruz.

Local authorities used community regulations to control workers, while others tried to redeem them through mutual aid societies and night schools designed to induce morality and discipline. Workers at times took over these institutions to use as vehicles for their own concerns, so that a few mutual aid societies pressed for improved working conditions and wages. Workers hungered for better earnings and also for the respect they believed was owed them as Mexican citizens. More than recalcitrance inspired them; their belligerence reflected the pervasive popular liberalism that had developed since the time of Benito Juárez. This attitude rested firmly on long-standing practices and the prevailing popular understanding of the 1857 Constitution, the example of the mythical Juárez, and the meaning of Mexico's victory over the French. Taken together, these attitudes resulted in folk liberalism that included festive and personal rights. The people believed, in other words, that they had the right to celebrate certain holidays and that they possessed a certain dignity as individuals bestowed on them by the constitution and measured by their personal honor.[13] In the eyes of the elite, such resistance merely proved the point. The truculent lower classes had to be forced to adopt modern values for their own good and that of the country.

FOREIGNERS AND THE SOCIAL STRUCTURE

A parallel group consisted of foreign entrepreneurs who, while not part of the social structure, functioned as a powerful supporting auxiliary. The modernizing elite profitably manipulated this group, although a certain amount of intermixing and even intermarriage occurred. If they individually became too powerful, such as the petroleum entrepreneurs and on occasion railwaymen and mining speculators, steps would be taken to cut them down to size, usually through competing contracts or concessions. In some areas foreigners appeared to dominate the economy. For example, in the coffee regions of Soconusco, German growers relying on German banks and shipping lines and the European market kept the industry functioning.

In Sinaloa, Mazatlán became a modern port, due to the economic impetus of the California gold rush of 1849 and the opening of many foreign commercial houses. Foreigners founded the Pacífico brewery in Mazatlán. German investors established the Moctezuma brewery in Orizaba in 1894 with an investment of 310,000 pesos. The reputation of its various brands, including Superior and Dos Equis, soon rivaled that of Carta Blanca produced by one of its competitors. The brewery became one of the most modern and efficient in Latin America with a number of subsidiary operations, all of which required other investors, both foreign and Mexican.[14] This type of activity might have made the founders rich, but it did not make them part of the Mexican economic or social elite. Selling shares to raise capital both diffused control and spread the return to a wide group of investors. Integration of foreigners into another culture requires several generations, facilitated by intermarriage and acculturation through birth. The Porfirian regime did not last long enough to absorb many of them into Mexican society.

European merchant-financiers dominated many major manufacturing companies. With capital generated in merchant activities and stock issues in Geneva or Paris, they possessed sufficient resources to invest in industrialization. Many large stockholders in Mexican industrial enterprises were Europeans from a merchant or lending background. Few had any extensive experience with actual manufacturing—they left that to foreign experts and managers. Their strong suit was in the administration of resources, manipulation of markets through their political skills, and other indirect ways of guaranteeing a profit. Spaniard Adolfo Prieto y Alvarez, for example, arrived in Mexico in 1890 to work in a Basque banking house with diversified holdings acquired as a result of banking activities such as textile and cigarette factories. Prieto may have been a relative of one of the company's principals. He in turn acquired stock in various enterprises.

Figure 5.4 Pacific Coast port of Mazatlán, Sinaloa, around the turn of the century. *Printed with permission, Research Collection, Annelisa Romero de MacLachlan.*

Prieto served on the board of the Fundidora Monterrey, becoming chairman of the board in 1917, and several years later held a controlling interest in the company. He directed affairs from his Mexico City office, remaining chairman until he died in 1945. He also served on the board of the Banco Hispano of Madrid. A man of great influence in financial and political circles, he nevertheless remained apart from the Mexican elite. French, Swiss, Germans, and other Europeans functioned in a similar manner.[15]

Early American entrants in the race to develop the fabled wealth of Mexico, while ambitious and energetic, could not be socially integrated into the elite. Promoters, rather than businessmen or administrators, blazed a trail leaving both success and failure in their wake. Many skirted the line between shady practices and cleverness—dream makers could become charlatans, depending on luck and results. Many lived in an ostentatious manner that exuded success even if they had to borrow money to maintain their prosperous façade. They represented the first generation—brash, insensitive, materialistic, but also path breaking. Major Robert B. Gorsuch arrived in Mexico in 1856 to supervise construction of the Veracruz railroad, fought for the Confederacy, and after the war returned to Mexico to construct railroads for Maximilian, then Juárez. He represented Collis Huntington and made a fortune speculating in Mexico City real estate. He remained an active member of the American community until his death in 1906. The archetype was Colonel William C. Greene, the developer of the Cananea copper mines, who started his career as a drifter, became a miner, fought the Indians (hence the title of colonel), hauled firewood on mule back for sale in Prescott, Arizona, loved to gamble recklessly, killed a man, raised money on Wall Street, hit it big, and died in bankruptcy. Alexander R. Shepherd, a more sedate individual, literally buried himself in the old colonial silver mines of remote Batopilas (Chihuahua), succeeding in squeezing out considerable wealth that went back into the modernization of the mines. Enrique C. Creel, then foreign minister, thought very highly of Shepherd and endeavored to help him. Unfortunately, the Batopilas enterprise did not survive the Mexican Revolution. Shepherd, an economic eccentric in Mexico, in the right setting would have been an outstanding success.

Albert Kimsey Owen combined utopian notions with capitalism in his attempt to transform Topolobampo (Sinaloa) into a major transpacific port, with rail connections to Norfolk, Virginia, through Austin, Texas. Lack of funds and supplies and community dissension among the disillusioned utopian settlers proved fatal. Nevertheless, Topolobampo seized the imagination of yet another railway promoter, Arthur E. Stilwell of Kansas City. A born salesman, he honed his skills hawking stationery, insurance, and finally stocks and bonds. His efforts delighted the Travelers Insurance Company of Hartford, but selling insurance did not provide the excitement he sought. As a result, he drifted from one sales job to another until he obtained his first railway concession. His interest in Mexico stemmed from his dream to link Kansas City with Asian markets. The grand scheme called for a rail line running from Kansas City across Kansas, Oklahoma, and Texas, into Chihuahua and finally Sinaloa. In the end, only bits and pieces of completed track on both sides of the border provided at least some substance to the dream. A hypnotic personality, elegantly dressed with a neatly waxed mustache, he traveled on a luxurious private Pullman car paneled with mahogany, along with all the conveniences, including an organ. He sometimes enticed his guests to sing Christian Science hymns along with him. Subsequently, after receivership, bankruptcy, and other disasters, the Mexicans referred to his "express route to the Orient," now a short, poorly maintained stretch with unpainted boxcars and unreliable locomotives, as "El Kansado" derived from *el cansado*—"the tired one", and one from Kansas.

Thomas Braniff, a more successful example, managed to die a millionaire. He began his career in the gold fields of California, where he met the English engineer Henry Meiggs. Meiggs's company, then involved in railway construction in Peru and Chile, provided the young adventurer with his first taste of the profit to be made in Latin American development. After his South American experience, Braniff went to Mexico to work on the rail link between Mexico City and the port of Veracruz. After the line was completed, he stayed on as general manager. Meanwhile, he began buying up enterprises along the rail line, including a textile factory in Orizaba that he traded to CIDOSA, eventually becoming a major stockholder in the French enterprise. Over the years, he acquired a controlling interest in some fifteen mining companies, banks, power companies, rail lines, real estate operations, and other enterprises. Admirers and the merely envious called him the "Midas of Mexico" because of his astute investments. As customary, he also served on the board of directors of numerous organizations, including the Bank of London and Mexico. Braniff carefully maintained close political allies in the government even helping to organize Porfirio Díaz's 1900 reelection rallies. When he died in 1905 he left a fortune worth four million dollars.

The lure of speculative wealth enticed an odd assortment of entrepreneurs. General John B. Frisbie, born in Albany, New York, began his career serving with a Tammany Hall volunteer regiment during the war with Mexico. Sent to California, he married the daughter of prominent Californio General Mariano Guadalupe Vallejo. Together they briefly owned Mare Island in San Francisco Bay. He went to

Mexico to represent Huntington's railway interest and later became an associate of Arthur Stilwell. He owned the only Mexican dairy producing American-style milk and milk products, as well as a sugar plantation in Guerrero. Like Stilwell, he traveled in his own Pullman equipped with a kitchen and bar. On occasion he allowed Díaz and other important Porfirians to borrow his private Pullman car. Another individual with Californio ties was Ignacio Sepúlveda, who was a prominent state judge before relocating to Mexico in 1883, where he established a thriving law practice and served as secretary of the United States legation in Mexico City in 1896. Sepúlveda Boulevard in Los Angeles, California, bears his family's name.[16] While not all of the early American entrepreneurs were as interesting or bizarre as those noted, they were not and could not be folded into the Mexican elite. They remained useful outsiders.[17]

The second generation of foreigners constituted a more sober group armed with formal training, often representing corporations as agents rather than flamboyant magnates of speculation. Many large foreign investors resided outside of the country. For example, Meyer Guggenheim, his seven sons, and their investment vehicle, the firm of M. Guggenheim's Sons, entered the smelting business and recognized new opportunities in Mexico. On October 9, 1890, scarcely a week after the McKinley Tariff became law, Daniel Guggenheim, the heir apparent as head of the family business, obtained from Porfirio Díaz a concession to build three smelters to foster the development of the Mexican mining industry. The Guggenheims later created the Gran Fundición Nacional Mexicana (the Great National Mexican Smelting Company), which erected works at Monterrey during the winter of 1891. A few years later, the family organized the Guggenheim Smelting Company, which built a plant at Aguascalientes in 1895 and a refinery at Perth Amboy, New Jersey. In a similar fashion, Robert S. Towne's Compañía Metalúrgica Mexicana, which by 1900 became the largest integrated mining and smelting firm in Mexico, drew capital from Boston, New York, and Europe. He acquired mines, erected a huge smelter at San Luis Potosí, and developed several ancillary firms, most notably the Mexican Northern Railroad. The connection between such investors and the Mexican upper class remained financial, not social.[18] Foreign enterprises functioned as corporations or partnerships whose capital came from Europe or Wall Street. Profits flowed out to those who put up the cash rather than creating a powerful foreign elite entwined in the regional culture and politics. Their representatives, agents, and managers, who constituted the American colony in Mexico City, formed a separate social entity with limited ties to Mexican culture. John W. Foster, the American representative in Mexico, encouraged

the 360 American residents to form a benevolent association, officially launched on July 4, 1875, an event that marked the formal
recognition of the American community in Mexico City. By 1910,
some 10,000 Americans made the colony the largest in Latin America. Most American residents lived in the then fashionable Colonia
Roma section of the capital.[19]

Wealthy Mexicans constituted the Porfirian elite. This reality explains in part their willingness to sacrifice foreign economic interests
and to encourage xenophobia when politically convenient. Foreigners
also tended to be associated with one economic activity, while Mexicans had diversified holdings. Because foreign entrepreneurs often
engaged in activities that required modern technology, they were very
visible. When a scapegoat for the changes brought about by modernization was needed, foreigners could be pushed forward. National and
regional elites directly controlled the climate of investment and development, yet they skillfully avoided much of the blame for creating the
conditions that made a revolution inevitable, and when it petered out,
they picked up most of the pieces. If a satisfactory arrangement with
foreign investors could not be established, the deal or project fell
through. For example, the powerful Guggenheim interests found their
plans to build a foundry and smelter in Saltillo blocked by a faction of
the state's elite; as a result, the plant had to be built in the neighboring state of Nuevo León, where Governor Bernardo Reyes cooperated.
The large-scale operation began production in 1892 in the city of
Monterrey.

Porfirian elites appropriated foreign cultural forms and made
them uniquely Mexican. The popularity of music for listening and
dancing demonstrates this pattern. Mexican composers took the
waltz form and using it as the frame to write Mexican songs. Of
these musical pieces, "Sobre Las Olas," became an international favorite that remains popular today. The young genius, Juventino
Rosas, who died tragically in Cuba at 26 years old, wrote the piece in
1891. This was only one of outstanding Mexican compositions.
Manuel M. Ponce, founder of Mexico's nationalistic school wrote
classical music primarily, but his 1886 song Gavota earned recognition through the musical world. In addition to waltzes and classic
music, Genaro Codina took the march form in 1892 for his tribute to
his home town. "Zacatecas" became so popular that still today it is
regarded as a virtual second national anthem. One Mexican characteristic of these popular songs was the instrumentation, characteristic of the *orquestas típicas* that appeared across the country,
especially the marimbas, or xylophones, and other percussion
instruments.

DEVELOPMENT AND UPWARD SOCIAL MOBILITY

All of the expectations for profitable businesses and the energetic spirit of enterprise found in Monterrey also existed in the towns of Sonora. Here the elite had most of the characteristics of the Mexican far north but had developed them in a unique pattern because of the state's isolation. The Porfirian years in Sonora saw the realization of plans that had been frustrated since the Bourbon years of the late colonial era. The "Notables," as elite families called themselves, had dominated Sonora for nearly a century and fostered a spirit of enterprise that awaited only the proper circumstances to explode into the economic development that they called progress. During the years between independence and the Porfirian era, urban notables, like their rural counterparts, relied on economic diversification as the way to survive the vicissitudes of weather, the destruction of incessant Indian wars, and the instability of markets along Mexico's Pacific Coast. A new era dawned in Alamos when the triumvirate of Luis E. Torres, Ramón Corral, and Rafael Izábal forged links to other notable families across the state and entered politics by hitching onto the Porfirian warhorse. The president rewarded their political cooperation with federal assistance to confront Indian hostilities and to promote sustained economic growth in the state. The Díaz government brought security, launching a major campaign against the Apaches that succeeded in 1886 and moving against the Yaquis and Mayos to seize their lands. Financial subsidies to railroads and tax exemptions stimulated regional development.

Corral, Sonora's administrative prodigy, soon built a treasury surplus that he believed should be used on public works and education. He also used state funds to promote Sonora's enterprises at the Paris Exhibition of 1889. His goal was to offer economic opportunity to all of the state's notables to draw them into compliance with triumvirate politics. A summary of his policy is "giving everyone a place, while at the same time making sure everyone remained in place." The notables did the rest, binding economics and politics together with family ties. Using the well-established pattern of forming joint businesses with outsiders (including foreigners), these entrepreneurs prospered as the economy boomed. Próspero Sandoval, a typical notable representing the Nogales business community, was the treasurer and resident manager of Tri-Metallic Mining, Smelting, and Refining Company, headed by Warren G. Harding.[20]

These self-satisfied Sonorans, in concert with their brethren across the country, had little interest in the classes a great many steps down the social pyramid. Meanwhile, the urban professionals—the managers of commercial, agricultural, and industrial enterprises, medium-sized shopkeepers, small family owned manufacturers, and government bureaucrats—lived in reasonable comforte and nursed the hope of upward mobility. This group expanded along with the growth of the economy and the federal and state government. Between 1876 and 1910, the government payroll swelled to 900 percent; as a consequence, by 1910 some 70 percent of the educated professionals depended directly on state employment or indirectly on government contracts and concessions. The direct link between economic policy and public employment determined the political loyalty of this class.[21] The lifestyle of the members of the professional class, in spite of their educational skills, remained modest and dependent. They were lawyers, medical doctors, engineers, and members of the bureaucracy, all quite respectable, but without an independent or a secure economic base and with little hope of achieving one. With effort, an individual could rise to this class but seldom beyond.

The United States, rather than Europe, increasingly attracted members of the professional class interested in a technical education. Supposedly, American institutes and universities emphasized practical application of knowledge, enabling a graduate to immediately enter a chosen profession and earn a living. In Europe, particularly in France, technical education allegedly indulged in elegant theories producing ineffectual thinkers rather than doers. Perhaps a more realistic attraction was the immigrant culture of the United States that made it acceptable to work one's way through school. Temporary work waiting tables, washing dishes, and other such activities carried no stigma in the United States; however, engaging in such activity in Mexico would embarrass the individual student and the family. Some twenty-five Mexican students studied at the Massachusetts Institute of Technology (MIT) between 1903 and 1910. Few of these students received scholarships. Of fourteen Mexican students at Northwestern University, twelve worked their way through school.[22] Those who could not afford to travel north of the border, or who chose for various reasons not to, struggled to acquire some professional preparation, preferably in Mexico City. To many, a technical education represented upward mobility and an occupational anchor in an otherwise frightening social structure. Caught between an all-but-impossible dream of entering the wealthy elite, and the all-too-possible nightmare of a downward plunge into poverty, they sought to find security in the process of modernization itself.

The Flores Magón brothers provide an example of the limitations, insecurity, and frustrations of the middle class. Their mother, Margarita Magón, moved from provincial Oaxaca to Mexico City and enrolled her sons in a series of schools and eventually in law school.

Limited resources required the boys to work. Jesús, the eldest, completed law training, while the other two, Ricardo and Enrique, dropped out after acquiring some educational polish. Ricardo, as will be noted subsequently, became a major opponent of the regime as well as of Mexican liberalism.

Small-scale entrepreneurs had more opportunity to move up in the early stages of modernization. The experience of a Poblano (native of Puebla) family of modest means is instructive. Leopoldo Gómez moved, along with his cousin Juan Miranda, a textile merchant, from Puebla to Mexico City as a result of the economic downturn caused by the bypassing of Puebla by the Mexico–Veracruz railroad that began functioning in 1873. A Mexico City store, set up with a group of Catalán businessmen, flourished. Leopoldo became manager, then partner, and subsequently started several textile factories with Spanish capital. By 1909, Leopoldo Gómez owned textile factories, lumber mills, banks, insurance companies, tobacco mills, and held shares in many other ventures, as well as rural and urban land. Other family members of more modest means also benefitted from the kinship network and moved up the economic and social ladder.[23]

In the northern state of Nuevo León modest middle-class families began the industrialization of Monterrey. Isaac Garza, one of the founders of the Cuauhtémoc brewery, married Consuelo Sada, thus creating a family alliance that soon dominated economic development in the state. The Garza-Sada family and others of similar origins pooled extended family resources, and many subsequently entered the elite in style. From the marriage of Isaac and Consuelo emerged the financial and manufacturing empire of the Monterrey Industrial Group—still a dominant economic force both within the state and nationwide. Nuevo León capitalists formed joint ventures with American investors, including David Guggenheim, and often ended up with a controlling interest.

In Chihuahua, Luis Terrazas, who started his career as a butcher in the 1850s, astutely used foreign capital (his first partner was a German) to expand his landholdings. With the cattle boom of the 1890s the family fortune exploded. An estimated half million to a million dollars derived from cattle exports went into a variety of other enterprises. The Terrazas bank, El Banco Minero de Chihuahua, provided profits and easy credit for family enterprises. Some 400,000 cattle, 100,000 sheep, and 24,000 horses grazed on the land of the patriarch himself, and among the father, his sons, and son-in-law Enrique Creel, they owned over fifteen million acres, including some of the best watered and most fertile land in the state. The Terrazas family owned textile factories, the state's first flour mill, a brewery, copper mines, insurance companies, and many other enterprises. The

Terrazas bank even loaned money to foreign mining companies, including Shepherd's Batopilas Mining Company and Colonel Greene's Sierra Madre Land and Lumber Company. Foreigners interested in investing in Chihuahua had to secure the family's permission and often took in family members as stockholders or partners. Luis Terrazas worked closely with American interests on the border. The Guaranty Trust and Banking Company of El Paso, Texas, functioned as a partnership between Terrazas and other border businessmen. Family members and foreigners often served on the board of directors of various concerns, regardless of who actually controlled the particular enterprises.[24] Terrazas would have been at home in the company of international entrepreneurial capitalists anywhere in the world. Duplicating entrepreneurial feats became harder as the modernization process matured and larger amounts of capital entered the competition. By the period 1906–1907, boom time economic and social mobility had passed. Because of the seriously constricted internal market, it then required more energy and ingenuity to continue to prosper let alone amass sufficient wealth to enter the ranks of the elite.

Middle to small farmers (*rancheros*) as a class occupied a social level somewhat lower than urban professionals and managers. Unlike the professional class, they had an independent economic base, but their status and influence, economic and political, were limited to their own immediate area. Their perspective appeared to be a quaint mixture of the past with an admiration of aspects of the modernization process. In some areas of the republic they enjoyed relative security, while able to profit from the demands of new markets. Nevertheless, as a group, they risked being swept away by an expanding agribusiness. While they tended to identify upward, they understood the distance between themselves and the top. They also appreciated the need to hang on to whatever resources they possessed. Fear of being driven into the lower classes as well as being deprived of their land haunted the rancheros. Subsequently, when the Mexican Revolution threatened their property, they tenaciously defended themselves. They had close contact with marginal workers of small agricultural plots (*medieros*) who often rented land from them as well as supplied day labor. Medieros participated in regional and local markets, but only in a sporadic fashion dependent on the climate and a good crop. Although this group represented several steps down from the ranchero class, their plight served as a constant reminder of the dangers that might befall farmers, many of whose own kinship networks included medieros.[25]

URBAN LABOR

Near the bottom of the social structure, the working class, divided into several subgroups, struggled to exist. A dependent class also, but without any resources in reserve, they lived from hand to mouth and day to day. Skilled workers, who were often literate, had some advantages and an ability to obtain better wages and conditions, but the gap between them and unskilled labor was not great, and new machines and technology threatened their existence. Indian workers could be skilled, unskilled, or marginal day laborers. Little of the fruits of progress fell into their hands. In 1895, over 90 percent of the Mexican population was found in the lower class.[26]

The urban-based workforce, unlike agricultural labor, had an important symbolic significance. New machinery and technology, including electricity, promised material abundance as well as a product revolution. Movement away from the production of handcrafted goods, which utilized natural materials, to industrially produced glass, iron, steel, and chemicals conjured up a future cornucopia of modern nineteenth-century products at inexpensive prices. As early as 1856 José María Lafragua, a prominent liberal who over the course of his career occupied high government positions under a series of presidents, including President Benito Juárez, urged the promotion of industrial development. Speaking at the opening of the Industrial Exposition that year, he emphasized the social benefits of industrialization, noting that it would "spread well-being to those less well off, lift thousands out of misery and vice, and by increasing public wealth form a society that will serve as a barrier to revolution." Lafragua's comments anticipated the creation of an urban proletariat that would be able to produce and consume.[27] In spite of such hopes, the number of workers employed in manufacturing increased slowly. In 1895, a mere 11.2 percent of the labor force belonged to the industrial category, and on the eve of the Mexican Revolution, 10.9 percent worked in industry. This contrasted sharply with 60.3 percent agricultural workers in 1895 and 64.4 percent in 1910.[28]

Gains in productivity as new machines went on line did not generate a broader distribution of wealth. The workforce had little power to withhold labor or negotiate improved wages. Use of child labor further undercut the economic power of industrial workers. A. J. Campbell, a British observer, noted that young children stood on boxes to reach the machines. Another individual estimated that 12 percent of all textile workers were children.[29] Working conditions for men, women, and children depended upon the employer as did the number of hours of work demanded. Twelve and a half hours from six o'clock in the morning to eight o'clock at night, with short food and rest breaks, constituted the norm. The El Mayorazgo mill in Puebla extended its work day to eleven o'clock or midnight. Others demanded sixteen hours from their employees. Sunday work also was common. Many companies paid in script, exchangeable only at the company store or at a high discount elsewhere. Employers conceded no paid holidays, sick leave, unemployment compensation, or responsibility for industrial accidents. Matías Romero in 1892 spelled out the government's position, as well as the general attitude that "work is submitted to the ineludible natural phenomena of the law of supply and demand."[30] Changes in wages and working conditions would come at a certain point when a balance eventually occurred, but meanwhile any artificial intervention constituted an obstacle to investment and a restriction on the use of capital, all of which ignored the fact that employers did everything in their power to circumvent the development of a competitive labor market.

Some changes became evident when the state of Mexico issued an industrial accident law in 1904 and the state of Nuevo León followed in 1906. Workers themselves collected funds for relief efforts and began the process of organizing. Illegal strike activity occurred in waves between 1878 and 1884, and again in the early years of the twentieth century. The government used troops and police powers to dampen such activity. The First Permanent Workers Congress was hounded out of existence in 1880 under Article 925 of the penal code pertaining to illegal associations. In 1891, the papal proclamation Rerum Novarum called for social justice and a Christian approach to labor. The Church's pronouncement gave the workers a moral basis for their demands, which could not be so easily dismissed by employers or the state. "White communism" emerged as a counterbalance to more radical proposals to address the problems of the workers. Some owners turned to industrial paternalism. Ernesto Pugibet, of the El Buen Tono cigarette factory, offered good wages and working conditions, extended fair treatment to women employees, and directed the construction of model homes with electricity and running water for workers along Calle Bucareli. The Scottish Robertson Brothers, owners of the Miraflores cotton mill that dominated Chalco in the south of the Federal District, offered their workers numerous benefits, including a well-equipped school, well-paid teachers, music training, and a theater. Ignacio Ferrer, owner of the Flor de Tabasco chocolate factory, improved the working environment by filling the patio with flowers; he also established a night school and presented prizes for achievement to the chocolate workers. The paternalism of Monterrey entrepreneurs has been noted previously.

Other paternalistic employers supported mutual societies, especially in response to the appearance of independent workers' organizations. Some fifty of them existed in Mexico City in 1906. The most energetic effort came when the governor of the Federal District, Landa y Escandón, attempted to create the Sociedad Mutualista y Moralizadora del Distrito Federal in 1910. He planned to provide workers with self-improvement and educational facilities, while encouraging them to keep away from vices. The society was formally inaugurated in the spring of 1911. Landa y Escandón himself donated $100,000 and succeeded in obtaining funds for the organization from most other industries throughout the district. The society attempted to keep the working class loyal to the regime at the outbreak of the Madero insurgency and even organized a voluntary battalion. The organization survived as late as 1913, but its energy dissipated when the governor left for exile in 1911 with Díaz.[31]

FEDERAL POLITICAL STRUCTURE AND NATIONAL CAMARILLA POLITICS

The politics of Porfirian Mexico followed the same pattern established by Benito Juárez, but were adjusted to reflect the new economic reality as well as advances in communication. While the national government had all of the accoutrements of a federal republic, in reality the executive dominated and directed the other branches. This system would remain in place until the 1937 crisis in the Cárdenas administration. The president viewed the federal government in its institutional entirety as his own political instrument and demanded loyalty and discipline. The selection process, more important than electoral formalities, fell to the president. A suggested representative might have little or no connection with his erstwhile constituents. Luis Pombo, elected deputy for Colotlán (Jalisco), expressed the commendable wish that "some day I hope to make the acquaintance of the Colotlanenses." He probably never did. A list of candidates for the national congress drawn up by the president went to each governor who then saw to their election. A foreign observer noted that in one particular instance, while not one voter came to the polling place, the election official tallied the appropriate and desired results.[32] Governors might suggest candidates provided they appeared to be compliant friends of the administration, willing to validate rather than legislate, but regional politicians understood that Mexico City constituted the president's own political turf—a national extension of the *camarilla* system within which they functioned. There appeared little to be gained from meddling with the president's wishes. Under normal circumstances, election to congress provided a title, financial support, and plenty of time to do other things. Only when the president allowed events to drift, or failed to maintain control, did congress rouse itself, but even then the executive's dominance decided the outcome of any dispute.

The federal judiciary, another theoretical counterbalance to the executive branch, also functioned as a subordinate instrument. The president exercised broad appointment and dismissal powers over judges. Nevertheless, district judges also responded to their immediate community, and as a result, a degree of conflict occurred between them and Mexico City. Issuing writs of *amparo* to release an individual from the forced military draft (*la leva*) at the request of local inhabitants or the unwilling recruit's family caused constant irritation, and at times such incidents reached the desk of the president himself.[33] Attempts to legislate restrictions on the use of writs of amparo proved only marginally successful. At the supreme court level, judges had to be elected, enabling the regime to select appropriate candidates. Both the legislative and judicial branches provided constitutional forms but with little independent political substance. The federal government in Mexico City needed to muster all of its strength to govern effectively and make the necessary political deals with the regional and state bosses. Unity, not constitutional balance, thus appeared more useful. By manipulating regional power blocks, the national government tilted the balance to suit its interests. It did not always succeed in doing so.

The government, and those who dealt with it, could not turn to the bureaucracy for assistance, support, or guidance. In spite of considerable expansion, the Porfirian bureaucracy remained protomodern. Characteristic of this stage of organizational development, regulations, often quite detailed and impressive, were drawn up at the top levels of government, but the lack of trained personnel at the functional level made implementation impossible. It was easier to order a cabinet minister to do something than to get the ill-trained and poorly paid clerk at the bottom to respond even partially. Regulations might be printed and widely distributed, but remained ideal statements.[34] In the absence of a strong regulatory bureaucracy, the burden of governing rested almost entirely on politics. Rather than exerting control through a bureaucratic network that reached into every corner of the republic, the national government manipulated a system composed of various political interests at the regional, state, and local levels. President Díaz, out of necessity, concerned himself with matters great and small as his correspondence indicates. This reality confused and frustrated foreigners who failed to come to grips with politics masquerading as bureaucratic regulation. Moreover, only modern and progressive property rights as defined by Mexican liberalism received total political support from the national and state government; everything else became subject to negotiation on an individual and case-by-case basis, regardless of law or printed regulations. Although President Díaz postured as the head of a modern government and the strongman of Mexico for credulous foreigners, in fact he coordinated more than presided over an oligarchy.

Camarilla politics at the national level functioned very much in the standard manner, with several significant differences. National political interests understood that instability at the level of the presidency made the country vulnerable to foreign intervention and possible annexation. Moreover, even the perception of instability discouraged investments and endangered established markets for export products. Foreign investors and those who depended on Mexican primary products needed constant reassurance. Even presidential elections caused anxiety as various interests moved to the sidelines to await events. As a means of providing more stable continuity, the presidential term was extended in 1903 to six years from the previous four-year term. Many politicians argued for an eight-year term. The six-year *sexenio* (the Constitution of 1917 restored the four-year term, subsequently changed to six years in 1928) with no reelection remains the term today. President Díaz in effect was the candidate of all national camarillas—the front man behind which furious and lively politics could be conducted without endangering the republic. The general outlines of such a system had been articulated by many, including Justo Sierra, in the late 1870s, as being the next best thing to a parliamentary structure. The president served as the symbol of stability while his ministers were accountable for governmental failure and thus were politically expendable. Sierra also advocated that the president's ministers be made accountable to congress, so political struggles would remain within the legislative chambers, making revolutions a thing of the past. The Porfirian system, however, relied upon the president's timely removal of individuals who had lost the public's confidence. Porfirio Díaz exercised an unofficial moderating power over the political process itself, while also functioning as an important player within it. The task required a high level of political skill, a delicate touch, and, on occasion, a calculated ruthlessness.[35]

National camarillas differed from state groupings in that they could not be excluded from the government even when they misplayed their hand. The regime needed their expertise and talents. This meant that all factions continued to have access to federal patronage. At the national level, three important camarillas functioned, each associated with one individual. *Los Científicos*, staunch defenders of Comtean development, recognized José Limantour, the secretary of the treasury, as their patron. The group included Francisco Bulnes, Romero Rubio

(Díaz's father-in-law), Justo Sierra, and on occasion state political figures such as Enrique Creel of Chihuahua. They exchanged favors, supported each other's objectives, and collectively hoped to influence the president to proceed as they believed most useful to themselves and to the nation. Due in part to the important position of Limantour, as well as to their catchy designation, Los Científicos came to symbolize the coldly dispassionate attitude of the governing elite toward development and the lower classes. In reality, their role within the political system was more complex, entirely human, and only vaguely definable.

Los Científicos, formed during González's presidency by Manuel Romero Rubio, who became Porfirio Díaz's father-in-law (1881) and attracted a loosely knit assortment of young intellectuals and professionals who gathered informally in Romero Rubio's law offices. José Yves Limantour attended, as did Justo Sierra. Discussions centered on the need for a new order to be implemented after Díaz returned to power. With strong leadership at the top the next step would be to strengthen the constitutional structure. They believed Mexico could become a stable constitutional republic. The group identified a broad and growing consensus awaiting the formation of a "Liberal Union"— in effect, a national constitutional political party. Such ideas constituted an attack on regional camarilla politics and sought a fusion of national camarillas into the projected party. As a major move in the desired direction, the group tied Díaz's reelection campaign with a National Liberal Union Convention (1892). The delegates to the convention hammered out what amounted to a political platform. A majority of the delegates to the convention also served in the Chamber of Deputies and wrote for newspapers and in other ways attempted to influence elite opinion. Federal Deputy Justo Sierra, also a convention participant, presented their program to the Chamber of Deputies as a constitutional amendment in 1893. Implicit in the reform program was the notion of a strong president within a progressively strengthened constitutional structure. Central to their reforms was an independent judiciary. Unfortunately for the Liberal Union, Porfirio Díaz did not share their optimism that Mexico hovered on the edge of political maturity. A debate carried on privately as well as publicly in the newspapers resulted in defeat for the reformers. The newspaper *El Siglo XIX* championed Díaz's antireform position and in the process coined the derisive term *Los Científicos*. The measure to make judges immovable sailed through the Chamber of Deputies, only to be entombed in a senate committee. In spite of their defeat, the reformers continued to urge reforms, albeit more gently.

Many *Científicos* assumed positions of power enabling them administratively to implement changes, although not in the constitutional fashion they had hoped for. Limantour, as secretary of the treasury, Roberto Núñez, another *Científico*, as subsecretary, and Justo Sierra, appointed to the Supreme Court (1894), then Mexico's first subsecretary of public instruction, all exercised tremendous influence over the national government. Other *Científicos* held lesser posts or served in congress. Newspapers such as *El Universal* (1893–1901) and after its demise *El Imparcial* and *El Mundo* provided access to public opinion. A second National Liberal Union convention (1903) dealt with the problem of Díaz's succession. The brief illness of President Díaz in 1901 had caused serious alarm. Institutional continuity, achievable through a strong party system within a constitutional framework, appeared to be the only solution. Francisco Bulnes observed that the country's political disorganization justified personal rule, making constant reelection necessary, but the country now needed to make Díaz's successor legal. Bulnes called for the creation of at least two political parties. Los Científicos functioned as a reform camarilla dedicated to moving beyond camarillas.[36]

General Bernardo Reyes provided the focal point for another camarilla, while the governor of Veracruz, Teodoro A. Dehesa, manipulated at the center of yet another network. Other less important individuals took part in subcamarillas that shifted their allegiances to suit their immediate advantage. The level of tension within national camarilla politics increased as Díaz aged. Each major camarilla hoped to guide the nation in the post–Porfirian era. Unfortunately, pressure to assure an orderly transition in case of the president's incapacity in office came at a time when no single national faction had emerged as the dominant one. As a result, Díaz, who agreed to the idea of a vice president in 1904, picked Ramón Corral, an individual few people respected, liked, or supported. All understood that Corral could not be the long-term successor to Porfirio Díaz. Limantour, Reyes, or Dehesa, in contrast, possessed the stature necessary to be a believable successor.

While Porfirio Díaz often is portrayed as a brilliant politician, playing one group against another, in fact he functioned by the rules of the camarilla system with the one great advantage of being the agreed-upon symbol of Mexican political stability. Porfirian Mexico had many master politicians—the president among them. As in all politics they, including Díaz, lost some struggles and won others.[37]

STATE CAMARILLA POLITICS

State political blocks revolved around an individual (*el gallo*) or a family linked through personal or economic connections with other groups in a camarilla. Within a state there might be three or four such groupings contending for political power and hoping to gain the national support needed to tip the balance in their direction. Those who failed lived on to try another time; the elite struggled bitterly among themselves but seldom practiced cannibalism.

A low-key yet excellent example of state camarilla politics occurred during the González administration. Mariano Martínez de Castro, a member of a distinguished Sinaloa family, replaced Francisco Canedo as governor of the state. It soon became apparent that the president preferred to limit Martínez de Castro's political ambitions and return Canedo to the governorship. President González instructed General Carbo, commander of the First Military Zone, to favor the Canedo faction without directly breaking with the governor. When Governor Martínez de Castro attempted to create a new congressional district, hoping to reward one of his own followers, General Carbo registered his opposition and to make the point sent a detachment of troops into the area. Martínez de Castro, acutely aware of the political process, attempted to ingratiate himself with Mexico City and General Carbo. In spite of public statements and even personal displays of friendship, Martínez de Castro failed to win the support of the federal government. Francisco Canedo returned to the state governorship, much to the satisfaction of Mexico City. The national political objective had been achieved in Sinaloa without violence or excessive public dissension, although all understood that the Martínez de Castro camarilla had lost. The effective combination of Canedo and his supporters, the military zone commander, and the national government determined the result.[38]

Few camarillas challenged Mexico City directly, but on occasion they successfully outmanipulated the national government. The Terrazas family, whose fortune had been acquired in the profitable export of cattle to the United States and who subsequently invested in a variety of different enterprises in their home state of Chihuahua, took over the state despite the opposition of Porfirio Díaz. Their successful strategy included financing small-scale revolts, as well as more standard forms of political manipulation. A large part of their success depended upon the skills of Enrique Creel. Creel, the son of a former American consul in Chihuahua and a Terrazas relative on his mother's side, married one of the daughters of Luis Terrazas. Ricky Creel, a bicultural northerner, proved to be an instinctive businessman and politician. With his help, the Terrazas camarilla drew in foreign entrepreneurs, other regional elites, and national interests. Foreigners liked Creel and believed he understood them and their needs. Mexicans viewed him as being more of an American than one of them and occasionally grumbled that he should not be allowed to occupy high office; nevertheless, he was a major family asset. He spent considerable charm placating Díaz's inner circle and became one of the Científicos of Secretary of the Treasury José Yves Limantour. Creel served as Mexican ambassador to the United States and governor of the state. The Terrazas camarilla manipulated Mexico City, Washington, Wall Street, and the state of Chihuahua.[39]

In a similar fashion, Olegario Molina in Yucatán headed a camarilla of some twenty to thirty families of the Molina–Montes clan, referred to as the "divine caste." As governor of the state, Molina and his group controlled all important political and administrative functions. His alliance with the International Harvester Company made him politically and economically supreme. After a term as governor, he joined Díaz's cabinet as minister of development.[40]

In Coahuila, the Garza Galín camarilla forged useful links with Manuel Romero Rubio, Díaz's father-in-law and a powerful national political figure as well as one of the Científicos. In spite of such contacts, contesting groups forced them out and the process of jockeying for power started again, giving Mexico City the opportunity to participate in a new deal. Camarillas had little interest in forming political parties. It is clear, nevertheless, that Porfirio Díaz realistically favored those with broad support. Too narrow an alliance could lead to troublesome instability, as well as reduce the chances of being on the winning side. Both the national and regional elites recognized the ability to control disorder as a paramount political skill. Thus, Manuel Alarcón, chief of the rurales in the newly created state of Morelos, became the *jefe político* (political chief) of Cuautla (1873) and finally rose to the governorship of the state in 1894. His political talents, undoubtedly honed as a jefe político, enabled him to hold the esteem and respect of large landholders as well as of rancheros and villagers.[41]

While Díaz's political strategy worked relatively well, it should be noted that the Madero camarilla in Coahuila eventually supplied the leader of the successful movement to force Díaz from power and into exile in 1911. Díaz mismanaged his relationship with the Madero clan. Evaristo Madero had refused to join with Díaz against President Lerdo. President Díaz, able to forgive others for their failure to back the Plan of Tuxtepec, entertained a lasting antipathy toward Evaristo Madero and the entire family in spite of their expressed willingness to cooperate. The political potential of the Madero family was well demonstrated during the regime of President Manuel González, a friend of the family patriarch, who helped engineer Evaristo Madero's elevation to the governorship. On Díaz's return to power, Madero was removed as governor. The president instructed General Bernardo Reyes to monitor the families' activities and block their political aspirations. Díaz had no interest in economically punishing the Maderos, but was determined to keep them out of state politics. When the balance could be tipped against them, he did so. In spite of Díaz's thinly veiled hostility, the Madero camarilla continued to profess its loyalty and willingness to play by the established political rules. When Evaristo's nephew, Francisco I. Madero, attempted to form a political party to oppose the regime, influential members of the family tried to dissuade him. Brushing aside prudence, Francisco Madero and Gabriel Calzada established the Club Democrático Benito Juárez in San Pedro, Coahuila, in 1904.[42] The subsequent disastrous failure of Madero as president stemmed in part from an attempt to fuse camarilla politics, which rested on elite interests, with social objectives that depended on mass mobilization.

MUNICIPAL POLITICAL CONTROL

At the municipal level, the jefe político theoretically placed municipalities under the direct influence of an individual appointed by the state governor. While the office had been created by the Spanish constitution of 1812 as a means of providing local political autonomy, it soon evolved into a control device of regional authorities. As a consequence, the jefe político and the municipal council, which still retained representation aspects, often became bitter opponents. At one time an elected office, in the 1880s it became part of the centralized state apparatus. The national government exercised only indirect influence, although in a serious situation, such as a revolt, Mexico City could intervene to remove or support the jefe político. Such a system enabled the state elite to reserve regional politics for themselves and minimize political pressure from below. Nevertheless, the jefe político had to gain the cooperation of the local population. An astute official tried to balance the demands of the state and national government with those of his constituents. He had to be perceived as being fair and sympathetic to local issues and concerns. The jefe político served in a formal as well as an informal judicial and administrative capacity, much like that of the *corregidores, alcaldes mayores*, and *subdelegados* of the colonial era. A skillful jefe político enjoyed the reasonable cooperation of his municipality as well as the esteem of higher authority, while an excessively harsh or corrupt one caused all sorts of trouble. Villagers offered cooperation or defiance, often leaving the choice to the jefe político. For example, the Tarascan villagers of Pahuatlán dispatched their brass band to serenade the jefe político of Tulancingo in a successful effort to persuade him to respect their autonomy.[43] Their spirited performance implied a potential battle if their needs were not addressed in some satisfactory manner. Zealous implementation of liberal objectives, particularly those involving land or other disruptive demands, could result in riots or even revolts. The jefe político served as the lowest-level political broker in a system characterized by manipulation and elite intergroup negotiation. As a result, he often seemed a pawn in a larger game. Ambitious individuals could prove their value and hone their nascent manipulative skills. Not surprisingly, Porfirio Díaz began his political career as a jefe político of Ixtlán in his home state of Oaxaca. He organized a semiofficial militia, used it to put down a threatening mob, and otherwise demonstrated his usefulness. When Benito Juárez became governor of the state, he authorized Díaz to organize a district guard. A man who needed little encouragement, Díaz assembled a group of armed retainers and thus started up the ladder of political success.[44] In Chihuahua, during the administration of Governor Enrique Creel, a new organizational law (1904) provided for a jefe municipal to be appointed by the governor. The new official replaced top elected municipal officers, and as a consequence, municipalities lost virtually all of their representative character.[45] Restoration of municipal autonomy became an important objective of the Mexican Revolution.

THE STRUCTURE OF THE PORFIRIAN ARMY

Overlaying the standard political divisions of the republic was a system of military administrative regions and designations. The political and military reorganization of the federal army began in 1877, and the following year President Díaz received wide authority from congress to reform the entire military structure. General González, while president, implemented many of the changes that remained in place, with only minor modifications until 1911. The new structure divided the nation into military zones, commandancies, and *jefaturas de armas*. A zone usually encompassed two or three states under an army general. Within the zone a subordinate division, the jefatura de armas, provided an actual military presence in a designated area, within a single city, an entire territory, or a state. The east coast port of Tampico functioned under a jefe de armas. Important or sensitive areas within a zone could be designated commandancies under the direct supervision and command of the secretary of war, unless he specifically ordered differently. The number of zones, jefaturas, and commandancies depended on the president, who also could determine the number of troops assigned.

According to President Díaz, this structure allowed for greater flexibility in order to respond to interior security needs. In fact, it divided up the army in terms of the chain of command and permitted the president and his secretary of war to respond to unacceptable political challenges, as well as control the power of individual officers. A sudden rearrangement or change in designation could leave a particular officer politically marooned. The structure reflected political more than military or internal security concerns. Nevertheless, the high-ranking army officer in charge of a military zone had the general responsibility of maintaining order in a broad interpretive sense throughout his jurisdiction. While theoretically under the direct command of the president, he in fact often developed his own political constituency. A military presence reminded the provincial elites that the national government possessed force—the ultimate political weapon. General Bernardo Reyes, appointed commander of the third military zone in 1885, became Díaz's proconsul in the north. Eventually Reyes acquired his own political persona and served as the focal point of a national camarilla.[46]

THE PORFIRIAN PERSUASION

President Díaz, in concert with his secretary of development and other high officials, spent considerable effort on manipulating international perceptions of Mexico. Always willing to meet personally with prospective foreign investors and even discuss details of some projected enterprises, the president functioned as an extremely effective salesman. John Hays Hammond, one of the era's foremost mining engineers, recalled an interview with Porfirio Díaz shortly after his arrival in Mexico City in 1900. Díaz struggled along with English, which he understood much better than he could speak, while Hammond did the same in Spanish. In spite of language difficulties, Díaz succeeded in charming the engineer. When Hammond mentioned the possibility of minor officials demanding bribes, Díaz indicated that should Hammond experience any difficulties, he must "Come to me and I'll settle it." Known access to the president functioned both to facilitate one's activities, as John Hammond noted, and to establish a bond of obligation and trust between an important foreign entrepreneur and the Mexican president. Díaz also used humor to captivate his guest. Hammond related an incident that occurred during a visit to Chapultepec Castle. As the men strolled in a light rain, the president expressed concern that Hammond's top hat would be ruined; calling for one of his own sombreros, he insisted that the engineer make the exchange, only to have the hat sink over Hammond's eyes much to their mutual amusement.[47]

In a similar fashion the president established an immediately warm relationship that matured into a strong friendship with Weetman Pearson, the international engineering and construction magnate. When the Mexican government signed an agreement with Pearson for the draining of the valley of Mexico, Díaz asked the Englishman for his word of honor that he would deal fairly with the government. Díaz in effect artfully suggested that they both shared a sense of personal honor that transcended a mere contract. From that instant, Pearson became a strong supporter of Porfirio Díaz, subsequently declaring that "He [Díaz] was absolutely my hero: I had the very highest affection and admiration for General Porfirio Díaz." The Englishman remained a lifetime friend of the family. After her husband's death, Carmen expressed her gratitude, as did the general's son. The personal bond between Pearson and Díaz influenced the Englishman's decision to invest in Mexican petroleum exploration, at the time still a risky and speculative business.[48]

Mexico City's American community provided a useful backdrop for Porfirian propaganda. Traditional American holidays served to glorify and publicly acknowledge Mexico's progress. Porfirio Díaz often attended ceremonial gatherings, including the Thanksgiving Day ball, to receive the applause of the American colony. Mexican military bands entertained Fourth of July crowds with appropriate patriotic marches, along with some favorite Mexican pieces. President Díaz and his wife succeeded in making the American residents into a political constituency eager to help instruct their ambassador and indoctrinate newcomers, journalists, and potential investors.[49]

To emphasize the regime's conquest of order, President Díaz presided over an annual banquet honoring the rurales. On the appointed day, elegantly dressed and mounted rurales lined a three-mile stretch of the Paseo de la Reforma. At noon, Díaz reviewed them from the balcony of a stylish restaurant, the Elysian Tivoli, a magnificently refined establishment that offered an exquisite garden and a popular casino. The Elysian Tivoli epitomized the good life that could only flow

Figure 5.5 The American community of Mexico City celebrates the Fourth of July in 1910. Observe the refreshment stand staffed by volunteers and the mixed U.S. and Mexican flags. *Printed with permission, Photography Collection, Harry Ransom, Humanities Research Center, University of Texas at Austin*

from order and progress. Generals, diplomats, intellectuals, novelists, poets, journalists, foreigners, and others made up the carefully selected guest list. At the conclusion of a sumptuous dinner around the horseshoe-shaped table, they joined the president to toast the rurales. Most of the guests then returned to try their luck at the gaming tables. Few if any could doubt that the government had an unbreakable grasp on domestic order. Impressed diplomats thus assured their compatriots that their investments could not be in safer hands.[50]

A large part of Díaz's success depended upon his exquisite sense of showmanship. A convincing performance covered up the essential fragility of the regime. On occasion, public relations provided short-term advantages, but at a high long-term price. For example, the policy of accumulating a substantial and highly publicized budget surplus came at the expense of infrastructure investment, including education. Image often outran substance, yet President Díaz succeeded in projecting the desired and calculated effect so soothing to foreign investors. Maintenance of an international reputation for stability and protection of private property rights was assiduously attended to by all high officials, with the president taking the lead.

The government stimulated the publication of books, articles, factual guides, and compendiums of commercial laws and regulations

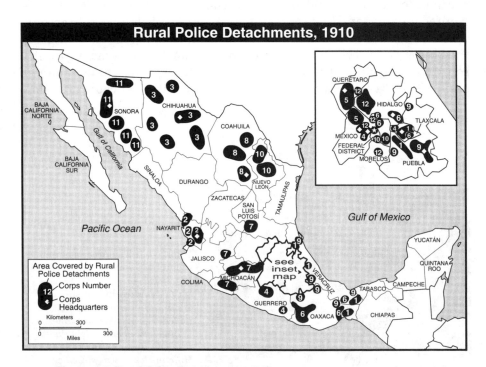

Figure 5.6 Rural Police Detachments, 1910

on the "Mexico of Today" to dispel the notion that Mexico remained on the far periphery of the modern world. Mexican commercial representatives and diplomats spent time, effort, and money to recast the nation's image. A virtual horde of publicists, both foreign and Mexican, worked in Europe and in the United States on the task. Newspapermen—Porfirian politician Manuel Zamacona and the tireless Matías Romero—became adept at manipulating Mexico's image in the United States. Travelogues, entertainingly written, captured the imagination of the general public, presenting a view of the "Republic to the South" as a fascinating country rapidly undergoing a process of fruitful modernization. In 1878, Edward Lestes, sought out by the Mexican foreign office, published his *The Mexican Republic* in New York. Englishman T. U. Brocklehurst published *Mexico Today: A Country with a Great Future and A Glance at the Historic Remains and Antiquities of the Moctezumas (1883)*, a title that made the point that Mexico had an ancient, impressive, pre-Columbian past as well as a yet to come brilliant future. Economists, engineers, metallurgists, and even historians contributed to the printed flood of laudatory works. Hubert H. Bancroft published his immensely popular multivolume *History of Mexico (1885–1893)* while maintaining a correspondence with President Díaz, who made comments on various details. Bancroft also published a biography of Díaz (1887) and a promotional work titled *Recursos y desarrollo de México in 1893*, drawing upon information gathered during paid excursions to Mexico. Bancroft dedicated his work to Porfirio Díaz and noted that in no other nation was life and property more secure. Moreover, he asserted that peace and abundance had created a Mexican "golden age."[51] The message was clear—the investor and his money were welcome in a stable, prosperous, secure, and profitable country.

Foreign expositions provided an opportunity to highlight in a material, physical, and concrete fashion Mexican development, as well as to boost the morale of the country's producers. Mexico could be counted on to participate enthusiastically in these events as it did in Paris, Berlin, New Orleans, Chicago, St. Louis, and a host of other cities. Expenditures to present displays totaled $200,000 in New Orleans (1884–1885) and $400,000 at the 1889 Paris exposition. The ministry of development lavished 10 percent of its budget on the French event; in return, Mexican exhibits won a gratifying 25 grand prizes of honor, 112 gold medals, 224 silver, 341 bronze, and 325 honorable mentions. Exhibit buildings often were reconstructed in Mexico City to the delight of the capital's inhabitants. Elaborate displays, such as a working model of the proposed Tehuantepec Ship-Railway used at the Cotton Centennial Exposition in New Orleans, made Mexican exhibits popular with the crowd. Expositions facilitated exchange of trade information, established contacts, and left a positive perception of the country's progress and future potential. Díaz invariably dispatched high-ranking officials to such events. As a thoughtful Porfirian observed, under Díaz Mexico acquired its "international personality." A financially important part of that personality rested upon the tireless activity of promoters. Bilingual Spanish–French and Spanish–English directories focused investor attention on opportunities in various states in mining and commercial agriculture. Illustrated books promoted a positive perception of Mexico as a country that had broken through into prosperity.[52] John R. Southworth edited and published guides to individual states, as well as *The Official Mining Directory of Mexico* and in 1910 *The Official Directory of Mines and Estates of Mexico*. The latter directory provided a brief history of Mexican mining, the names of leading officials of the ministry of development, government mining agents throughout the republic, and the mining laws and regulations. Southworth listed individual mines and agricultural enterprises, including information on the number of employees, capitalization, type of a production, and other useful information. He also served as managing director of the *Mexican Financier*, a weekly to be read by "all who have money to invest . . . all who have money invested . . . all who have investments to offer." The potential investor did not lack encouraging information on a wide variety of economic activity. He adopted as his motto *Siempre adelante* (onward and upward).[53] The government expanded its diplomatic relations with both trade and prestige in mind. In addition to an impressive number of representatives in the United States, Britain, France, Germany, Italy, and other European nations, Mexico had a consulate-general in Japan and two consuls in Russia. Treaties of friendship, trade, and navigation, postal conventions, and agreements covering other matters demonstrated Mexico's standing in the international community.[54]

Promoting Mexico, its natural resources, and its people as a commodity, boasting of the country's adhesion to a universal standard of nineteenth-century progress, and projecting a future identical to that of Europe and the United States implied a rejection of Mexican uniqueness. For the Porfirians, the path of progress in all of its features had been laid out by others. Emotional and cultural aspects of what it meant to be a Mexican were laid aside. The extent that the country's culture had been repressed only became evident after the Mexican Revolution, with its burst of artistic creativity, particularly the murals. Paris, Madrid, London, and other perceived cultural capitals provided Mexico's beacon. Few comprehended the cultural price of progress. Justo Sierra, one of the era's most brilliant intellectuals and a political actor, understood the dangers of the elites' cultural

Figure 5.7 Colonia Roma, the newest and most stylish district of Mexico City, around 1900. *Printed with permission, Photography Collection, Harry Ransom, Humanities Research Center, University of Texas at Austin*

abandonment of Mexico. He saw a process at work that began with the recasting of the nation's institutions to conform to foreign models. Under Díaz, the nation entered a period of "economic Americanism," totally intoxicated with visions of wealth and progress. The last stage, already looming, might well submerge the national culture under the weight of that of the United States—in effect, a "moral and intellectual annexation." Sierra identified Protestantism as a major threat to Mexico's Catholic culture. Paradoxically, he admired the United States and Protestant values, shared the anticlericalism of Mexican liberalism, yet feared cultural suffocation. Sierra viewed the United States with a mixture of admiration, disdain, and humor. In the account of his 1895 trip there, he noted, "This is the American people, a people who scarcely stay still to drink a beer and for that they do not sit. Moreover, they talk through their nose."[55]

The president's wife, Carmen Romero Rubio de Díaz, played an important role in smoothing over concerns, cultural or otherwise, that might impede progress. Doña Carmelita mobilized high society in support of her husband and his vision of modernization. Elite women and their families followed her lead in questions of fashion, polite manners, and public consumption of civilized products. She identified values and attitudes deemed compatible with a modern nation that had wide influence on society as a whole. Moreover, Carmen played hostess to prominent foreigners who went away impressed with Mexico as a result. The keen observer Henry Adams, for example, despite his reservations about Mexican programs of modernization and the capital city, spent a pleasant morning with the president's wife and her sister Sophia, and wrote in glowing terms about them.[56]

As a bearer of the new modern values, Carmen Díaz had a number of advantages, including her political and social position, her fluency in English, and a lively, intelligent mind. As an elite woman, she was not expected to observe traditional social norms that bound her middle- and lower-class counterparts. An important part of her activities centered on encouraging Mexican women to adopt a role closer to that of European and American women, a task that required a delicate touch. Her activities, coupled with the prominence of the Women's Club, founded by Americans, caused some concern among the more traditional elements of society. Fear that Mexican women would be influenced unduly by the apparent freedom accorded foreign women alarmed some and disquieted others. Priests attacked the Women's Club by name in their defense of traditional family values, while the newspaper *El País* warned "against an independence incompatible with their sex," noting with guarded relief that no Mexican women had joined the Women's Club or started their own. The elite, however, believed that a change in women's status had to accompany the entire modernization process. They varied in the degree of change they believed was required, but accepted the notion that the role of modern women went far beyond the home. At least six high Porfirian officials married American women, thereby breaking a series of traditional patterns in a highly personal and public way. Minister of Foreign Affairs Ignacio Mariscal and his wife, Laura Smith of Baltimore, often worked as a team. Sitting next to the targeted individual, perhaps an American investor or a politician, she presented the case for Mexico at innumerable banquets and receptions. Matías Romero's great diplomatic and social success in Washington depended in part on his wife Lucrecia (Lulu) Allen of New York, as he himself noted.[57] Carmen Díaz, at the public pinnacle of the social and political structure, represented the most important model for change. She delighted the avant-garde and nudged those who viewed the traditional role of women as a fixed part of Mexican culture to consider reasonable modifications. To foreigners she symbolized Mexico's ability to break with the past. Carmen's activities, behavior, and public statements constituted an important part of the Porfirian persuasion.

THE CHURCH

Carmen Díaz served as a political emissary between her husband and the Church. She provided an extremely effective alternate political channel that had the virtue of being both official and unofficial, depending on the circumstances. Any overly public modification of liberalism's strong anticlerical tradition always contained the potential for political embarrassment, even violence, as Juárez had earlier demonstrated. Nevertheless, hostility toward the Church complicated foreign relations and investments. A mutual working relationship between the Mexican government and the Vatican, however, could be established through the assurance of the president's wife without the need to revamp liberalism's theoretical anticlerical position. The program's success prompted Henry Adams to remark in 1894 that the ". . . Church and the Indian seem to be made for each other, and what we call superstition is a part of the natural order of railways and bicycles. . . ."[58] The de facto alliance between the regime and the Church began with the agreement to have Archbishop Labastida officiate at Díaz's wedding. Subsequently, clerics made a point of honoring the president's wife. Saint Carmen's Day (July 16) became an annual opportunity to emphasize the strong but informal connection between the Church and the state. Carmen Díaz became the focal point of an elaborate religious cult ceremony, ending in a public reception where she received greetings from the poor and humble. As *The New York Tribune* observed, Carmen "is loved by rich and poor alike, the latter holding her . . . in a state of veneration."[59]

The campaign to crown the Virgin of Guadalupe also constituted a political ploy as well as a religious pageant. The coronation necessitated papal permission, and in fact only the pope's designated representative could perform the act itself. The drive to crown the Indian virgin began in 1740 but met with success only after the archbishops of Mexico, Michoacán, and Guadalajara pressed for papal permission. Private encouragement by the Díaz administration was a major factor in the outcome. Pope Leo III granted their petition in 1887, ending a 147-year campaign. Carmen Romero Rubio de Díaz headed the committee to raise the funds to purchase an appropriate crown. Made in Paris, the thirty-pound crown of gold and silver incorporated symbols of both Church and state, highlighted with rubies and precious stones. It became a major event for the Catholic world in October 1895. The coronation stimulated public devotion to the Virgin. Pedro Rincón Gallardo, governor of the federal district, combined the old with the new when he decorated his home with electric lights on the day of the Virgin of Guadalupe (December 12). Other members of high society followed his example. The Indian virgin had been captured by the

Porfirians as their own symbol, shared in theory with the down-trodden, but spiritually and politically now one of them. The corona-tion sealed the all but official rapprochement between the liberal government and the Church, acknowledged the validity of the colo-nial religious experience—something the liberals had rejected previ-ously—and reassured the world that anticlericalism no longer posed a threat to political or social stability.[60]

Díaz also hastened to tie the Protestant churches to his regime. Still small in number, such groups had an important symbolic politi-cal function. Protestant missionary activity began in 1846, when a representative of the American Bible Society accompanied the Ameri-can army. By 1868, various Protestant missionary organizations had established themselves in the capital. Thanks to the dedication of peo-ple like Miss Matilda Rankin, who labored first in Texas then in Mon-terrey, missionary activity spread throughout the country, thus a modest number of adherents could be found throughout Mexico. With funds provided by the American Church Missionary Society, the Pres-byterian Church aggressively established itself in Mexico City and in several regions of the republic (1872). The Reverend Doctor Henry C. Riley directed their efforts. Some 385 Protestant churches had been founded by 1892, with 16,250 members. President Díaz, well aware that Americans often viewed Mexican Catholicism as a semipagan medieval throwback, made known his sympathy for Protestant ef-forts. The president, along with his cabinet, occasionally attended spe-cial memorial services in Protestant churches. Ramón Corral, Díaz's vice president, served as the honorary president of the YMCA in the capital. The Reverend William Butler (Methodist Episcopal Church), who met with Díaz along with other Protestant missionaries, reported that the president counseled them not to "be discouraged . . . keep on with your work." Ever the prudent politician, Díaz advised them to avoid "topics of irritation" but "continue preaching the gospel in its own spirit."[61] Religion, whatever the variety, would not be allowed to become an obstacle to the Porfirian program. Díaz, perhaps lulled by the small number of Mexican Protestants, ignored the philosophical implications that challenged the very nature of Porfirian society.

THE DRAMA OF STATE BUILDING

The funeral of Manuel Romero Rubio, Díaz's father-in-law, in 1895 was one of over 100 state burials, including the reburial of ten na-tional heroes, during this regime. These represented one of the most significant and frequently performed Porfirian rituals. Díaz's inaugu-ration of the Rotunda de los Hombres Ilustres (1877) and the marble mausoleum of Benito Juárez (1880) demonstrated his concern with promoting the cult of national heroes.

Romero Rubio died suddenly of a brain hemorrhage on October 5, 1895. As a signer of the 1857 Constitution, congressman under Sebastián Lerdo de Tejada, and Minister of the Interior under Díaz, at the time of his death, he was one of the nation's foremost statesmen and held a leading position in Mexico City's high society. His funeral, while it can be used as a lens to examine urban social relations between the elites and popular classes, will be viewed here as part of the process by which Díaz perpetuated himself in office, established his regime's legitimacy, and built the nation state.

Romero Rubio's prominence came in part from the significance of the marriage between his daughter Carmen, and President Porfirio. The arranged nuptials forged a political alliance among formerly competing liberal factions and provided access to capitaline society for the president and the other Liberal generals who surrounded him. The magnificence of Romero Rubio's state funeral testified to his prominence in politics and society.

Upon his death, the seat of national authority shifted temporarily from the National Palace to the Romero Rubio residence. Díaz, division generals, and cabinet members arrived at the home and immediately formed a junta to discuss funeral preparations. Meanwhile, cannons fired a solemn announcement of the death each half hour, and every prominent citizen rushed to the home to offer condolences. Romero Rubio's personal secretary, Rosendo Pineda, notified the state governors by telegram, and in the Chamber of Deputies Guillermo Prieto delivered a powerful call for national burial and the closing of sessions for three days, as part of nine days of national mourning. Mexico's most distinguished artist, Jesus Contreras, was commissioned to prepare the traditional death mask.

The official funeral arrangements called for the body to lie in state at the national legislative building, a funeral ceremony in the Chamber of Deputies, and burial, acquiescing to family requests, in their vault in the French cemetery rather than the Rotunda de los Hombres Ilustres. A cortege of 800 dignitaries, despite the miserable cold and wet weather, formed a procession with the casket from the home to the Chamber of Deputies. The most dramatic features of the funeral ceremony were the official ceremony in the Chamber of Deputies held for the governing class and a procession through the streets designed for the general public.

The funeral procession offered a visible display of the regime. Order resulted from the police, soldiers, rurales, and cadets who lined the parade route. This visible demand of order responded to the huge crowd, estimated at 100,000 to 250,000 mourners, about three-fourths of the city's population, who packed the route. The procession placed the Porfirian hierarchy on linear display. The president led the parade followed by the leaders of his regime, the family, then the bureaucracy, military representatives, and city government officials. Workers from various mutualist societies brought up the rear. The majority of the population, especially the poor and those from out of town, were relegated to the sidewalks. The spectators, screened from the parade by guards, were expected to illustrate order.

The public aspect of the funeral also illustrated the other major theme of the regime: progress. The organizers arranged the procession to move through the wealthiest streets of Mexico City and tour the city of palaces. The procession moved by streetcar, the urban version of modernity's icon, the railroad. Other less attractive features of progress and urbanization were represented by the numerous pickpockets and sneak thieves who joined the throng.

At the entrance to the French cemetery, the armed sentries gave way to an aisle from the gates to the family crypt formed by 400 students from the Orphan Boy's Industrial School that had been founded by Romero Rubio. Once the casket arrived it was consigned to its resting place with the assistance of a single priest, the only evidence of the church in the ceremony. Despite some hitches, the funeral served well as a public performance of Porfirian success. The regime tapped public emotion, and public participation reached such heights that one newspaper declared it was the grandest funeral since the burial of Benito Juárez in 1873. The Porfirian mythologizers used this funeral to reconstitute the social order, improve Mexico's international image, and coalesce civic ideology. The ceremony allowed the state to rewrite national history from the standpoint of its great men. During the heyday of progress, the state funerals succeeded in maintaining an illusion of strength and modernity. The processions in their constituent parts portrayed society's different segments, but the parts together equaled something much more—they combined to reveal the Mexican nation. Frequent, lavish, and orthodox, the ceremonies reminded citizens about the relationship between their heroes and Porfirio Díaz, the powerful leader who buried them all.[62]

Porfirian Diplomacy

Mexican diplomacy under Díaz struggled with the reality of economic and financial dependency. Attitudes and perceptions in the United States and Europe toward Mexico had to be carefully monitored. Moreover, the nation had to defend its sovereignty without jeopardizing market access and foreign investment by overly aggressive tactics. Anger could not be allowed to overcome prudence. Firmness without excessive public hostility had proven successful in securing recognition from the administration of Rutherford B. Hayes. Nevertheless, relations between the two countries continually hovered on the verge of becoming tense. A demanding and belligerent United States treated the Mexican government with scant respect. Problems involving extradition and extraterritoriality are characteristic of border regions. Unfortunately, the Extradition Treaty of 1861, signed by Abraham Lincoln and Benito Juárez, no longer served to resolve difficulties along an increasingly complex international boundary. Mexico attempted to be cooperative, while the United States appeared truculent at best. The ministry of foreign relations presented figures to demonstrate that Mexico had complied with at least half of all extradition requests, whereas the United States failed to honor even one.[63]

In any border incident, Washington and the American press assumed Mexico to be at fault. Rigid demands made it difficult to resolve problems quickly. For example, a legal incident arose with the arrest of Augustus K. Cutting in 1886 by Mexican authorities in el Paso del Norte for libel against another newspaper editor. American authorities allowed it to become a full-flown international issue and demanded that Mexico City override Chihuahua's legal code and release Cutting. In Texas, public sentiment demanded use of force, while an outraged Washington appeared more interested in posturing than in reaching a reasonable understanding. *The New York Times* editorialized in a most insulting fashion:

> The best proof of the worthlessness of Mexico for any purpose of ours is the fact that we have not annexed any part of the country since the treaty that closed the Mexican War.[64]

The *Times* went on to note that the United States could easily destroy Mexico. The Mexican government rode out the crisis by constantly and publicly indicating its willingness to be reasonable, but within a framework of respect for the law.[65] Grover Cleveland, in his 1886 State of the Union Address, warned Mexico to accommodate Washington or endanger the flow of capital and technology Mexico needed. In another case involving Chester Rowe, an Iowa county official who embezzled funds and fled to Mexico, the United States attempted to bully the Mexican government into an extralegal process. Díaz firmly resisted American pressure with reasonable arguments and explanations, including citing an opinion of a former chief justice, Roger B. Taney. A similar incident involving James Temple, a railway conductor who shot a Mexican bandit a mere several hundred yards within the state of Sonora, caused yet another uproar in 1898. Meanwhile, Mexico legally abrogated the 1861 treaty to force negotiations on a more useful agreement. Eventually, the Extradition Treaty of February 22, 1899, provided an acceptable process to resolve diplomatic conflicts over events on the border.[66]

Díaz worried that his inability to secure rapid cooperation from American federal and state authorities along the border posed a threat to his regime by undermining the all-important image of stability upon which everything rested. The esteemed intellectual and literary figure Vincente Riva Palacio, appointed Mexican diplomatic representative to Spain and Portugal, observed (1886) that the northern border region attracted the least desirable people of both republics. Such people, prone to disruptive behavior, endangered relations between Mexico and the United States. Matías Romero, an experienced and extraordinarily astute diplomat, agreed, as did the consul in Laredo, Texas, who warned that marginally employed migrant Mexican labor in south Texas constituted social tinder that at any moment could erupt in revolutionary violence. Mexican officials understood that unrest, racism, and poverty in the Río Grande Valley of Texas in particular endangered the Porfirian regime but not the administration in Washington, which seldom worried about social conditions in Texas until a crisis occurred.[67]

Díaz attempted to nip potentially revolutionary challenges in the bud. Thus he instructed Matías Romero to pressure Washington for assistance in dealing with Catarino Garza, Paulino Martínez, and Francisco Ruiz Sandoval, who, operating from the Laredo area, raided into Mexico in violation of American law. In Río Grande City, Catarino Garza recruited "revolutionaries." On Mexican Independence Day, September 15, 1891, Garza and Sandoval issued a "Plan Revolucionario" that demanded a new constitution, land reform, local political control, and no reelection. The *Laredo Times* referred to Garza as the "Moses of the Mexican Republic." Díaz requested permission to send troops under General Bernardo Reyes into Texas to track Garza down. Washington declined the request.[68] Garza's movement already had caused some damage to Mexico's all-important stable image. President Díaz personally responded to a report published in La Soleil of St. Nazarine, France, that Garza threatened the regime's existence. The government also monitored the reaction of London money markets to border problems. Mexican diplomatic representatives in Europe denied that Garza had set off a financial crisis in Mexico, or that he had any influence on popular opinion within the country. Matías Romero blamed the irresponsible and sensationalist tendencies of the American press for much of the public relations damage. Romero wrote an article for publication in American newspapers that explained the situation in terms of border social and economic conditions that had little to do with Mexico itself. He noted that while these bandit-revolutionaries spoke Spanish, they did so "incorrectly." In effect, they belonged to the border, not to Mexico. Most irritatingly, the San Antonio Express reported that Garza's group referred to itself as the "Constitutional Army." Even more chilling to Porfirian officials, the New Orleans Picayune published an article clearly setting forth the regime's vulnerability to border challenges. The Mexican government threatened legal action against the New Orleans paper. As a result, its editors apologized in print and, furthermore, predicted that Mexico would enjoy permanent peace and prosperity under Díaz's rule.[69] The battle of perceptions could not be lost by Mexican diplomats without fatal consequences.

To give the Mexican government some extraterritorial political leverage in Texas, consuls along the border attempted to protect the civil rights of the Spanish-speaking population. The case of Gregorio Cortez provides a good example. Cortez, a borderlander born in Matamoros, Mexico, moved at a young age with his family to Manor, Texas, and eventually settled in Karnes County. A series of events involving a groundless charge of horse theft resulted in the shooting of two Anglo law officers and widespread mob violence against Tejanos and Mexicans. The fugitive, eventually captured, would be defended in court as a Mexican citizen by the Díaz regime. Without pressure and money from Mexico City, he would have been lynched by a mob or sentenced to death in a Texas courtroom. Gregorio Cortez served eight

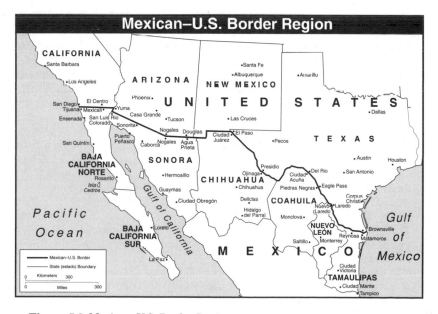

Figure 5.8 Mexican–U.S. Border Region

years in prison before receiving a full pardon from Governor O. B. Colquitt in 1913.[70] Less spectacular assistance to victims of various types of social and political abuse projected some influence north of the international line. Nevertheless, in the end, border vulnerability brought down the regime just as the Porfirians had feared.

Porfirio Díaz preferred not to bluntly refuse Washington's requests, no matter how outrageous they might appear to the Mexican government. At the same time, he understood that even if he maneuvered carefully he could not escape criticism. The objective could be only to minimize the degree of friction and avoid negative economic consequences. American investors often carped about the alleged favoritism shown other nationalities and sought to use diplomatic pressure for their own interests. Economic realism made it necessary for the government to placate American investors, while not losing sight of Mexican needs, including a limited balancing of American capital with European or Canadian investments. The delicate touch and a calculated response characterized Mexican–United States relations. Thus when the United States requested (1907) the permanent lease of Magdalena Bay on Baja's Pacific Coast, Díaz agreed to a three-year lease—a positive response, but on terms designed to derail the project. In the diplomatic game, Mexico held weak cards but usually played them with considerable skill.

NOTES

1. Salvador Novo, *Cocina mexicana: Historia gastronómica de la Ciudad de México* (México: Editorial Porrua, 1979), pp. 125–29.
2. Olive Percival, *Mexico City: An Idler's Notebook* (Chicago: Herbert S. Stone Co., 1901), pp. 121–51; Hale, Transformation, p. 181.
3. Wolfgang Vogt, "Influencias extranjeras en la literatura mexicana anterior a la revolución de 1910," *Relaciones* (spring 1990), p. 109.
4. This attitude is not unique in Latin America. Ariel, first published in 1900 by the Uruguayan intellectual José Enrique Rodó (1871–1917) and subsequently in numerous editions throughout the hemisphere, is the most famous literary expression of cultural apprehension. See the English edition with an enlightening foreword by James W. Symington and a prologue by Carlos Fuentes. José Enrique Rodó, *Ariel* (Austin: University of Texas Press, 1988).
5. Henry C. Schmidt, The *Roots of Lo Mexicano: Self and Society in Mexican Thought, 1900–1934* (College Station: Texas A&M University Press, 1978), pp. 38–40.
6. Saragoza, *The Monterrey Elite*, p. 81.
7. William H. Beezley, *Judas at the Jockey Club and Other Episodes of Porfirian Mexico* (Lincoln: University of Nebraska Press, 1987), pp. 61–62.
8. Ibid., pp. 20–26, 42, 63, 64.
9. Pletcher, *Rails, Mines and Progress*, p. 57.

10. Winter, *Mexico and Her People*, pp. 66–67.
11. Daniel Roche, *The People of Paris: An Essay in Popular Culture in the Eighteenth Century*, translated by Marie Evens (Berkeley: University of California Press, 1987), p. 272.
12. Exciting recent research on these topics includes Christiana Rivera-Garza, "The Masters of the Streets: Bodies, Power and Modernity in Mexico, 1867–1930 (Ph.D. diss., University of Houston, 1995); Ann S. Blum, "Children without Parents: Law, Charity, and Social Practice, Mexico City, 1870–1940" (Ph.D. diss., University of California, 1997); James Angus McLeod, "Public Health, Social Assistance and the Consolidation of the Mexican State, 1888–1940" (Ph.D. diss., Tulane University, 1990); Robert Buffington, "Forging the Fatherland: Criminality and Citizenship in Modern Mexico" (Ph.D. diss., University of Arizona, 1994).
13. See William E. French, "'Progreso Forzado': Workers and the Inculcation of the Capitalist Work Ethic in the Parral Mining District," in Beezley, Martin, and French, eds., *Rituals of Rule*, and French, *A Peaceful and Working People*. Alan Knight coined the term *folk liberalism* in his essay "Revolutionary Project, Recalcitrant People: Mexico, 1910–1940," in Rodríguez O., ed., The Revolutionary Process in Mexico, p. 233.
14. *Diccionario Porrua: Historia, Biografía y Geografía de México*, 4th ed., (México: Editorial Porrua, 1979), pp. 428–29.
15. Haber, *Industry and Underdevelopment*, pp. 69–72.
16. Schell Jr., "Integral Outsiders," pp. 59–64, 82.
17. For details on these individuals, see Pletcher, *Rails, Mines and Progress*. For more on Braniff, see Haber, *Industry and Underdevelopment*, pp. 76–77; Schell Jr., "Integral Outsiders," pp. 66–67.
18. Saragoza, *The Monterrey Elite*, p. 74; Fell Jr., Ores to Metals, pp. 198, 222.
19. Schell Jr., "Integral Outsiders," pp. 32–34.
20. Stuart F. Voss, "Porfirian Sonora: Economic Collegiality," unpublished paper presented at the American Historical Association Convention, San Francisco, 1978, pp. 17, 20.
21. Hansen, *Politics of Mexican Development*, p. 151.
22. Milada Bazant, "Estudiantes mexicanos en el extranjero: El caso de los hermanos Urquidi," *Historia Mexicana* (April-June 1987), pp. 739–58.
23. Larissa A. Lomnitz and Marisol Pérez-Lizaur, *A Mexican Elite Family, 1820–1980* (Princeton, 1987), pp. 22–23.
24. Wasserman, *Capitalists, Caciques, and Revolution*, pp. 43–70.
25. Jane-Dale Lloyd, "Ranchos and Rebellion: The Case of Northwestern Chihuahua, 1905–1909," in Nugent, ed., *Rural Revolt in Mexico*, pp. 87–111.
26. James W. Wilkie and Paul D. Wilkins, "Quantifying the Class Structure of Mexico, 1895–1970," in James W. Wilkie and Stephen Haber, eds., *Statistical Abstract of Latin America*, vol. 21 (Los Angeles: UCLA Latin American Center Publications, 1981), pp. 577–90. The authors allotted 8 percent to the middle class and 2 percent to the elite.
27. Sinkin, *The Mexican Reform*, p. 173.
28. Cosío Villegas, *Historia Moderna*, vol. 7, pt. 1, pp. 401–2.
29. Ibid., p. 405.
30. Ibid., pp. 420–21.
31. Morgan, "Proletarians, Políticos and Patriarchs," in Beezley, Martin, and French, eds., *Rituals of Rule*.
32. Pletcher, *Rails, Mines and Progress*, p. 13.
33. Robert Martin Alexius, "The Army and Politics in Porfirian Mexico" (Ph.D. diss., University of Texas, 1976), pp. 54–55.

34. Paul J. Vanderwood, "Explaining the Mexican Revolution," in Rodr íguez O., ed., *The Revolutionary Process in Mexico*, p. 106.
35. Hale, *Transformation*, pp. 52–53.
36. José Yves Limantour, *Apuntes sobre mi vida política* (Mexico: Editorial Porrua, 1965), p. 15; Jacqueline Ann Rice, "The Porfirian Political Elite: Life Patterns of the Delegates to the 1892 Union Liberal Convention" (Ph.D. diss., University of California, Los Angeles, 1979), p. 136; Hale, *Transformation*, pp. 107–38.
37. Francisco Madero conceded the success of Díaz as a politician and as a symbol of stable unity, noting that he could not be viewed as a vulgar dictator. Francisco I. Madero, *La sucesión presidencial en 1910* (Saltillo: Imprenta del Estado de Coahuila, 1958), pp. 297–301. On Reyes, see Anthony T. Bryan, "Mexican Politics in Transition, 1900–1913: The Role of General Bernardo Reyes" (Ph.D. diss., University of Nebraska, 1969). For Limantour, see B. W. Aston, "The Public Career of José Yves Limantour" (Ph.D. diss., Texas Technical University, 1972). Limantour's own *Apuntes sobre mi vida política*. For Dehesa, see Abel R. Pérez, *Teodoro A. Dehesa: Gobernante Veracruzano* (Mexico: Talleres Stylo, 1960).
38. Coerver, *The Porfirian Interregnum*, p. 78. For a discussion of camarilla politics, see William S. Langston, "Coahuila: Centralization Against State Autonomy," in Benjamin and McNellie, eds., *Other Mexicos*, pp. 55–76; Donald M. Coerver, "Federal-State Relations during the Porfiriato: The Case of Sonora, 1879–1884," *The Americas* (April 1977), pp. 567–84.
39. Wasserman, *Capitalists, Caciques, and Revolution*, p. 91.
40. Gilbert M. Joseph, "The United States, Leading Elites, and Rural Revolt in Yucatán, 1836–1915" in Nugent, ed., *Rural Revolt in Mexico*, pp. 167–97.
41. Langston, "Coahuila," pp. 58, 71; Illescas, "Agitación social," pp. 98–99.
42. Romana Falcón, "Raíces de la Revolución: Evaristo Madero, el primer eslabón de la cadena," in Rodríguez O., ed., *The Revolutionary Process*, pp. 33–56.
43. Guy Thompson, "Ceremonial and Political Role of Village Bands, 1846–1974," in *Ritual of Rule*, p. 39.
44. Vanderwood, *Disorder and Progress*, p. 32; Carreno, ed., Archivo del General Porfirio Díaz, vol. 1, pp. 51–55.
45. Wasserman, *Capitalists, Caciques, and Revolution*, p. 136; Romana Falcón, "Poderes y razones de las jefaturas políticas: Coahuila en el primer siglo de vida independiente," in Jaime Rodríguez O., ed., *The Evolution of the Mexican Political System* (Wilmington: SR Books, 1992); Romana Falcón, "Jefes políticos y rebeliones campesinas: Uso y abuso del poder en el Estado de México," in Rodríguez O., ed., *Patterns of Contention*, pp. 243–73.
46. Alexius, "The Army and Politics," pp. 4–7, 223–31.
47. John Hays Hammond, *The Autobiography of John Hays Hammond* (New York: Farrar & Rinehart, 1935), vol. 2, pp. 508–9.
48. Desmond Young, *Member for Mexico: A Biography of Weetman Pearson, First Viscount Cowdray* (London: Cassell, 1966), p. 68.
49. Charlotte Roehl, "Porfirio Díaz in the Press of the United States" (Ph.D. diss., University of Chicago, 1953), p. 191.
50. Vanderwood, *Disorder and Progress*, p. 134.
51. Paola Riguzzi, "México próspero: Las dimensiones de la imagen nacional en el Porfiriato," *Historias* (April–September 1988), pp. 137–57; Hubert Howe Bancroft, *Recursos y desarrollo de México* (San Francisco: Bancroft Co., 1893), prólogue, pp. v, vii.
52. Mauricio Tenorio-Trillo, *Mexico at the World's Fairs: Crafting A Modern Nation* (Berkeley: University of California Press, 1996); Gene Yeager, "Porfirian Commercial Propaganda: Mexico in the World Industrial Expositions," *The Americas*

(October 1977), pp. 235–39; Riguzzi, "México próspero," p. 149; Hale, *Transformation*, p. 10.

53. Justo Sierra quoted in Hale, *Transformation*, p. 10. John R. Southworth, ed., *El directorio oficial de las minas y haciendas de México (The Official Directory of Mines and Estates of Mexico: General Description of the Mining Properties of the Republic of Mexico, In Which Is Included a List of Haciendas and Ranches in Those States and Territories Where It Is Possible to Obtain Reliable Data)* (México: J. Southworth, 1910).

54. Lic. Rafael de Zayas Enríquez, *Los Estados Unidos Mexicanos: Sus progresos en veinte años de paz*, 1877–1897 (New York: H. A. Rost, 1899), pp. 216–17.

55. Hale, *Transformation*, pp. 242–43; Sierra, Viajes en tierra Yankee, p. 23.

56. Adams to William Hallett Phillips, Mexico, April 17, 1896, in J. C. Levenson, Ernest Samuels, Charles Vandersee, and Viola Hopkins Winner, eds., *The Letters of Henry Adams* (Cambridge: Harvard University Press, 1988), vol. 4, p. 381.

57. Schell, Jr., "Integral Outsiders," pp. 238–39.

58. Adams to Elizabeth Cameron, December 12, 1894, in Levenson et al., eds., *The Letters of Henry Adams*, vol. 4, p. 234.

59. *The New York Tribune* (July 16, 1898), p. 7.

60. William H. Beezley, "Holidays...Holy Days...Mexican Virtue on Parade," unpublished paper, pp. 34–35.

61. Bancroft, *Recursos y desarrollo de México*, p. 40. William Butler, *Mexico in Transition from the Power of Political Romanism to Civil Religious Liberty*, 3d ed. rev. (New York: Hunt & Eaton, 1893), pp. 300–05.

62. Matthew D. Esposito, "Memorializing Modern Mexico: The State Funerals of the Porfirian Era, 1876–1911" (Ph.D. diss., Texas Christian University, 1997).

63. Robert John Deger, Jr., "Porfirian Foreign Policy and Mexican Nationalism: A Study of Cooperation and Conflict in Mexican-American Relations, 1884–1904" (Ph.D. diss., Indiana University, 1979), p. 80.

64. Ibid., p. 88. *The New York Times*, July 28, 1886, p. 4.

65. *Caso del americano A. K. Cutting. Nuevas notas cambiadas entre la legación de los Estados Unidos y el Ministerio de Relaciones Exteriores de la República Mexicana* (México: Imprenta de Francisco Díaz de Leon, 1888).

66. Deger, "Porfirian Foreign Policy," pp. 100, 110.

67. Ibid., p. 127.

68. Ibid, pp. 141–43.

69. Ibid., p. 152; *Picayune* (New Orleans), August 15, 1893, p. 7; October 16, 1893, p. 4.

70. Américo Paredes, *With His Pistol in His Hand: A Border Ballad and Its Hero* (Austin: University of Texas Press, 1958), provides the dramatic story. Carlos Cortés, "El bandolerismo social chicano," in David Maciel and Patricia Bereno, eds., *Aztlán: Historia del pueblo chicano, 1848–1910* (México: Secretaria de Educación Pública, 1975), pp. 111–22.

Chapter 6

PRELUDE TO REVOLUTION

THE ILLUSION OF STRENGTH

The Porfiriato relied upon the appearance of strength rather than its
reality, perhaps more than most modern states. In a sense, the genius
of President Porfirio Díaz lay in the realm of the psychological. While
an effective politician, a valiant soldier, a clever manipulator of the
greed and ambitions of others, a loyal friend, an accomplished propa-
gandist, and a sincere patriot, he excelled at illusion. Indeed, the pipe
dream of Mexico's progress toward modernity seemed to have been
conjured into glorious existence through the strength of Díaz's persuasive personality. Understandably, the regime's enemies as well as
its friends confused calculated projection with substance. After all,
the instruments of state force must be as strong as Díaz himself. All
were aware that the army and rural police force, the rurales, patrolled
the countryside from the northern border to southern Mexico. Moreover, large-scale economic enterprises often had a detachment of rurales stationed on the premises ready to deal with any contingency.
The apparent importance assigned to order, deeply rooted in liberal-
positivist thought, reassured flighty investors and those opening up
new lands to plantation agriculture. Díaz's prompt reaction to internal disorder impressed outsiders and enhanced his reputation as a
strongman, but obscured the darker reality.

   The national government understood and responded to the historically fragile nature of order in Mexico. As virtually all officials instinctively understood, peace and tranquility could unravel quickly. In

Prelude to Revolution

1876–1911	The Porfiriato, the regime of Porfirio Díaz
1898	Apizaco textile strike
1900	Federal District Penitentiary, based on scientific penology, opens.
	Regeneración newspaper founded
1905	Mexican Liberal Party (PLM) founded by Ricardo and Enrique Flores Magón
1906	PLM plan issued in St. Louis, Missouri
	Cananea copper mines strike
1907	Río Blanco textile strike
1908	Díaz interview with James Creelman
1910	Centennial of Mexican independence

a socially fragmented nation with weak ties of loyalty and sympathy between the classes, few effective means of adjusting social conflicts without violence, coupled with a strong tendency to put local and regional interests above national objectives, the federal government could not and dared not temporize. Moreover, both the army and the rurales had a limited ability to sustain large-scale operations. They constituted an effective police force if they could be moved into action in the early stages—to nip disorder before it overwhelmed the relatively weak instruments of state force.

As a result of well-founded doubts that the army or the rurales could prevail in any given confrontation, armed clashes tended to escalate immediately to the maximum possible repressive level. Because these groups lacked the ability or self-confidence to apply restrained force in the degree necessary to control a situation, riots became major battles. Even strike breaking could be transformed into an instant social and political disaster as the strike at the Río Blanco textile factory (1907) demonstrated. Rioters contained at the factory moved on to burn the company stores in neighboring Nogales and Necoxtla. Six strikers identified as leaders were executed without trial in the charred ruins of the company stores. In the end, the toll reached approximately 100 dead and many more injured and imprisoned. Rumors reported railroad cars piled high with bodies were to be dumped in Veracruz harbor. Excessive force damaged the credibility of the regime. Río Blanco still signifies Porfirian harshness; in reality, it demonstrated the government's weakness.[1]

Plans to modernize the army, long under discussion, never moved beyond the planning stage. The huge investment that was needed and political ambivalence made army modernization difficult. Moreover, chronic shortages of recruits for the federal army weakened its strength and effectiveness. In the absence of sufficient volunteers, each state supplied a quota yet seldom delivered the number of recruits required by Mexico City. State officials used their *leva* (draft) to rid themselves of elements deemed undesirable; political troublemakers, vagrants, beggars, and those considered criminally inclined could be shipped off. Any group perceived to violate acceptable behavior became vulnerable. In 1910, for example, authorities seized forty-one transvestites attending a dance and dispatched them to Yucatán as army recruits. Use of military service as a means of political, social, or moral control did not provide willing nor dedicated soldiers. In truth, no group wanted a large, well-trained, and well-equipped professional army. Regional bosses preferred militias under their own control. Camarilla politics did not require overwhelming force, and in fact an effective as well as sizable military institution might unbalance the system. As a result, the illusion of the strength and control of the Porfirian regime marched far in advance of reality.[2] The trick was to make sure that illusion never met reality.

CRISIS IN FOOD PRODUCTION

The pressure on agricultural land to meet export needs had an effect on the quantity and quality of food production. Production for the internal market suffered as land use shifted to cultivation of more valuable export crops, driving out less profitable corn and beans. Maize (corn) and beans, traditionally grown and consumed by virtually the entire rural population, went to the local market and on occasion to a regional market, but seldom beyond. Because corn and beans represented the unneeded surplus of a self-contained system of production and consumption by the same individual, the prices of these items remained low, except during poor crop years. Commercial agriculture changed the situation. A metric ton of corn in Veracruz cost approximately 53 pesos in 1907, almost 200 percent more than in 1877. Sugar, however, returned 171 pesos, cotton 375, coffee 400, and tobacco 455 a metric ton.[3] A rational response to market forces made food crops virtually the last choice. Bits and pieces of marginal land continued to produce limited amounts of staples, but could not carry much more than a certain number of consumers. Corn production had to be supplemented by imports, and even then critical shortages occurred. In Sinaloa, the poor population in the Culiacán region desperately ate mescal roots and trunks to stay alive. A food riot in Durango involved some 4,000 people who attempted to storm warehouses and stores. Gunfire controlled them with difficulty. In Chihuahua (1877), worried individuals pleaded for donations of corn. The following year Mazat-lán's *beneficencia* (charitable association) solicited 20,000 pesos to buy supplies to meet the urgent needs of Sinaloa's poor. Distribution diffi-culties led to scarcity in some areas and abundance in others. High rail freight charges compounded the problem. In 1888, the state of Mexico suffered serious shortages while many other states enjoyed a surplus at reasonable prices. At times, the north and the southeast struggled with plentiful supplies of imported corn, while the rest of the land had exhausted its reserves. Generalized national shortages occurred with distressing and increasing frequency in 1884, 1892, 1896, 1900, 1904, 1909, and 1910. As *El Agricultor Mexicano* noted, at the turn of the century the government seemed unable to do much more than react. Crisis management required that 200,000 tons be imported during the period 1892–1893 and again three years later, and yet once more during the period 1910–1911. Shortages of beans, a traditional staple as well as a source of protein, caused particular re-sentment and anger. During the period 1892–1893, the government permitted tax-free importation and encouraged charitable organiza-tions to sell both beans and corn at cost. Removing structural obsta-cles that hindered distribution helped to a limited degree. Adjusting taxes and lowering freight charges alleviated the periodic scarcity of beans but did not increase actual production. Other food resources could not substitute for the three traditional components of the diet—corn, beans, and chile. Cultural and dietary factors made scarcity both a physical and psychological disaster. Other food items such as rice, beef, and garbanzo beans were drawn increasingly into the export market. Low wages made it impossible for the Mexican population to compete with export prices.[4]

Beginning in the 1890s, Mexico almost continuously imported staple foodstuffs from abroad. In 1905, the government sold food at subsidized prices in areas of extreme need, and in early 1909, it opened fifty subsidized outlets in the poor neighborhoods of Mexico City.[5] Food prices rose to a level that changed dietary habits and re-duced caloric intake to subminimal levels. The picture of rural Mexi-cans taking a siesta against a wall or tree, which many tourists thought so charming, in fact represented malnutrition and physical exhaustion. In 1910, estimated minimal demand for corn of fifty mil-lion hectares was met at best by production of some sixty million hectares—a margin of ten million over minimal demand, not enough to moderate prices or to carry through into the next year. Per capita production of corn fell from 282 kilograms in 1877 to 144 kilograms in 1907—virtually a 50 percent decline.[6]

Concentration of land ownership and loss of communal land made it impossible for unemployed worker peasants to retreat back

Figure 6.1 The President Porfirio Díaz puppet, used by the Rosete Aranda family in its productions across Mexico during the late nineteenth century. The puppet is now on display at the National Puppetry Museum in Huamantla, Tlaxcala, the hometown of the Rosete Aranda family. *Printed with permission, Meredith Main.*

into subsistence agriculture during difficult times. By 1910, 90 percent of the rural inhabitants of the central states of Puebla and Veracruz were landless.[7] Labor exploitation, malnutrition, and semi-starvation went together for a large percentage of the Mexican population. A sharp economic downturn brought real desperation. The more favored classes, while aware of the suffering, felt scant personal, physical, or emotional connection with the less fortunate. Hunger and social desperation remained abstract notions to be dealt with by paternalistic adjustments until progress brought society into balance. Mexican liberalism during the Porfiriato had little pressing moral or emotional content. Ideally, the response to suffering should be calculated to provide a cure rather than momentary relief. Liberalism philosophically rejected the supposedly mindless charity practiced by the Church over the centuries.

THE PATERNALISTIC IMPULSE

Porfirian paternalism had an ever-present ideological component. Those who received assistance were expected to use it wisely or forfeit consideration in the future. Paternalism had a sober, directed impulse, much different from what formerly might have been called charity. The liberal notion that the Indian had been rendered childlike and unproductive by Spanish colonial paternalism underlay the Porfirian approach, modified by Darwin, Spencer, Comte, and others to be sure, but an ingrained attitude nonetheless. While José Yves Limantour, who directed the economic program under Díaz, has been accused of being a believer in social Darwinism, in fact he reflected all the components of Mexican liberalism as it had evolved. Limantour and other Porfirians approached assistance very cautiously, intent on avoiding the creation of dependency. In his official capacity, Limantour abolished counterproductive taxes on the poor, did his best to soften the impact of declining silver prices on the lowest paid public employees, and supported the importation of corn and its sale, not free distribution, at subsidized prices. Limantour also played an important role in the establishment of the *Casa del Estudiante* (House of Students), opened in early 1910 to assist qualified and diligent students. He endowed the Casa with 168,732 pesos to fund poor students who had demonstrated the necessary virtues of hard work as well as aptitude.

Porfirian paternalism also could be used to offset negative propaganda. Olegario Molina, intent on countering Yucatán's reputation for harsh treatment of the lower classes, endowed Mérida with a modern hospital, including a free clinic for the poor. When Díaz toured Yucatán at the invitation of the elite, he officially opened the O'Haran Hospital, an asylum, and a new modern penitentiary. A carefully staged visit to the hacienda of Rafael Peón led Díaz to observe that the Yucatán elite had been slandered. Peón spent 200,000 pesos to transform his hacienda, including dressing "his" Indians for the occasion, to throw a lavish reception.

Model prisons captured the essence of the Porfirian approach. Reformers, abandoning previous liberal idealism that had inspired the 1871 Penal Code, sought practical solutions through isolation of prisoners and "scientifically" guided rehabilitation. Prisons, theorists argued, shared responsibility for social order with modern schools and factories. The morality of the workshop could redeem prisoners, not just punish them. For example, the Salamanca prison in Guanajuato included a primary school, offered lessons in drawing and music, and used workshops to teach the inmates a skill. When they left prison they received the small amount of money earned during their stay. Puebla's penitentiary had workshops that taught shoe making, among other useful skills. Social regeneration might also include labor on public works. The latest nineteenth-century European penal theories found an enthusiastic reception in Mexico. While the gap between theory and practice remained wide, the approach met with approval. Matías Romero, addressing prison conditions, had once observed that prisons could not be "as comfortable as palaces or hotels." They were not, but their functioning could at least be seen as a useful effort to remedy a perceived lower class problem. This preoccupation resulted in the construction of a new Federal District Penitentiary in 1900 and a new Pacific Coast island penal colony (Islas Marías) in 1908. The prison exhibited the modern architecture of the French-inspired radial design, and both institutions relied on a behavioralist administration, based on the Irish "Croffton" system of rewards and punishments. The new penitentiaries, along with the reorganization of federal prisons and the professionalization of the capital city's police force, represented the Porfirian commitment to a constructive order. Of course, theory often failed in the face of reality.[8]

RALLYING THE LOWER CLASSES

While the Porfirian oligarchy appeared able to arrange things more or less as they wished, the lower classes nevertheless remained part of the political equation. Denied access to political remedies and unable to profit from economic development, they responded by searching for an explanation as well as a solution to their growing misery. A reactionary nationalism provided the preliminary rallying point. Excluded in an economic, social, and psychological sense by the elite and their foreign cohorts and viewed as retrograde obstacles in the path of progress, the lower classes struggled to regain social value and a sense of validity in their own eyes. Ironically, they accepted the government's mythological Juárez but rejected the companion notion that the Díaz regime represented its continuation. Instead they chose to view Porfirio Díaz and his government as the corrupt betrayers of the sacred and pure principles of the *benemérito*. The soiled liberalism of the Porfiriato could not compete with the sanctified mythical Benito

Juárez. The lower classes looked back to the days of Benito Juárez, a time before they felt rejected by the elite notion of modern Mexico. Juárez depended upon the lower classes, campesinos, and workers in the great patriotic struggle to expel the French and the imposed emperorship of Maximilian.[9] The Reforma War and the Constitution of 1857 became mythical high points of lower class nationalism, and even today remain part of the myth. Restoration of the Constitution of 1857 emerged as a panacea in spite of provisions of the Constitution that directly struck at the well-being of the lower classes. What people constantly referred to as the spirit of the Constitution of 1857 in fact represented a mystical recreation of the initial motivating liberal impulse to construct a prosperous, stable, and modern republic encompassing the hopes and desires of all Mexicans within its benign embrace. The actual results of the Constitution could be seen as a perversion of original intent. They desired a philosophical return of the mythological Juárez rather than the reality. A self-validating nationalism, more emotional than analytical, became a feature of the Mexican Revolution of 1910.

A muted yet insidious challenge to the government came from an unanticipated source—Protestant missionaries. Protestantism, inherently antihierarchical and self-contained, posed a philosophical and political counterpoint to the actual functioning of the Porfiriato. Mexican liberalism under Díaz had become a screen behind which the elite ran the country and its various regions and enjoyed the early fruits of modernization. While they earnestly believed that all would benefit eventually, that notion provided cold comfort to those at the bottom. Protestant groups, however, preached the doctrine of immediate economic and social betterment, achievable through organization, individual effort within a civic community, combined with individual responsibility both toward the group and for one's self, at a time when the lower classes perceived themselves and their communities as being under siege. Protestant religious culture emphasized the need to reach the most benighted elements of society. Consequently, missionaries concentrated on conversion of the poor and humble. The lower classes, bewildered by change, often rootless and struggling in a new region to understand their changed status as worker peasants, had few options. For many, radical political ideas or radical religion provided the only haven.

Protestantism preached a form of civic religion that called for the restoration of an idealized liberalism that recognized the self-worth of all Mexicans, including the lower classes. Works represented words in action; thus, the vanguard of their efforts involved providing service to the community. Education, medical services, and immediate direct assistance would win respect first, followed by conversion. It did not always work as planned, but it did give them influence far beyond the number of adherents. The willingness of missionary groups to establish primary schools stimulated requests from rural areas across the republic. Comalcalco, Paraíso, Cárdenas, Frontera, Jalapa, and Tenosigue, all villages in the state of Tabasco, bombarded the Presbyterian headquarters in Mexico City in 1888 and 1889 with requests to establish schools. They understood that along with the school came a pastor. Tezontepec in Hidalgo offered the Methodists land for a church with the proviso that it include a school. Small isolated settlements often attracted an itinerant preacher looking for a challenge. Night school and prison programs hoped to teach potential converts to read the Bible. The number of Protestant schools rose from 96 in 1888 with some 2,940 students to 163 schools in 1911 with 11,682 students. High schools in the cities concentrated on the recruitment and preparation of teachers following the model of normal schools in the United States.

While small in terms of members, their influence, direct and indirect, loomed far out of proportion to their numbers. The popular perception associated American economic development and entrepreneurship with Protestantism, ignoring the reality of hordes of Catholic and Jewish immigrants who contributed to the northern republic's prosperity. An idealized view of Protestant values magnified their virtues, even among those formally attracted to Catholic beliefs and culture. Protestant acceptance of a mythical Juarezian purity complemented the needs of the lower classes and allowed them to pose as a depository of true Mexican values. They preached civic virtue amid the corrupted sea of Porfirian liberalism, including its accommodation with Catholicism. Perhaps an even more powerful source of Protestant influence stemmed from their approach to the class structure in general. Most Protestant pastors and teachers came from the lower middle class and tended to identify downward, viewing elite values as inherently suspect. The strong element of respect for the lower classes inherent in Protestant conversion efforts constituted an indictment of a hierarchical and an elitist society.[10]

Those buffeted by change also turned to cult beliefs to rally themselves. Folk cults divorced from society's formal structures became attractive as a last resort. Investing broad powers of social and economic salvation in an alleged supernatural cult figure challenged the claim of the governing structure as well as the Catholic Church to be the focal point of legitimate political and spiritual authority. Believers, in effect, created a rival higher authority and acted upon its presumed legitimacy. For example, the cult of Santa Teresa of Cabora constituted both a political and spiritual creation. Born into a ranchero family in Ocoromí, Sinaloa, Teresa Urrea moved to Cabora, Sonora, as a child. At the age of twelve she began to suffer epilepticlike attacks.

During one such incident, she appeared to be dead, only to suddenly and inexplicably come back to life. Witnesses believed that a miracle had taken place. Indeed the girl's voice, hand movements, and eyes seemed to radiate a special unearthly quality. A strange calm fell over those who came into her presence. News quickly spread that Teresa could perform miracles. A stream of the sick, lame, and troubled appeared at her door. Her father, don Tomás, originally among the scoffers, soon became a prosperous believer, supplying the multitude with food and refreshments. Devotees spread her fame throughout the borderlands and also carried home a little of the sacred soil of Cabora mixed with oil to prolong the benefits of their visit to Santa Teresa de Cabora.

Santa Teresa mingled politics, healing, and spiritual beliefs. She declared that "all the actions of the government and the clergy were evil." The inhabitants of Tomochic, reeling under the negative impact of commercialization, adopted Santa Teresa as their patroness. The rallying cry of their uprising was "Long live the Saint of Cabora—long live Saint Mary of Tomochic—long live liberty!"

Cult fanaticism created martyrs who fought to the bitter end, including two teenage boys who between them killed twenty-one soldiers. It required three days to bury all the dead. A similar outbreak of reactionary violence that drew upon the cult for legitimacy occurred in Temosachic. Believers attempted to seize customhouses on the border in order to buy weapons. Fifty armed men evoking Santa Teresa de Cabora attacked Palomas just across the international border from Deming, New Mexico. Santa Teresa, justifiably concerned that an alarmed government might take steps against her, moved to El Paso, Texas. Subsequently, she applied to become a naturalized American citizen. Her influence gradually faded and she died in Clifton, Arizona, in early 1906 at the same age as Christ at his crucifixion.[11]

Political radicalism also provided an alternative belief structure. A conscious, analytical protoradicalism attracted some elements of the lower classes in alliance with urban professionals. Anarchism arrived in Mexico as early as 1861 with the publication of the *Cartilla Socialista* by Plotino Rhodakanaty. Its immediate impact appears to have been minor, although the potential was evident in the political uprising of Chávez Lopez, discussed previously. In the 1870s, followers of Rhodakanaty took up the idea of anarchist Prince Peter Kropotkin. In Puebla, Manuel Serdán, father of Aquiles Serdán, who played an important role in the state of Puebla during the opening phase of the Mexican Revolution, participated in a number of anarchist-inspired revolts. His unexplained disappearance ended his activities. In Mexico City, anarchist workers established the Casa del Obrero Mundial in the early stage of the Mexican Revolution. Nevertheless, anarchism's potential contribution to the direction of the 1910 Revolution would not be realized, due in large part to tactical errors by its proponents.[12]

The American union movement, with its limited but well-defined working class goals, also influenced Mexican labor. Railways provided both a material and psychological link—an unintended and, as far as many were concerned, undesirable consequence of market ties with the United States. American railway unions helped organize Mexican workers in Nuevo Laredo in 1887, in Monterrey and Puebla the following year, and in Aguascalientes and Mexico City in 1900. As early as 1884, the Brotherhood of Locomotive Engineers founded a Mexican local, soon followed by the Order of Railway Conductors and the Brotherhood of Locomotive Firemen and Engineermen. American union locals initially excluded Mexicans, yet they provided organizational examples and eventually opened membership to all workers. Organized along craft lines, they constituted a conservative influence on the workers' movement.[13]

Unintended support for Mexican workers came from American industrialists, manufacturers, and organized labor, who believed low wages in Mexico threatened profitability and, from labor's standpoint, would undermine the wage structure in the United States. Fear of cheap imports brought organized labor and capital into an alliance. High tariff demands, coupled with well-publicized verbal attacks on low paid Mexican labor, had the same self-interested protective objectives in mind. Congress and the political system had to respond to such pressure. Congressman (later senator) Thomas H. Carter of Montana argued for a tariff against lead-content ores, citing as justification the "pauper" labor of Mexico that worked as virtual slaves. American citizens, their wages and working conditions, allegedly needed to be protected. Ironically, the high tariff of 1890 resulted in the building of Mexican smelters, along with the movement of more jobs south of the border. American Federation of Labor (AFL) leader Samuel Gompers subsequently and understandably came to view the international line as a device useful for capital that could only be countered by an internationalization of labor.[14] Meanwhile, Porfirian workers, aware of the negative characterization of Mexican working conditions in the American press, drew upon that view to rally more support for a reasonable share of the fruits of development.

A more radical American influence came from the Western Federation of Miners (WFM), which established a strong presence in the copper town of Cananea, Sonora, and organized Mexican miners in Colorado and Arizona. The WFM paved the way for the even more aggressively radical Industrial Workers of the World (IWW). The IWW aimed at one big union, encompassing skilled, unskilled, urban, and agricultural labor on a worldwide basis. Mexican and foreign employers feared the penetration of the IWW, particularly because of its appeal to unskilled and exploited agricultural workers. An IWW presence in the newly developed oil fields also caused considerable alarm. Both the WFM and the IWW, and to a lesser extent craft unions, adopted a non-nationalistic class orientation, worrisome to Mexican employers.

TRANSNATIONAL MOVEMENT: THE FLIGHT TO PROSPERITY

The development of a transnational labor force made possible by the railway system allowed workers to move back and forth depending on demand. As a consequence, concentrations of Mexican laborers were scattered throughout the Southwest. Some 70 percent of railway track crews in the American Southwest were Mexicans. Movement across the border in both directions appeared so natural and customary that records capture only part of the story. American rail companies in a six month period brought in 16,471 workers from Mexico. In 1908, the Southern Pacific and the Atchison Topeka and Santa Fe each recruited 1,000 Mexican track hands a month. As a result of the rail network connecting mining and commercial agricultural regions with northern manufacturing areas in the United States, a Mexican presence became evident in various rail centers such as El Paso, Laredo, San Antonio, Albuquerque, and as far north as Chicago, which today has one of the largest Mexican-American populations in the United States.

In Arizona, the copper camps northward to Prescott and Jerome attracted a substantial number of Mexican workers. Naco, Arizona, had a population of 2,010 Mexicans in 1908. Los Angeles and San Francisco depended upon a growing workforce from Mexico, as did the important agribusiness in newly irrigated regions. So many workers moved northward that Roberto Gayol, an engineer and avid proponent of state-sponsored irrigation projects, warned the government that the country risked losing its best agricultural workers who were drawn into the recently reclaimed and irrigated lands of California and the Southwest by job availability and higher wages. Newspapers in Monterrey complained of an exodus of labor from Mexico. The Porfiriato witnessed the merging in both an economic and a social sense of a modernizing Mexico and a developing American Southwest that blurred the actual importance of the international boundary for both labor and capital.[15] Movement back and forth across the border inevitably broadened the perspective of such workers. The obvious organizational progress of American laborers, especially railway and mine unions, that made them into an economic and political force impressed Mexican workers.

Figure 6.2 A funeral in Jerome, Arizona, around the 1890s, with Mexican miners lined up to pay their last respects. *Courtesy of Jerome State Historical Park.*

MODERNIZATION FALTERS

In spite of the evidence of working class radicalism and the change of attitudes toward the moral legitimacy of the government, prosperity and economic expansion kept the opposition in check. A disillusioning break in what had seemed like a brilliant and unstoppable movement toward modernization came with the economic downturn that dragged on from 1906 to 1908. Mexico, dependent on foreign markets, now suffered the consequences. The collapse of the silver market led to unsettling price fluctuations, inflation, a growing national debt, and budgetary shortfalls. The peso's value in relation to the dollar continued to slide. A worldwide financial panic in 1907 forced banks to call in loans and tighten credit. Copper prices fell to ruinous levels, and by the fall of 1907 unemployed miners in the states of Oaxaca, Hidalgo, Durango, Sonora, and Chihuahua roamed the streets in desperation. Thousands of laborers who had crossed into the United States to seek work returned to Mexico. All levels of Mexican society, from the unskilled day laborers to miners, merchants, farmers, entrepreneurs and the wealthy, felt the impact. The "Porfirian persuasion" had been shaken badly. While not necessarily ready to back a revolution, many believed a change might be beneficial. Díaz's advancing age also encouraged speculation about the future and the need for change. Díaz himself persuaded many to believe that a political change might be in the offing. In a 1908 interview with American journalist James Creelman, he expressed a desire to retire and his conviction that the Mexican people had matured to the point that a strongman might not be necessary. He ended the interview with a statement that he would welcome an opposition party. Creelman, confronted as well as enthralled with what he believed to be power, seemed almost hypnotized by Díaz. Subsequently, he wrote a glowing biography of the president. In the last chapter of his book titled *Will the Republic Stand?* he predicted that Ramón Corral would be the next president. Creelman did not understand the essential fragility of the Porfirian regime, choosing to see Díaz as the strongman of Mexico, or to use his term, "Master of Mexico."[16]

In the midst of political uncertainty, economic rationalization as defined by the elite continued. New legislation in the states of Morelos and Chihuahua sought to complete the transfer of community land that had escaped the laws of 1883 and 1894 into private hands. Chihuahua's Municipal Land Law of 1905 attacked the *fundo legal*, land set aside as far back as the colonial period for house lots and the town itself. Over the years much of the land had been divided into plots or rented to local *rancheros* and *medieros*. Enrique Creel, then governor of Chihuahua, explained the purpose of the law as another move to promote the creation of small landholdings by forcing the sale of municipal land. Private ownership and legal titles also would protect property from large landholders who might be tempted to incorporate municipal holdings. Proceeds could then be used for public improvements designed to integrate further these towns and villages into the broader regional economy. Consistent with one of the main tenets of Mexican liberalism, which sought to direct assets into the hands of those who would make best use of them, the state set the price of municipal land at such a level that only those with substantial assets could contemplate purchase. Many individuals who had farmed or built houses within the fundo legal had to pay to legalize title or lose possession.

The downward mobility that many rancheros had feared became a reality, as municipal land disappeared into private hands. While Galeana and Casas Grandes experienced widespread dispossession, Janos and San Buenaventura obstructed the law's implementation as much as possible. A small farmer, Porfirio Talamantes, who subsequently became a Villista revolutionary, organized resistance in Janos and went to Mexico City in a vain attempt to have the law annulled or changed. Nevertheless, by the end of 1908, land transfers began. Accused of revolutionary activity in support of the Los Angeles–based

Partido Liberal Mexicano (PLM), Talamantes fled across the border into the United States. The loss of access to land forced many to become salaried laborers on land owned by more fortunate Mexicans as well as by foreigners. Antiforeign hostility focused on Mormons who recently had purchased extensive properties in Chihuahua. The stark economic order of haves and have-nots, made even more glaring by the attack on municipal land, caused many to drift into violence and armed resistance under the loose direction and banner of the PLM.[17]

OPPOSITION FROM WITHIN

While the lower classes thrashed around for a means to alter their circumstances, opposition to positivism, though not necessarily its order and progress thrust, became evident among the professional class and some members of the elite. Krausism, the most important antipositivist philosophy, became popular in law schools. Among the elite, Francisco I. Madero became a notable devotee of the philosophy of Karl Christian Friedrick Krause (1781–1832), a contemporary of Auguste Comte. Krausism viewed society as a spiritual organism in which the state had the obligation to translate ethical, spiritual, and humanistic values into practice. Spiritual freedom would emerge from

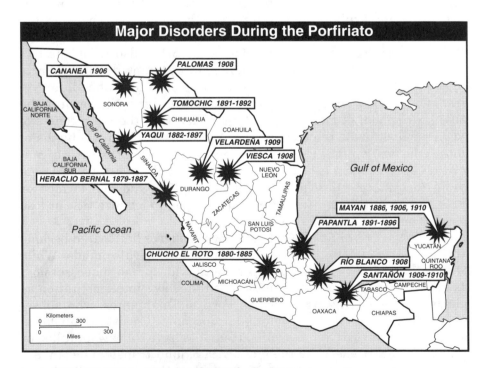

Figure 6.3 Major Disorders during the Porfiriato

the defeat of materialism. Like positivism, Krausism aimed at a transformation of society, but with a redemptive moral aspect.[18]

Attempts to modify the more objectionable aspects of the regime and to construct a new national political consensus resulted in several influential books. Andrés Molina Enríquez, a Yucatecan positivist, in *Problemas nacionales*, warned that if the country's problems remained unattended leadership would fall to radicals and anarchists. He defended the notion of private property as espoused by Mexican liberalism, but argued that ownership of property did not convey the right to treat workers as objects. In essence he believed that Mexico had not yet achieved a total separation between property rights and those of labor, thus the country suffered from a lingering feudal residue that had to be shaken off if Mexico hoped to enter the ranks of the more advanced nations.[19] Wistano Luis Orozco, in a similar fashion, connected property with the country's apparent social malaise. He criticized the concentration of land that he believed had created a degraded lower class. Orozco urged the government to purchase and break up haciendas, as well as change its land policies and the laws that favored unhealthy accumulation of agricultural land. He reflected some of the class concerns of his modest family background and his own uncertain middle-class status. His father worked as a mule driver, and he managed, with unknown difficulties, to earn a law degree in 1884. While he became involved in Jalisco state politics, Wistano Luis Orozco's historical importance rests upon being one of the first to assert that the Porfiriato's policies had created a serious agrarian problem.[20] Francisco I. Madero also put pressure on Díaz in the much-read book titled *La sucesión presidencial en 1910*. Madero believed the immediate problem was a question of a political structure that had outlived its usefulness and now needed to be reformed. His ideas appealed to those interested in preserving the social structure more or less intact while addressing the rigidity of the political system. Madero's philosophical notions, while not examined closely, were viewed as a generalized indication of his personal benevolence and kindness.[21]

Madero credited Díaz with bridging the "profound hatreds that had divided Mexicans" and putting into place a system that had given the country thirty years of peace. He also asserted that the process, while contrived at first, had now taken root in the national consciousness. Mexico no longer needed Díaz or an individual cut from the same cloth. Democracy to Madero meant elite camarilla politics, but without a permanent coordinator symbol at the top. A political rather than a social democrat, Madero believed that socioeconomic adjustments could be made within a reformed Porfirian process and system. Besides Madero's group, a number of different factions came up with candidates; however, in the end, President Díaz agreed to stay on for yet another term. An economic recovery, beginning in mining, favored Díaz. The presidential election of 1910 seemed a mere formality—in any event, the required votes could be arranged. The only serious opposition came from Madero and his Anti-Reelectionist party. Madero personally seemed an unlikely candidate for president.

The Madero family, in spite of Díaz's personal antipathy toward the clan, shared political power with other Coahuila camarillas in the standard fashion. José Limantour, a close friend of the family, assisted when possible. Immensely wealthy, they profited from Porfirian expansion. Francisco Madero, as a member of an elite family, went abroad to acquire a little polish. He attended St. Mary's College in Maryland, then went on to Paris and finally to the University of California, Berkeley. At St. Mary's, his youthful desire to become a Jesuit faded. The following year Panchito and his brother Gustavo sailed for Europe. Madero remained in Europe for five years (1887–1892), attending the School of Advanced Commercial Studies in Paris where he studied manufacturing, marketing, cost-price accounting, finance, commercial law, and other business-related subjects. In Paris he developed an interest in spiritualism and Oriental religions. The Hindu Bhagavad Gita (The Song of Heaven) deeply impressed the young student, who resolved to be useful to humanity in harmony with the divine plan. In 1889, virtually the entire family went to France to join the boys in discovering the delights of the Continent. Two years later, Panchito, his mother, and other family members toured Europe from France to Poland. Returning home, the boys soon went off again to the University of California, Berkeley, while two sisters attended a California convent school. At Berkeley, Madero studied agricultural techniques for the academic year then toured the state, including a visit to Yosemite National Park. He returned to Mexico with a fund of practical business and agricultural knowledge. He began his managerial apprenticeship with the family's agribusiness holdings and from all accounts established a reputation as a modern, progressive hacendado.

In 1903, Madero married a Mexican woman from an appropriate elite background. The wedding, with the archbishop of Mexico officiating, left no doubt that he came from a gilded family. About this time his interest in spiritualism became more passionate. He also began to study homeopathic medicine, experimenting with homemade remedies. In the gloom of the night at the bedside of an ill patient, Madero's hand fell under the power of the spirit world. He believed that he had made contact with the great minds of the past—a comforting thought and perhaps even useful for an aspiring politician. Madero subscribed to the notion that Mexican history went through long periods of quiet followed by a sharp adjustment. He suggested that after the calm of the Porfiriato the country hovered on the verge of just such an adjustment. Madero proposed to lead the country through the process into a new era. He believed that much depended on the restoration of the spirit and purity of the liberal Constitution of 1857. Influenced by Krausism, Madero believed that law could bring about ethical and spiritual change, while the economic factor represented only materialism. In a society where the distribution of wealth had gotten so out of reasonable social balance, Madero's concentration on politics denied reality.

Madero viewed spiritualism as a personal resource to be drawn upon for guidance as well as affirmation. In 1906, he attended the First National Spiritist Congress in Mexico City as an official delegate. Francisco Madero's romantic determination to serve humanity, coupled with more than sufficient financial resources, made him a backer of many charitable causes, including the political quest of Ricardo Flores Magón, discussed next. In many respects, he seemed ill suited for a political role. He was short of stature—his mother blamed his height on her maternal inexperience—and his voice became shrill when he became excited. Madero's interest in spiritualism and homeopathic medicine, viewed by many as offbeat notions, provided a source of amusement for the more skeptical. Porfirio Díaz failed to see the threat, ignoring contributing circumstances that would make future events wildly unpredictable.[22]

THE RADICAL OPPOSITION

In contrast to Francisco Madero's conservatism was the radicalism of Ricardo Flores Magón. Flores Magón symbolized in an intensely personal fashion the angry despair and frustration of the excluded classes. Those who struggled ineffectively with the results of what appeared to be a relentless process of modernization found in Flores Magón an eloquent, vitriolic spokesman. As one of the first individuals to take full political advantage of the new transnational social and economic environment, he now occupies a revered place in Mexico's revolutionary mythology; he also played a significant role in the radical movement in the United States. Flores Magón started his political career as a Mexican student agitator and ended it in 1922 in Leavenworth Federal Penitentiary as a transnational revolutionary under the concerned gaze of both the Mexican and American governments.

Flores Magón, a native of the state that produced the two major figures of nineteenth-century Mexican politics—Benito Juárez and Porfirio Díaz—reacted against Mexican liberalism and its harsh disregard for the less favored classes. His father, Lieutenant Colonel

Teodoro Flores, had fought with Juárez during the reform period, as well as against the French intervention, and subsequently rallied to Díaz's Anti-Reelectionist Plan of Tuxtepec in 1876. The provincialism that characterized Oaxaca and the simple life of its rural inhabitants formed Flores Magón's initial view of the world. Subsequently educated in Mexico City in spite of limited family resources, he never completed legal training, but in the process of acquiring an education discovered the force of polemic journalism.

In 1892 he joined demonstrations by students angered by Díaz's reelection. As a member of the Centro Anti-Reeleccionista, a student political organization, Flores Magón helped organize a short-lived antigovernment paper, *El Democrática*. He also understood the risks involved in anti-Díaz agitation and went into hiding after the paper fell victim to the government's policies. In August 1900, Flores Magón, along with others, founded the newspaper *Regeneración*, which attacked all aspects of the Porfirian regime. On January 1, 1901, Flores Magón attended the liberal congress in San Luis Potosí, held in response to Camilo Arriaga's manifesto, calling for respect for the liberalism of Benito Juárez and the neglected Constitution of 1857. Flores Magón and the romantic liberals functioned on different philosophical levels. While the attendees at the congress identified a political dictatorship, a situation that could be remedied by the restitution of an effective constitution, Flores Magón defined the dictatorship as one of class that required a revolution to smash the existing structure. Flores Magón's ideas had not yet solidified, but the move toward anarchism appeared obvious. His increasingly pointed radicalism separated him from the conservative opposition to the government, stripping him of any protection. As a consequence, he suffered repeated arrests and imprisonment as the regime sought the total suppression of Flores Magón's scathing journalism. He stepped out of Mexico City's Belén prison in October 1903, aware that he faced death if he persisted in attacking the regime. He went into exile in the United States. By the time Ricardo Flores Magón crossed the frontier into the United States, the formerly naive student protestor had become revolutionary.

From the American side of the border, Flores Magón reassessed his strategy. Aware that his radicalism frightened many, he decided to pursue more moderate objectives publicly while slowly moving toward more radical action. Francisco Madero, reassured, continued to offer some financial support, as did other traditional liberals. To provide a suitable structure, Ricardo, his brother Enrique, and a small band of fellow exiles announced the formation of the Junta Organizadora del Partido Liberal Mexicano (PLM) in St. Louis, Missouri, in 1905. Through their reestablished newspaper, *Regeneración*, they intended to encourage resistance to the Mexican government, first in the trans-border region and subsequently throughout the country. As a tactical move, the PLM issued a liberal manifesto in 1906 setting forth their goals, beginning with the reestablishment of the four-year presidential term and no immediate reelection. Reformist rather than revolutionary, the document advocated a minimum wage, the end of child labor, and the eight-hour workday. Privately, as an anarchist, Flores Magón envisioned a much more radical future for Mexico than timid reforms or restoration of the mythical liberalism of Benito Juárez.[23]

Flores Magón and the PLM influenced a generation of eclectic radicals and moderate reformers, including Emiliano Zapata and Felipe Carrillo Puerto. Alienated by the social and economic impact of Porfirian modernization, such individuals sought an ideological explanation and a plan of action. The PLM provided an introduction to radical alternatives from which they developed their own often unique revolutionary perspective. Like Flores Magón, such individuals had often experienced personally the negative weight of unbalanced economic progress. Carrillo Puerto, a mestizo born in Motul, Yucatán, in 1874, felt the impact of Yucatán's monocultural henequen industry, reacted with bitterness, then moved into action. The largely self-educated son of a small grocer, he began his independent existence as a minor landholder (*ranchero*) in the neighboring town of Uci. A largely Mayan town, Uci absorbed him into its Indian culture. He not only learned their language, but also understood them on a deep emotional level and sympathized with their problems. His Mayan friends called him Yaax Ich (green eyes). The relentless expansion of the henequen zone drove out small landholders, including Carrillo Puerto. He drifted into various salaried jobs, even working in New Orleans as a stevedore, yet he never forgot the suffering imposed on Yucatecan workers by the demands of henequen cultivation. He himself had been whipped by an outraged *hacendado* when he tried to help terrorized and abused Mayan workers. In 1906 he attempted unsuccessfully to establish a radical newspaper. Eventually he joined Zapata and served as the Zapatista agrarian commissioner in Cuautla (Morelos) along with Fidel Velázquez, then a seventeen-year-old student and subsequently the general secretary of the Mexican Workers Confederation (CTM). In the end, Carrillo Puerto became a socialist and a major actor in revolutionary Yucatán.[24]

MEXICO IN 1910: THE REALITY

Madero, Flores Magón, Carrillo Puerto, and others destined to play a role in the last days of the Porfiriato or in post–Porfirian Mexico emerged from the successes and failures of the regime itself.

Modernization and economic development created economic contradictions and social stresses; produced wealth; exacerbated class divisions; opened the way to social mobility; laid the basis of the modern middle class; led to the exploitation of workers, peasants, and Indians, along with the country's other resources; and demonstrated the possibilities of a grand and prosperous future. The republic under Díaz assured the territorial integrity of the nation, incorporated the north in both a psychological and political sense, and ended the fear of annexation by the United States. Mexican development and political stability became an object of international admiration, stimulating a sense of national pride. The positive international perception obscured the fact that the country did not have the resources to adequately fund education, public health, and other vital infrastructure investments. Most of the population could not read or write. In 1910 the illiteracy rate of 84 percent constituted a major national problem with negative social, economic, and political implications.[25] The highly publicized budget surpluses so admired by European and Wall Street bankers represented a propaganda expenditure, not an actual surplus, beyond the country's urgent needs. Deterioration of the standard of living of those at the bottom, as peasants became workers, seemed a regrettable but temporary imbalance that would be righted at some future point. That point constantly moved into the future as hope dimmed for most of the population. Railroads broke down regionalism and forged the modern Mexican and stimulated migration from the south and south-center to the north and the west in pursuit of economic betterment or survival, destroying the population's historical roots in the process.

Commercialization reduced all assets to commodities capable of becoming the foundation of individual and hence national wealth. The quick-witted and nimble left those unable to grasp the new reality far behind and resentful. Entire communities believed they had been sacrificed on the altar of change. Mexico's glittering industrial progress, without which it could not claim to be a modern nation, rested on a controlled market that forced consumers to subsidize national pride. The slightly more than a quarter century between 1880 and 1911 transformed the nation at such a pace that both progress and its problems could not be dealt with in an effective fashion. A breathless elite, pleased and shocked at the same time by headlong development, lost control and, in the end, legitimacy.

The most serious problem was the failure to match economic with political modernization. The elite fearfully clung to political stability and thus could not make timely and necessary adjustments. Unwillingness to move beyond the camarilla politics that had succeeded in reducing political violence to acceptable levels was understandable. Inaction could be justified by the vague notion of some sort of political

Figure 6.4 Night illumination of the cathedral in Mexico City during the centennial celebration in September 1910. Note the lavish use of electricity to symbolize technological progress. It subtly includes the Church in an important civic and political event. *Printed with permission, Photography Collection, Harry Ransom, Humanities Research Center, University of Texas at Austin.*

evolution—when the country appeared ready. Meanwhile, the need to debate national problems, including distribution of wealth and food resources, access to education, and political power itself, would not be addressed. Romero Rubio, Justo Sierra, Francisco Bulnes, Enrique Molinas, and others repeatedly warned of the dangers while still hoping for the "political evolution of the Mexican people." They feared that, in the words of Justo Sierra, "the political evolution of Mexico [had] been sacrificed to other aspects of [Mexico's] social evolution."[26] A complex society had emerged with new interest groups and organizations. As many were aware, the glittering coin of progress had two sides. Positives and negatives stemmed from the same source and only a responsive political structure could smooth over the inevitable social contradictions and make the continuous adjustments modern society demanded. In the end, the Porfiriato failed to keep up with change. All the Maderos, Flores Magóns, and Carrillo Puertos could not and did not destroy the Porfiriato; they represented only the symptoms of a self-inflicted malaise that eventually became fatal.

MEXICO IN 1910: THE FANTASY

Planning for the centennial celebration to mark Mexico's first hundred years as an independent nation began well in advance. A national commission designated on April 1, 1907, over three years before the event, planned and coordinated activities. In addition, each state had its own commission, as did every municipality in the republic. The Porfirian regime hoped to use the event and the positive publicity it would generate to accelerate Mexico's development. Carefully orchestrated, the occasion would be used to impress the outside world with the country's stability, progress, and even brighter future. Attracting ever-increasing investment capital to fuel industrial and agribusiness expansion had become even more important as a result of the Dublán Convention that mortgaged the nation's future. With the international press on the scene as well as world opinion leaders in attendance, the opportunity could not be missed. Skillfully managed, the investment climate might well be shaped in a favorable manner for at least the next decade.

Public construction projects timed to be completed or inaugurated in sequence starting on September 1, 1910, created the illusion that the entire country had moved into a new exciting stage of development that few foreign investors could afford to ignore. Perhaps as an unintended omen, one of the first ceremonies involved the official opening of the lunatic asylum in Mixcoac, presided over by the president surrounded by foreign representatives and high government officials. Pomp and ceremony also helped restore confidence among Mexican agriculturalists and industrialists that the best was yet to come. Recent economic hard times supposedly could be forgotten as the nation moved into the radiant future. While Mexico City received the bulk of these construction projects, every region and state would be involved. Many projects would have been initiated anyway, but would be made part of the centennial to maximize the public relations impact. From a modest fountain in Santa María del Oro (Territory of Tepic), a water pipe in Tonalá (Jalisco), a canal in Ciudad Ocampo (Tamaulipas), to a more impressive palacio municipal in Córdoba (Veracruz) and innumerable other local and regional construction projects, the face of Mexico appeared to be changing rapidly for the better. New streets, bridges, civic monuments, markets, and bandstands popped up throughout the republic.

In Mexico City an elaborate parade presented Mexican history and culture as a seamless movement through time from pre-Columbian societies into the present. The message could not be clearer—history linked all citizens together, regardless of race or class. Aztec nobles, warriors, Indian priests, Spanish friars, Fernando

Cortés, Pedro de Alvarado, and their captains marched down the street as if passing once again through history. Colonial officials with the royal standard of the city of Mexico, along with Agustín de Iturbide and units of his Army of Three Guarantees, moved to the stirring music of costumed bands—all were now sons of Hidalgo. To honor contemporary progress a civic procession composed of bureaucrats and business and professional associations walked through the streets in their suits and hats, indistinguishable from their counterparts in Paris, London, or New York. Photographs captured every movement, providing abundant material for a flood of commemorative editions. Critics referred to President Díaz as Porfiriopóchtli, a historical reference to the Aztec god Huitzilopóchtli's insatiable appetite for human sacrifice.[27] Don Porfirio, as the symbol of the country's progress, basked in international esteem. Scottish American steel magnate Andrew Carnegie, himself an icon of the new industrial age, praised the Mexican president's wisdom and steadfast character and held him up as an individual worthy of hero worship. Theodore Roosevelt, overcoming his own colossal ego, insisted that Díaz had done more for his country than any other individual and, moreover, was the greatest living statesman. Others compared him with George Washington, Abraham Lincoln, Robert E. Lee, Peter the Great, Frederick the Great, Otto von Bismarck, and Hannibal, among others. Such extravagant and fulsome praise temporarily banished all nagging fears of what might happen after Díaz.[28] Important nations dispatched representatives, and foreign journalists, with all expenses paid by the Mexican government, enjoyed deluxe tours, fine food, and the best wines in exchange for reporting the country's amazing progress to their eager and credulous readers around the world. Carefully selected groups of ladies and gentlemen met the special trains arriving with foreign delegates and conveyed them to luxurious lodgings, often in the homes of important officials. Fresh flowers, automobiles, carriages, and servants made their stay a delightful one.[29]

Spain returned the dress uniform of José María Morelos, one of the major independence figures, who had been executed by the royalists. Díaz himself received the prestigious Order of Carlos III. France, not to be outdone, sent back the silver key to the City of Mexico, acquired during their own Mexican interlude.[30] The high point arrived with the grand ball held in the central patio of the former viceregal palace, now the national palace. Thousands of electric bulbs, a radiant symbol of the new technology, lit the steps of the dancing celebrants. Brilliant arches of flowers highlighted the new red carpeting laid throughout the palace. Tables laden with red snapper from Veracruz, succulent oysters from Guaymas, shrimp from Campeche, turkey, and, most appropriately, roast suckling pig, awaited those weakened by the excitement. Liveried waiters poured French champagne into sparkling crystal goblets. Twenty carloads of imported champagne assured an endless supply. One hundred and fifty musicians played the most fashionable waltzes atop a flower-bedecked platform. As the clock struck ten, President Porfirio Díaz entered with the wife of the Italian ambassador on his arm followed by Señora Díaz and the special ambassador from the United States, Curtis Guild. The revelry went on until dawn. An overwrought journalist breathlessly exclaimed that it appeared to be a fairy tale—it was and would soon vanish amid revolutionary violence.[31]

NOTES

1. Anderson, *Outcasts in Their Own Land*, p. 167; Vanderwood, *Disorder and Progress*, p. 147.
2. For an assessment of the rurales, see Paul J. Vanderwood, *Los rurales mexicanos* (México: Fondo de Cultura Económica, 1982) and by the same author, *Disorder and Progress*. For the army, see Alexius, "The Army and Politics."
3. Schmidt, "Social and Economic Effects of the Railroad," p. 269.
4. Cosío Villegas, *Historia moderna*, vol. 7, pt. 1, pp. 8–68.
5. Clifton B. Kroeber, *Man, Land and Water: Mexico's Farm Lands Irrigation Policies, 1885–1911* (Berkeley: University of California Press, 1983), p. 182.
6. Pletcher, *Rails, Mines and Progress*, p. 20; Cosío Villegas, *Historia moderna*, vol. 7, pt. 1, p. 19.
7. González Navarro, *Estadísticas sociales*, pp. 218–19.
8. González Navarro, *La pobreza en México* (México: El Colegio de Mexico, 1985), pp. 137–54; Robert Buffington, "Revolutionary Reform: The Mexican Revolution and the Discourse in Prison Reform," *Mexican Studies/Estudios Mexicanos* (winter 1993), pp. 71–93.
9. Cuauhtémoc Camarena Ocampo, "Las luchas de los trabajadores textiles mexicanos: 1865–1907" (Escuela Nacional de Antropología e Historia, Tesis de Licenciatura, 1985), pp. 131–40; García Díaz, "La clase obrera textil," p. 89.
10. Jean-Pierre Bastian, *Los disidentes: Sociedades protestantes y revolución en México, 1872–1911* (México: Fondo de Cultura Económica, 1989), pp. 143–71; Deborah J. Baldwin, *Protestants and the Mexican Revolution: Missionaries, Ministers, and Social Change* (Urbana, University of Illinois Press, 1990), pp. 11–29.
11. Mario Gill, "Teresa Urrea, la santa de Cabora," *Historia Mexicana* (April-June 1957), pp. 626–44; Paul J. Vanderwood, "Santa Teresa: Mexico's Joan of Arc," in Ewell and Beezley, eds., *The Human Tradition*, pp. 215–32.
12. David G. LaFrance, *The Mexican Revolution in Puebla, 1908–1913: The Maderista Movement and the Failure of Liberal Reform* (Wilmington: SR Books, 1989), pp. 5–8.
13. John M. Hart, *Los anarquistas mexicanos, 1860–1900* (México: Secretaría de Educación Pública, 1974), p. 149; Lorena M. Parlee, "The Impact of the United States Railroad Unions on Organized Labor and Government Policy in Mexico (1880–1911)," *Hispanic American Historical Review* (August 1984), pp. 450, 453, 473; Richard U. Miller, "American Railroad Unions and the National Railways of Mexico: An Exercise in Nineteenth-Century Proletarian Manifest Destiny," *Labor History* (spring 1974), pp. 239–60.

14. *Romero, Mexico, and the United States*, p. 497; Samuel Gompers, "United States-Mexico-Labor-Their Relations," *American Federationist* (August 1916), p. 633; Gregg Andrews, *Shoulder to Shoulder: The American Federation of Labor, the United States, and the Mexican Revolution* (Berkeley: University of California Press, 1991), p. 190.

15. Kroeber, *Man, Land and Water*, p. 62; Saragoza, The Monterrey Elite, p. 90.

16. James Creelman, *Díaz, Master of Mexico* (New York: D. Appleton and Company, 1911), pp. 396, 414.

17. Hart, *Revolutionary Mexico*, pp. 94–95; Lloyd, "Ranchos and Rebellion," pp. 94–97; Vanderwood, *Disorder and Progress*, pp. 141–47.

18. William D. Raat, "Ideas and Society in Don Porfirio's Mexico," *The Americas* (July 1973), pp. 50–51, and by the same author, *El positivismo durante el Porfiriato* (México: Secretaría de Educación Pública, 1975), and "The Antipositivist Movement in Prerevolutionary Mexico, 1892–1911," *Journal of Interamerican Studies and World Affairs* (February 1977), pp. 83–98.

19. Abelardo Villegas, *México en horizonte liberal* (México: Universidad Nacional Autónoma de México, 1981), p. 94. Molina Enríquez's career spanned the late Porfiriato into post-revolutionary Mexico. He died in 1940, serving as a magistrate on the Superior Court of Justice in Toluca, state of Mexico. Moisés González Navarro, *Sociología y historia en México* (Mexico: Colegio de Mexico, 1970), pp. 40–52.

20. James L. Hamon and Stephen R. Niblo, *Precursores de la revolución agraria en México* (Mexico: Secretaría de Educación Pública, 1975), pp. 31–35.

21. Francisco I. Madero, *La sucesión presidencial en 1910* (Saltillo: Imprenta del Estado de Coahuila, 1958), pp. 296–314.

22. Stanley R. Ross, *Francisco I. Madero: Apostle of Mexican Democracy* (New York: Columbia University Press, 1955), pp. 3–19.

23. Colin M. MacLachlan, *Anarchism and the Mexican Revolution: The Political Trials of Ricardo Flores Magón in the United States* (Berkeley: University of California Press, 1991); Ward A. Albro, *Always a Rebel: Ricardo Flores Magón and the Mexican Revolution* (Fort Worth: Texas Christian University Press, 1992); Rosendo Salazar and José G. Escobedo, *Las pugnas de la gleba*, 1907–1922 (México: Comisión Nacional Editorial, 1953), p. 26; James D. Cockcroft, *Intellectual Precursors of the Mexican Revolution, 1900–1913* (Austin: University of Texas Press, 1968), pp. 91–97.

24. Joseph, *Revolution from Without*, pp. 191–92.

25. Vázquez de Knauth, *Nacionalismo y educación*, p. 93.

26. Justo Sierra, *Evolución política del pueblo mexicano* (México: Universidad Nacional Autonoma de México, 1977), p. 396.

27. *Memoria de los trabajos emprendidos y llevados a cabo por la Comisión N. del Centenario de la Independencia* (México, 1910); Jonathan Kandell, *La Capital: The Biography of Mexico City* (New York: Random House, 1988), pp. 396–97. Jesús Silva Herzog, *Una vida en la vida de México* (Mexico: Siglo Veintiuno Editores, 1972), relates the unreal aspects of the Europeanized celebration of modernity. Observer Frederick Starr, president of the University of Chicago, presented a more somber view in *Mexico and the United States; A Story of Revolution, Intervention, and War* (Chicago: Bible House, 1914).

28. American doubts about "the capacity of Mexico as a modern state" included concerns that after Díaz, order might collapse and the reverse worry that a strong Mexican state would encroach on Central America and threaten American interests in the region. See, for example, "A Diplomatist" (pseud.), *American Foreign Policy* (New York: Houghton Mifflin Co., 1909), p. 92.

29. María Robinson Wright, *Mexico: A History of Its Progress and Development in One Hundred Years* (Philadelphia: George Barrie & Sons, 1911), pp. 179–200.

30. *Recuerdo del primer centenario de la independencia* (México: Rondero y Treppiedi, 1910) provided photographs and emotional commentary.

31. *The New York Times*, 1910; *Picayune* (New Orleans), 1910.

Chapter 7

MAKING A REVOLUTION
The Borderlands Emerge
1905–1917

Borderlanders, inhabitants of a region already well defined by the latter half of the nineteenth century, especially the most populated strip from Ciudad Juárez–El Paso to Matamoros–Brownsville, began to shoulder their way into the national politics of both Mexico and the United States after the turn of the twentieth century. Statehood in 1912 for New Mexico and Arizona offered a means of political expression; revolution from 1910 to 1920 for Chihuahua, Coahuila, and Sonora brought presidential power and the chance to mold the rest of the nation in their image. Although the border remained a dividing line between nations, the borderlands comprised one zone for the people who lived there. Leaders in Mexico City and Washington looked on the region as a divided, desolate area; many residents, more often than not with family, friends, jobs, and political concerns that straddled the imaginary barrier, ignored the international division. As a natural consequence during the revolution, both sides of the Río Grande served as a zone for recruitment of rebels, provisioning of troops, refuge from national armies, and as a scene of significant battles.[1]

Until 1936 the revolution ushered in the national political domination of Mexicans from the border region. The political vitality of this region reflected the dramatic economic and demographic growth that had followed the arrival of the railroads and the subjugation of hostile Indians in the 1880s. This region, with the least integration of Indians into the dominant population, curiously reared men who ushered in the revolutionary era of Indian–mestizo politics. Looking for a

Making a Revolution: The Borderlands Emerge, 1905–1917

1910	Madero's presidential campaign against Díaz
	July: Madero placed under house arrest
	July–November: Anti-reelectionist junta organized revolution
	November 20: Outbreak of revolution
1911	May: Battle of Ciudad Juárez
	Rebel occupation of Torreón
	Porfirio Díaz resigns
	Emiliano Zapata's Plan of Ayala
1913	February: Tragic Ten Days
	Madero assassinated
1913–1914	Huerta dictatorship
	Constitutionalist and Zapatista rebellion
1914	Convention of Aguascalientes
	United States troops occupy Veracruz
	Treaty of Teoloyucan
1914–1915	Civil War between Constitutionalists and Conventionists
1915	January 6: National Agrarian Commission created

political banner, the soon-to-be victorious norteños championed *indigenismo* as a rejection of the Victorian eurocentrism of the Porfirian elites. The revolt fostered by these borderland leaders by 1917 had destroyed the central government, many state administrations, and most national institutions, including, ultimately, the federal army. Popular forces in countryside villages and local communities, as a consequence, recognized the opportunity provided by this political vacuum to make claims for agrarian, worker, and educational rights. They succeeded to the point that no Mexican national government can ever again ignore popular demands, and the character of the Mexican people will never again be the same.

SPUTTERING REBELLION, 1905–1909

What would become the tidal wave of northern politics that washed across the country began in the core of the country but soon moved to the borderlands. The efforts to provoke political fervor against the sclerotic presidency occupied the energy of three brothers, Ricardo, Enrique, and Jesús Flores Magón. Their newspaper campaign failed, at first because of the central government's suppression of newspaper critics, later because of the growing radicalism of the journalists that put off would-be supporters, and ultimately because the written word could affect few in a population in which eight or nine out of ten adults could not read. The sparks the Mexican Liberal Party (Partido Liberal Mexicano, PLM) made only smoldered, never catching fire, but the smoke—especially their demands for social reform—attracted other dissidents who succeeded with action where the printed words of the Flores Magón brothers could not.

Words, the magic conjured by newspaper writers, did not inspire the people to overthrow the president, regardless of how cleverly used and how precisely they outlined the abhorrent policies of Porfirio Díaz. Words led only to the closing of the newspaper, the jailing of the Flores Magón brothers, and the decision of Jesús to retire from radical politics and of Ricardo and Enrique to seek refuge across the northern border. Leaving their older sibling behind, the other two Flores Magón brothers moved briefly to San Antonio, Texas, but after an assassin hired by the Mexican government attacked their print shop and stabbed Enrique, who survived the assault, they fled to St. Louis, Missouri, in 1905.

Mexican opponents of the Porfirian regime gathered in St. Louis, where they organized an executive committee for their revolutionary movement, the Mexican Liberal Party, and proclaimed its 1906 Plan that expressed their vision of Mexico without the old praetorians, the Porfirian veterans of the French intervention. In the Plan, adherents expressed the sentiment that Mexicans, regardless of where they lived and what they did, including those in the greater Mexican neighborhood that stretched north of the border, were all part of a common community. The PLM called for the military overthrow of the Porfirian regime; in organizing their underground network, recruiting supporters, and arming their cadres, their base of operations shifted around, but remained for the most part within the greater borderlands zone. The Mexican government called on President William H. Taft to enforce United States neutrality laws against Mexicans trying to foment revolution from the haven of the United States and also called for the arrest and extradition of PLM members as common criminals wanted for a variety of trumped-up felonies in Mexico. The borderland community provided a haven for the PLM leaders who survived for several years, despite the aggressive pursuit of two national governments.

The PLM's transborder organization was hardly unique during these years. Entrepreneurs, workers, missionaries, and settlers paid little mind to the international boundary in their plans. Land speculators, lumber barons, oil wildcatters, and mine promoters all viewed the greater southwest and northern Mexico as their land of opportunity.[2] Job seekers and adventurers thought of the borderlands as a region of great opportunities. Railroad workers, miners, and lumbermen, managers and investors thought in regional, not national, terms of the U.S. southwest and the Mexican north. Unions such as the Western Federation of Miners and, more obviously, the Industrial Workers of the World, placed no boundaries on goals, recruitment, and membership. Protestant denominations and the Latter-day Saints (Mormons) in the 1880s began sending an increasing number of missionaries into the border region to proselytize a population that both religious groups believed ready to abandon its nominal Roman Catholic heritage.[3] Land developers, utopian visionaries, and schismatic church groups organized colonies to relocate to the borderlands. Restless energy, boundless optimism, and a ruthless sense of vigilante justice characterized the region—characteristics shared by Mexicans, Americans, and immigrants who moved into the area and breathed in these attitudes along with the thin, dry air.

MADERO'S AMBIGUOUS REVOLT

Francisco Madero, son of Coahuila and heir to old wealth, grew up in this atmosphere. The Madero family became disgruntled with competing against foreign enterprises favored by the Díaz government, especially in La Laguna's booming economy. Madero recognized the implications of economic contraction for Mexican-owned companies and sensed the end of a political era as Porfirio Díaz approached his eightieth birthday. Madero mused that Mexico after Díaz should be different. Open competition for political office, especially for the presidency, appeared to offer a method of change in administration and, through elected officials, economic and social practices as well. Madero's appeal for the restoration of the spirit of the 1857 Constitution spoke to the concerns of the elite and suggested that all Mexicans, that is, adult males, including those from the lower social groups, had a role, if only as voters, in shaping Mexico's future. His call appealed to the corporate sense of community characteristic of the north that had been forged from shared military duty based on the wars against the Indians and, above all, the heroic efforts against the French intervention.[4] His campaign paralleled the earlier efforts of such reform-minded governors as Emilio Rabasa of Chiapas, who, in the 1890s, wanted to establish a less personalistic regime and more democratic procedures without disrupting society or dismantling the economy.[5] Madero's nationalism had a redemptive quality that came from his commitment to popular liberalism and his acceptance of Krausian philosophical notions that rejected the social Darwinism of unregulated industrial and urban change. He preached evangelical, political democracy that did not extend beyond the ballot box.

Twisted together, his vaguely articulated sentiments became a steel cable of opposition to the Porfirian regime that pulled him further and further into a political campaign that challenged the aging president. At first, Madero flirted with the PLM, but rejected Ricardo Flores Magón's increasingly evident anarchistic goals and instead adopted a refurbished liberalism. Here he demonstrated, intuitively rather than consciously, a greater understanding of his countrymen than the Flores Magón brothers. He made a series of campaign trips to organize political clubs that sent delegates to a national convention. These political excursions allowed for face-to-face evaluation of Madero by those who could not read, but who could measure men and women by looking in their eyes, hearing their voices, and watching their demeanor when they appeared before an audience. As a member of an elite family, he had an air of authority and legitimacy that Flores Magón and Emiliano Zapata could not match. To those from the lower ranks who saw him and heard him speak, Madero became a trusted leader; to those from the distressed elite, he appeared as a leader drawn from the ranks of their camarilla, the traditional political network of patrons and clients.

Many opponents of President Díaz throughout Mexico and the southwest swung to Madero, especially after seeing and hearing him. His audiences recognized his sincere opposition to Díaz and saw him as a possible successor. As Madero put together his political organization, he surrounded himself first with men who, like himself, were from the border. The organization quickly grew to include dissatisfied younger men from across educational, occupational, geographical, and class lines, who found an opportunity in his movement to express their opposition. The organization soon suggested a national movement, rather than simply a regional development.

At first Díaz dismissed political challenges with little more than a wave of his hand. Although the old general had announced that he would welcome opposition parties in the 1910 election and that he had no intention of accepting reelection himself, he allowed his sycophants to persuade him to stand for a sixth term and decided to disrupt and then decapitate challenging political groups. Powerful opponents such as the Científicos around José Limantour and the followers of Bernardo Reyes collapsed as their meetings were broken up and their leaders were compelled to comply with the president's wishes. Reyes, for example, accepted a military assignment in Europe, making him ineligible under the residency requirements for the presidency. Díaz largely discounted Madero until the summer of 1910; then, suddenly aware that he represented more than a political caricature, he ordered his arrest.

MADERO CHOOSES INSURRECTION

Madero temporized in the early summer as he considered how to respond to Díaz, either by acquiescing or cutting a deal, abandoning political opposition and those with faith in his cause, or with contumacy, embracing violence and risking bloodshed. Madero chose rebellion.

He chose it, but in a haltering, half-hearted fashion, hoping to keep some options open. Díaz felt no need for accommodation and ordered Madero's incarceration. Under house arrest in San Luis Potosí, Madero had to make a clear unequivocal choice, one with which he would live and die; he decided to force Díaz's hand.

Madero escaped to San Antonio, Texas, and proclaimed his revolution. Unlike the Flores Magón brothers, natives of central Mexico who arrived in the United States for the first time when they fled Porfirian repressions and came without American friends or connections, Madero stepped down from the train in San Antonio, a town he knew as well as any city in Mexico. Here he banked with Franz Groos and Company and the Lockwood National Bank and shopped at businesses throughout town, particularly the Frost Brothers. His wife and her female acquaintances had accounts with the dressmakers at Joske Brothers, and his entire family placed its health in the hands of San Antonio doctors Ferdinand and Adolf Herff. Madero had long before become a part of the web of business, social, and political networks that stretched back to the time when his grandfather built the family fortune doing business with Texas Confederates in San Antonio. The Flores Magóns came to the United States as strangers and exiles in the borderlands; Madero was welcomed by social

Figure 7.1 Car crossing the Rio Grande to Mexico during the Revolution. *Printed with permission, Russell Lee Photograph Collection, Center for American History, University of Texas at Austin.*

acquaintances and business associates—other men and families of the border, who recognized him, his northern roots, and his cause.

For Mexicans throughout the borderlands, San Antonio, known as the Paris of the southwest, was the principal shopping and social center. The town comprised over thirty nationalities and ethnic groups, with Mexicans, Anglos, Germans, and blacks the largest representatives. San Antonio was one of only four cities in the United States in 1910 with a Mexican population of 5,000 or more. Its Mexican population had increased largely through immigration from 13,722 in 1900 (25.7 percent of the city's total) to 83,373 (30.5 percent of the city's total) in 1910, with most of these Mexicans crowded into the westside barrio. This neighborhood gave San Antonio the largest population of Mexican extraction in the United States until it was surpassed by Los Angeles in the 1930s.[6] Madero had left behind only the Mexican national state, not Mexican culture in its northern variation, nor the Mexican people.

Once settled, he established a revolutionary committee made up of his political allies, including a number of northerners. The exile committee began an ambitious campaign of raising money, recruiting fighting men, buying and smuggling arms, plotting an uprising in the central states, and planning an invasion of northern Mexico. The embryonic revolutionaries operated within a generally favorable climate in San Antonio where the local citizens and the newspapers supported them.

Abraham González assumed a prominent role, recruiting rebels in his native state of Chihuahua and smuggling arms and ammunition to them. From July to November 1910, the seemingly sun-drenched, placid society of the borderlands hid complex and contradictory crosscurrents. The rebels, still calling themselves Anti-Reelectionists, held clandestine meetings, raised money from countrymen on both sides of the line, recruited troops, and plotted strategy, while Mexican secret agents and private investigators in the hire of the Mexican administration followed every lead, staked out the homes of exiles, and called on the U.S. government for help. The United States relied on its consular officials along the border, military intelligence officers, Bureau of Investigation agents, postal inspectors, and well-intentioned informants. Everywhere, everyone bumped into one another and quickly looked the other way. The rebel committee faced enormous difficulties, including the efforts of Mexican government agents to eliminate them, U.S. and Texas government harassment, double loyalties, factionalism, intrigues, and, above all, inexperience.

Those in the circle around Madero differed from the PLM members who surrounded Flores Magón. United States secret service agent Joe Priest described the "many well-dressed" Anti-Reelectionist

Figure 7.2 A group of middle and upper class women supporters of Francisco I. Madero. It is unlikely that any of them intended to become involved in the armed phase of the Revolution. *Printed with permission, Photography Collection, Harry Ransom, Humanities Research Center, University of Texas at Austin.*

leaders who gathered at the Hutchins House, located on Main Street "among the Blue stockings of San Antonio."[7] A similar group of Anti-Reelectionists gathered in Arizona Territory. These men slipped easily into the community, with its large Hispanic population, because they knew the town well; they and their families often shopped there, and some sent their children to the new university. They met a sympathetic reception and shared a cordial camaraderie.[8]

In San Antonio, Madero's dapper council sent agents into Mexico with 5,000 copies of a proclamation, called the San Luis Potosí Plan, which set November 20, 1910, as the starting date of the revolution. The announcement also carried Madero's bland proposals for a new Mexico, which lamely ignored economic and social problems, emphasizing democratic politics and municipal autonomy as the keys to the appropriate reform of Porfirio's authoritarian manipulation. It sounded reasonable—and still does—but as a practical matter, rebel recruits wanted political power, not just elections; land and fair wages, not just laissez-faire economics; and social justice, not just well-meaning administrative paternalism. Madero made few promises to break. Echoes of Díaz's tactics in the Tuxtepec Plan could be heard in Madero's San Luis program.

Madero did not want to do anything that would lead to an uncontrollable general revolution. Beyond his own reserved nature, he knew that his organization could not afford the financial cost of a nationwide rebellion and that his backers feared such an insurrection would get out of hand, becoming a struggle for social and economic changes. Rather the organizers hoped that quick strikes in Pachuca, Puebla, and Mexico City, along with a general upheaval in the border region, would bring down the Porfirian regime. Madero, schooled in camarilla politics, did not forge a tightly knit coalition of revolutionaries, nor formulate a national scheme for revolution.[9]

His appeal aimed most clearly at Mexicans along the border. Calling for municipal autonomy (the *municipio libre*), he demonstrated his awareness of its importance in the north, while only dimly aware of its significance in the upland sections of the center, especially those sections peopled by rancheros. Madero knew the autonomous municipality served as the backbone of northern state camarilla politics in which local cliques ruled their own towns and bartered political loyalty to those above them in the hierarchy for economic preferment. This system began to break down in the 1890s, and especially after 1900.

Sonora offers an example. Here the triumvirate of Luis Torres, Ramón Corral, and Rafael Izábal began putting too much distance, measured in terms of authority and wealth, between itself and the other state notables. President Díaz, who earlier had followed Torres's suggestions of local candidates for congress, after 1890, began choosing presidential cronies who had no ties to Sonora. Moreover, the triumvirate after 1900 adopted its version of this policy, when it began to ignore family ties and impose its backers on the municipal governments, destroying local autonomy. The century-old camarilla of Sonora's notable families was disregarded and its members became embittered.

Moreover, the old camarilla politicians had felt some degree of paternalistic social responsibility expressed as concern for the popular classes—excluding Indians as beyond the boundary of civilization. Corral personified the values of the new successful Sonoran; he was intensely energetic and enterprising, and he had a deep antipathy toward the Indian peoples (resulting in deportation of Yaqui and Mayo peoples to Yucatán), based on the experience of the centuries of warfare. Along with these sentiments, Corral retained the old paternalistic sympathy of the older group of notables for the state's workers and campesinos, understanding that political discontent would result if some of the phenomenal profits did not trickle down to them. His departure to the national capital coincided with the final erosion of authority from Sonora's old notables and left the state in the hands of modernizers who lacked his sensitivity. After 1900 the state government shifted its expenditures away from public instruction and improvements to administration and law enforcement. This resulted in

the growing popular aversion to the regime that matched the vexa-
tions of the younger notables who wanted political power.[10]

In places like Sonora and Guerrero, dissatisfied and even desperate Mexicans found in Madero's appeal to arms the opportunity to
change their circumstances. The change they demanded varied
greatly from community to community. As the appointed day neared,
Madero, prepared to command the national government but not a revolution, headed for Mexico. He went, by way of Cotulla to Carrizo
Springs, Texas, with three others, expecting to meet his uncle
Catarino Benavides with 400 to 500 men on the bank of the Río
Grande near the outskirts of Ciudad Porfirio Díaz (now Piedras
Negras), Coahuila. His selection of Benavides demonstrated that family ties to Madero at times overcame sound judgment. His uncle was
widely known throughout Coahuila for his follies. In the most widely
repeated story, people recounted his claim to have invented a "flying
machine," whose wing size he determined using the proportions he derived by measuring the wings of hundreds of canaries that he kept in
his home. His reputation possibly hurt his recruiting efforts. When
Madero joined his uncle, he found only a handful of expectant rebels.
They were all mounted, but between them they had only four car-
bines, some pistols, and little ammunition.

This meeting persuaded Madero that his uprising was stillborn
and he quickly returned to San Antonio where he made plans to go
into European exile. He soon departed by train on the roundabout
route to New Orleans through Dallas. Once in the Crescent City, he
spent a good deal of time sleeping, planning to go to Europe, considering membership in the YMCA so he could undertake a physical fitness
program, and attending the rather new spectacle of motion pictures
each afternoon. He disrupted his regular routine on one occasion, perhaps with Uncle Catarino preying on his mind, to attend an air show,
which left him unimpressed with the flying machines, and he concluded they had not been developed to the point that they would be of
much value.

What Madero and the San Antonio organizers had witnessed and
dismissed as failure was only the tranquil eye of the cyclone of rebellion. In the fall of 1910, neither Díaz nor Madero recognized in countless small uprisings the revolution to come. Madero even more than
Díaz looked but could not see the revolution sputtering to life. Several
leaders, such as Aquiles Serdán in the core region of Puebla, Tlaxcala,
and Veracruz, had already been killed. Nevertheless, in the borderlands, and above all in Chihuahua, Pascual Orozco, Jr., and Francisco
"Pancho" Villa, both recruited and armed by Abraham González and
the rebel committee in El Paso, made lightning strikes on the mountain villages of Guerrero and San Andrés and successfully occupied

them. Success attracted a trickle of new recruits that grew in the next few weeks, as both commanders won additional skirmishes. Echoes of the small successes in Chihuahua soon could be heard from other parts of northern Mexico and even the interior. Despite Serdán's death, fighting soon broke out in the villages and towns of Puebla and the surrounding states.[11]

The U.S. ambassador Henry Lane Wilson, with accidental and uncharacteristic perspicacity, cautioned the minister of foreign relations Enrique C. Creel, "There is evidence of great unrest on both sides of the frontier." The commanding general of the army in Texas, on the other hand, believed the flash point was in the interior of Mexico, to which Ambassador Wilson responded that the general's opinion was "erroneous," adding, "The obvious point of danger . . . is on the border where substantial victories of revolutionists would gravely embarrass the government owing to the encouragement, derived thereby, to disaffected elements in other parts of the Republic."

The committee in exile became the headquarters for information, recruitment, and supply. After his return from New Orleans, Madero ordered more intense efforts at financing the campaign and gaining popular support in the United States. Pro-revolutionary newspapers popped up in profusion in the Alamo city. Of special interest was the effort of Andrea Villarreal, who edited *La Mujer Moderna*, a journal that espoused incipient feminism for Mexican readers. Her efforts so impressed the editor of the *San Antonio Light* that he dubbed her the "Joan of Arc of Mexico."[12]

Growing pressure from Mexican agents, U.S. government officials, and Texas authorities persuaded the committee to move to El Paso because it was more centrally located in the borderlands, closer to the successful rebel troops in Chihuahua, and the pivot point of competing political jurisdictions. (El Paso is located in the remote corner of Texas, abutting both the Mexican state of Chihuahua and what was then the federal territory of New Mexico.) The complex legal jurisdictions provided ample space for rebel maneuvering in and around international, federal, state, and territorial laws. Moreover, the twin cities of Juárez–El Paso (with a combined 1910 population of 114,280)[13] constituted by far the largest, most dynamic cross-border metropolitan center, and El Paso alone in 1910 was the largest city between San Antonio, Texas, and Los Angeles, California. Moreover, the binational urban area served as the dispersion point for thousands of Mexican immigrants coming north in search of work. Together these two towns formed the unofficial but popularly recognized economic center of the borderlands.

In early 1911, the revolution seemed on the verge of encompassing all of Mexico. Although there existed large zones completely untouched by fighting, rebels had appeared and attacked towns across the nation; insurgent bands had increased tenfold and then doubled. Revolutionaries appeared in Morelos (the state that bordered the federal district), Veracruz, Puebla, Sonora, and Yucatán. Even the undaunted warrior Ricardo Flores Magón, released from a U.S. federal prison, organized and directed an invasion of Baja California. The impression of general upheaval grew. As the insurgency multiplied, Ciudad Juárez became the prize of the borderlands and the fulcrum to overthrow the so-called "Díaz-potism."

The showdown for the city and the sideshow for the spectators on the north side of the river began in late April 1911. Pascual Orozco, supported by Pancho Villa, led rebel troops from the south and west toward Juárez, while Madero hemmed and hawed with worry that the impending battle might spill into El Paso, thus provoking a response from the U.S. troops stationed at Ft. Bliss. The rebels established a perimeter just out of gunfire range but close enough for strutting and taunting.

As the armies readied for battle, federal troops, who had been conscripted from the core of the nation, were isolated within Juárez, beyond relief from the federal garrison in the city of Chihuahua. The border character of the Maderista troops could be seen clearly. Orozco's men were largely from the mountain villages of Chihuahua, augmented by volunteers who had crossed the border for jobs in the mines and fields of the southwest and had returned to the revolution.

Once the insurrection began sputtering to life, refugees in Arizona prepared to return to Mexico to regain their country. One gave notice to Tucson's Mexican consul by planting a sign on the front lawn of his office one night that announced, "Good-bye, Arturo Elíaz. 47 of us are going back to Mexico to join the revolutionists. Hurrah for Madero, death to the tyrant Díaz." In a newspaper interview, the consul tried to laugh off the message, but it clearly indicated that border sympathies lay with the revolutionaries.[14]

Besides recruiting throughout greater Mexico, Madero also had created a foreign legion of vagabond mercenaries who joined the rebellion because of political commitment (Giuseppe Garibaldi, grandson of the Garibaldi who unified Italy), military careerism (Benjamin Viljoen, veteran of the Boer War, who eventually became the Mexican consul in Breslau, Germany),[15] wanted posters at home (Sam Dreben, "the Fighting Jew," wanted in San Francisco for bank robbery, who received the medal of honor in World War I),[16] youthful exuberance (Tom Mix, who later successfully tried his hand at making cowboy movies), or the boredom associated with traditional jobs ("Dynamite" Oscar Creighton left his position as a Wall Street stockbroker to join the revolution). Creation of the foreign legion seems completely counter to a nationalistic revolution, unless one recalls that Madero was a product of bicultural, transborder community. He had looked for friends and support on both sides of the border his entire life; certainly he would not change during his revolution.

Madero deliberated and negotiated with his advisors in El Paso. Curious borderlanders rushed to Orozco's camp to admire the rebels and offer advice. Newspapers reported as many as 1,500 "Kodak fiends" in a single day, snapping pictures of the revolutionaries.[17] After smuggling in large numbers of arms and supplies and wringing his hands at the prospect of difficulties with the U.S. government, Madero decided to order a withdrawal rather than risk a battle that might splash into El Paso. Orozco and Villa received the orders but could not retreat before shouts and gestures between their troops and the federal army had resulted in some gunfire. Once shots were fired on May 8, there was no backing down. The commanders disregarded Madero's orders and attacked the federal positions. Fighting their way from house to house for the next two days, rebels steadily forced regulars toward the center of town. United States and Mexican spectators clamored for lookout spots atop the El Paso buildings that fronted the Río Grande. Some vendors quickly appeared, creating a holiday atmosphere that remained, despite the accidental death and wounding of seventeen spectators from ricocheted bullets.

Federal Colonel Juan J. Navarro, fearing the massacre of his troops, on May 11, 1911, surrendered his sword to Giuseppe Garibaldi, commander of the foreign legion. The victory immediately created controversy among the rebels as Mexican officers believed they, not the foreign legion, had won the battle and deserved to receive the surrender of the federal army. Garibaldi and Madero compounded the slight to Orozco and Villa, when they decided to permit Navarro to go into exile across the border without consulting the other officers.

Díaz, watching as rebels appeared everywhere, experienced a renewal of the vitality and genius that had brought him to office in 1876; historians have discounted his capacity to rule in 1911, because of his advanced years, declining health, and the increasing pain caused by dental problems, but on inspection, Díaz demonstrated a sense of realpolitik. He understood the burgeoning importance of the borderlands region, especially Ciudad Juárez–El Paso. Mexican elites had developed financial interests on the border; both Mexican and U.S. workers moved back and forth across the line. Madero's recruiters had reversed the flow of Mexicans northward to mines and fields in the United States and brought them back to El Paso to enlist in the revolution. Díaz recognized that thousands of impoverished Mexicans were returning to their homeland to oppose his government.[18] Moreover, the United States had developed a new sensitivity to disorder along the frontier, and, above all, U.S. investors had been flooding into the region. These U.S. entrepreneurs had become the touchstone of Díaz's policies. From the perspective of landowners, railroad promoters, and oil men, Ciudad Juárez was the gateway as well as the key to Mexico. Díaz recognized that Madero's victory fatally damaged his legitimacy.

CRISIS IN THE SHOWCASE

Shortly after the battle of Ciudad Juárez, events took a major turn in Torreón, the principal town in the Laguna, the showcase of Porfirian modernization. Understanding revolutionary events in this region requires a review of its economic development through cooperation with foreigners and management of wage labor that epitomized the Díaz regime. Madero himself had moved to the Laguna in 1893 to manage family properties and investments in the midst of a boom. Serious social and economic strains became apparent in the 1907 depression. Moreover, beginning in 1909, a number of complex economic and political disputes sprang up. These included controversies over water rights, especially involving the Tlahualillo Company; guayule monopolies, notably the Rockefeller's Continental Rubber Company; contractual cottonseed sales to the cooperative soap factory; and intrazone, intercity, Coahuila–Durango, and Científico–Reyista rivalries. Díaz only managed to paper over them by imposing outsiders to accomplish his decisions. The 1907 economic crisis had revealed glaring problems in the Laguna and offered the social disruption that invited Ricardo Flores Magón's PLM to organize throughout the region and in June 1908 to attack the railroad village of Viesca. This crisis accentuated foreigners' privileged position, and anti-U.S. and anti-Chinese activity united Mexicans. Generally, they agreed with *El Nuevo Mundo,* June 8, 1908, that "There is prosperity in Mexico, but it is Yankee prosperity; there is poverty and misery in Mexico and that belongs totally to Mexicans." The PLM, then Bernardo Reyes, and then Madero drew active and vocal support in the Laguna. Díaz's failure to resolve the economic and political problems in this region combined with his willingness to meddle in local affairs created a general hostility toward his regime. The sentiments that would create rebels in this region clearly reflected the economic downturn and the growing anti-U.S. hostility but received the strongest stimulus from the president's unsuccessful manipulation of local affairs and his unwillingness to restrain foreign privileges there. When Madero called for revolution, insurgents fed on the volatile conditions of the Laguna.

The Madero followers in the Laguna came from all segments of society, and in the town of Gómez Palacio those who plotted military

action for November 20, 1910, included the manager of the local
smelter and the town's organizer of the government's centennial celebration, as well as workers and PLM veterans. When the time came,
Jesús Agustín Castro, a streetcar conductor, led forty to eighty men in
an attack that captured the police station, released prisoners, and
seized arms, ammunition, and horses. Other small uprisings occurred
in Matamoros and Concepción del Oro. The movement continued to
grow, and by February 1911, some 1,200 insurgents had nearly para-
lyzed the Laguna. Federal commanders abandoned the countryside
and tried to hang on to the cities. These forces developed independently for the most part from rebel committees in San Antonio and El
Paso, Texas. Madero sent representatives to try to unify these bands
in March 1911 and to coordinate their activities. The insurgents
moved against towns in April, capturing San Pedro, Mapimi, and
Gómez Palacio by the end of the month.

The fall of Ciudad Juárez encouraged rebel preparations against
Torreón. On May 17, 1911, federal officers, fearing the worst, abandoned the town. Rebels, after several months in the field, were spoil-
ing for a fight. Frustrated, and with no enemy to punish, they

Figure 7.3 Women followed men
into revolutionary campaigns and
provided the commissary for the
troops. *Printed with permission,
Aultman in the Southwest Collection, El Paso Public Library.*

unleased an outburst of violence against Torreón's Chinese population. Town residents, whose hostility had developed over the years against high prices and high credit costs, joined the looting and killing. A massacre of Chinese residents resulted, which continued until Madero's brother Emilio restored order the next day.

The fall of Torreón and with it the Laguna moved Díaz to resign. But the armed conflict in this region did not end. The revolution opened an era of violence that continued unabated for the next twenty-six years, until Cárdenas nationalized the cotton plantations and established the state-run cotton *ejidos*.[19]

Personally troubling to Díaz, no doubt, although much less serious than the loss of Ciudad Juárez and Torreón, was the rebel capture of Tula, his wife Tamaulipas', birthplace, also in May.[20] He could survive the embarrassment of the rebel victory at Tula, but even if his armies defeated the growing rebel forces in the central part of the nation, he could not weather the long-term political and economic implications of Madero's capture of Juárez and Torreón.

Díaz pragmatically approved negotiations with Madero, who also wanted to halt the fighting. These talks resulted on May 21, 1911, in the resignation and self-imposed exile of both the president and his vice president. Perhaps the old president acted to preempt a general lower class uprising,[21] recognizing that if such a struggle gained momentum he would not be capable of putting it down, even if he defeated Madero. More certain was the concern shared by most Mexicans over President William H. Taft's deployment of 20,000 United States troops along the border. Neither Díaz nor Madero wanted to tempt fate and a U.S. intervention into Mexico. Consequently, a negotiated peace quickly followed the onset of negotiations. As Díaz departed for Paris, he grasped that Madero had won a far from complete victory and that an unwanted revolution might overtake the inexperienced new leader. According to Mexican folklore, Díaz is said to have departed with the words, "Madero has unleashed a tiger, now we'll see if he can ride it." It would be more accurate to say that Madero had unleashed a brace of tigers and he stood with a foot on each one. How long could he remain upright, balancing between popular revolutionary demands from his rebel troops and residual complacency from the bureaucrats and soldiers who remained in place?

Popular groups, whether members of Madero's insurgent army or associated with one of the myriad armed bands that had sprung up after November 1910, embraced the rebel victory. They saw it as the opportunity to gain or regain land, obtain living wages, retain independence from intrusive government, hacienda, or military institutions, or seize the advantage or get revenge against rivals. These individuals shared an exuberance based on an end to the dangers of fighting and the rise of expectations about what the victory meant. Madero wanted them to put down their arms and go home.

Madero had agreed in the peace agreements of Ciudad Juárez that only Díaz, Corral, and a few governors would have to resign. Madero wanted a transition government to hold elections so he could run a democratic campaign not based on his authority as the provisional president. Francisco León de la Barra, diplomat and minister of foreign affairs, became the head of this acting government, and he relied on the federal army to maintain order and discharge the rebel troops.

A NORTHERNER IN OFFICE

One or two battles do not make a revolution. Madero's unexpectedly quick victory left little time to hammer out or define political goals.[20] Thus trying to discover Madero's program becomes an exercise in opening Chinese boxes. His army won one major battle and claimed victory. Yet opening this, the largest Chinese box, leads only to another box, the treaties of Ciudad Juárez, which baffled Madero's followers and represented a camarilla negotiated settlement providing for a transitional government that continued the Porfirian regime without Porfirio. Upon opening this box, there appeared no strong direction to the transitional government, because Madero's differences with the previous regime were political not philosophical. The De la Barra regime simply drifted. The optimism and enthusiasm that followed the rebel victory dissipated, for the most part, as self-serving veterans claimed the political spoils customary in the Porfirian political system.

Madero's insistence on free elections for the presidency also became a policy that hid more than it revealed, as he insisted on the same policy in gubernatorial races in the states, but as leader of the national camarilla he intervened in the same manner as Díaz had done to ensure the election of men who had supported him. This intervention, like discovering still another smaller box, confused those who misinterpreted his democratic statements as an attack on camarilla politics. He succeeded Díaz as head of state, but had no desire to demolish his institutions of authority.

The treaty of Ciudad Juárez reflected the camarilla politics of the elite. For Madero, the first step in the process required an agreement between opposing elements of the elite as to which group should be permitted to control the existing political structure. The notion of destroying the structure did not enter his mind; it was a question of political control. Leaving the Porfirian bureaucracy and army intact, as

well as most of the government, appeared quite rational to him. In effect, a new national camarilla had emerged—a reality made even
clearer as the new president brought in his relatives to help run the
government. Democracy to Madero meant the traditional play of regional political blocks, coupled with reasonable elite competition for
national office; it did not mean mass participation.

Local elections, the crucial test of the *municipio libre,* became occasions for the imposition of Porfirians in Maderista clothing. The
veterans of the brief armed struggle were ignored in favor of what the
Maderista leadership regarded as more solid citizens. The historian
of Tula, Tamaulipas, concluded that ". . . despite the rhetoric associated with Madero's call for democratic procedures, the arbitrary
imposition of local elites and other townsfolk in municipal offices, instead of holding local elections, represented a continuance of the old
boss system." Tula's Maderista hero, Alberto Carrera Torres, received
a commission as a general, but had his troops discharged. His efforts
to gain a local elected office failed in an election for state deputy that
the Maderista government fixed against him. Madero's revolution in
Tula meant the destruction of the community's corporate unity and the
institution of Telésforo Villasana's *cacicazgo* with the backing of the
state governor.[23]

The elections in Chihuahua demonstrated the same political
process. Madero named his political assistant Abraham González as
provisional governor of Chihuahua and also encouraged him to run for
regular election to the office. Others persuaded Pascual Orozco to
campaign for the office, since González in theory could not succeed
himself. Madero had no way out of this box; he had already ordered
the discharge of Orozco's troops, and now he intervened to defeat
Orozco's campaign to become governor. Not surprisingly, Orozco's loyalty to the new president, which was already shaky, withered, and he
became the target of counter-revolutionary politicians who cajoled
and flattered his unhappiness into hostility against the new regime.

Meanwhile, in Puebla state, Madero, consistent in his reliance on
the more favored elements to reestablish government, ignored those
who had supported him in revolution to impose more conservative
politicians in office, discharged troops loyal to him to placate the federal army, and kept up his democratic rhetoric. But the mobilization in
the countryside, the vision of changes for a better life, and the decision
to take risks had all taken hold in Puebla, and after 1911, people in
many communities pushed ahead to demand local autonomy, land redistribution, and worker reforms, in spite of Madero.

Farther south in Oaxaca, the Madero rebellion offered the opportunity for local politicians to rearrange power and settle old scores.
Thus in what was reported as a threatened Indian uprising and what

became known as the Mixteca millennium for eleven days in Pinotepa, Juan José Baños established a cacicazgo built firmly on his private army, largely of African descent, from the coast of Oaxaca.[24]

Similar policies characterized the gubernatorial campaigns that put Venustiano Carranza in office in Coahuila, and other Maderistas in Sonora, Puebla, Chiapas, and Veracruz. Madero's maintenance of the Porfirian bureaucracy and army, his acceptance of traditional political methods, and his lack of action on the land question resulted in widespread criticism. One antagonist dubbed him, "Díaz the Little."[25] To Madero, Emiliano Zapata, leader of the insurgent movement demanding land in Morelos state, and Ricardo Flores Magón appeared to be peripheral figures without acceptable claims to high national office. As a patrician, Madero found it impossible to escape his class and its restricted perceptions of Mexican reality. While he recognized the emotional attachment to Flores Magón and Zapata, he failed to understand their social appeal to workers and peasants. Nor did he grasp the fact that traditional Mexican politics was increasingly just a metaphor for a deeper social malaise. Madero marched forward with his face turned toward the past, while the lower classes saw hope in an as yet unspecified redemptive future. Both sides eventually saw themselves as victims of perfidy. Madero, lacking principles that would inspire his following—that is, finding the last Chinese box empty, clung to what he knew. Yet many Maderistas rejected the camarilla system. The revolutionary fighting and the possibility of death, inspired an elision of deeply held opinions and ideals, but ultimately Madero failed because he and his followers during the struggle against Díaz had found no folie à deux.

Reacting to his own misperceptions, Madero attempted to placate Flores Magón and Zapata in a paternal and condescending fashion that enraged them. In June 1911, he sent Ricardo's brother Jesús Flores Magón and Juan Sarabia, the PLM's long-imprisoned and largely honorary vice president, to Los Angeles, California, to arrange for a settlement of differences and to initiate some form of political cooperation, perhaps even creating a place for him in the new government. An angry Flores Magón resented Madero's attempt to neutralize the PLM. The soon-to-be president already had indicated to the U.S. government that he favored Flores Magón's arrest for neutrality law violation. The American government, convinced that the PLM leader posed an internal security problem, issued indictments in early July, and Flores Magón soon found himself in the federal penitentiary at McNeil Island, Washington.

Emiliano Zapata, whose armed peasants had played only a marginal role in bringing about the end of the Díaz regime, received similar treatment from Madero, who even offered him some land as a personal reward for cooperation. Madero's misunderstanding of the social problem rather than simple ineptitude on his part precipitated disaster. In Morelos, the men who had taken up arms to support Zapata and reclaim their village lands lost to commercial agricultural estates had no intention of surrendering their arms when Madero called for disarmament before they saw evidence that the fighting would actually result in some benefit for their communities. Skirmishes soon followed, and within weeks Zapata's men were again fighting the federal army—however this time the commander-in-chief was not Díaz, but his successor. Madero believed that taking away property from its owners to deliver to others constituted illegal and arbitrary expropriation. He suggested that patience and due process through the courts would take care of illegal land seizures. While the court system had been used to facilitate illegal land seizures under the old regime, Madero naïvely envisioned a less corrupt system whose fairness could be accepted by all parties.

Zapata and his advisors responded in the November 8, 1911, Plan of Ayala, saying, ". . . we declare the said Francisco I. Madero unfit to realize the promises of the Revolution of which he is the author, because he is a traitor to the principles...which enabled him to climb to power . . . and because on orders of the *científicos, hacendados,* and *caciques* who enslave us, he has crushed with fire and blood the Mexicans who seek liberties."[26] Zapata initially sought to press Madero into a revolutionary reform program, but predictably Madero, the traditional liberal politician that he was, refused to move beyond rhetoric. Failure to manipulate Díaz's successor forced Zapata to change tactics and attempt to recast the ousting of the old regime as a revolutionary struggle now betrayed. Thus the popular leaders identified their own struggle with that of the PLM and its leader Ricardo Flores Magón and with that of the Maderista movement as one great revolutionary effort. In doing so, Zapata and his allies established the legitimacy of Díaz's removal and Madero's assumption of power, while at the same time reframing the movement in such a way as to destroy Madero's personal integrity as its leader. Zapata, in a manner similar to Ricardo Flores Magón, played a crucial role in the elaboration of the revolutionary ethos that postrevolutionary politicians had to scramble to co-opt and control.

WORKSHOP OF REVOLUTION, I

Madero, consistent with camarilla politics, believed that reform and social experimentation remained a prerogative of state governments. Thus the president pushed for decentralization of his revolution and did have some short-lived success in the northern states of Coahuila and Chihuahua. This policy must not be oversimplified. By Madero's reckoning, he had reinvigorated the office of state governor, at the same time rejecting what he saw as Porfirian centralization and adhering to his liberal ideals—in particular, the federal system of government espoused in the 1857 constitution. Meanwhile, a nervous army and an insecure federal bureaucracy shied away from any change. From the perspective of political practice, his genuine liberal ideals cloaked the insurgency's real patron–client system, replacing the old cacicazgos with his own. The self-delusion of Madero and some advisors did not extend to everyone.

Nevertheless Madero appeared to redeem the authority of state governors, delegating to them the responsibility for state reform programs. This scheme renewed their political autonomy within strict limits imposed by the patron–client relationships that constituted the new national cacicazgo. Governors—now under Madero as earlier under Díaz—retained their independence of action as long as they stayed within the limits prescribed by the president. For some governors, this delegation of power gave them the opportunity to institute reform programs.

Governors Abraham González in Chihuahua and Venustiano Carranza in Coahuila both instituted legislation that drew heavily on earlier efforts to forge middle class identity and morality. Their initiatives focused on the moral betterment of society by restricting the sale of alcoholic beverages, regulating prostitution, and prohibiting gambling, which debased poor males, wrecked their families, and sustained their poverty. Both governors believed that reform paternalism could produce a better society immediately, but for the future they placed their faith in general public education, particularly literacy. González and Carranza opened new schools, which included adult literacy classes, and attempted to increase operating revenues, raise teacher salaries, and expand teacher training programs with mixed success. The curriculum, course content, and goals remained the same mixture of liberal faith in civic virtue, patriotism, and literacy developed during the Porfirian years.

The governors also attempted reforms that benefited solid, hardworking, middle-class residents of these northern states. Revision of tax laws and property assessments took aim at large, especially non-resident, landowners and corporations. New rules for utility and other privileged corporations imposed regulations—such as railroad and street car schedules—that benefited the society rather than the company. They also extended some assistance to rural and urban workers; both attempted to end company stores and support strikers. Their efforts extended only to safer, improved working conditions, however, and rarely to increased wages or benefits.[27]

Figure 7.4 Boy revolutionary. *Printed with permission, Russell Lee Photograph Collection, Center for American History, University of Texas at Austin.*

POLITICAL CONFUSION

Generally Madero and his governmental agents failed to understand the feeling of entitlement of those who had joined the violent phase of the struggle against Díaz. Many fought to defeat Porfirio in order to gain upward mobility. Madero, in his recruitment campaign, had promised permanent military rank to those who joined his revolutionary army. With victory, he reneged on his promise, discharging armed followers in central and southern Mexico with little formality. Insurgents from the border to Puebla received the option of being discharged or becoming part of his newly created Cuerpo de Rurales de la Federación—essentially a paramilitary police force. The regular army remained undiluted, neither strengthened nor weakened. Madero intended to manipulate the military as Díaz had previously done. As president, he underestimated the dangers of a demoralized but dangerously untrustworthy army and a large number of resentful ex-partisans. It proved to be one more fatal misunderstanding of the new Mexican reality.[28]

Other aspirants to power misread the circumstances as well. Bernardo Reyes, one-time presidential candidate in the 1910 elections, returned from Europe and quickly renewed his poorly conceived grasping for presidential power. Once his campaign against Madero foundered, he showed the courage to rebel that he lacked when Díaz held power in Mexico City. In December 1911, Reyes, who had well-established ties in the north, tried to provoke his own northern uprising that he hoped would carry him to national command. Instead he was arrested by loyal Madero troops and jailed in a Mexico City prison. In a rather comfortable cell, Reyes spent his days conspiring to bring about an army coup d'état.

Meanwhile, Orozco, unable to convert his revolutionary service into political opportunity, decided that indeed his contributions had been so neglected and his talents so overlooked by the Madero–González crowd that he would return to the battlefield to claim the recognition and power they had denied him. Thus Madero faced an uprising against his government from his most successful and most popular rebel general. Villa, on the other hand, believed Orozco had succumbed to the entreaties and bribes of old Porfirians, and he remained loyal to Madero. The Orozco rebellion, once ignited, raged across Chihuahua; Governor González was forced to flee, and federal troops had to begin a difficult and bloody reconquest of this northern state. Beyond the threat of Orozco's forces, many feared the insurrection would provoke a U.S. intervention. This dread reached the point that Bishop Echavarría in Saltillo, Coahuila, called for special prayers during all masses in the diocese, asking for divine assistance against the Orozco rebellion to prevent the arrival of foreign troops.[29]

Madero found himself under growing pressure from foreigners who wanted reassurances that their privileges would continue unchanged. When firm commitments did not appear, they became apprehensive. Madero gave some evidence that he supported Mexican workers against foreign companies and sought to encourage Mexican companies against foreign competition. Businessmen from the United States and Europe withdrew their support and began to campaign against him. As world war loomed on the horizon, German espionage agents began trolling in these troubled political waters, further complicating matters.

And if Madero did not face enough difficulty, he found himself at odds with the Roman Catholic Church, which wanted not only to have its actual position in society confirmed, but also wanted the legal, theoretical disabilities of the Constitution of 1857 removed so it could take a more active role in the reformation of society. Inspired by

Rerum Novarum, the 1891 papal encyclical that called on the Church to accept industrialization and urbanization and to work for social justice, and by the example of European Catholic political parties and unions, Church leaders cautiously created a Mexican Catholic Party. They even offered a vice presidential candidate in Madero's successful 1911 presidential campaign.

BARRACKS REVOLT

Without underestimating churchmen who had become both more aggressive and self-righteous, rebels who had bewitched themselves with their own hopes and felt betrayed by Madero, bureaucrats whose drudging and inert lives they believed guaranteed their survival despite all political convolutions, or foreigners whose wealth they believed indicated cultural, moral, and political superiority—without underestimating any of these interests—the old Porfirian praetorians proved the most treacherous. Madero trusted in the national army, whose officers dressed in epaulets and perfidy. General Bernardo Reyes, imprisoned in a luxurious apartment cell, conspired with General Félix Díaz, the exiled president's nephew, also under arrest for what Madero had generously called insurrection rather than treason. These military políticos planned to overthrow the Madero regime, call elections in the Porfirian manner, and alternate in power. The intrigue failed because of the two generals' overconfidence and Díaz's vanity.

Rather than suborn all the officers possible (who were certainly eager for revolt), the two generals had limited their conspiracy to just a few. Neglecting, for example, several commanders of Madero's personal guards cost Reyes his life and Díaz the presidency. February 10, 1913, was fixed as the evening of the coup d'état. Guards released the two generals, but before they could leave for the presidential palace to arrest Madero, Díaz insisted on making a thorough toilet so his appearance, properly shaved, combed, and lotioned, befitted a presidential aspirant.[30] The delay proved fatal as the presidential guards who were prepared to hand over President Madero were relieved by sentries who knew nothing of the plot. Reyes led a charge against these loyal guards and was shot to death by their first volley.

Fighting dragged on for ten days between loyal and mutinous troops, with hundreds of Mexico City's civilians the victims of the conflict. The Tragic Ten Days (February 9–19, 1913), as Mexicans call it, ended only after Díaz had arranged another plot with an officer initially excluded from the plan, Victoriano Huerta. The two met with the complicity of United States Ambassador Henry Lane Wilson, who also encouraged them with talk of U.S. recognition and investment. Huerta arrested Madero and his vice president José María Pino Suárez, and, through procedural manipulations, made himself first minister of war and after a spate of imposed resignations, by constitutional succession, the president of Mexico. Félix Díaz, expecting to replace Huerta in prompt elections, feared a groundswell of support for Madero if he were allowed to go into exile, especially in the borderlands. The old president's nephew and his followers, with Huerta's connivance, arranged on the night of February 22, 1913, for the murder of Madero and Pino Suárez. The triggerman was Captain Francisco Cárdenas, who learned his trade in the Porfirian rurales.[31] Probably Félix Díaz correctly assessed Madero as a threat, but he underestimated Huerta. Perhaps Díaz believed his rank gave him precedence and his lineage gave him command. He was wrong and never claimed the office he coveted so much for the rest of the decade.

As for Madero, he had been wrong about nearly everything. His view of what was right and wrong about Mexico was cockeyed (he proposed keeping the Científico economic programs as a great success, yet by 1908 they had dragged the nation to the brink of bankruptcy), naïve (he believed the right to vote for genuine candidates would make selfless, disinterested Mexicans out of people connected by the web of clientalistic networks), and misguided (trusting to the professional standards of the national army and bureaucracy). These views constituted both a personal and national disaster. Madero's idealism never struggled free of the old habits of camarilla manipulation. His vision, although wrong, made the march to revolutionary drums inevitable, demonstrating once again history's law of unforeseen consequences.

General Huerta's seizure of the government cannot be viewed as a simple barracks revolt. Virtually everyone believed Madero had been miscast as president and could not be expected to endure much beyond a certain transition stage. Calls for the replacement of the weak president by a strong individual came from all sides, including the foreign community. Huerta ushered in what many believed was the inevitable; he believed he had a mandate to reestablish governmental direction and social order. Like Félix Díaz, he also was wrong.

Knowledgeable about the north, Madero had less understanding of the nation. Despite his apparent success in defeating the old regime, Madero's undoing came less than three years after launching his revolution. Because he tried to hedge on his choice of insurgency, he established no purposeful national program. He refused to recognize that his decision to revolt, like a leap from a ten-story building, had unleashed social forces that could not be reversed. He chose for himself, for Mexicans, and for the borderlands. Some others might slip, almost unintentionally, into revolution; some others might announce their insurrection for a time; some others might become rebels of convenience, turning with the winds of politics. This led to Madero's death, but also resulted in the greatest strength of the Mexican Revolution through 1937, the ability of people to negotiate programs and policies for their benefit. Politically it was disastrous in the short run, yet it was vital for the nature and character of the revolution that occurred under the northerners and that was then revised under Cárdenas and was completely concluded in the last days of the Alemán regime. The absence of a rigid national project offered the opportunity to experiment, fail, and experiment again. Unfortunately, with each experiment came a cost paid in the lives of Mexicans.

NORTHERNERS RECAPTURE THE CAPITAL

Once Huerta connived at Madero's assassination and duped Félix Díaz out of national power, the violent reaction to him and his regime dragged the nation and the borderlands into the revolutionary conflict deeper than ever before. This *camarazo* or coup d'état by a camarilla, in this instance of military officers, ushered in a much greater mobilization of the Mexican people.

Huerta's assumption of power gave him and his military co-conspirators control of only part of Mexico. He took command of the army and the government bureaucracy in Mexico City. But his actions provoked Mexicans to take up arms against him and enlist in the armies of other factions or camarillas, such as the Zapatistas, and made emphatic the revolutionary character of the borderlands, as armies appeared in Sonora, Chihuahua, and Coahuila.[32]

In the United States, those cities with large Mexican communities witnessed demonstrations of outrage at the assassination and the involvement of the U.S. ambassador.[33] In the borderlands, both Mexicans and Americans began to experience total warfare. Both sides of the boundary were marshalled to war standing, each serving as recruiting and provisioning zones. Most of the gunfire took place south of the Río Bravo, but occasional raids compounded the intense contest of intrigue and espionage that occurred to the north of it. Invaders struck both sides of the river, claiming to be in pursuit of outlaws.

The Constitutionalists, those who were outraged by Huerta's violation of the spirit if not the letter of the constitution to assume presidential power, organized and armed in the states along the northern border, led the challenge to the new dictator. Once again the federal army, now directed by Huerta, fought against civilian revolutionaries, and once again it faltered. Northern insurgents under the leadership of Venustiano Carranza, the constitutional governor of Coahuila, and the military command of Alvaro Obregón and Francisco Villa raced south for Mexico City, also threatened from the south by Zapata's troops. The intrusion of these northerners into the life of central Mexico made an indelible impact on their fellow Mexicans. Historian Daniel Cosío Villegas who, as a boy, watched them enter his hometown of Toluca in 1914, recalled the spectacle. These men from the north, he noted, ". . . whom we did not know, who did not wear the uniform of the regular Mexican Army (which was the only one we knew), who, furthermore, wore Texas-type hats, which are used in northern Mexico, whose khaki-colored uniforms were very similar to those of the American Army, who used American weapons—the famous 30-30. In sum, people who were entirely different physically from the ones we knew."[34]

Moreover, the U.S. government took a hand in opposition to Huerta. President Woodrow Wilson, determined to teach "Mexicans to elect good men," decided to prevent the delivery of machine guns to Huerta. He ordered marines and sailors to occupy both Tampico and Veracruz, on the flimsiest of provocations. The U. S. president expected Mexican gratitude and short of that at least no more than a rude reception. On the contrary, Mexicans reacted with a surge of indignant nationalism and volunteers from as far away as Guadalajara organized companies to join the battle. Mexicans made a fierce defense. Fighting became so intense in Veracruz that when U.S. troops had finally subdued the Mexicans and occupied the city, the commanders awarded fifty-five Medals of Honor, including the first of two presented to Major Smedley Butler.[35] Mexicans, too young or too distant to defend their country, managed to express their outrage. Students discontinued their classes in English; youngsters gave up fashionable U.S. cigarettes for Mexican brands; and anyone who owned one threw away the Texas-style hat previously made popular by the northern revolutionaries.[36] Huerta simply could not withstand the three-pronged advance from the north and the assault from the south, partly because he became short of weapons and ammunition, cut off by the United States embargo and occupation of Veracruz.

At the threshold of success, rivalry split the Constitutionalists; *norteños* Carranza (from Coahuila) and Villa (from Chihuahua) agreed only on the elimination of Huerta; they disagreed on the former's supreme command, his call for restoration of the 1857 Constitution, and his neglect of social and economic reforms. The latter, at this time, offered no specific suggestions, but he recognized the need for revolutionary changes. The conflict resulted in Carranza slowing Villa's campaign to the south so his more trusted General Obregón could direct his troops in taking the capital city. After sixteen months of general fighting against the Constitutionalists, Huerta fled into exile. Once revolutionary officers had sensed victory over Huerta (1914), they began preparing to ensure that veterans, mostly northerners, would exercise authority.

The revolutionary forces splintered even further.[37] Military leaders held a convention in Aguascalientes the same year and made this point. Delegates had to have command of a least 1,000 troops to attend the meeting, where Eulalio Gutiérrez, the pro-Villa revolutionary general and governor of San Luis Potosí, was selected as provisional president. More powerful generals had permitted this, but with no intention of dealing themselves out of politics. For tactical reasons, at that time Obregón had remained an adherent of the Carranza regime. After this convention, General Villa moved his troops south to threaten Mexico City. Joined by Zapata and Pánfilo Natera, Villa fielded a combined force of some 72,000 men.

The struggle among the victorious Constitutionalists and choosing sides between Venustiano Carranza and Pancho Villa in bellicose alliances fractured the revolutionary movement and resulted in some concern for social problems as a recruiting ploy. Carranza, as a matter of wartime expediency, issued a series of decrees on the nation's social problems, with some vague plans for land reform and a promise of strict application of Benito Juárez's reform laws and the 1857 Constitution. Obregón recruited workers from the Casa de Obrero Mundial, affiliated with the Industrial Workers of the World, into "Red Battalions," with promises of support for labor organization and other reforms. The most significant, in the long run, of these exigent measures came in Carranza's creation of the National Agrarian Commission on January 6, 1915, which became the Secretariat of Agrarian Reform. These crisis decisions enabled the Constitutionalists and other revolutionaries to attract recruits, and they offered the mechanisms by which popular groups—workers, agrarians, Indian villagers—would demand, and sometimes obtain, dramatic improvements in their lives.

THE INSURGENTS

The insurgents following each leader fought for a variety of motives and convictions; some were accidental or impressed recruits. Nevertheless, each rebel army had a particular character. The so-called Conventionists, after the Aguascalientes Convention, of Villa and Zapata most clearly represented the popular, dispossessed elements of the population—although intellectuals, former Porfirian soldiers, shopkeepers, and ranchers could be found in their ranks as well. The Zapatistas, including first-generation workers, came from peasant backgrounds. Many practiced subsistence agriculture on village-owned lands or sharecropped on estate properties, supplemented their family income with seasonal labor on commercial estates, and adhered to their own brand of popular Catholicism (that stressed identification

Figure 7.5 Mexican federal border guards at Matamoros, Tamaulipas. *Printed with permission, Russell Lee Photograph Collection, Center for American History, University of Texas at Austin.*

with the Virgin and the saints) and folk liberalism (that emphasized local autonomy and community self-defense).[38] Others came from the cities, including the capital, where they had found work in the textile mills or other jobs, but they held a nostalgic view of an idealized, idyllic agrarian past that resulted in demands among these workers for higher wages or plots of land. These Zapatistas became masterful guerrilla fighters, capable of defending their homeland but incapable of offensive warfare. They wore down their opponents by never conceding the struggle.

The Zapatistas combined with the forces of Pancho Villa. These Villistas, for the most, epitomized Mexico's transient population. Many, before the revolution, had abandoned their villages and headed north, where they became wage workers in the mines, fields, lumber camps, and railroad construction camps. Others became migrant workers, working beyond the northern boundary of their own country in the south and west of the United States. Indigenous peoples, especially groups who had lost their properties, augmented their numbers for the chance to fight against their long-standing enemies. The rootless, mobile character of most Villistas tended to reduce their participation in formal religion, although most remained culturally Catholic.

Their experience as wage earners generated the expectation that they should be rewarded for their time and effort, and their mobility inculcated a greater awareness of Mexico as a nation.

The Constitutionalists were no more homogeneous than their opponents, but Carranza appealed especially to those northerners who had been engaged as entrepreneurs and managers in commercial undertakings, agriculture, ranching, mining, and rubber production, which had brought them into competition with foreigners. Others had experience as town or village officials and bureaucrats who often encountered the intrusion of the national regime. He and his closest advisors wanted to provide capitalistic opportunities for Mexicans, without foreign competition. Generally higher up the social ladder than the troops of the Convention, the Constitutionalists resented outside meddling in their affairs, whether the outsider came from a foreign country or Mexico City. Nevertheless, the Constitutionalists added at least a paternalistic concern for the Mexican people and their well-being to their nationalistic interests.[39]

Obregón's followers represented perhaps the most mixed of all of the legions. He had recruited an army of northern shopkeepers, schoolteachers, ranch foremen, and businessmen. These men felt their place in the social order was threatened. Many knew the United

Figure 7.6 Destruction of alcoholic beverages in Ciudad Juárez on the orders of General Francisco "Pancho" Villa. *Printed with permission, the Southwest Collection, El Paso Public Library.*

States and, with the experience of international travel, more sharply defined the Mexico they wanted in the future. They stressed Mexico's heritage of resistance to outsiders, of defense against foreigners, free-booters, and hostile indigenous peoples, and of achievement against the odds of distance, harsh climate, and difficult economic conditions. Because they came mostly from small towns, their ideas and experiences with social relationships differed from the village community of the Zapatistas, the transience of the Villistas, and the urban orientation of the Carrancistas.

In all of these groups, women participated in the revolution not simply as silent witnesses and mourners; the *soldaderas* followed their men who joined the popular armies. Campesino women recreated the rural household in the field or in boxcars or wherever necessary, always with the same backbreaking labor of making tortillas; women from the towns and construction camps earned wages for providing food and clean clothing to the men; other adventuresome women became combatants. The federal officers, with only limited success, tried to keep women away from their troops. The largest numbers of women could be found in the popular forces.[40]

Other male rebels appeared who made up bands that maintained their autonomy. Some represented peasants who refused to align with

Figure 7.7 Railroads served as transportation, homes, and weapons during the Revolution. A *soldadera* boards the train in the right foreground. *Printed with permission, Aultman Collection in the Southwest Collection, El Paso Public Library.*

any of the national figures. Campesinos in the state of Tlaxcala, for example, endured throughout the decade, fighting for the distribution of communal lands to their villages and political autonomy for their local councils. They joined the fray against Huerta, but would recognize no outside leader. Still other rebels, who lived the tough, independent, although economically marginal life of rancheros, joined the rebellion to preserve their personal freedom of action. Some joined the fighting because a friend did, or their boss recruited them, or because they hoped to settle the score with a local landlord, shopkeeper, or bully backed by government authorities.[41]

REVOLUTION WITHIN A REVOLUTION

The murder of Madero had ushered in a chaotic period in which no government ruled. The conflict focused at first on driving Huerta from the country, and then the disparate rebel forces turned on each other to determine what political, social, and economic changes would occur. The struggle from July 1914 until July 1915, when the Constitutionalists claimed military victory in the core, resulted in more than 200,000 deaths and represented a revolution within the revolution.[42] Serious guerrilla fighting continued through 1917.

Figure 7.8 Train derailed in Northeastern Mexico during the Revolution. *Printed with permission, Russell Lee Photograph Collection, Center for American History, University of Texas at Austin.*

As the Constitutionalists broke up, Obregón, still backing Carranza, retreated to Veracruz (relinquished to him by the U.S. troops, who left behind a warehouse of arms and ammunition), allowing Villa and Zapata to occupy the capital. The Zapatistas also briefly held the city of Puebla. Eventually regrouping, Obregón forced Villa and Zapata out of Mexico City and subsequently defeated the Villistas in several major engagements, most notably El Ebano and then Celaya.[43] This struggle served to shake out the generals who insisted on a role on the national stage. Obregón, after 1915, controlled the most powerful armed camarilla in the country.

Following their victories at Celaya and León that brought a semblance of peace to the country, the Constitutionalists hedged on social and economic programs, especially land reform and labor benefits for popular groups. At the same time, Carranza sought to avoid the mortal errors committed by the martyred Madero. He had to deal with his own armed revolutionary followers. The Constitutionalist officer corps, as did all of the revolutionaries, had learned their military skills on the job. Slow learners often paid with their lives, while others became successful tacticians. Mostly drawn from the middle sectors of society, they came from a variety of different occupations. Salvador Alvarado was a druggist, Juan Barragán a student, and Plutarco Elías Calles a schoolteacher. Others such as Lucio Blanco and Alvaro Obregón came from ranchero families. Francisco L. Urquizo, Panfilo Natero, and Francisco Villa, all from more popular origins, represented exceptions. Urquizo rose from the lower ranks, Natero was an Indian peon who had previously fought for Madero, along with Villa, who sprang from a murky background of banditry. Their participation complicated Constitutionalist politics. The revolutionary army, loosely controlled by Carranza as the First Chief, numbered approximately 200,000 by 1916, and the commanders expected to be involved in political as well as military struggles.

The federal army posed another problem. With victory over Huerta in 1914, Carranza insisted on its total destruction. Self-trained Constitutionalist General Obregón met with Federal General José Refugio to sign the Treaty of Teoloyucan, which provided for surrender of arms, military installations, and discharge of all officers and enlisted men. Demobilized federales formed a floating pool of recruits to be drawn on in future conflicts by one side or the other.

The armed force that remained had more in common with the militias of regional caciques than with a professional army. Fragmented by personal loyalties to their immediate revolutionary leaders, they became political units useful in the primitive politics of the early revolutionary period. They perceived themselves as armed citizens, the paladins of the nineteenth-century liberal folk nationalism, not institutional soldiers. As a result, politics, personal gain, and status quickly came to the fore. Although the federal army had disappeared, political discourse continued to have streaks of armed violence. Post–Porfirian politics had a deadly character that endured at least through 1937. For many it came to represent the northern way of administration.[44]

NOTES

1. Josiah McC. Heyman, *Life and Labor on the Border: Working People of Northeastern Sonora*, Mexico, 1886–1986 (Tucson: University of Arizona Press, 1991), discusses in detail this transborder culture.
2. John M. Hart presented an exhaustive analysis of the extensive activities of U.S. entrepreneurs in the southwest and Mexico in *Revolutionary Mexico: The Coming and Process of the Mexican Revolution* (Berkeley: University of California Press, 1987).
3. For a discussion of the missionary movement after 1880 in Mexico, see Jean-Pierre Bastian, *Los disidentes: Sociedades protestantes y revolucíon en México, 1872–1911* (México: Fondo de Cultura Económica,1989), and Deborah Baldwin, *Protestants and the Mexican Revolution: Missionaries, Ministers, and Social Change* (Urbana: University of Illinois Press, 1990).
4. Victor O. Story, "Genesis of Revolution in the Tamaulipas Sierra: Campesinos and Shopkeepers in the Carrera Torres Uprising, 1907–1911" (Ph.D. diss., University of North Carolina, 1991), pp. 121–22, offers a significant and suggestive discussion.
5. For a discussion of Rabasa, see Thomas Benjamin, *A Rich Land, a Poor People: Politics and Society in Modern Chiapas* (Albuquerque: University of New Mexico Press, 1989), pp. 39–54.
6. Richard A. García, *Rise of the Mexican American Middle Class: San Antonio, 1919–1941* (College Station: Texas A&M University Press, 1991), pp. 18–19, 28–29, 33. Laredo, El Paso, and Los Angeles each had a population of 5,000 or more Mexicans in 1910. El Paso had the largest concentration of Mexicans in the United States in 1910.
7. David Nathan Johnson, "Exiles and Intrigue: Francisco I. Madero and the Mexican Revolutionary Junta in San Antonio, 1910–1911" (M.A. thesis, Trinity University, 1975), p. 39.
8. Anne Pace, "Mexican Refugees in Arizona, 1910–1911," *Arizona and the West* 11:1 (spring 1974), pp. 6, 7.
9. Johnson, "Exiles and Intrigue," pp. 79, 86.
10. Stuart F. Voss, "Porfirian Sonora: Economic Collegiality" (Paper presented at the American Historical Association meeting, Dec. 28, 1978), pp. 46–49, note 11.
11. David G. LaFrance, "Many Causes, Movements, Failures, 1910–1913: The Regional Nature of Maderismo," in Thomas Benjamin and Mark Wasserman, eds., *Provinces of the Revolution: Essays on Regional Mexican History, 1910–1929* (Albuquerque: University of New Mexico Press, 1990), pp. 18–28.
12. Johnson, "Exiles and Intrigue," pp. 97, 121; the quotations come from pp. 107 and 185–86.

13. Oscar Martínez, *Border Boom Town: Ciudad Juárez Since 1848* (Austin: University of Texas Press, 1975), Tables 1 and 2, pp. 158–59.
14. Pace, "Mexican refugees," p. 9.
15. See Richard Medina Estrada, "Border Revolution: The Mexican Revolution in the Ciudad Juárez–El Paso Area, 1906–1915" (M.A. thesis, University of Texas at El Paso, 1975), pp. iii, 75–76.
16. See the Dreben file at the Institute of Texan Cultures, University of Texas, San Antonio.
17. Shawn Lay, *War, Revolution and the Ku Klux Klan: A Study of Intolerance in a Border City* (El Paso: Texas Western University Press, 1985), p. 18.
18. Estrada, "Border Revolution," pp. 67–71.
19. Meyers, *Forge of Progress*, pp. 5–6, 197–98, 256, 278, 283, 349–51, 354–60, 365.
20. Story, "Genesis of Revolution," p. 23.
21. Hart, *Revolutionary Mexico*, p. 249, says about Díaz, "He understood that the Revolutionary process had to be terminated before mass participation went too far and could no longer be controlled by either his regime, the interim government or Madero's narrowly based leadership circle."
22. See David G. LaFrance, *The Mexican Revolution in Puebla, 1908–1913. The Maderista Movement and the Failure of Liberal Reform* (Wilmington, Del.: SR Books, 1989); William H. Beezley, "Madero: The 'Unknown' President and His Political Failure to Organize Rural Mexico," in George Wolfskill and Douglas W. Richmond, eds., *Essays on the Mexican Revolution: Revisionist Views of the Leaders* (Austin: University of Texas Press, 1979), pp. 1–24.
23. Story, "Genesis of Revolution," pp. 124, 309, 313, and 323–41.
24. This nearly incredible episode is examined in Francie R. Chassen-López and Héctor G. Martínez, "Return to the Mixtec Millennium: Agrarian vs. Rancher Revolution on the Costa Chica of Oaxaca, 1911," paper presented at the Rocky Mountain Council on Latin American Studies, El Paso, Texas, February 1992.
25. Emma Goldman gave Madero this sobriquet in *Mother Earth* (February 1912), cited in James A. Sandos, *Rebellion in the Borderlands: Anarchism and the Plan of San Diego, 1904–1923* (Norman: University of Oklahoma Press, 1992), p. 46.
26. James W. Wilkie and Albert L. Michaels, eds., *Revolution in Mexico: Years of Upheaval, 1910–1940* (New York: Alfred A. Knopf, 1969), p. 45.
27. William H. Beezley, "State Reform during the Provisional Presidency: Chihuahua, 1911," *Hispanic American Historical Review* 40: 3 (August 1970), pp. 524–37, and "Governor Carranza and the Mexican Revolution in Coahuila," *The Americas* 33: 1 (July 1976), pp. 50–61.
28. Edwin Lieuwen, *Mexican Militarism: The Political Rise and Fall of the Revolutionary Army, 1910–1940* (Albuquerque: University of New Mexico Press, 1968), p. 12.
29. Pastoral Circular No. 4, March 12, 1912, Archivo de la Catedral de Santiago, Saltillo, Libro de Gobierno, vol. 5.
30. William F. Buckley Sr. recalled in a letter to Henry Lane Wilson that Díaz had delayed the expedition over fifty minutes as he finished shaving. See the accounts by Buckley and Wilson of the Tragic Ten Days in W. Dirk Raat and William H. Beezley, eds., *Twentieth-Century Mexico* (Lincoln: University of Nebraska Press, 1986), pp. 105–14.
31. Michael C. Meyer, *Huerta: A Political Portrait* (Lincoln: University of Nebraska Press, 1972), esp. pp. 45–63 and 70–82. On Cárdenas's career in the *rurales*, see Paul J. Vanderwood, *Disorder and Progress: Bandits, Police, and Mexican Development*, revised and enlarged edition (Wilmington, Del.: SR Books, 1992).

32. John Tutino, "Revolutionary Confrontation, 1913–1917: The Regions, Classes and the New National State," in Thomas Benjamin and Mark Wasserman, eds., *Provinces of the Revolution: Essays on Regional Mexican History, 1910–1919* (Albuquerque: University of New Mexico Press, 1990), pp. 42–43.

33. José Vasconcelos, *A Mexican Ulysses: An Autobiography*, translated and abridged by W. Rex Crawford (Bloomington: Indiana University Press, 1963), p. 79.

34. Wilkie and Michaels, eds. *Revolution in Mexico*, p. 6.

35. *Above and Beyond: A History of the Medal of Honor from the Civil War to Vietnam* (Boston: Boston Pub. Co., 1985), p. 333. Nine marines (all officers) and forty-six sailors received the award. Butler earned a second Medal of Honor at Fort Liberté, Haiti, in 1915.

36. Roderic A. Camp, interview with Ernesto Robles Levi, Mexico City, May 21,1985.

37. Berta Ulloa, *La revolución escindida* (Mexico: El Colegio de México, 1979).

38. Tutino, "Revolutionary Confrontation," pp. 45–47.

39. Alan Knight, *The Mexican Revolution: Counter-revolution and Reconstruction* (Lincoln: University of Nebraska Press, 1986), vol. 2, pp. 232, 239, 274, 283–85.

40. Elizabeth Salas, "The *Soldaderas*," in Salamini and Vaughan, eds., *Women of the Mexican Countryside*. (Second citation)

41. Raymond Buve, "Neither Carranza Nor Zapata: The Rise and Fall of a Peasant Movement That Tried to Challenge Both: Tlaxcala, 1910–1919," in Friedrich Katz, ed., *Riot, Rebellion, and Revolution: Rural Social Conflict in Mexico* (Princeton: Princeton University Press, 1988), pp. 338–75; Knight, *Mexican Revolution*, vol. 2, pp. 50–51, 188; Romana Falcón, *Revolución y caciquismo: San Luis Potosí, 1910–1938* (México: El Colegio de México, 1984); Dudley Ankerson, *Agrarian Warlord: Saturnino Cedillo and the Mexican Revolution in San Luis Potosí* (DeKalb: Northern Illinois University Press, 1984).

42. Tutino, "Revolutionary Confrontation," pp. 41, 55.

43. Berta Ulloa, *La encrucijada de 1915* (México: El Colegio de México, 1979).

44. Lieuwen, *Mexican Militarism*, pp. 21, 24.

Chapter 8

MAKING A REVOLUTION WORK
Part I, 1917–1927

The revolutionary violence of the years to 1917 had destroyed the national government, brought the northerners to Mexico City to preside over reconstruction, and removed many restraints on popular groups, especially rural villagers and urban workers. The fighting had not completely ended, the contradictions among revolutionary leaders continued, and the economic difficulties worsened for much of Mexico. Thousands of Mexicans remained in self-imposed exile in the United States, having fled the violence and chaos of the revolution. In these circumstances, the revolutionaries struggled with a number of different programs, marred by political succession and economic disruption, as they faced the challenge of reconstructing Mexico and making the revolution work.

SAN DIEGO PLAN

Nothing serves better to demonstrate the revolution in the border region, in all of its convolutions of politics and military actions, than the 1915 Plan de San Diego and the 1916 Pershing Punitive Expedition. Both of these episodes continued the revolution within the revolution that began with the defeat of Huerta and represent aftershocks of Obregón's victories in July 1915.

    The history of the San Diego Plan has a surreal quality. The signers claimed they issued the plan in the small Texas town of San Diego. Although the true authorship and its place of creation remain in doubt, the fact that it bears the name of San Diego, signatures of

Making a Revolution Work, Part I, 1917–1937

1914	Decree ends debt servitude in Yucatán
	Unión Mexicana Benito Juárez founded
	in Kansas City, Missouri
1915	San Diego Plan
	Radical labor law adopted in Yucatán
	California Home Teacher Act
1916	Pancho Villa raids Columbus, New Mexico
1916–1917	Pershing Punitive Expedition
1916–1920	Presidency of Venustiano Carranza
1917	Deportation of Mexican workers from Bisbee,
	Arizona Constitution of 1917
1918	Workers convention in Saltillo creates the
	Confederation of Mexican Workers (CROM)
	Lill report
1919	Zapata assassinated
1919–1920	U.S. Senator Fall conducts hearings on Mexican
	affairs
1920	Plan of Agua Prieta
	Carranza assassinated
	Interim presidency of Adolfo de la Huerta
1920–1924	Villa agrees to retirement
	Obregón administration
	Law of Ejidos
1921	Independence Centennial
1923	De La Huerta Revolt
1929	"Aztec Gold" exhibit in New York City

border Mexicans, and appeals to Mexican Americans and other minorities has significance. The immediate official reaction in Washington and by later historians has been to describe the episode much like the flea that attacked an elephant, that is, to characterize it as the height of pretension. Nine signatories called for an uprising to overthrow the U.S. government in Texas, New Mexico, Arizona, California, Oklahoma, and Colorado and to establish an independent republic in the southwest that would seek annexation to Mexico. The signers envisioned a Liberating Army of Races and Peoples that would end the subjugation of Mexican Americans, Blacks, Indians, and Japanese residing in the borderlands. The appeal to Indians, offering to restore their lands, clearly echoed the PLM's 1906 promise to return lands to the Yaquis. Later versions of the plan went further with a proposal to assist blacks in seizing several states in the Old South that would become a separate, independent republic.[1]

San Diego lies a fraction less than 200 miles from the Texas state capital in Austin and about 1,600 miles from Washington, D.C.; it is situated only slightly over 200 miles from Monterrey, the Nuevo León state capital, and about 800 miles from Mexico City. Its population in 1915 numbered about 2,500, with a substantial Mexican or Mexican American majority, and the same ethnic proportion characterized the rest of Duval County.

Ethnic conflict had marred the border country since the 1911 shoot-out at the Duval courthouse in San Diego, when three Anglos from nearby Alice killed several Mexicans. Local Democratic party boss Archie Parr sided with the Hispanics and laid the basis for a south Texas political machine that survived until 1975 and dramatically provided the recount ballots for Lyndon B. Johnson's tainted 1948 election to the U.S. Senate. Not everyone in the lower south Texas counties after 1911 sided with Parr, the self-styled Duke of Duval, but outside officials left local matters to him.[2]

Figure 8.1 A Mexican family dwelling built between two boulders on a hillside near Polvo in 1916. Notice the individual cooking over a campfire, probably a guest whose bedding is in the forefront. *Printed with permission, Photography Collection, Harry Ransom, Humanities Research Center, University of Texas at Austin.*

Only the arrogance born of distance and ethnic disrespect allowed officials in Washington and Austin to disregard events in Duval County such as the San Diego Plan. Although both location and population offered an attractive opportunity to stir up trouble in San Diego, neither president nor governor gave much attention to the call for revolution there at first. Only if the rebels had been inspired with funds and encouragement from Germans—an enemy representing a modern nation—would the Wilsonians take the threat seriously. Contempt for the demands of a handful of Mexicans and Mexican Americans in south Texas encouraged unthinking bureaucrats and army officers to ignore the possibility that the scheme had the backing of Mexico City.

This pronouncement, which one U.S. federal judge characterized as the work of lunatics because it was proclaimed in the borderlands, soon took on a significance that no one—not the signers, nor government officials in either country, nor local officials in border Mexican or southwest states—anticipated. Only Venustiano Carranza, whom political desperation and international exigency made a master manipulator, grasped the plan's potential. In Carranza's hands, it became the cat's-paw for a succession of his provocateurs as he tried to

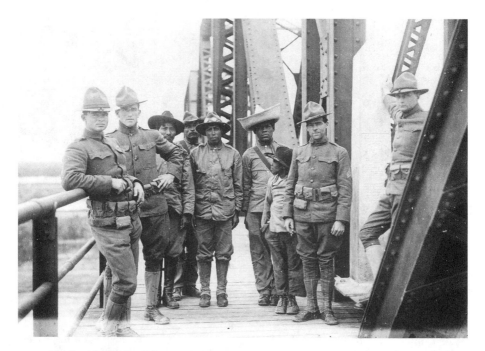

Figure 8.2 U.S. soldiers with Mexican irregulars on the Brownsville (Texas)–Matamoros (Tamaulipas) bridge. *Printed with permission, Russell Lee Photograph Collection, Center for American History, University of Texas at Austin.*

manipulate events along both sides of the border. Just as Porfirio Díaz understood the importance of the borderlands when he negotiated the end of the regime and his exile after Ciudad Juárez and Torreón fell, so did Carranza. He used the explosive character of the borderlands to his advantage.

German espionage agents, the Kaiser's troublemakers, found marvelous opportunities for their handiwork along the border. They had been active in giving monies, weapons, encouragement, and promises of even more to the schemes to restore Victoriano Huerta to power. The San Diego Plan unfolded while Huerta was in exile in Spain, but his co-conspirator Pascual Orozco haunted the region, skipping from side to side of the border as necessary. Carranza seized on the San Diego Plan and exaggerated the efforts of German agents and their support for Huerta to make the point that Mexico needed a strong government to control border incursions.[3] He hoped to maneuver the United States into extending diplomatic recognition to his government, and he dangled the prospect that his government could end the German espionage and eliminate borderland raiders by reasserting order along the border.

The Plan offered a cover for his efforts. The details Carranza left to his favorite military commander, the rather unsuccessful Pablo González, who knew the south Texas region well and saw in the plan an opportunity to order raids across the river into the area. The incursions were supposed to encourage the putative Liberating Army into further military actions, thus demonstrating to the United States that the German-Huerta threat had grown and that only diplomatic recognition of the Carranza government would lead to a return to order along the river. A number of raids occurred in the lower Rio Grande Valley that had only the most nominal U. S. military and Texas Ranger protection. Some 20,000 U.S. servicemen patrolled the 1,745 miles from the Gulf of Mexico to the Colorado River and about thirty state troopers, three-quarters of the entire force, operated in the lower Río Grande Valley.

Local Mexican Americans (coldheartedly encouraged by Carranza's activities) had reason to support the plan's demands. While they represented the majority of the population in south Texas, they had little political or economic clout. Until about 1900, the society in the southernmost counties had achieved a delicate balance, based on intermarriage of Anglo and Hispanic residents, common use of English and Spanish, and mutual respect for cultural traditions. A unifying culture had emerged, but the railroad and irrigation attracted large numbers of Americans and Mexicans from outside the region in pursuit of economic opportunities. By 1910, outsiders had overwhelmed the border society and two conflicting ethnic groups were emerging. Some Hispanics lost land, others suffered from labor discrimination, and all lost respect. They sought to reassert their rights, some early on through association with Flores Magón and others through the San Diego Plan.

Manipulation of events in Texas seemed natural to these borderlanders. Violent provocation began on July 4, a date calculated for maximum reaction, when forty Mexicans crossed the river and ambushed and killed two Anglos near Lyford, Texas. Revenge against Mexicans swiftly followed, with two killed the next day. Both sides began settling scores with what the Hispanics regarded as "bad" Anglos and with what the Anglos considered "bad" Mexicans. One such victim was A. L. Austin, who prided himself on handling the "Mexican" problems in the town of Sebastian. He used the toe of his boot to deal with malingering and administered lynch laws through the local Law and Order League for more serious breeches of ethnic relations. Following the outbreak of violence, raiders captured both him and his son and shot them to death. Retaliation occurred in sporadic fashion and resulted in the killing, in execution style, of fifteen local Hispanics near Ebenezer.[4]

Raiders struck the symbol of authority and wealth in the region, the King Ranch, and on another occasion derailed a passenger train just eight miles from Brownsville. But the most provocative incident came on September 23 when eighty uniformed Mexican soldiers crossed the river into Texas and looted a store near La Toluca, taking arms, liquor, food, and mules. A U.S. army patrol surprised the raiders and a skirmish followed in which U.S. Private Richard J. Johnson was taken prisoner. Covering gunfire from south of the river allowed the Mexican troops to escape with their prisoner and booty. Safely in

Figure 8.3 A Mexican woman and her young son selling chino grass to soldiers of the Sixth Cavalry stationed along the border in 1916. *Printed with permission, Photography Collection, Harry Ransom, Humanities Research Center, University of Texas at Austin.*

Mexico, they tortured Johnson by cutting off his ears, then decapitating him. They posted his head on a spike and paraded it along the river.

Unpredictable political violence drove both Anglos and Hispanics from the lower valley. Mexicans headed south to Tampico, most dramatically from the two southernmost counties of Texas, where some 40 percent of the Mexican population left in 1915. The Anglos went north to Corpus Christi, some even returning to the Midwest.

Carranza's plan succeeded but came perilously close to disaster. The combination of provocations in 1916 brought Mexico to the edge of war with the United States. Bloodshed seemed inevitable as Mexicans made raids throughout the lower valley. The best organized and most well equipped band was the Fierros Brigade of 450 Mexican and Mexican American troops with six Japanese volunteers that infiltrated the region north of Nuevo Laredo and headed toward San Antonio. General Pablo González coordinated these activities and directed the Fierros. Once Carranza had obtained all he could from pressing the United States with these troops, he disappointed González by allowing the invasion plans to wither in the valley region. A few cadres continued rogue actions, but the war threat declined as the Carranza government quickly moderated its tactics in Texas.

Figure 8.4 Wagons loaded with firewood and hay (chino grass) crossing the Rio Grande in 1916 near Lajitas, site of an American army camp from 1916 to 1920. *Printed with permission, Photography Collection, Harry Ransom, Humanities Research Center, University of Texas at Austin.*

The San Diego furor subsided once the U.S. government extended recognition to the Carranza government. General González halted his incursions across the river. The call for social revolution, real or contrived, was now ignored by the Constitutionalist commanders. Both national governments, in uncoordinated programs, began decisive campaigns against those borderlanders involved in the San Diego Plan.

Unrequited social demands left Hispanics north of the border vulnerable. Anglo-Texans turned on them. They found in the Plan, especially its exhortation to slay all Anglo males over sixteen years old, a clarion to race war in the borderlands. Anglos used this possibility as a rationalization for vigilante strikes. They abused and, in some instances, murdered Mexican Americans. The Texas rangers turned on Hispanics, who were regarded as troublemakers, were disrespectful of Anglo authority, were independent in their actions, or were simply in the wrong place at the wrong time. A wave of repression swept across the counties of deep south Texas.[5]

The brief but bloody Anglo rampage in the lower valley soon ran its course. Although the death toll officially reached 150, it was probably much higher. One witness reported finding on several occasions the corpses of Mexican Americans who had been lined up, executed, and left to rot in the chaparral. The failure of long-standing Anglo political bosses (with the exception of Archie Parr in Duval County) to protect their Hispanic supporters from ranger vengeance broke boss rule in south Texas, allowing a new breed of politicians posing as reformers to seize political control and develop their own economic interests in these southern counties.[6]

COLUMBUS RAID AND PERSHING EXPEDITION

The lower Río Grande Valley offered the opportunity for the Carranza government to demonstrate that it could maintain order, justifying diplomatic recognition. Meanwhile, events at the western end of the river boundary challenged the authority of both Mexican and American regimes along the frontier.

Norteño Pancho Villa utilized the borderlands as the scene for his efforts to influence the course of events. He sent a raiding party on March 7, 1916, across the international boundary to attack Columbus, New Mexico. The town, little more than a cavalry outpost defended by a skeleton force, could offer little resistance to the lightning strike of Villistas.

The raid resulted in the call-up of 150,000 U.S. militia troops, leading to the first total mobilization of military forces after the Spanish-American War, and served as a prelude to World War I.

European events forced President Wilson, beyond activating troops, to respond cautiously to the raid, eventually dispatching only a punitive expedition into Chihuahua after Villa.

Villa's raid and Pershing's expedition, like the San Diego Plan, convulsed the borderlands. The amphitheater of revolution, international intrigue, slippery diplomacy, and, on occasion, violence and terror again demanded the attention of both Mexico City and Washington. Retaliation meant violence directed against one's nationals or their property deep in the interior.

Carranza objected strenuously to Pershing's intervention in Mexico, and again the wily old revolutionary resuscitated the San Diego Plan and encouraged its Texas adherents to foment violence, who included in this outburst some African Americans and some Japanese recruited in Mexico by Pablo González. The possibility of a war between Mexico and the United States again loomed, until both sides peered eye to eye, then each side blinked. Pershing withdrew; the United States extended complete recognition to Carranza; Mexico's president backed away from the San Diego rebels; and he silently refused to acknowledge any association with German provocateurs or Prussian grand designs, such as the Zimmermann note,[7] to involve Carranza's government in alliance against the United States.

Figure 8.5 Texas rangers posing with dead Mexicans. *Printed with permission, Russell Lee Photograph Collection, Center for American History, University of Texas at Austin.*

In practical international politics, Carranza benefited from the Columbus raid and Pershing expedition, but in popular mythological recollection Villa triumphed. His reckless attack on the United States and masterful evasion in Chihuahua of the pursuing foreign army for virtually a year gave him national stature as the avenger of wrongs against Mexico and made him the greatest protagonist of popular revolutionary folklore. His raid on the United States became the subject of perhaps the most successful of all corridos, "La Persecución de Villa," which celebrates Villa's ability to elude an exaggeratedly huge American army in pursuit. The corrido remained a top-selling song into at least the 1950s.[8]

WORKSHOP OF REVOLUTION, II

As the norteño revolutionaries battled for a national military victory, individual military commanders also fomented state policies to put revolutionary programs into practice. These northern outsiders arrived with their troops in the central and southern states and took political control as well. Constitutionalist proconsuls included General Cándido Aguilar, the son-in-law of Carranza, in Veracruz and General Salvador Alvarado in Yucatán. These two outstanding commanders ordered the initiation of revolutionary changes.

Exemplary was the administration of General Alvarado, because Yucatán had weathered the storms of revolution with little disruption. Madero's campaigns provoked insurgent shudders in the peninsula (in Valladolid and in Mérida's so-called La Candelaria plot and other abortive efforts in 1910 and 1911), but despite sporadic political instability the society remained largely quiescent. The lack of popular rebellion in response to the opening created by Madero's insurgency reflected the unique circumstances of Yucatán. Isolated from revolutionary campaigns, remote from arms smuggling, removed from rebel threats, the small, weak middle class and the disorganized popular groups had little success in making a local rebellion. Moreover, rival elite factions, for all their willingness to use any campaign, including violence, to gain political leverage, would not attempt a full-scale mobilization of popular groups such as plantation workers, villagers, and stevedores. These notables remained haunted by the nineteenth-century Caste Wars, Maya uprisings that had threatened the annihilation of all *dzules* (or whites). Their northern brethren feared creating the opportunity for U.S. military intervention. This concern at times made them act with caution and circumspection; but they acted. The Yucatecos, dreading a race war, refused to organize. Thus the thrust toward revolutionary changes came from outside, with the arrival of a norteño army.[9]

The Constitutionalist *huaches* (the pejorative nickname given to people from interior Mexico), an army of some 7,000 men, arrived in Mérida in March 1915 with orders to tighten control of the soaring profits from henequen or sisal exports for Carranza's war effort. The responsibility rested with the borderland commander Alvarado, the one-time druggist, shopkeeper, and small farmer from Sonora who had experience in Flores Magón's PLM, participated in the Cananea strike, lived in Arizona exile, and emerged during the revolution as a powerful, adept general. Determined to build a committed following for the Constitutionalists, Alvarado granted amnesty to those who opposed his troops, courted and married a Yucatecan woman, and generally respected the traditions of the peninsular culture. Nevertheless, he left no doubt that the revolution had arrived. He froze assets and expropriated the properties of old rulers who had fled, dismantled the old regime's repressive institutions, including the militia, secret police, and jefes políticos, and placed thirty-seven of the most prominent former officials still in Yucatán under close supervision. Before undertaking further reforms, Alvarado directed an investigation of social and economic conditions that required six months to complete. His careful policies enabled him to build a strong coalition that cut vertically through peninsular society, attracting support from all social levels for his revolutionary undertaking.

Determined to make Yucatán a workshop of revolutionary change, Alvarado created a hurricane of reforms (later claiming responsibility for more than 1,000 decrees), of which two had transcendent force in changing the lives of peninsular peoples. He ended slavery. This action came as he enforced a 1914 decree that ended debt servitude; domestic and field labor would never be the same. Some 100,000 field hands were said to have abandoned the plantations, although most left only briefly, exercising their new freedom. The general softened the economic disruption by importing several thousand contract workers from central Mexico for agricultural labor.

Reflecting his Liberal commitments, his northern rearing, and his understanding of U.S. development based on widespread education, Alvarado launched a school reform program that focused on teaching literacy and citizenship. His campaign resulted in the building of more than 1,000 rural schools, the training of Maya teachers for rural areas, and the teaching of literacy (reputedly some 12,000 rural people learned to read and write Spanish during Alvarado's tenure) and civics. The lessons in citizenship taught civic responsibility (voting), patriotism (loyalty to the Constitutionalists), and personal rights (especially the end to forced labor). This campaign also made the rural schoolteacher a primary voice for revolutionary actions and a receptionist for local responses to proposed changes. The efforts to develop a curriculum that stressed rational education, that is, collectivist and anticlerical principles for village life, failed.

Social class, rural or urban residence, and ethnic identity mattered little on the religious issue—Yucatecans rejected the anti-Church policies, refusing to cooperate with the closing of churches, exiling priests, and defiling temples. Demonstrations against these actions spontaneously occurred, displaying popular feelings about the kind of revolutionary change the local people did and did not want in the peninsula. The negotiation between northern decrees and southeastern acceptance continued on Church issues until early 1917, when Alvarado acknowledged through his actions that he had changed his campaign. He began a policy tolerating some priests and opening some churches.

Reflecting the middle-class roots of his experience, the paternalistic policies of the general-governor prohibited prostitution, alcoholic beverages (except for beer with a 5 percent alcoholic content), and gaming (bullfights, lotteries, cards, and other gambling games). His concern for labor, sharpened by his association with the PLM and honed by Constitutionalist promises, led to his support for the organization of urban workers, first in unions and then for politics, in the Socialist Workers Party. In December 1915, Alvarado issued his labor law. One of the most radical in Mexico, it served later as a model for the labor provision in the 1917 Constitution. Above all, it legitimated workers' demands for reasonable hours and wages, the right to organize and strike, regulation of child and female labor, and the establishment of minimum safety standards in the workplace. It also gave support to worker mutualist organizations that became increasingly important at the end of the decade.

Agrarian programs focused on the development of a society of small landowners, but with one eye on the profits of henequen exports. Alvarado's decrees aimed at the redistribution of unused lands. He had a personal dislike of both the huge, exploitative henequen plantations and the communal ejido properties. The growing financial demands of the constitutional campaign required funds from the lucrative henequen exports. This economic motive combined with Alvarado's intense nationalistic hostility to the monopolistic activities of the International Harvester Corporation. He confronted this transnational business by reviving and reinforcing the Comisión Reguladora del Mercado de Henequén. Alvarado required all planters to sell their harvest to the Reguladora, making it the sole marketing agent for the fiber. Aided by the World War I disruption of other sources, the general succeeded in increasing the price of Yucatán's fiber in 1915 by over 400 percent to slightly over fifty cents a pound. This policy prospered as long as these world conditions prevailed.

Alvarado's programs initiated the widespread mobilization of popular groups, but he ensured that these emergent organizations remained under his control nevertheless. The revolution came from outside and from above, and he intended to keep it that way. He carefully erected a political apparatus, the Yucatecan Socialist Party, which consisted largely of urban unions, now renamed *ligas de resistencia,* or resistance leagues, and campesinos mobilized by rural schoolteachers and military prefects (the *comandantes militares,* who replaced the jefes políticos). By November 1918, when Carranza recalled Alvarado from Yucatán, no doubt existed that the revolution had come to the peninsula. Forced labor had ended, rural and urban workers had received the right to organize and had gained respect, women had received special recognition (including job opportunities in the state bureaucracy, acknowledgment of civil rights, and hosting of a feminist congress), and an enduring educational system had been initiated. Although the changes had been promoted from the top down, the people of Yucatán made themselves a part of the revolutionary process, rejecting such programs as the anticlerical attacks on religion and priests.[10]

In Exile

Rejecting the prospect of new revolutionary social, economic, and political programs, or simply fearing for the lives of their families and themselves, thousands of Mexicans went into exile. Once they crossed the border into the United States, they faced another decision. If they remained in the greater southwest, they found security in the extension to that area of Mexican food, customs, religion, and language. If they stayed in the region, they found as well that the revolution had intruded there with raids, recruitment, and espionage. Most chose the southwestern United States and the certainty of their culture. Unfortunately, Mexicans increasingly became objects of suspicion and even greater discrimination in the southwestern United States. Middle- and upper-class refugees had arrived north of the border in 1911, but in the fall of the year and from then on the largest number of refugees were poor workers. Madero's followers had been welcomed, the Porfirian expatriates (who brought money and possessions) also were well received, but the poor and destitute found little comfort and much hostility. Workers who fled the revolution's disruption and violence in their homeland arrived in the tumultuous labor scene of the borderlands. The unstable circumstances resulted from the competition among rival unions, the unstable market, and worker unhappiness with working conditions; these conditions soon produced strikes, especially in the Arizona mines. Mine owners and local law officers often reacted harshly to the disputes. The most dramatic example followed the return of the Pershing expedition and the lingering fear of Villista raids. Anti-Mexican hostility provoked the deportation of 1,200 striking miners from the Copper Queen mine in Bisbee, Arizona, in 1917. The workers were packed into railroad cattle cars, shipped first to Columbus, then on to Hermanas, New Mexico, where the cars were unhitched from the engine and the strikers abandoned in the desert.[11] The borderlands community had splintered into hostile factions.

Many more middle-class refugees after 1911 chose to move farther north to escape completely from the revolution's demands and violence. These exiles, chiefly from the states of Guanajuato, Jalisco, and Michoacán, followed railroad routes to Kansas City, St. Louis, Chicago, and other midwestern cities. Confronted with an alien environment, an unfamiliar language, and different customs, these Mexicans often established organizations to promote patriotic, social, and mutualist activities, created ethnic churches, and started Spanish language newspapers. In Kansas City, for example, Mexicans were excluded from many churches and recreational facilities, so many congregated at pool halls, bars, and brothels. The middle-class members of the colonia responded in July 1914 by establishing the Unión Mexicana Benito Juárez, probably the first Mexican patriotic society in the Midwest, and a few weeks later by founding the newspaper *El Cosmopolita*. The society sponsored patriotic celebrations, especially on September 16 and May 5, organized a night school that offered English classes, and constantly lobbied the city council to end police harassment of Mexicans, to end the segregation of Mexicans with African Americans, and to improve the quality of public education in the colonia. The society also worked to restrict alcoholic beverages, prostitution, and gambling in their neighborhoods.[12]

Once the United States entered World War I, popular attention in the colonia turned from the border with Mexico. Refugee Mexicans and Mexican Americans participated in the effort against the Central Powers, enlisting in the U.S. armed forces and working in war industries. A small indication of Mexicans involved in the war effort appeared in Nashville, Tennessee, at Old Hickory Powder Plant, where some 1,300 Mexicans (no doubt including many U.S. citizens) found employment, along with Anglo and black workers, with each group separated into its own compound.[13] The ebb and flow of anti-Mexican politics often reflected the needs of the local economy for workers.

LATENT MILITARY THREAT

Simultaneously with the Villa guerrilla threat and the intervention of U.S. troops in Chihuahua, Carranza confronted another military

Figure 8.6 A border home overlooking the Rio Grande on the Texas side between Polvo and Presidio, around 1924. *Printed with permission, Photography Collection, Harry Ransom, Humanities Research Center, University of Texas at Austin.*

problem, the Constitutionalist forces. He understood that his survival as president rested on transforming revolutionary soldiers and their officers into an institutional army under his control. Once he accomplished that, he could draw on the historical antipathy toward the military institution, firmly grounded in nineteenth-century liberalism, to keep the force small and relatively weak. In his efforts to control and reduce the army, he also could rely on the support of regional caciques, who preferred their own personal militias. Carranza's concern for the military coincided with that of Alvaro Obregón, the minister of war. Obregón began the process of dissolving competing armed revolutionary camarillas by incorporating them into the national army, establishing a table of organization, and determining the number of troops. Peacefully retiring officers required ingenuity. He offered the bait: Officers who agreed to leave active service and enter the Legion of Honor of the National Army retained their rank and full salary. Those who did not do so risked forced retirement at half pay and were subject to recall. The message could not be misunderstood—cooperate and retain status and lifestyle; resist and, at best, retain half pay. The revolutionary soldier, now considered an enlisted man, went into the reserve without pay. The delicate political task conducted behind the façade of organizing the National Army demonstrated Obregón's remarkable political skills. Once he accomplished his goal, he resigned from the cabinet, on May 1, 1917. Understandably, he expected to succeed Carranza in the presidential chair, and he returned to Sonora to bide his time.

THE 1917 CONSTITUTION

Meanwhile, Carranza and his northern cohorts, even while negotiating the withdrawal of the Pershing expedition and grappling with the discharge of rebel forces, turned their attention to national reconstruction, that is, to making their revolution work. The president, as he attempted the reconstruction of the national government, chose to present himself as the embodiment of the revolution. His ego prompted him to claim credit for it—and at the same time he became the target of all those who had some complaint, whether an irksome sleight or major grievance. Carranza was determined to rely on his own judgment and cast aside the suggestions of others. Many examples exist of Carranza's obdurate behavior, but there is none better than his involvement in the creation of a new constitution. He believed that the 1857 Constitution (the legal echo of the Juárez Liberal idealism) needed to be revised because a half century and a revolution had occurred since the promulgation of the document. Thus, he convened a convention at Querétaro, where delegates wrote the 1917 Constitution.

The delegates, all certified by their association with Carranza's campaign against Huerta and Villa, divided into general blocs: those who agreed with Carranza that the revolutionaries generally could maintain the Porfirian national economic structure with its strong modernizing orientation; and those, especially Obregón and Francisco Múgica, who insisted that added to this national structure there must be a popular base (whether this would move toward a new hierarchy or an egalitarian society remained in contention).

The populists, the latter group, won, but it did not matter. Carranza ignored the document once it was written, largely because he had wanted to have a revised nineteenth-century constitution, not to establish a set of revolutionary fundamentals. For all his rejection of the document, the 1917 Constitution drew on the First Chief's decrees, the December 1914 "Additions to the Plan of Guadalupe," and the January 1915 "Law of Restoration and Dotation of Ejidos," which Carranza had improvised to broaden his popular support during the fighting. Múgica successfully campaigned with the delegates to incorporate these decrees and include sweeping new provisions in other areas, so that the new document placed special emphasis on "public education, land distribution, labor guarantees, and regulation of religious organizations." These statutes were loosely wrapped in an eclectic ideology that manifested itself in "nationalism, secularism, anticlericalism, and social consciousness. . . ."[14] Both revolutionaries and later historians have emphasized the importance of these provisions in articles 3 (church and education), 27 (land) and 123 (labor). The extensive document included provisions that foreshadowed significant later developments. Of these, article 28 stands out. This provision directed the government to prevent "ruinous competition" in industry by limiting producers. President Lázaro Cárdenas, in the 1930s, and his successors expanded this article, enabling the administration to direct industrial development through investment, prices, profits, and wages.[15]

The new document had three major sources of inspiration: national needs, the Constitutionalist (that is, Carranza's) revolutionary goals, and the legacy of the Juárez Liberals. The latter two drew on the borderlands inheritance that Carranza recognized as his own; the first he rejected because he would not accept something outside of his own conception of what was good for the country. Continuity could be found in provisions such as article 18 on prison reform that reiterated Porfirian views on the penal system (rehabilitation, social defense, and reform from the top), but called for decentralized control to prevent the abuses attributed to Díaz and made possible by centralized control.[16] Despite all of the changes in the new charter, the delegates wanted to affirm the continuity with the Liberal past of Juárez, so they approved the document on February 5, 1917, in Querétaro, the same day in the same city where the Liberals had ratified the 1857 Constitution.

Symbolic relationship notwithstanding, the president would have nothing to do with the constitution. What Carranza scorned, other revolutionary veterans championed. He talked about "Mexico" and they "La Mexicanidad," or, Mexican-ness. The former was static and structured, the latter dynamic and functional; both looked to the national government to achieve its ends. The constitution, although Carranza refused to see it, contained both views.

The 1917 Constitution, a document four times the length of the U.S. charter, trumpets the Mexican as a citizen and an individual. It refers fifteen times to the family and more than fifty times to the working class. Because of its specificity, the constitution is regularly being revised to bring it into line with national practices. Between 1917 and 1980, some 350 amendments were added, but each one is incorporated directly into the document, so the original wording and provisions disappear and the new language simply appears without notice.[17]

The president's pinch-nose reaction to the constitution left to others the task of putting it into practice. Despite the provisions in support of working people, for example, Carranza did nothing. In this void, Gustavo Espinosa Mireles, the governor of Coahuila, acted, calling a labor convention in his capital of Saltillo in early 1918. This border state served as the focus for a major convention, which included a friendly observer representing Samuel Gompers and the American Federation of Labor. The delegates, with a majority from the north and from a variety of unions, especially those organized along craft lines, created the Regional Confederation of Mexican Workers (CROM), led by Luis M. Morones. This organization quickly became the most powerful voice of labor in the country.[18] Morones seized the opportunities to enrich himself in the name of the 1917 document.

THE LILL REPORT

The constitution represented the victory of one group of revolutionary veterans within the Constitutionalist forces. Other veterans had to claim their due in the risky politics of the emerging Mexico or in shaky opportunities of the shattered economy. Many relied on their wartime experience and used force as their investment capital. These officers directed their personal armies to seize estates, mines, and lumber camps, control the railroads, and enter business. Others found that revolutionary military rank now made them socially acceptable to old Porfirian families, eager to parlay the marriage of a daughter into the preservation of economic and social standing.[19] New men everywhere grasped for political and economic opportunities offered by the revolution. Many were veterans, but others had merely skulked around the rebel camps and battles looking for some angle of advancement. Many reckless victors by association claimed the spoils.

Not all rebels and rebel hangers-on focused on personal gain as the reward for successfully making a revolution. They took up the most difficult of tasks, making the revolution work. Idealism and revolutionary fervor met head on with the reality of the government's near bankruptcy, the people's appalling shortages of food and work, and the ravages of the 1918 Spanish influenza epidemic. Dreams might offer solace and inspiration, but economic recovery promised jobs, full bean pots, and ample tortillas. Carranza, despite the enormous pressure of these circumstances, maintained his commitment to Mexico first. He stopped the export of gold, keeping the great majority of its production for national reserves to repair revolutionary damage and launch programs in education and public health. Moreover, he made it clear that his administration placed the needs of Mexicans above any obligations to foreigners, whether investors, property owners, or governmental representatives. The insurgents had driven Díaz from Mexico, but not his legacy, in terms of tangled and nearly over-whelming foreign debts, further increased by loans obtained by the rebels themselves.

The Carranza regime announced that it wanted to resume debt payments, reestablish its international credit, and renew national economic development. As the first step, Carranza wanted a deter-mination of actual debts, so his treasury secretary Luis Cabrera arranged for an impartial audit by bringing New York banker Henry Bruére and certified public accountant Thomas R. Lill to Mexico City in 1917. Simultaneously, talks between treasury officials and Thomas Lamont, representing J. P. Morgan, resulted in the creation of the In-ternational Committee of Bankers on Mexico, with representatives of four French, six British, and seven U.S. (New York) banks. Bruére re-turned to New York after three' months, but his colleague stayed on for another six months completing a summary of Mexican debt. Lill and Lamont were destined to have a major role in the financial affairs of subsequent Mexican regimes.

Lill completed his audit and published a report that calculated the Mexican debt at $864,942,598, including the loans obtained by the Huerta dictatorship. The figure represented the Mexican govern-ment's projected income for approximately eight years. Although Car-ranza and other Mexican leaders rejected the Huerta loans, the Lill audit became the basis for future financial discussions, particularly those between the treasury department and the International Com-mittee of Bankers on Mexico. The Lill report defined financial negoti-ations and international agreements until the 1970s.[20] Adolfo de la Huerta and Thomas Lamont, through informal negotiations, made this report the basis for long-standing agreement on the debt.[21]

Don Venus in Eclipse

Despite successful programs in some states, Carranza and those around him provoked a growing popular revulsion against their in-cumbent regime. Corruption resulted from the mingling of the new revolutionary elite with the former Porfirian hierarchy, as Carranza's favorites grabbed fortunes and paraded before the public. The reality of greed was little different. The *mordida,* the bite, was put on every-one attempting to do business with the government. Zapata, before his death, appealed to Carranza as a "Mexican" who must feel at some moments "the anguish of mothers, the suffering of orphans," to step down and end the orgy he called a revolution. Zapata charged that the Constitutionalist army "steals seeds, cattle and beasts of burden in the countryside. In the small villages they burn or sack humble dwellings, and in the big cities they speculate . . . with stolen grain. . . . They murder in broad daylight; they assault automobiles and commit crimes in the street during business hours on the main avenues. . . ."[22]

This system of payoffs reached new levels during these years as the president himself began accumulating so much personal wealth that when he fled the national capital, the locomotive and freight cars hauling his personal possessions were referred to as the "Golden train." This personal enrichment led to the widespread use of the newly created verb "Carranzar," that is, "to carranza," meaning "to steal." When Constitutionalist troops or bureaucrats took over the town, the people soon referred to the effects of a "carranclán," a play on words merging Carranza and hurricane, at the hands of "conlasuñaslistas," a neologism alluding to the Constitutionalists, but describing them "with their claws ready." This popular evaluation reached out widely across the countryside, so even in the Maya communities of Chiapas, villagers used the modified noun "Carranza Ch'o" or the "Carranza Rat" to refer to the rodents that entered their homes, bringing disease, biting children, and stealing food.

The president ignored the profiteering of his administrators and army officers. Carranza, while guilty of personal peculation, continued to face problems with foreigners, especially U.S. Senator Albert Bacon Fall of New Mexico. Carranza and Fall represent a curious pair of politicians from the borderlands. Carranza built on his experience along the border to achieve national power and manipulated politics to acquire international recognition. Fall also seized the opportunities provided by New Mexico's location to garner personal wealth and national office. Both men ultimately failed because they misjudged their countrymen, as a consequence of the vanity that resulted from their personal successes. Arrogance as surely as pride precedes a fall. Carranza thought he could rule indefinitely through marionette presidents and Fall believed he could bring down the Mexican government and later manipulate U.S. President Warren G. Harding.

Senator Fall's ambition to destroy the revolutionary government and replace President Carranza with Félix Díaz led him to inspire schemes calling for an invasion of Mexico and to indulge in such embellished accusations against Mexican revolutionaries that he discredited his own campaign. His Senate subcommittee on Mexican relations became the focal point of the effort to be the king maker in Mexico. Hearings from August 1919 until May 1920 set the stage. By the time it had finished its deliberations, the committee, consisting of Fall, Frank Brandegee of Connecticut, and Marcus Smith of Arizona, had heard the testimony from 257 witnesses, most of whom recited atrocity stories and other allegations. Fall badgered witnesses favorable to Mexico, petted those who made accusations against Carranza, and neglected accounts he could not magnify as proof that there existed a heinous government in Mexico. The final report exaggerated the number of U.S. citizens killed and the extent of U.S. property lost from 1910 to 1920.[23]

The rhetoric to discredit Carranza became so strident that the general public in the United States, including Fall's fellow senators, in the end discounted the subcommittee's report in its entirety, thus, missing among other things, the information on Carranza's manipulation of the San Diego Plan.[24] Fall failed in his effort to have the United States withdraw its recognition of the Carranza government. This son of the border soon faced problems of his own in the Teapot Dome Scandal, an effort to exploit U.S. navy oil reserves in Wyoming, which made him a political outcast as the first presidential cabinet member sentenced to prison and left him in disgrace. Despite all of his achievements, Carranza's reputation suffered as well, and this other son of the border lost not only his political position but also his life in the struggle with Obregón.

Obregón in Waiting

What of Obregón during these episodes? The champion of the wars against Huerta, Zapata, and Villa, recovering from the loss of one arm at the Battle of Celaya, seems strangely absent from the events from 1917 until 1919. Certainly he watched the border cockpit closely. Making ready to emerge in the presidential contest of 1920, he enriched himself after 1917 with exclusive War Industries Board contracts for food exports (garbanzos) to the United States during World War I. Then he resigned from his position as minister of war and took refuge in Sonora.

Obregón represented the opposite side of the borderlands coin from Francisco Villa. Rather than the popular and flamboyant, Obregón expressed the bourgeois and businesslike visage of border character. Pragmatic, individualistic, opportunistic, and ambitious described both men, but in Villa these traits combined with his impulsive nature and led to banditry, smuggling, violence, womanizing, and, oddly, teetotaling, while in Obregón they joined a methodical quality to foster commercial farming, reliance on the law, although not always adherence to it, and exporting business, dour monogamy, and, no surprise, a taste for his liquor neat and in large quantities. Both men established a political base along the border in their native states. Ultimately Villa's campaign for control of all of Mexico failed (at the hands, primarily, of Obregón), while Obregón eventually became the most powerful revolutionary during the decade of the 1920s. But his prospects at first looked bleak, although not altogether hopeless.

Favoring Obregón or any revolutionary veteran who challenged Carranza was the popular reaction against him. But the president controlled the government, including the electoral machinery. Carranza's insistence on civilian primacy over participants in the armed phase of the revolution also caused bitterness. After all, as many observed, the civilian citizen who risked his life on the field of battle and in the process earned military rank should not be subordinated to those who remained out of harm's way. Incredibly, such noncombatants sought to establish some sort of proprietary hold on politics and its benefits, excluding those who had been willing to sacrifice their lives in battle. Revolutionary veterans refused to be pushed aside in such cavalier fashion. In their minds, battlefield credentials established one's right to engage in politics.

Carranza bypassed Obregón as his official presidential candidate in 1920 for another son of Sonora. He decided in favor of a more compliant, malleable choice, Ignacio Bonillas, who had spent virtually the entire decade in the United States, missing the battlefield, while representing Carranza, first on the 1916 Mexican-American Joint Commission and later as the First Chief's representative in Washington, D.C. In the United States, he married a North American woman, adding to his reputation of having become a Yankee. Despite the public's hostility to someone they called "Mister" Bonillas in the newspapers and in theaters, and the veterans' opposition not only to a civilian but also to someone who sat out the revolution in the United States, Carranza's choice expected victory.

In military, financial, bureaucratic, and idealistic terms, a new era, framed by the 1917 Constitution, began in 1918. The great multitude of Mexicans had been given the means to demand the advantages offered in this constitution by the exigency measures (e.g., the Agrarian Commission) decreed during the fighting. These laws and agencies should have given Carranza national repute for his efforts to achieve it. His personal excesses undercut his public successes. Moreover, Carranza misjudged another northerner; he better than anyone else should have known Obregón, but he did not. Perhaps Carranza's success in wringing recognition from the U.S. government, pushing aside Villa, and withstanding the intrigues of foreigners, especially Fall, explains his casual dismissal of Obregón's ambition.

SONORANS ASCENDANT, 1920–1927

In a strange kind of revolutionary meteorology—perhaps revealing the distance between capital city developments and the general public—this 1918 lightning flash was not followed by its political thunderclap until 1920. The rumble came from the Sonora Triangle, so-called for its three leading members, Obregón and his home state henchmen, Adolfo de la Huerta and Plutarco Elias Calles. Understanding that the election would be an affirmation of the president's choice, rather than the casting of votes, the Triangle chose rebellion. They proclaimed this stage of the revolution from the small border-town of Agua Pricta, Sonora, with little in the way of promises except to hold elections for Obregón once they replaced Carranza.

They moved quickly to eliminate the three other contending forces from the Convention of Aguascalientes. The triangle might just as well refer to the successful manner in which this Agua Prieta movement on May 21, 1920, decapitated the Carranza forces with Venustiano's assassination at Tlaxcalantongo, Puebla, co-opted the Zapata troops by reaching agreement with Emiliano's successor, Gildardo Magaña, and compromised the Villista legions by persuading Villa to go into retirement. Eliminating the three most prominent competitors for national power cleared the way for Obregón and his fellow Sonorans to establish their version of a northern regime.

The Sonora Triangle seized power in 1920, confirming northern control over the national government for the next sixteen years. Beyond installing their personal authority, these Sonorans dedicated their energies to making the revolution work. They were committed to carrying out the goals of the revolution, articulated primarily in the 1917 Constitution, largely through agrarian and educational reforms. The Sonorans faced the torturous process of establishing the procedures for presidential succession and arranging for the administration of the revolution. They confronted the Porfirian elites, who survived either in Mexico or in exile, and the techniques they used to reemerge in the society and economy.

The Sonorans had to overcome monumental obstacles in their efforts to make the revolution work. The task of reviving Mexico was a staggering undertaking. These leaders had to rebuild after the revolutionary destruction, resuscitate the economy, and restore confidence in government, constructing a new relationship between the government and the people. These campaigns required the efforts of the Mexican people, who had endured a decade of fighting, food shortages, worthless money, erratic employment, disease, and the death of relatives and friends. The Sonorans needed to inspire an exhausted people if they hoped to make the revolution work.

Brittle Hopes of the 1920s

As the new decade dawned, those who survived the revolution's feroc-
ity shared a sense of exuberance about the revolutionary future and
exhaustion that followed the chaotic conditions created by its misery
and violence. Their horror at the time of the death and destruction reflected sentiments in both the United States and Europe. Mexicans
accepted the high cost in lives and property in the belief that national
uniqueness now could become manifest, provided Mexico shed the
Porfirian-embossed veneer of Europe and disavowed the campaign to
ignore its indigenous people and traditions. The decade revealed that
at the moment Mexico become more conscious of its ethnic diversity, it
also shared more and more of the culture of Western Europe and the
United States. Many Europeans, reacting to the end of the World War,
dismissed what they regarded as wartime insanity. Some acted out a
peaceful madness of their own in the "Roaring '20s"; others turned to
pacifist movements to prevent it from happening again. In the United
States, many preened at the success of the doughboys, took satisfaction in providing women with the vote, and tried to balance a high
moral tone that led to the prohibition of alcohol with a thirst that led
them to speakeasies in the evening. Moral hypocrisy and unpopular
statutes created disrespect for the law and gangsterism. Generally,
Americans indulged in the culture of flappers and Ford flivvers.

The new Mexico was not immune to these currents of excess and
exaggeration from abroad. While Europeans struggled with the reality of 8.3 million dead in the World War, Mexicans had the equally
hideous task of acknowledging 500,000 to two million persons killed
or immigrated as a result of the internecine violence (representing
from 4 percent to 15 percent of the population). The tragedy of
Gallipoli or the slaughter at the Somme remained horrible memories
for Europeans, but similar grisly events had been repeated time
and again in the Mexican struggle at Zacatecas, Durango, Torreón,
Querétaro, and elsewhere. At Celaya (1915) 40,000 men fell upon each
other in the bloodiest slaughter in Mexico's history. Obregón, borrowing tactics from the Great War then reaching new heights of destruction in Europe, used trench warfare and barbed wire against the
Villista cavalry, cutting down 7,000 men in three days. Several months
later, he came close to duplicating his feat at León. As a consequence,
Villa went from a Division General to an elusive guerrilla never again
able to mount a large-scale campaign.[25]

Mexicans, like Europeans, mourned the loss of a generation;
poets, authors, painters, politicians, fathers, brothers, and lovers had
died in what seemed to be endless slaughter. Perhaps the revolution
was fairer than the World War. The European conflict weighed heaviest

on young men of the lower classes; Mexicans killed each other without regard for age, rank, title, or social position. It was a terrible loss for the nation to bear, made even more bitter by being self-inflicted. Just having survived the national upheaval that lasted until the inauguration of Obregón in 1920 gave Mexicans of energy and intellect an incredible feeling of euphoria.[26]

Mexicans combined revolutionary politics and social extravagance with extreme cultural efforts. The muralists turned to monumental art and authors resorted to "vanguardism" in literature. Cultural giants emerged in music, while José Vasconcelos and his literary campaign attempted to raise national interest in the fine arts. All of these artists and cultural representatives drew on the euphoria that followed the fighting and the emerging popular culture.[27]

Efforts to express the meaning of the revolution extended to architecture as well. Following the aesthetic leadership of the muralists, architects turned first to neocolonialism then to functionalism. Venustiano Carranza, while president from 1916 to 1920, offered tax exemptions to those who built homes in the neocolonial style as an expression of the new revolutionary society. As a result, Porfirian era neoclassical and early colonial buildings were destroyed to make way for neocolonial construction. Secretary Alberto Pani in 1922 enlisted Carlos Obregón Santacilia to renovate and expand the building of the ministry of Foreign Relations. He revised the building in the neocolonial style. But the greatest and most ironic inspiration for neocolonial public architecture came from José Vasconcelos, who promoted the style as the decolonization of Mexico. The public buildings in the capital that reflected his influence and Obregón Santacilia's designs included the Benito Juárez elementary school in Colonia Roma, Escuela "Gabriela Mistral," Instituto Tecnico Industrial, and Centro Industrial Nocturno.

Later, young architects would reject the ornamentation, among other things, of neocolonialism and in 1925 turn to the functionalism of Walter Gropius and Le Corbusier. As a practical matter, this new style received vigorous support from Mexican cement companies, because they relied heavily on this construction material. Obregón Santacilia switched design styles and joined with Juan O'Gorman and José Villagrán García, who became the leaders of functionalist architecture. This style of construction represented the revolution of President Calles. The modernization of the revolution could be seen clearly in the newly constructed high-rise buildings that towered over the previous limit of eight-story buildings.[28]

Other Mexican attitudes found expression in the street corner music of corridos, the most plaintive of which called out "The Wish for a Peace Tortilla."[29] Beyond hopes, Mexicans had to cope with their reality. The death toll demanded new behavior on the part of both women and the young of both sexes. The fact that about one in ten adult men had been killed created new spaces and opportunities for others, resulting in social mobility and expanding options for previously marginal groups.[30]

Nearly everyone had felt the brush of death. Thus, many had the compulsion to live life with as much zest as possible. The jazz age, with of its commotion, intensity, and frivolity, appeared in Mexico, as did gangsters, lured by the disrupted social conditions in the cities and the countryside and the profits from smuggling alcoholic beverages along the northern frontier. The romance of these criminals soon appeared in stories and movies, especially those concerning the Grey Automobile Gang. Along the northern boundary, saloons, gambling houses, and nightclubs became social centers for Mexicans and tourists alike. The jazz age temples in Ciudad Juárez, for example, the Tivoli, Jimmie O'Brien's, the Palace, the Baghdad, and the Central Cafe No. 2, featured the gangland liturgy of shootings and payoffs. Cafe society in the capital roared around the city in imported cars, sported flashy suits and bopped hair, and drank martinis.[31]

The new national leaders had shared the battlefield experience; a majority of these politicians from 1914 to 1934 were combat veterans. Their level of participation equals that of the post–insurrection leaders of revolutionary China and Cuba or the membership of resistance veterans in the post–World War II parliaments of France.[32]

General Alvaro Obregón had survived the decade from 1910 to 1920, but he did not escape unscathed; a wound during the battle of León cost him most of his right arm. He also had dodged death despite the orders to arrest and execute him from both Villa and Carranza (no doubt Zapata would have given the same command had he the chance to get his hands on Obregón). Obregón was a northerner who had breathed in deeply the airs of borderland survival, capitalism, and individualism.

OBREGÓN ASCENDANT

This son of Sonora was more than a profit seeker; he was a capitalist consumer as well. That is, the winds of reform capitalism or Progressivism had blown across his face. He expected value for what he paid. He had no illusions about what the rebellion had accomplished in Mexico and no grand ideals about what it might do, but he did have some specific plans for what Mexicans should receive as payment for the tens of thousands of lives the nation had lost. He also had business relations with the U.S. government and American entrepreneurs. Based on his experience, he knew when a handshake made a better deal than an elaborate contract. (The Bucareli agreements, in which both sides could claim what they wanted but agreed to work things out, are a perfect example.) Historian Howard Cline used a different analogy—with Spain's Bourbon reformers—to describe much the same set of characteristics. Thus he dubbed Obregón and the northerners the "Neo-Bourbons."[33] Above all, the new president represented a set of middle-class values, especially of the noneconomic sort, which included "an emphasis on national as against local concerns; a familiarity with urban life, associated with a commercial, entrepreneurial spirit and an awareness of the role of organized labour; an indifference, or more often a hostility to the Church, a capacity for bureaucratic organization—of army or civil institutions—which was personal, universalistic and meritocratic."[34]

Obregón, as a survivor, had a quiet but determined confidence, confirmed in the presidential election of 1920. With Obregón's ascension, the Mexican social revolution abandoned its self-destructive phase and turned to more constructive programs. His policies fit within the general framework created by the 1917 Constitution, and the new president used his opportunities to the utmost, tempered with a realistic assessment of the strength of the national government and a preference for responding to popular demands. His government benefited from the general surge toward peace and tranquility that followed the popular revulsion against violence after the assassination of Zapata in 1919 and the retirement of Villa in 1920 (during the interval of de la Huerta's interim presidency). De la Huerta had done much to create the conditions for national reconciliation when he declared a general unconditional amnesty for all insurgent partisans.

Obregón's regime also benefited from the sense of community that had developed through the fighting, the wartime comradeship that created a kind of brotherhood often mistaken for nationalism. This camaraderie overcame the intense parochialism of the soldiers when they were forced to change sides after losses in battle. Thus Juan the Chamula fought for Huerta (as a conscript seized in a Chiapas jail and taken to the front), then for Carranza, and finally for Villa before being retaken by the Carrancistas and demobilized. Marcelo Caraveo joined Orozco in 1910 to battle Porfirio, then followed a topsy-turvy career soldiering for Huerta, then Zapata, then Félix Díaz, then Peláez, and finally Obregón.[35] The experiences of these veterans were typical of many revolutionaries.

Fighting shoulder to shoulder with men from across the republic, enduring the agony of war with men of different ethnic groups, and sharing what little food there was with those of different classes helped engender both a sense of *lo mexicanidad* among veterans and a soldier's disregard for civilians. With this as a basis, the assassination of first Zapata and then Carranza could be understood as a loss, not just to one faction but to the entire pueblo. Brothers in arms wanted an end to the bloodshed. In that sense, enough death was enough. These veterans constituted a political generation that made revolutionary participation a key to political success through World War II, when the political recruitment patterns returned to gathering novices in the major universities, including the National Military College, a practice that began in the last years of the Porfirian regime. From 1920 through 1946, more than three times the number of politicians were combat veterans as during the Porfirian years. For its moment in power, this generation shared the revolution as its defining experience.[36]

Obregón faced desperate economic problems in Mexico, brought about by the revolutionary devastation and successive droughts and crop failures. Moreover, he had problems that extended beyond the nation's boundaries. Wartime economic expansion had ended in the United States in late 1920, causing an abrupt collapse of the demand for Mexican workers. By early 1922, some 20,000 workers and their families, stranded north of the border, were on the verge of starvation. Despite severe hardships at home, Obregón's government spent more than one million dollars trying to alleviate the crisis by repatriating workers. But those who returned to Mexico had difficulty finding employment at home, and by the middle of 1922, when the United States economy improved, emigration northward began again. Obregón faced economic and social circumstances that harbored potential danger. These repatriated unemployed workers returned home with expanded political awareness and a willingness to criticize the government. Many left Mexico in the first place because they opposed the revolutionaries and did not like them any better when they came back.

Transborder problems, which received great emphasis by the existence of starving Mexican workers in the United States, gave impetus to Obregón's effort to secure American recognition and promote economic recovery. His efforts to achieve normal diplomatic relations suffered from the U.S. government's excessive concern with radicalism that resulted in Obregón's being labeled in the press as a Bolshevik. To counter this concern, the Mexican foreign affairs ministry spent nearly two million dollars in a publicity campaign to persuade influential U.S. political and business leaders that the time had come to reestablish mutually beneficial commercial and diplomatic ties with the Obregón regime.

Obregón did not want to scare off resurgent foreign investors and owners, alarm restive Catholic priests and lay leaders, or mobilize regional warlords and foot-dragging villagers by hasty or radical change. Within this complex of inducements and impediments, Obregón recognized both the constraints and the political advantages arising from the reconstructive phase of the revolution.[37] His pragmatism encouraged the elite (whether created by the revolution or survivors from the Porfirian era) to resume their productive economic activities, repatriate the money removed from the country during the earlier stages of the revolution, and act as a magnet for renewed American investment. Luis Terrazas, who had fled first to El Paso and

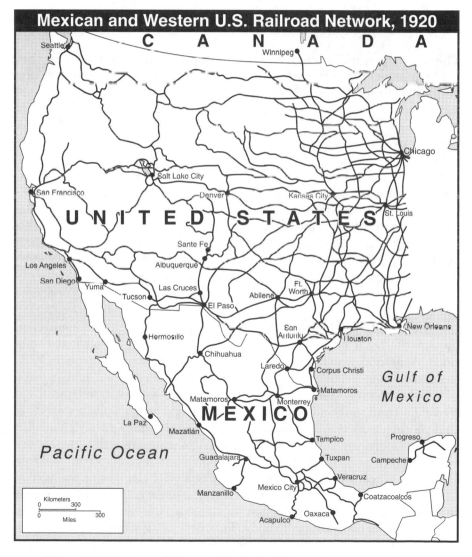

Figure 8.7 Mexican and Western U.S. Railroad Network, 1920.

then to Los Angeles, along with at least five million pesos, returned in 1920. He accepted thirteen million pesos in settlement for expropriated land, allowing the family to reestablish its economic position in Chihuahua. His son-in-law, Enrique Creel, with his immense fortune built during the Porfirian years, returned in the 1920s from Los Angeles exile to establish his own banking firm in Mexico City and to become an important economic advisor to the president. Creel's network of friends and associates within the international financial community served Obregón well.

OLD ELITES ACCOMMODATE

The Terrazas family and other Porfirians found circumstances they could master. The violence of the previous decade had largely prevented the appearance of new self-sufficient state and revolutionary local elites. Although badly damaged (Creel, for example, claimed to have lost $5,502,222.76 from 1913 to 1921), the Porfirians had not been destroyed. Those with diversified holdings recovered the quickest; those who had limited their pre-Revolutionary holdings to land suffered the most. The Monterrey group, ignoring rural properties, was hardly damaged at all. Although these reemerging oligarchs could not reenter directly into politics, they recovered indirect influence through interaction (including intermarriage) with the new revolutionary elite and through the exercise of economic power. As early as 1918, Carranza had desperately sought to rebuild the economy and to develop political allies; consequently, he approved the return of many estates to oligarchs, such as Guillermo Muñoz, Terrazas's grandson.[38]

Local administrations during the decade 1910–1920 had witnessed the least change of all levels of government. Political conditions remained much the same in the municipalities, especially in isolated areas. Porfirian caciques and families retained power—and where new men seized offices, this probably resulted more from local rivalries than national revolutionary allegiance. Representative of this pattern was the Rascón family. The family dominated Uruáchic, in the western mountains of Chihuahua, throughout the nineteenth century until the revolt against the Porfirian regime. From 1910 to 1920, the office of municipal president changed hands ten times; five times its occupants were Rascón family members. The rebels threw them out in 1911. They returned as Orozquistas in 1912 and continued to fight as counterrevolutionaries until 1914, when the family accepted the Villa amnesty but lost political control until 1918. They recovered the office and retained it through the 1920 election.[39]

Figure 8.8 A festive gathering of post–revolutionary upper middle class in Guadalajara, ca. 1925. Note the army band in the background. *Printed with permission, Research Collection, Annelisa Romero de MacLachlan.*

The survivors of the Porfirian elite in larger towns often took their first step back into Mexican society through the networks established by their wives. Oligarchic women joined charitable organizations, especially the Mexican Red Cross, where they were socially reintegrated into the community, and the family's men soon followed them to the Casino and other elite clubs.

The old elite in Chihuahua soon emerged again as important cattle ranchers and gradually reasserted its influence in industry and finance. Although they never regained direct political power, they used intermarriage with the new elite and their own economic importance to exert strong, if indirect, influence. In this way, these persistent oligarchs helped shape the course of Mexican history in the post-Revolutionary era. No member of these emergent and reemergent families during this era (through World War II) served as representative or intermediary of foreign companies. These old and new elites came together in the state's cattlemen's association and the formation of the Banco Comercial Mexicano, the flagship of the Vallinas empire. Eloy Vallina, through banking, real estate, and a host of other investments, acted much as Enrique Creel had during the Porfiriato as the engineer of enterprise.

The Samaniegos of Ciudad Juárez and El Paso offer a striking example of a family that recovered its influence through intermarriage with revolutionaries. Dr. Mariano Samaniego had bossed city politics from the 1860s until his death in 1905 and had appeared eleven times in the state legislature and many times as interim governor. His son-in-law Inocente Ochoa emerged as the richest man on the border. During the 1920s, five different relatives served as the political boss of Juárez.[40]

Similar merging of old and new elites took place in other states as well. In Oaxaca, the ranching families, especially in the Costa Chica, constituted the most dynamic sector of the society throughout the nineteenth century. Rancheros began contesting for political influence around the turn of the century and seized on the revolution to push forward their claims to authority. By 1902, twelve ranchers shared the Baños family name in Pinotepa; in 1911, the family established a cacicazgo in the region; and in the 1990s, the family remains dominant in the region.[41]

JUGGLING CAUDILLOS AND CACIQUES

Despite the emergence and reemergence of local and state camarillas, Obregón managed to exercise national authority. His strength as president came from his ability to tolerate this development and use it to benefit his regime and Mexico. He accommodated widely divergent social elements within his government and harnessed their energy and political potential. Moreover, he had earned prestige with the army, which his predecessors in the previous decade lacked: neither the civilians Madero and Carranza nor the unpopular General Huerta received much in the way of recognition from the army. On the other hand, Obregón had a brilliant military career and he proved willing to do what was necessary to incorporate private armies into the national armed forces. Summing up this program he stated, "If a man calls himself a general, he must be one." In this way, he brought warlords and their followers under his command, using what he privately called a "cañonazo de pesos," that is, a cannon blast of money. In exchange, he repeatedly tried to restrict officers on duty from working for opposition political candidates. The largely futile program did result in the cashiering of some officers and the confiscation of their property. He also resorted to the policy of creating military zones and then rotating officers to limit the growth of loyalty between commanders and their troops. In these ways, he began the process in which the revolution's military leaders transformed themselves into political authorities, eventually making the armed forces subservient to the state. The success of this effort has made Mexican civil-military relations unique in Latin America and one of the most crucial and enduring results of the revolution. Obregón's policies and those that followed under Calles and General Joaquín Amaro succeeded because both political and military leaders shared the same revolutionary experience.[42]

Obregón's sense of humor enabled him to defuse awkward and dangerous political confrontations as well as establish bonds of sympathy with both his supporters and detractors. The general's willingness to poke fun at himself peremptorily turned aside the deadly satirical barbs of Mexico's political humor. He established a sense of personal camaraderie through laughter—a skill that made him one of the boys, while at the same time his past exploits and obvious sense of control confirmed his leadership status. The loss of his right arm during the fighting became the focus of many of his jokes. Normally, body intactness is essential in revolutionary politics where strength often is more inferred than real. Obregón observed that the only reason the other revolutionary generals trusted him to be president was that with a missing arm he could only grab half as much money. On another occasion he supposedly attended a play with the Spanish ambassador who also had lost an arm—in this case, on the opposite side. Sitting side by side, Obregón, suddenly afflicted with a back itch, turned to his companion and said, "Lend me your arm." Humorous stories, whether apocryphal or authentic, circulated with appreciation throughout the country.

Obregón's technique of metaphorically firing a cannon blast of pesos at groups he wanted to bring into his national organization worked with laborers as well as it did with soldiers. Obregón supported workers by endorsing efforts to create unions and backing strikes. He brought them under his authority by bringing their union leaders into his government. The Regional Confederation of Mexican Workers (CROM), under his aegis, acquired its first real power. Nevertheless, article 123 remained little more than an ideal and, even with the president's support, real wages improved only slightly, remaining well below the three peso minimum daily wage that the national labor commission reported as being necessary for subsistence. Moreover, Obregón backed programs that resulted in arbitration boards that tied the workers more tightly to CROM and to the Obregón administration.

The pragmatic impulse of the revolution and its institutional architects can be found most clearly in the agrarian reform program. Politicians understood that land redistribution demanded by agrarian leaders needed to be addressed. Not to do so risked the creation of a formidable opposition that had seized upon the issue. With proper handling, a useful alliance could be established. Resurrection of the concept of communal land as a viable socioeconomic arrangement promised the mass mobilization of a significant number of people. Thus the ejido served as a political grouping as much if not more than an economic one. While individual land titles created individual voters, the ejido delivered organized numbers and even armed support if necessary. Moreover, reassigning land to communal entities made it possible to mix bottomland with infertile rocky stretches without creating dissatisfied peasant owners stuck with essentially useless plots. While it would not be possible to avoid individual titles, the ejido made political mobilization much easier. Whatever the arrangement, communal or individual, the new landholders provided a powerful political base. Access to credit, markets, and technology made land recipients dependent on the government.

To gauge the needs and the advantages of redistribution of land in any given region, an elaborate procedure emerged. The decree of January 6, 1915, provided for restoration of land improperly taken under the Lerdo Law and its supplements. Quasi-judicial bodies decided the issue and, if the governor and state agrarian commission agreed, a provisional grant of land could be made. Final approval depended on the president. Under this decree, lawyers could stall the proceedings indefinitely, exhausting a petitioner's limited financial resources. While little land was restored under this decree, it laid out the basic political process. Article 27 of the 1917 Constitution subsequently imbued land with a social function that transcended its propriety uses. National and community needs could override individual ownership.

The Carranza regime, unwilling to implement what it believed to be unnecessary radical procedures, had confused the issue with a 1919 decree that required villages to pay for transferred lands. As a result, the government avoided all but a few minor reassignments of property. Obregón's Law of Ejidos of December 28, 1920, set up a procedure without time limits and a process so cumbersome that it had to be discarded. Finally, the Agrarian Regulatory Law of April 10, 1922, provided an effective political mechanism. This law required the formation of village executive committees that could draft a petition for reassignment of land and have it signed by all those in the agrarian census. Only communities with a population of at least 500 could make an appeal based on the economic needs of the community. The local agrarian commission composed of state, peasant, and landholder representatives had four months to make a decision, at which time the case passed to the governor and then on to a special executive committee. The decision had to be reached within four months at each step in the process. At this point, a provisional title could be made permitting cultivation of the land. The law established the minimum size of plots. Finally, the National Agrarian Commission in Mexico City made its decision within the four-month period and then the president, if so inclined, would sign it and pass it to the secretariat of agriculture for final disposition. The entire process could take as long as two years. In the end, the president might personally hand out titles to the grateful peasants.[43] The process tested the strength of all sides before a decision was made and allowed for extensive political negotiations before a deal was struck. Miscalculation leading to dangerous countermoves could be minimized. In the end the government posed as the champion of the strongest party, which in turn understood its political obligation to the state's executives.

Obregón fulfilled the land amendment of the constitution to the extent necessary to bring the agrarian forces that had supported Zapata back under political control and into the mainstream of national life. During his term, some three million acres went to 624 villages. Nevertheless, the president avoided a comprehensive land distribution program that would have destroyed the agricultural production needed in the burgeoning capital and other cities. For Obregón, land was a commodity, while in many parts of central Mexico it was emblematic of a way of life. No reconciliation of these views proved possible. He left office with some 320 million acres still in the hands of a few large hacendados. Villages that received land remained dependent on the state. Campesinos who received land found they lacked seeds, implements, credit, and even agricultural training. Still Obregón did organize campesino leagues and arm many of their members. Political cooperation preceded serious and sustained governmental assistance.

Yet this agrarian program cannot be seen as a revolutionary process directed solely from the top. More important than the amount of land distributed by Obregón and then Calles was its location. Mexican presidents had political motivations in their land programs, but they also responded to the demands of the agrarians, who insisted on their right to land. Obregón coined the phrase "Life before Property," meaning he preferred to wait for the popular demand for property to develop, rather than for his administration to push a distribution program.[44] Those villages, communities, and groups of agrarians who recognized their opportunities had a chance of claiming property and getting it. The local representatives of the agrarian commission not only represented governmental political projects but also presented popular demands to higher authorities. Scattered local agrarian leagues were first organized in 1921 and 1922 by agents of the National Agrarian Commission under Secretary Armando Mendoza

López in the states of Jalisco, Zacatecas, Puebla, Michoacán, and Guanajuato. Peasants in Mascota, Jalisco, on July 18, 1921, held a meeting that resulted in a petition for land. Local landowners and community leaders fought the petition for the next thirteen years, when the peasant organization finally achieved success.[45] These peasant leagues became crucial institutions for the articulation of popular demands, provided a mechanism to petition for land grants, and defended communities from landowner coercion.

WORKSHOP OF REVOLUTION, III

Obregón's campaign to reduce the number and regulate the authority of revolutionary generals could not succeed against the most powerful of these chieftains. Several of the latter had seized on the disintegration of national government from 1913 to 1917 to create personal state or regional fiefdoms. In these instances, the president wisely chose to put aside his programs of centralization for a patient policy of accommodation, allowing caudillos and camarillas to govern their own territories. This policy reflected Obregón's genuine support for local autonomy, realistic assessment of the relative strength of the central government compared to several regional armies, and purposeful support for several governors who were developing agrarian and worker organizations that would exist beyond military or caudillo control. The rise of these latter organizations ultimately would reduce the president's dependence on the army. Moreover, Obregón knew that shortly after the Sonora Triangle claimed power, Provisional President Adolfo de la Huerta had forced the resignation of Governor Esteban Cantú Jiménez of the federal territory of Baja California del Norte and appointed fourteen provisional state governors. The majority of state-level officials owed their positions to the Sonorans. Thus as long as the governors did not challenge this national authority, Obregón declined to interfere in state affairs, tolerating governors who ranged from reactionary to radical in their policies. Several of the latter established "experimental laboratories" of the revolution.[46]

As the federal government maintained its distance, several governors, especially the civilian appointees, but warlords as well, developed programs to institute social change. Where these programs coincided with popular needs and demands, the policies made the revolution work and resulted in popular organizations, especially agrarian and worker groups. In these states, revolutionary changes occurred as a result of the revolutionary principles of innovative governors, the demands of popular forces seizing the opportunity provided by the revolution, and the support, or at the least the measure of independence to negotiate local policies, offered by the national regime.

One experiment occurred in Veracruz, where Colonel Adalberto Tejeda secured the governorship with Obregón's support. Finding the military linked to landlords in the state, the new governor attempted to build his political base by turning to workers and campesinos. When he experienced difficulties with labor groups, he appealed to the agrarians. He and Ursulo Galván established the League of Agrarian Communities and Peasants Syndicates. Tejeda's program gave these agrarian leagues greater attention and authority than elsewhere, and they soon became a model adopted by other state governments. For Obregón, his program's importance became apparent in the 1923 de la Huerta revolt, when Tejeda and Galván mobilized the agrarians in defense of the Obregón government and assisted in the recapture of Veracruz. The military actions of the leagues in turn guaranteed the agrarian reform program in the state and the political ascendance of Tejeda.

Another state laboratory for social reforms appeared in Tamaulipas under Governor Emiliano Portes Gil, appointed to the post by Provisional President de la Huerta in 1920. Obregón's hands-off policy foiled Portes Gil's first efforts, when he supported a general strike that included oil workers in Tampico opposed by the regional strongman Manuel Peláez. But Portes Gil made a political comeback in 1924 with the support of the Border Socialist Party (Partido Socialista Fronterizo) that he created as a coalition of agrarian leagues. During the next three years, Tamaulipas became a revolutionary showcase. The governor, with the assistance of Marte R. Gómez, carried out a moral reform program reminiscent of the efforts by middle-class Porfirians and some of Madero's governors against alcohol and an anticlerical campaign that presaged later anti-Church policies. The state administrators promoted the establishment of workers' cooperatives and initiated a vigorous agrarian reform program sustained by the state organization of agrarian leagues. But, to some extent, all of the revolutionary programs nurtured by these state regimes could be termed "fragile revolutions," because these popular organizations relied too greatly on the patronage of state administrators who could change or could be removed. Their opponents—landlords, regional strongmen, and ambitious army officers—during the early 1920s were not vanquished.[47] Nevertheless, the northern revolutionaries had identified a major program for change, the education campaign.

EDUCATING THE MASSES

Perhaps at no other point did the goals of the northern revolutionary leaders and the popular forces across the country coalesce to such a degree as on the question of education. The nature of the education program, however, resulted in intense contests for control over the local schools and subject matter.

The most successful program of the Obregón years came in the area of education. Achievements here were primarily due to the initiatives of José Vasconcelos, the secretary of education, who received unprecedented federal appropriations with which to work. He began his campaign unofficially as soon as Obregón began his term, while the congress debated the creation of a ministry of education. Liberals at the 1917 constitutional convention had eliminated this bureau, leaving education in the hands of the states. The congressmen, under pressure from Obregón, acted with unusual speed to reestablish the agency to be directed by Vasconcelos. He had developed a national plan for education while he was in exile in Los Angeles during the last year of the Carranza era. His scheme rested on the new principles of education developed in the Soviet Union by Lunacharsky[48] and called for a ministry with offices across the country, divided into three departments with two areas of responsibilities. The divisions were schools (providing all scientific and technical instruction), libraries (books and classes for adults and special students), and fine arts (specialized instruction in singing, drawing, and physical education in all schools). The two special areas of responsibility called for acculturating monolingual Indians, following closely the methods of the early Catholic missionaries, and teaching literacy to the masses. Under this plan, he succeeded in building nearly 1,000 rural schools and in prescribing a program that subsequent governments would follow. The minister looked at the school not merely as an agent of literacy but as an educational nucleus in the broadest sense of the word. He wanted the rural teacher to replace the priest in the work of acculturating, that is to say Mexicanizing, the rural population. Teachers were directed to promote cultural values through arts, literature, and music, including the folk dances of Mexico, Spain, and Latin America, while eliminating jazz and other foreign forms. The schoolteacher's new responsibilities included changing the worldview of country people, including what they ate, how they reared their children, when and how they relaxed, how they understood their work, and how they imagined their community and their country.[49]

The program required dedicated, selfless teachers, and to find them, Vasconcelos turned to the teachers of the old regime, those trained in the normal schools created by Justo Sierra, and to new recruits trained by his ministry. He wanted nothing to do with the teachers of the Carranza era, whom he regarded as conceited agents of North American methods. (Carranza had sent 100 young teachers to Boston, Massachusetts, for a one-month training seminar.) In the minister's opinion, the older normal school teachers were the best. Some foreigners also served as teachers, such as Chilean Gabriela Mistral, who in 1945 received the Nobel Prize for her poetry.[50]

According to one federal school inspector in Puebla, Jesús H. González, this crusade would transform the "undernourished, alcohol-weakened, materially and culturally deprived creatures into market-oriented yeoman farmers and productive citizens." This goal was nearly Porfirian in its desire to mold the lower classes. The teachers were supposed to introduce inoculation against diseases, new foods and recipes to improve nutrition, and hygienic measures, including disposing of garbage, eradicating flies, constructing latrines, purifying water, and more frequent bathing and washing of clothes. Vasconcelos held regular seminars to exhort his teachers to achieve these goals that would create modernity, which Michel Foucault defined as capturing ". . . the mind and body to make them more efficient, healthier, and more productive."[51]

Still, the success of the educational programs must be tempered with the understanding that a national campaign presupposed a national regime that could organize, staff, and finance such a program. Such a nation-state did not exist in the 1920s and, despite some impressive successes, rural schools developed differently than Vasconcelos and other national leaders had hoped and anticipated.

Figure 8.9 An inside view of a Tejano home in the Big Bend area of Texas in 1924. The iron range and sewing machine indicate a relatively well-off family. *Printed with permission, Photography Collection, Harry Ransom, Humanities Research Center, University of Texas at Austin.*

Rural schools, poorly funded and weakly controlled from the capital, became the educational expressions of villagers, who built them, selected the teachers, and supported their activities. In this respect, the educational campaign seems primarily to have resulted in the revival of nineteenth-century Liberal schemes of secular, state-controlled schools rather than the creation of revolutionary cultural missions. Tlaxcala offers an example. In 1923, the state had 120 elementary schools, fewer than twenty years earlier. The curriculum had been simplified, not replaced, by revolutionary programs, with some emphasis on science and the elimination of classes in morality.[52] National publicity linked rural literacy and agrarian reform as complementary programs. The residents of different communities, however, developed different priorities—land or schools—and campaigned for what they wanted.[53]

CALIFORNIA'S EDUCATIONAL PROGRAM FOR MEXICANS

The educational campaigns in the countryside saw women as a target second only to the young. A simultaneous program across the international border in California had as its primary purpose an instructional campaign among Mexican immigrant women to Americanize the state's burgeoning population from Mexico.[54] Pushed by the violence of the revolution and pulled by work opportunities, the Mexican population (by birth or descent) in the United States grew from 100,000 in 1900 to 1.5 million in 1930. Of the latter number, 64 percent had immigrated since 1915. During the 1920s, the population of the barrio in Los Angeles tripled, making it second only to Mexico City in population of Mexicans. The numbers increased in the same ratio in such traditional United States barrios in San Antonio and El Paso, and new Mexican communities appeared in the Midwest.

These recent arrivals became the target of educational programs in the midst of restrictions on immigration, fear of foreigners, and promotion of nationalism. In some respects, the education campaign reflected the same reform zeal that motivated Vasconcelos, but in the California case the impetus came from Progressivism, the genuine desire to improve the lives of people through learning. The 1915 Home Teacher Act in California created a group of instructors who would work in the homes of students to teach hygiene, diet, domestic skills, literacy, English, and Americanism. Like Vasconcelos, the directors stressed language as the key to the rest of the program. The Great Depression beginning in 1929 abruptly cut short this campaign, as funding ended and general efforts followed to repatriate Mexicans rather than integrate them. During the fifteen years of its existence, the Home Teacher Program failed if measured simply in terms of literacy and the English-speaking ability of Mexican women. But just as rural Mexicans drew from the Vasconcelos program what they wanted and needed, Mexican women in California learned lessons of hygiene and diet that proved helpful. Moreover, pressured to become Americans, they responded by becoming more self-consciously Mexican American.

SPLINTERING EL PASO'S BICULTURAL SOCIETY

Not everyone in the American Southwest saw education as the solution to the growing Hispanic population. A nasty form of nativism appeared, hidden under the sheets of the Ku Klux Klan, that gave ethnic interaction a racist, violent quality. El Paso become one focal point of this development. A center of revolutionary adventurers, ambitious gunrunners, and foreign conspirators, El Paso had remained free of most ethnic battles and racial violence. From the time of the arrival of American troops in 1846, the city had become an ethnic mosaic of Mexican residents, American frontiersmen and women, a sprinkling of native Americans, and U.S. forces that after 1868 included black troops. Texas had been a member of the Confederacy and its leaders regarded themselves as southerners. Nevertheless, racial harmony, if not equality, prevailed in the town until 1915. The only exception to racial tolerance occurred when two black troopers were jailed in February 1900 and several of their friends attempted to break them out. A gunfight followed in which one black soldier and one white deputy were shot to death. Fears of a black uprising or an Anglo lynching party racked the town, but thoughtful town and military leadership combined with restrained newspaper coverage kept the incident under control, and it eventually ended in a long, tedious trial that sent one trooper to prison for ten years.[55] Compared with ethnic conflict in the lower valley, in fact most of the country, El Paso seemed a model for others until 1916.

Francisco Villa brought the revolution to El Paso on January 10, 1916, when he ordered the execution of sixteen mining engineers taken off a train at Santa Ysabel, Chihuahua. The engineers had been en route to reopening a mine in the Sierra. The wave of indignation in the United States focused on El Paso because many of the victims had maintained residences there. Friends and relatives in El Paso received a second jolt several days later when the mutilated bodies arrived by train. That evening the city experienced a race riot as a crowd of three to four hundred people, including soldiers from Fort Bliss, assembled at the closing time of the bars and then moved through the streets beating up any Mexicans or Mexican Americans the mob happened to encounter. Local police and General J. J. Pershing cooperated and used two companies of infantry to disperse the crowd after three hours of rioting. The quick, decisive action of local leaders prevented rioting on the scale of that in south Texas associated with the San Diego Plan.[56]

The rioting shattered the community that existed in El Paso and, in many ways, lapped over into Ciudad Juárez. From the Anglo conquest onward, isolation, danger, and hardship had created a community of necessity that became one of mutual respect. Even after the railroads brought a steady flow of Anglos to El Paso, there remained a clear recognition of the need for Mexican workers that muted ethnic conflict. Even after the rioting related to the San Ysabel massacre, leaders in El Paso managed to control mounting anti-Mexican feeling, despite the provocation of Pancho Villa's Columbus Raid. The damaged sense of community between Anglos and Hispanics remained for the time intact.

World War I put new strains on the borderlands community. The city continued to grow, and the new arrivals brought intolerance with them that tension created by the revolution and the Villa raid compounded. These new arrivals never learned the shared values of the older community. The war exacerbated these attitudes with its demands for total support of the war effort, campaigns to confirm individual loyalty, and fears of German espionage and resulted in vigilante actions. This jingoism survived the war and split the Anglo community between the more tolerant traditional residents and the intolerant more recent arrivals. The two groups clashed over the question of the Ku Klux Klan and the Hispanic population.

The Klan arrived in El Paso in 1921, where it achieved some political and social success, focusing its campaign of hate on local Hispanics. But by 1923 it had been thoroughly beaten in local politics. The Klan's antiforeign, anti-Catholic, and anticolored campaigns, on reflection, quickly alienated the bicultural community of El Paso. Later, in the early 1930s, more strident racism would emerge against Hispanics, when the force of women's suffrage diminished the importance of the Hispanic vote and the depression destroyed the need for Hispanic workers.[57]

CULTURAL DIPLOMACY AND INTERACTION

The tensions between the United States and Mexico required mending and Obregón and Calles after him, devoted attention to the problem. The end to the general fighting and the energetic reform campaign provided the circumstances for a good deal of cultural interchange between Mexico and its northern neighbor that culminated in widespread interest in Mexican folk and high cultures in the United States. This vogue endured from 1920 until the next world war diverted attention away from Mexico.

Obregón's nationalistic culture seemed to find its voice in the centennial celebration of the achievement of independence in 1921. This national holiday had a self-consciously national and popular character that provided ordinary Mexicans with the opportunity to see a major folk art exhibition, a charro demonstration, and the distribution of toys and candy to 10,000 needy children. The month-long series of events ended in a Mexican night at Chapultepec Park, featuring Mexican fireworks, music, and dances.

A highlight of the cultural relations between the two countries occurred at New York's Madison Square Garden in 1929 with the presentation of "Aztec Gold." This benefit pageant showed off a cast of a thousand representing such diverse characters as Fernando Cortes, Montezuma, and a Hopi Indian chief. Mexican artists Miguel Covarrubias and José Clemente Orozco participated, as did Alma Reed and Frances Flynn Paine, well-known patrons of Mexican art. The pageant represented the zenith of the cultural relations between Mexico and the United States. Before the 1920s, there had been only limited artistic interaction. Mexicans knew little of the United States, beyond its economic and political expansion, and Americans knew no more about Mexican cultural life than could be drawn from a few foreign travelers. The revolution, of course, earned Mexico the reputation of being home to flamboyant rebels (such as Villa), cowardly traitors (such as

Figure 8.10 Mexican Independence Day celebration in the copper mining town of Jerome, Arizona, in 1925. *Courtesy of Jerome State Historical Park.*

Huerta), and anonymous insurgents (featured in photographs and reports by John Reed and others). Prior to the 1920s, Americans, unless they were border residents, had little opportunity to encounter Mexican culture. For some, the motivation to know Mexico came from the new position of the United States following World War I; the nation's global interests demanded that citizens become acquainted with other world cultures. At the same time, there was an awakening of interest in Native American life in the United States as part of the pursuit of genuine national culture that dominated intellectual life until World War II. Mexico after 1920 had great appeal, especially its archaeological zones, those mute witnesses of long-departed cultures. Moreover, many Americans admired the way in which the Obregón administration had initiated a cultural renaissance.

While the government promoted its authentic Mexican culture, many Mexicans looked to the United States and its popular culture. Jazz, the hit parade, and the saxophone, expensive cars, weekends, and the beach all attracted Mexican men. Women discovered chewing gum, sports, and, above all, hairstyles and clothing fashions.[58]

Americans, especially those with sympathies for the political left, turned an admiring gaze southward to Mexico. These eager political pilgrims[59] found the revolutionary Mexico they expected in the artistic, especially the mural, program initiated by the minister of education, José Vasconcelos, or in the *indigenista* program that recognized the indigenous peoples, especially those that had mobilized during the revolution.[60]

NOTES

1. Sandos, *Rebellion in the Borderlands,* pp. xv–xvi.
2. See the Associated Press story, "Facing Up to the Past: Duke of Duval Display Puts a New, Old Face on History," *Ft. Worth (Texas) Star-Telegram.* May 5, 1991, Sec. B, p.2. Archie Parr served as the state senator for the area for twenty years; then his son George became the second Duke of Duval. In 1948, former governor Coke Stevenson appeared to have beaten Johnson by around 100 votes in a runoff election. But a recount found an additional 203 votes, all but 1 for Johnson, from the thirteenth precinct in Alice, Texas (10 miles from San Diego). This box 13 gave Johnson the election. Today there is a county historical museum in San Diego that hopes to obtain the ballot box and provide exhibits on such events as the Plan of San Diego.
3. Michael C. Meyer, "The Mexican-German Conspiracy of 1915," *The Americas* 23: (July 1966), pp. 76–89, and Allen Gerlach, "Conditions Along the Border—1915: The Plan de San Diego," *New Mexico Historical Review* 43 (1968), pp. 195–212, stress the Huertista and German background to the plan, based largely on the statements of a captured signer. More recent studies with access to German archives and U.S. Bureau of Investigation and military intelligence documents not available to Meyer and Gerlach find no evidence of direct German or

Huertista involvement. See Charles H. Harris III and Louis R. Sadler, "The Plan of San Diego and the Mexican-United States War Crisis of 1916," *Hispanic American Historical Review* 58 (August 1978), pp. 381–408, and Friedrich Katz, *The Secret War in Mexico: Europe, the United States and the Mexican Revolution* (Chicago: The University of Chicago Press, 1981), pp. 339–44.

4. This discussion relies on Sandos, *Rebellion in the Borderlands,* especially chapters 4 and 5.

5. Sandos, *Rebellion in the Borderlands,* chapter 6.

6. Evan Anders, *Boss Rule in South Texas: The Progressive Era* (Austin: University of Texas Press, 1982), passim.

7. In the Zimmermann note, the Germans offered Carranza an alliance that, if the Central Powers won the world war, would return the lands lost in the U.S.–Mexico War to Mexico. The complex, at times contradictory, German activities in Mexico represent a major theme in Katz, *Secret War in Mexico.*

8. Ilene V. O'Malley, *The Myth of the Revolution: Hero Cults and the Institutionalization of the Mexican State, 1920–1940* (New York: Greenwood Press, 1986), pp. 96–97.

9. Gilbert M. Joseph and Allen Wells, "Yucatán: Elite Politics and Rural Insurgency," in Thomas Benjamin and Mark Wasserman, eds., *Provinces of the Revolution: Essays on Regional Mexican History, 1910–1929* (Albuquerque: University of New Mexico Press, 1990), pp. 93–131.

10. Gilbert M. Joseph, *Revolution from Without: Yucatán, Mexico and the United States, 1880–1924* (Durham: Duke University Press, 1980), pp. 1–10; 93–148.

11. Linda B. Hall and Don M. Coerver, *Revolution on the Border: The United States and Mexico, 1910–1920* (Albuquerque: University of New Mexico Press, 1988), p. 40.

12. Michael M. Smith, "Social and Political Dynamics of the Kansas City *Colonia* during the Mexican Revolution: The Role of the Unión Mexicana Benito Juárez and Middle-Class Leadership," in Virginia Guedea and Jaime E. Rodríguez O., eds., *Five Centuries of Mexican History* (México: El Instituto de Investigaciones Dr. José María Luis Mora; Irvine: University of California Irvine, 1992), vol. 1, pp. 384–401.

13. Lou Cretia Owen Diary, October 1, 1918–January 25, 1919, Tennessee State Library and Archives, Owen Diaries, Box 1.

14. Wilkie and Michaels, eds., *Revolution in Mexico,* p. 113.

15. Mary Angeline Watrous, "Fiscal Policy and Financial Administration in Mexico, 1890–1940," (Ph.D. diss., Washington State University, 1991), pp. 184–85.

16. Robert Buffington, "Revolutionary Reform: The Mexican Revolution and the Discourse on Prison Reform," *Mexican Studies/Estudios Mexicanos* 9: 1 (winter 1993), pp. 71–93.

17. Dick J. Reavis, *Conversations with Moctezuma: Ancient Shadows Over Modern Life in Mexico* (New York: William Morrow, 1990), pp. 52–53, 57.

18. Douglas W. Richmond, *Venustiano Carranza's Nationalist Struggle, 1893–1920.* (Lincoln, 1983). Gregg Andrews, *Shoulder to Shoulder: The American Federation of Labor, the United States and the Mexican Revolution* (Berkeley: University of California Press, 1991), pp. 82–83.

19. This is the subject of Carlos Fuentes's novel *The Death of Artemio Cruz,* translated by Sam Hileman (New York: Noonday Press, 1966).

20. See Thomas R. Lill, *National Debt of Mexico: History and Present Status* (New York: Report for the International Committee of Bankers, 1919).

21. Watrous, "Fiscal Policy," pp. 73, 96, 213–20.

22. Wilkie and Michaels, eds., *Revolution in Mexico,* pp. 116, 119–20.

23. United States Senate, Committee on Foreign Relations, *Investigation of Mexican Affairs.* Report and Hearings before a Sub-Committee on Foreign Relations, Senator Albert Fall, Presiding, Pursuant to Senate Resolution 106. 66th Cong. 2d Sess. (Washington, D.C.: Government Printing Office, 1919–1920), 2 vols.

24. Mark T. R. Gilderhus, "Senator Albert B. Fall and 'The Plot against Mexico,'" *New Mexico Historical Review* 48 (October 1973), pp. 299–311. For the "core of truth" in the Fall committee hearings, see Harris and Sadler, "Plan of San Diego," pp. 406–08.

25. Lieuwen, *Mexican Militarism,* p. 34.

26. Wilkie and Michaels, eds., *Revolution in Mexico,* p. 28.

27. John S. Brushwood, "Innovation in Mexican Fiction and Politics (1910–1934)," *Mexican Studies / Estudios Mexicanos* 5: 1 (winter 1989), pp. 69–88, esp. pp. 70, 85.

28. See Patrice Elizabeth Olsen, "Issue of National Identity: Obregón, Calles and Nationalist Architecture, 1920–1930" (Ph.D. diss. in progress, Pennsylvania State University).

29. John Womack Jr., "The Mexican Revolution, 1910–40: Genesis of a Modern State," in Fredrick B. Pike, ed., *Latin American History: Select Problems* (New York: Harcourt, Brace & World, 1969), p. 319.

30. Fowler Salamini and Vaughan, eds. *Women of the Mexican Countryside* p. 16.

31. The new intellectual community expressed Mexico's Roaring 'Twenties. See, for example, Bertram D. Wolfe, *The Fabulous Life of Diego Rivera* (New York: Stein and Day, 1969). For a recent effort to create Mexico City of the 1920s as the setting for his mystery plot, see Paco Ignacio Taibo II, *The Shadow of the Shadow,* translated by William I. Neuman (New York: Viking Penguin, 1991). Edward Lonnie Langston, "The Impact of Prohibition on the Mexican–United States Border: The El Paso–Ciudad Juárez Case" (Ph.D. diss., Texas Tech University, 1974), pp. 93–101.

32. Roderic A. Camp, *Political Recruitment across Two Centuries: Mexico, 1884–1991* (Austin: University of Texas Press, 1995), chapter 3.

33. Howard C. Cline, *The United States and Mexico* (Cambridge: Harvard University Press, 1953), pp. 192–94.

34. Knight, *Mexican Revolution,* vol. 2, p. 231.

35. He finished as a brigadier general and became governor of Chihuahua in 1928, before making the wrong choice in favor of Escobar in 1929 and being forced into exile. See Mark Wasserman, *Persistent Oligarchs: The Political Economy of Chihuahua, Mexico* (Durham: Duke University Press, 1993), pp. 40–41.

36. Camp, *Political Recruitment,* chapter 3.

37. Stuart F. Voss, "Nationalizing the Revolution," in Benjamin and Wasserman, eds., *Provinces of the Revolution,* p. 281.

38. Wasserman, "Persistent Oligarchs," pp. 21–23, 75–76.

39. Wasserman, "Persistent Oligarchs," p. 47. Also see Miguel Angel Giner Rey, *Uruáchic: 250 años de historia* (Chihuahua: Centro Librero La Prensa, 1986).

40. Wasserman, "Persistent Oligarchs," pp. 11–12, 82, 138.

41. Chassen-López and Martinez, "Return to the Mixtec Millennium," pp. 23, 26, 37.

42. Roderic A. Camp, *Generals in the Palacio* (New York: Oxford University Press 1992), pp. 9, 37, 478.

43. Paul Friedrich, *Agrarian Revolt in a Mexican Village* (Englewood Cliffs, N.J.: Prentice Hall, 1970), pp. 95–97.

44. Carleton Beals, *Mexico: An Interpretation* (New York: B. W. Huebsch, 1923), pp. 235–38.

45. Jean Meyer, *Estado y sociedad con Calles* (México: El Colegio de México, 1977), p. 93; Carlos B. Gil, *Life in Provincial Mexico: National and Regional History Seen from Mascota, Jalisco, 1867–1972* (Los Angeles: UCLA Latin American Center Publications, 1983), pp. 131–32.

46. Carleton Beals, in *Mexico: An Interpretation* (pp. 74, 102), first called these state programs the Laboratories of Revolution in 1923. For this section, also see Alvaro Matute, *La carrera del caudillo: Historia de la Revolución Mexicana, 1917–1920* (México: El Colegio de México, 1980), pp. 150–54; David C. Bailey, "Obregón: Mexico's Accommodating President," in Wolfskill and Richmond, eds., *Essays on the Mexican Revolution,* pp. 81–99.

47. Thomas Benjamin, "Laboratories of the New State, 1920–1929," in Benjamin and Wasserman, eds., *Provinces of the Revolution,* pp. 71–90; Heather Fowler Salamini, "Tamaulipas: Land Reform and the State," in ibid., pp. 185–217; and Heather Fowler Salamini, *Agrarian Radicalism in Veracruz, 1920–38* (Lincoln: University of Nebraska Press, 1971).

48. Vasconcelos, *Mexican Ulysses,* pp. 145, 151.

49. Mary Kay Vaughan, "Women School Teachers in the Mexican Revolution: The Story of Reyna's Braids," *Journal of Women's History* 2: 1 (spring 1990), pp. 143–68.

50. Vasconcelos, *Mexican Ulysses,* pp. 160–61, 163, 168, 170.

51. Mary Kay Vaughan, "Rural Women's Literacy in the Mexican Revolution: The Case of Tecamachalco, Puebla," MS, pp. 23, 28–29.

52. Elsie Rockwell, "Rural Schooling and the State in Post–Revolutionary Mexico," in Gilbert M. Joseph and Daniel Nugent, eds., *Everyday Forms of State Formation: Revolution and the Negotiation of Rule in Mexico* (Durham: Duke University Press, 1994), pp. 1–2, 7, 8.

53. Vaughan, "Rural Women's Literacy," pp. 15–17, finds a negative correlation between literacy and agrarian reform beneficiaries in Tecamachalco, Puebla; Rockwell, "Rural Schooling," p. 13.

54. The information on California's "Americanization" program relies on George J. Sanchez, *"Go After the Women": Americanization and the Mexican Immigrant Woman, 1915–1929,* Center for Chicano Research, Working Paper Series, 6 (Stanford: Stanford University Press, 1984).

55. See the chapter titled "Black Fort Bliss," in Garna Loy Christian, "Sword and Plowshare: The Symbiotic Development of Fort Bliss and El Paso, Texas, 1849–1918" (Ph.D. diss., Texas Tech University, 1977), pp. 159–233.

56. Christian, "Sword and Plowshare," pp. 368–70; Lay, *War, Revolution and the Ku Klux Klan,* p. 25.

57. Lay, *War, Resolution and the Ku Klux Klan,* passim.

58. Paraphrase of Henry C. Schmidt, *The Roots of Lo Mexicano: Self and Society in Mexican Thought, 1900–1934* (College Station: Texas A&M University Press, 1978), p. 98.

59. This is the term coined by sociologist Paul Hollander and adopted by Helen Delpar in *The Enormous Vogue of Things Mexican: Cultural Relations between the United States and Mexico, 1920–1935* (Tuscaloosa: University of Alabama Press, 1993), p. 21 and note 1, p. 289. Hollander developed the term in *Political Pilgrims: Travels of Western Intellectuals to the Soviet Union, China, and Cuba, 1928–1978* (New York: Oxford University Press, 1981).

60. Delpar, *Enormous Vogue of Things Mexican,* pp. 21, 34.

Chapter 9

MAKING A REVOLUTION WORK
Part II, 1927–1937

CURSED BY INVESTORS AND SUCCESSION

Despite the progress toward reform and the implementation of the constitution, Obregón still faced two problems that plagued every president after 1828 and that threatened to undo all of his achievements. These obstacles were foreign investors and presidential succession. The foreign capital question resulted in the United States and Great Britain refusing to grant diplomatic recognition to the Obregón government when it came to power in 1920. The reservations, especially of the United States, concerned the protection of foreign-owned property in Mexico and the repayment of the debt owed to foreign (New York and London) bankers. Besides diplomatic recognition, the Obregón government felt a surge of urgency about the foreign capital issue because of the high cost of its social programs. Oil properties in the Huasteca region (the zone from Veracruz to Tampico) constituted a difficult problem, not only for Mexican authorities but also for Anglo–U.S. negotiators. These issues were settled in 1923, in the Bucareli agreements, which discounted article 27 of the 1917 Constitution, making it clear that it would not be applied retroactively against oil companies and that oil production taxes would be paid to the Anglo-American bankers' committee on the foreign debt. This agreement resulted in diplomatic recognition and the subsiding of demands in the United States for military intervention in Mexico.

Social progress halted as the government confronted the traditional crisis of presidential succession. Military commanders divided

294

Making a Revolution Work: Part II, 1927–1937

1923	Bucareli agreements
	Villa assassinated
	De la Huerta Revolt
1924–1928	Calles presidency
1925	Banco de México founded
1926	Military promotions law
1926–1929	Cristero Rebellion
1927	Gómez-Serrano Revolt
1928	Obregón reelected and assassinated
1928–1930	Interim presidency of Emilio Portes Gil
1929	Escobar Revolt
	Official Party (National Revolutionary Party or PNR) created
1929–1935	U.S. deportation programs
1930–1932	Presidency of Pascual Ortiz Rubio
1932	Escuela Superior de Guerra founded
1932–1934	Interim presidency of Abelardo L. Rodriguez
1933	PNR six year plan
1934	Grito de Guadalajara
1934–1940	Cárdenas presidency
1936	Calles exiled to the United States
1937	National economic crisis
1939	Cárdenas converts the PNR into the Mexican Revolutionary Party (PRM)

in their support between Adolfo de la Huerta, secretary of the treasury and former interim president, and Plutarco Elías Calles, the governor of Sonora. Obregón had to choose a successor from the other two members of the Sonora triangle. Rumors circulated that Pancho Villa, from retirement in Durango, expected to play some role in the selection process and might even reemerge on the national scene. The threat he represented to the presidential process caused shivers of both anticipation and anxiety, especially in the northern states. But the concerns ended abruptly when Villa was assassinated on his way home to Durango from Parral.

Villa's murderers confessed to the crime, claiming he had ordered the execution of their father during the years of bitter revolutionary fighting. Few in Mexico accepted such a simple answer. The bravado of the murder and its timing suggested to many a conspiracy. The street analysis of the grisly affair was summed up in the popular riddle, "¿Quién mató a Villa?" With the answer, "¡Cállese y pórtese bién!"—

Who killed Pancho Villa? Be quiet and behave yourself!—making the pun with the name of presidential aspirant Calles.

Despite Obregón's agile manipulations and lavish use of money, the government confronted a serious armed rebellion that almost succeeded in toppling his regime during the period 1923–1924. As so frequently happened in these years, the issue involved presidential succession and the right of the incumbent to impose his successor. Obregón chose his fellow Sonoran Calles much to the anger of other *divisionarios* who outranked Calles and, moreover, controlled large numbers of troops. Adolfo de la Huerta believed that he had a claim on the presidential office. Because Obregón controlled the electoral machinery, rebellion appeared to be the only option. Some 20 percent of the army's officers, including 102 generals commanding 40 percent of the troops, declared against the government. The desperate president quickly called up military reserves and rallied thousands of workers and peasants to defend his regime. He astutely painted his opposition as wealthy landowners and discredited, corrupt Carrancista generals. In three months, 7,000 died. Obregón, while eliminating many generals, ended up with a new crop, indeed, a larger number of generals than before the revolt. Thus he had to press ever harder to professionalize the army, an objective that soon provided some proof of success when the government had to put down a similar revolt in 1927. Meanwhile, the government's success in mustering worker and peasant support confirmed the usefulness of establishing semicorporate interest groups.[1]

Obregón and Calles won with the aid of the armed workers and campesinos. Obregón, who had appealed to the Casa de Obrero Mundial during the struggle against Villa and had extended benefits to organized labor after 1920, received the support of these cadres. Moreover, his agrarian reform policies, including the arming of peasants, also garnered support during the campaign against de la Huerta. Finally, the fact that Obregón had reached an accommodation with the United States meant that the U.S. government placed an arms embargo on weapons for de la Huerta's forces and allowed Calles to import what he wanted. Consequently, de la Huerta fled into exile to the barrio of East Los Angeles, where he settled into the life of a teacher of voice and violin, while his erstwhile colleague Calles was duly elected president of Mexico.

Another victim of the de la Huerta revolt proved to be the revolutionary program, initiated by the Carrancista governors in Yucatán, that had created largely from above the socialist state of the southeast in response to the pressures and demands from the peasants of the peninsula. First Salvador Alvarado and then Felipe Carrillo Puerto brought revolutionary programs to the suppressed population of this peninsula. For rather muddled reasons, Carrillo Puerto sided with de la Huerta and his opponents seized the opportunity to execute him and his advisors for treason. Carrillo Puerto's betrothed, Alma Reed, chose to continue living in Mexico as a testament to his revolutionary convictions and as a visible indictment of his enemies. She became over the years the symbol of unrequited true love and the bittersweet nature of Mexican life.

CALLES INCUMBENT

Once in office, Calles gave the reform programs a push forward, but he also redirected the goal of the government's primary effort, as he gave new emphasis to the anti-Church provisions of the constitution. His program for social reform required strong political support, so the president weeded the regime of governors whom he found to be faint-hearted, less than fully committed, and independent minded. From 1925 to 1927, he deposed twenty-five governors.[2]

Calles continued to support the union movement, giving the Confederación Regional Obrera Mexicana (CROM) the advantage in organizing labor and making Luis Morones, its boss, a member of the presidential council. Efforts at labor organizing reached massive proportions, as most urban and industrial workers joined a union, including the capital's cadre of prostitutes. Reforms in agriculture received a new sense of urgency as agrarian agents distributed over eight million acres of land to 1,500 villages and paid former owners 10 percent over the tax valuation prices. Distribution led to reduced agricultural production, so the government instituted irrigation projects, agricultural credit, and agricultural schools to intensify production through higher yields from each acre.

Public health, especially sanitation, was improved. The building of over 2,000 rural schools encouraged education. This dramatic growth of the federal school system, however, probably did not result from the central direction of the education ministry; rather, if Tlaxcala is representative, the impetus came from rural villagers themselves. Residents of villages without schools could request teachers from either the federal or the state systems after 1923. Some towns, at the urging of teachers, asked to be transferred to the federal system. By 1926, Tlaxcala had thirty-four one-room rural schools and four urban primary schools. This action was taken independent of local authorities and created links to the national regime, opening new channels for other programs initiated by the state to intrude into rural Mexico.[3]

The high cost of the Calles social programs was partially met by cutting the military budget as the president ordered the discharge of some units (estimated at 50,000 to 100,000 men) and placing officers on the half-pay retirement list, reducing graft, and cutting expenses. The remaining troops received stiff discipline and good equipment under the direction of the sphinxlike minister of war, Joaquín Amaro. The president's efforts to raise professional standards resulted in improvements in training offered at the Colegio Militar and in a new promotions law in 1926 that replaced many irregular procedures with a new emphasis on professional training as the requirement for advancement. These programs paid dividends later in both the smashing of the 1927 Gómez–Serrano adventure and the quick defeat of the 1929 Escobar revolt. The 1929 revolt measured professional development; it was the first time substantial numbers of military units under regional control chose loyalty to the national government over their regional officers.[4]

But anticlerical legislation based on the constitution emerged as the darling of the Calles program and resulted in the Church-state confrontation that burst into civil conflagration in 1926. The president resolutely opposed the intrusion in any way of the Catholic Church in Mexican secular affairs. He intended to end, once and for all, the secular activities of that organization. One proposal called for a National Catholic Church that would incorporate practices to express Mexican patriotism, such as substituting tortillas and mescal for communion wafers and wine. This proposal failed. As Calles began to implement his anticlerical laws, the Church responded by declaring that Mexican Catholics would not accept the anti-Church provisions of the constitution (especially articles 3, 5, 27, and 130). The Church statement elicited a hostile response from the Calles regime. Anticlericalism quickly became anti-Catholicism. The president placed all primary education under secular supervision, ordered the registration of all clergy, demanded the deportation of foreign-born priests, and closed seventy-three convents.[5] State governors received new powers to restrict the number of religious in their states (often resulting in only one priest per 30,000 confessions as in Veracruz, for example) to prohibit the wearing of ecclesiastical garb in public, and so forth. This anti-Church program has been portrayed by Graham Greene, a convert to Roman Catholicism, in his novel *The Power and the Glory*.

CRISTEROS: TAKING UP ARMS AND TAKING FLIGHT

The faithful matched militancy with militancy. In July 1926, a general religious strike was called that continued for three years, suspending the Mass, confessions, and sacraments. A few priests and several lay leaders, most notably Miguel Palomar y Vizcana, in 1926 added to the tension by encouraging their Catholic supporters to take direct action, especially against the new symbol of the revolutionary regime in rural

Mexico, the school. The National Religious Defense League responded by burning school buildings and intimidating and sometimes murdering teachers. Centered in the western states of Jalisco, Michoacán, and Colima, the crisis escalated in April when Catholic insurgents dynamited a government troop train. Full-scale guerrilla warfare followed, called the Cristero Rebellion, because of the battle cry of the insurgents, "¡Viva Cristo Rey!" Calles and his ministers banned bishops, ruthlessly dealt with guerrillas, and turned churches into stables. The Catholic insurgents constituted a grave military and political threat, one that impelled the Calles regime to look to foreign investors for the capital desperately needed to finance the struggle against the rebels. Despite the intensity of the conflict, the effects of the Church-state struggle were not felt everywhere. Tlaxcala, for example, was spared the violence, as it had always lacked both priests and rancheros, the two groups deeply involved in the rebellion. In the west, where the struggle continued with gathering fury, the two sides had reached positions from which they could no longer deal with each other. Before it ended, 65,000 to 80,000 Mexicans died in the violence and an uncounted number fled the country.

The exiles escaping the Cristero wars represented different segments of the population—practicing Catholics, war-weary workers and peasants, wealthy who had lost faith in the country, and disheartened rebels. Among the refugees, the Company of Mary abandoned its novitiate house in Aguascalientes when the rebellion began for safety in Douglas, Arizona. Local Knights of Columbus helped them locate a house there in a neighborhood of Mexicans and Mexican Americans, mostly workers at the local copper smelters. Douglas, a town that once shared a transborder community, by 1926 had become divided; its population of 15,800 split into Anglo, Mexican, Chinese, and black groups, with segregated parks and schools. The Hispanics were concentrated in the southern and western sections of town. Most of the residents were Protestant. The majority of Catholics were Hispanics, who in 1926 heard the Mass said by a French priest. Nevertheless, the convent soon became the center of Mexican culture, and the sisters worked to preserve the way of life left behind by the immigrants, especially the holiday customs and language. Mexican mothers found in the convent a place to reinforce the lessons of the home in their daughters, especially modesty in dress and respect for the family, church, and elders. The entire Hispanic community found it a place to celebrate both Church and Mexican civic holidays. But the convent soon faced a crisis: the modest incomes of Mexicans in Douglas, the economic depression in the United States that restricted immigration from Mexico, and the availability of well-established public schools, even though segregated, combined to place in jeopardy the vocation of the sisters to educate girls with the same rigor that their male counterparts in the Company of Jesus taught boys. Necessity became opportunity, as the nuns redirected their activities to meet the needs of local Mexicans. They opened a kindergarten with a totally Spanish curriculum until 1940, when it became the first bilingual school in Douglas. They also offered lessons in needlework, painting, piano, business, and English. Moreover, they taught the catechism as preparation for the sacrament of First Holy Communion. These classes became especially important to the Hispanic community because the sisters taught the lessons with numerous allusions to Mexico and its history. They also sponsored celebrations, especially Corpus Christi and Mexican independence, that grew each year. By mid-1935, their efforts had reached outside of Douglas to the surrounding region. The Mexican character of their effort became especially visible in 1949, when the sisters successfully arranged to place an image of the Virgin of Guadalupe, taken from their convent, in the parish church.[6]

Back in Mexico, the Cristero Rebellion represented more than an armed outburst by countryside religious fanatics. The uprising became the expression of pent-up tensions revolving around land distribution and rural education. During the Calles years, rural communities built over 2,000 new schools. The schools imposed added pressures on villages, as law required that the community furnish a plot of land, the income from which was supposed to support local education. This requirement took precious land away from extremely poor villagers and increased the suspicions that someone was draining off the school profits. The educational missions in some areas added demands that had no relationship to the already overwhelmed resources. The schooling program called for teaching improved hygiene through more frequent bathing, laundering of clothes, and washing food, when in some communities in Puebla, for example, there was not enough water for drinking or the fields.[7] Calles's education minister Moisés Sáenz focused on teaching children practical skills and attitudes to replace Catholic values. He declared the difference between his goals and the general liberal education of Vasconcelos, saying it was "as important to rear chickens as to read poetry."[8]

Former teacher Calles held stubbornly to the importance of education for the future of the revolution and the Mexican nation. He declared in his Grito de Guadalupe that Mexico had entered into the "psychological revolutionary period."

> we must . . . take control of the consciousness of the youth, because it . . . must belong to the revolution. . . . The reactionaries mislead us when they claim that the child belongs to the home, and the youth to the family; . . . it is the revolution which has a compelling obligation towards the consciousness, to banish prejudice and to form the national soul.[9]

   Thus the Cristero Rebellion had a fury born of unrelenting demands on the rural population, especially through the national educational campaigns that directly challenged traditional Catholic customs. On the other hand, there is scant evidence about the reactions of the persons most involved—the children who attended the schools. Students helped build classrooms and defended teachers as best they could during the Cristero Rebellion. In one account, students in a Durango village were the only ones who dared to bury teachers murdered by Cristeros.[10]

DEVELOPMENTALIST PROGRAM

Calles desperately needed a program that in the long run would unite Mexicans, create loyalty to the revolutionary regime, improve the economy, and preempt future insurgencies against the national administration. He hoped to accomplish all of these goals with a major road-building program. Roads and education, like railroads for the Porfirians, offered a method to create a modern society, but unlike Díaz's approach to railroad construction, Calles intended that Mexico would use internal financial resources to build the roads and Mexicans would direct the construction. The new highways would demonstrate Mexican financial independence and technological ability.
   Calles's commitment to this Developmentalist program and faith in technological solutions to questions of national order reflected his upbringing in the borderlands. There he had witnessed both the successful programs of U.S. development and Porfirian expansion (with few benefits for workers). He summed up this program, saying, "What I am trying to do is to demonstrate that the country possesses the necessary resources to sustain itself and to develop itself. . . ."[11] Under this plan, Mexicans would build the roads themselves, thus providing employment to Mexican technicians and unskilled labor and creating transportation routes where Mexicans wanted them. The roads would improve opportunities in mining and agriculture by opening the way to markets. Further, the president intended that the roads improve communications throughout the nation to promote nationalism, transform the people and their backward customs and economy (to Calles, this meant undermining Catholicism), and build a modern state. Improved highways implied the more rapid and effective deployment of troops to maintain order. These roads, along with the schools, were to create a New Mexican, with a technical education, capitalist notions of production and consumption, and a nationalistic sense. Between 1925 and 1927, the federal government completed 2,000 kilometers of roads.[12]

This expansive road program received publicity throughout Mexico. Newspapers, especially those in the capital city, the semi-official Excelsior, in particular, discussed highway construction programs in United States, Canada, and Europe, noting its positive impact on tourism (the U.S. population owned 17 million automobiles in 1925), on the development of extractive industries, and on educational programs in the countryside. Reporters then extolled the Mexican program that would soon bring tourists south and would promote industry and education. Road construction required a community effort by rural Mexicans to achieve the national goals and supplement the federal highway network. The Porfirian railroad campaign had demonstrated the problems of foreign financing, so Calles intended to use only Mexican revenue.

Strong national leadership in developing roads also would contribute to autonomous economic and fiscal programs. The protagonist of the revolutionary fiscal program was Alberto Pani, finance minister for both Obregón and Calles. He moved to streamline the bureaucracy, generate revenue through sales and property taxes, and recognize foreign debts by making interest payments. A government-controlled central bank held the key to Pani's national economic programs. Such national banks were being created across Latin America during this decade. They had first been proposed for Mexico by a Carranza-appointed fiscal commission in 1916 and were implied in article 28 of the 1917 Constitution. Pani managed the creation of the Banco de México in 1925.[13] His action laid the groundwork for later Cárdenas reforms and the economic miracle.

Pani's bank and treasury programs succeeded to the point that a federal treasury surplus existed in 1925. Supplementing these resources, the government also decreed luxury taxes on gasoline and tobacco to finance road building. These tax monies went directly to the National Road Commission, so although the first appearance of recession in the economy cut other public works programs in 1926, road building continued. The road construction program demonstrated to federal developmentalists that Mexico could forge a nation autonomously. It offered a precedent for the formulation of future programs during the Cárdenas regime.[14]

The administration's attention to the road program and the Cristero Rebellion was somewhat distracted midway through Calles's presidential term by the question of succession. The issue acquired urgency when placed in perspective: eleven presidents had held office in the fourteen years since the defeat of Porfirio Díaz. Each succession had been attended by insurrection. The question of who should accede to the presidency initiated an episode of debate and actions that had a transcendent effect on Mexico.

TRANSCENDENT PRESIDENTIALISM

Two early favorites for the 1928 presidential campaign were General Francisco Serrano, former minister of war, and General Arnulfo Gómez, steadfast adherent of Calles, especially during the de la Huerta revolt. Neither excited much popular support outside of their immediate circles of friends. Neither had any backing in the large blocs of workers or campesinos. Politics had the impending feel of the air before a summer cloudburst.

The thunder crashed: Obregón appeared on the scene again as the Calles term approached its end. The former president decided that the "No Reelection" provisions of the 1917 Constitution meant only no immediate reelection. Consequently, through the legislators he controlled in the national congress, he arranged for the election law to be written in January 1927 to allow for his candidacy for another term. The following year, the compliant congressmen also created the six-year presidential term that stipulated no reelection.

Calles had no intention of playing Manuel González to Obregón's Porfirio Díaz, foresaw alternating terms with his mentor, and quickly backed Obregón for the office. Others, perhaps more aware of the former president's plans, glimpsed an action that seemed uncomfortably close to the Porfirian pattern in which Díaz returned after the González interregnum to remain as the perpetual president. Skillful politician that he was, Calles also made preemptory moves against those politicians who were both suspect and vulnerable. Chihuahua governor José Antonio Almeida became a victim as he was overthrown in 1927. Although no direct link has been found to Calles, the arrival of presidential associate Senator Nicolás Pérez in the state capital prompted the coup d'état the next day. The local CROM official rationalized the overthrow, saying the governor had been the head of "an inexpert, weak government, dominated by a *camarilla*." Almeida ended two trends in Chihuahua; he was the state's last independent political boss and the last major leader from the Sierra (a group that emerged during the revolution) as political influence swung back to groups representing a Ciudad Juárez-Chihuahua-Parral axis, clearly linked to the national regime.[15]

An unexpected interest group appeared in the presidential campaign. Young Mexicans, graduates of the national preparatory school and the national university, entered politics for the first time and became a pressure group whose education and patrons encouraged two principles: no presidential reelection and return to civilian rule. These university faculty and students formed a loose bloc around the best-known and most active educator of the years of the Sonoran dynasty. These were the disciples of José Vasconcelos.[16]

The 1927 maneuvering by presidential candidates initiated an episode with long-term political ramifications and led to another interlude of violence that continued into 1929. Once the violence ended and the political dust settled, Mexicans learned that Calles had emerged victorious from the struggles from 1927 to 1929 and that their politics had been placed in the hands of an official monolithic party, the National Revolutionary Party (Partido Nacional Revolucionario, PNR), which he had created. Moreover, they discovered that disenchanted Vasconcelista students were forming the principal opposition political parties. Manuel Gómez Morín established the Partido Acción Nacional (PAN) and Octavio Béjar Vázquez had a major role in the organization of the Partido Popular (later the Partido Popular Socialista). This university bloc had lost the election, but did not intend to lose the war. The loosely organized interest group was determined to win political power, although they disagreed over the best method to achieve it. The largest number entered the government with plans to capture and dominate the Calles system and the others followed Gómez Morín and Béjar Vázquez, who organized the principal opposition political parties for the next half century in Mexico.

Although it may appear curious that Vasconcelos had served as the teacher and mentor of many of the politicians who would one day dominate Mexico and of the politicians who would challenge that domination, this pattern became a precedent. The university, especially the law school, became the center of political recruitment and the creation of enduring political alliances (often around a favorite instructor).

Immediately during the period 1929–1930, this episode of presidentialism created a deep-seated desire for revenge for the dead and the humiliated and for their own defeat among this potentially powerful group. Angel Carvajal in 1957 and Manuel Moreno Sánchez in 1963 shared this ambition and advanced to the round of presidential preliminary candidates. Two others who harbored this passion were Miguel Alemán, whose father, a brigadier general and Anti-Reelectionist, was killed in the 1929 campaign, and Adolfo López Mateos, who was personally marked by the 1929 defeat and the humiliation of his friends. Calles and his party established the practice still prevalent today, in which the ruling party recruits university students who prove their abilities in the ranks of university politics by challenging the incumbent regime. In addition to those Vasconcelista adherents already mentioned, the PNR recruited seven other student activists for their speaking ability who later served as orators in official presidential campaigns. Despite all of the focus on revolutionary generals and General Calles's formation of the official party, the essential conclusion emerges that a civilian, university-trained group laid the foundation for modern Mexican politics during the period 1927–1929. These Vasconcelista activists had the future; for others from 1927 to 1929, the future was bleak and short.

Arnulfo R. Gómez and Francisco R. Serrano organized a splinter political party comprising both ambitious and idealistic veterans of the revolution. They formed the "Anti-Reelection Party" to challenge Obregón, whom they dubbed "Alvaro Santa Anna," after Antonio López de Santa Anna, who had held the presidency on eleven occasions. When Gómez won the nomination, Serrano's followers walked out of the party. Both generals became persuaded that they had no chance for victory in voting that was "regulated" by Calles, so in October 1927, they reunited and revolted. Their effort proved less popular than the earlier de la Huerta revolt, as this time only one-fourth of the federal army joined the uprising. Their brief armed challenge ended in death. Federal troops, commanded by General Claudio Fox with written orders from Calles, captured Serrano with thirteen collaborators on October 3, 1927, at kilometer 47 of the Cuernavaca highway and shot them to death in what became known as the Huitzilac Massacre. On November 5, they also arrested and then executed Gómez and an aide, Colonel Francisco Gómez Vizcarra, in the cemetery at Coatepec, Veracruz.

Obregón won easy reelection to the presidency. Full of self-confidence, during the interval before his inauguration he hosted a series of galas to celebrate his upcoming administration. The president-elect had earlier boasted to Calles when he turned the presidential office over to his protégé, "I have proved that the presidential palace is not necessarily the ante chamber of the cemetery." He proved himself wrong.[17] At a lavish dinner on July 17, 1928, at a fashionable San Angel restaurant in suburban Mexico City, a sketch artist made his way around the table. Once he reached Obregón, he drew a revolver and fired five shots, all of them hitting the president-elect. Obregón died within minutes.

José de León Toral, the assassin, was nearly murdered by irate Obregón supporters at the inn, but cooler heads prevailed and he was taken to a military prison. Interrogators determined he was deranged, a supporter of the Cristero movement and a devotee of the charismatic nun Madre Conchita. The nun was quickly arrested and the trial of the two became a public spectacle that intensified both Catholic and anti-Catholic feelings. The defense tried to justify the actions of the defendants with a plea that they were acting on behalf of their God. The claim of divine inspiration did not bring divine intervention. The court ordered the execution of León Toral and sentenced Madre Conchita to thirty years imprisonment at the Islas de Tres Marías federal prison off Mexico's Pacific coast.

In addition to Obregón, the presidential contest proved costly for revolutionary veterans. The two Anti-Reelectionist candidates, Generals Serrano and Gómez, died for confronting Obregón. The presidential succession also resulted in the assassination of other lower-ranking officers, including Colonel Crispiano Anzaldo, General Agapito Lasta, Colonel Aurelio Manzao and all the officers of the 16th battalion (Torreón), General Arturo Lasso de la Vega (Pachuca), Generals Alfredo Rodríguez and Norberto C. Olvera (Zacatecas), Luis T. Vidal (governor of Chiapas), General Alfredo Rueda Quijano (Mexico City), General Oscar Aguilar (Monterey), and Generals Francisco R. Bertani and Horacio Lucero (Minatitlán, Veracruz). Engineer Luis Seguara Vilchis used dynamite in an assassination attempt on Obregón, who escaped unhurt. The engineer and his collaborator, Antonio Tirado, were shot to death in the company of Humberto Pro and his brother, Father Miguel A. Pro, S.J., who had nothing to do with the attempt (Mexico City, November 23). Obregón's assassin, Toral, faced a firing squad in Mexico City on February 9, 1929. The death toll from the crisis created by presidential succession in 1927 included ten generals, a governor, thirteen co-conspirators, all the officers of the 16th Battalion, and a priest subsequently beatified as a Christian martyr.[18]

Obregón's death was the last murder of a major leader of the revolution. When Obregón joined Madero, Carranza, Zapata, and Villa in death, the revolution had consumed its greatest leaders. His assassination created a political crisis for the regime in which Calles had to devise some solution to the presidential succession. He and nearly all other Mexicans hoped he could develop something that would replace the process of presidential selection by violence that had characterized the nation for virtually its entire independent history.

Calles wanted to remain in office, but the hostility raised by Obregón's decision to reclaim the presidency persuaded him that he could only hold office by force. Moreover, he recognized the threat that the Cristeros, who had achieved a military stalemate in west-central Mexico, might align with the powerful opposition campaign coalescing in the cities around José Vasconcelos. The outgoing president needed to act quickly and decisively, so he improvised a way to rule through others.

First he arranged for the congressional selection of General Emilio Portes Gil as interim president, from 1928 to 1930, and then he established a party to secure the selection of General Pascual Ortiz Rubio in the 1929 election for the president who would complete the Obregón term.

Calles devised the structure of what became the "official party" in an effort to end the succession crisis and to resolve his immediate desire to continue exercising power. Rather than to say he created this party, it is more exact to explain that he gave formal endorsement and administrative structure to the system that had been in place since the Madero rebellion. From the time of Madero, Mexico was ruled by a revolutionary clique of leaders that has been referred to as "the revolutionary family." The revolutionary clan actually rules the nation and this can lead to the situation in which the president is not the head of the family, so that a puppet presidency occurs.

Calles gave the revolutionary family an institutional structure when he formed the Partido Nacional Revolucionario (PNR), the progenitor of the present-day Partido Revolucionario Institucional (PRI). Although the temptation exists to interpret this action as part of the bureaucratization of the revolution that occurred in France and the Soviet Union, among other revolutionary regimes, it should be recognized that in Mexico, the Calles government created a party. In other instances, the revolutionary party created a government. Thus, in a unique way, the Mexican government shaped and has continued to shape the party, instead of the reverse. Moreover, the party became the instrument of the state to implement its own programs. Increasingly, since the founding of the party, the state developed interests of its own and used the party to popularize, implement, and complete these programs.[19]

He organized the party to heal the divisions among Callista and Obregónista followers, limit the influence of the military in politics, and institutionalize the existing political situation. Power was given to four sectors of society (labor, campesinos, civil servants, and the military); business and church leaders were excluded. The interaction of these four monolithic groups in theory was supposed to provide a system of one-party democracy. The result was the PNR, resting on two basic principles: first, party discipline, created through vertical organization, and second, all-encompassing ideology, established by claiming the nineteenth-century Liberal heritage and the ideals implicit in previous revolutionary programs enlarged by incorporating the revolutionary mythology of Zapata and Flores Magón.[20]

In a nice historical touch, the PNR was formally inaugurated in March 1929 in the city of Querétaro, birthplace of the 1917 Constitution. The party's neat vertical structure did not emerge at first, but rather in its first incarnation brought together military and civilian chiefs. Among the most notable regional bosses were "Rodríguez in Sonora, Cárdenas in Michoacán, Cedillo in San Luis Potosí, Maximino Avila Camacho in Puebla . . . Portes Gil in Tamaulipas, Adalberto Tejeda in Veracruz and the party of the recently deceased Felipe Carrillo Puerto of Yucatán."[21]

At this point, Calles intended to corral all of the regional, labor, and campesino caudillos. Some proved difficult; strongmen in the border region often had greater financial resources than many of their contemporaries because of the economic opportunities provided by Prohibition in the United States. The Mexican side of the border had tremendous opportunities to produce alcoholic beverages to smuggle across the line or serve to thirsty tourists, even though Calles, Pancho Villa, and Adolfo de la Huerta had all been staunchly pro-temperance while serving as governors. The lure of beer or liquor combined with the chance to gamble or enjoy other illicit nightlife soon made Mexican border towns important tourist and convention attractions. Perhaps no one recognized this opportunity better than General Abelardo Rodríguez, at that time serving as governor of Baja California del Norte, who developed the attractions of Tijuana for tourists. He made his fortune in Tijuana before being called to the presidency.

Profits made along the border financed powerful camarillas that had the income to remain autonomous from Mexico City and Calles. Ciudad Juárez serves as an example of the way profits from the sale of alcoholic beverages and lurid nightlife financed local politicians. The Juárez Brewery, opened two years after Prohibition began, soon had customers supplied with bottles of light or dark Richelieu beer in "Big Kid's" Palace, Harry Mitchell's Mint Bar and Oasis Cafe, or the best-known Jimmie O'Brien's bar. The Waterfill and Frazier Distillery also kept busy. Gambling became big business once the Obregón administration brought more settled conditions to the border. Thus city

Figure 9.1 Smuggling alcohol (sotol) across the Rio Grande in 1930. Although made in Mexico, sotol was sold mostly across the river in Texas. *Printed with permission, Photography Collection, Harry Ransom, Humanities Research Center, University of Texas at Austin.*

Figure 9.2 A small celebration on the border around a keg of sotol. *Printed with permission, Photography Collection, Harry Ransom, Humanities Research Center, University of Texas at Austin.*

officials and the state governor, with substantial sources of license and tax revenue, often operated independently from the national regime.[22]

Tijuana's growth directly resulted from the opportunities created by Prohibition along the border. The town's population increased from 1,000 to over 8,000 during the decade of Prohibition from 1920 to 1930. Baja California del Norte's strongman governor Abelardo Rodríguez profited handsomely. Nevertheless, strong Prohibitionist lobbies in San Diego managed to get a 6 P.M. border closing that limited somewhat both the drinking and gambling industries. The border crossing between Calexico and Mexicali (also in the jurisdiction of Rodríguez) remained open until 9 P.M. because the communities were more tightly integrated, even sharing one fire department.[23] Calles had to find ways to deal with these caudillos, with access to substantial funds of their own, whom he could not coax into the party.

JEFE MÁXIMO AND THE PNR

Calles's new party was immediately tested by three challenges, and it prevailed. The military suppressed the Escobar Revolt (March 1929), negotiators finally concluded the Cristero Rebellion (1929), and party supporters backing the army ended the Vasconcelos electoral campaign. With their defeat in 1929, revolutionary generals never again succeeded in mounting a major assault on the government in Mexico City, although an anti-northern legacy remained, waiting to be tapped in the future. Calles had emerged as the undisputed Jefe Máximo. Successfully handling these challenges established political stability, but critics such as Jesús Silva Herzog declared that Calles's authority from 1929 to 1934, the years of the Maximato, rested on the triangle of "assassination, corruption and the PNR."[24] In reality, it constituted a much more complex mix of both positive and negative tactics.

The army's handling of the Escobar Revolt, however troubling, caused little public outcry, but scandal erupted with the discovery on the outskirts of Mexico City of around 100 bodies of persons who had supported José Vasconcelos. Vasconcelos had served as a catalyst for student activists, who entered politics in a much more direct and organized way than they had in the 1927 campaign. He accomplished this because, more than an opposition politician, he had become the embodiment of the new Mexico to university-trained Mexicans. Having served as the director of the National Preparatory School, the rector of the National University, and the secretary of public education, he had tremendous influence on Mexico's students in the decade of the 1920s. His candidacy attracted the support of the survivors of the 1927 Anti-Reelection Party and eager student-faculty activists. Their political ideals remained the same, no reelection of individuals and return to civilian rule, although broadened by their opposition to the continuation of the northern dynasty.

Violence continued to etch starkly on Mexican politics. Only a year and half after the assassination of Obregón, an assassin ambushed newly inaugurated President Ortiz Rubio, firing six shots at him in his car. The bullets hit the president's wife in the right ear, before entering Ortiz Rubio's jawbone. Shattering glass caused multiple wounds to his niece. The assailant, Daniel Flores, was alleged to be a disappointed Vasconcelos supporter. General Eulogio Ortiz, the military commander for the Valley of Mexico, without any collaborative evidence, launched an intense harassment campaign, including arrests of followers of Vasconcelos. After interrogating and torturing these prisoners, Ortiz ordered that some sixty persons be taken to Topilejo, about halfway between Mexico City and Cuernavaca, where they were forced to dig their own graves, then were hanged and buried. The military refused to give out any word on the persons who had been arrested. The victims disappeared without a trace, until the bodies were accidentally discovered about a month later.[25]

The Topilejo Massacre commanded headlines until the government silenced the newspapers with a campaign against sensationalist journalism. Still, demands for investigation of the incident surfaced periodically, and the episode showed clearly the violence involved in establishing the PNR's rule. Vasconcelos refused to forgive the official regime; in 1959, anticipating his death, he wrote his son-in-law unequivocally stating his opposition to any attempts to bury his remains in the Pantheon of Illustrious Men, saying, "I have not even accepted friendly banquets because justice still must be done to those who died in the electoral campaign of 1929. . . ."[26]

The 1929 campaign demonstrated not only the failure of students yet to enter the political forum but of women as well. The revolution in many ways provided new opportunities to females but it also empowered the macho characteristics of violence, strength, and manliness that limited women's public activities. Vasconcelos's female voice in the 1929 campaign was Antonieta Rivas Mercado, who recorded the presidential effort in short stories and articles. The daughter of a well-known Porfirian architect, she had the personal wealth to finance the first avant-garde theater in Mexico, publication of experimental fiction, and reports of the Vasconcelos campaign. In her accounts of the campaign, she repeatedly referred to him as a messiah on his way to the Mexican Jerusalem. Before the presidential defeat, she left for the United States where Vasconcelos, in defeat, joined her and then they continued on to Paris. Rivas Mercado committed suicide in France, using Vasconcelos's pistol. For many, her experience and death demonstrated that Mexican women could not live through powerful men, but had not yet identified an independent life and career beyond the traditional expectations of mother and wife. The new careers, such as teachers, had opened only limited spaces for women. Their emancipation from the home was yet to come,[27] just as the incorporation of university students more fully into national life remained in the future.

Others survived the Escobar debacle only by quick thinking and a light step. Marcelo Caraveo, born in western Chihuahua in 1884, had joined the revolution in 1910, fighting with Orozco; he then in succession changed sides with the political winds and emerged a brigadier general in 1920. Five years later, he arrived back in his native state as chief of military operations for Chihuahua and Durango. In 1928, he became governor of Chihuahua with widespread support in the state. But he joined the Escobar revolt, and only a quick step into El Paso and exile saved him. The exiled executive, highly regarded for his devotion to principles, was the last of the home-grown governors and independent caudillos in Chihuahua.[28]

Throughout the 1920s, despite the efforts of Obregón and the Sonorans at pacification, three major insurrections—the de la Huerta revolt, the Cristero Rebellion, and the Escobar rebellion—challenged the national regime. Beyond these national campaigns, political instability remained a part of life at the state and local levels for many Mexicans. In Chihuahua, for example, not one governor served his entire term until Rodrigo Quevedo held office from 1932 through 1936.[29]

The success of the PNR, partially relying on this violence, enabled Calles to establish himself as the Jefe Máximo, guiding the nation's next three presidents. Emilio Portes Gil (1928–1930), Pascual Ortiz Rubio (1930–1932), and Abelardo Rodríguez (1932–1934) each served a biennium as president with responsibility but with varying degrees of power. While Péleles I–III—Dummies I–III as the public called them—sat in the presidential chair,[30] actual authority remained chiefly with Calles, who chose cabinet members, suggested policies, and dictated the selection and resignation of presidents. He handled most national business from 1930 to 1934 from his palatial home in Cuernavaca, located on what quickly became known as "street of thieves."

During his presidency, during the period 1934–1936, Abelardo Rodríguez drew on his Sonora heritage with knowledge of the borderlands and his experience as governor of Baja California del Norte. Jefe Máximo Calles continued to manage politics and the official party, but Rodríguez developed independent administrative programs for land reform, education, labor, and development of the nation's infrastructure. As he pushed these programs, he replaced government officials who supported the ideological position of Calles; in this way, he provided a transition to the Cárdenas administration. Rodríguez favored agrarian reform based on small holdings rather than ejidos; lay, not socialist, education; physical education programs promoting participation in sports, including American football; a minimum four-pesos-daily wage for workers; and construction of the Mexico City–Nuevo Laredo highway to encourage internal markets and automotive tourism. His moderate programs did contain proposals to place mining, oil, and electrical production under national corporations to guarantee that profits and services would remain in Mexican hands. When he left the office, he returned to Baja California to run his economic, rather than political, cacicazgo until his death in 1967. Nevertheless, his presidential policies influenced the PNR's six-year plan.[31]

In addition to the creation of the PNR during the rule of the so-called puppets, there were a number of other developments. Most dramatic was the professionalization of the army. The successful reduction of the number of officers and enlisted men on active duty also allowed the government to reduce military spending. Curtailing the military had a stabilizing effect on the government, with the decrease in the possibility of revolt at each election. Just as important as regulating the finances of the military was the increased professionalization of the officers through improved training. General Joaquín Amaro recognized the need for improved training and created the Escuela Superior de Guerra or Superior War College in 1932. Company and field grade officers attended the college to receive training for battalion and higher command. Major Luis Alamillo Flores, who had a diploma from the Higher War College in Paris, visited U.S. military staff schools before designing the curriculum at the Superior War College. Between its creation and the establishment of the Colegio de Defensa Nacional in 1981, graduation from the Escuela Superior de Guerra offered the surest route to eventual promotion to general rank.[32]

Moreover, mediation finally emerged from the outside to end the Cristero stalemate. United States President Calvin Coolidge, in 1927, appointed Dwight Morrow as the ambassador to Mexico. Because of Morrow's ties to Wall Street and his reputation as an investment banker and full partner in the J. P. Morgan firm, his appointment was at first resented by Mexicans. But he proved to be one of the best received and most revered diplomats ever to represent the United States in Mexico City. Immediately following his appointment, both he and his wife began taking Spanish language lessons. He made it a point to become acquainted with prominent Mexicans, including Calles, on an informal, friendly basis. He promoted Mexico, by arranging visits by world celebrities to Mexico City. He arranged for Charles Lindbergh, for a time the world's most popular hero after his solo flight across the Atlantic Ocean, to appear in Mexico. And, as an unexpected outcome, Morrow's daughter Anne fell in love with the dauntless pilot and the couple was married shortly after the visit. Morrow also arranged for a visit to Mexico by the most popular humorist in the United States, Will Rogers. Soon Morrow and Calles were meeting regularly for breakfast to confer on international events as the Mexican chief dined on popcorn lightly dusted with chocolate. Discussing the Cristero Rebellion, a Spanish waiter commented to a journalist that the cause of the crisis had been wives. "It is mostly the doing of the women. When it was profitable to make revolutions and to persecute the Church, the politicians had their pockets full. They could take up with gay and expensive women from the theaters and cabarets. But now that Señor Morrow has insisted on a budget and honest accounting here in Mexico, there is an end to the grafting. The politicians have to return to their wives. But the wives, who are good devout women, won't stand for any more nonsense about the Church."[33] This trenchant comment gave a role to Morrow that neither he nor any foreigner had and could have in Mexico.

Still Morrow's prestige abroad and in Mexico allowed him to arrange for negotiations and serve as the go-between to resolve the Cristero fighting. He secured an invitation from Calles for Father John Burke to come to Mexico and meet with the Cristeros. Obregón's assassination interrupted these efforts, but they resumed in 1929,

Figure 9.3 An oil company office in Mexico around 1920. *Printed with permission, Research Collection, Annelisa Romero de MacLachlan.*

when Morrow arranged for prelates exiled in the United States to return to Mexico for negotiations. The critical issues were religious education and anticlerical legislation. New president Portes Gil said he would not attack the spiritual functions of the Church, would allow religious instruction in churches, but not in schools, and, finally, pointed out that proper channels existed for campaigns to repeal any legislation. In June 1929, the government's position was accepted and the rebellion ended. Although the Church-state struggle was not resolved, it never again resulted in actual civil war. The 1929 accord stopped the fighting that had cost Mexico perhaps as many as 100,000 lives and permitted the nation to move on.

Fear of another Cristero rebellion came in 1934. Minister of Education Narciso Bassols moved to introduce what his ministry called Socialist Education, limiting the Church's role in education and promoting coeducation and instruction in sexual hygiene. Heightened tensions broke into violence in a few rural areas. Handbills in Puebla threatened parents with excommunication if they allowed their children to attend school; small armed bands stole horses and called for revolution; and villagers in Tenango, Puebla, murdered local teacher Castulo Meneses González. The crisis abated quickly, when the newly chosen president abandoned the anticlerical parts of the new thrust of schooling.[34]

The presidents during the Maximato sustained good relations with the United States; these amiable feelings were largely due to the Morrow ambassadorship and were continued by J. Ruben Clark after 1930. Only one incident marred the generally good relations. One of Calles's relatives, a young boy living in Oklahoma, was murdered in a racist incident. Clark handled the rather complicated issue and arranged for the payment of an indemnity and a personal apology from President Herbert Hoover to Calles.

MEXICANS AND THE GREAT DEPRESSION

Government reform programs moved to the right under the extended Calles regime, from 1928 to 1934. Economics and general international uncertainty made Calles less willing to indulge in radical rhetoric. Moreover, the severe weather patterns of 1929 resulted in extremely poor harvests with potentially dangerous political consequences. Agricultural difficulties were accentuated by the impact of the great world depression that severely reduced government revenues. Mexican exports of raw materials faced a glutted market and weak demand. Declining silver exports contributed to the downward spiral that saw Mexico's purchasing power from exports fall to 47.2 percent of their 1929 value by 1934. This collapse sent shock waves throughout the economy. Declining tax receipts and falling reserves reduced money in circulation. Faced with this crisis, the Calles government responded with a balanced budget proposal, along with other steps dictated by orthodox economic principles.

His officials resorted to orthodox solutions because of their training, his own observations in Europe, and encouragement from the U.S. ambassador and the International Committee of Bankers on Mexico.[35] After a trip to Europe in 1929, Calles concluded that further land reform would create the rural difficulties he found in France. He believed the French land reform program had created such a large number of smallholders on minuscule plots of land that French agriculture could not take advantage of modern agricultural machines and techniques. Another push to the right, at least according to many observers of the Mexican situation, came from the United States Ambassador Eyler N. Simpson, who advocated the ejido as the cradle of democracy, while he denied passing judgment on Morrow's activities, declared "... coincident with his [Morrow's] presence in Mexico the life went out of the revolution."[36]

Whatever the mix of domestic and foreign pressures, from 1929 to 1934, the federal government distributed little land as it became clear that the policy decreased total agricultural production. Nevertheless, land reform retained some life as three governors, Lázaro Cárdenas of Michoacán, Agustin Arroyo Ch. of Guanajuato, and Adalberto Tejeda of Veracruz, continued agrarian reform programs. Even these persistent efforts did not equal the land programs in Chihuahua, which by 1933 had distributed more land (2.54 million acres) than any other state, although most of it during the tenure of agrarian commissioner Gustavo L. Talamantes, from 1920 to 1924.[37] A national agrarista policy that included education and machinery thus slowly developed.[38]

Workshop of Revolution, IV

State governments appealed to some insurgents as an appropriate level at which to direct the remaking of society. Madero first had attempted, rather unsuccessfully, to locate the revolutionary impetus with the state governors; dynamic state executives emerged again under Carranza after 1917 and again under Obregón in the early 1920s. Creative, zealous governors again seized the initiative under Calles to establish what came to be called laboratories of the revolution, pushing the ambitions for social justice, a secular society, and socialist ethos to their limits in Mexico. These revolutionary leaders shared what has been called a Developmentalist ideology that included the belief that only by molding minds, by creating "new men"— modern, dynamic, secular, and educated—could they found a new Mexican society.[39] Plutarco Elías Calles, Francisco J. Múgica, Tomás Garrido Canabal, Salvador Alvarado, Adalberto Tejeda, Lázaro Cárdenas, and Rodolfo Calles identified the major obstacles as religion and the Roman Catholic Church, which they held responsible for promoting backwardness, superstition, and fanaticism. This led the revolutionaries, primarily at the state level, to attempt to effect their cultural revolution from above. The most forceful of these governors were Tomás Garrido Canabal, Lázaro Cárdenas, and Rodolfo Calles in the states of Tabasco, Michoacán, and Sonora.

Garrido Canabal dominated Tabasco state, either serving as governor or placing a lieutenant in the office, from 1922 to 1935. His success rested on mobilized popular groups—workers organized into Ligas de Resistencia and producers and consumers in two or three hundred cooperatives. Students formed the Bloque de Jóvenes Revolucionarios or "Red Shirts," and membership quickly became compulsory for all males between the ages of fifteen and thirty. Members had to memorize the "Hymn of Youth" and wear the uniform of black pants, red shirt, and the black-and-red military cap.

This state jefe maintained that the revolutionary regime should regulate public morality and personal habits of the citizens. For example, the regime ordered all children under the age of eight to be in bed before 8 P.M. each night; prohibited female teachers and other women state employees from using color on their faces or wearing short hair; and issued laws that at first regulated then prohibited the sale of alcoholic beverages. Education was given a great deal of attention in the form of "rationalistic schools" that were free, compulsory, and coeducational. As an aspect of the education program, Garrido launched his statewide campaign against religion in 1925, decreeing that all priests must be married. He also closed all churches and despoiled them of all valuables. As a result, his cadres destroyed many church buildings and burned the images of saints, usually while singing atheistic songs. Writing in red ink, as he did for all official actions, he outlawed all religious holidays. Before he departed in 1934 to become the minister of agriculture under Cárdenas, he arranged a great "firing of saints" in which thousands of women participated.[40] Garrido Canabal's extreme religious persecution attempted to eliminate, according to Cárdenas, that "idolatrous cult which had subjugated the masses."[41] Later, Cárdenas government dropped him from the cabinet in 1935 and forced him out of state government and into exile on diplomatic assignment in Costa Rica. The state decrees were shortly declared unconstitutional.

Michoacán had produced more Cristeros than any other state. The rural people remained restive under a peace they had not made (the Church hierarchy who had not participated in the fighting had arranged the peace), and antigovernment sentiments remained high. Cárdenas tried to control agrarian policy, institutional politics, and anticlericalism through the construction of a popular idiom of agricultural symbolism, the ceremonial imagery of the Catholic Mass, and fragments of the Tarascan Indian language that survived.

During the Cárdenas governorship (1928–1932), his followers reached agreement on the state's problems: the great majority of the population was landless, governed at the village rather than the state level, and avowedly Catholic. Once they recognized this they began programs to redistribute land, replace local political officials with state authority, and remove Catholicism with an anticlerical education program. For this state program, Cárdenas relied on teachers, village politicians, and agricultural agents.

At the moment the Cardenistas learned they had to speak the vernacular of the region and local spokesmen had to use the argot of the official regime. Both Cardenista officials and campesinos used language to negotiate the revolutionary programs. Obregón had first used Zapatista language to advertise the Constitutionalist land policy in Morelos. By suggesting that the land redistribution met campesino demands, they were able to pacify the countryside. This does not imply that the Zapatistas were deceived by Constitutionalist propaganda. Rather, it seems clear that exhaustion, poverty, and defeat in the revolution led Zapatistas to accept land despite the fact that they did not control the terms. The Constitutionalist land reform program bore little resemblance to the Zapatista vision of land reform, since the government decided size, location, and quality and government agents decided which campesinos would receive land. Cárdenas planned to use the techniques of the sixteenth-century Catholic missionaries, but this approach clashed with villagers (both Tarascans and mestizos) who envisioned a life in which campesinos controlled land, politics, and religion. Cárdenas learned from this experience; he ignored the campesino clamor for control of political and economic affairs, but yielded on the anticlerical policy.[42]

Cárdenas's role as state governor was disrupted by the Cristero Rebellion that halted the land reform and educational programs. He took a leave of absence to lead government troops against the Cristeros in Michoacán. The experience led him to create special committees of students and local caciques in 1929 called the Confederación Revolucionaria Michoacana de Trabajo (CRMDT), and he placed them in local leadership positions. These men provided land and arms to campesinos for participation in the anticlerical crusade, fighting Cristeros when necessary. At the same time, the CRMDT teachers were to teach basic literacy, encourage adults to apply to the government for land, and support the secular government over the Church.[43]

Governor Rudolfo Elías Calles, possibly influenced by Tomás Garrido Canabal as well as his father, embarked on a fierce campaign of religious persecution in Sonora. The crusade included the expulsion of all priests and ministers; the closure of churches and chapels; the extirpation of religious symbols and images (i.e., the burning of "fetishes," novenas, crucifixes); a campaign of de-Christianization by means of education and mass propaganda, including speeches, songs, civic ritual, and anticlerical satire; and the repression of worship. This radical anticlericalism ultimately provoked widespread Catholic and ethnic subterfuge, civil disobedience, riots, and, finally, armed revolt.[44] This campaign to win the hearts and minds of the Sonorans involved anticlerical satire, the performance of secular civic ritual, the formation of anticlerical organizations such as the Liga Anticlerical and the Juventudes Revolucionarias (Revolutionary Youth), a radical group comparable to Garrido's "Red Shirts" or Cárdenas's Bloque de Jóvenes Revolucionarios, and a concerted effort to inculcate youth with rationalist attitudes.[45]

During the Cárdenas and Garrido administrations, educational expenditures comprised 40 percent of the state budgets.[46] Likewise, Calles spent between 35 percent and 37 percent of Sonora's budget on education.[47] Ultimately, Cárdenas as president moved against this state regime, as part of his well-coordinated policy to meet the rural population halfway, by ending the cultural campaign against their folk religion.

GOVERNMENT BY THE PNR

As government policies moved to the right, in compensatory moves the PNR tried to promote programs of cultural nationalism and national identity. One aspect of this design was the glorification of revolutionary myths, in other words, the replacement of reforms with metaphors. Thus the official party seized on Zapata as one of its symbols. In 1924, Calles had found it convenient to deliver an "I am a Zapatista" speech, but then let the memory of Zapata fade until 1929, when civic celebrations in his honor returned. With Calles making decisions in the background, in 1930 the national government organized a full-scale memorial in Mexico City, marking Zapata's total co-option by the official party as an official national hero. This new status received official sanction the following year, when Zapata and ironically Carranza both received the vote of the Mexican congress as national heroes whose names would be inscribed in gold on the wall of its chambers. Celebration of Zapata included the fabrication of a suitable personality. This consisted primarily of making the Morelos revolutionary the precursor of agrarian reform. On the one hand, this seemed long overdue recognition of Zapata's rebellion, but on the other hand, making him the precursor meant that the actual revolution came after him. Of course, it was Obregón and Calles who followed Zapata, and because they had accomplished the revolution, agrarian resistance was no longer necessary. At the very time agrarian reform subsided, official party celebrations informed rural Mexicans that their cherished values represented by Zapata had been achieved: they did not have to take up arms because they could apply to a sympathetic government for lands. Not everyone accepted the new Zapata because of the connection of the old hero to the problems in the countryside. The government faced a constant battle of co-option, symbolized in its unsuccessful effort to move Zapata's remains from a grave in Cuautla to Mexico City.[48]

As another result of this policy of cultural nationalism, the party in 1930 established a Confederación Deportiva Mexicana to sponsor and regulate national sports activities. The hoopla surrounding the announcement of the new bureau stressed the importance of the physical fitness of Mexico's population. Despite all of the expression of concomitant issues, little was done about this concern until the 1934 election of a new president.

The Depression and Greater Mexico

Mexicans suffered during the Depression, but none more than those who had crossed the northern border into the United States in search of economic opportunity or political stability. Many had found only hardship. San Antonio, Texas, had a large Mexican and Mexican American population, many of whom worked by shelling the ubiquitous pecans for candy production. This industry dated back to the United States Civil War when Gustave Duerler, a Swiss candy maker, bartered with Indians for nuts and hired Mexicans to crack them with railroad spikes and pick the meats with tow sack needles. By 1926, Julius Seligmann had created the Southern Pecan Shelling Company, and during the depression he surged ahead of his competitors by relying on poorly paid hand labor instead of mechanization. His company kept prices down by paying next to nothing ($10 to $12 a week) and providing only primitive working and sanitary conditions in plants concentrated on the west side of San Antonio, where some 65,000 Mexicans lived in a four-square-mile area, creating one of the worst slums in the United States. With the depression, the management cut wages to $2.50 a week and then to $1.50. The National Industrial Recovery Act (NRA) provided the first step in organizing these workers that led to an effort to raise wages to $11 a week for men and $7 for women. Seligmann responded with the Southwestern Pecan Shellers' Association that kept wages at $7.50 for men and $5.60 for women, as the NRA code remained ineffectual. When wages were cut almost 20 percent at the peak of the 1938 season, smoldering worker frustration burst into flames when nearly 5,000 workers spontaneously walked off the job. When Donald Henderson of the Congress of Industrial Organization's (CIO) United Cannery, Agricultural, Packing, and Allied Workers of America arrived, San Antonio's political machine felt threatened and moved against the strikers. The city officials hired scab workers, threatened workers who did not return to work, and jailed more than 1,000 strikers (twice putting 300 strikers in a county jail designed for sixty persons). After thirty-seven days, both sides agreed to arbitration that resulted in new wages, but federal government representatives would not grant an exception to the $.25 an hour minimum sought by the companies and the union. As result, when the companies mechanized in 1939, 5,000 unskilled workers lost their jobs, the largest displacement of workers as a result of the minimum wage law. By 1941, the labor force at Seligmann's plant dropped to 600. The union expired in 1948.[49]

The pecan shelling industry brought hardship to Mexican workers but others suffered even more during the Depression. Municipal and county governments throughout the southwestern United States

Figure 9.4 Rental announcement for west side one-, two-, and three-room houses at $2 per room, San Antonio, Texas. *Printed with permission, Russell Lee Photograph Collection, Center for American History, University of Texas at Austin.*

dealt with the financial exigencies of the Depression by removing Mexicans, even Mexican Americans, from the relief rolls, then arranging deportation trains to ship Mexicans back to Mexico. Representative Martin Dies led the attacks on undocumented Mexicans in the United States. Eventually, Representatives John C. Box and Albert Johnson endorsed legislation aimed at returning Mexicans, Canadians, and Filipinos to their native countries. From 1929 to 1933, the annual deportations exceeded 30,000 a year, with the practice continuing until 1937, when more than 8,000 persons were repatriated. A total of more than 400,000 Mexicans and U.S. citizens of Mexican heritage were returned from the United States.[50]

The Mexican and Mexican American population was largely concentrated in the states of Texas, New Mexico, Arizona, California, and Colorado, as well as in enclaves in all major U.S. cities. Each of these political units devised repatriation programs to ship Mexicans out of their jurisdictions, with the most elaborate repatriation effort, combining city, county, and national programs, established in Los Angeles, California, with a Mexican population second only to Mexico City in 1930. The newly appointed Secretary of Labor William N. Doak, in 1931, wanted to create jobs for Americans by deporting aliens, and he launched a vigorous campaign against foreigners, although most of those rounded up were unemployed and most were on relief rolls. Los Angeles officials created two special relief committees, one for the city and one for the rest of the county. The coordinator of the city committee, Charles P. Visel, in early 1931 issued sensational press releases announcing his plans to send all foreigners home. He made it clear to federal and city authorities that he intended to intimidate aliens into leaving the country and encourage the arrest of illegal aliens. Federal

TABLE 9–1   REPATRIATION REGISTERED IN MEXICO FROM 1930
THROUGH 1933

Months	1930	1931	1932	1933
January	3762	6627	9394	3216
February	3446	6216	6501	3291
March	3367	7719	6151	3278
April	3817	7448	6229	5058
May	3719	7616	8594	3120
June	5102	9959	7927	3175
July	5662	8465	8266	2042
August	5522	8624	6291	2550
September	6957	9398	4302	1944
October	8610	17092	5368	2552
November	9679	21055	5686	2816
December	9927	14742	5939	3466
TOTALS	69570	124991	80648	36508
Total for the four years:				311,717

Source: From James C. Dilbert, "A Field Study in Mexico of Mexican Repatriation Movement," M.A. (University of Southern California, 1934).

and local officers undertook raids in El Monte, the City Plaza, and
Brawley. From February to April 1931, numerous Mexicans, with their
money, property, and possessions, returned to Mexico. Pablo Baca,
president of the newly organized Mexican Chamber of Commerce in
Los Angeles, reported that by May 1931 some 10,000 Mexicans (many
with children who were U.S. citizens) had left the city. The county
repatriation program focused specifically on persons of Mexican heritage on the relief rolls. The county paid out over $2 million in 1930 for
relief. Officials believed they could substantially reduce this amount
through the repatriation of Mexicans and Mexican Americans on relief, as well as those with jobs, thus could create jobs for unemployed
Anglos on relief. The county program resulted in fifteen repatriation
trains from March 1931 through 1933, carrying 3,145 relief cases
that totaled 12,668 Mexicans and Mexican Americans at a cost of
$182,575. One Los Angeles County Commissioner calculated that the
program saved the county $435,000 in relief payments.

The number of persons who chose to return to Mexico during the
Great Depression and their motives for leaving are difficult to as-
certain. Some Mexicans, with their possessions, returned home at
the end of the Cristero Rebellion. Others left the United States

intimidated by the campaign against undocumented and unemployed foreigners, but clearly the largest numbers were either deported by the U.S. federal government or repatriated by local government bodies or charitable agencies. Mexican statistics reported that some 415,000 Mexicans and Mexican Americans returned to Mexico from 1929 to 1935; other records give a breakdown that includes 132,639 from Texas, 52,926 from California, and 18,520 from Arizona for the period 1930–1932.

The Mexican government attempted to provide assistance to repatriated citizens. Andrés Landa y Piña, chief of the migration service in the department of the interior, headed a short-lived National Repatriation Committee. The most successful programs located some 500 repatriated persons in San Luis Potosí and allowed others to join the new agricultural colonies, such as the don Martín Project, located forty miles west of Nuevo Laredo, Tamaulipas. The government committee attempted to create special agricultural colonies for the repatriated persons at El Coloso, Guerrero, and Pinotepa Nacional, near Minizo, Oaxaca, but in less than a year, both these settlements failed because of harsh conditions and disease. Author Carey McWilliams asserted that most of the repatriated Mexicans from Los Angeles eventually came back to California,[51] but no investigation has been undertaken to determine the fate of these persons.

Not all Mexicans left the southwestern United States. Mexican workers fought back against depression era wage cuts and in the 1930s participated in a wave of strikes, including coal mine conflicts in New Mexico, demonstrations in Arizona, organizing efforts in Texas, and major agricultural strikes in California, with 7,000 workers stopping work in the San Joaquin Valley in 1933 and in the same year, another strike in the Imperial Valley. Berry pickers in southern California walked off the job in 1933 rather than accept a $.09 an hour wage offered by the Japanese owners, despite talk of arresting and repatriating the workers. Other strikes in San Antonio involved bakers, tobacco rollers, and many other piecework enterprises that relied on cheap Mexican labor.

While the CIO made some efforts to assist these workers, it had little success (as with the pecan shellers). Later in the 1930s, Vicente Lombardo Toledano and the Confederation of Mexican Workers (Confederación de Trabajadores Mexicanos, CTM) made some overtures to Mexican workers in the United States. The most successful effort was the formation of political, rather than labor, groups. This approach resulted in a meeting in Corpus Christi, Texas, in 1929 of several Mexican groups that joined together as the League of United Latin American Citizens (LULAC), which remains the largest Mexican American organization in the United States.

TABLE 9–2   REPATRIATION REGISTERED IN MEXICO FROM 1931 THROUGH 1933, WITH DIVISION OF SEXES

Months	1931		1932		1933	
	Male	Female	Male	Female	Male	Female
January	4161	2496	5443	3951	1971	1245
February	3899	2317	3736	2765	1966	1325
March	4747	292	3558	2593	1931	1347
April	4630	2818	3731	2498	3002	2056
May	4913	2703	5011	3583	1919	1201
June	6357	3602	4672	3255	1997	1178
July	5235	3230	5010	3256	1186	856
August	5107	3517	3752	2539	1493	1057
September	5716	3682	2577	1725	1180	764
October	10178	6914	3229	2139	1553	999
November	12375	8680	3574	2112	1699	1117
December	8531	6211	3569	2370	2090	1376
TOTALS	75849	49142	47862	32786	21987	14521

Note: The figures given in the above table represent both adult repatriates and their children. If it were limited to adults, there would probably be a greater discrepancy between the masculine and feminine element.

Source: James C. Dilbert, "A Field Study in Mexico of Mexican Repatriation Movement," M.A. (University of Southern California, 1934)

In the wave of strikes involving Mexicans and Mexican Americans, at least in San Antonio, Texas, women took leading roles. Emma Tenayuca, called "La Pasionaira," proved to be a fiery organizer and an impassioned speaker. Ultimately she enlisted in her husband's community group in the Alamo city.[52] Mexican strikers, whatever their gender, discovered that the local law enforcement agents quickly called on the U.S. Immigration and Naturalization Service (INS) for help. The infamous "migra" appeared at all of the strikes mentioned. Mexican American organizers found themselves targets of INS investigations and many, including Jesús Pallares, the leading organizer in New Mexico, Paul J. Arias, leader of Colorado beet sugar workers, and Jess Govea, an organizer in California's Imperial Valley, were investigated and deported for illegal entry into the United States.[53]

THE SIX-YEAR PLAN AND THE PRESIDENCY

Calles, as head of the revolutionary family, had two guidelines for the selection of the official presidential candidate for the 1934 campaign:

first, he expected the person to be puppet number four and, second, responding to more radical members of the party, he wanted a more activist platform for the next administration.

Calles decided in 1933 to create a six-year plan to guide the next presidential administration back to a more revolutionary program. He called for a six-year policy to be developed for every department of government, based on "concrete facts" and the revolutionary regime's "ample experience."[54] He also wanted to deal with the international debt problem; Mexico and the rest of Latin America (with the exception of Argentina and Venezuela) were technically in default on bonds totaling nearly one billion dollars.[55] Calles directed that Mexico's representatives at the Seventh International American Conference planned for December 1933 propose a debt moratorium—the so-called Mexican Initiative. The initiative rested on the background paper prepared by Luis Sánchez Pontón and was proposed by Mexican ambassador Dr. José Manuel Puig Casauranc.

The debt issue could not be resolved easily because it formed a part of the complex of issues between the United States and Mexico. There existed the emotional issue of Mexican land and oil held by foreigners and the equally emotional issue of the deportation of some 300,000 Mexican citizens between 1930 and 1933 from the United States back to Mexico.[56] Despite the strident, bombastic nationalism on both sides, behind closed doors the groundwork was established for working out most problems.

The PNR met in its national convention in December 1933 in Querétaro to approve the six-year plan. Agrarian party members, just as the delegates to the 1917 Constitutional Convention in Querétaro had seized the initiative, grabbed control of the meeting and forced the adoption of a radical provision in the six-year plan, insisting that the land distribution program be renewed and expanded. This move helped promote the agrarian reform policies of the next administration. Radical delegates also forced consideration of education, believing that the Roman Catholic Church remained a dangerous enemy because it competed with government teachers for the minds of children. Arnulfo Pérez H., representative from Tabasco and self-styled "Personal Enemy of God," demanded that the state require the teaching of "scientific truth" to challenge the Church's "dogma and superstition." In an emotional appeal for the PNR to extirpate religion from Mexico, he lashed out, demanding that the delegates modify the constitution to establish a more militant school system, one that would challenge religion. In his words, the state school must "be able to combat the clergy, religion, and—let us say it frankly—in order to combat 'God!' Yes, gentlemen, the Revolution has the imperative duty of combating that false divinity that is venerated in every temple and that has many altars in the hearts of the people. We must fight this outdated and absurd belief, inspired only by the fear and ignorance of humanity. We must fight 'God,' the maximum myth from which the greatest lies have been derived to exploit humanity and keep it on its knees throughout the centuries. 'God' does not exist."[57] Pérez's passionate speech resulted in the inclusion of an aggressive education program in the six-year plan. Calles supported the program, perhaps with the perverse thought of creating a problem for the next president. The delegates ended their Querétaro meeting by nominating as presidential candidate Lázaro Cárdenas.

Calles's personal choice for president was another northerner, Manuel Pérez Teviño from Coahuila, who had backed Calles in his move to the presidency and the creation of the party, becoming in the process the party's president and power broker. But Calles forsook his personal preference and tapped Cárdenas as his official candidate. According to a widely circulated joke at the time, Cárdenas was as surprised as everyone else by his selection. The story goes that Calles called Cárdenas to a meeting.

> Calles tells Cárdenas, "We have you in mind to occupy the presidency of the Republic because of your revolutionary stock."
> Cárdenas, imperturbable, answers, "Pardon my ignorance, General, but what do you mean by 'stock'?"
> Don Plutarco, surprised by the question, and scratching his head, says to him, "Well, 'stock' is. . . who the hell knows? The important thing is that you are going to be the next president of Mexico."[58]

Cárdenas was both an extremely prescient man and an extremely lucky one—he indeed had come from excellent revolutionary stock. He was born in Michoacán, where he joined the Madero revolt, opposed Huerta, backed Carranza until 1920, supported the Sonora Triangle (which earned him promotion to brigadier general) and followed Calles against de la Huerta. He correctly followed the twists and turns of revolutionary turmoil. He served as governor of his native state, and in 1929, as the protégé of Calles, he became the first president of the newly formed PNR.

Immediately after his formal nomination, Cárdenas developed a campaign strategy to reach voters in all parts of the nation, even though his election was assured by the PNR. He toured the nation, recalling in some ways the campaign of Madero, and continued to travel during his term of office (while president, he spent 489 days outside of the capital, visiting some 1,028 cities, towns, and villages). The candidate also made use of the radio for the first time. He relied on Guillermo Morales Blumenkron, a native of Puebla, who had joined the PNR at age twenty-six as head of state radio station XEFO. Morales B. (as he was known) developed successful radio programming as a powerful part of his presidential campaign. The strategy created a tremendous surge of support for Cárdenas that he would find useful later in putting an end to Calles's rule of the party. He gained political support from the general disenchantment with the long reign of the Sonora dynasty, from the popular unrest especially with Calles as jefe máximo, and from those, such as Adalberto Tejeda in Veracruz, threatened by the PNR's attack on regional autonomy.

CÁRDENAS IN POWER

As Cárdenas took office for the presidential term, from 1934 to 1940, he inherited a political structure that included regional caudillos such as General Juan Andreu Almazán, a revolutionary echo of Bernardo Reyes, in Nuevo León. The six-year plan, created by Calles in May 1933, was a legal brief by the official party to return to revolutionary policies. Cárdenas summarized the program developed in Querétaro by saying that together the agrarian movement, the cooperative movement, and the educational movement would be the chief focus of his administration.

After his inauguration, before attempting to implement these goals, he took the first steps to consolidate his power. Selection of advisors required immediate attention and, although he turned to his comrades in arms from the revolution, he also named civilians, who had missed the fighting because he wanted their expertise. At least fourteen of his closest advisors—such as General Francisco Castillo Nájera, named ambassador to the United States; Gabriel Leyva Velázquez, who became governor of Sinaloa; and Benecio López Padilla, who had the most important military commands, including the Federal District, during this presidency—had shared the battlefield experience with the new president. The second group of advisors included civilians, some of whom Cárdenas had met through his administrative experience, especially while governor of Michoacán. The most prominent example of the latter group was Gabino Vázquez Oseguerra, who became the secretary of agrarian reform.[59] The new president drew on his personal popularity generated during the campaign. He also had done much to establish rapport with the ordinary Mexican by arranging for free telegrams to his office from noon to 1 P.M. each day to make complaints that needed immediate attention. Moreover, he moved out of the residence at Chapultepec and made the palace a national museum, while he lived in middle-class surroundings.

The military also attracted the new president's attention. Cárdenas moved to make the military dependent on him. Units were separated from their longtime commanders by injecting junior officers in strategic positions between enlisted men and senior officers. Other junior officers received promotions and battalion commands as older officers (allied to Calles) received highly visible but insignificant military goodwill tours abroad, or went into retirement. These changes resulted partially from a change in the maximum age limits and maximum career span for officers below the rank of general, thus opening positions for younger men. He also encouraged recruitment of cadet officers from the popular classes and from the ranks of enlisted men. These policies, for the most part, elaborated programs first devised by Calles. Cárdenas, in an original decision, split the ministry of war and navy into two cabinet offices, the secretariats of national defense and navy. He also introduced the first significant criterion for promotion since the revolution, when he ordered all infantry officers to take a comprehensive examination in military science. Those who failed had the option of undergoing remedial training or of retiring.[60]

The new president had to deal with the remaining strongmen, their private armies and personal sources of income that had been built up since 1910. Several of these formed alliances with him in opposition to Calles. Of this group, the most important was Cándido Aguilar, Carranza's son-in-law, who had spent a decade in exile because of his support for de la Huerta, but who had returned to become a senator from Veracruz. By 1934, most of the former regional caciques had been replaced or had reached some accommodation with the revolutionary government. The long-standing financial autonomy offered to bold caudillos also was greatly diminished through the combination of two events: the U.S. government's decision to end Prohibition, which in turn brought an end to that windfall source of dollars, and, ostensibly in reaction to at least twenty gangland murders in Ciudad Juárez, Cárdenas prohibition of legal gambling along the border, curtailing another substantial source of money.[61] Exceptions existed, most notably Saturnillo Cedillo of San Luis Potosí, who remained independent. Cárdenas dealt with Cedillo by bringing him into the cabinet in 1938, where he could be stroked by the administration and closely watched. Moreover, Cárdenas built his political authority by recognizing those camarillas—led by new-style caudillos who ran regional, union, or campesino groups.

Calles moved too late to counteract the tilt of power to the new president. He charged Cárdenas with trying to create a dictatorship of the proletariat. Cárdenas ended the Calles challenge in 1938 when he placed the ex-president, known as the Jefe Máximo, on a plane to Brownsville, Texas. Cárdenas also moved to clip the wings of Luis Morones, head of a major but fading labor group, the CROM. The personal corruption of Morones was well known, and that knowledge was used to break his and his union's power. He sent Morones to Texas with his old mentor.

With Calles gone, Cárdenas turned to his program of reform. One spokesman explained the final goal of the administration, saying, "We have dreamt of a Mexico of agricultural cooperatives and small industrial communities, electrified, with sanitation, in which goods will be produced for the purpose of satisfying the people; in which machinery will be employed to relieve man from heavy toil, and not for so-called over-production.[62] Cárdenas used the opportunity of Calles's exile to purge his supporters in the party. In 1938, he had the PRN abolish itself, and then the president created the Mexican Revolutionary Party (Partido Revolucionario Mexicano, PRM). The new party was divided into components representing labor, peasant leagues, military, and civil servants. These four formal groups replaced the amorphous agglomeration of individuals, officers, labor bosses, caudillos, and jefes that had formed the PRN.

Agriculture received immediate attention. Cárdenas distributed twice the amount of land of all other revolutionary presidents before him. By the end of his term, one-third of Mexico's population of 45 million persons had received some land from the government. Most of it had been distributed as communal property, that is, ejidos. The lands of the Yaqui Indians were returned in a major reparation for the Díaz regime's attack on indigenous properties. The Cárdenas administration represented the apex of land reform. The most ambitious single program was the Laguna cotton ejido of over one million acres, which included government schools, implements and machinery, cooperative mills, and a hospital located in Torreón. Still, over 300 haciendas encompassing over 100,000 acres remained in existence at the end of the Cárdenas administration.

Despite the shaky beginning because of the educational issue, the Church-state struggle cooled as both sides retreated from hardline positions. This development allowed the administration to focus on other questions, including labor. The president backed the emergent Confederation of Mexican Workers led by Vicente Lombardo Toledano, and with government backing, this umbrella union quickly filled the vacuum left by the CROM. The CTM was similar to the CIO in the United States with its industrial or sectoral organization. The success of the union received international recognition in 1938, when the Inter-American Labor Congress met in Mexico. At this meeting, the delegates formed the Confederation of Latin American Workers that became a Communist front during World War II.

Vicente Lombardo Toledano tried to improve wages for workers. He instituted a survey that showed that four pesos a day was the absolute minimum for subsistence, but that the average wage in Mexico was only 1.6 pesos a day. He dedicated his term as minister of labor to reaching the four pesos a day wage. Industries, both Mexican and foreign, blocked and harassed his efforts, resulting in a wave of strikes. In the first year of the Cárdenas administration, 202 strikes involving 14,685 workers occurred and the next year, 642 strikes resulted with some 145,212 workers participating. At the end of his presidential term, the average wage had reached 3.5 pesos a day. The CTM had other functions as well, including social, sports, and political activities for members that made the organization a potent force under the Cárdenas administration.

Cárdenas attempted to make everything seem revolutionary. Public health and hygiene became a national campaign. Village clinics were adorned with banners, posters, and placards that urged peasants to regard cleanliness as a nationalistic act. Unlike nineteenth-century reformers who molded the lower classes allegedly for their own good, the Cárdenas bureaucrats tried to enlist them as an important part of the grand cause that went beyond the individual. Signs asserted that "Hygiene is an act of social fraternization" and "Cleanliness [is the] pride of the working class." Health teams traveled around the country. In 1938, 300 interns received rural assignments and public health officials urged physicians to relocate outside of Mexico City in areas of greater need.[63]

Other programs included a new focus on education for Mexico, in which the government insisted upon a scientific emphasis. This led to some collisions with religious fundamentalists, but the Church hierarchy and high government officials resolved these difficulties. Schooling during the Cárdenas term emphasized the weekend patriotic fiesta. The revolution's schoolteachers revised the Liberal pantheon, adding new figures, such as Emiliano Zapata, and new ideals, such as equality, social justice, and agrarian reform. The fiestas also featured athletic competition, such as basketball, baseball, and foot races that fostered community pride through competition with other villages. These contests involved boys almost exclusively, but the preparation of a collective meal drew females into the festival.[64] The physical activities reflected the plans drawn up by Luis Obregón for the ministry of public education and expressed in the slogan, "Play in exercise and exercise in the form of play should be the formula for education in the countryside." This program aimed at creating community interest and support for the schools, reducing alcoholism and other social ills, and promoting nationalism. This led to the Juegos Deportivos Nacionales de la Revolución during the Avila Camacho years. Under Cárdenas, the government established a separate department of physical education (1935), whose director, General Tirso Hernández García, led the campaign to create the Normal School for Physical Education established in 1936 at the Venustiano Carranza Sporting Center in the Federal District. Thus the campaign saw the number of physical education teachers grow from fifty-eight to 300, with an additional fifty-eight pianists called on to accompany exercise classes. The Cárdenas government made every effort to incorporate physical education into the national educational program. The regime extended education to military families, beginning in 1935 with the construction of elementary schools for the children of soldiers.

The intellectual backing for this program remained almost exactly the same as that used to support sport during the Porfirian years. The experience, according to Carlos González Peña in 1938, promoted the mental and physical well-being of the individual in modern society. Others added that it contributed to friendships and offered alternatives to bars and other immoral traps.

CRISIS OF 1937

The Mexican leadership found its regime convulsed in a crisis in 1937 that had two sides to it. First, Mexican governments virtually since independence had tap danced on the thin ice of financial collapse, but in 1937 the ice broke and the government sank into the cold waters toward bankruptcy. Second, Cárdenas and his supporters interpreted the Spanish Civil War as the outbreak of a second world war, so Mexican foreign relations acquired an urgency impelled by international crisis.

The economic crisis in the spring of 1937 accelerated the downward spiral of the economy. The eye of the maelstrom was the most severe increase in the cost of living index in the twentieth century. After the 1925 and 1926 surpluses, the federal treasury overextended itself. Land redistribution resulted in declining production of food for the burgeoning urban population, forcing the government to import corn and beans, the expense of which reduced public spending on social programs. Private credit collapsed, and with a strike by oil workers the petroleum companies transferred bank deposits abroad, unleashing a general flight of Mexican capital. The Mexican treasury ran out of money.

The crisis of 1937 forced the leaders of the revolutionary party to adopt emergency policies and make difficult decisions about the direction of the nation, industrial development, and, as the election of 1940 approached, the selection of a successor for Cárdenas. The short-run policies averted collapse; their implementation as the bases of Cárdenas's programs reshaped revolutionary goals (or, as some would have it, meant the end of the revolution).

Immediately, Eduardo Suárez, treasury minister, using the cotton and sugar harvests as collateral for bonds, instituted a 3 percent income tax and reinstituted corporate taxes. He then worked out new deals with the petroleum company El Aguila for concessions in Poza Rica and with other independent oil producers for loans to finance public works. In his most daring action, he issued bonds on the previously untouched and sacrosanct reserves of the Bank of Mexico. His dramatic action combined with his long experience in working with representatives of U.S. banks and the U.S. government enabled him to gain the support of the Franklin D. Roosevelt administration.

Suárez was a disciple of John Maynard Keynes and spoke the economic language of many U.S. government officials. He had their respect and their support. The U.S. president moved swiftly to reassure Suárez that the U.S. government would continue monthly silver purchases from the Bank of Mexico, despite efforts in Congress to block this. And, at year's end, when it appeared Mexico would be unable to maintain the peso exchange rate, the Roosevelt administration in a dramatic gesture made a one-time purchase of 35 million pesos of Mexican gold to deliver the Cárdenas regime out of the crisis.

Deficit spending reached 120 million pesos by the end of the year, but the program devised by Suárez saved the regime in financial terms. At the same time, this policy, combined with the effects of the petroleum strike, ended the Cárdenas government's ability to finance its social programs. Political support for the regime rapidly eroded as peasants and workers joined businessmen in their opposition to the government.

Domestic concerns mounted along with international difficulties. Cárdenas's government had to balance its economic and political links to the United States with its cultural-ideological ties to Spain. Foreign policy had an urgency because the Spanish Civil War seemed to be a terrifying preview of Mexico's future if the president could not reunite Mexico's disparate groups. Cárdenas and his closest advisors understood clearly that the greatest threat to Cardenismo did not come from Nazi German or Fascist Italian activities, but instead from the growing Mexican conservative groups that saw in Franco the personification of the Hispanic tradition favoring family, Church, and anti-Communism. Thus the revolutionary government that had escaped economic collapse in 1937 faced an equally profound crisis of shaping Mexico's future social and economic direction in order to avert a Spanish Civil War kind of political paroxysm.[65]

In evaluating the Cárdenas regime and the Mexican revolution to 1937, we must measure it as Cárdenas and his advisors did—through small, actual improvements for real people, not through the statistics that can easily belie social change. For roughly half of the population, the revolution did next to nothing. Women had few political rights, although for the first time in 1938 a woman addressed the national congress and women gained the vote in some state elections, but they were not permitted to vote in national elections until 1958. Cárdenas's reform program did make a special appeal to women. He and his administrators encouraged women to engage in sports, social work, and public affairs.[66] The revolution did open the teaching profession to hundreds of women from poor and rural backgrounds, giving them an opportunity to develop as individuals beyond the roles created for them by their fathers, brothers, husbands, and sons.

The educational campaign to bring about the sociocultural reconstruction of the countryside began in the late Porfirian years and was subsumed in the revolutionary mission initiated by Vasconcelos in the 1920s. Teachers contributed to two basic changes in the community: inoculation and the raising of the hearth from ground to waist level. Teachers persuaded parents that inoculations helped people, especially young children, survive epidemics. The rural schoolteachers were not solely responsible for this change in attitude, but certainly contributed to it. Likewise, teachers encouraged by moving the hearth from the hard-packed earth to waist level. All of those involved in public health advocated the change, along with the construction of chimneys to carry smoke out of the room, tables for the families to eat on, and the use of utensils at meals.

The schools performed an important role in rural communities by teaching basic literacy to children, promoting sports for better physical health, and encouraging patriotic celebration of the new revolutionary values. Between 1910 and 1940, the literacy rate[67] nearly doubled for males, rising from 26.4 percent to 50 percent, and climbed from 24 percent to 42 percent for females, although the literacy rates in rural sections of the country were lower, especially for women. The education campaign was eminently successful at least in the outer forms of physical education (basketball backboards and hoops stand in mute testimony throughout rural Mexico). The educational crusade directed from Mexico City evolved from a revolutionary program for social transformation to a program desired by villagers themselves for teaching literacy and social betterment, not only because the Mexican state had become more conservative but also more responsive. It was because communities had whittled down the federal school's pretensions and shaped them to meet their own needs in a changing world. By that time, the teacher had negotiated a secure and respected position in the community. Over the years, teachers had demonstrated their staying power, their ability to compromise, and their utility. Many had lived in the communities and gained local trust. The fact that most of them came from modest provincial backgrounds, just a notch above the villagers, helped them as cultural brokers and communicators. They themselves were experiencing social mobility through the revolution and preached an optimism about the future and the state.

The secret to the teachers' success was precisely their lack of training and resources to carry out the transformation they proposed. They improvised. They taught what they knew from their own backgrounds. The women introduced the recipes and remedies they had learned from their mothers, along with the information they received from the federal public health program. In their own homes, the school, or the orchard, they demonstrated the benefits of a new crop or two. Some of the things the teachers promoted proved their worth. They had entered communities at a vulnerable moment of disorganization and became part of the process of reconstruction.

Villagers themselves often insisted on certain changes. Nothing demonstrated this more clearly than inoculation against smallpox and other contagious diseases. In communities constantly ravaged by epidemics before the 1930s, mothers, having learned that vaccinated children had a better chance to survive, asked for shots. The local healers and midwives began to give inoculations, incorporating them into a synchronous repertoire of knowledge, skills, and services. In the village of Mascota, Jalisco, epidemic death had formed a natural part of the peoples lives for as long as anyone remembered or records had been kept, until the inoculation campaign began in 1936. The process of change and negotiation was generational as well.[68]

The revolution, some would say the market and the schools that represented two faces of the revolution, promoted labor-saving devices for domestic work: the corn-grinding mill eliminated spending hours at the metate; the stove brought cooking from the ground to waist level; the introduction of manufactured cooking utensils meant they no longer needed to be made; in many areas the introduction of potable water eliminated the necessity to walk to streams carrying heavy buckets.[69]

These were changes the villagers eventually accepted. The rural education program became one created by villagers. They rejected the teachers they did not like, the schools and the lessons they found irrelevant, and accepted those elements of the program that worked. In this sense "it was the peasants . . . who 'created' rural teachers."[70]

Many believed that Cárdenas after 1937 did what was necessary to save the revolution by making concessions to more conservative domestic and foreign interests. Others believed his action "was not saving the life of the Revolution, it was merely preserving its corpse." This judgment is too harsh. The dominant groups might still exploit the masses, but not with impunity. The fact that the people had to be reckoned with has been called "something of a hollow victory for the masses,"[71] but this is not quite so. Now the people, in fact, must be part of any governmental equation—a small, but real victory. Lázaro Cárdenas's skill at manipulating the myth and ethos of the revolution accounts for his continuing popularity and his own inclusion into the larger myth of the institutional revolution and accounts for interpretations that identify the end of the revolution with the end of his regime. In fact, the revolution of the northerners ended in 1937, when Cárdenas led Mexico in a new direction.

NOTES

1. Lieuwen, *Mexican Militarism*, pp. 27–29.
2. Meyer, *Estado y sociedad*, pp. 182–83.
3. Rockwell, "Rural Schooling," pp. 9, 11.
4. Camp, *Generals in the Palacio*, pp. 38–39; Gordon C. Schloming, "Civil-Military Relations in Mexico, 1910–1940: A Case Study" (Ph.D. diss., Columbia University, 1974), p. 289.
5. Wilkie and Michaels, eds., *Revolution in Mexico*, p. 159.
6. Raquel Rubio Goldsmith, "Shipwrecked in the Desert: A Short History of the Mexican Sisters of the House of Providence in Douglas, Arizona, 1927–1949," Vicki L. Ruiz and Susan Tiano, eds., in *Women on the U.S.–Mexico Border: Responses to Change* (Boston: Allen and Unwin, 1987), pp. 177–95.
7. Vaughan, "Rural Women's Literacy," pp. 26–27.
8. Jean A. Meyer, "Revolution and Reconstruction in the 1920s," in *The Cambridge History of Latin America*, vol. 5 (New York: Cambridge University Press, 1986), p. 163.
9. Adrian A. Bantjes, "Burning Saints, Molding Minds: Iconoclasm, Civic Ritual and the Failed Cultural Revolution," in Beezley, Martin, and French, eds., *Rituals of Rule*.
10. Rockwell, "Rural Schooling," p. 16.
11. Plutarco Elías Calles, *Mexico Before the World*, translated by Robert H. Murray (New York: Academy Press, 1927), p. 92.
12. Enrique Krauze, *La reconstrucción Económica* (México: El Colegio de México, 1977), pp. 98–106; Wendy Waters, "Calles at the Crossroads of Mexican History: New Roads, Old Directions" (Honors Thesis in History, University of British Columbia, 1992), passim.
13. Watrous, "Fiscal Policy," pp. 134, 144, 150–51.
14. Meyer, *Estado y sociedad*, pp. 158–62, 180.
15. Wasserman, "Persistent Oligarchs," pp. 39–40.
16. This discussion of the emergence of university students and alumni in politics relies on the provocative work of Roderic A. Camp. See his "La campaña presidencial de 1929 y el liderazgo político en México," *Historia Mexicana* 23: 2 (1977, pp. 231–59.
17. Quoted in Bertram D. Wolfe, *Portrait of Mexico* (New York: Covici, Friede, 1937), p. 190.
18. Reavis, *Conversations with Moctezuma*, pp. 118–19.
19. Roderic A. Camp, *Politics in Mexico: Democratizing Authoritarianism* (New York: Oxford University Press, 1993), pp. 26, 246.
20. This argument is based on Voss, "Nationalizing the Revolution," pp. 285–88.
21. Wilkie and Michaels, eds., *Revolution in Mexico*, p. 175.

22. Langston, "Impact of Prohibition," pp. 91, 227.
23. Robert Buffington, "Prohibition on the Border: National Government–Border Community Relations," *Pacific Historical Review* (forthcoming).
24. O'Malley, *Myth of the Revolution*, p. 153.
25. John W. F. Dulles, *Yesterday in Mexico: A Chronicle of the Revolution, 1919–1936* (Austin: University of Texas Press, 1961), pp. 484–89.
26. Vasconcelos, *Mexican Ulysses*, p. 11, citing the letter published in Novedades, July 1, 1959. He had died on June 27, 1959.
27. Vasconcelos refers to Antonieta in his *Autobiography* by the pseudonym Valeria. See Jean Franco, *Plotting Women: Gender and Representation in Mexico* (New York: Columbia University Press, 1988), chapter 5, "Body and Soul: Women and Postrevolutionary Messianism," pp. 102–29, 214–18.
28. Wasserman, "Persistent Oligarchs," pp. 40–41.
29. Wasserman, "Persistent Oligarchs," p. 56.
30. Schmidt, "Humor and Politics," Appendix A, "Political Nicknames."
31. Barbara Allen Kuzio, "President Abelardo Rodríguez (1932–1934): From Maximato to Cardenismo" (M.A. thesis, Portland State University, 1997).
32. Camp, *Generals in the Palacio*, p. 365 ff.
33. William F. Sands, *Our Jungle Diplomacy* (Chapel Hill: University of North Carolina, 1944), p. 156.
34. Vaughan, "Rural Women's Literacy," pp. 30–31.
35. This discussion relies on Robin Ann King, "Confrontation and Accommodation: A Multi-Action Approach to Mexican External Debt Policy and Macroeconomic Management" (Ph.D. diss., University of Texas, 1991), pp. 78–155; and, her "Propuesta mexicana de una moratoria de la deuda a nivel continental (1933)," *Historia Mexicana* 38: 3 (January-March 1989).
36. O'Malley, *Myth of the Revolution*, p. 167.
37. Wasserman, "Persistent Oligarchs," pp. 43, 82–83.
38. The best introduction to the agrarian question is John M. Hart, "Agrarian Reform," in Raat and Beezley, eds., *Twentieth-Century Mexico*, pp. 6–17.
39. Knight, *The Mexican Revolution*, pp. 69–70.
40. Dulles, *Yesterday in Mexico*, pp. 611–24; 656–58.
41. Carlos Martínez Assad, *El laboratorio de la revolución: El Tabasco garridista* (México: Siglo XXI, 1979), pp. 54–55.
42. Marjorie Becker, "Torching la Purísima, Dancing at the Altar: The Construction of the Revolutionary Hegemony in Michoacán," in Gilbert M. Joseph and Daniel Nugent, eds. *Everyday Forms of State Formation: Revolution and Negotiation of Rule in Modern Mexico* (Durham: Duke University Press, 1994), pp. 143, 237, 245, 248.
43. Marjorie Becker, *Setting the Virgin on Fire: Lázaro Cárdenas, Michoacán Peasants, and the Redemption of the Mexican Revolution* (Berkeley: University of California Press, 1995), pp. 71–73.
44. See the Michael C. Meyer Prize-winning volume, Adrian A. Bantjes, *"As If Jesus Walked on Earth:" Cardenismo and the Political Culture of the Mexican Revolution in Sonora, 1929–1940* (Wilmington, Del.: SR Books, 1998).
45. Manuel S. Corbalá, *Rodolfo Elías Calles. Perfiles de un sonorense* (Hermosillo: n. p. 1970), pp. 154–55, 158.
46. Adrian A. Bantjes, "Burning Saints, Molding Minds: Iconoclasm, Civic Ritual and the Failed Cultural Revolution," in Beezley, Martin and French, eds., *Rituals of Rule*, pp. 159–60.
47. Bantjes, "Burning Saints, Molding Minds," p. 183.

48. This discussion draws on O'Malley, *Myth of the Revolution*, chapter 3, "The Public Image of Emiliano Zapata," pp. 41–70.

49. George Green, "The Pecan Shellers of San Antonio," *The Compass Rose* (Special Collections Division, University of Texas, Arlington) 6: 1 (spring 1992), pp. 1, 3, 6, 8.

50. This discussion of Mexican repatriation relies on Abraham Hoffman, *Unwanted Mexican Americans in the Great Depression: Repatriation Pressures*, 1929–1939 (Tucson: University of Arizona Press, 1974), esp. pp. 3, 39, 41, 43, 71, 85–86, 91, 106, 120, 139, 141.

51. Carey McWilliams, *North from Mexico: The Spanish-Speaking People of the United States* (Philadelphia: J. B. Lippincott, 1949), p. 193.

52. García, *Rise of the Mexican American Middle Class*, pp. 54–71.

53. D. H. Dinwoodie, "Deportation: The Immigration Service and the Chicano Labor Movement in the 1930s," *New Mexico Historical Review* 52: 3 (July 1977), pp. 193–206.

54. Wilkie and Michaels, eds., *Revolution in Mexico*, p. 188.

55. King, "Confrontation and Accommodation," p. 10.

56. King, "Confrontation and Accommodation," p. 31, n. 71.

57. Wilkie and Michaels, eds., *Revolution in Mexico*, p. 198.

58. Schmidt, "Humor and Politics," p. 130. This is a joke apparently told about other official candidates. For example, José Vasconcelos tells the following version about the 1929 candidacy of Ortiz Rubio: "The story was going the rounds that when they recalled Ortiz from Brazil, where he had been shipped [as Mexican ambassador] soon after the death of Obregón, he thought he was being fired. Arriving in New York, he was told, 'Prepare yourself'; you are going to occupy an important position.' And he asked, incredulously, 'Minister?' 'No, President!' He couldn't get over it." Vasconcelos, *Mexican Ulysses*, p. 232

59. Camp, *Political Recruitment*, chapter 3.

60. Camp, *Generals in the Palacio*, pp. 44, 418.

61. Wasserman, "Persistent Oligarchs," pp. 165–66.

62. John Womack Jr., "The Spoils of the Mexican Revolution," *Foreign Affairs* 48, no. 4 (July 1970), p. 679.

63. J. H. Plenn, *Mexico Marches* (New York: Bobbs-Merrill, 1939), p. 322.

64. Vaughan, "Rural Women's Literacy," pp. 32–33.

65. The discussion of the crisis of 1937 draws on Friedrich E. Schuler's dissertation, "Cardenismo Revisited: The International Dimensions of the Post–Reform Cárdenas Era, 1937–1940" (Ph.D. diss., University of Chicago, 1990), chapter 2. It also relies to some extent on King, "Confrontation and Accommodation."

66. Plenn, *Mexico Marches*, p. 322.

67. The census defined literacy as the ability to read and write Spanish by those over twelve years of age in the 1900 and 1910 censuses and those over ten years of age thereafter.

68. Vaughan, "Rural Women's Literacy," pp. 33–34; Gil, *Life in Provincial Mexico*, p. 81.

69. Vaughan, "Rural Women's Literacy," p. 35.

70. Adolfo Gilly, *La revolución interrumpida; México, 1910–1920: Una guerra campesina por la tierra y el poder* (México: Ediciones El Caballito, 1971), pp. 67–68.

71. O'Malley, *Myth of the Revolution*, pp. 68, 132.

Chapter 10

THE REVOLUTION BECOMES
THE MIRACLE, 1937–1946

Mexicans dreamed of La Jauja,[1] the utopia vaguely imagined in the early revolution, given dimensions in the 1917 Constitution, and described in immediate terms in the party's 1934 six-year plan. But Mexico in 1937 was not utopia; with its splintered society, shattered economy, and wretched people the future appeared more likely to resemble Picasso's Guernica than a revolutionary Shangri-la. Cárdenas had tried the old revolutionary prescription with his agrarian and labor programs, but for every Mexican who received a share of land another moved to the city in search of work and both fertile land and jobs soon ran short. Acknowledging that revolutionary programs called for reclaiming Mexican resources and then more equitably dividing them among the people, Cárdenas and his advisors admitted that national wealth was inadequate to the task. They turned to developmental programs to accomplish what simple redistribution of resources could not. These erstwhile revolutionaries, especially for domestic reasons but international ones as well, used the official party to guide Mexicans toward new hopes for what shape the future would take. The economic crisis created domestic exigencies and the international circumstances, if Cárdenas were to adhere to the principles he espoused, required Mexican action. Responding to the urgency of both demands, the Cárdenas regime decided to forsake the essence, as defined for two decades, of the revolution.

The Cárdenas administration in 1937 largely abandoned hallowed revolutionary policies, retaining only the rhetoric. Domestic

The Revolution Becomes the Miracle, 1937–1946

1934–1940	Cárdenas presidency
1936	Leon Trotsky granted asylum in Mexico
1937	Department of Press and Publicity created
	Properties expropriated to create the Laguna cotton ejido
	Nationalization of the railroads
1938	Nationalization of the oil industry
	Cárdenas replaces the PNR with the Mexican Revolutionary Party (PRM)
1940	Presidential campaign; Juan Andreu Almazán challenges official party
1940–1946	Presidency of Manuel Avila Camacho
1941	U.S.–Mexican agreement on oil compensation
1942	Mexico initiates Japanese relocation program
	May 22: Mexico declares war on the Axis
	Bracero agreement between Mexico and the United States (continued until 1964)
	Suárez–Lamont debt agreement
1943	Zoot-suit Riots
1944	Qualifying Commission for Illustrated Publications and Magazines established to censor publications
	April 10: Attempted assassination of Avila Camacho
	The siesta ended by presidential decree

programs turned away from reform of agriculture, especially redistribution of land, preferential backing for labor, and endorsement of village, chiefly indigenous, Mexico. International policies replaced the neutral, disinterested Carranza doctrine, opposition to economic and political intervention in Latin American affairs, and automatic recognition of governments in power, whether or not they were born of revolution. Cárdenas expressed support for Republican Spain, quiet cooperation with President Franklin Roosevelt, and growing opposition to Fascist and Nazi aggression. His new programs combined a developmentalist economic project and an assertive, partisan foreign policy under the rubric of the old revolutionary litany. Cárdenas and his government relinquished the revolution, but not its revolutionary propaganda, for what was soon to be called the Mexican miracle.

CÁRDENAS THE POLITICIAN

Extraordinary revolutionary, supreme nationalist, humble populist, and father to his people—Cárdenas was indeed each of these, but often observers forget that he was the most artful of politicians and a pragmatist. He came to power by dominating the unorganized, disunited, inarticulate groundswell of politicians clamoring to push their way into power by pushing out the northerners. For a quarter century, revolutionaries from the border, beginning with Madero, had thrust brash northerners on the rest of the government, dominating the national regime and sending generals and governors throughout the republic. Cárdenas, from the core, became the cutting edge of the revanchist movement that in no systematic way united the survivors and the heirs of both the major 1927 and 1929 challenges to the Sonoran dynasty, as well as scores of lesser state and local defeats. Cárdenas claimed the first victory for the center against the north when he ordered the exile of Plutarco Elías Calles. Miguel Alemán (president, 1946–1952) would restore the vanquished from 1929, and this inarticulate, but inexorable movement reached high tide in 1958 when Adolfo López Mateos (president, 1958–1964) returned the remnants from the 1927 group to government.[2] Cárdenas's governmental advisors, free of northerners and impelled by crisis, formulated policies that focused on industry and the city after 1937.

The enhancement of the revolutionary mythology proved both necessary and useful; it coincided with the rise of the mass media. Mass culture had become a possibility in the 1920s with the arrival in Mexico of modern technology, but, with the exception of the movies, Mexicans did not seize on the commercial or propaganda possibilities of the widespread, especially urban, audience until the mid-1930s. Then entrepreneurs, seeing the success of movies, promoted radio, photographic magazines, recorded music, and, above all, comic books, each had been influenced to some extent by U. S. versions of the same medium, but during the 1930s Mexicans imposed their own cultural character on them all.

The borderlands predictably early seized on modern broadcasting. Here promoters recognized radio as a way to create consumers for an impressive variety of goods and services. Beamed across the border, radio stimulated tourism, attracting the thirsty and adventuresome. First, the powerful XEJ appeared, and it was soon followed by other border broadcasting stations.[3]

The mass media facilitated the administration's program to create the myth of the revolution. With the exception of Villa, all of the heroes of the decade of destruction—Madero, Zapata, Carranza, and Obregón—found a place in the official history, with their actions and

Figure 10.1 Youngster reading a comic book at the San Antonio public market. *Printed with permission, Russell Lee Photograph Collection, Center for American History, University of Texas at Austin.*

principles bent into acceptable shape. The closest Cárdenas's government came to offering an official interpretation of Villa was Fernando de Fuentes's 1935 production of the first movie made by Cinematográfica Latino Americana (CLASA), the government film company, titled *Vámanos con Pancho Villa.* The government established CLASA in 1935 to promote a national film industry; it premiered this Villa film in Mexico City on December 31, 1936. The movie drew on portions of Rafael M. Muñoz's novel, received direct government subsidies through CLASA, and was provided with federal troops and military equipment for the majestic battle scenes. The film, through its selection of chapters from the book, delivers a brutal condemnation of the meaningless sacrifice of lives through loyalty to Villa. Director Fuentes denied the popular myth of Villa, the macho who challenged the United States on its side of the Río Grande and daily laughed at death, when he ended the movie by having the demigod Villa, afraid of the contagion of smallpox, abandon one of his most loyal generals in the desert, who may have been infected with the disease. The film redeemed Villa by carrying the story through the Columbus Raid, but it never achieved commercial success, probably because it did not give the public the Villa it knew from popular mythology.[4]

Thus the regime could not reconcile Villa to its conception of the revolution and its alignment of revolutionaries. He remained the people's rebel and bandit chieftain, almost forever hopping in and out of the newly emerging mass media of sensational tabloids (such as *Mujeres y Deportes*), comic books, movies, songs, and stories. This personification of daring and adventure eluded the national government until the 1960s, when the official party finally made him a national hero and brought his remains to a tomb in the national capital.

The president clearly recognized the political potential of the mass media. He, as did many other leaders in the 1930s, understood the power of organized propaganda. Consequently, in 1937, he established the Department of Press and Publicity to manage relations with the press. The new agency issued news releases, suggested articles to journalists, developed radio presentations, published posters, booklets, and leaflets, and organized school events, all in support of government programs. Radio station XEFO of the official National Revolutionary Party could broadcast significant events throughout the country by means of a nationwide network of radio stations. On September 15, 1938, the station broadcast the Independence Day ceremony from the national palace. Mexicans across the nation could hear the reenactment of Father Hidalgo ringing the bell of independence and shouting the *grito* to his countrymen.

The Department of Press and Publicity used various devices to enlist support. With a handsome budget, even in tough economic times, it attempted to mobilize all sectors of the population, from the lower classes to the intellectual community. It could choose to patronize

Figure 10.2 Arnulfo Yriarte, a young junior officer, around 1930. *Printed with permission, Research Collection, Annelisa Romero de MacLachlan.*

artists and intellectuals or exclude them. Directly subsidized magazines could be counted upon to be sympathetic while others who ran government-paid advertisements or propaganda announcements could be expected to trim their criticism down to acceptable levels. The system of payments to journalists and radio commentators allowed the regime to claim that Mexico supported a free press and communications systems. Some myths of the Cárdenas era linger today because of new methods of mass communications in the late 1930s and the success of the propaganda campaign that for the first time used the national communications system made possible by modern technology and advances in advertising and distribution.[5]

This burst of mass communications creating a mass culture coincided with the Mexican miracle, a time roughly from 1937 to 1972, when Mexico's population, economic growth, political leadership, and social demands seemed to be largely in harmony. The social construct engineered by Cárdenas began to collapse in the mid-1960s, illustrated most dramatically by the student demonstrations and the Tlatelolco massacre in 1968, followed by severe shortages in foods, especially beans, and declining exports. The repression and the recession combined in a pervasive loss of confidence in the government that resulted in the flight of capital out of Mexico to south Texas and California. A final shock came with the Corpus Christi massacre on June 10, 1971, when paramilitary antiriot squads trained by the police killed fifty student demonstrators.

Before it ended, the national government's developmental project, initiated by Cárdenas, was truly miraculous. Ready to take advantage of the government's new developmental programs were the revolutionary elites. These new men, hardy veterans of the revolutionary wars, had achieved their places, occasionally by resorting to the "clumsy and primitive" methods of "seizing a hacienda, marrying a daughter of the Porfirian aristocracy, taking irredeemable loans from state banks, selling their influence in government circles, embezzling government funds or dealing in the food of their soldiers."[6] Having once established themselves by whatever means, they looked for new enterprises, opportunities, and respectability.

Beginning in 1937, they found them all. During the next three and a half decades, Mexico grew from 19.6 to 50.4 million people, while the urban population grew from 22 percent to 42 percent, and the capital tripled in size, jumping from 3 million in 1950 to 9.2 million in 1970. While difficulties implied in such population growth became apparent, for the historical moment that endured some quarter-century after 1937 the Mexican regime recovered from the near fiscal collapse of that year, seized on the opportunities provided by the circumstances of international politics and world war, and built an administration and economy that grew by 6 percent a year that was rightly called the Mexican miracle.

RECOVERY FROM THE 1937 CRISIS

The 1937 crisis threatened national economic collapse and the possibility of social dissolution. The former was rather quickly relieved through foreign assistance and the adoption of Keynesian national economic programs. The latter required more dramatic public action. The most controversial and visible aspect of these years was Cárdenas's promotion of economic nationalism. Emphasis has been placed on the economic side of this equation but it properly belongs on nationalism. Cárdenas wanted, in fact desperately needed, to unite a people deeply splintered by the economic disruption of the Great Depression, especially the 1937 crisis, and grave threat of dissolution caused by the inability of the government to continue the social programs of the revolution. Cárdenas combined the benevolent rhetorical paternalism of Franklin D. Roosevelt with the strident nationalism of European Fascism to achieve a nonimperialist nationalistic populism that psychologically rallied the Mexican people.

Economic nationalism permeated the government and its actions at all levels. For some it was an opportunity, in a more specific program, to play off the Germans, who after all had never invaded or blockaded Mexico, against other world powers, especially the United States. For the president and his associates, it was a program to mobilize the people in support of the regime. It replaced the rough unity provided through the camaraderie of revolutionary veterans who had died or had become increasingly irrelevant to the times.

A test case of this program came in the north. The Laguna region had experienced continuous armed conflict since Madero's call for revolution on November 20, 1910. Radical popular movements continued for more than two decades and climaxed in a general strike in 1936. The president could not avoid dealing with the crisis that included the leading cotton-producing zone and the northern transportation center at Torreón. In 1937, Cárdenas acted decisively by expropriating the cotton plantations and creating a huge state-run ejido.

Others saw this program as a chance to break free the major sectors of the economy from foreign regulation. Cárdenas began the promotion of pride in being Mexican with the nationalization of the railroads in 1937. The dream of Mexican ownership of the railroads had begun when the Porfirian regime purchased a controlling interest in the major lines. Cárdenas realized the scheme first formulated by Limantour, assumed total ownership, and then went a step further than many could imagine when he turned the railroad management over to the workers. Although following a succession of spectacular accidents, he had to reclaim management of the rail industry. The entire episode looked more radical than it was in fact.

Oil became the focus of the major nationalistic episode. This industry from 1936 to 1938 boiled with controversy between workers and management of the British- and United States-owned oil companies in Mexico. Laborers went on strike several times protesting their low wages in contrast to the huge profits of the companies. The May 1937 strike was the most serious: 17,000 workers walked out, demanding higher wages, housing, hospitals, and schools. Cárdenas ordered arbitration. The arbiters, responding to the climate of economic nationalism, ruled against the oil companies and the companies turned to the courts. Once the Supreme Court upheld the ruling of the Arbitration Board, the companies had no other legal recourse. Nevertheless, they simply refused to accede to the ruling, transforming the issue into a challenge to the sovereignty of the government.

Several issues influenced Cárdenas's thinking. Although the grave 1937 economic crisis had been survived, the government still faced severe financial problems that resulted in ejido and worker banks suspending all loans in early 1938. Fiscal disaster pushed worker and peasant groups into growing hostility. Shortages sparked stories (that may have been true) that the government was dipping into the retirement funds of oil workers and the postal savings program. The economic shredding of the social fabric invited comparisons with pre-civil war Spain.

In the frantic search for monies for social programs to buy peace and cooperation, there existed two possibilities as collateral for loans: minerals and petroleum. U. S. companies controlled the former and Anglo-Dutch companies much of the latter. Both the British and the Dutch were distracted by the rise of Nazi Germany and Fascist Italy, so that a Mexican move against the petroleum industry had acceptable political costs with major economic benefits because both countries wanted access to Mexican oil in case of war. On the other hand, Mexico needed to preserve as much as possible its friendly relationship with the Roosevelt government in Washington.

Government policy shifted after 1937 from a socially distributive one back to the traditional Liberal goal of economic modernization. The perceived need to create wealth rather than distribute the finite resources inherited from the nineteenth-century process of development seemed evident. President Cárdenas believed the strong centralized state the revolutionaries had been attempting to construct since 1920 would be able to regulate in the interests of the broader nation. Acceptance of federal regulations and imposed social obligations would be required of private enterprise in exchange for the freedom to function economically in their own best interests. The government's proven ability both to mobilize labor and peasants and its willingness to support popular groups that organized themselves provided the threat of force and economic nationalism the moral justification. This combination had been successful in the nationalization of land in the Laguna and in the case of the railroads. It remained to be seen if it could be applied to resolve the issue of Mexican oil. This return to full-blown developmentalism, not complete until the war years of the early 1940s, soon appeared to have been beneficial.

The Cárdenas government had a clear understanding of its diplomatic and economic options because of the successful professionalization of the major ministries of the federal government. The modernization of these bureaus resulted from the efforts of Calles during his presidency to reorganize the federal administration to achieve efficiency and professional standards.[7] The secretariats of foreign relations under Eduardo Hay and finance under Eduardo Suárez[8] adopted high standards that inspired pride and professional commitment from their bureaucrats. Suárez, Mexico's premier Keynesian, received authority from Cárdenas to act as the arbiter in allocating funds to other agencies and to state governors as part of the regime's revenue-sharing program. Thus the treasury secretary not only determined the direction of governmental financial policy but allocated economic resources as well.[9] The two Eduardos and their ministries became rivals with each other and with the defense ministry of Manuel Avila Camacho. This rivalry did not result in disruptive bickering but rather in higher professional standards and greater efficiency.

Cárdenas, well informed of his options and the risks of each, on March 18, 1938, expropriated the oil companies under article 123 (the labor provision) of the 1917 Constitution. He announced his action on nationwide radio, and public opinion rallied instantly behind the decision. Land ownership was not in question; that issue had been resolved by the Bucareli and Calles-Morrow agreements. Cárdenas presented his action as the preservation of the rights of labor as well as upholding the jurisdictional integrity of the Mexican Supreme Court. Expropriation of the petroleum industry propped up the pro-Cárdenas social alliance by promoting ardent patriotism. Moreover, it immediately helped alleviate fuel shortages and allowed the regime to place the blame for a wide variety of economic problems on foreigners. Equally important, it gave Cárdenas a source of collateral income. The president gambled that expropriation eventually would provide the income necessary to modernize agriculture and finance industry.[10]

Immediately, national pride thrust out its chest in Mexico. Standing tall, Mexicans hailed the expropriation as their declaration of economic independence. "It was a marvelous movement for all the people," remembered Socorro Rivera, a schoolteacher in Puebla's textile district near Tehuacán, ". . . [for] the workers, the campesinos, the children, the merchants, everyone. The moment was precious—precious to remember, I cry thinking about it. Every Monday morning, the children came to school with their centavitos to pay for the oil. Everyone helped. We organized fiestas, kermesses, and dances. We made wreaths of flowers, confetti, and streamers. The *señoras* prepared *chalupas* and *tamales*. We sold them to pay for the oil. And the workers! You cannot imagine with what *cariño* they came to give their money! It was so moving because you saw people so poor, who had no money, not even for their daily needs, but with what cariño they brought the little they had to pay the national debt!"[11] The people's emotional affirmation contrasted sharply with the objective political and economic reality of the governmental position.

Consternation, counternationalism, and then anger appeared in the United States. Oil producers and their allies made scathing attacks against what several called the "Communist" or "Bolshevik" leaders of Mexico. Widespread rumors of intervention circulated on both sides of the border. Old stereotypes of Mexican bandidos suddenly returned full blown as oil companies sought to harness nationalism to their own advantage in the United States. A declaration endorsing a U. S. military invasion of Mexico passed both houses of Congress, but President Franklin D. Roosevelt ignored the call for war.

Once intervention fever subsided, the struggle began to fix a price for petroleum. The oil companies demanded payment of $450,000,000. Mexicans said the value of the oil properties and installations reached only $200,000,000. Mexico's resistance to international pressure and its limited ability to pay eventually resulted in a price of $130,000,000. The negotiations demonstrated the diplomatic skill of Cárdenas, Múgica, Suárez, and Isidro Fabela, who split British oil interests away from the Americans and left Britain virtually unrepresented in Mexico. The original multinational question involved Great Britain, the Netherlands, the United States, and Mexico, but the situation changed when Mexico recalled its ambassador from London (the first time in a century that a country chose to break relations with the British), and of course the British retaliated. The United States then refused to act for the British oil companies, and the Dutch became their rather desultory representatives. In essence, Cárdenas succeeded in restricting the petroleum issue to Mexico and the United States.

Cárdenas created a state corporation, Petróleos Mexicanos (PEMEX), and by 1940 oil production had recovered. Faced with efforts by U.S. and British companies to block sales and withhold tankers, the problem became finding a market for the oil. The initiative of Suárez and his rivals in the foreign ministry provided the solution as Mexico bartered oil to the Axis powers for industrial goods, especially Italian rayon and German manufactured products. Technically, Mexico sold the oil to independent U.S. agents who resold it in Europe. Cárdenas traded with Germany and Italy out of economic necessity, but he could only bend his political principles for so long. In May 1940, Mexico suspended this oil trade in reaction to Italian military actions in support of the German invasion of France.[12]

The reform programs of Cárdenas, especially the oil expropriation, gave him an important place in the mythology of Mexico's national history. Many divide Mexican history into the struggle for political independence against Spain initiated by Hidalgo, the struggle for religious and social independence against the Church directed by Juárez, and the struggle for economic independence against foreign companies led by Cárdenas. Consequently, until his death in 1970, Cárdenas remained a potent political force in national affairs, and his son Cuauhtémoc inherited at least part of his father's mystique.

The desire of Lázaro Cárdenas to unify the population, using the oil expropriation to create national pride, for example, was reflected in the reorganization of the official party as well. Institutionalizing the groundswell of patriotic feeling that embraced the oil expropriation resulted in a political unity much like that which followed the expulsion of France from the country in the nineteenth century. Cárdenas moved to give structure to this sentiment by reforming the official party. He had already called, in December 1937, for the National Revolutionary Party (PNR) to transform itself into a new, more representative organization, although there was no immediate movement in this direction. About three weeks after the oil expropriation in March 1938, Cárdenas decided to capitalize on the sense of nationalism, and he replaced the PNR with the Mexican Revolutionary Party (Partido de la Revolución Mexicana, PRM). This new corporatist-structured organization comprised popular, agrarian, labor, and military sections (the latter eliminated in December 1940). These sectors broadened the party's base of support to workers, agrarians, public employees, and soldiers, replacing the clearly self-interested organization of powerful leaders. Cárdenas envisioned the official party as being more reflective of blocs of popular interests (labor, agrarians, public workers) than of individuals (the old caudillos). Moreover, he believed the new structure brought political conflict and competition more directly within the party and therefore under control. This did not mean that the camarillas, strongmen (caudillos), and family networks (caciazgos) disappeared, but rather that they played out their struggles within the party structure and were forced to recast their objectives in broader social terms. Reform, for workers, agrarians, and caciques, remained a political tool; they had to mobilize support to achieve their socioeconomic objectives.

Some military men believed the president had taken a step backward from the program of subordinating the military to civilian authorities and restricting their political activities. The new party structure brought the armed forces directly into politics again. Some scholars believe the military brought to the official party its ethos of discipline, hierarchy, and loyalty and made them elements of its value system.[13]

The crisis of 1937 and the decisions it demanded brought Cárdenas face to face with the fact that Mexico was nothing like the utopia envisioned in the party's six-year plan devised only three years earlier. He had turned the nation toward new development programs to secure the fiscal resources required to meet the demands of mobilized groups, which included political elites on the move. The nation's financial problems combined with the need for international markets compelled his government to take action. The programs represented a new government emphasis, based on previous experience. Cárdenas took the developmental programs of the Calles regime that stressed Mexican financing and technology, especially the Banco de México, the Nacional Financiera (an industrial investment institution created in 1933), and road building, and expanded them, creating a national infrastructure.

Secretary of the Treasury Eduardo Suárez, a committed Keynesian who had worked closely with Eduardo Villaseñor, was named subsecretary in 1938 and then director general of the Banco de México in 1940. Suárez and Villaseñor drew upon Keynesian analyses of global economic policy after World War I. Their developmental program established a precedent for creditor nations dealing with monumental foreign debts and foreshadowed the programs of import substitution. Mexico should export more and import less. *Hecho en México* (made in Mexico) stamped on various domestic products enlisted the nationalism of consumers. Their willingness to pay semi-monopolistic prices had to be encouraged emotionally. Economic nationalism required consumers to make sacrifices that directly affected their standard of living. The Eduardos provided government encouragement and aid to Mexican industries entering new product areas. Calles had pushed for electric power production and auto assembly plants (starting with Ford Motor Company in 1925); the Cárdenas government supported expansion of the glass and beer industries and moves into chemical production.

Mexico had to increase its international debt to free assets to support import substitution industries. The Dawes and Young plans relating to British, French, and German World War I reparations and debt payments offered an example clearly understood by Mexican treasury officials. Along with the two Eduardos, Luis Sánchez Pontón, another long-time government bureaucrat, recommended that Mexico suspend debt payments (in 1934) in order to put pressure on the U. S. bankers for a new debt convention.

Cárdenas and his closest advisors, especially Suárez, understood that as Latin America's largest debtor nation, Mexico had become the uninvited partner in the world's most powerful financial institutions. The Cardenistas lived the aphorism, "If you owe the bank $1,000, it owns you; if you owe the bank $1 million, you own the bank." Empowered with this understanding, Cárdenas initiated a new policy toward foreign debt payments: his government acknowledged the debt, but refused to use monies allocated to developmental programs to make payments. Mexican officials adopted the radical view of foreign investors ". . . as partners, not all powerful dispensers of capital" who had to cooperate with the government so all could benefit.[14]

The situation, especially in 1937 and after, as Cárdenas understood it, demanded other changes in foreign relations. Here also the president moved in decisive ways. During the first years of his administration, Cárdenas allowed Germany, Great Britain, and the United States, each to believe that he favored one above the rest. The Mexican executive skillfully inflated the competition among all three and used it to his advantage. In theory, the Mexican government opposed no foreign political entities, but Cárdenas opposed the Soviet Union. Mexico had broken diplomatic relations with that nation during the Calles presidency. Cárdenas continued the policy and harassed the Communist Party in Mexico. He insulted the Soviets and their hard-line followers by granting political asylum to Leon Trotsky in 1936. The decision split the Mexican Communist Party. Cárdenas and his advisors also recognized that the changing European situation made Great Britain vulnerable to Mexican nationalistic interests and used this knowledge skillfully in dealing with the oil question.

Spain was the crucial state in the international crisis of the late 1930s. Cárdenas interpreted the Spanish Civil War, as has been noted, as the beginning of another world conflict, and for ideological reasons, he pushed his government in every way possible to aid the Spanish Republic. Thus the Mexican government shipped medicines, doctors, and nurses to the Republicans until the "nonintervention" program of the United States and Great Britain interrupted that policy. Later he welcomed exiles from Spain, including those academics who founded El Colegio de México.

SECURITY, BOTH HEMISPHERIC AND MEXICAN

Changing world conditions by 1939 made the modernization of Mexican military a common interest of both the United States and Mexico. The United States, increasingly concerned about the prospect of war, looked upon Mexican preparedness as one aspect of the defense of the hemisphere. Although Cárdenas had moved the military out of domestic politics, officers became actively involved in foreign affairs, especially in questions with the United States of common defense. From the fall of 1939 into the spring of 1940, Mexican national security became a more pressing issue. For the Cárdenas regime, the security question revolved around the impending 1940 presidential election. His government feared both the radical right and the radical left in Mexico (temporarily cooperating because of the Hitler-Stalin Pact) and Nazi provocateurs, suspected of trying to instigate an armed uprising before the election. Cárdenas especially worried about the possibility that such an insurrection might provoke intervention into Mexico by the U. S. military in a prescriptive effort to prevent the collapse of the regime. For the Roosevelt administration, the security issue primarily concerned reports and rumors of growing Nazi fifth column activities in Mexico. Roosevelt wanted cooperation with Cárdenas to halt Nazi espionage and permission for some independent action, such as U.S. Army Air Force reconnaissance missions over Mexico.

Cárdenas moved decisively to thwart possible disruption of the 1940 presidential election. Both he and his high command made several administrative decisions: the military incorporated the federal police in October 1939 and then all immigration and customs officials in June 1940; Mexico's few coastal patrol boats were organized as an independent navy; and the government in May 1940 instituted national conscription to train military reserves.

The United States for its part tried to pressure Mexico into joining a bilateral defense pact. But Cárdenas maintained that Mexico should only participate in multinational arrangements, and he did not want to give the radical Hispanista right nor the official party's left the chance to make a political issue of collaboration with the United States. Meanwhile Finance Minister Suárez wanted to develop the closest possible economic cooperation with the United States to take advantage of U.S. dependence on Mexican raw materials during the war to come. And still another policy opinion came from the war department, suggesting Mexico's fate was linked to the United States and that Mexico would have to enter the war when the United States did. Therefore, the minister of war argued that Mexico should create an army that could participate in combat, requiring bilateral cooperation to obtain military equipment. The desire to build a strong army was seconded by several government advisors who believed it would be necessary to confront what they anticipated would be the postwar imperialistic policies of the United States.

Thus the Cárdenas administration abounded with contradictory policies in late 1939 and early 1940, resulting from earlier programs overlapping with new policies: the regime attempted to avoid entanglement in U.S. defense efforts and to stay out of the war at the same time it tried to create the closest possible economic cooperation to supply the U.S. war effort; the military was seeking bilateral cooperation with the United States to acquire modern military equipment to protect Mexico from the United States once the world war ended. Some contradictions continued until well after the 1940 presidential elections in both Mexico and the United States. Of course, in trying to build Mexican security, Cárdenas relied on his revived popularity as well. He remained well liked by most of the rural and urban masses, but he faced strong opposition from the elite.

CHALLENGE FROM THE BORDERLANDS

The challenge to the national government came in the traditional manner from a regional elite. Because borderlanders were abruptly removed from national power with Calles's exile, the north attempted to rally its political resources. Agrarian reform and the revolutionary propaganda that accompanied land distribution served to undercut the moral legitimacy of those who retained large rural tracts. Attacks on latifundios, whether merely rhetorical or actual, constituted a major element in the political mobilization of the masses. While vast stretches of land remained in private hands, prudence dictated a non-confrontational approach by landowners toward the government. To do otherwise risked becoming the target of redistribution programs. Only the industrial elite possessed both the resources and the legitimate moral claim on property. Industrial enterprises could not be viewed as the natural patrimony of the nation. Peasants born on the land might have a moral claim to the land they worked, but such a claim could not be transferred to manufacturing enterprises. Industrial employers might be cast as heartless exploiters of labor, forced to recognize independent unions and made to improve wages and working conditions, but seizure of their property required a specific pretext. Of the manufacturing elite, the best organized and most powerful nucleus controlled the northern city of Monterrey. This group's obvious contributions to the economy, capital resources, and international connections made it a formidable opponent, as President Cárdenas soon discovered.

Monterrey's industrialists had weathered the earlier stages of the revolution shaken but still in control. Local newspapers and radio stations filtered revolutionary events through an acceptable interpretive screen. With the growing radicalism of the revolution under Cárdenas from 1934 to 1937, businessmen became obsessed with preservation of the social order, as they perceived it. A concerned inner circle gathered at Monterrey's Rotary Club. The emergence of this group as the most important political organization in the city was consistent with the international and transborder orientation of this elite. The two major participants, Luis G. Sada and Roberto G. Sada, had been educated in the United States, at the Massachusetts Institute of Technology and the University of Michigan, respectively. The Rotary movement's international pro-private enterprise commitment appealed to Monterrey's business community. The local Chamber of Commerce brought the elite into contact with middle-class businessmen, enabling them to develop an impressive degree of solidarity from the top down. Revolutionary politicians might be skillful at organizing the peasants and workers, but Monterrey's industrialists easily matched these organizations within the business community. Networks linked Monterrey's industrialists with like-minded entrepreneurs throughout Mexico and the United States. Newspapers and magazines such as *Actividad* glorified capitalism and private business enterprise. One example of the men who made up this effective business network was Manuel Barragán, who managed the local Coca-Cola bottling plant, served a term as president of the Chamber of Commerce, managed *Actividad*, and in the late 1920s, edited *Excelsior* in Mexico City. Such high-profile activities maintained the unity of fellow businessmen and served to counter revolutionary rhetoric.

Just as the industrialists of the region had worked closely with General Bernardo Reyes during the Porfirian years, they now moved to establish useful alliances with revolutionary generals. People like General Juan Andreu Almazán, a man keenly interested in acquiring wealth, could be drawn into cooperation with the elite as was his successor Aarón Sáenz, who served as governor of Nuevo León. The Monterrey group, as early as the crisis caused by the 1928 assassination of Obregón, moved to capture the national presidency. Sáenz had served as Obregón's presidential campaign manager, and the Monterrey group saw him as a logical person to succeed interim president Portes Gil in 1930. It had only remained for the Jefe Máximo Calles, the determining voice behind the scenes, to arrange the nomination. The Regiomontanos (people of Monterrey) had their expectations dashed as Calles pushed forward Pascual Ortíz Rubio, recently returned from obscurity as Mexico's ambassador to Brazil. This unexpected reversal forced a change in antirevolutionary strategy and tactics.

The implementation of the 1917 Constitution's labor provisions (article 123) offered the first test of the Monterrey group's new strategy. This long-pending issue, involving the elaboration of a labor code, would determine the balance between labor and capital. Depending on the nature of regulations, employers would retain or lose control over their workers. Monterrey's elite had established a private-sector pressure group called the Confederación Patronal de la República Mexicana (COPARMEX) to lobby against worker interests. Despite the Monterrey opposition, the code had gone into effect in August 1931. The industrialists, battered by the worldwide depression that began with the stock market crash of 1929 and still with their backs to the wall, decided to resist the statutes. Their decision to do so rested on their belief that if they went under so would the Mexican economy, leaving the revolutionary government to preside over a ruined and bankrupt nation. The election of Cárdenas to the presidency in 1934 resulted in a no-holds-barred struggle for control. President Cárdenas, able to put together strong popular support, due to the distribution of land, the creation of a new powerful labor bloc, the CTM, and the general public's weariness with the northerners (the Sonorans), prevailed. Monterrey's factories now came under union pressure. The Cuauhtémoc Brewery and its supporting glass factory became targets. Labor disturbances became endemic. In early 1936, the labor arbitration board in Monterrey declared the company union at the Fundidora steel work illegal. Ruling against company unions undermined the ability of employers to use paternalistic methods to control workers.

Employers responded by closing up their businesses and bringing the entire city to a standstill. The lockout, complete with organized demonstrations, came close to an act of civil rebellion. Industrialists also recast the struggle in terms of "Mexicanism against Communism." They linked Vicente Lombardo Toledano and Cárdenas to the foreign ideology that allegedly sought to undermine Mexican family values. In doing so, they adroitly contested Cárdenas's claim to being the champion of Mexican values against an immoral ideology drew support from religious groups, the Church, and the United States. Financial support for conservative anti-Cárdenas organizations from student groups to women's organizations to the Fascist Sinarquistas kept up the pressure. A barrage of propaganda cast government officials as either dupes or agents of Moscow. Cárdenas, now willing to compromise, encountered a totally obstinate business community out for total victory. In this environment, violence became inevitable. Acción Cívica, the main anti-Cárdenas organization, came under a barrage of gunfire and rocks as workers attempted to disrupt a meeting (July 29, 1936). Police arrested some 600 people who attended and

Figure 10.3 Sonoran state basketball championship (February 7, 1943). *Printed with permission, Research Collection, Annelisa Romero de MacLachlan.*

held them overnight as the governor attempted unsuccessfully to dissolve Acción Cívica.

In the end, Cárdenas backed away from the confrontation without receiving any quid pro quo as he steered his administration in the new direction adopted in 1937. Only a new president to be elected in 1940 could heal the bitterness. Within the official party, now called the Partido de la Revolución Mexicana (PRM), conservative elements pressed for a candidate who was able to deal with the Monterrey elite in a realistic manner. Their choice and Cárdenas' was Manuel Avila Camacho, who publicly acknowledged the importance of Monterrey's industrialists and their contribution to Mexico. To keep maximum pressure on the PRM, the Monterrey group backed its own presidential candidate. Shortly after the elections, the government announced a series of incentives and subsidies for Mexican enterprises—a deal had been tentatively struck.[15]

Manuel Avila Camacho, the Unknown Soldier, as he was called, is usually represented as an unexpected choice, one that many Mexicans

Figure 10.4 World War II veteran, holding his medal presented to survivors of the Bataan Death March, squats in front of his home on the west side of San Antonio, Texas. *Printed with permission, Russell Lee Photograph Collection, Center for American History, University of Texas at Austin.*

believed stood too far to the right. But Cárdenas thought it was necessary to consolidate governmental decisions. He wanted someone to continue the far-reaching economic programs that he and Suárez had initiated. He also sought unity. The choice of Avila Camacho appeared to challenge this plan, but the revolutionary party and its mythology proved strong enough to make the selection work. The PRM announced Camacho's candidacy at the 1939 ceremony paying homage to Madero and Pino Suárez. Joining Avila Camacho at the celebration as the principal speaker was Francisco Múgica—the popular choice for president as the champion of agrarian reform, labor rights, and leftist politics. Both men demonstrated their support of the party's selection. Múgica's participation in the ceremony clearly illustrated how successfully politics and politicians had been co-opted and institutionalized within an official party.

Industrialists, on the other hand, challenged Avila Camacho. General Juan Almazán resigned from the army and the party to launch his own political adventure, supported by the Monterrey group, which ultimately failed. Avila Camacho won the presidency. His overwhelming majority resulted from blatant manipulation of the vote count. It confirmed the direction of the Mexican government first adopted in 1937 and continued the move away from redistribution to creating wealth.

The new president had a solid domestic base in 1940. The successful recovery from the worst of the economic crisis and the consolidation of the revolutionary state, through the ministries of finance, education, and foreign affairs, permitted further emphasis on development and industry. To preserve the momentum, Avila Camacho left Suárez in his position as treasury minister. This decision reassured many entrepreneurs, including those in Monterrey.

NEW PRESIDENT AND THE RADIO

Manuel Avila Camacho, as president, attempted to create a populist political following (a populist cacicazgo, rather than one based exclusively on patron-client relationships) by using the mass media to appeal to nationalistic sentiments and the interests of a new, urban generation. The outbreak of World War II, of course, aided this appeal to the former. The president and his aides, drawing on the experience of Maximino Avila Camacho's dominant cacicazgo in Puebla, used both culture and the media to build popular support. They relied particularly on the radio, popular and classical music, film, architecture, and public education. They wanted to overcome Mexico's regional and political differences to mold a unified national sentiment that would preempt the social disintegration that ripped Spain to tatters and, in part, allowed Fascism and Nazis to come to power in Italy and Germany. Of course, they also aimed to create a broad-based political following for the president.

This campaign resulted in official funding for the arts. Avila Camacho's government sponsored the national film industry, the national ballet, the national symphony, the radio symphony, and the national school system. It also continued the financial support and overall direction of La Hora Nacional on the radio. Of these, radio and education merit particular attention.

Radio stations broadcast to the more than 300,000 receivers across the nation. Guillermo Morales Blumenkron, program manager of the nation's most powerful station, XEW, initiated youth-oriented programming with new music and new, sometimes film, stars. (He also inspired the mass media approach to musical programming on La Hora Nacional.) The most widely listened to programs featured music in the "popular style, reflecting the preferences of three groups: *danzón* (probably originating from Cuba) and *bolero* tunes that represented urban music of the era, ranchero music from the countryside, and older forms such as *sones huastecos* expressing regional traditions. Radio broadcasts created stars such as singer Jorge Negrete and arranger Alberto Domínguez, whose versions of "Perfidia" and "Frenesí" for Tommy Dorsey and Artie Shaw were giant hits in both

Mexico and the United States, and the comic Cantinflas. These shows brought these new stars to the widest possible audience of Mexicans.

By playing orchestral music, radio enhanced the popularity of ballrooms that had opened during the 1930s. Salon Mexico presented a variety of popular music (and inspired Aaron Copland to compose his Salon Mexico suite). Entertainers like Toña la Negra and the Noé Fajardo orchestra played there. The Smyrna, another popular club, stirred the imagination of listeners, who each week listened to live broadcasts on station XEW from the orchestras of Amparo Montes, Enrique Byron, and Abel Domínguez and his orchestra.

Not everyone enjoyed or approved of the radio programming. Announcers played songs with lyrics that shocked many older Mexicans. Agustin Lara, Consuelo Velázquez, and Juan Charrasqueando composed and sang "Besame mucho," "Diez minutos más," and other songs that offended traditional sensibilities. Groups organized to preserve their version of traditional culture, such as an association of Catholic parents, which demanded censorship of song lyrics, comic books, and films. These groups felt their way of life, in which identity had been defined by family, village, region, and religion—the institutions seriously disrupted by the Revolution and its aftermath—now seemed further endangered by popular culture.

Despite efforts at censorship, the radio brought a new world of politics, ideas, and entertainment to the population. Villagers at night shared the same world as urban Mexicans. Listeners participated in a new music-centered popular culture that appealed especially to young people. The administration recognized the importance of the radio and the potential of musical programming to mobilize national support.[16]

EDUCATIONAL CAMPAIGN

After two decades of the education crusade, the state and the villagers reached a consensus in the countryside about the efficacy of schooling. The education program helped create more receptive attitudes toward change and mobility defined as progress. The schools encouraged optimism about improvements in the future and pride at being a part of the Mexican national modernization project.[17] Thus the school served as both an agency of domination and advancement that taught values that facilitated political stability and state allegiance. It also provided a useful and valued tool for personal and community betterment.[18] Nineteenth-century Liberals would have been pleased at the result.

The Avila Camacho government modified the revolutionary culture that previous regimes, especially that of Cárdenas, had fabricated and attempted to inculcate throughout the country. His predecessors had given an "official" character to the revolution that would

Figure 10.5 Miner Dimas Hernández and helper at the United Verde copper mine in Jerome, Arizona, in 1940. *Courtesy of Jerome State Historical Park.*

be subsumed in schoolbooks, in monumental art, and in the political party's presentations. By 1940, all of the great figures of the decade of the 1910s, with the exception of Villa, had their characters and their contributions redefined and homogenized into one revolutionary cause. A semimythical Madero, Carranza, Zapata, and Obregón served the state in numerous civic celebrations. Avila Camacho backed away from the missionary effort to convert the rural population to an anticlerical belief in the state. He officially altered the anticlerical educational campaign and the government's anti-Church stance; these actions confirmed the reality that these programs had gone as far as popular groups would allow them to proceed.

Educational programs underwent major changes but remained a primary concern. Avila Camacho pushed through changes in the educational amendment of the 1917 Constitution, replacing socialist programs with directions that teachers give instruction in democracy, moderation, and national unity. These goals were ignored by Minister of Education Octavio Véjar Vásquez, who swaggered around the ministry with six-shooters on his belt and exercised his arch-conservative sentiments, closing schools he considered too far to the left, shifting teachers at will, and returning some school properties to the church. This eventually forced the president to remove the pistol-toting minister from office in 1943. His replacement, Jaime Torres Bodet, had served an apprenticeship under José Vasconcelos, and he eagerly undertook a new literacy campaign in his mentor's style.

The Torres Bodet program received major encouragement from the Law for the Elimination of Illiteracy of 1944. This required all illiterate Mexicans to register and all literates (ages eighteen and sixty) to teach one illiterate (ages six to forty) to read. This educational offensive included informing the population of the campaign through radio broadcasts and leaflets dropped by the air force and relied heavily on popular culture and the mass media for success. The government offered rewards for those teaching and learning to read. Anyone teaching fifty illiterates received a medal from the president. Students could earn college tuition and others could earn bus and theater passes good for a year for educating twenty-five other Mexicans. Some agencies offered students a kilo of corn for every session attended, and others installed sewing machines in the literacy centers to lure women there. States received funds so they could give attractive prizes to the best teachers. Oaxaca set up over 3,000 instruction centers, many in converted canteens. Participants in the program had their names announced on the radio. Education department officials offered villages that sent enough people to study prizes of radios, band instruments, movie projectors, record players, and cases of soft drinks. This law, among other things, called for bilingual teaching attempting to recognize the cultural differences of Indian peoples and to teach them Spanish. Of course, the administration ordered the construction of hundreds of new schools.[19]

WARTIME PRESIDENT

Avila Camacho, despite serving as Mexico's president during World War II, took major steps to complete the transition to civilian control of the armed forces and to limit the military's participation in politics. He responded to both the civilian and military dissatisfaction with the military sector in the official party and removed that group from the organization. During his administration, he reduced from 21 percent to 15 percent the portion of the national budget allotted to defense (made possible in part because of military assistance from the United States) and retired many revolutionary generals because of the new technical demands of warfare during the Second World War. He, in fact, implemented the Cárdenas decree on time in grade and retired 550 officers in 1941. A different kind of policy resulted from the president's decision to end the recruitment of enlisted men for officer training in 1944. Ending this highly successful Cárdenas program of "mustang" officers closed a major channel for social mobility within the armed forces. The decision seems to have resulted from the apparent failure of the wives of mustang officers to make the social transition.[20]

The president faced a new urgency in the security talks with the United States because of the Nazi military blitzing through France, driving the British army off the Continent and prompting the Italian government to join Germany by declaring war. Axis victories increased U.S. concern about hemispheric defense, especially the capabilities of the Mexican military. These concerns resulted in a series of Mexico-United States military meetings in July 1940. General Tomás Sánchez Hernández and Major Eduardo Huttich Palma went to Washington to meet with Colonels F. S. Clark, E. M. Almond, and Matthew B. Ridgway. At these meetings, officers on both sides made clear the position of their military: the United States wanted to establish bases for its troops in Mexico, and Mexico wanted to obtain as much economic aid as possible from the United States. The officers demonstrated a willingness to sidestep the diplomatic concerns in the United States about the oil expropriation and in Mexico about bilateral cooperation. In separate financial negotiations, a United States–Mexican accord in 1941 settled the oil expropriation issue with an allotment from Mexico of $24,000,000, with all but $2,015,192 of the sum going to Standard Oil.[21]

The December 1941 Japanese attack on Pearl Harbor provoked the United States to declare war against the Axis powers. The Mexican government moved in a series of steps against the Axis powers during the six months following the Japanese air assault against the United States. Avila Camacho's government froze Japanese banking and property assets, halted the naturalization of all Axis nationals, ordered all axis nationals out of coastal and defense zones, and broke diplomatic relations. The Mexican government declared war on Germany, Italy, and Japan on May 22, 1942, when German submarines sank the Mexican tankers *Potrero del Llano* and *Faja del Oro* in the Gulf of Mexico.[22] After both Mexico and the United States entered the war, Mexican officers had three goals: closely cooperating with the United States, participating in combat, and obtaining modern equipment. Proof of their political acuity was the fact that they achieved these goals, despite the opposition of Mexican politicians and U.S. high commanders. Temporarily, a brotherhood of soldiers emerged that transcended the border between the two countries.

The military cooperation resulted in the decision that Mexicans in the United States could be drafted by the United States and U.S. citizens in Mexico could not be conscripted there. The United States even opened recruiting stations in Mexico. The U.S. armed forces provided monthly reports to Mexico on its citizens inducted into the service. All told, about 250,000 Mexicans served in the U. S. military. Of the latter number, some 14,000 saw combat, 1,000 received the Purple Heart, and one received the Medal of Honor. Some borderland families saw nearly all the males go off to war. Socorro Félix Delgado of Tucson, Arizona, recalled that fifteen members of her immediate family served. Those who remained behind had a weekly prayer service, and at the end of the war the family and neighbors organized a procession of thanksgiving to San Xavier de Bac mission.[23]

Newspapers also carried stories about Mexicans in the war. Excelsior, for example, carried photographs of United States Army Corporal Luis L. de Guevara and his brother, Navy Seaman Arthur L. de Guevara, the sons of Sr. and Sra. Luis L. de Guevara of Mexico City. Mexican officers visited every theater of the war, observing and meeting Mexican servicemen fighting with units of the U.S. Army, Navy, and Marines. Film and radio stars toured on behalf of the government. Rosita Moreno, for example, logged over 30,000 miles in the Pacific theater, entertaining allied troops and visiting Mexican soldiers.

The great majority of Mexicans rallied in support of the Allied cause. Nothing better symbolized their unity in the war effort than the appearance on Independence Day, 1942, of Avila Camacho and five former presidents on the balcony of the national palace. They

Figure 10.6 The "Pancho Pistolas" pilots of Squadron 201, the Mexican Air Force in the Philippines during World War II. *Printed with permission, Colonel Carlos Garduña.*

appealed for national unity.[24] At the beginning of the war, Mexico had only a small military force of 70,000 men and 65,000 trained reserves, supported by another 20,000 CTM Union members who had received military training. Avila Camacho, acting quickly, created a Supreme Council of National Defense, promulgated an Obligatory Military Service law, established local Councils of Civilian Defense, and called for a voluntary reserve army of two million. The new service law registered men between eighteen and forty-five. Mexicans quickly responded and army officers were soon leading weekend drills in village plazas such as Tlacolula, Oaxaca, and in urban public spaces such as Mexico City's Chapultepec Park (reportedly some 120,000 men paraded in the Federal District), and in Chiapas, for Chamula Indians. The mobilization included women. Among the many nursing units established, in 1943, the army recruited fifteen women between the ages of twenty and twenty-four for a brigade of parachute nurses. This was the first women's airborne unit in Latin America. Another group, comprised of young women recruits, was trained to work in Mexico City's first airplane factory (they built the Teziutlan, a training plane named for Avila Camacho's birthplace). Recognizing the danger of a Japanese attack on their exposed western flank, Avila Camacho recalled Lázaro Cárdenas to active duty in charge of the newly organized Pacific Military Zone. In January 1942, the U.S.-Mexican Joint Defense Committee was created and by March, the U.S. Lend Lease programs were in place for Mexico.[25]

President Avila Camacho and Mexican military officers wanted their troops to join the U. S. armed forces in the war effort. After much consideration, President Franklin D. Roosevelt suggested that an air force squadron join the Allies. In spring 1944, the Mexican military created the *Fuerza Aérea Expedicionaria Mexicana*, a 300-man unit. Designated as Squadron 201, the men came to the United States to train at Foster Field, Victoria, Texas, Pocatello Air Base, Idaho, and Majors Field, Greenville, Texas. The pilots and support personnel shipped out in spring 1945 for the Philippines.

Squadron 201, whose pilots called themselves "Pancho Pistolas," flew fifty-nine combat missions against Japanese positions before the war ended. Five 201 pilots died during their Pacific service. They returned home on November 18, 1945, to a tumultuous welcome. Their experiences had been widely publicized in newspapers and in a joint Mexico City-Hollywood film named for the squadron.[26]

Mexicans contributed industrial and agricultural labor and critical raw materials to the war effort against the Axis powers. Contract workers (called braceros) arrived in substantial numbers in the United States, especially in the Southwest. Although their efforts in the fields are generally known, in fact, by the end of the war, more braceros were working on the railroads (69,000) than in agriculture (58,000). The railroad braceros worked primarily in the western states, with over half of them employed by the Southern Pacific or the Santa Fe lines, but others could be found employed by thirty-five different railroads. Agricultural workers found jobs in the fields of twenty-four states, with the largest number in California.

Mexico's strong bargaining position during the war resulted in a sweeping agreement that provided more protection to braceros than the United States extended to its own agricultural laborers. The 1942 treaty required written contracts between workers and employers. The employer or the U.S. government covered transportation, living, and repatriation expenses. Contract workers would not be eligible for U.S. residence nor service in the U.S. military. They could not be employed to replace U.S. domestics or receive reduced wages, and a single incident or racial discrimination against a bracero (including segregated buses or businesses) would be cause for excluding workers from that community. The best indication of Mexico's bargaining position was the Avila Camacho government's refusal to permit braceros to go to Texas because of its history of discrimination against and maltreatment of Hispanics. Texans created a Good Neighbor Commission and lobbied throughout the war to be included in the bracero program, but had no success until March 10, 1947. Of course, undocumented Mexican workers continued to cross the Río Grande into the Lone Star state during the war.

PACHUCOS AND THE ZOOT-SUIT RIOTS

The bracero program represented by far the most important cooperative program between the two governments. Both administrations participated in public displays of unity and mutual assistance. Public reports made clear that the armed services of the two countries had established collaborative programs, including the training of Mexican naval officers in San Diego, California. Officials in Los Angeles, California, hosted a parade to honor Mexico's military holiday of Cinco de Mayo in 1943, which featured Mexican soldiers parading through downtown.

Mexican Americans enthusiastically joined the war effort. In Los Angeles, community organizations such as Cultura Pan América, the Coordinating Council for Latin American Youth, the Mexican Welfare Committee, the American-Mexican Victory Youth Club, and the Cleland House Athletic Club became centers of patriotic meetings and support programs. Nevertheless, below the surface, ethnic hostility and wartime apprehension damaged cooperation.

The deeply felt tensions, especially in the western United States, following the attack on Pearl Harbor, resulted in the internment of Japanese Americans amid fears that the Japanese air force would bombard cities in California. In one such case, on February 26, 1942, stories circulated that Los Angeles was under attack. The same apprehensions aroused suspicion of anyone whose behavior or appearance deviated from the norm. The popularity of the zoot suit among young Hispanics provides an example. These flashy, baggy suits, with their wide, padded shoulders and peg trousers, incited hostility in a community seeking wartime conformity in the face of fear. Enmity first surfaced in August 1942 with the discovery of the body of José Díaz near a pond, called the Sleepy Lagoon, frequented by Mexican American youths who could not use the segregated public swimming pools. Reports that the night before the discovery of the body a group of pachucos had been fighting near the pond resulted in mass arrests, followed by the trial and conviction of seventeen zoot-suit gang members. An appeals court subsequently overturned the convictions in the Sleepy Lagoon case. The hysteria, indicative of the level of insecurity evident in the early years of World War II, damaged relations between Mexican Americans and the general community. Like the Japanese air raid on the city, a murder may never have occurred at Sleepy Lagoon.

It may not be too farfetched to suggest that for young Anglos, zoot-suiters represented an enemy whom they could defeat immediately. Zoot-suiters became a convenient target, especially for servicemen waiting to be shipped out to the front lines and for the older population upset by the appearance of what would soon be called a teenage culture. Many Americans learned about the "zoot-suit craze" through Al Capp's comic strip dealing with "Zoot-suit Yokum" and the "conspiracy" to dress all men in these clothes, which appeared in Sunday newspapers nationwide in April and May 1943.

A series of clashes occurred over a ten-day period, June 3–13, 1943, in Los Angeles, collectively known as the Zoot-suit Riots. Anglo soldiers, sailors, and civilians came into Hispanic East L.A. to fight with young Mexican Americans dressed in zoot suits, in particular to strip off their pants and jackets and destroy them. Freudian explanations aside, the fights increased the level of apprehension among the Southern California population; nevertheless, no one was killed, no major injuries resulted, and little property, other than the suits, was damaged. The riots remained largely symbolic actions, especially when compared to the series of violent race riots that occurred across the country in the summer of 1943, such as in Detroit, where thirty-four died in fighting between blacks and whites. Nor, did the fear-inspired riots display the blatant racism of the beating of Medal-of-Honor winner Sergeant Macario García in Richmond, California.[27]

Ironically, the Zoot-suit Riots helped ensure that braceros would not go to Texas, a state with a reputation for having more severe discrimination than California against Hispanics. Mexican policy may not have improved the treatment of Hispanics in Texas and elsewhere, but it forced embarrassed U.S. officials to acknowledge the problem. This wartime labor program continued until 1964 and became an important safety valve for the Mexican working population and a significant source of dollars for the Mexican economy. Under the terms of the contract labor agreement, more than 200,000 braceros worked in the United States from 1942 until 1947, earning $205 million.[28]

Wartime prosperity galvanized all sectors of the Mexican economy. High demand for agricultural, mining, and industrial products returned handsome profits and created jobs. Mexican exports, especially raw materials, reached a level in which the country accumulated over twenty million dollars a month during the period 1942–1943, even after having reduced its external foreign debt.[29] The bracero program further increased prosperity as Mexican agricultural and railroad workers flooded into the American Southwest and California. Unrelenting demand for labor gave the lower classes higher wages and new buying and consuming power.

DANGEROUS ALIENS

The security of the home front concerned both Mexican and U. S. leaders. Both governments appointed experienced federal police officers to handle counterespionage and countersabotage activities. Roosevelt sent Gus Jones, an FBI agent who had specialized in border and Mexican questions since 1921, to Mexico City, where he worked closely with the Minister of the Interior Miguel Alemán, Colonel Alvaro Basail of the Mexican Secret Service, and the president's brother, General Maximino Avila Camacho.[30] United States agents from the Federal Communications Commission traveled to Mexico and successfully tracked clandestine radio stations that had been relaying messages to German submarines in the Atlantic. The information led to the arrest of Nazi spies.

Internal insecurity fed on fears of Axis nationals who were suspected of plotting military actions. The Interior Ministry estimated that 6,500 Germans, 6,900 Italians, and 4,300 Japanese citizens lived in Mexico. Graciano Sánchez, the secretary general of the National Confederation of Campesinos, wrote to the president on August 28, 1942, demanding that all of these enemy aliens, without exception, be placed in internment camps. Mexico, following the lead of the United States government that had adopted Canadian procedures, began the surveillance, deportation, and internment of enemy aliens. The

Japanese in Mexico constituted a rather small group (20 percent of the number that migrated to Peru, for example) scattered across the nation; nevertheless, their deep sense of solidarity caused fears of espionage and sabotage. The United States had worried since early in the century about Japanese naval interest in Baja California. As a result, the Mexican and U. S. governments cooperated on the alien question.

Actions against Japanese residents and Japanese Mexicans had begun on January 2, 1942, with orders to relocate those living in coastal areas and in the region bordering the United States. Within three months, this program had carried out the forced removal of 2,100 Japanese from Baja California, Colima, Sonora, Chihuahua, Sinaloa, Veracruz, and Nayarit to relocation centers in Guadalajara and Mexico City. The fate of 100 Japanese from Ciudad Juárez appeared typical: 80 were eventually sent to a camp at Santa Rosalía, a former copper mining town in Baja California, and the other 20, who seemed the most threatening, were imprisoned in Mexico City. The last relocation occurred in March 1943, when the Japanese residents of Chiapas were sent to Mexico City, and the most suspicious were later transferred to the main Axis detention camp at Fortaleza de San Carlos in Perote, Veracruz. Mexico also began a program to repatriate Japanese who could not prove Mexican citizenship.

Government agents arrested German residents and German Mexicans and impounded their assets in Mexico. Notably, the government seized the property of Boker y Cía., known as the Sears of Mexico, the retail company that had dominated hardware sales in Mexico since the Porfirian years. Curiously, the founder, Roberto Boker, had emigrated from Germany to the United States, where he had become a naturalized American citizen. In Mexico, Boker and his family had chosen to associate with the German colony.[31]

Fear of espionage rationalized the relocation programs. Before the Japanese legation was closed and its officials sent back to Japan, well-documented reports revealed efforts by the Japanese to organize an espionage network to gather intelligence on roads and ports of military significance. Yet the absence of any widespread Japanese plan and the fact that the FBI apparently knew the residence of every Japanese in Mexico explained why the Roosevelt government did not insist on the relocation of these Japanese to the United States. The Roosevelt administration had been instrumental in the creation of the Emergency Committee for Political Defense, in Montevideo, Uruguay, charged with oversight of hemispheric security. This agency had established the policy that called for preventive detention of dangerous Axis nationals and the deportation of such persons to another American nation if local facilities were inadequate. Guided by this resolution, the Peruvian government sent 1,300 Japanese Peruvians to camps in Kenedy, Crystal City, and Seagoville, Texas, Missoula, Montana, and Santa Fe, New Mexico. Nevertheless, the U. S. government made no such demands on the government of Avila Camacho.[32]

The Mexican government seized some 346 Axis properties at the beginning of the war and placed them under the control of the Junta de Administración y Vigilancia de la Propiedad Extranjera, headed by Luis Cabrera. Pressure (allegedly from Minister Alemán of Gobernación himself) failed to return confiscated properties to the German owners. Eventually 39 of these properties reorganized under Mexican ownership and the state sold 38 others. The other 249 remained in the hands of Cabrera's Junta and earned an average of a 16.55 percent profit a year during the war.[33]

Governmental cooperation between Mexico and the United States on programs to promote security in the Western hemisphere resulted in the collaboration of the U.S. Department of State, the Hollywood movie industry, and the Mexican film industry. This activity was encouraged by the U.S. Agency called the Office of the Coordinator of Inter-American Affairs (OCIAA), directed by Nelson Rockefeller. Mexican cinema received a boost from the OCIAA and Hollywood, allowing it to surpass Argentina as the leading producer in Latin America. Mexican movies promoted the war effort in a nationalist call for unity, disseminated anti-Nazi propaganda, and encouraged tourism. The relationship with Hollywood reached its extreme point in the collaboration with Walt Disney and the production of the propagandistic "The Three Caballeros." The United States, through OCIAA, helped modernize Mexican studios and encouraged the partnership between Emilio Azcárraga and RKO that resulted in the construction of Estudios Churubusco. The cooperation would result in continuing propaganda films during the Cold War.[34]

New demands and opportunities for the Mexican military offered the president the opening he needed to reduce further its direct political role by removing the military as a separate sector of the PRM. He asserted that national defense required the military's undivided attention. This action placed the party completely in the hands of civilians.

THE HOME FRONT AND POPULIST POLITICS

On the home front, radio programs, movies, music, and popular culture generally began to reflect war-related and nationalist themes. Mexico City station XEW alone had six programs devoted to hemispheric unity and war news, and the station made Felix F. Palavicini the radio voice of the national war effort. Of the programs, Palavicini hosted the widely popular "La verdad es (The Truth Is)" and

"Interpretación Mexicana de la Guerra (Mexican Interpretation of the War)." The owners of movie houses flashed civilian defense instructions and propaganda messages on the screens, the post office issued stamps extolling the war effort, and newspapers printed advertisements (including those of U.S. companies) reflecting war themes. Government officials commissioned artists and artists' cooperatives to create war posters—inspiring a wave of popularity of this colorful "heroic style" art form. Popular musicians composed songs invoking the war effort; one hit by Fernando Rosas demanded that Mexicans must unite under the banner of the Virgin of Guadalupe to defeat the enemies of Liberty.

Government statistics revealed that in 1940 there were 446 licensed motion picture theaters that grew to nearly 1,100 by 1946, with the numbers growing rapidly. In 1940, Mexicans spent 49 million pesos on personal entertainment and in 1946 more than 100 million, with 80 percent spent on tickets to movie theaters. Of the total amount, 54 percent was spent in Mexico City. Clearly, by 1946, the cinema was playing a significant role in the lives of ordinary Mexicans. Many of the films the audiences enjoyed, as noted earlier, resulted from Hollywood-Mexican cooperation.[35]

Economic cooperation offered yet another opportunity to restructure the foreign debt. Negotiations between the Mexican authorities and the International Committee of Bankers on Mexico resumed (they had met during the period 1937–1938) in early 1941. They concluded on November 5, 1942, when Eduardo Suárez, secretary of finance, representing Mexico, and Thomas W. Lamont, on behalf of the committee, signed an agreement on the direct (nonrailroad) debt. The Mexicans hoped to reach an agreement that would provide access to credit markets after the war. Under the agreement, the Mexican government required all bondholders to register their bonds with its financial agent in New York, thus preventing the transfer of funds to the Axis powers and in the process saving approximately $50 to $60 million (U.S.). Mexico agreed to pay in dollars or pesos at the discretion of the bondholders at the rate of 4.85 pesos to the dollar (no matter how the exchange rate changed). Little overdue interest was paid, and the agreement reduced the Mexican debt by approximately 90 percent, with the principal being converted into pesos at one peso for every dollar and unpaid interest almost entirely forgiven. Negotiations succeeded in 1942, in part because Mexico had not made regular payments for many years and the market value of Mexican bonds was low. Roosevelt's Good Neighbor policy encouraged a quick and favorable resolution that reflected the Mexican government's ability to pay. The Suárez-Lamont agreement, favorable in every sense to Mexico, reduced the external debt from $1,066,600,000.00 to $116,900,000.00.[36]

Questions of security inspired the zealous to undertake the protection of Mexican culture from all threats, including the perceived challenge to national identity and morals by comic books. A growing concern had developed since the initiation of the commercial comic book in 1934 with the first publication of *Paqin*. The Mexican Legion of Decency sponsored by the archdiocese of Mexico City and conservative Catholic parents' groups such as the Family Action Section of the Union of Mexican Catholics began a popular campaign to restrict the tremendously popular comic books, from those defined as racy to translations that could be seen as artifacts of cultural imperialism. These efforts resulted in the creation of a government office of censorship in 1944, which exists today as the Qualifying Commission for Illustrated Publications and Magazines. Readers, publishers, and censors from this point on used nationalist rhetoric to justify their activities. In the process, the censors effectively, although inadvertently, protected the Mexican comic book industry from foreign competition as they worked to block cultural imperialism. The commission assumed a mediating role between comic book publishers and conservative parents' groups, especially the Parents Association, during later censorship campaigns during the periods 1953–1955 and 1973–1976. Moreover, the censorship crusade foreshadowed similar campaigns in Cuba (1954) and Peru (1972) against United States and, ironically, Mexican comic books.[37]

By 1942, Mexico embraced the main domestic and international policies it would follow for the next four decades. Among Mexican postrevolutionary governments, the Cárdenas administration was the first one to use foreign policy on a bureaucratic, professional level as an effective means to achieve political, economic, and social objectives. The deepening interplay of domestic and international politics linked Mexico to the broader world and in particular to the United States. Conservative economic and social ideas inside the administration emerged during the Avila Camacho presidency as official policy. The interference by Axis and Allied interests in Mexican internal affairs contributed significantly to this process. However, they also created economic and political opportunities that Mexican policy makers exploited skillfully.[38]

The political calm abruptly ended when an assassination attempt was made on Avila Camacho on April 10, 1944, as the president arrived at the patio of the National Palace. Artillery lieutenant Antonio de la Lama, a longtime friend of the president, approached Avila Camacho and fired his .45 revolver at the chief executive. The bullet struck the president's vest and coat, but missed his body, and Avila Camacho escaped unharmed except for powder burns. Thinking he had hit the president, the assailant turned to fire at the president's companion, and as he did, the president grabbed him and pinned his arms to his sides. Three bodyguards then manhandled de la Lama and disarmed him. Papers in his possession linked him to a Nazi-Fascist organization. The one-time seminary student-turned-army officer told the president he had made the attempt on his life because of the November 16, 1943, presidential decree that prevented the military from attending religious services in uniform. That evening, according to official reports, guards shot de la Lama as he tried to escape from custody; badly wounded, he died two days later. Investigating the assassination attempt, Mexico City's chief of police Miguel Z. Martínez uncovered another plot to kill Avila Camacho, two cabinet members, and former president Calles. Martínez ordered the arrest of fourteen persons, including a Serbian bomb maker.

One week later, Vicente Lombardo Toledano, head of the major labor union, the CTM, reported that the assassination attempt had been the conspiracy of a military Fascist group masquerading as a soldiers' relief organization. According to Lombardo Toledano, the group included some Catholic priests and had links to the Sinarquista movement. The officers planned to overthrow the government and establish a regime on the Argentine model. Despite these charges, the investigation turned up nothing more and public attention shifted away from the incident.[39]

Mobilization of the war effort changed Mexican life. While the initiation of national conscription affected some Mexicans and a number of foreign males, everyone felt the effects of the presidential decision to eliminate the siesta on June 1, 1944. Government offices and private businesses were ordered to end their afternoon closings. Avila Camacho, in his proclamation, explained the action as an effort to reduce the use of the buses from four to two times daily and to reduce the use of hydroelectric power for lights for evening business. Only those enterprises with two or three shifts were exempt from the decree. Mexicans had to endure wartime rationing, including reduced voltage as well as a two-hour reduction per day of electrical current. Austerity measures also included new regulations; for example, one decree prohibited the custom of discarding the soft doughy center of the popular breadroll, the *bolillo*.[40]

Mexico faced a disastrous food problem when nature and the war effort combined to create an alarming scarcity of corn by early 1944. With the rush to plant crops that could be exported to the United States for the war effort (for example, various oil-producing plants, such as cottonseed), only 3,048,317 hectares had been planted in corn in 1943 and scarcity of rain resulted in an average yield of only

528 kilos per hectare for a total production of 1,775,200 tons of corn. To make matters worse, an outbreak of hoof-and-mouth disease occurred that resulted in the killing of cattle and the burying of carcasses in lime. Faced with the prospect of famine, several state governors threatened to prohibit the export of corn beyond state borders. The governor of Durango seized railroad cars loaded with corn for Mexico City to feed his state.

Because of wartime restrictions in the United States, it was virtually impossible for Mexico to import staples to make up the shortage. United States Ambassador George Messersmith called on Nelson Rockefeller and Will Clayton to press the U.S. government to provide corn, lard, and sugar for Mexico. Most Mexicans remained unaware of how desperately they needed Messersmith's efforts. Even with U.S. government approval, transportation problems existed. For example, through a complicated swap of Canadian grain purchased by Mexico that went to the United States, the American government arranged for the shipment of Australian wheat to the west coast of Mexico. Barely escaping the teeth of famine, the Department of Agriculture issued a decree on September 21, 1943, that identified corn-growing regions, forbade the planting of crops other than corn, and set confiscation of crops as the penalty for violating the order.

Ordinary Mexicans faced an increasing cost of living throughout the war years, called the *carestía*. President Alemán had a private cost of living index prepared in 1946. It revealed that a stunning deterioration in real wages—twice the publicly released figures—had occurred. Real wages had increased from 100 in 1939 to 316 in 1950, and the cost of living for the working class increased in 356 in the same period. Inflation rose as well, beginning in 1942, and an index of eighteen basic foodstuffs increased by 59 percent over the next two years. The government announced price controls on March 2, 1943, but many merchants simply ignored them, especially in the countryside.

Meanwhile, the wealthy, who were able to take advantage of the wartime boom, accumulated enormous profits. They soon moved to the new suburbs in Lomas and then to the Pedregal in Mexico City; they danced and relaxed in the night clubs that proliferated throughout the capital or enjoyed the new racetrack, the Hipódromo de las Américas.[41]

Mexicans felt the greatest wartime pride in Air Squadron 201. This air force unit of 300 men, including thirty-five pilots, served in Luzon as part of the Pacific campaign. Two pilots died in training and five others in combat. Despite Mexican political and U. S. military resistance, the Mexican military succeeded in taking an active role in the fighting. The members of the Squadron became national heroes.

Avila Camacho continued some highly visible social reforms. Despite the demands created by the war effort, he encouraged the continuation of the development program. Most important, the president established the national social security system.[42] Throughout the regime, the dominant theme repeated by the administration was the elimination of extremism. The president set the stage for less strident public posturing. He defused the religious question when he simply announced during his presidential campaign, "I am a believer." Moreover, the president restored the financial ties between the National University (UNAM) and the government, reasserting a significant relationship. The 1944 statute somewhat reduced student and faculty authority and strengthened that of the rector and board of governors. Financial support and administrative dominance stabilized the university for the next twenty-four years.

Wartime brought social changes, perhaps more thoroughgoing than revolution programs. Women, who enlisted in the army or worked in wartime factories, all wore slacks rather than skirts—a fashion change that would become a social issue once peace returned. Strong women appeared in cultural fields who acted as role models and challenged gender stereotypes. Lola Alvarez Bravo, Gloria and Nellie Campobello, Frida Kahlo, Maria Izquierdo and, perhaps above all, Maria Felix became role models for young women. Some women also influenced advertisers, who sought to affect females between the ages of twelve and twenty-five in the areas of fashion, cosmetics, lifestyle, music, and personality.

Besides the new activities of women, the Avila Camacho administration directly influenced mass culture in its efforts to create a populist regime. The government encouraged music, films, records, and radio and subsidized the development of technology useful to these media. This government support inspired what today is recognized as a "golden age" in film, radio, and popular music. The promoters of these forms took the emerging urban culture of Mexico City and popularized it on radio and in films, giving it a uniform shape for the masses in all parts of the nation. The styles, dances, songs, and action films used in the process appealed especially to the young.[43]

Wartime developments enabled the government to consolidate programs launched during the second half of the Cárdenas regime. The revolution, as remade during the period 1937–1938 and carried forward by Avila Camacho, was now an urban, developmental campaign. As a result, the miracle continued through the decade of the 1950s and papered over many of the difficulties of the decade that followed.

NOTES

1. This is the mystical country of ideal happiness, the Promised Land.
2. The revolution as a northern adventure for social justice had its final gasp during the López Mateos administration.
3. One borderland pioneer broadcaster was Harry Mitchell. This Englishman who had immigrated to the United States joined the army, serving at Ft. Bliss, where, after his discharge, he took advantage of the opportunities presented by the border during the American experiment with prohibition. In 1923, he became the managing partner of the Mint Cafe in Ciudad Juárez. His imagination soon made it the top nightspot on the border. Above all, he recognized the value of advertising, and in 1931 he began broadcasting live shows on XEJ from the ballroom of the Mint cabaret. Langston, "Impact of Prohibition," pp. 109, 111.
4. O'Malley, *Myth of the Revolution*, p. 110, reaches this conclusion. See her discussion of the film and its multiple endings (pp. 103–12) and the valuable notes (pp. 171–74).
5. Plenn, *Mexico Marches*, pp. 28, 372.
6. Héctor Aguilar Camín, "The Relevant Tradition: Sonoran Leaders in the Revolution," in D. A. Brading, ed., *Caudillo and Peasant in the Mexican Revolution* (New York: Cambridge University Press, 1980), pp. 120–23; Alicia Hernández, "Militares y negocios en la revolución mexicana," *Historia Mexicana* 34 (1984).
7. Meyer, "Revolution and Reconstruction," p. 172.
8. Suárez attended the National University's law school from 1913 to 1917 and taught there during the periods 1916–1917 and 1919–1932. These two Eduardos, to some extent, were in the tradition of Alberto J. Pani, who held major offices under seven consecutive elected presidents between 1910 and 1933. See a discussion of his career in Allen Haynes, "Orden y Progreso: The Revolutionary Ideology of Alberto J. Pani," paper presented at the Sixth Conference of Mexican and U.S. Historians, Chicago, September 1981.
9. Antonio Carrillo Flores in the introduction to Eduardo Suárez, *Comentarios y recuerdos, 1926–1946* (México: Editorial Porrúa, 1977).
10. Schuler, "Cardenismo Revisited," pp. 28–29, 31–32.
11. Mary Kay Vaughan interviewed Socorro Rivera and published her recollection in "Women School Teachers," pp. 143–68; the quotation is from pp. 159–60.
12. This is an important revision of chronology made by Schuler in "Cardenismo Revisited," pp. 140–49. The usual interpretation declares that Cárdenas and the Mexicans only ended the oil sales to the Axis in the wake of the Pearl Harbor attack. Schuler shows that Cárdenas made it clear to Roosevelt that Mexico would immediately suspend all European sales the moment Mexico regained access to the U.S. market.
13. Camp, *Generals in the Palacio*, pp. 46–48, 176, n. 6, 226, 121–22, 140, 161.
14. Watrous, "Fiscal Policy," pp. 2, 4.
15. This discussion draws on Stephen R. Niblo, "Mexico in the 1940s" (Wilmington, Del.: SR Books, forthcoming); Michael Miller, "Forging the Nation; Avila Camacho and the Emergence of Modern Mexico (Ph.D. diss., Texas A & M University, 1996); and, Yolanda Moreno Rivas, *Historia de la música popular mexicana* (Mexico: Alianza Editorial mexicana, 1979).
16. Alex M. Saragoza, *The Monterrey Elite and the Mexican State, 1880–1940* (Austin: University of Texas Press, 1988), p. 152, 179, 193.

17. Mary Kay Vaughan assesses the success of revolutionary education programs in Puebla in "Women School Teachers," pp. 158–59, and "Rural Women's Literacy," p. 2 and Appendix Table 1, p. 11.
18. Vaughan, "Rural Women's Literacy," pp. 36–37.
19. Shirley Brice Heath, *Telling Tongues: Language Policy in Mexico, Colony to Nation* (New York: Teachers College Press, Columbia University, 1972), pp. 123–29. Eric Vane, "Required Reading," *Inter-American Magazine* 5, 8 (August 20, 1945), p. 12.
20. Mustang generals (one-fourth of the general officers) dominated the armed forces for the three decades after 1960. A version of the program was reinstated in 1955. Camp, *Generals in the Palacio*, pp. 51, 261, 266, 303.
21. Watrous, "Fiscal Policy," pp. 232–33.
22. Blanca Torres Ramírez, *Historia de la Revolución Mexicana: México en la Segunda Guerra Mundial* (México: El Colegio de México, 1979); Stephen R. Niblo, *War, Diplomacy, and Development: The United States and Mexico, 1938–1954* (Wilmington, Del.: SR Books, 1995), pp. 103–04.
23. Victor Alba, *The Mexicans: The Making of a Nation* (New York: Pegasus, 1967; originally published by Praeger), pp. 213–14; Patricia Preciado Martin, *Songs My Mother Sang to Me: An Oral History of Mexican American Women* (Tucson: University of Arizona Press, 1992), p. 70; Niblo, *Setting the Rules*, p. 125.
24. *Excelsior*, January 6, 1945; Howard Cline, *United States and Mexico* (New York: Athenaeum, 1963), p. 29.
25. Niblo, *War, Diplomacy, and Development*, pp. 120–22, 124. See *El nacional*, May 20, 1943. The five young women, whose uniform consisted of battle dress and slacks, were Squadron Chief Enriqueta de Leal (who became the first woman professional parachute jumper in Mexico), Blanca Lastiri, Margarie Galvan, Norah Gonzalez, and Violenta de Torres.
26. W. G. Tudor, "Flight of Eagles: The Mexican Expeditionary Air Force *Escuadrón* 201 in World War II" (Ph.d. diss., Texas Christian University, 1997).
27. The Sleepy Lagoon incident is the subject of two artistic treatments, Luis Valdez's play titled *Zoot Suit*, also made into a movie starring Edward James Olmos, and Thomas Sánchez, *The Zoot-Suit Murders: A Novel* (New York: Dutton, 1978). Mauricio Mazón, *Zoot-Suit Riots: The Psychology of Symbolic Annihilation* (Austin: University of Texas Press, 1984), esp. pp. 1, 4–5, 15, 20, 28, 34, 78. Only in 1945 would interest develop in Mexico proper with the Pachuco style of clothes and language popularized by Germán Valdés, known as Tin Tan, in a series of cabaret-like moves; Niblo, *Setting the Rules*, p. 212.
28. See Manuel García y Griego, "The Importation of Mexican Contract Laborers to the United States, 1942–1964: Antecedents, Operation, and Legacy," in Peter G. Brown and Henry Shue, eds. *The Border That Joins: Mexican Migrants and U.S. Responsibility* (Totowa, N.J.: Rowman and Littlefield, 1983), pp. 49–98; and Richard B. Craig, *The Bracero Program: Interest Groups and Foreign Policy* (Austin: University of Texas Press, 1971), p. 43.
29. Niblo, *War, Diplomacy and Development*, p. 164.
30. Based on William D. Raat, "Gus T. Jones and the FBI in Mexico, 1900–1947," paper presented at the American Historical Association Meeting, San Francisco, December 29, 1989; and Gus T. Jones, "The Nazi Failure in Mexico," Hoover Institution Archives, Stanford University.
31. William Schell Jr., "Integral Outsiders: The Role of Mexico City's American Colony in the Making of Porfirian Mexico," (Ph.D. diss., University of North Carolina Press, 1992), pp. 42–43.

32. Information on the Japanese in Mexico draws on the unpublished research of Daniel Masterson, U.S. Naval Academy, and John Bratzel, Michigan State University, in "Unknown Internees: Hemispheric Security and the Latin American Japanese during the Second World War." Masterson offered some preliminary information for Mexico and Peru at the Conference of the Association of Third World Studies, Temple University, Philadelphia, October 1991.

33. Niblo, *War, Diplomacy and Development*, pp. 88, 111, 143.

34. Seth Fein, "Hollywood and United States–Mexico Relations in the Golden Age of Mexican Cinema" (Ph.D. diss., University of Texas, 1996), chapter 5.

35. Carl Mora, *Mexican Cinema: Reflections of a Society, 1896–1988* (Berkeley: University of California Press, 1988; 2d ed.), p. 20.

36. King, "Confrontation and Accommodation," pp. 47–51; the analysis of the final agreement is based on the evaluation by Suárez's son, Francisco Suárez Dávila; Niblo, pp. 82–83.

37. Anne G. Rubenstein, "Comic Books, Censorship, and the Invention of Cultural Imperialism in Mexico, 1936–1976," (Ph.D. diss., Rutgers University, 1995).

38. Schuler, "Cardenismo Revisited," pp. 2, 8.

39. *The New York Times*, April 11, 12, 13, 18, 1944.

40. *The New York Times*, May 4, 1944; Niblo, Setting the Rules, pp. 113, 205.

41. Niblo, *Setting the Rules*, pp. 185, 189, 190, 196, 202, 211–12.

42. Daniel Levy and Gabriel Székely, *Mexico: Paradoxes of Stability and Change* (Boulder: Westview Press, 1983), p. 35.

43. See Miller, "Forging the Nation

Chapter 11

THE MIRACLE

Its Zenith and Decline, 1946–1972

REDEMPTION OF CENTRAL MEXICO AND CIVILIANS

Miguel Alemán took the oath of office in December 1946 as the first civilian president since Francisco Madero thirty-five years earlier. Although not a revolutionary veteran, he had been reared in a revolutionary family; his father had been a revolutionary general, who chose correctly at every political crossroads until 1929, when he opposed Plutarco Elías Calles—a fatal deviation. The younger Miguel got his chance with the ouster of Calles in 1936. He learned his politics in Veracruz, holding several positions, including governor (1936–1940), and in the official party, as Avila Camacho's campaign director and then as interior minister (1940–1946).

The election of Alemán realized in part the revanchist goal of many one-time partisans of the 1929 Vasconcelos campaign, especially their desire to see Mexico ruled by a civilian. For his part, Alemán redeemed his father's memory and, as the first president to come from the national school of law, he promoted his classmates. The "Alemán generation" shifted the official party's recruitment away from the army and the bureaucracy to an emphasis on the National University (UNAM). Apprentice political camarillas appeared in the National Preparatory School and became more vigorous at the university level, developing into channels to political power. A study of degree holders who obtained high government office from 1935 to 1974 revealed that over 80 percent earned their diplomas from the national university

The Miracle at Its Zenith and Decline, 1946–1972

1946–1952	Presidency of Miguel Alemán
1946	PRM converted into the Party of the Institutionalized Revolution (PRI)
	Ciudad Nezahualcóyotl settled
1948	In *Delgado v. Bastrop Independent School District*, federal court declares segregation of Mexican American students unconstitutional
1952	Bombing of Mexican airliner
1952–1958	Presidency of Adolfo Ruiz Cortines
1954	Women receive the right to vote in national elections
1958–1964	Presidency of Adolfo López Mateos
1959	Railroad workers strike
	National Commission for Free Textbooks created
1962	Rubén Jaramillo and family murdered
1963	Chamizal question resolved
1964–1970	Presidency of Gustavo Díaz Ordaz
1968	Student demonstrations
	Tlatelolco massacre
	Mexico hosts Olympic Games
1969	Carlos A. Madrazo dies in airplane crash
1960s	Chicano civil rights movement
1970–1976	Presidency of Luis Echeverría
1971	Corpus Christi massacre
	Avándaro music festival

and over 60 percent from the national law school. This shared experience was a major step toward overcoming the regional differences in a nation as diverse as Mexico. Of the 107 men who came to office with the new president, 88 of them had college degrees, 45 overlapped in their education with the president, and 13 were in his 1925 law school class. Several government appointees who did not attend UNAM had been classmates of Alemán at the National Preparatory School. They were indeed the Alemán generation.[1] The basis of recruitment for leadership positions shifted from revolutionary veterans to university graduates. This emphasis on the university as the place of initial recruitment remains unchanged today although a foreign graduate degree is becoming a useful step to political power. This recruitment policy included an emphasis on university-trained men from the core of the country.

Through 1970, this region, especially the Federal District and Veracruz, contributed nearly four out of every ten high party and government officials, while the northern states had no high party officers. Once Alemán restructured the party, he gave an institutional basis to regionalism that the center could dominate.[2] His revanchist project not only resulted in a major changeover in administrative and party personnel, but also in national organizations, especially the ruling party.

The new president continued the developmentalist programs initiated during the Cárdenas regime after 1937, by emphasizing industry and large-scale agriculture. Political pundits expected great things from him. He disappointed them because of his penchant for the architecturally grandiose, statistically impressive, and personally profitable. He continued the push toward manufacturing, inviting foreign investors to reestablish themselves in Mexico. Shortly, Mexicans again became familiar with U.S. companies and their products, such as General Motors, Ford, Chrysler, Goodyear, Firestone, Colgate, Palmolive, Sears, Woolworth, and Coca Cola, among others.[3] In agriculture, there was hardly even a cursory tip of the hat to agrarian reform, although the government encouraged large-scale irrigation projects, especially the Papoloapan project in the south modeled on the Tennessee Valley Authority. These programs received support from Nacional Financiera, the government finance corporation.

In the general postwar euphoria, few worried or even noticed that industry became even more capital rather than labor intensive. The identical tendency evident in the pre-revolutionary industrialization process of employing the latest technology seemed quite sensible and desirable. Government policy encouraged capital-intensive development as the best means of reducing the importation of finished products and promoting domestic goods at the best possible price.

The development programs ignored environmental concerns as well. Wartime plans for industrial expansion in the central valley had recognized that locating factories near the railroad yards on the north side of Mexico City would result in "inconvenient gasses and smoke" that would bother and perhaps endanger capital city residents. Nevertheless, the planners decided to go ahead with the development, trusting to future technical innovations to "avoid injuries and annoyances to the inhabitants."[4]

Industrial development marked a switch away from the concerns of labor, at least for the short run. The reduction in the rate of job creation along with the need for technically trained workers, however, began to have a negative impact on the labor force. New workers could not be absorbed quickly enough while the skills of other older workers became only marginally useful. CTM leader Vicente Lombardo Toledano suggested a labor-management agreement of cooperation,

TABLE 11–1   INSTITUTIONAL CAMARILLAS

Fifteen Principles

1. Every major national figure is the *"political* child," grandchild, or great grandchild of an earlier, nationally known figure.
2. The structural basis of the camarilla system is a mentor-disciple relationship that shares many similarities to the patron-client culture throughout Latin America.
3. The camarilla system is extremely fluid, and camarillas are not exclusive but overlapping.
4. All successful politicians are the product of multiple camarillas at different points in their careers, that is, rarely do politicians remain within a single camarilla from the beginning to the end of their career.
5. Mexicans who successfully pursue politics as a profession initiate their camarillas simultaneous to their membership in a mentor's camarilla.
6. The larger the camarilla, the more influential is its leader, and similarly, the more influential are his disciples.
7. Most significant camarillas today can be traced back to two major political figures, Lázaro Cárdenas and Miguel Alemán.
8. Some camarillas are characterized by an ideological flavor, but generally other personal qualities determine disciple ties to a mentor.
9. Disciples often surpass the political careers of their mentors, thus reversing the benefits of the camarilla relationship and the logical order of camarilla influence.
10. Camarillas with institutionalize features, that is, largely formed within an institutional environment, have become increasingly significant as decision making, especially in the economic realm, has become more complex. The single most important public

but Alemán, in the early stages of the Cold War, did not want any ties to Communist leaders in Mexico. With the president's backing, Fidel Velázquez forced Lombardo out of the union. Velázquez and four associates, together called the Five Little Pigs because of their stoutness, split with the Communist-controlled Confederation of Latin American Workers (CTAL) and cooperated with the presidential development program. In turn, Alemán pushed the expansion of the Social Security Institute so workers would not be deprived of all benefits during the intensifying economic growth.[5] The Mexican Export-Import Company (Compañía Exportadora y Importadora Mexicana, S.A.), which later became the CONASUPO program, was established to provide basic goods at low cost to the public, especially workers.

institution representative of this trend, especially relative to its size, is the Bank of Mexico.

11. Kinship and educational companionship are the major sources of camarilla loyalties today, but professional merit, contrary to popular assumptions, has become increasingly important.

12. All politicians automatically carry with them membership in an educational camarilla, represented by their preparatory, professional, and graduate school generation.

13. Politicians with kinship camarillas have advantages over peers without such ties.

14. Politicians who are most adept at building camarillas on the basis of professional merit have the largest and most successful groups over time, but are not necessarily the most likely to achieve the presidency.

15. Because of the overlapping quality of camarillas, some politicians have shared loyalties. Normally, most politicians, at a given time, can be identified with a specific camarilla. It is acceptable to shift your loyalties when the upward ascendancy of your political mentor is *congelado* (frozen).*

---

*A frozen politician will not receive "important tasks, he will not be called to the leader's office, he will not participate in high level consultations; he is 'frozen.' " David Schers, "The Popular Sector of the Mexican PRI," Unpublished Ph.D. dissertation, University of New Mexico, 1972, p. 39; and Martin H. Greenberg, *Bureaucracy and Development: A Mexican Case Study* (Lexington: D.C. Heath, 1970), p. 118.

Adapted from Rodric A. Camp, "Camarillas in Mexican Politics: The Case of the Salinas Cabinet," *Mexican Studies/Estudios Mexicanos* (winter 1992), pp. 85–86, reprinted with permission.

Nevertheless, the development program created a dual economy leading to a dual society, one modern and technological and the other marginal, labor-intensive, and archaic. Reasonable wages characterized modern workers while subsistence levels marked the marginalized workforce. As an inevitable consequence, squatter settlements began to surround virtually every city in the country. Redundant workers sought out employment as domestics, casual laborers, street vendors or entertainers, prostitutes, and in various criminal pursuits—jobs that provided subsistence, but without social or occupational mobility. Ciudad Nezahualcóyotl, adjacent to Mexico City in the eastern part of the state of México, offers the largest and best example of the development of a dual society and economy. Previously a dust bowl created by the draining of Lake Texcoco, it provided a sanctuary for displaced and homeless workers. The area began to attract a permanent population in 1946; a little over ten years later, 10,000 people lived on the lake bed, and today the population is 2 million.[6]

Alemán continued the reduction of the military budget initiated by his predecessors, cutting it to only 7 percent of government expenditures. But diminished financial support does not reveal the complete picture of civil-military relations. As the first civilian president elected since the revolution, Alemán felt a need for reliable security forces. Several factors accounted for this attitude: he may have been particularly conscious of Madero's fate; he certainly remembered his father's death at the hands of the military in 1929; and he had escaped the same end only because a friend of his father's who remained loyal to the government gave him safe conduct. As a result, he created the presidential guards by reorganizing the 28th Infantry Battalion from Puebla and designating it the presidential guard battalion on February 1, 1947. Alemán also adopted an extravagant approach to promotion, politicizing the process, while becoming the only president after 1946 to name more generals than colonels.[7]

His most notable successes came in a dramatic foreign policy that included an active role in the activities of the United Nations. The administration also expanded education and science programs. Good diplomatic relations with the United States grew even better as Alemán became the first Mexican president to visit the United States during his term of office. A border summit meeting between Alemán and Truman coincided with the centennial of the U.S.-Mexican War. Consequently, the two chief executives returned many but not all of the battle flags and trophies taken during the war. A curious exception was the case of Santa Anna's artificial leg, captured by Illinois Volunteers at the Battle of Cerro Gordo. The state governor refused to return the trophy, housed today at the museum in Springfield. Despite these achievements, the administration was deemed morally bankrupt in its last two years and is still regarded as a failure by many analysts.

Corruption, at least allegations of it, damaged the Alemán regime. Construction programs offered ample opportunities for buying up property cheaply before building and road projects were announced, skimming off construction costs, taking kickbacks from builders, and collecting bogus reimbursements for materials and services. These practices did not originate in Mexico or with Alemán. For example, outrage echoed across the Laguna in February 1910, when Coahuila's state government directed Torreón's city council to pay an exaggerated price for the installation of a new water system, and the public learned that the contractors, from Mexico City, included prominent Científicos and Porfirio Díaz Jr.[8] Nevertheless, during the

Alemán years, corruption became more visible, more apparent. Fortunes based on illegal largess appeared and became the subject of
public gossip, engendering both envy and hostility. Allegations about
the source of income of the new rich became the stuff of daily street
corner and coffee shop conversations.

Stories were widely repeated about Jorge Pasquel. Gossip named
Pasquel as the "hit man" of the Alemán regime, who personally had
murdered six recalcitrant members of the government and arranged
the demise of others who refused to provide kickbacks from official
funds. The job paid well, according to allegations, netting him some
800,000,000 pesos, enough that he bought various enterprises, among
them a string of newspapers, including *Excelsior*. Reputed to be the
world's third richest man, he traveled in style; he could fly on his personal DC-6, DC-2, or super Constellation, or drive one of the six Cadil-
lac convertibles that he paid cash for in New York City. Pasquel began
construction in 1956 (just before his death at a weekend getaway in
San Luis Potosí) of a cluster of buildings decorated with 20- to 30-foot
murals, with a master bedroom compared to that of Egypt's King
Farouk. Pasquel achieved notoriety as the promoter of the ill-fated
and scandal-ridden Mexican baseball league that shook major league
baseball in the United States.

Construction projects on the colossal scale popped up across the
country as monuments to the Alemán presidency. The University City
was perhaps the best known, but his associates, who benefited from
inside information and skimming contracts, built their monument to
the president in the new ultraexpensive real estate development, the
Pedregal. The neighborhood became one of the showplaces of the capital city, called "Processed Gardens" by architect Juan O'Gorman because of the sprayed volcanic stones, which he suggested might be
referred to as "French boudoir rocks" and house styles he labeled
"Convent Modern."

One street in Cuernavaca where a number of Alemán's bureaucrats had homes was popularly known as the Avenue of Forty Thieves.
Calle de Las Casas had a number of garden houses remodeled by
the architect Fred Davis during the late 1920s—one for himself, another or U.S. Ambassador Dwight Morrow, and others for the Calles
coterie. This street during those years also had been called the Street
of Forty Thieves.[9]

Ramón Beteta, who served as secretary of the treasury during
the Alemán administration, explained the opportunities for corruption. He stressed that many people think that government officials
simply stuff pesos into their pockets and take them home. Rather, he
described the legal but unethical ways public officials acquire wealth,
usually taking advantage of inside information (such as the future

location of roads or public buildings) or receiving a percentage of profits from a state corporation (such as PEMEX) on whose board the individual sits. Top administrators have had no need to resort to the petty corruption of accepting tips (the *mordida*).

Lower level officials continued the practice without interference during the Alemán years. Government officials took a tip to speed up administrative procedures or to slow them down or to allow illegal activities (such as smuggling).[10] The mordida was rationalized by many as the necessary complement of low wages for government officials.

Corruption, according to some, also contributed to economic expansion during this administration. Victor Alba, for example, argued that "proceeds of corruption were invested in the country, capital was created and Mexican capitalism grew strong enough to offset the damaging effect of the influx of foreign investment." He viewed the Alemán sexenio as Mexico's gilded age, one in which corruption served as an alternative form of capitalization. This works, he claimed, "provided that it does not last and is confined to small segments of society that invest their profits in the country, and provided that it does not lower the standard of living of the weakest economic groups." Alba believed those conditions existed in Alemán's Mexico.[11]

For the people in the street corruption formed the stuff of humor—because they could do little about it, and it pervaded all aspects of their lives. Mexicans told each other,

> The President sends one of his trusted aides to represent Mexico at the World Cup of Corruption. The aide calls him and says, "I have good news Mr. President, we got second place." "That's not good news," responds the President. "Well, we were in first place, but we fixed it so we came in second."[12]

General agreement spread across Mexico that Alemán permitted politicians to become millionaires through public graft and then to ship their money off to foreign banks. This perception of ill-gotten wealth extended to the president himself. Stories reported that he had made his original fortune as governor of Veracruz shaking down refugees from Republican Spain, and it was widely believed he had obtained landholdings that approached half of Baja California. These allegations, years later, still stung Alemán.[13]

To some extent the criticism of corruption was misdirected. While the practice did not begin with the Alemán years, the scale and the different nature of the corruption caught the public's attention. Crime generally appeared to increase during these years, yet it was the nature of the crimes, rather than their frequency, that changed. New heinous felonies, not previously possible, appeared, such as the attempted destruction of a Compañía Mexicana de Aviación passenger

Figure 11.1 Rául Cortez, president of the Spanish language radio station in San Antonio, Texas, interviewing General Matías Ramos Santos during his goodwill tour of U.S. military establishments. *Printed with permission, Russell Lee Photograph Collection, Center for American History, University of Texas at Austin.*

plane in September 1952. Although the effort failed, during the trial that lasted until August 1956, the public reacted to testimony that two criminals, Emilio Arellano Schtelige and Paco Sierra, husband of the well-known opera star Esperanza Iris, had tried to blow up the plane in a scheme to collect the flight insurance policies of seven persons they had recruited for jobs in Oaxaca.[14] As Mexico's first airline crime, with only four previously known cases of airline sabotage throughout the world, the case created a sense of horror. The public reaction intensified in May 1953, when a bomb exploded in the airport of Mazatlán. The investigation revealed that José Alfredo del Valle had planted the bomb in his luggage and had planned to blow up the plane to La Paz, simulating his own death so his wife would collect 850,000 pesos in insurance. The new communications technology and its unsettling impact appeared to threaten values—a perception symbolized by sensational crimes made known to every radio listener in the country. Information ended the blissful ignorance that prevailed before the revolution in communications.

Summing up the Alemán sexenio, one businessman concluded, "We learned quickly that the old-time general, with his pistols, his *tequila* and his whores, was less costly to Mexico than the new 'administrator type' with his flowered shirts, his imported whiskey, and his water skis."[15] Popular reaction to the regime could be found in the mass media. The cinema industry witnessed the rise of a new genre, the cabaret film that charted the tragic fate of a succession of bar girls as a savage indictment of the breakdown of family and social values under the Alemán economic programs. The best of these was *Los Olvidados*, directed by the internationally recognized Luis Buñuel in 1950.

Perhaps the most insidious side to the Alemán era was the switch from real numbers (hectares distributed, miles of road constructed, water pumps delivered to villages) to statistical averages (average income, average caloric intake, average plot size). Statistics too easily hide reality. An anecdote that went around about duck hunters demonstrated that not everyone could be deceived by the fallacy of averages. A hunter, spotting a flight of ducks, fired at one and saw the pellets go behind the target. Adjusting his aim, he fired again and saw the pellets go in front of his prey. Before he could shoot again, the birds had flown to safety. The hunter turned to his friend and said, "A little behind and a little in front; on average, I shot the duck." And, on average, Alemán made great strides for the Mexican people. The Alemán construction campaign resulted in a developmental program for Mexico that nearly every Mexican could see, but only a few got to share.[16]

Alemán's appointments raised some eyebrows as they excluded virtually all northerners. One exception came when the president named Antonio J. Bermúdez as the director of PEMEX in 1946. Bermúdez had built his fortune in the 1920s supplying liquor to the tourists who rushed to Ciudad Juárez and bootlegging it across the border during Prohibition in the United States. He started as a liquor wholesaler, then bought D & E Distillery and an ice plant in the border town. Marrying into an old family, he soon became an influential member of the community, especially the Chamber of Commerce in Juárez. He entered local politics after serving as chamber president in 1926 and eventually served as municipal president from 1942 to 1943. From there, he was selected to head PEMEX from 1946 to 1958.[17]

Alemán left an enduring legacy in national politics. Between 1946 and 1976, his camarilla produced 102 disciples, spread across four political generations. This group had been created through the president's network of primary school friendships (61), associates in state government (13), and the federal bureaucracy (12). His camarilla remained one of the most significant sources for leaders in the 1990s.[18]

Figure 11.2 West side barrio, San Antonio, Texas. Houses built in 1913 had outdoor flush toilets in 1949. *Printed with permission, Russell Lee Photograph Collection, Center for American History, University of Texas at Austin.*

After his departure from the presidency, Alemán eventually devoted his efforts to the promotion of tourism, notably developing Acapulco into a resort destination. The creation of playgrounds for the rich entailed land seizures, construction contracts, and payoffs with directorships. A widely reported example was the 1970 creation of the Tres Vidas en la Playa multi-course golf resort on the Guerrero coast. The ministry of tourism assisted U.S. developer Troy Post in locating an ideal site, and the government sent in troops to drive squatter families off the land. Investors in the development included Post, Alemán, Antonio Patiño, Count Ferdinand von Bismark, Prince Franz Joseph II of Liechtenstein, Prince Rainier of Monaco, and representatives of Sears, the New York Stock Exchange, and National City Bank.[19] For many, these associations clearly indicated the ex-president.

Alemán seemed to live out a Mexican myth. Despite the corruption, this Mexican Midas turned everything he touched to gold. And those who followed, the other political thaumaturgists or miracle workers, the two Adolfos, Díaz Ordaz, and Echeverría, continued the miracle of political stability, industrial growth, and large-scale social programs. Yet the Midas story had its catch, as did Mexico's version. Opposition at first foundered, without leadership or direction, but surfaced sporadically in the next two decades. The prevalence of the muted sentiments expressed in the assassination attempt against Avila Camacho can only be guessed. Then in the late 1950s and early 1960s, waves of strikes occurred that were quickly and harshly put down. Among the first persons to be imprisoned was Demetrio Vallejo Martínez, chief of the railroad workers, and he was soon followed by one of the big three muralists, David Siqueiros. Opposition in the countryside met greater repression. In May 1962, the government carried out a series of assassinations, including that of rural guerrilla Rubén Jaramillo, his wife, and two sons.

Because of the indiscreet corruption of the Alemán administration, the party selected Adolfo Ruiz Cortines to straighten out the accounts and clean up the scandal. The "old man" or "Griz Cortines," as he was called, insisted on inspecting plans and specifications for new construction projects. According to one businessman, the effect was reduced corruption and economic slowdown in the construction industry. Even with that, suspicion marred every project in the capital. When Mayor Ernesto Uruchurto initiated a project to beautify the city by planting beds of gladiolus down the center of major streets such as Insurgentes, his opponents, in cynical suspicious comments, charged that the program was simply a way to have the government finance the search for the graves of his parents.[20] Commentators generally credit Ruiz Cortines with little during his term of office beyond promoting women's suffrage and, above all, reducing the level of corruption remaining from the Alemán era.

THE MEXICAN AMERICAN GENERATION

From the immediate post–World War II era through the decade of the 1950s, new leaders emerged as the voices of Mexican Americans and Mexicans in the United States.[21] Mostly from the Hispanic neighborhoods of borderland cities, these individuals drew on their shared experiences during the Great Depression, World War II, and the Cold War to demand full rights as U.S. citizens. They represented a population, many of whom were children during the great migration of more than a million Mexicans between 1900 and 1930, and many of whom had shifted from agriculture into more urban and service occupations, which combined pride in their U.S. citizenship with respect for their

Mexican heritage. In recent years, these leaders often have been dismissed for accommodating Anglo society, yet a closer look shows that they remained uncompromising in their demands for first-class citizenship.

World War II provided the greatest impetus to the movement, as thousands of Mexican Americans displayed their patriotism in the struggle against the Axis powers. The armed forces brought together Mexicans and Mexican Americans from across the United States and made them conscious of each other and their diversity in language (ability to speak Spanish and use of different slang), experience, origin, and occupation. The result was a greater awareness of the Mexican community in the United States.[22]

The most persistent, broad-based organization for the three decades before 1960 was the League of United Latin American Citizens (LULAC), founded in 1929 in Corpus Christi, Texas. Led by men such as M. C. González, LULAC wanted to create both a "new Mexican" and a "new politics" goals that sprung from the south Texas origins of the organization and aimed to end anti-Mexican discrimination throughout the Southwest in public schools, public facilities (restaurants, movie theaters, swimming pools, and barbershops), "white man's" political primaries, housing, and juries. By eliminating discrimination, LULAC leaders planned to achieve the full rights of U.S. citizens. Consequently, leaders agreed at their founding meeting to limit membership to U.S. citizens and to make English the official language of the group. The LULAC expanded quickly and by the outbreak of World War II had groups in Texas, New Mexico, Arizona, California, and Kansas.

LULAC and other Mexican American organizations rejected Anglo efforts to segregate Mexican Americans as a nonwhite people. They challenged discrimination in theaters (e.g., Upland, California, 1939 and San Angelo, Texas, 1940), in public swimming pools (e.g., San Bernardino, California, 1943), in housing (Chino, California, 1949), in prisons (e.g., Texas State Prison, Huntsville, 1954), and on juries (e.g., The Hernández case in Jackson County, Texas, that resulted in the U.S. Supreme Court decision of May 3, 1954, which stated that the absence of Mexican Americans on the Jackson County jury deprived Hernández of his civil rights under the Fourteenth Amendment). Above all, LULAC, from its inception, focused on discrimination in education, achieving its first major legal victory in 1946 in a Westminister, California, case. An even more significant victory came two years later in Texas in *Delgado v. Bastrop Independent School District*; the federal court went beyond the Westminister decision, declaring it unconstitutional to segregate Mexican American students or to put them in separate classrooms within integrated schools.

Figure 11.3 Restaurant sign in Dimmit, Texas, in 1949. Because this wheat town had no permanent Mexican or Hispanic American residents, migrant workers arrived each year for the harvest. *Printed with permission, Russell Lee Photograph Collection, Center for American History, University of Texas at Austin.*

The struggle for integrated schools took place on a community-by-community basis. An outstanding example of the struggle against school segregation was the campaign led by Eleuterio Escobar and the School Improvement League in San Antonio, Texas, from 1934 to 1956. For New Mexico, George I. Sánchez, in his study of Mexican Americans, titled *Forgotten People* (1940), demanded equal education and criticized de facto school segregation and overreliance on IQ tests given in English to Spanish-speaking children.

Participation in politics resulted in many defeats for Mexican American candidates in the early years, but in time led to success. An early victor was Griff Jones, who in 1932 became the first Mexican American county commissioner of Maverick County in south Texas, but the political benchmark was the election of Raymond L. Telles as mayor of El Paso in 1957. Telles received support from the Mexican side of the border from René Mascarenas, the mayor of Ciudad Juárez and many Juárez merchants, and he used the Juárez radio stations (at reduced cost) to reach Spanish-speaking voters. Telles served four years (wining reelection) and later was named ambassador to Costa Rica by President John F. Kennedy.

Despite successes in fighting segregation and organizing political campaigns, the Mexican population barely recognized its economic power. One instance in which Mexicans did exercise this power came in 1939 when Josefina Fierro de Bright organized the Los Angeles barrio to boycott the Eastside Brewery for refusing to hire Mexican workers even though Mexicans consumed most of its beer. The boycott succeeded, due in part to financial support of Hollywood stars Orson

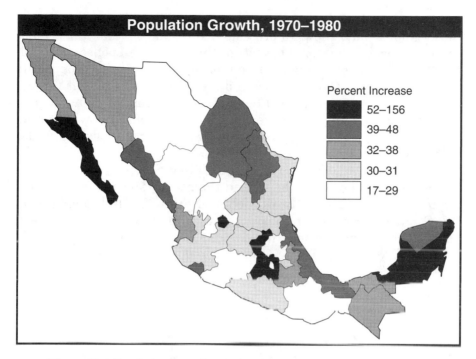

Figure 11.4 Population Growth, 1970–1980.

Welles, Anthony Quinn, and Dolores Del Río. In general, Mexican Americans of that generation did not use economic techniques to achieve their political and social goals.

Only seldom did Mexican workers turn to organized work actions and strikes to demand proper treatment and equal wages. The El Paso local of the International Union of Mine, Mill and Smelter Workers of the CIO, for example, challenged the Guggenheim American Smelting and Refining Company and the Phelps Dodge refinery policy of creating so-called "Mexican" jobs, dead end, low-wage, manual labor positions occupied by Mexicans. The result was a union-led strike. The CTM, across the border in Ciudad Juárez, cooperated, promising not to allow scab workers to cross the border. The strike began in February and continued until May 1946, when the Office of Price Administration intervened, allowed an increase in the price of copper, and participated in the negotiations that resulted in a wage increase of 18.5 cents per hour.

The Asociación Nacional México-Americana (ANMA), organized by radical members of the Mine Mill union in Denver, Colorado, in 1950, focused its struggle in the area of popular culture and attacked the stereotypes of Mexicans projected in the mass media, in particular, the lazy, stupid character named "Pedro" featured on the Judy Canova radio show. To protest, ANMA and several allied labor unions launched a national boycott of the program's sponsor, the Colgate Palmolive Peet Company. Two months later, Colgate dropped its sponsorship of the Canova show and NBC canceled it. Other targets of media stereotyping included Peggy Lee's hit song "Mañana," which imitated the way Anglos believed Latinos spoke, and the widespread use of the image of a Mexican sitting against a cactus asleep under his sombrero.

Ironically, while Mexicans in the United States expressed pride in their cultural heritage, they found themselves in conflict with new Mexican arrivals. The LULAC's policy of extending full membership to U.S. citizens resulted in constant friction between Mexican Americans (citizens) and Mexican immigrants, a group constantly replenished by new arrivals. The relationship remains unresolved.

Figure 11.5 Organization meeting of the Pan-American Progressive Association, San Antonio, Texas. *Printed with permission, Russell Lee Photograph Collection, Center for American History, University of Texas at Austin.*

THE MILITARY DURING THE MIRACLE

The military entered a new period of professionalism during the era of the Mexican miracle. Civil government established the parameters of military activity by controlling the budget and size of the armed forces and maintained good relations by leaving internal questions completely to officers.

Alemán reduced the number of military appointees to political office to fewer than 10 percent, a figure not equaled again until 1964. His antimilitarism and that of his civilian colleagues stemmed from the presidential campaigns of 1927 and 1929. The murder of Alemán's father and the massacre of Serrano's entire campaign party had sent a chilling message to ambitious civilians willing to associate with military political opponents. As a student, Alemán had supported General Gómez. When Alemán and his peers emerged as national leaders from 1946 through 1970, they determined to alter the role of the military in politics.

Alemán, however, made changes that could be viewed as promilitary. He created the post of military liaison between the chief executive and the armed forces. Moreover, the president had the secretary of defense select four or five young officers to organize the Federal Security Department (DFS). General Marcelino Iñurreta, who studied with the United States Federal Bureau of Investigation, became its first director. Until it was disbanded in 1985, an active duty or a retired officer holding the rank of colonel has headed the DFS. Alemán, while reducing the military's overt role in politics, provided the means for ensuring its involvement in national security issues.

The sense of loyalty to the president on the part of the military deepened after Alemán's departure from office. From 1952 to 1968, civil-military relations changed little. The presidents relied on the military to handle conflicts with workers and students. For example, troops were used to occupy the National Polytechnic Institute in 1956 to replace striking telegraph operators in 1958 and to suppress striking railroad workers in 1959. During the military action in the railroad strike, Military Camp No. 1 served as a virtual political prison.[23] These events notwithstanding, civil-military relations remained remarkably stable until 1968.

During these years, the recruitment of officers had a distinctly regional character. Regular officers who reached the rank of general came from three important regions—the Federal District, the North, and the Gulf. The west central region was noticeably underrepresented. The regional character of the officers perhaps reflected the residual bitterness of the Cristero wars. The army continued to encounter general distrust and often hostility in the region through the 1980s. On the other hand, the region has provided a large proportion of Mexico's bishops, who grew up amidst general antimilitary sentiments.[24]

THE MIRACLE AT ITS ZENITH

The economic wizardry that produced the Mexican miracle was contained in the development programs inspired after 1937 by Eduardo Suárez, who served under two presidents, and other officials of the ministry of the treasury. Endorsed by Presidents Cárdenas, Avila Camacho, and Alemán, these programs reached their apogee during the recent years of Adolfo López Mateos (1958–1964). The economic progress began to decline after his term, but Mexicans both publicly and privately ignored the warning signals for nearly a decade. The refusal to recognize the growing danger signs in part resulted from the high international opinion of Mexico. For example, the International Olympic Committee named Mexico the host of the XIX Games, scheduled for 1968. (López Mateos served as head of the organizing committee after his presidency, until poor health caused his resignation.)

During the sexenio of López Mateos, the Suárez program of deficit spending, government promotion of the economy, and bureaucratic involvement in industry reached its highest levels. The new president had served in the ministry of the treasury under Suárez during the Cárdenas years where he came under the influence of the secretary's economic views and the president's belief in using economic programs to promote political causes. Like Cárdenas, López Mateos utilized economic themes to instill national pride. He proposed nationalistic legislation—the 1959 petrochemical law, the 1961 mining law, and the 1962 automotive industry law—to demonstrate that he took seriously the Mexicanization provisions of the constitution that required at least 51 percent native ownership of industry. As a result, he nationalized the telephone system, motion picture distribution to 365 theaters,[25] electric power, mining, petrochemicals, raw materials and basic products, and automotive parts. Despite Mexico's increasing urban and industrial character, land distribution remained the bellwether of revolutionary idealism. Thus, to merit mention in the same breath with Cárdenas, López Mateos distributed some 40,000,000 acres of land to 128,000 families.

These programs all served as rallying cries to reunite Mexicans following the events, early in his administration, that splintered society. Old political bosses, the caciques, still clung to power in a few states. Two days after settling down in the presidential chair, López Mateos faced a strike against corrupt local officials in San Luis Potosí, namely the state cacique, Colonel Gonzálo Natividad Santos. Like his role model Cárdenas, who had moved against political bosses, López Mateos intended to deal with Santos and his nefarious peers— Leobardo Reynosa in Zacatecas, Margarito Ramírez of the federal territory of Quintana Roo, and Fausto M. Ortega, representative of the Avilacamachista crowd in Puebla. For eighteen years, Santos, backed by his gunmen, dominated state and municipal politics in San Luis Potosí. His granite-hard grip on the state for nearly two decades made him a powerful member of the inner circle of the official party. Students, workers, and businessmen went on strike, demanding the removal of the Santos's handpicked governor, Manuel Alvarez. The strike reached such proportions that Alvarez went into hiding in Mexico City and Santos requested and received army assistance in San Luis.

The state capital became a ghost town with businesses, schools, government offices, factories, and even gasoline stations closed. Strik- ers shut down the railroad stop at this critical north–south junction and successfully disrupted a part of the telephone system. The first twenty-three truckloads of soldiers were soon joined by reinforce- ments, and together they battled the strikers, using rifle butts and truncheons. Local police, less prepared for this kind of confrontation or perhaps more committed to Santos, fired into the crowed, killing one person. In addition to suppressing the strike, the president used the opportunity to remove Santos, a regional embarrassment to his party and the most infamous of the state's officials. Governor Alvarez found it expedient to resign and Santos received a minor, but reputation- saving, appointment as federal fisheries supervisor. He remained in this post long enough to salve his blistered ego, then entered private life to enjoy the millions of dollars he had accumulated through graft and corruption. Within months, the other longtime caudillos Reynosa and Ramírez left office as well.[26]

ENDURING CACICAZGOS

Elsewhere, old-style caudillo regimes remained. The Avilacamachista cacicazgo brought authoritarian political stability to Puebla for 35 years, from 1937 to 1972. In contrast to the national pattern, during the 1920s, instability reigned in Puebla. Nineteen governors, almost all imposed and several from outside the state, held the office from 1920 to 1930, and partisans constantly resorted to violence in strug- gles among agrarians who controlled the southern half of the state, labor groups that held sway in many cities and towns, powerful busi- nessmen in the state capital, and the warring clans in the sierra. The presage of change came when Cárdenas, as part of his move to con- solidate power, sent General Maximino Avila Camacho, a native of

Tezuitlán, Puebla, back to his home state to serve as military commander. Two years later (in 1937), the general ran for governor and claimed victory in elections marked by fighting between locals and busloads of pro-Avila Camacho voters from Mexico City. The PNR president Portes Gil dismissed strong protests from Puebla and endorsed Avila Camacho's election. President Cárdenas ignored the 30,000 Pueblans who protested in Mexico City's streets and announced his support for the new governor, the brother of his minister of war, Manuel Avila Camacho.

Once Maximino took office, he appointed friends, relatives, and fellow Teziutecos to important positions in the state and party. To illustrate his firm commitment to establishing his power, he had all state legislators from 1937 to 1940 sign a Pact of Honor—a statement of principles and a set of by-laws for the cacicazgo. The pact called for: (1) recognition of Maximino Avila Camacho as the exclusive leader, (2) coordinated action in social and political affairs, (3) collective action with a willingness to sacrifice, if necessary, the individual, and (4) the exclusion of all non-Pueblans from state politics.

Like earlier camarillas, the cacicazgo relied on the patron-client system of reciprocity, but Maximino added to it the manipulation of popular culture and attitudes through the mass media. He gained control of the leading newspapers in the state, had close connections with Emilio Azcárraga, who added the state's first radio station (1939) to his national network, and managed to influence movie distribution through his working relationship with William O. Jenkins and his Pueblan protégé Gabriel Alarcón Chargaoy. In addition to manipulating the mass media, the cacique dominated Puebla's educational system. The revolutionary educational missions had sent teachers into Puebla, but they received little support before 1937 because of the political disruption. Owing to Maximino Avila Camacho's ties with the Roman Catholic Church, the Cárdenas administration experienced little success in promoting its program of socialist education. The personal ties between the president and the cacique and the economic importance of Puebla's industry prevented Cárdenas from instituting his national program. Although Avila Camacho had little interest in the specifics of the educational program, he recognized the importance of the teachers, thus rapidly dismantled previous, radical teachers' organizations and formed a new state teachers' union under his control. Puebla's state boss also reopened and reorganized the University of Puebla, with the intention of making it another agency of his cacicazgo.

Governor Avila Camacho's cacicazgo achieved dramatic success. So productive was its system of promotion into the official party that two of its stalwarts, Manuel Avila Camacho and Gustavo Díaz Ordaz, became president of the republic. So effective were the linkages welded together that the cacicazgo survived the sudden death of Maximino at a political rally in 1945.

The Avilacamachistas, then, protected by one of their own, Gustavo Díaz Ordaz, minister of the interior under López Mateos, for the moment proved more than the president could handle. López Mateos had other, more pressing difficulties.

A serious labor outbreak occurred when workers in major cities protested skyrocketing prices and low wages. A general strike threatened when Demetrio Vallejo Martínez led his railroad workers' union off the job, calling for increased pay, more democratic union procedures, and worker participation in the management of state enterprises. Living conditions and worker demands soon brought other unions to the picket lines, such as electricians, telegraphers, telephone operators, oil workers, and others. Student groups stoutly supported these strikers and the radical left, especially Marxists. The president overreacted. Deciding in March 1959 that the action threatened national security, he ordered the army to break the strike and apprehend union leaders, notably Vallejo.[27]

Again in 1960 and 1961, demonstrations rocked the cities, becoming pitched battles in the capital. President López Mateos called on Mexico City's riot police to disperse students, workers, and the unemployed who had taken to the streets. He tried to squelch trouble by jailing leaders and spokesmen, a strategy that prompted the arrest of several prominent Communists, including the famous muralist David Alfaro Siqueiros.

The railroad strike and the president's reaction revealed deep social divisions that seemed especially threatening in the context of the Cuban Revolution and the outbreak of national liberation movements. In Mexico, the threat of agrarian rebellion swirled around the peasant leader Rubén Jaramillo, who inspired comparisons with Zapata. The government decapitated the radical movement in the countryside. In May 1962, men purporting to be federal troops took Jaramillo, his wife, and two sons as prisoners. Later the four were found shot to death. Although the agrarians in the south were temporarily repressed, rural troubles persisted as squatter movements broke out in the north. Campesinos occupied land in Sinaloa, Sonora, Chihuahua, Coahuila, and Durango. Federal troops, under presidential orders, evicted some 5,000 squatters in early January 1963. Ghastly murders and ruthless evictions fractured Mexican society even more profoundly.

Confronting this crisis, López Mateos offered to distribute small plots to families, provided they would colonize the sparsely settled south, especially Quintana Roo. But most farmers wanted to remain in their own villages, and if they had to move, they wanted to go to the cities.

Federal troops arrested Communists, disciplined workers, agrarians, and students. The deepening divisions in society spurred López Mateos to find policies that would reunite Mexicans. He resorted to nationalistic programs. Besides those aimed at industry, the president dusted off the agrarian program, distributing more land than any president since Cárdenas, enforced the constitutional provision calling for industrial profit sharing for employees, and dealt as an equal with the United States. Promoting national unity required action— not lip service—in the countryside and among the urban masses. Thus numerous government programs took on a populist character: social security coverage was increased and extended outside of the towns and CEIMSA change its name to CONASUPO, to become a national supplier of heavily subsidized low-cost food and basic necessities to the poor. And Jaime Torres Bodet, an acclaimed poet and former director of UNESCO, became minister of public education and initiated a massive campaign of school construction and literacy training. The National Commission for Free Textbooks was created in February 1959 to provide free, standard texts for all schoolchildren.[28]

Mexican-United States relations reached a new level of mutual understanding. The Cuban and Chamizal questions clearly illustrated the ability of the two administrations to agree to disagree. The Kennedy administration favored hemispheric sanctions against the Castro regime, but the Mexicans refused to condemn the Cuban Revolution. Mexico recognized the new Cuban government and maintained travel and economic relations. López Mateos's tolerance of Castro did not extend to the installation of Russian-supplied offensive missiles. He joined the hemispheric condemnation of Cuba during the 1962 missile crisis. Denunciation of the United States by workers and students did not alter the close relations between the two governments, nor between the two business communities. John F. Kennedy was extremely popular in Mexico, even among those who publicly attacked the Yankees. The Cuban disagreement did not intrude on Kennedy's reception in Mexico City, however, when he took the first steps to settle the Chamizal question.

The Chamizal issue, a century-old border dispute resulting from the shifting waters of the Rio Grande,[29] was resolved on July 18, 1963, when the U.S. government turned over to Mexico 437 acres, formerly a part of El Paso, Texas. In turn, Mexico relinquished title to the United States of about one-third of Cordova Island in the Rio Grande. The López Mateos administration also agreed to pay $4,676,000 as its share of the cost of relocating and reimbursing some 3,500 persons living in El Chamizal.[30]

López Mateos traveled extensively to promote Mexico's international image and to diversify its economic relations, so much in fact that he was soon called López "Paseos," or his "rambles." These trips took him on goodwill visits to the United States, Canada, Europe, India, Japan, Indonesia, the Philippines, and South America. Moreover, he hosted India's Jawaharlal Nehru and Charles de Gaulle of France, along with President John F. Kennedy.

López Mateos was not alone in his efforts to heal the deepening social divisions. Within the PRI, conservative party members, concerned about the upsurge of strikes, land seizures, populist administrative programs, and student activism, organized the Frente Cívico Mexicano de Afirmación Revolucionaria. The members of this self-styled civic front, which included former presidents Miguel Alemán and Abelardo Rodríguez, viewed the challenges to the government and the ongoing social changes as a Communist threat. To combat this peril, the front called for cooperation and financial support from the business community. Rodríguez became especially active in 1961, urging national and regional business organizations to seize the initiative and create propaganda centers throughout the country to counteract the Communist threat. The centers, he said, could be used for recruiting storm troops of young men who had completed their military service to combat acts of vandalism and social subversion.[31] His exhortation offered an eerie premonition of the Corpus Christi massacre.

Outside the party, others opposed the López Mateos programs. Church leaders, aggressively searching for issues around which to develop a political base, seized on the free textbook initiative. They mobilized lay support against the program through the Unión Nacional de Padres de Familia (National Parents Union) and conservative entrepreneurial groups and achieved notable success in Puebla and Monterrey.

LOCAL CHARACTER OF THE MIRACLE

From the second half of the Cárdenas administration through the López Mateos presidency, the Mexican miracle built to a crest. To a great extent, the achievements of the 1940s and 1950s resulted from the articulation of national programs in relation to local circumstances and interaction between local residents and representatives of the national government. Some national programs—socialist education, for example—failed, because the localities rejected them. Others succeeded because the intent of revolutionary rhetoric (expressed in the mass media, civic fiestas, and school curricula), the goals of national programs, and the needs of communities coalesced. Although neither the national government nor the official party delivered participatory democratic politics, together they provided Mexicans with a better life. Improvements benefited everyone in the community: new roads, cheap buses, potable water for residents and deep wells for crops with irrigation canals, mechanical corn grinders, and inoculations against epidemic diseases. The mass media promoted national cohesion, while educational and sport programs encouraged regional and local loyalty. Mexicans lived better, left their villages in fewer numbers, and shared pride in national achievements. These changes had perhaps their greatest impact on women. For example, the mechanical grinding mill gave a woman time to devote to other tasks and the bus gave her mobility, thus she was able to contribute more to satisfying the family's economic needs. Outside of the home and outside of the community, women began tossing aside other traditional restraints in favor of machine-made dresses, greater interaction with men, more conspicuous involvement in public activities, and increased educational attainment.[32]

Few realized the miracle had already been undercut. The inability of the state to devise acceptable means to moderate conflict between those that appeared to be getting richer, workers who struggled with low wages and high prices, and peasants whose expectations went beyond potable water, public health programs, and national pride, became increasingly damaging. Strains apparent during the López Mateos regime verged on shattering society and negating the positive advance of the miracle years. Violence appeared to be the state's only response to social conflict. Reliance on force represented a massive failure of party legitimacy and political imagination.

The policies of the administration of Gustavo Díaz Ordaz (1964–1970) underscored well-established political, economic, and social programs. His blatant disregard of issues of importance to the countryside and his enthusiastic support of business and industry indicated that the government had traveled full circle, back to a Porfirian-like regime. For example, the twenty-two members of his cabinet were called neo-Científicos, referring to the Porfirian ministers. An analysis revealed that in 1964, despite the prevalence of law degrees among the secretaries, their singular characteristic in common was government experience and training that had made them technicians, specialists, or experts in particular aspects of government. The Porfirian goal of better administration through the use of technocrats seemed to be a reality. The people in the street called the president "Porfirio Díaz Ordaz."[33]

Thus early in his administration, Díaz Ordaz used troops against striking doctors and nurses and put students on notice that the government would tolerate little direct confrontation. He also decided that the PRI needed to undergo some cosmetic changes. Early discussions focused on creating a fourth sector in the party to represent business interests, but this notion was abandoned in favor of a plan to bring youth into the party and to increase the party's popularity among the people. Díaz Ordaz named Carlos A. Madrazo to devise a new image. Madrazo promptly advertised several shocking propositions: conduct open party primaries to nominate candidates for local elections; appoint university students to prominent party posts to attract youths to the party; and establish a Commission for Honor and Justice to expel racketeers from the party. Yet even more shocking was the fact that Madrazo acted to carry out his proposals. Rhetoric suddenly gave way to action. At once, he outraged the establishment and embarrassed the president. Forced to resign in 1965, he would not properly retire from politics. Continuing to politic around the country, flattering youth, bewailing economic inequities, fishing in the troubled waters of student rebel politics, Madrazo, until he died in a suspicious plane crash near Monterrey in 1969, remained a trial to the regime. Díaz Ordaz's problems with Madrazo coincided with the student uprisings that began in the summer of 1968.

TLATELOLCO AND ITS AFTERMATH

Student demonstrations had occurred sporadically before the 1910 Revolution and became increasingly common in Mexico City and other cities after World War II. Inspired by the civil rights movement of the 1960s and protests against the Vietnam War in the United States and concurrent demonstrations in Paris, Amsterdam, London, and Tokyo, Mexican students, many of whom came from the lower and middle classes, yearned to take an active part in national political and economic life. In July 1968, an alarmed federal government called out the *granaderos* (riot police) to break up a fight among students representing rival prep schools. Student protests against the police intervention provoked further confrontations with the authorities. Huge demonstrations at the National University and the National Polytechnical Institute (IPN) resulted in the formation of a National Strike Action Committee and the articulation of demands to end the repression of demonstrators. Attempting to gain the support of workers through rallies, street drama, and speeches, the university students discovered that they needed to learn the language of the street. Salvador Martínez de la Roca of the Action Committee recalled, ". . . I soon noticed that when guys from the faculty of political sciences, Paco Taibo for instance, came in contact with working-class people, in the beginning especially, they would talk to them about the class struggle, the means of production in the hands of the bourgeoisie, the class in power, and all that stuff, and nobody understood them."[34]

The students organized a mass movement that attempted to force the government to reform the official party to expand opportunities for political participation. So the students learned to communicate. Military commanders feared the movement might even attract cadets at the military, so they ordered the entire corps of cadets to Chetumal for the summer.[35] Student leaders organized a silent march to express their commitment and discipline, which brought an estimated half million people to the zócalo, Mexico City's central plaza.

President Gustavo Díaz Ordaz would neither negotiate with the students, nor risk disruption of the Olympic Games. His stepped-up repression of the demonstrators climaxed on October 2, 1968. Some 10,000 students met in peaceful protest against police repression, illegal arrests, and violations of human rights at the Plaza of Three Cultures, or Tlatelolco. Suddenly, army and police squads opened fire on the students. The *Manchester Guardian* reported that 325 persons were killed. More than 2,000 reportedly were wounded and at least 2,000 more were jailed, beaten, and tortured. Thousands more spent the night, the next day, and the days after searching for family and friends in the morgues or on lists at hospitals and prisons. Five years later, more then seventy protesters remained in prison. With helicopters and machine guns, the troops defeated the young people and destroyed a generation's youthful idealism.

According to most accounts at the time, the decision to call out the military against the demonstrators was attributed to the president through his Defense Secretary General Marcelino García Barragán or Interior Minister Luis Echeverría. Subsequent interviews with persons involved in the decision produced two different versions. One reported that President Díaz Ordaz went to Michoacán to avoid responsibility for what might happen. General Barragán took command, telling Interior Minister Echeverría to stay out of military affairs. The other account claims the president was indeed present but unable to make a decision, so Barragán issued the order to clear the plaza. Both accounts agree that General Barragán, disgusted with the handling of the episode by the civilian leadership, used force to suppress the students to clean up what he regarded as a political mess.[36]

The 1968 student movement served as a catalyst to changes in the lives of many young women. Males supplied most of the leadership in the central strike committee and generally provided the voice of the movement. Young women joined the movement and many found themselves relegated to traditional female activities, running kitchens and performing secretarial duties. Others jumped out of these roles: Some young women joined guerilla theater troupes and others demanded places in the guards that defended against further violations of school autonomy. In less obvious ways, female protestors ignored previous restrictions on their behavior: they disobeyed their parents and spent the night at campus without chaperons, they joined in heated discussions of political ideas, theories, and strategies, and a few even spoke in public rallies, such as Roberta Avendaño, who addressed thousands in the zócalo. The political opportunities had a counterpart in women's personal lives. The same year as the Tlatelolco massacre, the birth control pill was introduced in Mexico. The ability to make choices about their bodies and sexual relationships encouraged women to consider new roles and activities, ignoring traditional gender and family, economic, and political practices, creating a feminist movement. The Mexican government successfully suppressed the student movement, but it could not destroy the ideals and interests of the time. Mexico 1968 remains an expression of Cuba, Vietnam, Paris, rock'n'roll, youth culture, and the sexual revolution.[37]

Mexicans reflected on what the country had become. For marginal families, urban laborers, rural workers, and university students, the powerless and the marginal, the massacre confirmed that the PRI had discarded the revolution. For businessmen and bureaucrats, the incident demonstrated that the masses needed greater discipline. The incident at Tlatelolco forced Díaz Ordaz and his Minister of the Interior Luis Echeverría to recognize that administration had to be more effective. Meanwhile, intellectuals claimed the massacre indicated a bankrupt revolution.

Intellectuals attacked the PRI. Octavio Paz, essayist, poet, and dean of the intelligentsia, resigned his post as ambassador to India and from self-imposed exile in the United States wrote an indictment of the government titled *The Pyramid*. Others castigated the regime in novels, essays, painting, and poetry.

Faced with a national outcry against the events in Tlatelolco, military leaders determined to avoid the suppression of their countrymen in the future. For the officers, this decision meant an expanded role in developing preventative measures and greater participation in national security. Moreover, the officers extracted a high price from government leaders for the damage done to the military's reputation. The president created a new zone command, three additional battalions, another company in the presidential guards, reequipped the nation's combat troops with modern weapons, and purchased thirty-seven new airplanes for the air force. In addition, the president named forty new generals and thirty-one new colonels, more than doubling the promotions to those ranks of the previous two years.[38]

Ordinary Mexicans, who already sensed that the glamorous statistics disguised morbid reality, were now convinced. Gross national product, price index, production report, and profit margin marked the four corners of statistical Mexico. The Mexican miracle and modernization meant more than increased manufacturing, miles of paved roads, kilowatt hours of hydroelectric power, and acres of land distributed.[39] Mexicans learned it also meant low wages, zooming birth rates, burgeoning slums, increasing food imports, and paralyzing pollution.

TRANSBORDER PARALLELS

The 1960s will forever be known as the decade of popular movements, especially the mobilization of university-age youth. North of the border, persons of Mexican heritage, motivated by the strategies of Vietnam War protestors and African Americans demanding their civil rights, organized to call for their own political, economic, and civil rights. Many, calling themselves Chicanos, undertook political and economic efforts that succeeded to some degree. The established groups, such as LULAC and the G.I. Forum in Texas, remained in existence, but many younger Chicanos agitated for immediate involvement in the political process. As early as the unsuccessful Texas gubernatorial campaign of Henry B. González in 1958, Tejanos began to mobilize and carried the movement into the presidential campaign of John F. Kennedy, forming the Political Association of Spanish-Speaking Organizations (PASO). In 1963, PASO joined forces with the Teamsters Union to gain control of the city council of Crystal City, Texas, electing an all-Chicano board that held power for two years, a hint about future developments in south Texas.

By the mid-1960s, LULAC having adopted a more activist political and economic program, organized a farm workers' strike in the lower Rio Grande Valley in the summer of 1966 and a sixty-five-day, 490-mile march from Starr County to the capitol building in Austin. The march galvanized numerous Mexican American groups into a solid movement with militant objectives that continued into the 1970s. Members of the most militant component, the Raza Unida Party (RUP), won control of the school board in Crystal City in 1970 and implemented a new curriculum and a free lunch program. Similar efforts took place across Texas.[40]

Education concerns resulted in a student strike at seven Los Angeles, California, high schools in March 1968. At issue was the failure of the schools to offer adequate education to Chicanos in Eastside schools. Many Chicanos never bothered to enroll in high school and among those who did, less than 50 percent graduated. Of those who finished high school, few went to college. The University of California, Berkeley, in 1966 enrolled 26,083 students, of whom only 76 were of

Mexican descent. In part inspired by the Black Power movement and the 1965 riots in the Watts section of Los Angeles, Sal Castro, a teacher at Lincoln High School, advised students to demand improvements from the board of education. Instead, students turned to "blowouts," walking out of classes in two high schools in East Los Angeles on March 6, 1968. The next day the strike spread to two more high schools with a majority of Chicano students and to a number of other high schools, including several predominantly black schools. The Los Angeles board of education agreed to grant amnesty to the students and to hold hearings at Lincoln High School in East L.A. The blowouts caused little violence and resulted in only thirteen arrests. There was one conviction, eventually overturned, and all other charges were dropped. The largely peaceful protest could claim few victories, beyond a greater awareness of Hispanic culture and language in the school district.[41]

Militant Chicanos joined the Brown Berets, founded in Los Angeles in late 1967 by David Sánchez, Carlos Móntez, and Ralph Ramírez, which eventually had chapters in twenty-seven other cities, including Denver and San Antonio. The Brown Berets operated the East Los Angeles Free Clinic with a staff of volunteer professionals who offered free medical, social, psychological, and legal assistance. But this community effort was overshadowed by the Brown Beret's alleged involvement in a number of incidents, among them: an arson

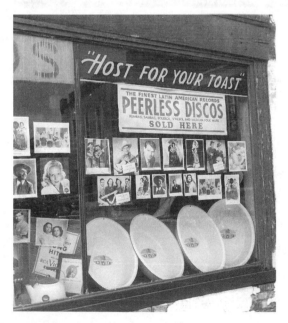

Figure 11.6 Record and housewares store, San Antonio, Texas. *Printed with permission, Russell Lee Photograph Collection, Center for American History, University of Texas at Austin.*

at the Los Angeles Biltmore Hotel (April 24, 1969); a demonstration against the Vietnam War during the Chicano Moratorium at Obregón Park and a confrontation with police (December 20, 1969); a Coachella, California, riot (April 5, 1970); and a Brown Beret demonstration in Pomona, California, in May 1970.[42]

In addition to the efforts of the Brown Berets and Chicano leaders such as José Angel Gutiérrez and the Raza Unida Party in Texas, Reies López Tijerina and the Alianza Federal de los Pueblos Libres in New Mexico, and Rodolfo "Corky" González and his Crusade for Justice in Colorado, the symbol of the Chicano movement became César Chávez, who led the United Farm Workers' movement in California and Arizona. Through a national boycott of California table grapes that began in 1965 in Delano, California, Chávez focused attention on the plight of farm workers and their families (averaging eight persons) who lived in severe poverty, with annual incomes of less than $2,000, with no unemployment or health insurance or social security benefits. The United Farm Workers of California demanded contracts with growers that guaranteed wages and improved working conditions and collective bargaining agreements. Chávez's death in 1993 resulted in widespread tributes and renewed appreciation of his efforts to win recognition of the rights of farm workers.

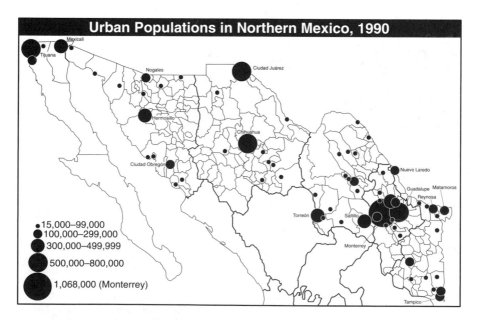

Figure 11.7 Urban Populations in Northern Mexico, 1990.

Figure 11.8 Mexican American shoeshine boy in front of a bilingual movie playbill at a theater in San Antonio, Texas, in 1949. *Printed with permission, Russell Lee Photograph Collection, Center for American History, University of Texas at Austin.*

THE FADED MIRACLE IN THE COUNTRYSIDE

Back in Mexico, even those who praised the government for its handling of the student demonstrations of 1968 were in for a shock. First, the country faced overwhelming population problems—an accelerating birthrate and an even higher rate of urbanization. Second, economic growth had begun to decline. All at once, it seemed, Mexicans above and below the "average" experienced real problems, and the government only tinkered with solutions. The optimism and confidence that had rested since 1937 on prospects for economic development and the promises of revolutionary rhetoric evaporated.

Rural Mexico suffered most. Administrators responsible for implementing development policies of the miracle years had turned their backs on the countryside. At first they appeared to be taking a logical step, but later they seemed to have forgotten that national well being, not be separated from the well being of all of the nation's people. Beginning in the 1930s, technocrats in Mexico and abroad recognized that in modernizing societies an economic gap existed between urban and rural areas, but assumed in a manner not much different from nineteenth-century Liberals that the disparity eventually would narrow through what economists called the equalization theorem. The imbalance would be corrected through the countervailing actions of capital, goods and services, and labor. The prevailing view of rural societies held them to be stagnant, overburdened with surplus workers, and unable to generate savings. Thus, the countryside, populated by lethargic campesinos resigned to marginal life, received little attention.

Economist Manuel Avila claimed, however, that "in the main, these notions are not supported by facts."[43] He examined the conditions in the countryside, roughly from the Cárdenas turnabout in 1937 to 1968 and found the campesino stereotype inaccurate on every count. In fact, when Cárdenas shifted government assistance away from rural Mexico, the same supporters of the revolution who had inspired rural economic growth by seizing on government programs continued to press for government assistance in land reform, road and school construction, and the delivery of potable water; these local stalwarts kept alive the hope of a better life. The popular nature of the revolution inspired the populist reformism that continued into the post–World War II era. The loss of dynamism in village and urban Mexico could be explained in large part by the passing away of the revolutionary generation. The transfer of revolutionary enthusiasm from one generation to the next has yet to be mastered.

Avila found that between approximately 1937 and 1964, Mexico's villages had a relative growth rate higher than cities. Moreover, campesinos possessed a keen interest in markets and prices and accumulated savings. He found no evidence of a labor surplus and concluded that equalization might help close the traditional–modern gap. Transferring rural labor to industry or modern agriculture would not solve the problem. Most crucial, he warned that, "Growth at the national level will be more apparent than real unless it encompasses growth in the traditional sector." From 1919 to 1930, Mexicans planted more land in corn than in all other crops combined, yet productivity ranked thirty-ninth in the world, with yields for each hectare amounting to less than half of those in the United States, Argentina, Spain, and Italy, and less than a third of those in Canada.[44] Woefully low production, compounded by poor transportation and communication networks, resulted from primitive technology. The only contact with the modern world in many communities remained the schoolteacher. Seeming to prove the point, three decades later, the length of the road network had increased thirteen times and the number of irrigated hectares under cultivation had more than doubled, while corn production had tripled. Mitla, Oaxaca, for example, was joined by a four-kilometer paved road to the Pan American Highway in 1951, then received bus and local taxi service to the state capital. Between 1930 and 1964, the number of bicycles increased from 100 to 200, and motor vehicles increased from one truck to thirty-two vehicles. Radios had become commonplace.

Tepoztlán, Morelos, had one road in the 1930s, which served as the community's link to modernization. By the 1960's, a new superhighway linked Tepoztlán to the capital. The first telephone had been installed in 1956 with six subscribers; by 1964, the number had climbed to twenty-three. Radios, from only four in 1943, could be found in all but the poorest homes, while televisions were already being purchased by the more well to do. Tepoztlán's residents built an enviable school system, with a good deal of outside assistance acquired through the hard work and initiative of the townspeople. The town's largest elementary school, built with federal funds, served as a war memorial. When the president called together the nation's World War II veterans, the members of the air squadron who fought in the Philippines, and asked what the government could do for them, an airman from Tepoztlán asked for a school building. Tepoztecos designed educational programs such as free breakfasts for the poorest pupils, high school classes for the highly motivated students, and scholarships for high-achieving graduates. Villagers requested aid from the federal government, approached the nationally known poet Carlos Pellicer, and sought out private sponsors.

The industriousness of the rural population matched their resistance to programs, policies, and reforms that conflicted with their way of life and their visions of the future. Dr. Spencer Hatch, who came to Mexico from India, where he had directed rural reconstruction programs, described the villagers' proactive role in rural programs: "Stubbornness is a virtue with them. They cannot be induced to do something they do not want to do or do not believe in."[45]

An Era Closes

Faced with the need for reforms, Díaz Ordaz extemporized, that is, he fiddled and jawboned. He granted the right to vote to single men and women between the ages of eighteen and twenty-one. Student pacification with empty reforms failed to hide the fact that the government had repressed them, which he called political reform. He borrowed heavily to finance public works, which he called fiscal policy. He encouraged calm in the face of rising prices, which he called inflation control. And he ignored alarming census reports, which he called population planning. Not since 1920 had difficulties seemed so pressing nor hostility so articulate as in 1970. Many saw the presidential elections as a crossroads. The PRI temporized. Announcing a campaign to march onward and upward with this makeshift program, the party chose Luis Echeverría as president and marched in place for two years.

Echeverría tried to continue the politics of revolutionary rhetoric and the economics of deficit spending. Neither worked. Far more successful was his policy of repression directed toward university student groups. Echeverría stepped up surveillance and disruption of student organizations in Mexico City and the provincial universities, tactics that culminated in the Corpus Christi Massacre of June 10, 1971. This violent clash occurred within the context of renewed guerrilla activity. The campaigns of Genaro Vázquez's Asociación Cívica Nacional Revolucionaria and Lucio Cabañas's Partido de los Pobres had flared into violence in rural, western Guerrero, Mexico's poorest state despite the presence of the international resort of Acapulco. Small, short-lived urban terrorist groups, such as the Fuerzas Revolucionarias Armadas del Pueblo and the Movimiento de Acción Revolucionario, created tensions and fears of social upheaval in Mexico City, Guadalajara, and Monterrey.[46] In support of these organizations, students resorted to revolutionary rhetoric to demand social improvements and announced a strike in Monterrey, the capital of Nuevo León.

Mexico City students called for a demonstration in support of the strikers. Responding to the call, some 10,000 students from the Polytechnic University marched on the Monument of the Revolution, expressing support for the students in the north and demanding the release of political prisoners still being held since the 1968 demonstrations. The rally became the focus of several ambitions. Student leaders hoped to reorganize and invigorate their movement, which had remained in disarray since the events of 1968. President Echeverría hoped to improve his reputation and gain respect as a populist by negotiating with the students. Mexico's conservatives in the PRI, in the Mexico City bureaucracy, and in the business circles of Monterrey all wanted to embarrass the president and discipline the students. Echeverría's implacable political rivals, especially the director of the Federal District, Alfonso Martínez Domínguez, saw an opportunity to humiliate the new president.

This stew of ambitions and motives boiled over in violence and brutality, because no prominent leader firmly opposed the paramilitary forces. Ex-president Abelardo Rodríguez had encouraged business groups to finance such troops, thus giving them an aura of official party backing. The Monterrey Group financed one such outfit, the Falcons, and the Department of the Federal District provided training and equipment. Two other squads, the Pancho Villas and the Olympic Battalion, had inglorious reputations among university students because of their participation in the 1968 Tlatelolco massacre.

Uniformed police patrolled the parade route. The student demonstrators marched peacefully until they approached the Monument of the Revolution. Then some 900 special service police sealed off the area and riot patrolmen fired tear gas among the demonstrators. At that point, the Falcons passed through the cordon attacking the students with batons, guns, and cattle prods, following the fleeing demonstrators into stores, movie theaters, churches, and hospitals where the injured had been taken. Witnesses estimated that approximately fifty students were killed in the assault.

The Corpus Christi massacre, so known because it occurred on the feast of Corpus Christi, resulted from the ambitions of several individuals and groups. No one involved escaped without stain. Student leaders failed to recreate their movement, although they again became martyrs. The Monterrey industrialists successfully broke the student strike, but at great cost to their public reputation. Conservatives in the PRI humiliated the president, but coincidentally discredited their own party faction. Echeverría challenged the Avilacamachista cacicazgo in Puebla, which still identified with Gustavo Díaz Ordaz, in order to strengthen his authority, but in the process contributed to social upheaval in the state. The president blamed party conservatives, especially in Monterrey, for trying to sabotage his "democratic opening," and he used the opportunity to move against his rivals. Although Echeverria had not forgiven the military for the violent repression at Tlatelolco, he assembled the senior army commanders to secure their support before he forced the resignations of the head of the federal district,[47] Martínez Domínguez, and the capital's police chief, Rogelio Flores Curiel. Both reappeared in PRI politics a few years later as the governors of Nuevo León and Nayarit, respectively. Despite this action, he could not escape public censure for authorizing the police repression.[48]

The social malaise that accompanied the repression found confirmation after 1968 in economic decline, peso devaluations, and capital flight. What could one make of so-called revolutionary government that no longer supported agriculture, even when it was incapable of feeding its people? After the 1976 and 1982 peso devaluations, Mexicans sent their savings north to be invested in secure properties. Monterrey families flooded into South Padre Island, Texas, to buy condominium and resort properties modeled on those of Miami Beach.[49] The most glaring contradiction appeared in the visible dual economy and society.

What ideological vitality remained in the political party of the revolution dissipated. Paco Taibo, the political science student who learned to converse with the general population in the student movement, turned to writing fiction about Mexico's future because, after several years of trying, he could imagine no real remedy for the nation's hopeless state. The ordinary Mexican could effect no change in national life, so Taibo imagined a solution based on the magical realism of contemporary Hispanic American literature in his fictional memoirs, titled *Calling All Heroes*. In this story, the protagonist, help-less in a hospital bed, in the early 1970s called the world's great mass cultural heroes to the old Aztec capital to save the Mexican people: Sherlock Holmes with the pup from The Hound of Baskervilles (En-gland); Doc Holliday, Wyatt Earp, and several other frontier gunmen (United States); the Light Brigade (Great Britain); the Three Muske-teers (France); Yáñez de Gómara; Sandokan, the Prince of Borneo and his Tigers of Malaysia (Malaysia); the Mau-Mau (Kenya); Dick Turpin (English highwayman); and Norman Bethune, doctor for Mao's troops (China). They all arrive to destroy President Gustavo Díaz Ordaz's government and save the country. No doubt many Mexicans addicted to radio, TV, and comics agreed that the national malaise clearly had reached the point where the revolution's ideals and idealism could only be resurrected in fantasy.

While Mexico's productivity gap with the United States had closed slightly, the social gap widened. The quality of life deteriorated in the 1960s and worsened in the next decade. The miracle had de-ceived many, but in real terms there were more impoverished Mexi-cans in 1970 than there had been in 1937. Income distribution had become so skewed that the lowest tenth of the people were getting poorer, while the upper tenth got richer. Meanwhile, middle-class Mex-ican youth turned from politics to rock and roll. Demonstrating their membership in the counterculture, 250,000 gathered at Avándaro, State of Mexico, in September 1971 for a Mexican Woodstock.[50]

But above all, the spirit was gone; it died at Tlatelolco. One mother spoke for many Mexicans when she said, "Not since the mili-tary uprising against Madero led by Victoriano Huerta in 1913 had there been anything that had damaged our image so much as Tlatelolco . . . that had filled our mouths with the taste of blood, the blood of our dead."[51] Government troops vanquished the soul of the revolution at Tlatelolco and battered even its memory on Corpus Christi. Politicians, technocrats, and bureaucrats scattered the tat-tered shreds of the revolution on the winds of self-interest and per-sonal profit. The miracle ended in the nadir of despair. La Jauja became La jaula de melancolía,[52] as political and economic visions of Shangri-la became the cage of melancholy. Of course, most of the com-mon people continued on as they had before, doing the best they could to survive and getting as much out of life as they could.

NOTES

1. Roderic A. Camp, "Education and Political Recruitment in Mexico: The Alemán Generation," *Journal of Interamerican Studies and World Affairs* 18: 3 (August 1976), pp. 295–321. In comparison, Cádenas, in his administration, relied on revolutionary experience as the most important requirement (34 percent) and Alemán, who had no revolutionary veterans, looked to the university (85 percent) for recruits. See Camp, *Mexico's Leaders, Their Education and Recruitment* (Tucson: University of Arizona Press, 1980), p. 22.

2. Paul W. Drake, "Mexican Regionalism Reconsidered," *Journal of Inter-American Studies and World Affairs* 12: 3 (July 1970), pp. 401–15, esp, pp. 401, 405.

3. Patrick Oster, *The Mexicans* (New York: William Morrow, 1989), p. 124.

4. Niblo, *Setting the Rules*, p. 236.

5. Alba, *The Mexicans*, pp. 217–18.

6. Carlos G. Vélez-Ibañez, *Rituals of Marginality: Politics, Process, and Culture in Central Urban Mexico, 1969–1974* (Berkeley: University of California Press, 1983), pp. 17–32.

7. Camp, *Generals in the Palacio*, pp. 82, 423, 457–58.

8. Meyers, *Interest Group Conflict*, p. 338.

9. Selden Rodman, *Mexican Journal: The Conquerors Conquered* (Carbondale and Edwardsville: Southern Illinois University Press, 1965), pp. 4–6, 84, 176.

10. Beteta interview with James and Edna Wilkie, December 17, 1964, quoted in James W. Wilkie, *The Mexican Revolution: Federal Expenditure and Social Change Since 1910* (Berkeley: University of California Press, 1967), pp. 8–9.

11. Alba, *The Mexicans*, p. 218.

12. Schmidt, "Humor and Politics," p. 69.

13. Dale Story, *The Mexican Ruling Party: Stability and Authority* (New York: Praeger, 1986), p. 29. Schmidt, "Humor and Politics," p. 134, n. 10, describes Aleman's concern about these allegations in 1982.

14. Margaret Larken and her daughter were passengers on the ill-fated flight. She devoted herself to following the investigation and trial. See Larkin, *Seven Shares in a Gold Mine* (New York: Simon and Schuster, 1959).

15. Robert Lasalle, a Mexican businessman, to Rodman, *Mexican Journal*, pp. 141–42.

16. This conclusion paraphrases Levy and Székely, *Paradoxes of Stability*, p. 4.

17. Bermúdez married the daughter of Manuel Mascareñas Jr., Chief Collector of Customs in Ciudad Juárez, in 1927. The marriage provided social connections to powerful groups in both the state and national capitals. During the 1930s, he led the Juárez Chamber of Commerce in policing the alcoholic beverage industry in the city to prevent sales of poison whiskey and to stop children from purchasing drinks. Despite his efforts to regulate the industry, the conjecture remains that the shadow of liquor smuggling, border town racketeering, and Prohibition gangsterism fell across Bermúdez and prevented him from receiving the presidential nomination in 1952. See Langston, "Impact of Prohibition," pp. 233–38 and n. 41; Wasserman, *Persistent Oligarchs*, pp. 116, 132.

18. Roderic A. Camp, "Camarillas in Mexican Politics: The Case of the Salinas Cabinet," *Mexican Studies/Estudios Mexicanos* 6: 1 (winter 1990), pp. 96–97.

19. Edwin R. Shrake, "Rich Way to Make a Getaway," *Sports Illustrated*, August 31, 1970, pp. 29–30. In response to the outrageous actions that led to the resort's construction, campesinos grazed cattle on the fairways and washed laundry in

the water hazards. When security forces failed to prevent these activities, membership (costing in the thousands of dollars) began declining, and in 1975, Post closed the $10,000,000 resort. Squatters quickly returned. See Ronald E. Whitten, "Mexican Golf: Turf on the Rocks," *Golf Course Management* (July 1983), pp. 28–32; "Paradise Lost," Time (November 10, 1975), pp. 88–89.

20. Rodman, *Mexican Journal*, pp. 56, 85, 142.
21. This section draws on Mario T. García, *Mexican Americans: Leadership, Ideology, and Identity, 1930–1960* (New Haven: Yale University Press, 1989).
22. Raúl Morín, *Among the Valiant: Mexican-Americans in WW II and Korea* (Los Angeles: Borden Publishing Company, 1966), pp. 29–30.
23. Roderic Camp reports that the Federal Security Directorate was in league with the drug cartels. It was disbanded in an effort to root out corruption and repair Mexico's intelligence image. See William Brannigan, "With Friends Like These, Who Needs Enemies," *Washington Post, National Weekly Edition*, July 23–29, 1990, p. 31.
24. Camp, *Generals in the Palacio*, pp. 57–58, 254, 278, 281–82.
25. This involved buying out the Puebla-based United States millionaire William O. Jenkins. See Time (December 26, 1960), pp. 25–26.
26. Paul P. Kennedy, *The Middle Beat: A Correspondent's View of Mexico, Guatemala, and El Salvador*, edited by Stanley R. Ross (New York: Teachers College Press, Columbia University, 1971), pp. 53–55.
27. Wil Pansters, *Politics and Power in Puebla: The Political History of a Mexican State, 1937–1987* (Amsterdam: Center for Latin American Research and Documentation, 1990), pp. 49–52, 63, 65, 74, 102.
28. Enrique C. Ochoa, "Feeding Mexico: The State, The Marketplace, and Social Policy Since 1934" (Ph.D. diss., UCLA, 1995).
29. Story, *Mexican Ruling Party*, p. 32.
30. Daniel Cosío Villegas, *American Extremes (Extremos de América)*, translated by Américo Paredes (Austin: University of Texas Press, 1964), note pp. 28–29. Also see Sheldon Liss, *A Century of Disagreement: The Chamizal Conflict, 1864–1964* (Washington, D.C.: University Press of Washington, D.C., 1965).
31. Pansters, *Politics and Power*, pp. 105–06; this is a paraphrase of Panster's translation of Rodríguez's letter. See *Declaración, discursos y cartas del Sr. General de División don Abelardo L. Rodríguez* (Mexico 1961), p. 13.
32. See Mary Kay Vaughan, "The Construction of Patriotic Festivals in Tecamachalco, Puebla, 1900–1946," in Beezley, Martin, and French, eds., *Rituals of Rule*, 1994.
33. James D. Cochrane, "Mexico's 'New Cientificos': The Díaz Ordaz Cabinet," *Inter-American Economic Affairs* 21: 1 (summer 1967), pp. 58, 62, 65; Samuel Schmidt, "Humor and Politics," p. 166.
34. Elena Poniatowska, *Massacre in Mexico* (New York: Viking Penguin, 1975) quoted in Raat and Beezley, eds. *Twentieth-Century Mexico*, p. 258.
35. Camp, *Generals in the Palacio*, p. 62.
36. Camp, *Generals in the Palacio*, pp. 57–61, draws on Michael J. Dziedzic, "The Essence of Decision in a Hegemonic Regime: The Case of Mexico's Acquisition of a Supersonic Fighter" (Ph.D. diss., University of Texas, 1986), p. 113, and "Mexico's Challenges: Problems, Prospects, and Implications," unpublished paper, United States Air Force Academy, April 21, 1989, p. 9.
37. Elaine K. Carey, "Women and Men on the Threshold of Modernity: A Cultural History of 1968: (Ph.D. diss., University of New Mexico, forthcoming 1998).
38. Camp, *Generals in the Palacio*, pp. 62–64, 421, 439.

39. Niblo, *War, Diploma and Development*, pp. 38–52, examines various statistical indicators.

40. Robert A. Calvert and Arnoldo De León, *The History of Texas* (Arlington Heights, Ill.: Harlan Davidson, 1990), pp. 390–93.

41. Kaye Briegel, "Chicano Student Militancy: The Los Angeles High School Strike of 1968," in Manuel P. Servín, ed., *An Awakened Minority: The Mexican Americans*, 2d ed. (Beverly Hills: Glencoe Press, 1974), pp. 215–26.

42. Christine Marín, "Go Home, Chicanos: A Study of the Brown Berets in California and Arizona," in Servín, ed., *An Awakened Minority*, pp. 226–46.

43. Manuel Avila, *Tradition and Growth: A Study of Four Mexican Villages* (Chicago: The University of Chicago Press, 1969), pp. 9–15.

44. Avila, *Tradition and Growth*, pp. 18–19, 23, and n. 11.

45. Avila, *Tradition and Growth*, pp. 71, 73–74, 78–79, 86, 88, n. 33.

46. Pansters *Politics and Power*, p. 194, n. 46; also see Jaime López, *10 años de guerrilla en México, 1967–1974* (México: Editorial Posada, 1974).

47. Camp, *Generals in the Palacio*, p. 66.

48. Judith Adler Hellman, *Mexico in Crisis* (New York: Holmes & Meier, 1978), pp. 161, 206, n. 28, 208, n. 30 and 31; Alan Riding, *Distant Neighbors: A Portrait of the Mexicans* (New York: Vintage Books, 1986), pp. 88, 112.

49. Alan Weisman, *La Frontera: The United States Border with Mexico* (New York: Harcourt Brace Jovanovich, 1986), p. 6.

50. Paco Ignacio Taibo II, *Calling All Heroes: A Manual for Taking Power*, translated by John Mitchell and Ruth Mitchell de Aguilar (Kaneohe, Hawaii: Plover Press, 1990); José Augustín, *Tragicomedía Mexicana 2: La vida en México de 1970–1988* (México: Editorial Planeta Mexicana, 1992), pp. 21–28; Eric Zolov, "Containing the Rock Gesture: Mass Culture and Hegemony in Mexico, 1955–1977," unpublished Ph.D. diss., University of Chicago, 1997.

51. Poniatowska, *Massacre in Mexico*, p. 266.

52. This is the title of Roger Bartra's evaluation of Mexican national character. See Bartra, *The Cage of Melancholy: Identity and Metamorphosis in the Mexican Culture* (New Brunswick: Rutgers University Press, 1992); also see David E. Lorey, *The Rise of the Professions in Twentieth-Century Mexico: University Graduates and Occupational Change Since 1929* (Los Angeles: UCLA Latin American Center, 1992) and his *University and Economic Development in Mexico Since 1929* (Stanford University Press, 1993).

Chapter 12

AFTER THE MIRACLE
"A Day without the Revolution, 1972–1996"

Economists turned magicians called the period from 1937 to 1972 a miracle. The government-inspired economy grew by over 6 percent each year, while the same government held the inflation rate to under 5 percent nearly every year. The national oil corporation became a major exporter of oil and hydrocarbons, while industry expanded to the point that the World Bank proclaimed Mexico, along with Taiwan, Hong Kong, Singapore, and South Korea, one of the new industrialized countries. Despite their well-known tunnel vision, economists could not continue chanting about a miracle after 1982—a year when the inflation rate reached 100 percent. The persistence of economic speculation and growth based on new oil discoveries during the decade after 1972 only intensified the despair of those who knew the miracle had ended as Mexico became notorious for its inequitable income distribution.[1]

The Cárdenas-Suárez programs after 1937 stimulated industrialization that flourished during World War II, free from outside competition, and even began to export such goods as textiles. The project's success by the 1940s began to attract foreign investors, who brought venture capital (hailed as one aspect of the miracle), but it also encouraged the purchase of foreign technology and took profits out of Mexico (a fact ignored, for the most part, until after 1972). A comparison of direct foreign investment with capital taken out of the country by multinational corporations from 1940 to 1970 reveals that in only seven of these thirty-one years did Mexico receive more money than it sent to foreigners.[2]

After the Miracle: "A Day without the Revolution"

1963	Kalimán first appears on radio and two years later in print
1965	Maquiladoras establish operations
1970–1976	Presidency of Luis Echeverría
1973	Minimum voting age changed to eighteen
1976	Peso devaluation
1976–1982	Presidency of José López Portillo
1977	Congressional election reforms
1979	Pope John Paul II visits Mexico
1980s	Economic "Lost Decade"
	International drug trade expanded
1982	Nationalization of the banks
	Peso devaluation
1982–1984	Combined Mexican–U.S. drug enforcement campaign
1982–1988	Presidency of Miguel de la Madrid
1985	Mexico City earthquake
1986	Mexico joins General Agreement on Tariffs and Trade (GATT)
	Electoral law reforms
1987	Super Barrio appears
1988	Presidential candidate Cuauhtémoc Cárdenas challenges the PRI
	Cananea Copper Company privatized
1988–1994	Presidency of Carlos Salinas de Gortari
1989	National Action Party (PAN) victory in Baja California del Norte
1992	PAN victory in Chihuahua
	Mexico City imposes one day per week without a car program
1994	North American Free Trade Agreement (NAFTA) goes into effect
	EZLA revolts
	Presidential candidate assassinated

Thus behind the glitz a great many Mexicans had been battered by declining purchasing power during the waning years of the miracle, while the highest income groups continued to increase their share of the national income. Commentators referred to the 1980s as the "Lost Decade" because of the severe economic crisis that followed

1982. The abysmal distribution of wealth (as real wages plummeted and the real numbers of those living in poverty skyrocketed) required social repression, resulting in serious human rights abuse of those who challenged the economic and social hierarchy.[3]

The Mexican political regime was mired in structural stagnation. The revolutionary framers, especially Obregón, Calles, Cárdenas, and Alemán, created a political party and an administrative bureaucracy that incorporated workers, agrarians, and public employees. Initially hailed as providing populist groups with political access, while denying a direct political voice to the representatives of business and industry, this structure had also co-opted such groups, making them dependent on the official party. Meanwhile, business and industry leaders had developed unofficial channels to government and, the threat of nationalization notwithstanding, remained the most autonomous group in Mexican society. The exclusion of the chambers of commerce and industry from the party from 1929 to 1946 benefited workers, but as the developmentalist programs initiated in 1937 accelerated and succeeded, the party and the administration lost control but would not bring these groups into the formal structure for fear of abandoning a tenet of the revolution. Ideological inflexibility proved costly, but was repeated time and again, demonstrating the dangers of freezing a revolution in place.

Beginning in the 1970s, the government sought to regulate the economy but found that the businessmen it had failed to incorporate were independent and difficult to control. Nor could the government demand their loyalty and assistance. Tensions increased between government and business, especially as the Echeverría administration began buying privately operated enterprises. Growing discomfort culminated in outright hostility in 1982, when then-president José López Portillo announced the nationalization of the privately owned banks—an action that had little to do with nationalism and much to do with the failure of the government's efforts to resolve economic matters. Later, President Miguel de la Madrid would undertake a major effort to repair government-business relations, but reversing the effects of mismanagement proved difficult.[4]

Some PRI leaders tried to strengthen the regime's image by breathing life into electoral politics through grudging recognition of traditional opposition parties and midwifing the existence of others. They hoped the latter would identify new initiatives attractive to popular groups that later could be co-opted by an official party that seemed incapable of generating its own ideas. These PRI reformers wanted to provide incentives and political rewards to opponents of the regime willing to campaign, but they did not want to offer the possibility of actually winning significant elections. As these mild reforms moved forward, as though by sleight of hand, they inevitably resulted in demands for genuine electoral change that would eventually lead to victory by opposition parties.

The miracle's children and orphans inherited a capital-weak economy, bankrupt revolutionary rhetoric, and a top-heavy regime manipulated by bureaucrats and managed by technocrats. Their birthright was to shoulder a huge foreign debt, to mouth the praises of the revolution while abiding its promises turned to dust,[5] and to endure a *licenciadocracia*, or government by degree holders (perhaps one might say, college boys). Many Mexicans, no doubt, characterized their government as administration by *licenciadillos*. The presidents from 1937 to 1970 all had experience as elected governors or congressmen. The new breed of president, beginning with Echeverría, had never run for an elected office before the presidential campaign. López Portillo, De la Madrid, and Salinas rose to positions of influence through the bureaucracy rather than through the party.[6]

SEARCHING FOR THE CÁRDENAS MANTLE

In this era of technocrats, decisive bold actions occurred only when the president had reached a point where he had no other options and little

Figure 12.1 Manufacturing Labor Force, 1990.

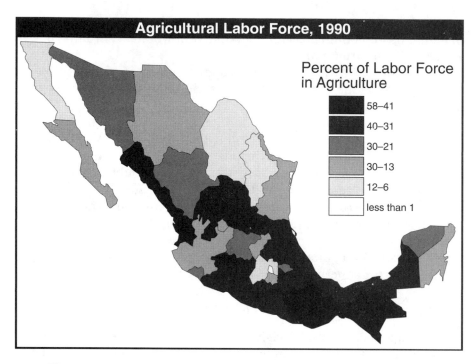

Figure 12.2 Agricultural Labor Force, 1990.

time for extemporizing. The presidents since 1972 have been the most revolutionary during their last year in office, when the next chief executive has been identified but has not yet taken office. This lame duck era from the July presidential election until the December inauguration is sardonically called *el año de Hidalgo*. Miguel Hidalgo's portrait appears on large currency bills, and in the final year of the presidency, it is widely asserted in jokes and street corner conversations that officials uncertain of their future enrich themselves.[7] For the president, this period also is the last chance to gild his reputation. Thus in his last months, Echeverría set a torrid pace for land redistribution to create the self-image he had announced at the beginning of his term. His successor, José López Portillo, his lame duck period, nationalized the banking system, his boldest and most irresponsible presidential stroke. The administrations of the last few presidents lurched from crisis to crisis and ended in a frantic series of actions during the closing months of the term.

Luis Echeverría aspired to be the new Cárdenas, a populist president who would reinvigorate the revolutionary tradition and enjoy public esteem. Of course, he meant the Cárdenas of 1934 to 1937. He made constant references throughout his term of Cárdenas, in the hope he would become a populist by association.[8] But, by the end of his sexenio, Echeverría had driven Mexico into political and fiscal crisis. While he could not be held solely responsible because international circumstances also had an impact on the situation, nevertheless the president's policies contributed to "bankrupt steel works, increased unemployment, a balance-of-trade deficit, and a decline in the output of basic foodstuffs." By 1976, the inflation rate was more than 30 percent and the public debt had reached $20 million. Echeverría, grasping at straws as he left office, devalued the peso by 60 percent, altering the exchange from 12.5 to 22 pesos to the dollar. Moreover, he had abandoned the official party's usual methods of governing by turning his back on several sectors of society. Most clearly, he moved away from organized labor. The president tolerated the activities of independent labor organizations to promote his image as a populist leader and undermine the efforts of Fidel Velázquez of the CTM. This policy had its greatest success among the automotive workers of Ford (Mexico City), Nissan (Cuernavaca), and Volkswagen (Puebla).[9] However much the president's reputation improved, the people benefited little from his populist approach.

After the miracle turned to mud, northerners seized the opportunity to reassert their regional political character. This northern displeasure with the politics of Chilangos, the disparaging nickname for Mexico City residents, and the PRI in general, resulted most often in support of the opposition Partido de Acción Nacional (PAN) and reverberated dramatically in the 1989 gubernatorial victory of Ernesto Ruffo in Baja California del Norte and of Francisco Barrio Terrazas in Chihuahua in 1992.[10] For the first time since Cárdenas recaptured the party and the government for the central states, the northerners in the 1980s reasserted borderlands regionalism in politics.

These events set the stage for the emergence of Carlos Salinas de Gortari. His new administration at first inspired great hope, but its waning years and afterward caused despair then disgust with his governmental and family corruption.

URBANIZATION: CERRADA DEL CÓNDOR AND CIUDAD NEZAHUALCÓYOTL

Echeverría and the PRI found Mexico's population growth to be their greatest challenge (3.4 percent a year in 1970), even though the president had told the press during his first year in office that Mexico had no population problem. The urban crush had actually begun well before the end of the Mexican miracle, but only became apparent around 1970. Population movement into the cities reached major proportions after World War II. After 1950, Mexico City's population began to lap over the boundaries of the Federal District into the surrounding State of Mexico. Between 1940 and 1970, some four and a half million Mexicans moved to cities. Of its residents during these years, 43 percent were first-generation migrants. By 1975, some 2,600 persons arrived in Mexico City each day, looking for a home and a job. Once there, for many, dreams of employment faded and hopes for a home ended in cardboard boxes and tin cans. In 1974, 5.7 percent of the capital's population was unemployed and 35.3 percent was underemployed. Studies revealed that most unskilled workers in the capital regularly earned less than the monthly equivalent of the minimum wage because of job instability. Nevertheless, opportunities seemed greater in the city and living conditions better than in the countryside.[11]

According to experts, Mexico has the potential, using current technology, to feed a population of perhaps 200 million. But in 1970 the nation did not take advantage of this capability and could not adequately feed its fifty million people. The Echeverría government had to import basic foodstuffs, including corn and beans. Even with imported food, fifteen million Mexicans had never tasted milk. Nutrition experts reported that over half of the population should be classified as undernourished.

The increasing population first strained, then simply overwhelmed, the supply of available housing. Owners of old downtown residences seized the opportunity to create slums as they subdivided the buildings into one-room units (called *vecindades*). Despite the overcrowding, the new occupants had access to such services as water, sewerage, public transportation, electric power, garbage collection, schools, and sometimes rent control. The government also provided low-cost housing, for example, the apartments that border Tlatelolco Plaza, but generally these were only available to industrial workers and government clerks.

With the slums congested and public dwellings occupied, new arrivals had to search for housing elsewhere. The mushrooming towns that surrounded the capital offered some attraction. Ciudad Nezahualcóyotl, for example, first settled in 1946 by persons displaced from the capital city, by 1971 was the fourth largest city in the Mexican republic (today it covers sixty-four square kilometers). The State of Mexico made and continues to make attempts to introduce and extend water and sewage lines, but such efforts are immediately overwhelmed by population growth. In 1959, the State of Mexico Development Law established basic conditions for land development, such as the provision of sewerage, water, and electricity. Land developers, assisted by the authorities to obtain legal titles, became responsible for orderly development. Would-be squatters could no longer select a vacant lot and proceed to build a hut, but rather had to purchase tracts from developers. This development system floundered on a number of realities. In alliance with politicians, developers seldom bothered to introduce any of the required improvements and simply charged for lots that previously cost nothing. Moreover, legal title rested with a developer who promised to make the necessary improvements and without them the title remained invalid. In effect, the marginalized population had to fight off developers who functioned merely to extort money from them. Ciudad Nezahualcóyotl became integrated into the political system when it was recognized as a municipality in 1963 and acquired all of the necessary officials and a federal deputy. The state did not appear to become any more socially useful, however. Police and other officials responded to developers while requiring many of the locals to pay protection money and bribes. In fact, the city continued to function in many cases in spite of the state.

The pattern of survival for newcomers, in squatter settlements, slightly over 50 percent of who came from the federal district, changed little since 1946. A new arrival would identify a lot and erect a hut on the rear of the parcel. Building materials for the hut included everything from cardboard to tin cans hammered flat, or whatever could be found. As money became available, the squatter poured a permanent foundation and slowly a cement block structure would take shape. The original *jacal* (or hut) remained as an auxiliary building, perhaps to sleep relatives or serve as the kitchen. During the rainy season from June to October, life became especially difficult. Mud made most of the streets into treacherous bogs. Going to work outside of the city meant walking long distances to a paved road where buses could still run. Raw sewage and garbage floated through the flooded streets and into the houses and huts, bringing disease and pestilence. During the dry season, life improved, although the wind swept up dust from the lake bed mixed with dried fecal matter that entered every crevice, irritated noses and throats, stung the eyes, and contaminated food and water. In spite of sick, dying children, chronic illness, and substandard diets, the inhabitants struggled to make life tolerable. Low wages and continuous economic insecurity remained major obstacles. Nevertheless, over time, these early mushroom cities around the capital city became settled neighborhoods. Catholic and Protestant churches were the site for weddings, burials, and some social life. Movies became a welcome diversion, especially adventure love stories and those with "underdog makes good" plotlines. Wrestling matches provided relief from daily routine and a source of heroes for young and old. While residents had virtually no respect for state officials and the police, they generated a broader sense of self-worth from nationalism. This folk nationalism evoked the names of Emiliano Zapata and Ricardo Flores Magón and reassured town residents that they were the "real Mexicans."[12]

Others seeking opportunity on the fringes of the capital became cave dwellers. They dug homes in the banks of gullies and arroyos that surrounded the capital city, and the best the government could manage for them was to provide cement fronts for the caves and send tank trucks daily to dispense drinking water. Others found space to build shacks in the interstitial lots of decaying sections of the city. Far more turned to Mexico City's suburban barrancas, the "steep ravines, reclaimed mudflats, and dusty slopes in the volcanic badlands." This wasteland was home to between two and three million people in 1970 (about 40 percent of the city's population). Residents of the shantytown of Cerrada del Cóndor, whose existence went unnoticed for some time by city authorities, were typical of the growing marginal population whose survival hinged on the informal economy. Marginality, as described by United Nations analysts and social scientists, has two basic features: (1) lack of formal articulation or insertion in the urban industrial process of production, and (2) chronic insecurity of employment. In the informal sector, these people operated in the part of the economy not directed by the law; in general, they were self-employed, without licenses or social protection, and they did not pay taxes.

Cerrada del Cóndor contained about 200 dwellings in a section about ten blocks by two blocks in size. The residents did not regard themselves as squatters. Like the residents of the capital's other shantytowns, they formed a symbiotic relationship with middle-class neighborhoods. The settlers used the services (transportation, utilities, schools, markets, and social security centers) of the middle class, and the middle class employed the settlers as gardeners, maids, and servants, without paying a minimum wage or providing mandatory worker benefits.

Life in this *colonia popular* was extremely hard. It demanded the minimum consumption and maximum recycling of resources. In the never-ending struggle to make ends meet, shantytown residents relied on the unpaid work of family members, forming a system of reciprocal exchange networks that drew heavily on the free contributions of wives, children, and the elderly. A large family was an economic asset in the shantytowns. In meeting their challenge, these marginal people became masters of recycling.

Migrants to Cerrada del Cóndor typified the new Mexican, a recent arrival in the capital or other urban center. The new city dwellers did not immediately assimilate to urban society. Upon arrival, they generally lived in one of the rural islands of the city. They remained rural marginal residents in an urban setting for many years, usually a decade, before accommodating to the city. And, no matter how quickly they adopted the ways of the city, migrants maintained rural contacts for many years, usually through a regular schedule of visits.

Their scheduled trips to the countryside often coincided with holidays or feast days, such as the village saint day. The maintenance of urban–rural ties served as a safety net for family members and friends. Long-term urban unemployment could be dealt with by a trip to the country; crop failures could be overcome with a visit and a job in the city for a short time. The second generation, born in the city, also maintained its rural ties.[13]

In 1970, unskilled workers regularly earned less than the monthly equivalent of Mexico's mandatory minimum wage, even though the employers of contract labor, including construction companies, usually met the standard. The difficulty for most workers was that they could not find regular work. Yet they managed the purchase of certain luxury items demanded by urban life. The homes of the Cerrada del Cóndor had electric appliances, purchased on credit, and usually a portable transistor radio. One third of them had a television set. Another major expense was the purchase of religious objects for a home altar. These possessions indicated that social stratification existed, based on appliances, in this and other shantytowns and slums.

Residents made do. One system, called a *tanda*, served as a convenient practical savings and credit mechanism. Four to ten people each contributed a fixed number of pesos every month. On a rotating basis, each member received the entire amount accumulated to use for his or her needs. The system required no treasurer because there was no accumulation of capital and also eliminated the risk that someone's savings might be stolen.

In the shantytowns, strict gender divisions applied to labor, leisure, friendships, and affections. Male friendship, called *cuatismo*, was the key to male behavior. Drinking bouts developed the bond, called *confianza*, between men. *Cuates*, or drinking companions, shared leisure activities, including sports. Most households consisted of extended families, and a man's effective community included relatives living nearby and his cuates who represented the reciprocity networks on which he relied. These networks responded to scarcity and made a maximum use of limited resources.[14]

The urban slum and shantytown residents did not join political, social security, worker, sport, or other national associations. The few who did become incorporated into the social security system, or enrolled in a union, remained passive members. Many shantytowns lacked any kind of local authority, so members belonged to the invisible, but effective, informal exchange organizations. Marginal urban dwellers functioned outside of local and national organizations and were thus beyond government control. The PRI had no control over the growing self-reliant urban population that believed the state had little to offer.

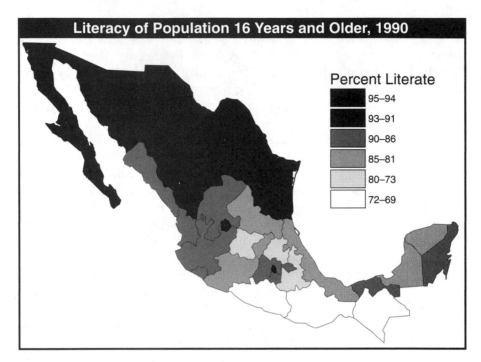

Figure 12.3 Literacy of Population 16 Years and Older, 1990.

The urban poor also constructed their own Catholicism, beyond the control of the Church. They recognized Church ceremonies (such as baptism) and erected home altars. In Cerrada del Cóndor, each residence had an altar that usually included images of the Virgin of Guadalupe, Saint Martin of Porras, and the Sacred Heart of Jesus.

Those on the edges of the city and the margins of urban life learned about national culture through public education and the mass media. In the early 1970s, perhaps as many as 80 percent of the children living in the slums attended school at least until the age of twelve. An equal percentage of households had a radio and 40 percent had a television set. By 1973, the potential Mexican television audience had reached roughly twenty-five million.[15]

POPULAR CULTURE AND MASS MEDIA

Private commercial television companies, buttressing the status quo, dominated the mass media. The public education channel focused on basic instruction and civics programs that attracted only limited audiences. Echeverría tried to improve public broadcasting by buying an ailing private channel to convert into a more innovative public channel. The powerful Monterrey Group of industrialists responded to what they saw as a threat to the private sector. The Monterrey Group merged its channel with Mexico's major private network to form Televisa. This new, powerful network rarely covered events embarrassing to the incumbent president or directly criticized his administration's policies. Nevertheless, its existence and political potential was not lost on the government. Network television affirmed preferred political, social, and economic values through soap operas, comedies, and variety programs. Never did these programs question the circumstances of life in contemporary Mexico. Nor did radio broadcasts, which reached probably four out of every five Mexicans across the nation, offer more than "safe" programming.

This style of television and radio programming resulted from broadcasters being ever mindful of the delicate balance between their own interests and the state's concerns, backed by the bureaucratic potential for censorship. The government had the authority to regulate broadcasting in the "public interest" and could insist on specific programs such as the "National Hour." Music, soap operas, sports, and public service announcements, rather than analytical reporting, comprised the major part of television and radio programming.

Figure 12.4 Basket vendors in the Oaxaca market. Handicrafts such as these continue to form a part of Mexico's popular culture. *Printed with permission, Cheryle Champion.*

Moreover, the barely literate population enjoyed an ample supply of comics, foto-novelas, and sports publications. These outlets reinforced the values, norms, and aspirations of the urban national culture. Most comic books were rather conventional and apolitical, but a few have vigorously attacked government policy on an array of issues. Eduardo de Río, for example, popularly known as "Rius," creator of Los Supermachos (the supermachos) and Los Agachados (the stooped over ones), directed his scathing satire at the presidential administration and its policies. The Los Supermachos claimed a circulation of nearly 200,000, before the cartoonist, a brash Marxist, was forced to abandon the characters (claimed by the publisher he worked for). Soon he created Los Agachados, and from 1968 to 1977 this new comic book claimed a circulation of roughly 150,000. In both, Rius used Mexico's villages and their residents to declare repeatedly that the Emperor–President had no clothes. Thus he juxtaposed the "Noble Villager" against the alleged agents of U.S. imperialism, the Vatican, the new rich, private enterprise, and the official party and government.

Besides satirical comic books, no-holds-barred discussion of government issues occurs in scholarly journals with limited circulation. Both of these have little influence outside of intellectual circles and do not form a part of the popular culture transmitted by the mass media.

On rare occasions, the question of censorship has become public. In 1974, the federal government forced the demise of the weekly leftist journal *¿ Por Qué?* after six years of publication. The Baja California state government in 1977 suppressed the *El ABC de Tijuana* because of its hypercritical columnists.

The most prominent example of government censorship in contemporary Mexico was in the 1976 *Excélsior* case.[16] Editor Julio Shearer García, beginning in 1968, made the newspaper into a progressive voice of dissent that soon earned international respect. He recruited well-known intellectuals, including Daniel Cosío Villegas, Gastón García Cantú, Ricardo Garibay, Pablo Latapí, Vicente Leñero, and Rodolfo Stavenhagen as columnists. The paper's columns and editorials critically examined presidential domestic and international policies, called for greater opportunities for genuine political participation by Mexicans, and demanded a more equitable distribution of wealth and concerted government action against corruption. Both Shearer and *Excélsior* earned plaudits for their outstanding journalism.

President Echeverría at first supported the newspaper as evidence of his administration's liberalism. He even used government funds to buy advertising space when business leaders had become angry with Shearer, resulting in lost advertising revenue. Then in

1976 the president dropped his support and moved to change the editorial policy. *Excélsior* had attacked the president and questioned the regime's progressive (that is, revolutionary) character. These lines of criticism touched two nerve centers in the administration: (1) the president remains beyond written condemnation while in office and (2) the administration represents continuing revolutionary idealism. Charging that the president ignored the middle class in his populist campaign for rural people, that he fostered closer ties with Castro's Cuba, or that he endorsed the demands of labor unions strengthened the myth of revolutionary continuity. The claim that the president had abandoned the revolution, on the other hand, would not be tolerated.

Rather than resorting to bludgeon blows and closing the editorial offices and jailing the writers, the Echeverría administration conducted a skillful and imaginative campaign against Shearer and the newspaper. As a way to increase the newspaper's independence, the *Excélsior* corporation had purchased land on the outskirts of Mexico City and in 1976 began building a middle-class housing development to generate needed revenues. On June 10, 1976, the Echeverría administration initiated a major media campaign alleging that *Excélsior* had become the enemy of peasants and slum dwellers. One politician from the PRI's agrarian section led squatters in seizing the property in question. Government officials offered assistance to the squatters by bringing in more peasants for support, while rejecting the newspaper's efforts to expel them.

The Echeverría campaign also reached the newspaper's workforce. The company was a cooperative, and the government identified and financed a dissident group of rank-and-file workers. This anti-Shearer group, on July 8, 1976, charged Shearer with ineffectual management of the squatter issue, forced him and his supporters out, and seized the printing presses. The following day, *Excélsior* appeared as only another of the lackluster capital city dailies. Shearer's supporters quickly established the weekly *Proceso* and many of his columnists moved to the daily *Uno Más Uno*.

The erratic character of media censorship and presidential whim were soon demonstrated once again. Echeverría made some efforts to influence *Proceso* but his authority was already diminishing as his term approached its end. The incoming president, López Portillo, regularly remarked that there would be complete freedom of the press beginning with his inauguration on December 1, 1976. Once in office, López Portillo not only reduced pressure on *Proceso*, but also encouraged Shearer to return to *Excélsior*. The editor and his associates accepted the president's proposal, but events took a further turn. Shearer went to New York City to receive a journalism award and *The New York Times* used the occasion to break a story about his return to the paper. The *Times* story was used in Mexico City as evidence of U.S. involvement in restoring Shearer as editor, and the entire initiative fell apart.

Generally the regime relies on the agency that imports and distributes the necessary newsprint (Productora e Importadora de Papel—PIPSA) to encourage self-censorship among editors and reporters. Since its creation in 1935, PIPSA has allowed those newspapers that present favorable reports of the government to operate on nearly unlimited credit to obtain newsprint; opposition newspapers often find paper is not available. Government advertising also provides assistance to supportive newspapers. Other forms of subsidy paid to journals and reporters include *gacetillas*, paid stories that are presented as news, and *igualas* or *embutes*, stipends paid directly to reporters and editors for favorable coverage.[17]

Despite these inducements to self-censorship, some reporters have attacked the official regime. A wave of violence against hostile reporters occurred in the years from 1971 to 1989, which resulted in the deaths of fifty-one journalists. Of these, forty-eight were newspaper reporters, two were radio broadcasters and one a television employee. The number of murders at a time when Mexico was regarded as one of the most stable nations in the hemisphere prompted investigations by the Inter-American Press Association and Article 19, the human rights committee of the International Centre on Censorship. Corrupt money associated with projected oil fields and with drug trafficking seem to have paid for the murders of journalists who pressed on the corruption and narcotics issues.

The investigations found that no more than two (only one for certain) of the murders related to the person's journalistic activities, despite government reports to the contrary. Moreover, forty-four of the fifty-one murders occurred in the provinces, outside of the glare of public interest focused on the national capital. The murder of Manuel Buendia in Mexico City on May 30, 1984, finally focused international concern on the issue. More typical of the gangland-style murders were the deaths of Ernesto Flores Torrijos and Norma Moreno Figueroa, the owner and columnist of the Matamoros newspaper *El Popular*. Both had received numerous death threats and scurrilous insults, including widely distributed posters charging that Moreno Figueroa was a dangerous lesbian. They were killed by machine gunfire on July 17, 1986, as they arrived at the newspaper offices. Investigations revealed that all three murders resulted from the reporter's incessant stories on corruption. For the most part, all of these murders remain unsolved.[18]

The conditions of both urban and rural Mexico, the manipulation of the mass media to preserve the status quo, and the president's encouragement of populist programs induced militants to act. Terrorism, kidnappings, bank robberies, army ambushes, and student unrest jostled Mexico's one-time image of stability. A wave of both urban and rural insurgent terrorism lapped over the country. These circumstances in turn provoked a military and paramilitary response. Many assumed the virus of the Cuban and Chinese revolutions had again invaded the minds of the young and poor as they believed it had in 1968. But old ideologues of the left such as Fidel and Che lacked the appeal their detractors imagined. Thus in the capital city shantytown called Campamento 2 de Octubre, founded in 1972 in memory of the victims of Tlatelolco, leaders linked themselves to the tradition of the Mexican Revolution of Zapata and Villa and refused to allow Marxist representatives the opportunity to organize the community. Rather than Marxist ideology or revolutionary doctrine, many populist insurgents found the expression of their aspirations and needs in public mass culture.

Mexico's desperation reached the point that the heroes of fiction and comic books served many as actual guides to behavior. A settler in Campamento 2 de Octubre talked about his experience as a *paracaista* (land squatter) in the Huasteca region near San Luis Potosí. He recounted how, after the squatters had seized the land, the state police arrived and arrested the speaker and two others. After driving awhile, the driver stopped and one campesino was taken off into the brush, a shot was heard, and the policeman returned alone. The police van continued for some distance, stopped again, and the same events occurred with the second campesino. The speaker remembered, "They started driving again. I was afraid. I didn't know what to do. Then I told myself, 'What would Kalimán do?' . . . they took me out and made me walk over some ridges, and down into a little dry creek. I tried to act like I wasn't afraid, because that's what I think Kalimán would have done. And when one of those cops looked at his shoe, I did what I think Kalimán would have done. I hollered real loud, to scare them, and I ran up over the bed of the creek. They fired their guns behind me, but they fired into the air." Later the campesino learned that the police had not shot either of his companions, but the most revealing aspect of his testimony was his decision to act based on his understanding of how a comic book superhero would react to the circumstances.[19]

Kalimán, by far the most popular comic book hero, was a role model to a great many Mexicans. In the 1970s, the estimated monthly consumption of comic books was approximately 2.5 million, the world's highest comic book readership. Readers turned most often to Kalimán, which had a weekly circulation of between 1.5 and 3.5 million. Kalimán first appeared on radio in 1963, and two years later emerged as a comic book hero, one whose appeal stretches across class and gender boundaries and over rural and urban divisions. He dresses all in white, from his form-revealing Nehru jacket and tights and cape with red lining to his turban. He confronts supervillains and defeats them through a combination of strength and magical powers, but above all through, his extraordinary intelligence. This caped hero repeatedly stresses that the human mind, when properly trained and disciplined, can overcome physical needs, but one must ignore personal cost and remember that simply to be alive is a victory.[20]

PROBLEMS IN THE MIRACLE'S WAKE

In an effort to undercut the appeal of terrorists and the reaction of paramilitarists, Echeverría authorized a huge wage increase of 33 percent for urban workers. By 1973, inflation had climbed to 11 percent, low compared to most of Latin America but high enough to create near panic in Mexican commercial and industrial centers. Powerful Mexican businessmen believed the president was constricting profits, hindering economic recovery, and paving the way for inflationary disaster.

After riding the high tide of the miracle, when it completely receded Echeverría was forced in 1973 to institute emergency anti-inflation policies. He ordered stricter price controls, redirection of public investments into short-term productive projects, especially agriculture; an increase in foreign exchange through expanded exports and reduced imports; and a tighter grip on monetary policy. These measures did little except provoke attacks on the administration from both the left and the right. Assurances to American, European, and Japanese businessmen that his government did not have an expropriation mentality angered those on the left who accused Echeverría of selling out. Relations with the private sector deteriorated as the result of the government's ceiling on profits. Business was upset by tighter controls on the booming private investment banks that they used to offset the damaging effects of short-term government policies.

External pressures pushed inflation to 40 percent in 1974. Recession in the United States had an adverse effect on the Mexican economy. Declining tourism reduced Mexico's source of dollars, and dollar devaluation weakened the peso's purchasing power. A new 10 percent U.S. surcharge on imported goods had severe results because the United States remains Mexico's largest customer and supplier.

Echeverría launched a campaign to reduce imports, but had little success in 1974. Major floods decimated the wheat harvest and again the government had to buy grain abroad at a time when world prices for food had soared. Equally damaging was the failure of the petro-chemical industry to meet the domestic demand for petroleum. The government imported oil when the energy crisis suddenly burst upon the world. The administration managed enough assistance to agriculture to increase production so it could stop importing corn and beans in 1976. But Mexico will be unable to feed its people in the year 2000 unless the government achieves a more equitable distribution of income in rural areas and has some success with its new national population policy. There is a limit to Mexico's capacity to produce food.

The foreign debt emerged as a major problem in the mid-1970s. The Díaz Ordaz administration had borrowed heavily to finance major public works projects. These investments were essential to sustain rapid economic growth, but at the same time they caused the national debt to swell to more than $3 billion. Just before the conclusion of his term, Echeverría announced he was ending the twenty-two-year-old exchange rate of 12.5 pesos to the dollar. Devaluation was a desperate effort to stem Mexico's raging inflation and strengthen the country's economy. Following the announcement, unfounded rumors of military coups and peasant uprisings crisscrossed the country. The central bank tried to hold the exchange rate at 20 to 1, but in October the rate dropped to 25 to 1. Then the central bank decided to float the peso again. The exchange rate dropped again, falling to more than 28 to 1, and continued to decline. A predictable flight of pesos crossed the border. Devaluing the peso about 40 percent was intended to boost tourism and exports by making Mexican goods and services cheaper in relation to other currencies.

The second major theme of the Echeverría government was political and administrative reform. The president reacted strongly to the increasingly strident opposition to the party and his regime. Moreover, he portrayed the militant opposition, especially the events associated with the Corpus Christi massacre, as justification for bringing his associates into government. He installed a new group of technocrats in the government to replace the aging "revolutionary" generals and party bureaucrats. He also promoted a cadre of junior officers in the military. Approximately 354 generals retired during Echeverria's six-year term. Nevertheless, the president only promoted 192 colonels to the rank of general. This presidential policy thus brought a new generation into government.[21]

The president determined to change the image of the PRI by altering the party's personnel. In the 1973 congressional elections, the party's candidates were not the traditional party henchmen but well-educated middle- and lower-middle-class young men. He particularly encouraged those from the public and agrarian sectors, dealing a hard blow to the labor section of the party. These efforts generated little enthusiasm for the PRI. Only 60 percent of Mexico's twenty-five million voters cast ballots in the congressional elections.

Attempting to create excitement for his regime, Echeverría launched a well-publicized foreign relations campaign that journalists called *guayabera* diplomacy. Throughout his administration, he met with the presidents of Central American nations to improve diplomatic relations as well as to search for new markets for Mexican products. Echeverría gave each official he met a southern Mexican peasant shirt, called a *guayabera*, as a gift, hence the name of his diplomatic offensive. Mexicans contributed to the international changeover that began in 1971. They withdrew recognition of the Chinese government on Taiwan and in February 1972 became the fifth nation in the Western Hemisphere to recognize the People's Republic of China. In humanitarian actions, Echeverría accepted exiled Chileans, Argentines, and Uruguayans fleeing military regimes tolerating so-called dirty wars to eliminate the Left. He also accepted exile governments from Nicaragua and El Salvador and created the Third World University. The president sought potential markets throughout the world, having his greatest success in Japan. The growing cooperation between the two countries resulted in several joint ventures in Mexico, involving Mitsubishi, Ishikawajima, Yamaha, Nissan, Datsun, Mitsui, and others.

The Echeverría government also found it necessary to develop policies to deal with the belatedly recognized population problem. The president inaugurated a major publicity campaign calling for family responsibility and encouraging Mexicans not to have more children than they could afford to feed and educate. By the end of Echeverría's sexenio, birth control information and devices were available to women through the social security offices. By then, the campaign had become more aggressive. Mexican women were told that they could choose whether or not to become pregnant.

The administration also devised plans to combat the pollution that accompanied urbanization and industrialization. Mexicans had passed laws against noise and uncollected garbage in the capital city but did little to enforce them. Two major programs were initiated to rehabilitate Mexico City. The first, a six-year project to restore the dry lake and reforest the surrounding hills, was designed to prevent the dust storms that contributed to the city's air pollution and to increase the oxygen supply in the capital where traffic policemen had begun carrying gas masks as part of their regulation equipment. The second project proposed the decentralization of industry, in the hope that it would decentralize the population. The plan called for twenty-five dispersed industrial cities, the first of which was inaugurated in

Durango. A short-lived feasibility study even investigated relocating the nation's capital.

As his term ended, Echeverría hoped to become the first Latin American secretary general of the United Nations. But Mexico's vote to condemn Zionism as a racist policy dashed any chance Echeverría had to become secretary general, and also sparked a tourism boycott by U.S. Jews at a time when Mexico badly needed tourists. Still hoping to become the spokesman for the Third World, Echeverría launched his Third World University in Mexico City. His last major presidential act was an effort to establish revolutionary credentials. He confiscated nearly 100,000 hectares of land belonging to seventy-three families in the border states and distributed them to 9,000 landless peasants. In doing so, he forged a reactionary alliance between the two major northern interests, the Monterrey industrialists and the northwest commercial agriculturalists.

Echeverría selected his finance minister José López Portillo as his successor. That López Portillo was the son of a career army officer no doubt strengthened civil-military relations. Again the election proved disappointing, as the PRI faced no opposition—a necessary element for the sake of democratic appearances—and some 30 percent of the voters abstained. López Portillo, who had written a book about the plumed serpent Quetzalcóatl, adopted this Toltec bearer of technology as his symbolic mentor. According to legend, Quetzalcóatl had introduced improved agricultural techniques, such as irrigation and fertilization, to central Mexico. López Portillo, who named his official airplane and bus after this cultural hero, also planned to bring to Mexico the benefits of technocracy.[22]

The new president and his successor de la Madrid both adopted the practice of ignoring PRI politicians in favor of recruiting technocrats for their governments. The shift away from the traditional cabinet selection process seemed to be confirmed when López Portillo chose as secretary of tourism Rosa Luz Alegría, the first woman to serve in a presidential cabinet. For their other appointments, both presidents looked to individuals who held degrees from prestigious universities. Thus López Portillo delegated most economic policy decisions to his two Cambridge University-trained advisors, José Andrés de Oteyza and Carlos Tello Macías. Later, de la Madrid would rely on Ivy League-trained economic counselors Carlos Salinas de Gortari and Jesús Silva Herzog, educated at Harvard and Yale universities, respectively. The successful technocrat needed more than just a degree. The international reputation of the institution became an important factor after 1970. Moreover, these appointments represented "the grandchild generation," descendants of antirevolutionaries. For example, José López Portillo himself is the grandson and namesake of Victoriano Huerta's secretary of foreign relations, and Miguel de la Madrid is related to both Miguel and Enrique de la Madrid, Porfirian governors of Colima.[23]

Mexicans took a roller coaster ride as the economy enjoyed a breathtaking rise to new heights following the 1978 discovery of new oil fields, which inspired reckless government disbursements, a surge of confidence in the private sector, and frantic consumer spending. From atop the petroleum-producing world, in 1982 Mexico's fortunes plummeted in the face of declining oil prices, staggering foreign debt, and an astonishing balance of payments deficit. López Portillo again devalued the peso and turned to the United States and the International Monetary Fund (IMF) to rescue his country.

In 1982, the price of the bailout was high. Mexico agreed to deliver the bulk of its prospective gas and oil to the United States at a "favorable" price, and to multiple exchange rates in the future (a series of mini-devaluations interspersed with periods when the peso's exchange rate was frozen). The government also agreed to an IMF austerity program that meant: (1) wage controls and a reduction in government spending; (2) price increases for goods and services provided by government agencies such as CONASUPO; (3) a move toward opening markets to international competition and eventually seeking membership in the General Agreement on Tariffs and Trade (GATT); (4) promotion of exports via the maquiladora industry along the border; (5) a flexible interpretation of the 1973 Foreign Investment Law to encourage foreign investment; and (6) an agreement to reduce by more than 40 percent the number of public sector firms. On September 1, 1982, a desperate López Portillo nationalized the private banks.

This administration also saw a greatly expanded social role for the military. Through a policy that gave the armed forces greater public presence, army commanders received presidential encouragement to expand their security activities through increased responsibility for utility and petroleum installations. At the same time, the former army brat who had become president supported military modernization through high-tech weaponry. He expanded professional education by creating the Colegio de Defensa Nacional (CDN) in 1981, under the direction of General Félix Galván, and allowed it to award master's degrees. By 1988, a third of the thirty-one staff officers in the ministry of defense had earned master's degrees at CDN.[24] Moreover, the president consulted with the secretary of defense on all major policy decisions.

The IMF austerity program worked for the new president, Miguel de la Madrid, who was inaugurated in December 1982. De la

Madrid generated considerable favorable reaction because of his ad-ministration's anticorruption campaign and efforts to heal political wounds. With a flurry of publicity, de la Madrid launched a program to investigate complaints of corruption against civil servants. He re-ported in his sixth state of the union address that as a result of this program his government had investigated 1,571 allegations and had recovered some 19.5 trillion pesos ($470 million dollars at the time) for the national treasury.[25] The long-standing issue (especially since 1968) of political prisoners received some resolution when de la Madrid freed some 2,000 individuals he claimed were the last of Mexico's political prisoners.[26]

Other de la Madrid programs, however, had their down side. Mexico enjoyed a favorable balance of trade in 1983, the inflation rate had fallen, and between 1983 and 1984 the country's international reserves increased by over $4 billion. Then a devastating earthquake hit Mexico City in September 1985. Rescue workers found bodies throughout the city. In the rubble of the basement beneath the attor-ney general's office, searchers recovered the bodies of four Colombians and several Mexicans who showed signs of torture. The PRI congress-men and the attorney general successfully stonewalled, avoiding all demands, including that of the Colombian embassy, for a formal in-vestigation.[27] Then in 1986 oil prices fell dramatically, resulting in a massive drop in oil revenue for Mexico.

Paying the rest of the price of the economic downturn, Mexico joined GATT (General Agreement on Tariffs and Trade) in July 1986. Most surprising, the Mexican government sold, liquidated, or trans-ferred over 200 "low priority" state enterprises to private concerns. During the 1970s, the number of parastate enterprises had increased dramatically. A host of businesses—including smelters, sugar refiner-ies, grocery stores, hotels, shampoo factories, bottling plants, and a bi-cycle factory—had been acquired in a great rush by the government. In 1975, 14 percent of the workforce were government employees and by 1985, the figure had risen to 22 percent.[28] Pressured by the IMF, de la Madrid removed some enterprises from government control, espe-cially such visible businesses as the National Hotel chain, the auto-mobile corporation jointly held with Renault of Mexico, Mexicana Airlines, and the Monterrey foundry. In 1988, the state-owned copper mine at Cananea, site of the historic strike of June 1906 that helped undermine the Porfirian government, went into the hands of an in-dustrial conglomerate for some $910 million.

By 1987, the debt amounted to three-fourths of the gross national product. Most Mexicans, who exercise prudence when purchasing on credit, could not comprehend the magnitude of the national debt. Many do not meet credit requirements and others will not assume debt obligations. One popular aphorism states that, "It is better to go to bed without supper than to wake up in debt." Apart from the elite, Mexicans live on a cash-and-carry basis. They oppose government borrowing from foreign bankers, although much of this opposition focuses on the corruption associated with the loans and the debt. As the government struggled to deal with economic realities, many, unable to voice their distress, responded with sarcasm. In an ironic reference to the nation's Angel of Liberty, the monument to independence, people used the first name of Angel Gurría, de la Madrid's director of public credit, and called him the "Angel of Dependency." They labeled the economic advisors "the Eunuchs" and the technocrats at the national petroleum corporation (PEMEX) "the Smurfs."[29]

The fleeting oil bonanza served as a cruel prelude to the economic crisis that followed in 1982. During the boom, corruption reached new levels. Purchasing costs were inflated on every project or activity by two or three times. Oil workers rented their union cards, union leaders received gifts to prevent work actions, construction contractors earned huge kickbacks, and ingenious managers devised daily new ways to pad accounts, siphon funds, and receive bribes. The economic crisis required government action and brought a new attitude among the middle sector of the population.

The rampant inflation provoked official decisions symptomatic of deep problems. The government imposed a 15 percent retail sales tax. Facing an inflation rate of 60 percent to 150 percent, officials at the national mint abolished coins valued at one centavo and introduced twenty-one coins, with the highest valued at 5,000 pesos (worth about $2 at the time).

TABLE 12–1   COMPARISON OF THE DEBT AND THE GROSS NATIONAL PRODUCT (IN MILLIONS OF DOLLARS).

Year	Debt	GNP
1980	41,250	189,155
1982	59,651	163,815
1983	81,565	140,089
1984	86,022	165,962
1985	88,446	175,494
1986	90,912	122,162
1987	98,484	132,987
1988	86,492	165,308
1989	80,256	186,704

Many Mexicans viewed corruption as a tradition of national life and saw the campaign launched by de la Madrid as a "battle between novitiate priests of financial abstinence and the invincible forces of sin. Not many Mexicans believed that their nation could be cleansed." On the one hand, for many corruption was an indelible aspect of machismo in which the macho exercised his dominance through extortion or bribery.[30] On the other hand, after the overwhelming economic problems of 1982, the middle classes began to blame government corruption for the crisis and their declining standard of living. In response to this growing attitude, de la Madrid launched an anticorruption campaign to generate support for his administration in its waning months. The government jailed Jorge Díaz Serrano, the former head of PEMEX, the state oil corporation on charges of defrauding PEMEX of about $30 million. But the campaign backfired as the public saw the arrest as the result of political rivalry.

The Año de Hidalgo offered de la Madrid the opportunity to make his mark, which he did by ignoring the swelling opposition of those concerned about the environment. In October 1988, he authorized the on-line operation of Mexico's first nuclear power plant, the Laguna Verde plant in Veracruz. His action climaxed a six-year struggle in which opponents of the plant demanded a meeting with the president. In desperation, in 1988 they blockaded the main coastal highway four miles north of Laguna Verde and forty miles north of Veracruz at Palma Sola. When Echeverría discovered that Mexico risked losing its energy independence because in 1971, for the first time in its history, Mexico imported more oil than it exported, he agreed to a plan to convert the national electrical industry from thermoelectric to nuclear generation. The plan approved the construction of a nuclear plant at Laguna Verde to solve a problem—the energy shortage from 1971 to 1974. But the problem had disappeared before the first part of the foundation was poured in 1976. Mexican ecologists claimed Laguna Verde was unnecessary and said it was identical to the plant in Zimmer, Ohio, which had to be abandoned because of defects in construction. Opponents of the plant made it clear that they did not want a Mexican Chernobyl. Others protested on nationalistic grounds, saying the new electric power would be used in the U.S. and Japanese-owned maquiladoras along the northern border and that Mexicans would not benefit directly. After eighty-six hours, the military and state police ended the blockade without violence.

Other Mexicans, in increasing numbers, turned to the formation of opposition groups to vent their frustration with the PRI and the government. Among the political opposition in the north is the Movimiento Constitucional Mexicano (MCM), formed in 1983 in Monterrey by Herminio Gómez, who said at the outset that the group's purpose was implementation of the 1917 Constitution. Members of MCM, who have been called ". . . bristling activists, an ACLU with bullhorns," have staged ". . . sit-ins, hunger strikes, marches, and rallies . . . protested election-rigging, clamored for releasing street vendors from jail, and decried hikes in utility rates." In 1985, Gómez, a master of attracting attention for popular issues, went to Europe and unfurled a banner that read "In Mexico There Is No Democracy" at fetes where Mexico's president spoke. In early 1988, he walked from the Guatemalan border to the Rio Grande, a distance of some 2,000 miles, on what he billed as a "March for Democracy." His forays on behalf of the MCM have landed him in jail a dozen times, but never for long enough to suit him. Brushes with the law are a tonic for Herminio, who pictures himself as a prophet calling a wayward nation to the path of righteousness.[31]

Political pressure from a variety of corners and a growing awareness of global economic developments generated an increasing interest in a North American economic bloc. In early 1990, President Carlos Salinas de Gortari agreed to consider Mexico's entry into a North American Common Market, a notion considered ludicrous a decade before.[32]

THE GLOBAL PROBLEM OF DRUG TRAFFICKING

Recent focus on national economic measures does not mean serious international problems do not exist. Cocaine and derivative drugs have become a social issue as Mexico became a transmission point to major drug markets north of the border. To some extent, shipments followed routes established during the revolution, when some producers and shippers provided Mexican opium and marijuana to the United States. Opium production, legalized during the Second World War, resulted in a well-established heroin industry in Sinaloa, Durango, and Chihuahua. Reports suggest that a cocaine-smuggling empire was developed, perhaps by someone in the national security police, at the same time. Both industries declined after the war but acquired new life with the emergence of the drug culture in the United States during the 1960s. Confronting a national crisis, the U.S. government created the Drug Enforcement Agency (DEA) in 1973. Seeking help from the Mexican government, the United States pressured the Echeverría administration to assist its antidrug campaign by sending money, supplies, fixed-wing aircraft, helicopters, pilots, and DEA agents to join Mexican officials in the eradication campaign known as Operation Condor.

A few drug patriarchs became known to the public: Jaime Herrera Nevares of Durango reportedly directed heroin shipments

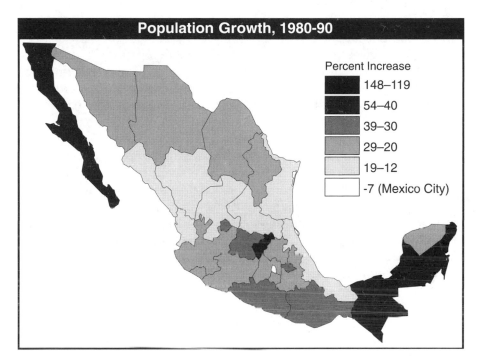

Figure 12.5 Population Growth, 1980–1990.

from northern Mexico through Ciudad Juárez–El Paso to large U.S. cities, especially Chicago.[33] Pedro Aviles Pérez in Sinaloa had the reputation as chief of the marijuana network reaching to Southern California. A series of raids in the late 1970s and early 1980s apparently forced the marijuana industry to relocate to the area of Guadalajara, where its production on large plantations using modern equipment and fertilizers became big business.

The international nature of the drug business became evident by the early 1980s, when DEA officials successfully cut off the flow of cocaine through Miami, Florida. The Colombian dealers sought new routes to the U.S. market through Puerto Rico and northwestern Mexico. In Mexico traffickers channeled their cocaine through the established networks that moved marijuana and heroin. The narcotics traffic made multimillionaires out of the cartel members and generated huge sums of money that could be used to bribe enforcement officers or to buy assault weapons to protect the illegal industry.

Between 1982 and 1984, a combined force of the Mexican army, members of the Mexican federal judicial police, and U.S. DEA agents raided marijuana fields in Zacatecas, San Luis Potosí, and Chihuahua. The success of these forays drove growers away from the exposed foothills to the less accessible uplands of the Sierra Madre in Chihuahua and Sinaloa.

Seeking revenge in February 1985, the members of a drug ring kidnapped, tortured, and murdered DEA agent Enrique Camarena outside of Guadalajara. Camarena's death, the torture of another DEA agent, and the initial unwillingness of Mexican authorities to investigate led to a public outcry in Mexico. The United States Congress in 1986 passed legislation enabling the president to refuse financial aid, including loans, to any country unwilling to participate actively in pursuing drug traders. Mexican officials responded to both the popular indignation and the financial leverage. Rafael Caro Quintero of Guadalajara was arrested and convicted for crimes related to drug trafficking. Subsequently, nineteen others were charged with kidnapping, drug trafficking, and murder in connection with the Camarena slaying. The investigation resulted in the firing of several hundred federal police officers and the dissolution of some major enforcement agencies.

But the major dilemma remained: the problem was as much one of demand as supply, as the street value of drugs in North American cities continued to decline, indicating that supplies were more available than ever to meet what was evidently a rising demand. (The single exception was marijuana, for which demand was declining, while sinsemilla was being grown in greenhouses, basements, and attics, and national forests across the U.S. countryside.) Even when the cocaine supply was temporarily limited during the summer of 1990, the immediate result was not less drug use but more gun smuggling and gang fighting in inner-city America. During the decade of the 1990s, drug trafficking has resulted in a growing list of problems. Difficulties began with an increasing flow of drug money to corrupt public officials, then incessant squabbles between the Mexican government and the United States Congress over enforcement issues (called "decertification" in the United States) and the growing concern with the increasing militarization of the countryside with armed men— narcotrafficantes, police, army, and drug enforcement agents—seemingly everywhere.

President Salinas de Gortari in 1989 promised Mexican cooperation in the struggle against the drug lords, noting for the first time the national security concerns related to drug kings who can field their own armies and threaten the integrity of the state, either through military action or bribery of public officials. Although drugs have been a recent focus of corruption, police corruption has been a long-standing and more pervasive problem. The symbol of police corruption is the *mordida* (bite), the payment of a fee to a policeman to avoid a traffic citation, a trip to the precinct office, or some other inconvenience.

Mexicans often perceive the police bribe as nothing more than the need for the officer to make a decent living, to compensate for his low wages and the fact that he may have had to pay a bribe to get a police job. Another form of corruption, although few regard it as such, is the *propina*, paid for services, and not for profit, in which the amount is never mentioned. The most iniquitous form of bribery is the *soborno*, arranged, usually in advance, for financial gain on both sides.

Stories about corruption pepper discussions of the Mexican experience among travelers and businesspeople. Journalist Dick Reavis recalled an incident on July 4, 1984, when he drove his car into Mexico at the Matamoros border crossing. To cope with heavy traffic, the immigration officers established different border crossing lines: the free line for those who wanted visa applications processed without paying a tip, which meant at least a two-hour wait; the ten-dollar line, which took about thirty minutes; and the twenty-dollar express lane. Reavis explained that without the bribery option, everyone would have been subject to delay.[34]

Nevertheless, evidence of major incidents of police corruption in the last two decades has appeared. Arturo "El Negro" Durazo Moreno,[35] the Mexico City police chief, became the symbol of corruption, especially racketeering under the protection of government officials. Durazo was born in Sonora but grew up with Echeverría and López Portillo in the Del Valle section of Mexico City. Although his friends turned to politics, he chose police work as the avenue to wealth and power. He first became aware of the possibilities by working as a bodyguard, gunman, and smuggler, before joining the secret service. Later he directed the graft-ridden police unit at Mexico City's airport until his childhood friend, President Echeverría, named him head of the capital's judicial police force in 1971. Durazo's rise continued under another old friend, López Portillo, who placed him in charge of security for the presidential campaign and then, despite information that a Miami grand jury had charged him with conspiring to export cocaine to the United States, named him head of all police forces in the capital city.

Durazo seized the opportunity to build an unprecedented racketeering empire. He demanded kickbacks on the purchase of police vehicles, a personal $40 tax on each of the 1.6 million license plates issued in the capital, a daily take from the *mordida*, and profits from the cocaine trade. When a gang of Colombian drug dealers challenged the arrangement, their bodies were found in the Tula River. The detectives of the Department for the Prevention of Delinquency acquired a public reputation for widespread extortion.[36] Until this newly named four-star general fled the country in 1982, the public could only guess at his excesses. When Durazo went into hiding, his former aide José González published *Lo negro del Negro Durazo*, an account of the chief's corrupt enterprises and police abuses, which was an immediate best-seller.

Readers learned that the police chief, who officially earned about $1,600 a month, in six years acquired real estate and other assets in Mexico, the United States, and Canada of $200 to $600 million. Beyond his palatial houses and foreign bank accounts, his other possessions—a gymnasium, discotheque, casino, racetrack, and man-made lakes—demonstrated his excesses and his disregard for public opinion. Once Durazo fled Mexico, authorities launched perhaps Mexico's most extensive manhunt, but the elusive ex-police chief, using at least a dozen different passports, dodged agents of 140 countries. Officials finally arrested "El Negro" in 1984 in San Juan, Puerto Rico, on allegations of murder, drug and arms trafficking, extortion, fraud, and tax evasion, as well numerous minor crimes. Following his arrest, Durazo was secretly jailed under heavy guard near Los Angeles, perhaps at Terminal Island in suburban San Pedro, until extradited to Mexico City. He was formally sentenced on a succession of minor charges in September 1989, but at seventy years old and in declining health, it seemed unlikely that he would outlive his prison term.

Although *Lo negro del Negro Durazo* sold more than a million copies, most Mexicans learned about Durazo's crimes through the comic version of the book with the same name. Additional numbers of the comic book, replete with exaggerated and invented details about the former police chief, quickly appeared and an irregular adult comic series called *El infierno de Durazo* produced perhaps as many as fifteen issues. Nearly eighty issues of another comic, *Picardías del Negro Durazo*, portraying Durazo as a roguish rather than sinister character, appeared between 1984 and 1986 before the government halted its publication.

Commercial-market movies and popular music also brought Durazo to the public. Alberto and Benjamin Escamilla, despite threats and legal and financial obstacles, translated González's best-seller for the screen. The film's brief life, in 1985, created a lingering suspicion that pressures beyond the film's lukewarm reviews caused its quick departure from theaters. At least three songs made their appearance on the radio: "Duro, Duro, Durazo," performed by Tropa Loca in both tropical and rock-and-roll renditions and by Francisco "Charro" Avitia in the ranchera style; "El sustazo del negrazo" by Chico Che and Las Crisis; and "La cumbia del duro negrazo" by Pagochito. Sales in 1984 for all three songs totaled over 150,000 singles, LPs, and cassettes.

Throughout the mass-market depictions of Durazo's exploits, several themes prevailed: the close connection between Durazo and more prominent government officials; the decadence and corruption of the police; the common recourse to violence and torture; the insistent sexism of society; and the general corruption of the regime. A public opinion poll in 1984 found that 47 percent believed that the publicity given the Durazo case was an effort by the government to divert attention away from Mexico's severe economic problems. Others believed the campaign against Durazo served to prop up the new de la Madrid administration by placing as much distance as possible between itself and the previous presidency. Everyone—readers of sensational books and comic books, moviegoers, and those humming popular tunes—agreed that Durazo represented only part of the general government corruption.

The Camarena and Negro Durazo affairs confirmed that President Salinas's apprehensions about outlaw police and corruption in the highest level of government were all too real. In June 1989, further evidence became public in reports implicating José Antonio Zorrilla Pérez, ex-chief of the federal directorate of security, in the murder of Mexico's leading journalist. Manuel Buendía, whose daily column appeared on the front page of *Excelsior*, was shot to death on May 30, 1984, as he left his downtown office. He had been highly critical of the CIA and the DFS, an internal security "political police" force assigned to the ministry of interior and at that time under the direction of Zorrilla.[37]

Again, on February 1, 1990, Manual Ibarra-Herrera, the former head of the Mexican federal judicial police (a secret police force under the attorney general's office that specializes in espionage and arms and drug trafficking), was indicted by a federal grand jury in Los Angeles on charges of murder in the 1985 death of DEA agent "Kiki" Camarena. Whatever the constitutional issues and legal rights involved, the fact remained that the security forces were out of control and police corruption had penetrated the inner circle of the Mexican government. Corruption among the police or other groups remained the major political issue of the 1980s, in both the gubernatorial and senate elections of 1985 and 1986 and the presidential election of 1988.

Allegations of corruption and gangland practices continue into the 1990s. Assassins, on May 21, 1990, killed Norma Corona Sapiens, the president of the Sinaloa state bar and head of the Commission on Human Rights in Culiacán. Widespread stories hinted at some federal judicial police involvement in her murder. Also in May 1990, the governor of Jalisco charged the attorney general and former governor with drug trafficking.

While technocrats, corruption, debt, and drugs have dominated the public side of the Mexican government since 1972, the PRI and its leaders have undertaken a kind of self-censorship that has involved placating some dominant figures within the party. Of these, none stood taller in party councils than labor boss Fidel Velázquez. It was Veláquez who was selected by López Portillo in 1981 to announce that the PRI had chosen de la Madrid as its presidential candidate. Others, including the president of the PRI, Javier García Paniagua, fumed at the choice.[38] Attempting to streamline cabinet involvement in policy making, de la Madrid organized subcabinet groups along policy lines, including an economic cluster.[39] Increasingly, the PRI and its leaders have been blamed for the nation's problems.

SUPER BARRIO TO THE RESCUE

Super Barrio Gómez first appeared on June 12, 1987, to lead a crowd of thousands to demand help from the government to rebuild their homes destroyed in the 1985 earthquake.[40] He has since become a Mexico City folk hero who makes the street his office. He often arrives in the barrio mobile, with his appearance announced by his own theme song "La Cumbia de Super Barrio." He is the symbol and spokesman for a grassroots organization that speaks out for the poor—especially on the subject of housing. Super Barrio assists individuals in qualifying for low-interest loans to rebuild or buy homes, and leads the fight against rent gouging.

Super Barrio emerged from the popular reaction to the 1985 earthquake. Four political activists created the Asamblea de Barrios (the Congress of Barrios) to aid those left homeless by the natural disaster. Other grassroots groups appeared as well, but the Asamblea became the most effective because of Super Barrio, who attracted newspaper, radio, and television coverage and whose appearance and bluster resonated with that of Mexico's tremendously popular professional wrestlers, especially the legendary El Santo, who built on the widespread popular images of comic book heroes.[41] Previous experience as the professional wrestler "the Black Prince" prepared Super Barrio for this role. His wrestling career ended with a back injury following his defeat by El Diablo.

Over the past seven years, Super Barrio Gómez, the masked hero, has organized five or six high-profile demonstrations a year that have resulted in the construction or rebuilding of more than two million low-cost government housing units, and government assistance in opening more than 5,000 individual bank accounts for persons trying to save money to purchase a home. Above all, a dialogue now exists between government officials and the poor. Confident that Super Barrio can help them, more than 160,000 persons have brought their housing problems to the Asamblea. They ask for housing to be made available at a reasonable price, for rent control, and for more government rental

Figure 12.6 Super Barrio, a former Mexican wrestler, now a spokesman for the poor, frequently meets with high government officials dressed in full costume. For many he is a comic book hero come to life. *Photo by Danny Turner.*

homes. When a landlord tries to evict a family, the family summons Super Barrio with a three-bottle-rocket signal, attracting neighbors who block the eviction. Someone then contacts Super Barrio, who rushes to the scene in the barrio mobile if it is running, or on a city bus. The call also alerts the news media who quickly appear to report the event. The caped hero claims he has prevented more than 1,200 evictions. Other efforts on behalf of housing for the poor have included leading fifty homeless families to the offices of the federal ministry of urban development and ecology, where they camped out for a week, until the agency agreed to consider them for low-interest home loans.

The campaign for the poor receives continuing publicity as Super Barrio performs periodic street melodramas. In a wrestling ring erected in a public square, the hero battles other masked wrestlers representing the nuclear industry ("Nucleosaurio"), or most often, the greedy landlord Catalino Creel (based on a popular soap opera's villainous landlady, Catalina Creel). These popular events consistently draw large crowds and receive widespread media coverage.

The life of this comic hero typifies that of many residents of the capital. While he was growing up, his family was twice evicted from their substandard home. He abandoned school after the elementary grades and began earning a living on the street by selling candy and cigarettes. The 1985 earthquake destroyed his family's home but created the opportunity for change. One morning as he started for work, ". . . a red-and-yellow light started flashing and a strong wind rushed in. . . . I was very afraid. But when the light diminished and the wind died down, I discovered myself dressed the way you see me now. And I heard a voice say, 'You are Super Barrio, the defender of the pobres, the poor tenants.'" He identifies with Robin Hood, who took from the rich to give to the poor, and Batman, who defended "Ciudad Gothica."

The barrio knight has not gone unchallenged. Some government officials decided to respond with a superhero, Super Pueblo, who challenged, contradicted, and taunted Super Barrio. Without public support, however, Super Pueblo quietly disappeared. Super Barrio continued to grow in popularity. Soon he led home seekers into government offices, the legislative chambers, and meetings with presidential aides. Despite an initial effort to make him remove his mask, for fifteen minutes he addressed the chamber of deputies, with his face still covered in red and gold. He called for cooperative action and urged the deputies to do more than give speeches and write plans. His address ended in shouts and applause from his followers and the deputies.

The campaign on behalf of everyday Mexicans has taken Super Barrio to the Mexico City exhibition in the Netherlands and to Los Angeles, California, where he appealed for better treatment of Mexican nationals. His effort to speak to the Los Angeles City Council ended when the *migra* (the Immigration and Naturalization Service, INS) arrived and demanded to see his papers—without pockets in his costume, he carried none. He then endured the experience shared by many of his countrymen; arrest by the INS, interrogation, and time in a holding cell until a Los Angeles lawyer could arrange for his release.

For all of his tawdry glitter and luster soiled by air pollution, and for all of his garish comedy and comic book solutions to real problems, Super Barrio personifies the volunteer, self-help organizations that emerged from the ruins of the 1985 earthquake. These groups meet with bureaucrats to discuss community needs and to develop government solutions. Beyond just talk, this interaction, known as *concertación*, has resulted in reasonable solutions to community problems. Super Barrio and the Asamblea have kept the dialogue alive since the days of the earthquake to emphasize the effectiveness of negotiation followed by action. Evaluating the impact of the man in the comic book costume, Asamblea activist Marco Rascón declared, ". . . Super Barrio creates a state of debate. His humor enables the government and the homeless to discuss their differences. He's good for everybody."

POLITICAL CHALLENGES AND REALISTIC CHANGES

The movement to broaden the right to vote in national elections culminated in 1973. The 1918 enabling legislation based on the 1917 Constitution provided the franchise to literate, married males at least eighteen years old and to literate, unmarried males at least twenty-one years old. In 1954, women gained the right to vote, and a 1975 law lowered the minimum voting age to eighteen, without regard to gender or marital status. The next step would be to allow honest elections.

Early reform efforts pertaining to representation of opposition parties in the congress culminated in 1964 with a system that gave the opposition between thirty and forty seats in the chamber of deputies, beyond what they might win in congressional district elections (these are called majority districts and each chooses a deputy to represent it). The seats were assigned based on percentages received in the national voting. During its life span, the opposition averaged about 17 percent of the deputies' seats and none in the senate. The system remained in place through 1976.

López Portillo's secretary of government Jesús Reyes Heroles introduced new election legislation in 1977 that increased the number of congressional districts to 300 and specified that an additional 100 seats be assigned to opposition parties through a complex mathematical system proportionately based on the national vote. Allocating all 100 seats to the opposition guaranteed that opponents of the PRI would hold a minimum of 25 percent of all seats. The reforms also allowed opposition parties greater access to the media. The impetus behind these changes withered when Reyes Heroles left his post. The effort of both reform efforts to create a plurinominal deputy system resulted in stabilizing opposition representation at 17 percent and 26 percent. In effect, the PRI froze its opposition at these levels.

De la Madrid introduced his revision of the election laws in 1986, and the first test of the charge occurred in 1988. The new code includes the following provisions: the majority party may never hold more than 70 percent of the seats in the chamber of deputies; the seats allotted on the basis of proportional voting will number 200 (an increase of 100); the party winning the greatest number of district seats will retain a simple majority in the entire chamber; this majority will be maintained by allotting sufficient proportional seats to establish an absolute majority in the chamber; and senate elections will be held on an alternating schedule (half of the seats face election every three years, instead of renewing the entire senate every six years.) This

1986 reform reduced the PRI's control of the deputies to 70 percent and diminished the importance of the districts. But the fact remains that in all of these reform efforts, the government allocates seats to the opposition, rather than the opposition winning its positions.

The declining legitimacy of the president, the government in general, and the PRI began to take its toll by the 1985 and 1986 elections. Although small parties on the left gained slightly, the most consistent opposition and greatest beneficiary of these trends was the National Action Party (Partido de Acción Nacional, PAN).[42]

THE 1988 ELECTION

The 1988 campaign for the presidency began its six-year renewal cycle in August 1987 with the introduction of six leading men from whom the president would choose his successor. The group included five cabinet members and the mayor of Mexico City. On October 4, 1988, Energy Secretary Alfredo del Mazo told reporters that the president had chosen Attorney General Sergio García Ramírez. Despite the leak to the press, two hours later the PRI's chairperson, Jorge de la Vega Domínguez, called a press conference and informed reporters that the choice was Carlos Salinas de Gortari. The políticos in the PRI reacted in dismay when the choice of Carlos Salinas de Gortari was announced. Labor leader Fidel Velázquez walked out of the press conference in protest. For the fourth straight time the party had chosen a technocrat with no experience as an elected official. Salinas had bureaucratic experience and a master's and doctoral degrees from Harvard University. He also had a reputation as a pinch-penny conservative, no doubt a reflection of the common perception of those from Monterrey being stingy.

The políticos fumed at the selection of Salinas, a representative of Mexico's young professionals. They blamed the technocrats for dragging the party further and further away from the people, thus holding them responsible for the PRI's mounting problems. The technocrats, however, supported de la Madrid's position that it was the políticos and their "old boyism" that created the economic and politic difficulties that plagued the nation since 1972. Still another group in the PRI decided that enough was enough. Led by Porfirio Muñoz Ledo, former labor secretary, party chairperson, and ambassador to the United Nations, and Cuauhtémoc Cárdenas, son of the revolutionary president, the group called itself the "Democratic Current." Opposed to de la Madrid's economic policy and his timid approach to political reform, they decided to attempt reforms within the party. Other PRI leaders quickly grew impatient with the constant criticism directed at the party by the Democratic Current, and in 1987, they revoked the membership of its two leaders.

Cárdenas, Muñoz Ledo, and other PRI dissidents responded by organizing the Democratic Front for National Reconstruction (FDN) and eventually selected Cárdenas as its presidential candidate. The FDN appeared too late to have its credentials legally recognized, but the Authentic Party of the Mexican Revolution (PARM), one of the PRI's tiny splinter parties, named Cárdenas as its presidential candidate to place him on the ballot.

Cárdenas, like his father, had served as governor of Michoacán, where he established his reputation as a reformer by cracking down on prostitution and excessive drinking of alcoholic beverages. His name, not his reputation, mattered. The legend of his namesake, the heroic defender of the Aztec Empire against Cortés, is taught in schools and honored by an elaborate statue at the intersection of Insurgentes and Reforma avenues erected during the Porfirian years, street names throughout the republic, and his image on the 50,000 peso bill. Moreover, the elder Cárdenas was remembered for his revolutionary concern for the ordinary Mexican and for the expropriation of foreign owned oil that remains intact today. Despite his historical name recognized, Mexicans wondered about his candidacy. Many, for example, did not understand the support he received from Joaquín "La Quina" Hernández Galicia, the infamous labor boss, and raised the specter that Cárdenas had ties to corrupt unions.[43]

The campaign focused on the role of mass media as never before. More than any previous presidential candidate, Salinas recognized the importance of public opinion and mass culture. Consequently, he relied heavily upon the head of social communication, a more powerful counterpart to the American presidential press secretary.[44] The PAN complained that Televisa, Mexico's private television network, slandered and ignored the opposition. In particular, PAN aimed charges at Jacobo Zabuludovsky, Mexico's Walter Cronkite, and his program *24 Horas*. The PAN alleged that 90 percent of the program's airtime devoted to the campaign consisted of reports on the activities of Carlos Salinas. A Televisa special program about the opposition superimposed footage of Mussolini and PAN candidate Manuel Clouthier, and another report associated Cuauhtémoc Cárdenas with images of Castro, Khrushchev, and Salvador Allende.[45]

In 1988 the low level of public esteem for the government and the PRI plummeted even further with the selection of Carlos Salinas de Gortari, the least popular of all of the preliminary candidates. These circumstances strengthened Cárdenas's widespread appeal among voters. The PARM candidate, according to official tallies, received

31.1 percent of the vote, the highest proportion ever won by an opposition presidential candidate. Salinas received only 50.7 percent, barely a simple majority, and the PAN standard bearer, Clouthier, 17 percent, the party's typical winning percentage in presidential elections. Contrary to the expectations of most pundits, the Left, not the Right, altered the election. The voters who had defected from the PRI since the 1982 presidential election cast their ballots for Cárdenas, not the PAN candidate.

Crucial for Mexico's political circumstances, the 1988 election took place under the 1986 reform law. The PRI needed to invoke the provision of the law that increased its representation so it would have a majority of seats in the chamber of deputies. The dominant party obtained only 233 district seats; it needs twenty-seven plurinominal seats to have a slight majority in the chamber of deputies.

Upon review, most observers believe Salinas indeed won the election, even taking into account large-scale corruption, but not with the 51 percent of the votes claimed by the party. The victory exacted a high price in electoral fraud and political manipulation. The president and his party made changes so these maneuvers will not be required again.

The PRI's response to its victory notwithstanding, the 1988 election had three effects that made the year a turning point. First, Cuauhtémoc Cárdenas, pushed out of the PRI, launched a major independent presidential challenge that encouraged opposition to the official party; second, the victory of numerous opposition candidates created the prospect that the national congress could become a vital branch of government; and third, the election campaign was so fraught with fraud and charges of fraud that it brought the presidency and the official party to a striking low, adding to its tottering legitimacy. All three developments made 1988 a political benchmark.

The significance of the 1988 presidential election has been obscured by the 1991 senate elections, where Cárdenas's party did not win a majority in a single state (including those it had dominated in 1988—Michoacán, México, Morelos, and the Federal District). The vote total for the PARM was nearly a third in the 1988 presidential election, declining to only 8 percent in the 1991 senate election.

The low level of respect for the new administration affected civil-military relations, forcing the new president to reconstitute the ruling coalition. In so doing, Salinas gave generals a greater role in implementing decisions. For example, in 1989, he bypassed the police and sent the armed forces to move against drug kingpin Miguel Angel Félix Gallardo. Again, troops were dispatched to break the strike at the Cananea mining property. In addition, the president assigned the armed forces to supervise local, state, and national elections.[46] The expanded enforcement and security roles of the armed forces gave rise to fears of a new politicization of the military.

Mexico's proximity to the United States also played a role in the presidential and senate elections. In 1988, the government became increasingly sensitive to charges from abroad of massive election fraud, especially in the U.S. media. And in 1991, the conduct of the Mexican elections came under scrutiny as the U.S. Congress debated the proposed North American Free Trade Agreement. The pluralization of Mexican politics appears permanent. As Delial Baer argues, "Two aspects of the 1980s democratic ferment are unlikely to be reversed. The first is the relatively greater importance of elections in the legitimation of power. The second are the more rigorous public expectations about the cleanliness of the electoral process."

The most important variables in determining the opposition's effectiveness in challenging the PRI are location, relations with the government, level of development, and urbanization. The location of opposition has some baffling characteristics: the seven states where the opposition has won at least 30 percent of the vote in presidential elections (1946, 1952, 1982, and 1988) are Baja California, the Federal District, Guanajuato, Jalisco, México, Michoacán, and Morelos. In the elections of 1991, the opposition in these states (with the exception of Jalisco and Morelos) won more than 40 percent of the vote, and in the Federal District and Baja California, the opposition actually outpolled the PRI. One reason the opposition has done well in these states is an economic one. Baja California, the Federal District, and México are among the six states with the highest per capita income in the nation. Since 1976, the PRI's total percentage of votes in high-income states (the northern states of the Californias, Chihuahua, Sonora, and Nuevo León, and México and the Federal District) has been much lower than its nationwide average.

The PRI is better organized in rural areas, and lower income states typically are Mexico's most agrarian. More educated Mexicans, who are more likely to vote for the opposition, tend to live in higher income states. In addition, fraud is less of a problem in urban centers than in the rural countryside.[47] Wage earners who represent a potentially important political force are the low-wage assembly plant workers in the border regions.

The Salinas administration continued to assert the importance of camarillas, "the cement of the political system." Like all recent ones, the president's cabinet had its roots in the Alemán presidency, which brought the professional civilian politician to power. Although many were surprised by Salinas's nomination, his rise to power followed a traditional and predictable path. For major economic cabinet positions, he selected technocrats with graduate degrees from leading foreign universities. In this case, Yale University predominates. Yale graduates include Secretary of Commerce Jaime Serra Puche, Secretary of Planning and Budgeting Ernesto Zedillo de León, and Secretary of Treasury Pedro Aspe, as well as Gustavo Petricioli, ambassador to the United States, and Miguel Mancera, director of the Bank of Mexico. For other cabinet positions, however, Salinas broke with this practice of choosing technocrats and turned to experienced politicians. Especially noteworthy was his choice of Fernando Gutiérrez Barrios as the secretary of interior, the first graduate of the national military academy to hold a nonmilitary cabinet position since Alfonso Corona del Rosal (today regarded as the leader of the dinosaurs, the Party group opposed to reforms) served as secretary of national properties and head of the Federal District under Díaz Ordaz. The appointment of Gutiérrez also created much stronger ties between Salinas and the military than his predecessor ever had.[48]

STAY-AT-HOME BRACEROS

In the borderlands, the controversial maquiladora program represents an analog of industry–labor developments under the proposed North American Free Trade Agreement. Primarily U.S.-owned, these assembly plants began operations in 1965 and have been criticized for contributing to Mexican labor dependency on U.S. companies and for taking jobs away from union workers in the United States. The number of plants grew quickly, and by 1984 there were 680 factories employing 184,400 workers. Like the earlier Bracero program, the maquilas pay wages much lower than what U.S. workers will accept. Despite criticism, the maquiladora program has been a qualified success; it has stimulated the Mexican side of the border economy and has provided a large number of jobs to women. Female maquiladora employees have the following characteristics: median age is twenty-five; more likely to have secondary education than other women their age, while the nonmaquiladora worker is more likely to have some vocational training; the majority are single; and are more likely to be migrants, but are primarily (55 percent) from a bordering state, rather than the core. A great number of the female workers migrate from within Chihuahua to the border, a finding not shown in earlier studies.

Although many women find their factory jobs alienate them from family expectations, they enjoy a regular paycheck and health insurance. They also experience a change in their relationships to men in their families. Some indicate that they would prefer a job more compatible with their role in, and obligations to, their families. When women leave a job in the maquiladoras, it is usually because of family obligations rather than personnel conflicts, transportation difficulties, or dislike for the job.

Critics of the maquiladoras claim that these factory jobs do not contribute in any way to women's commonly expressed desires for self-expression. They also cite health hazards. The assembly lines, however, do not seem to threaten family cohesion. It is generally a younger daughter who works in the plant, and not the main caregiver and nurturer. Many young women give their wages to their mothers, keeping only a small amount for themselves. Some women do become financially independent and therefore personally independent. That women assembly plant workers contribute an average 40 percent to household expenditures has a disruptive effect on their relationships with men in the patriarchal Mexican family. Nevertheless, these young women continue to act like other young women their age. They wear their good clothes under their smocks so they can socialize after work. They are perhaps a little more independent than others their age, but the family continues to exercise a great deal of control over

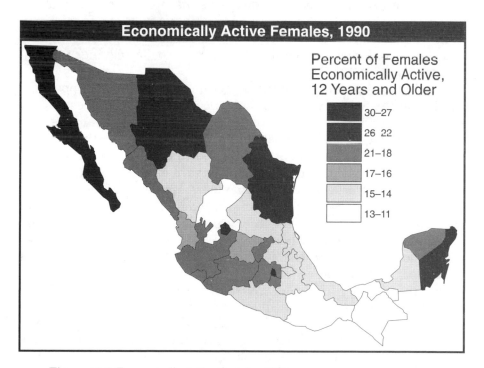

Figure 12.7 Economically Active Females, 1990.

them. Because interaction between men and women on the factory floor is limited, the large number of female employees has not significantly altered gender attitudes. Although most assembly line supervisors are female, generally women did not seek out these positions. Accepting a supervisory role moves the women out of the work group and creates suspicion about her association with management. At the same time, management, exclusively male, does not recognize the female supervisor as being part of the management team.

The most common reason women give for taking a job in the maquilas is to keep other family members in school and to enroll the family in the health care program (the whole family receives health insurance coverage). Generally these women also express a desire to have a higher level of consumption. A household has to have sufficient resources to enable one of the daughters to work in the maquila. For example, the family must be able to replace the woman at home and provide transportation. Despite the efforts of management to create a sense of loyalty or community among workers, few women have their identity wrapped up in their work. The mass media has a much greater impact on women in the borderlands. Telenovelas and situation comedies that frame television culture influence attitudes, consumer desires, and leisure interests. The bars that cater to maquila workers, for example, have fashion shows that feature evening gowns based on telenovela styles. The money maquila workers earn stimulates the economy on both sides of the border. Increased consumption and the desire for a more comfortable life come before savings for most of these workers.

As the prospect of a free trade agreement approached, opponents cited what they perceive as economic inequities in the proposal. They stressed the imminent loss of jobs for workers if U.S. companies set up plants in Mexico, where the per capita wage is one-seventh of that in the United States. Proponents responded that the agreement would serve as a major step, in the long run, toward eliminating the disparity, as Mexican workers become consumers. While real differences existed between what can be characterized as a rich nation and a poor one, there were nevertheless other converging problems, opportunities, and attitudes. The authors of the 1990–1991 World Values Survey of forty countries representing the spectrum of wealth and politics found that widespread concern about the environment had emerged in both countries during the 1980s. Moreover, they determined that many concerns crossed political and economic lines as well. These include availability of natural resources, production of foodstuffs, level of inflation, access to health care and adequate housing, and distribution of wealth. These issues reach beyond national borders and in many instances require multinational responses.

   If U.S. labor leaders and others distrust the motives of the U.S. government, many Mexicans have reservations about the North American Free Trade Agreement. Nevertheless, despite understandable reservations about the United States, according to a 1989 *Los Angeles Times* poll, 34 percent of Mexicans said that what they liked most about the United States was its "economic opportunities." Of course, NAFTA's goal is to extend these opportunities throughout the region. America's level of "culture" (15 percent) and "democracy" (14 percent) were admired as well, suggesting a strong foundation for the convergence implied in the treaty.[49]

TRANSBORDER NATIONALISM

Beginning in the twentieth century, new forms of Mexican self-identification appeared as a result of a changing perception of nationality and culture. Mexicans began to understand their identity as extending beyond national borders. At the same time immigration became and remains a contentious issue in the United States.

   Culturally, immigration is an element in many issues that confront the United States and Mexico. The "English Only" movement came about largely as a response to the rapid growth of the Hispanic

Figure 12.8 Virgin of Guadalupe mural at Ochoa and Seventh streets in south El Paso, Texas. The city's Junior League, Le Fe Clinics, and city representatives Tony Ponce and Jesús Terrazas sponsored the restoration of the mural in 1991 as a memorial to youths killed in gang violence. *Photo by Lisa M. Murillo.*

population and the visible immigration of Mexicans and Central Americans to the U.S. Southwest. Immigration, therefore, is perceived as a cultural threat. It becomes part of the debate on the local, state, and even national issues voters are eventually asked to decide. In Mexico, whole villages have become ghost towns as younger men and women leave for better opportunities in the United States. Their departure has serious cultural implications. Children are often left in the care of grandparents, or their father, altering the traditional family structure. Discouraged by the violence in American cities, many migrant Mexicans who brought their children to the United States have sent them home—along with their newly acquired American values, threatening the integrity of Mexican culture at the community level.

The issue of immigration has numerous implications, both subtle and obvious. The physical proximity of Mexico and the United States makes each country a prisoner, to some extent, of the other's domestic economic and political problems. Nevertheless, Mexico labors under a condition of some dependence on the United States. Mexico's political leaders must give careful consideration to domestic issues that have an impact on the bilateral relationship, as well as policy responses to them. The United States does not exercise veto power, directly, over Mexican politics, but its presence creates a permanent shadow over Mexico, a shadow that Mexican political leadership cannot ignore.[50]

FAMILY, CHURCH, AND SCHOOL

Optimism about the future of the Mexican people and Mexican culture can be drawn from the stability of the government created by the revolution. Despite major challenges in 1923, 1927, and 1929, the political leadership has survived. This record is unmatched by any Third World regime. The Mexican government surpasses in longevity those of Italy, Germany, and Japan.

Looking back over the lurching movement of the Mexican experience, how striking it is that Mexicans today express widespread respect for three institutions, not one of them a political or an administrative entity. Unlike the United States and Canada, where some governmental institutions received over 50 percent positive evaluation, Mexicans identified the family, church, and school as their most revered institutions. The first two are reminders of Mexico's colonial heritage, and the third is a product of the revolution (although it certainly was foreshadowed by Porfirian educational programs). The high regard for the Catholic Church may result from its autonomy and probably also reflects the respect that churchmen have earned for their actions. Parents, priests, and teachers are identified as the most

Figure 12.9 Winner of the "Miss Ciudad Obregón" (Sonora) beauty pageant (1943), Gloria Symanski, daughter of Elisa Romero Calderón and Manuel Yriarte Symanski. Selection process eventually resulted in the naming of "Miss Mexico." *Printed with permission, Research Collection, Annelisa Romero de MacLachlan.*

respected individuals in Mexico. Mexican attitudes toward education are important because the system is largely public, and a government team the elementary school textbooks writes. This is an area of government legitimacy and revolutionary achievement. Teachers have importance for another reason—they form the largest component, the National Teachers Union (SNTE) of the CTM, the official labor umbrella organization.

Mexicans regard themselves as being religious and more than eight out of ten report that they received religious training in their homes. Moreover, while the percentage of those who attend church services has declined since the turn of the century, the number of practicing Catholics remains quite high. In 1991, about 45 percent of Catholics reported that they attended Mass at least once a week, and another 14 percent to 19 percent go to Mass at least monthly. This commitment notwithstanding, the overwhelming majority of Mexicans oppose Church intervention in politics. Even those who regularly attend Mass reject the idea of political activity by the Church. President Salinas's initiative to allow priests to vote, to grant legal recognition to the Church, and to establish diplomatic relations with the Vatican was not a response to a groundswell of popular opinion, but rather reflected the president's own convictions. The conclusion must be made that Mexicans, while they are religious, do not allow the Church to affect their political behavior or commitment. It must be remembered that the Church does not speak with one voice. The Catholic Church in Mexico is decentralized to the diocesan level, and there are sixty-nine dioceses.[51]

Indicators of religiosity appear across the country. For example, some twenty million Mexicans responded enthusiastically with an outpouring of emotion when Pope John Paul II visited in 1979. Given the example of the Poles, who preferred their Pope over their premier, and the new role of reform-minded priests, especially in Brazil, Chile, and Central America, both the government and the PRI felt threatened. The era of inevitable alliance between Latin America's conservative states and the Church has ended. The Church in Mexico now has an active minority, spearheaded by the "red bishop" of Cuernavaca and the progressive bishop of San Cristóbal de las Casas, who argue that the masses deserve a better material fate now, not in the afterlife.

In state and local surveys throughout Mexico, the police consistently receive the lowest approval rating of any institution. They are perceived as being dishonest, often involved in criminal activities, and abusive of their authority, especially among lower income and rural groups. From another perspective, in a 1991 poll pertaining to confidence in public services, schools received the highest rating (67 percent), followed by medical services and then trash disposal. Again, the police came in last (24 percent).[52] Mexicans have maintained this low level of confidence over the past decade, while in contrast, in the United States during the 1980s, confidence in governmental services remained at a high level.[53]

Low ratings of the government notwithstanding, Mexicans expressed a favorable opinion of society and confidence in each other. The 1985 earthquake provided a good test case. Government relief efforts, or lack of, were heavily criticized, while neighborhood volunteers, who devoted days to the rescue effort, especially searching the rubble for survivors, inspired an esprit de corps among workers and popular pride at the local level. The earthquake left some 200,000 persons homeless. At first, the government proposed moving people to new housing projects outside the capital city, but barrio residents would not leave their neighborhood communities. Grassroots organizations sprung up across the city and successfully organized to effect a change in the relocation proposal. These volunteer groups united to force the government and the World Bank to reverse several programs, including housing relief plans, and to accelerate reconstruction programs.[54]

This increased confidence in one another on the part of Mexicans serves as a critical indicator of the potential for democratic political institutions that require high levels of personal trust. It seems then that individual Mexicans have been moving more quickly toward democratization than their institutions. This attitude (and confidence in the Salinas reforms) revealed itself clearly in the 1991 congressional elections, when 42 percent believed that the vote would be respected, compared with 23 percent who voiced the same confidence in the 1988 presidential fiasco. Moreover, since 1981, political participation has more than doubled, an increase that reflects changing attitudes among the younger generation and a portent for the future of a society in which teenagers and children make up over half of the population.[55]

An important indicator of a Mexican's involvement in society and politics comes from the level of individual participation in various organizations. As Larissa Lomnitz found shortly after World War II, few Mexicans join in organized activities. A little more than half (58 percent) belong to no organizations; church groups attract the greatest number (17.6 percent), followed by unions (10.3 percent), charities (7.8 percent), and educational or artistic organizations (4.1 percent). Only 2 percent of Mexicans in the late 1980s belonged to political organizations.[56]

After the northern elections in 1986, the clergy threatened to shut down masses if the government did not agree to recount votes. The state's archbishop, Adalberto Almeida, directed the campaign against voter fraud in Chihuahua. Although the Pope intervened to halt the bishop's threat, such public action by Church leaders, in direction violation of the Constitution, illustrated their political potential.

Nearly twice as many college graduates as nongraduates support the National Action Party (PAN). Little relationship exists between the PAN, the party of the right, and Catholicism. Survey data for the 1980s and early 1990s identify only a tiny group who attend Mass daily and belong to PAN. Those who express no religious belief are the strongest supporters of PAN and are weakest in their support of the PRI. Moreover, contrary to popular wisdom, studies reveal that women are no more committed to PAN than are men. The party ran its own presidential candidate for the first time in 1958 and since then has elected a candidate for every election except 1976, when it opted to protest the PRI monopoly and electoral fraud by withdrawing from the presidential contest. The PAN elected its first governor in Baja California in 1989. Its future strength seems to lie at the local and state levels rather than the national level, and especially in the north, as many small- and medium-sized businessmen press for an increased voice in partisan politics.

The only other major political voice in Mexico today is the Democratic Revolutionary Party (PRD). The PRD has a short history, although it built upon the foundations of smaller leftist parties that emerged during the 1970s. The party has found it difficult to maintain cohesion. Making the accusations of electoral fraud in 1991, many active supporters were physically threatened, injured, or killed. In fact, PRD members constitute the largest group of victims cited in national and international human rights commission reports. The party has been unable to transform its 1988 election success into grassroots labor and agrarian organizations.

Opposition political parties face another problem; they can challenge the PRI—but the PRI does not control the government. The government controls the PRI. To gain power, the opposition must control the government. The election process has remained essentially unchanged since its development in the 1940s. The potential presidential candidates somehow emerge during the last two years of a sexenio. They generally come from the presidential cabinet and quickly attract adherents from the bureaucracy and the party. The president ultimately names the candidate who will succeed him in office. In the recruitment process, the most important institution continues to be the university, as it has been since the time of Miguel Alemán. After only one generation, the university replaced the revolution as the training laboratory for political leaders. The federal bureaucracy, dominated by *chilangos* (residents of Mexico City), serves as another leading source of recruits. By the time of Echeverría, one-fourth of national political figures claimed Mexico City as their place of birth, while of the total population, only one in ten Mexicans were born there. The proportion of Mexico City natives in the federal bureaucracy has continued to grow. In the Salinas administration, one-half of those holding national office for the first time came from Mexico City. Moreover, between 1970 and 1988, one in eight national politicians was the offspring of a prominent political figure. Salinas's father, for example, had served in the cabinet in the 1960s. Considering extended family ties, between one-fifth and one-third of all national politicians came from prominent political families during these years.

Recent survey data reveal that Mexican women have yet to insist on their own liberation and to adopt nontraditional roles. Among female government officials between 1989 and 1991, twelve were legislators and five were executive branch office holders. Women have shown slightly different recruitment patterns. They have generally been recruited from the ranks of the party and bureaucracy, rather than from the university, since they have not, traditionally, achieved the same level of education as their male counterparts. Changes have occurred in the pattern. Cárdenas had no female cabinet officers; Avila

Camacho had one; López Portillo had nineteen. More women will occupy high-level government positions as they enter the university in larger numbers and become active in the personal political associations there.[57]

A unique Mexican political characteristic, essential to understanding the recruitment process, relies on the clique, or camarilla. The camarillas, formed on regional and family bases in the nineteenth century, then among revolutionary veterans, and, during the 1920s, among labor, agrarian, and student groups, have become the foundation of politics. Cárdenas promoted veterans and also turned to labor and agrarian camarillas, while Alemán made the university camarilla preeminent. The camarillas of these two presidents have exerted long-term influence on the shape of Mexican politics. Cárdenas's personal following spawned four generations of camarillas, who held at least 144 national offices, with his most important disciple, of course, his son Cuauhtémoc. Historically, a university education (especially from UNAM), urban birthplace (especially Mexico City), a career in national politics and the federal bureaucracy, and a law degree and entrance into public service at a young age have been the prerequisites for a high-level national office.

This profile, however, has begun to change in recent years. Seventy percent of high-level officials in the Salinas administration received graduate training, and many have doctoral degrees. Graduate study outside of the country, usually in the United States, has become more common. Also, and perhaps most important, economics has replaced law as the most popular discipline. Salinas became the first Mexican president with an economics degree. Moreover, study at a private university has become more important than a public education to aspiring políticos.

The most important groups in the structure remain the military, the Catholic Church, business, organized labor, and intellectuals. In contrast to the military in the rest of Latin America, where it intervened politically and seized power in the 1970s and 1980s, the Mexican military forms a part of the government apparatus, within which it operates primarily as an internal police force, devoted to national security rather than national defense. Civilian control of the military can be readily demonstrated in the system of promotions. Promotions of career military officers above the rank of colonel require action by the president with the approval of the senate. In the early 1950s, the senate on occasion actually disapproved of, as an abuse of presidential authority, the promotion of officers who had not completed the required time in grade according to military law.[58]

Nongovernmental organizations function as informal channels of information and influence in the Mexican political system. Of these,

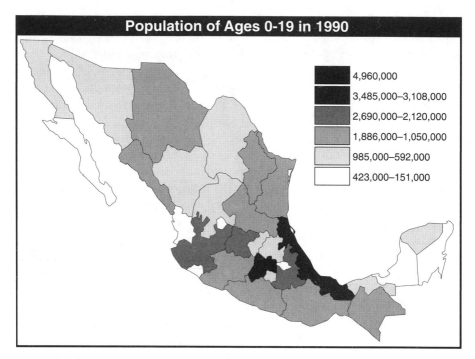

Figure 12.10 Population of Ages 0–19 in 1990.

the most important are business organizations. Businessmen created the Businessman's Coordinating Council (CCE), but this group does not exercise much political influence. A far more important organization is the semisecret Mexican Council of Businessmen (CMHN), a group of some thirty prominent capitalists who meet frequently with cabinet members and the president himself, to not only deliver collective demands but to deliver individual requests.

The labor movement, dating to the 1920s, achieved its greatest expansion during the 1930s, when membership increased from 5.6 percent to 15.4 percent of the economically active workforce. Labor groups have not increased in percentage terms since 1940, and by 1970, the number of members began to decline. The largest group, the teachers union (SNTE), organized partial strikes, meetings, marches, and demonstrations to express their demands.

Another influential group within Mexican society are the intellectuals. They appear prominently in government, academia, and print media, and unlike their counterparts in the United States, Mexican intellectuals have a long history of employment in public life, as ministry officials, cabinet members, governors, and party leaders. They express their opinions regularly in the print media, often establishing magazines as outlets for their writing. Intellectuals pay particular attention to those executive actions that indicate presidential character and the direction of a presidential administration.

Establishing a major precedent, Salinas intervened in state politics when he removed from office the newly elected governor of San Luis Potosí in 1991. He appointed his former mentor and majority leader in the 1988–1990 legislature, Gonzalo Martínez Corbala, as interim governor, a difficult assignment requiring superior negotiating skills.[59] The PRI leadership had little role in this or any other major decisions of the regime. The president centralized decision making and, as economic problems have overshadowed other issues, the influence of the economic cabinet expanded over that of party leaders.

For the heirs to the miracle and the revolution, the quality of life in Mexico City itself has become a major issue. Home to more than a fifth (some 20 million people) of the total population, it suffers from the world's worst air pollution. Atmospheric contamination rose approximately 50 percent in 1979 alone. The automobile is the major culprit. Moreover, drivers endure traffic far worse than anywhere in the United States, despite the efficiency and convenience of the metropolitan subway system, which moves some two million passengers daily.[60] In 1992, to deal with Mexico City's deteriorating condition, the government imposed a system (based on license plate numbers) to control the number of cars in the capital. The publicity campaign for the "One Day without a Car" program quickly provoked sarcastic variations of the slogan, such as "One Day without the Revolution."

REVOLUTION-WEARY NORTH

During the 1980s, as an aftereffect of the collapse of the Mexican miracle, the decline of government influence owing to widespread corruption, and the recovery from the earlier revanchist campaign, northerners renewed their challenge to the government. The return of northern regionalism built on the developments of the early 1970s, noted earlier, such as Echeverría's campaign to become a neopopulist. Northerners interpreted this as Marxist posturing and claptrap. Moreover, they saw Echeverría's expropriation of northern lands as a naked power play to undercut their economic power. When López Portillo nationalized the banking system in the midst of the economic crisis, the northerners felt totally alienated from the ruling administration. The crisis of the early 1980s reignited historic antagonism between the regions. Northerners blamed the politicians from Mexico City for the economic collapse, and their own rapid recovery in 1986 inspired northern insolence.

The resurgent politics reflected the north's prospering economy, confident society, and hostility to such a new programs as the *impuesto de valor adicional* (IVA), or value-added tax of 6 percent to 20 percent. Northerners saw the tax revenue go south, never to return in the form of any programs for their states. All along the border, *Norteños* complained that their value-added taxes subsidized Mexico City's massive transportation system, especially the modern subway with its extremely low fares. The first political evidence of the northerner's resolve came in the 1982 elections, when record numbers of voters participated, resulting in victories for the PAN presidential candidate in several towns. Voters responded to opposition parties and to the nonpartisan efforts of the Asociación Cívica Feminina (The Women's Civic Association), organized in September 1982 to encourage female participation in the voting process. This campaign set the stage for local elections in 1983. The political challenge benefited from the commitment of PRI governor Oscar Ornelas Kuchle to honest elections, which immediately resulted in a confrontation with CTM labor boss Fidel Velázquez. The PAN won municipal victories across the state and in the towns of Delicias, Meoqui, Hidalgo del Parral, Camargo, and Casas Grandes, among others; the dramatic win came

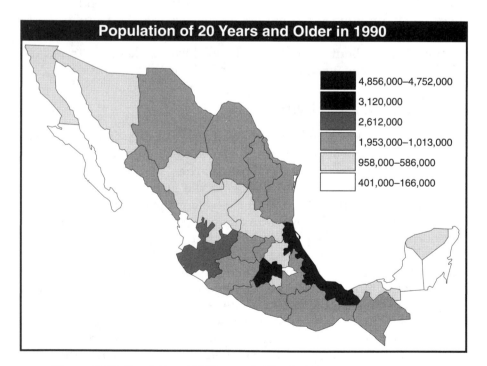

Figure 12.11 Population of 20 Years and Older in 1990.

in the victory of Francisco Barrios Terrazas as mayor of Ciudad Juárez. Other opposition parties claimed victory in Cuauhtémoc, Ignacio Zaragoza, and Gómez Farías.[61] The municipal results in Chihuahua provoked stern reaction within the official party. Veláquez held the state governor responsible for the defeat of his PRI candidates and began to arrange for the removal of Ornelas in 1985, as the official party worked to ensure 1986 state electoral victories, particularly in gubernatorial races.

The PAN retaliated with a strategy of civil disobedience. Party members defaced one-thousand-peso notes with the words "Respect for the Vote," covered license plates, and refused to pay utility bills. The PRI's representative, Fernando Baeza, won the governorship by (officially) a two to one margin over his PAN opponent. The PAN members launched hunger strikes, blocked the Pan American Highway south of Juárez, and occupied the Cordoba international bridge between Juárez and El Paso, Texas. The action disrupted the Juárez economy to the point that PAN leaders altered their tactics and took their case across the border.

The actions of U.S. Senator Jesse Helms served as a red herring, diverting attention from the understandable interest in the Chihuahua elections on the part of five other senators from states with large Hispanic populations. These senators knew that, according to estimates, one in every two Mexicans in the United States comes from Chihuahua. During the summer of 1985, Helms blustered about U.S. intervention to guarantee free elections in Chihuahua and to halt the drug trafficking. His colleagues, including Dennis DeConcini, a Democrat from Arizona, wanted the Senate to request formally that President de la Madrid nullify Chihuahua's elections. Also during the summer seven leading PAN officials from Chihuahua unsuccessfully sought political asylum in the United States. The PAN demonstrators traveled to New York City to make their case during de la Madrid's visit to the city and moved to present their charges of fraud to the Organization of American States.

The voices of outrage against the 1986 elections soon included those of other political parties and Chihuahua's bishops, but increasingly the opposition to the PRI was recast as northern antagonism toward the capital city. The state's bustling economy, booming population growth, and regional arrogance reinforced the political opposition to the PRI. Expressions of regional jingoism appeared on bumper stickers and public walls in messages such as "Chilangos go home" and "I am a barbarian of the north.[62] Such attitudes also accounted in part for the 1989 election of opposition Governor Ernesto Ruffo in Baja California Norte and the gubernatorial victory of PAN candidate Francisco Barrio Terrazas, former mayor of Ciudad Juárez, in Chihuahua.

POLITICAL CRISIS

The northern bishops failed in their efforts to overturn the 1986 elections in Chihuahua. But these state elections mobilized the Mexican episcopate who began to advocate civic responsibility and fair elections to the faithful in their dioceses. The bishops expressed an unequivocal position against electoral fraud and human rights abuses. The elections in Chihuahua turned church leaders into a powerful ally of those demanding a democratic opening in the political system.

As a result of the general political crisis incited by disputed elections and the resurgence of the north (often through the PAN), the administration had no choice but to discard some revolutionary rhetoric and programs, not just for a day, but for good. The agrarian programs had done little to resolve actual food shortages and raised the specter of even greater problems in providing corn and beans for Mexicans. The restrictions on the civil rights of churchmen served simply to aggravate old wounds that need not be reopened. Other aspects of the hallowed revolutionary myth needed revision, not the least of which made hostility toward the United States an unwritten tenet of foreign policy. The possibility of a North American Free Trade Agreement dismissed this hoary attitude.

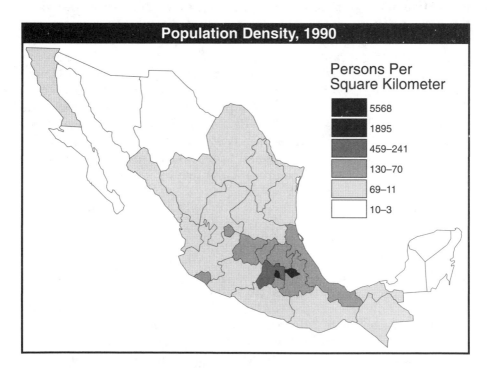

Figure 12.12 Population Density, 1990.

Those who described the Salinas regime as nothing more than the echo of the Porfirian era, however, ignored several differences. The PRI uses "a smaller stick and a larger carrot than the Porfiriato did." This means that the government relied less on repression, exclusion, and narrow elitism. The peasants and workers fared better than did their ancestors at the turn of the century. The middle class had grown significantly and enjoyed significant economic opportunity, while the prospect for both social and political mobility for all Mexicans improved. The Mexican revolution succeeded in replacing the old oligarchy with a much more broadly based ruling elite. Popular participation in the formulation of government policy, such as local development and community education, continued to rise. Workers formed a major institutionalized component of the political system. The new political order rested on civilians who were educated, patriotic Mexicans.

Mexico experienced a cultural revolution in the twentieth century. With roots in nineteenth-century expressions of nationalism, Mexican elite and popular culture incorporated elements from the United States and Europe but with a Mexican twist. The revolution reduced the overtly European attitude of the Díaz regime, nourished Mexico's indigenous roots, and set in motion the movement back to the United States orientation of the pre-Porfirian Liberals.[63]

The crisis in the political system since the miracle years has been explained in several ways. Alan Riding, correspondent for *The New York Times*, believed that the presidential system combined a "ritualistic sense of hierarchy with an enormous capacity to negotiate." Since 1970 he found that the "system has ignored its own rules of pragmatism, reflecting the caprices of the President rather than the natural dynamics of society, the country has become less stable. . . . For the system to work, then, the President can enjoy absolute power so long as he does not wield it absolutely."[64]

The actions of President Salinas suggested, on the other hand, that he and his advisers had decided that the revolution had indeed passed and that even revolutionary rhetoric had become counterproductive to the kind of programs Mexico needed to adopt and the reforms it had to undertake. The Cárdenas regime abandoned the revolution as being inappropriate to the needs of the Mexican people in 1937; the Salinas administration began to discard the revolutionary rhetoric. This action offered two significant opportunities to the Mexican people: (1) to honor the revolution for what it was and what it achieved and (2) to free the Salinas regime and its successors from the need to continue an inappropriate revolutionary rhetoric that only reinforced a deepening dichotomy between official pronouncements and actions. The heritage of the revolution had become a part of the culture of the Mexican people, but it was only a part.

RECOGNIZING THE END OF THE REVOLUTION

The Salinas administration, in a series of remarkable decisions in 1991 and 1992, implemented several constitutional reforms, some essential for the national economy and others indicative of the new political era. Nothing signified the Salinas government's departure from longstanding revolutionary rhetoric more clearly than the constitutional changes that he initiated. Of these, virtually no public attention focused on what arguably represents the most dramatic change. The Salinas government redefined national identity. Revolutionary programs promoting and glorying the Mexican as an ethnic synthesis, the Mestizo, once dominated revolutionary statements and programs. The Salinas government abruptly abandoned the mestizo identity with a revision of article 4 of the national constitution. The new article redefined Mexicans as a people with "a pluricultural composition, sustained originally in its indigenous population." Salinas also altered the constitutional restrictions on the Roman Catholic Church, that represented the government's victory in which a century-long church-state struggle. The revisions to article 3 allowed the church to hold public celebrations and bring foreign priests to Mexico, and most dramatically to operate its own school and to own property. Salinas and Pope John Paul II also agreed to restore Mexican-Vatican diplomatic relations that had been broken since the Liberals came to power in the 1860s.

In an impressive departure from revolutionary rhetoric, Salinas proposed on November 7, 1991, to amend the land provision (article 27) of the 1917 Constitution. Abandoning a government program that had been established some seventy-four years earlier represented an entirely new direction in policy toward the countryside. The policy would not only permit but also encourage private ownership of the previously sacrosanct community-owned ejido properties. His declaration affected half of Mexico's arable lands held by 3.1 million persons in 28,000 ejidos. The president formally withdrew government commitment to land distribution first contained in Carranza's 1915 decree. To some extent, the action simply ratified some long-standing practices (e.g., renting ejidal lands), but its more striking provisions constituted a bold presidential move. The nearly unanimous congressional support for the initiative, even among the opposition, demonstrated widespread recognition that the stagnant agricultural sector needed to modernize.

The resulting enabling legislation ended the government's constitutional obligation to continue redistributing land, assured private owners that they could make capital improvements without fear of reclassification of the property (in the past, reclassification had implications for the land's redistribution), and created new agrarian tribunals to settle disputes between private and ejidal owners rather than requiring the intervention of the national agrarian ministry. The legislation gave ejidatarios the right to sell, rent, sharecrop, or mortgage their land parcels as collateral for loans (if two-thirds of the ejido membership agreed). They no longer had to work their own land. To prevent excessive concentration of land, the government continued to limit property size. One goal of these changes was to open ejido lands to as much as 49 percent foreign investment.

The new law acknowledged what agrarian and political experts had claimed since 1986—that the ejido system was dead. Moreover, this constituted an effort to end illegal, informal, and clandestine practices by ejido owners. It also reflected the conviction of many technocrats that Mexico must reduce the more than two million subsistence corn growers and move them into urban-industrial and service employment. With the new law, experts anticipated a 16 percent to 26 percent reduction in the population engaged in agriculture over the next decade. How the Salinas government expected to implement the legislation remained vague, perhaps because the strategy rested almost exclusively on the success of the Solidarity program and the outcome of debate on the North American Free Trade Alliance.[65]

SOLIDARITY

Clearly, Salinas had undertaken an effort to break with the labyrinthine bureaucracy that handicapped the national government by empowering the individual on the local level—once the dream of such revolutionaries as Madero. The model for what one person can accomplish working through local groups was Poland's Solidarity movement. The Salinas government created a National Solidarity program of its own called El Programa Nacional de Solidaridad (Pronasol). The president's announcement of the initiative on December 2, 1988, his second day in office, was his first official presidential act. Shortly afterward, he declared that the targets of the program were the poorest Mexicans, including indigenous groups, inhabitants of the arid regions, and squatter settlers in the cities, and that the proposal would concentrate on health, education, nutrition, housing, and employment projects. Intended as government policy to harness economic growth for social equity, an essential by-product of the initiative was the construction of political consensus. No one, not even the most ardent supporters, predicted the positive popular reaction. The presidential program that abandoned the emphasis on parastate economic growth, without returning to neo-liberal government deregulation, touched a responsive chord within the general population. The program's appeal stemmed from its recognition that local-level groups could best rally community resources to deal with the economic and social dislocations that followed the collapse of the miracle, especially after the peso devaluation of 1982.

The grassroots Solidarity program rested on several principles: (1) the need for a closer relationship between the state, society, and the economy; (2) the promotion of decentralized politics; (3) the implementation of a social program at the community level that built upon mutual aid systems common among indigenous, rural communities, and those in urban neighborhoods; (4) the creation of new programs for social betterment; and (5) the adoption of qualitative assessments of government spending. Pronasol and its 80,000 local committees have given a new life to community groups, enabling them to select improvements that meet their own needs. At the same time, it should be noted that Solidarity groups had to enroll their members in the PRI before they had any chance of receiving federal funding for local projects. At its best, this program provided a structure for community negotiations and a means of access to government programs. It also supplied a mechanism to obtain national funding for local projects.[66]

THE NORTH AMERICAN FREE TRADE AGREEMENT

The North American Free Trade Agreement (NAFTA) received governmental endorsement on August 12, 1992, when representatives of Mexico, the United States, and Canada signed the 2,000-page agreement. Although the three nations had to approve it formally, the signing of the agreement after two years of negotiations indicated recognition of the cultural and economic convergence in North America. The treaty creates a market of some 360 million people, with an estimated $6 trillion in production. The treaty raised many as yet unresolved issues, such as differences in environmental protection laws and the level of their enforcement in the three countries. In the United States, opposition focused on the potential loss of U.S. jobs to Mexico, where wages are much lower. Mexico in turn worried that its entrepreneurs would be overwhelmed and put out of business by U.S. companies.

Predictably, most of the optimism about the free trade agreement came from the border region. Those who support the treaty believe that it will stimulate trade across the three-nation region. An end to Mexico's tariff barriers should permit increased U.S. sales in Mexico (including the products of the maquiladoras).[67] Mexicans anticipate the growth of industry, greater ability to acquire industrial technology,

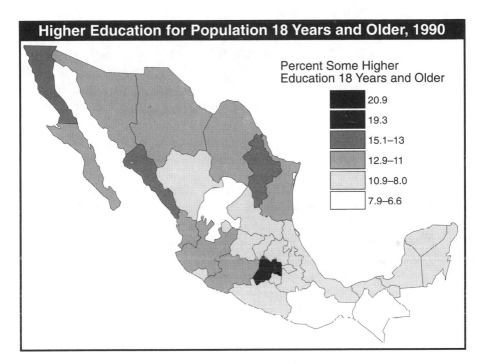

Figure 12.13 Higher Education for Population 18 Years and Older, 1990.

and dramatic expansion of jobs. To obtain the November 1993 ratification in the United States, President Clinton insisted that the Salinas government negotiate on issues of health, environmental protection, and labor.

Meanwhile, the convergence of Mexican and U.S. economic interests was most dramatically evident in the field of marketing. Wal-Mart and a Mexican counterpart, CIFRA, S.A., opened the first Club Aurrera, a Mexican Sam's Wholesale Club, a warehouse market in Mexico City that sells goods in bulk for about one-fifth of their Mexico City prices; a second store opened in February 1992. Other cooperative marketing enterprises have been negotiated in the field of insurance (Aetna Life and Casualty and VAMSA), food and beverages (in October 1991, Pepsico, Inc. acquired an 80 percent interest in Empresas Gameas, parent company of Mexico's largest cookie maker), financial services (Banco Nacional de México [Banamex] and American Express have jointly begun to issue "Gold" credit cards), oil (Houston's Triton USA became the first foreign company to be granted drilling leases since 1938), and many of the fast food chains, including Taco Bell, now have Mexican outlets.[68] One major challenge to this economic integration came on January 1, 1994, the day NAFTA went into effect.

ZAPATISTAS IN CHIAPAS AND THE PRESIDENTIAL ELECTION

On New Year's Day, 1994, the Zapatista Army of National Liberation (EZLN), a movement of indigenous guerrillas, attacked army posts around San Cristóbal de las Casas, Chiapas, and seized several communities in the region. Salinas responded with military force, but the reaction of both domestic and international media representatives excoriating the troops for excessive force mobilized Mexican and foreign public opinion against the government policy. The EZLN's spokesperson, calling himself Subcomandante Marcos, scholarly appearing with his pipe and philosophical sounding in his statements, quickly became a media celebrity—in newspapers, on television, and on the Worldwide Web.

Marcos and the EZLN demanded recognition of indigenous peoples and programs to aid the nation's indigent. The Zapatistas wanted autonomy from government, increased spending on education and health, and the redistribution of agricultural lands. This confrontation between the guerrillas and the soldiers quickly shifted to negotiations, mediated by the Catholic Church. Government officials, urban Mexicans, and foreigners also expressed shock at the sudden appearance of the EZLN and the demands for recognition of indigenous peoples. Yet, programs addressing the indigenous had waxed and waned throughout the decades after the outbreak of the revolution in 1910. Most dramatically, during the Cárdenas presidency the government promoted a series of indigenous congresses, beginning with the Primer Congreso Regional Indígena (the First Regional Indigenous Congress) held in Ixmilquilpan, Hidalgo and established the Departmento de Asuntos Indígenas (the Department of Indigenous Affairs) that survived until the end of 1946. Other important expressions of indigenous cultures sporadically emerged, such as the Congress of Indigenous Peoples in 1972. These expressions of both national and grassroots concern with indigenous issues and peoples should have obviated any surprise with the appearance of the EZLN, but they did not.

The EZLN drew national attention, in the first months of 1994, away from the presidential election. That changed dramatically on May 23, 1994, with the assassination in Tijuana, Baja California, of PRI candidate Luis Donaldo Colosio. Many believed the assassination and the Chiapas revolt were the first shocks of widespread that would overturn the government or provoke a military overthrow of the administration. Colosio's replacement as presidential candidate was Ernesto Zedillo. The party, already deeply divided, argued over this choice that many regarded as a lackluster technocrat. The candidate ignored the dissident voices in his party and called for the decentralization of administration, reduction of presidential authority, and strengthening the judicial and legislative branches of government.

The campaign featured Mexico's inaugural presidential debate on May 12, 1994, before a television audience estimated at 30 million. The television cameras surprised everyone, and the popularity of each candidate changed. The PAN candidate, the charismatic congressman Diego Fernández de Cevallos, overwhelmed both the PRI candidate Zedillo, who tried to appear statesmanlike, but seemed stiff and dull, and completely disconcerted PRD candidate Cuauhtémoc Cárdenas by attacking his record as a state governor. Polls after the debate showed that Fernández had a slight lead over Zedillo, and Cárdenas plunged to a distant third—from which he never recovered.

Zedillo and the PRI nevertheless won the election. Voters, unnerved by national instability, chose the devil they knew (the PRI) over the devil they did not know (the PAN) in a close election in which the victor received only slightly over 50 percent of the votes cast. The new president took office as the last of the purely technocratic-bureaucratic PRI selections. He witnessed the creation of vastly new political circumstances; electoral changes no longer guaranteed the winning party a majority in Congress, and the Federal Electoral Institute (IFE), with eleven independent citizens as members, was selected to oversee elections. The PRI acted as well in 1996, taking a slap at both Zedillo and Salinas, requiring that all future party candidates for the presidency must have won an elective office and must have served in a party office as well. These party reformers attacked the technocrats who had been ruling the country.

The new president had greater immediate concerns than the political system. A crisis of finances and corruption challenged the chief executive. Just before Salinas left office, in September 1994, José Francisco Ruiz Massieu, the PRI secretary general and former brother-in-law of President Salinas, had been assassinated. Subsequently, the president's brother, Raúl Salinas, had been arrested for inspiring the assassination and for laundering millions in drug monies. The investigation of both the Colosio and the Ruiz Massieu murders soon led to the high offices of the Salinas administration. The efforts to trace drug and protection money also reached into major government positions. Out of office, Salinas soon fled the country for the United States, Canada, and Ireland. He remained in exile, as stories of his association with corruption and allegations of his peculation mounted.

Worse for Zedillo, on December 1, 1994, the administration faced a serious run on the peso, leading to extraordinary levels of capital flight and domestic financial crisis. Foreign investors and Mexican capitalists withdrew billions of dollars from the economy, sending Mexico into a nosedive. The situation required the joint financial intervention of the United States and the World Bank to stabilize the currency. President Bill Clinton used his executive powers to create an emergency rescue package of $50 billion to stabilize the currency. But this assistance came at the high cost of a severe austerity program.

By the end of 1995, Zedillo and his advisors faced a negative economic growth rate and a rise in inflation of 50 percent. The angry public charged that many individual capitalists were the direct beneficiaries of the reprivatization program, while ordinary people endured the loss of jobs, a huge increase in interest rates on bank loans, and numerous bankruptcies. The austerity strategy did reduce inflation, restore stability to the peso, and strengthen banks, but only after two years of economic deprivation for most Mexicans, which had an enormous political price for Zedillo's presidential popularity.

Life deteriorated for the great majority of Mexicans. A crime wave, with an estimated increase of 20 percent of violent crime in Mexico City, swept the nation. Crime became the preoccupation of the general public, who saw it as an indication that order and authority had broken down. Mexicans also experienced unemployment at unprecedented levels, with over one million layoffs. These problems were compounded by a public health crisis in which the nation endured epidemics of cholera and dengue fever. Even more serious was widespread malnutrition. The United Nations agency UNICEF ranked Mexico with Ethiopia, Kenya, and Nigeria in terms of nutrition—only nations at war had worse malnutrition. Finally, Mexicans felt the constant abrasion of the drug culture on their society; the narco-traffic brought increased violence and corruption to all areas of Mexico.[69]

"NADA PERSONAL"

Ordinary Mexicans have responded to the crisis, worse than the Great Depression of 1929–1930, in a variety of ways. A few have turned to insurgencies such as the EZLN and the Popular Revolutionary Army (ERP). Many more joined "El Barzón"—the national movement that refuses to pay outrageous interest charges on loans and mortgages by withholding payments. Others have voted against the PRI, so that in the near future, an opposition party will govern more than half of all Mexicans at the local or state level.

Moreover, while official investigations of murders and corruption attributed to officials of the Salinas administration appear stalled, the acrid national humor tried and convicted the former president, his brother, and others in the streets. When sensational stories from northern Mexico reported the activities of a bat, reputedly exposed to nuclear radiation, which killed and sucked out all of the blood of ranch animals, especially goats, the public developed great interest in this "chupacabra." Vendors quickly began selling T-shirts, models, pictures, and comic books of this "chupacabra," and many of the images showed the bat with a Salinas face (especially emphasizing his ears). On almost any downtown street corner, vendors also sold Salinas masks, Salinas rats, and an array of sarcastic Salinas items, none more biting than the chupacabras.[70]

The disrespect Salinas brought to the presidency and his brother brought to government officials resulted in widespread criticism of them and all public institutions. Even television soap operas have been openly critical of prominent political figures. The hugely popular "Nada Personal" opened with a political assassination reminiscent of the 1994 assassination of Ruiz Massieu. This telenovela featured a love story against themes of government corruption and political assassination, drawn from the daily newspapers. A favorite game over

Figure 12.14 The Alamo movie theater on the west side of San Antonio, Texas. *Printed with permission, Russell Lee Photograph Collection, Center for American History, University of Texas at Austin.*

morning coffee in many Mexico City offices was to identify the actual politicians in the previous evening's show. "Nada Personal" inspired a new generation of telenovelas that do not hesitate to feature previously sacrosanct politicians. The shows include "Lagunilla," after the barrio in Mexico City, "Tijuana," filmed on location near the international fence, and "Las Hijos de Nadie," (No One's Children). For President Zedillo, the public injunction based on these television programs was to restore some dignity to the government.

NOTES

1. Story, *Mexican Ruling Party*; pp. 2–3.
2. Pansters, *Politics and Power*, p. 187, n. 21.
3. David E. Lorey and Aída Mostkoff-Linares, "Mexico's 'Lost Decade,' 1980–1990: Evidence on Class Structure and Professional Employment from the 1990 Census," in James W. Wilkie, Carlos Alberto Contreras, and Christof Anders Weber, eds., *Statistical Abstract of Latin America*, vol. 30, part 2 (Los Angeles: UCLA Latin American Center Publications, 1993); Camp, Politics in Mexico, p. 10.
4. Camp, *Politics in Mexico*, pp. 231–32.
5. The clearest statement of this malaise was the belief that the individual could do nothing to influence things in society; this attitude was held by 81 percent of the lower and poorly educated segments of the population of Jalapa, Veracruz, in the 1970s. See Richard R. Fagen and William S. Tuohy, *Politics and Privilege in Mexico City* (Stanford: Stanford University Press, 1972), p. 117. No doubt it increased as Mexicans entered the "Lost Decade."
6. Rafael Bernal, *El complot mongol* (México: Joaquín Mortiz, 1975), p. 191; *licenciadillo* is a colloquialism referring to ridiculous little bureaucrats. Also see Riding, *Distant Neighbors*, p. 107.
7. Reavis, *Conversations with Moctezuma*, p. 34, identifies this period as the "year of the gentlemen." But a more persuasive discussion can be found in Stephen D. Morris, *Corruption and Politics in Contemporary Mexico* (Tuscaloosa: University of Alabama Press, 1991), pp. 85–86.
8. Edward J. Williams, "The Resurgent North and Contemporary Mexican Regionalism," *Mexican Studies/Estudios Mexicans* 6: 2 (summer 1990), pp. 299–323; Manuel A. Machado, *Barbarians of the North: Modern Chihuahua and the Mexican Political System* (Austin: Eakin Press, 1992).
9. Riding, *Distant Neighbors*, p. 21.
10. Charles L. Davis and Kenneth M. Coleman, "Structural Determinants of Working-Class Politicization: The Role of Independent Unions of Mexico," *Mexican Studies/Estudios Mexicanos* 5: 1 (winter 1989), pp. 89–125.
11. Larissa Lomnitz places 70 percent of the population below the poverty line in rural Mexico. See *Networks and Marginality: Life in a Mexican Shantytown*, translated by Cinna Lomnitz (New York: Academic Press, 1977), pp. 18, 70.
12. Vélez-Ibañez, *Rituals of Marginality*, pp. 17–32.
13. This discussion of Cerrada del Cóndor is derived from Lomnitz *Networks and Marginality*, passim.
14. Lomnitz, *Networks of Marginality*. These patterns are developed and then confirmed by *compadrazgo*, rather than the other way around, as many have assumed. In fact, Lomnitz concluded that "... *compadrazgo* as practiced in

Cerrada del Cóndor is an example of a ritual institution harnessed to the needs of a new social situation. The formal duties of a *compadre* are mostly of a ritual nature; they are definitely shrinking in importance besides the informal duties as contained in the prevailing ideology of mutual assistance" (p. 173).

15. Lomnitz, *Networks of Marginality*, pp. 108–81.
16. Levy and Székely, *Paradoxes of Stability*, pp. 88–89, 94–99.
17. Richard Cole, "The Mexican Press System: Aspects of Growth, Control and Ownership," *Gazette* 21 (1975), pp. 65–81.
18. For the discussion of the arrest of the alleged murderer of Buendia, see later note. Stephen F. Jackson, "Killing of Mexican Journalists," and "Journalism in Mexico," *Editor & Publisher*, October 7 and 14, 1989; William Stockton, "Journalism in Mexico Can Turn into a Risky Craft," *The New York Times*, July 23, 1986, I, 2; Cheryl Allen, "Una Prensa . . . ¿Libre?; Freedom of the Press in Mexico from 1968 to 1991," (Honors Essay, School of Journalism and Mass Communication, University of North Carolina, 1992).
19. Reavis, *Conversations with Moctezuma*, pp. 212–13.
20. Harold E. Hinds Jr., "Kaliman: Mexico's Most Popular Superhero," *Studies in Latin American Popular Culture* 4 (1985), pp. 27–42.
21. Camp, Generals in the Palacio, pp. 408, 440–41; Riding, *Distant Neighbors*, p. 88.
22. Riding, *Distant Neighbors*, p. 21.
23. Camp, "Camarillas in Mexican Politics," pp. 96–97; Riding, *Distant Neighbors*, pp. 113–14.
24. Camp, *Generals in the Palacio*, pp. 69, 384–86.
25. *Excelsior*, September 8, 1988, p. 4.
26. On the other hand, Reavis reports the assertion by one soldier that he had participated in the execution of more than 100 political dissidents from 1978 to 1983. See *Conversations with Moctezuma*, p. 44.
27. *The Wall Street Journal*, October 15, 1985.
28. Reavis, *Conversations with Moctezuma*, pp. 133–34.
29. Schmidt, "Humor and Politics," p. 167.
30. Reavis, *Conversations with Moctezuma*, pp. 65, 67. Reavis hints at this machismo connection in his discussion of corruption as an outcome of relationships characterized by the verb chingar. See pp. 68–69.
31. Reavis, *Conversations with Montezuma*, pp. 21–25, 39–44, 46–48, 51–52.
32. Jacqueline Roddick, *The Dance of the Millions: Latin America and the Debt Crisis* (London: The Latin America Bureau, 1988), p. 116; Niblo, *War, Diplomacy and Development*, pp. 253–55.
33. The Juárez–El Paso gateway for heroin flowing along the traditional marijuana route from Mexico to Denver is the subject of the novel *The Alvarez Journal* by Rex Burns (New York: Harper & Row, 1975; Penguin Books, 1991). The Mystery Writers of America awarded the book its 1976 Edgar Award as the best mystery of the year.
34. Reavis, *Conversations with Moctezuma*, p. 74.
35. David G. LaFrance, "The Myth and the Reality of 'El Negro' Durazo: Mexico City's Most-Wanted Police Chief," *Studies in Latin American Popular Culture* 9 (1990), pp. 237–48; Alan Riding examines the question of corruption in the political system in *Distant Neighbors*, pp. 163–93.
36. Riding, *Distant Neighbors*, p. 171.
37. Robert A. Pastor and Jorge G. Castañeda, *Limits to Friendship* (New York: A.A. Knopf, 1988), p. 213.
38. Riding, *Distant Neighbors*, p. 102.
39. Camp, *Politics in Mexico*, p. 285.

40.   Mark Seal, "Super Barrio," *American Way* (September 1, 1992), pp. 45–48, 82, 84, 86–90; David Brooks, " 'We Are All Superbarrio,' " *Zeta Magazine* (April 1980), pp. 85–91.

41.   Professional wrestling's place in Mexican popular culture received official recognition with the dedication of a special exhibit at the Museum of Popular Cultures in 1992. The television program "Discovery," produced by the National Geographic Society, featured a program on Mexican professional wrestlers in early 1992.

42.   Camp, *Politics in Mexico*, pp. 283–90, 292, 295.

43.   Reavis, *Conversations with Moctezuma*, pp. 129–30, 132–33, 138.

44.   Camp, *Politics in Mexico*, pp. 260–61.

45.   Reavis, *Conversations with Moctezuma*, p. 139.

46.   Camp, *Generals in the Palacio*, p. 74.

47.   Camp, *Politics in Mexico*, pp. 296–99; Baer quotation on p. 297.

48.   Camp, "Camarillas in Mexican Politics," pp. 96–97.

49.   Camp, *Politics in Mexico*, pp. 18, 81, citing Los Angeles Times poll of August 1989.

50.   Camp, *Politics in Mexico*, pp. 86, 89–90.

51.   Camp, *Politics in Mexico*, pp. 25, 103–04, 226. Table 3–1, "Legitimacy of the Mexican State: Confidence of Citizens in Institutions," shows that Americans generally have more confidence in institutions, giving at least an 80 percent rating to church, schools, the army, businesses, congress, and the police, with no data on the family, law, or politics. Only Canadians rated the police this highly. In contrast, Mexicans are clearly suspicious of their institutions, with the police and politicians receiving just over a 10 percent confidence rating; no other institution received more than a 33 percent approval rating, including television, unions, and so on. Also see p. 105. This information comes from the Cross-Cultural Values Survey.

52.   Levy and Székely, *Paradoxes of Stability*, p. 42, 107–09.

53.   Camp, *Politics in Mexico*, p. 110, world values survey reporting 1980–1990.

54.   Sheldon Annis, "Giving Voice to the Poor," *Foreign Policy* 84 (fall 1991), p. 100; Camp, *Politics in Mexico*, p. 111.

55.   Camp, *Politics in Mexico*, pp. 114, 117, 174.

56.   Lomnitz, *Networks and Marginality*, p. 120, p. 140, n. 15.

57.   Camp, *Politics in Mexico*, pp. 125, 163–64, 198, Chart.

58.   Camp, *Politics in Mexico*, pp. 220–21, 224, 266–67; citing Senado, *Diario de los debates*, 1953, pp. 5–6.

59.   For background on the rise of programming and budgeting, see John J. Bailey, "Presidency, Bureaucracy, and Administrative Reform in Mexico: The Secretariat of Programming and Budgeting," *Inter-American Economic Affairs* 34 (summer 1980), pp. 27–59.

60.   Levy and Székely, *Paradoxes of Stability*, p. 5.

61.   Machado, *Barbarians of the North*, pp. 78–83, 87.

62.   Machado, *Barbarians of the North*, pp. 111, 120–26, 187–94.

63.   Levy and Székely, *Paradoxes of Stability*, pp. 28, 34.

64.   Riding, *Distant Neighbors*, p. 95.

65.   Wayne A. Cornelius, "The Politics and Economics of Reforming the Ejido Sector in Mexico: An Overview and Research Agenda," *LASA Forum* 23, No. 3 (fall 1992), pp. 3–10.

66.   *El Cotidiano: Revista de la Realidad Mexicana Actual* devoted its July–August 1992 issue to a discussion of the Solidarity program.

67. Robert Barnstone, "Border Bonanza," *Texas Monthly* (January 1993), pp. 44, 47–49.
68. David Lida, "Making for Mexico," *Sky Magazine* (July 1992), pp. 81–89.
69. Roderic A. Camp, "The Time of the Technocrats and Deconstruction of the Revolution," in Michael C. Meyer and William H. Beezley, eds., *The Oxford History of Mexico* (New York: Oxford University Press, forthcoming); David Lorey, "Zedillo's Presidency: the Status of Social Development," Presentation, Tulane University (April 12, 1996).
70. Rosario Manzanos, "Una verdadera 'salinasmanía,' la invasión callejera de objetos con la imagen del expresidente," *Proceso* (December 25, 1995), pp. 50–57; Sam Quiñones, "Nada Personal," *Fort Worth Star-Telegram*, February 14, 1997.

CONVERGING CULTURES: NEW CENTURY, NEW PRESIDENT

Mexicans entered the new century with a sense of anticipation and astonishment. Both sensations reflected the popular response to the victory of Vicente Fox in the presidential elections, July 2000. Mexicans were becoming increasingly aware that in spite of international events and national policies they were experiencing a converging of cultures with their northern neighbors in the United States and Canada. This occurrence was resulting at the community level rather than as the result of some grand policy.

Mexico in the 1990s, following a trend evident more than 100 years earlier, became an increasingly important trading partner of the United States. Moreover, recent changes in economic policy have spurred a surge of American investments. Soft drink giant Pepsico announced (1993) plans to invest $750 million in Mexico, and a large retail chain proposed some thirty-nine additional stores. Anheuser-Busch and Modelo brewing companies developed joint marketing and brewing facilities. Much of the new investment was in retail and services, all of which depend directly on a rising standard of living. Mexican enterprises in marketing (to take advantage of the existence of Greater Mexico), communications, and manufacturing firms are making similar investments in the United States. For example, Pan Bimbo bought controlling interest in Mother Beard's Breads. The desperate hope of nineteenth-century liberals, that economic development would benefit all Mexicans, now appears to be an actual possibility.

New issues continue to challenge Mexico's leadership as well as the people themselves. The realization that the nation's political system needed adjustment has stimulated public debate and caused considerable soul-searching within the official party (PRI) and the various opposition groups. Underpinning the debate was the fact that urban dwellers were increasingly attracted to opposition parties. As material conditions and educational standards improved, the public was demanding more and more influence over the political process. The PRI's success in balancing demands unleashed by the Mexican Revolution laid the groundwork for positive change. To what extent Mexico will become a standard representative democracy remains unclear. Nevertheless, a consensus emerged that some type of modification of the current system was required. Closely linked to the issue of political reform is the problem of corruption. Long tolerated as a part of the political process, it was becoming less acceptable, particularly to the middle class. At the same time, illegal drug money posed a growing danger to the integrity of all levels of government.

Environmental protection, never high on the priority list of a government that placed development above other considerations, had become a major, difficult, and suddenly immediate task. Seriously deteriorating air quality, pollution of inland waters and coastal seas, and uncontrolled development in physically fragile areas threaten the quality of life of the population, health standards, and the tourist industry. The federal government, in reacting to the crisis with determination, has taken dramatic steps, even at the expense of the economy. Closure of the oil refinery in Mexico City signified the government's intention to elevate environmental concerns to a level equal to that of development. New projects, industries, and other types of development must be harmonized with strict environmental considerations. Establishment of biospheres by President Carlos Salinas de Gortari, including one (1993) protecting a coastal stretch near Puerto Peñasco, Sonora, on the Sea of Cortez, has brought the environmental message to every region of the republic. It is evident that the Mexican government understands the importance of safeguarding land, water, air, and the natural habitat of plants and animals. While much remained to be done, the problem was for the first time addressed. Promising birth control programs, which are showing positive results already, also will relieve pressure on the environment.

Another relatively new threat to the well being of the country was the drug traffic. Vast amounts of illegal money make it possible for criminal elements to corrupt police, judges, army officers, and high-ranking political officials. An estimated 50 percent to 70 percent of all cocaine passed through Mexico (as of 1993) into the United

States. South American narcotic rings poured vast resources into the country to keep the Mexican route open. In addition, Mexican suppliers of illegal drugs had become powerful in several regions and increasingly challenge the state. The brutal murder of Cardinal Juan Jesús Posadas Ocampo, his chauffeur, and five others in the parking lot of the Guadalajara International Airport (May 24, 1993) brought the danger posed by the illegal drug industry into sharp focus. Local television crews captured parts of the incident as panic-stricken people dashed for safety while the police shot it out with gunmen armed with high-powered weapons, including AK-47s. Narcoterrorism suddenly became a public affair. The cardinal, an outspoken critic of drug dealers, was widely believed to have been the target. President Salinas proposed the formation of an elite antidrug unit reinforced with tougher laws—in his words, "a grand national crusade" against the drug dealers who "corrupt and rot everything they touch." The government was anxious to prevent the emergence of narco-caciques able to control a region and powerful enough to force the state to negotiate with them.

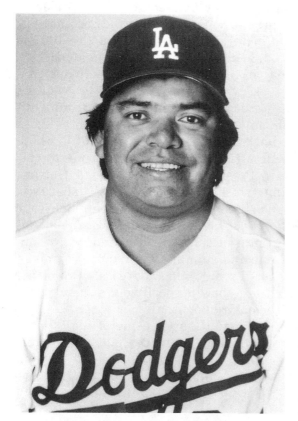

Figure CC.1 Fernando "El Toro" Valenzuela led the Los Angeles Dodgers to the World Championship of baseball in 1982 and ignited Fernando-mania across the borderlands. *Printed with permission, Los Angeles Dodgers.*

While the challenges and dangers of the problems facing the Mexican people were obvious, the republic was in a strong position to deal with them and prevail. The strength of 1990s Mexico was rooted in an intellectual clarity, evident among influential opinion makers as well as politicians at the top of the political structure. A highly rational, calculating (occasionally to the point of cynicism) approach governed decision making. Historically, Mexico is a nation with well-articulated goals and a firm notion of how to achieve them. While not exempt from errors, missteps, and even disastrous mistakes, the republic has followed a remarkably consistent and successful course. The perceptive talents of the country's leadership served the nation well in the nineteenth century and continued to do so in the 1990s. The government found ways to preserve the positive aspects of the Revolution by instituting programs that continue to pursue revolutionary goals without counterproductive rhetoric. President Salinas de Gortari's cabinet consisted of technocrats in economic positions and, in a reversal of recent trends, individuals with party experience in political posts. He thus combined the strengths of political experience and technical training. Beyond the efforts of the Mexican government to promote free trade, the administration made special efforts to recognize the activities of Mexicans residing outside of the country and their need to vote in national elections. The widespread campaign, using sophisticated advertising, to publicize Mexican programs throughout Greater Mexico, and the frequent visits by government officials to Los Angeles, California, Dallas, Texas, Phoenix, Arizona, and other cities provided the regime with greater visibility and legitimacy.

Perhaps the most accurate indicator of government thinking is found in the official school textbooks. A commission in 1992 revised the official elementary school texts, presenting a more positive image of Porfirio Díaz. While still seen as a dictator, Díaz is portrayed as the father of modern Mexico because of his economic development programs. The authors thus tied together developmental currents that continued to be present, despite the political upheaval of the Revolution, and recognized the time of tremendous economic growth throughout Greater Mexico. The new texts represent no simple endorsement of the official party. For the first time, for example, the textbooks report the army massacre of students in 1968 and remark on the efforts of indigenous peoples through the colonial years to resist the Spanish colonizers. A hesitant ambivalence led the education ministry, after initially accepting them, to withdraw the new texts. Whether the government eventually will permit distribution remains to be seen, yet their existence and the frank portrayals of painful events they contain are significant. The reevaluation of the Mexican past and the Revolution has resulted

Figure CC.2 An effigy of Carlos Salinas in the trash bin in Oaxaca City, 1996. The sign reads, "The Dump of History. Deposit Here: Political Corruption, Drug Politics, Bosses and Gunmen, and Country Sellouts." *Printed with permission, Roger Pierce.*

in a vigorous debate among Mexicans about their history and their government. This public debate is an important step toward political, economic, social, and educational justice for all Mexicans and it climaxed in the 2000 presidential election.

THE PRESIDENTIAL ELECTION

Mexicans and Mexico watchers agreed that the 2000 presidential election represented a test of the PRI, the official party, and the governmental system. The two dramatic electoral trends of the 1990s—

increasing victories at the local and state level by the opposition PAN and PRD parties and the apparent PRI fixing of election results at the national level—were headed for a collision. The campaign matched the popular, recently elected mayor of Mexico City, Cuauhtémoc Cárdenas of the PRD, the personable, casual governor of Guanajuato and successful businessman Vicente Fox of the PAN, and the PRI's official candidate, Francisco Labastida. Questions abounded. Would the official party permit honest and open elections? Would the PRI claim victory despite election results? Would Cuauhtémoc Cárdenas claim the office many believed he won in 1994? Would the PRD emerge as the dominant national party? Would the PAN, regarded as a rather conservative party on the Right, continue the string of election victories it had achieved since the 1980s? Would the PAN candidate, Vicente Fox, if he won, be a PAN president or go his own way as an independent?

In spring and early summer the campaign witnessed heightened excitement and expectations. Despite Cárdenas's earlier success in attracting voters, he quickly dropped to a distant third place, as the other two candidates shared the lead in the political polls. International observers and journalists flooded the country to watch the campaign that featured the impromptu style of Fox, whose causal dress, religious references, and open dialogue with his audiences, represented a populist break from the formal, formulaic PRI campaign. For the first time, the candidates debated each other on television. The debate highlighted the differences in the leading candidate's style. Fox came across as a dynamic, innovative leader, while Labastida seemed hesitant and apologetic.

Then suddenly the seemingly endless political commentary and prognostications ended. Mexicans in record numbers went to the polls to determine if the next president would be the fourteenth official party representative or the representative of an opposition party. Political commentators and many voters seemed to hold their breath, waiting to see if the PRI would resort to creative vote counting or some other fraudulent way to obtain the victory. Then came the results, in an astonishing victory, Fox, with 42.8% of the votes to Labastida's 35.7%, won the presidency. Outgoing President Ernesto Zedillo, in a gracious address praising the voters and the system his party had created, promised a smooth transition to the new administration. Mexicans, many teary-eyed, danced in the streets as 70 years of official party rule ended through democratic elections.

As events calmed down and the transition began, other aspects of the election emerged. Fox and the PAN had won the presidential election, but no party was close to a majority in Congress. Not only would there be a new president, but one that for the first time since the revolutionary 1920s did not control the congress. Nevertheless, the exuberant President-elect Fox promised to see the Chiapas issue and root out the corruption that rotted away civil society.

THE NEW ADMINISTRATION

The new president's honeymoon with public and press proved short, as Fox faced a "presidential towel crisis" (over the cost of towels for his official residence), increasing Catholic moral outrage over his female companion (ultimately resolved with marriage), and secular outrage when he kissed Pope John Paul II's ring during the papal visit to Mexico to make Juan Diego a saint. Nevertheless, Fox has moved ahead and the administration appears to be generally successful despite the fact he has no unqualified success in ending corruption or healing indigenous issues. The U.S.-Mexican relationship benefited from the good personal relationship between Fox and George W. Bush and their wives. While national level policies have been largely shelved in the face of international terrorism concerns in the U.S. and domestic distractions, the papal hoopla surrounding San Juan Diego, for example, in Mexico, at the local community level the border is disappearing as the cultures are converging.

During the Fox era, all three major political parties, the PAN, the PRI, and PRD, have recognized the Mexican population in the United States as an untapped political, economic, and educational resource. Intense political debate continues about how to permit Mexicans and binational Mexicans in the United States to cast votes in Mexican national elections. Exact numbers of potential voters in the United States do not exist, but analysts estimate 8 million eligible individuals, a substantial number that could swing Mexican presidential and gubernatorial races.

CONVERGING CULTURES

Nevertheless, the most significant development during the Fox years has occurred in spite of policies of both the Mexican and United States national governments. At the state, local, individual, and business levels, the border is dissolving, despite the U.S. government's efforts to tighten regulation of border crossings, redoubled after the terrorist attacks of September, 2001, and the Mexican government's efforts to secure amnesty for the four to five million undocumented Mexicans in the United States. The numbers of people legally and illegally crossing from Mexico have dramatically increased. In the absence of a Mexican-U.S. agreement on documentation for many of the Mexicans now in the United States, Mexican consuls have begun offering identity cards, called the matricula consular, and are working to gain their acceptance at the community level. The consuls have presented their case to local law enforcement officials, local health agencies, local educational administrators, and local banks. This policy has begun gaining acceptance one municipality at a time. By the end of 2002 more than 800 police departments and 66 banks, including Wells Fargo and Citibank, recognized the ID cards. In numerous cities, notably Los Angeles and Chicago, officials recognize the card for access to public buildings, obtaining a driver's license, and opening utility accounts.

Moreover, United States citizens and Mexicans in the U.S. during the past two years have increasingly crossed the border to purchase prescription drugs. The U.S. Federal Drug Administration would prefer that U.S. citizens, who buy prescription drugs outside the country, choose Canada. However growing number of individuals have instead begun purchasing in Mexico. U.S. consumers especially cross the border for amoxicillin and penicillin. Pharmacies in Mexican border cities have an increasing number of generic drugs available, and bargain priced drugs from Merck, Rhone-Poulenc-Rorer, Inc. and Arents. Since 2000, Blue Shield of California has offered its clients the opportunity to select "Access Baja," an HMO that allows them to be reimbursed for medical services in Mexico. Most of the 2,500 members in 2002 were Mexicans who commute to work in California, but a significant number are U.S. citizens willing to go to Mexico for medical care and prescription drugs. The American Association of Retired Persons estimates that over half of the 50,000 retirees in Tucson, Arizona travel at least once a month to buy prescription drugs in nearby Nogales, Mexico. Many travel on a weekly bus service RX-Express. A U.S. pharmacist travels with the group to certify that prescriptions have been filled properly. As a result of increasing sales to U.S. citizens, estimated at $100 million in 2002, Mexico's largest pharmacy chain, Farmacias Benavides, has begun to target U.S. customers along the border. This strategy includes an English-language webpage that allows on online orders.

The widespread bilingual nature of the borderlands best indicates the disappearance of the border. Automatic bank tellers, state and local government documents, recorded business telephone messages, and countless other examples are appearing across the U.S. Of course those businesses on the Mexican side that cater to U.S. residents have English speaking clerks and salespersons. A further, dramatic demonstration came in 1999 when the Kansas City-based Hallmark Cards introduced a line of holiday, anniversary, birthday, and wedding cards in Spanish. This line has grown since then and other companies introduced competing Spanish-language greeting cards. In a particularly, ironic marketing development, bodegas (small grocery stores) in Brooklyn, New York in 2002 began advertising Coca Cola®—once universally regarded as the symbol of U.S. cultural imperialism—from Mexico for sale to Latinos who prefer the sweeter taste.

Mexican state governments have also begun to ignore the border. Leaders from Jalisco have long sought out the migrant Tapatíos (as residents of the state are known) in the United States, assisted in the formation of Jalisco social clubs where officials can call for political and financial assistance for the home state. Lately the government officers from Michoacan have provided over $100,000 for the construction of the Michoacan Social Club in Chicago and have assisted other groups in Garden Grove and other California cities. The Guanajuato state government from the time Vicente Fox served as governor has been particularly active in meeting with its citizens, especially in Texas, and seeking their political, financial, and marketing advice. Oaxacans have been most active in local communities activities, from California's central valley back to the seven regions of Oaxaca. Taken together all of these developments are making the border disappear at the local community level and a convergence of North American cultures is well underway.

The economic cooperation and the North American Free Trade Agreement served as specific expressions of the converging cultures of Mexico and the United States. The roots of the process, now far advanced, go back into the nineteenth century. Today this phenomenon can be seen in the extent of human exchange as well, with the steady flow of U.S. tourists and retirees to Mexico and the influx of Mexicans moving north across the political boundary. As a result of Mexican legal and illegal, temporary and permanent migration, and the tremendous number of daily workers (green card holders), the influence of Mexican culture on the Southwestern United States has mushroomed. Mexican women domestics occupy the bottom of this economic ladder in the bordertowns and throughout Greater Mexico. Nevertheless, such employment offers obvious advantages, such as five times the wage paid in the maquilas, although without benefits. On the U.S. side, Mexican domestic labor has become a part of the lifestyles of Anglos and Mexican Americans, so much so that in 1953 El Paso housewives organized to lobby, albeit unsuccessfully, for a federal "Bracero Maid" program. These domestic employees are regularly detained by the border patrol and returned to Ciudad Juárez. For the Immigration and Naturalization Service, such apprehensions receive a low priority and have no punitive action. Nevertheless, "La Migra," or immigration agents, have become one of the villains in the popular culture along the border.[1]

The emergence of an Anglo-Hispanic culture can be seen in food and beverages, language, sports, and other amusements, and the rise of Santa Fe, New Mexico, as a Sunbelt capital. So-called Mexican food, including regional Mexican, Tex-Mex, New Mexican, Az-Mex, and Cal-Mex cuisine, boomed in the 1980s. Restaurant franchises and chi-chi cafes popped up everywhere, Mexican food products filled grocery store shelves, and menu suggestions and recipes by prominent chefs such as Dianne Kennedy appeared in all of the gourmet and kitchen magazines. A sign of the success of Mexican food was the Tortilla Wars. Tortillerías (tortilla shops) traditionally had been family businesses. The popularity of Mexican food beginning in the 1960s created a mass market for tortillas, with the emphasis on low unit cost rather than subtlety in taste. The result was a price war and battle among tortilla makers to capture the Anglo market as far away as Boston and New York. Pioneer companies in Texas, such as Houston's Fiesta, San Antonio's Amigo, and Austin's Fiesta, went out of business as other companies flourished, adopting marketing plans that included national distribution channels and consumer-sensitive tortilla descriptions such as "all natural," "no preservatives," and "no salt." El Galindo, based in Austin, Texas, produces 35 tons of tortilla chips, 50,000 dozen flour tortillas, and 160,000 dozen corn tortillas a week. The world's largest tortilla factory, in East Los Angeles, operates twenty-four hours a day to meet local demand. The market is largely Anglo. Success such as this has caused such giants as Frito-Lay, Borden, Beatrice, and Pet to move into the market so that today tortillas are a mainstream grocery product in the United States.[2] Even General Mills has moved into Greater Mexico with a special product, Buñuelitos, a breakfast cereal that tastes like popular Mexican pastry for sale in the Southwestern United States.

Athletes and sports promoters barely notice the national boundary between the United States and Mexico. The Mexicanization of major league baseball reached a high point with the period of "Fernando-mania" when the Mexican pitcher Fernando Valenzuela starred for the Los Angeles Dodger in the 1980s. Mexican first-division professional soccer teams play regularly in Los Angeles, California, and Dallas, Texas. Mexicans, traditionally fans of baseball and soccer, have followed the Dallas Cowboys in increasing numbers. National Football League games are telecast throughout the republic on cable television.

Another major source of strength is the recognition of Greater Mexico, not only by the authorities in Mexico City and in Washington, D.C., but more important by the people on both sides of the international line far beyond the border region. Mexicans have adopted a more flexible state of mind, discarding many old attitudes and archaic limitations. Previous notions of isolation, whether real or perceived, tended to constrict innovative thinking and hence made it difficult to conceive of workable options and alternatives—particularly in economic and political relations with the international community. The apprehension that accompanied a narrow parochial mind-set undermined the nation's self-confidence. Mexicans throughout much of their history as an independent entity have struggled to define themselves for themselves. Mexico's place in the wider context of a broader world could not be contemplated when survival seemed in doubt. That stage has now passed. Mexico today is one component, albeit a central and an important one, of the larger transnational entity of Greater Mexico. The reservoir of talent, wealth, and sympathy, now greatly expanded, has strengthened as well as changed the Mexican Republic.

The development of Greater Mexico as a consequence of the annexation of Texas, the subsequent acquisition of territory following the war, the emergence of the importance of the transborder region, and a series of demographic movements has created a vast transculturalization zone. Constant interchange, not the least being the tremendous impact of Spanish- and English-language television, melds cultures together. Mexicanization and Americanization, the two extremes of the process in theory, in reality meet somewhere in the middle, creating a hybrid. This process, identifiable in the nineteenth century, has become self-sustaining in the twilight of the twentieth century. It is a reality that binds together the fate of Mexico and the United States.

NOTES

1. Vicki L. Ruiz, "By the Day or the Week: Mexican Domestic Workers in El Paso," in Ruiz and Tiano, eds., *Women on the U.S.–Mexican Border*, pp. 61–76. Poet Pat Mora has written searing poems on La Migra and its relations with border residents, especially women. See her *Chants and Borders* (Houston: Arte Público Press, 1984 and 1986).
2. Richard Zelade, "Masa Marketing," *Texas Monthly* (May 1989), pp. 132–41. *Fort Worth Star-Telegram*, October 20, 1993.

Glossary

agrarista   Peasant militia, agricultural squatter; more generally an individual sympathetic to peasant or agrarian interests.

alcabalas   Excise tax.

alcalde   Magistrate; sometimes in reference to a mayor of a village or town.

Alemán, Miguel   First postrevolution civilian president; assumed office in 1946; shifted political recruitment away from the army and the bureaucracy toward university graduates and technocrats.

amparo   Judicial stay of execution from an act of the executive.

Article 27 of the Constitution of 1917   Imposed restrictions on private landownership with need to serve a useful social function as determined by the state; provided restitution of illegally acquired land.

Article 123 of the Constitution of 1917   Provided for an eight-hour day; six day work week; minimum wage and equal pay for equal work, regardless of sex or nationality; right to strike, organize, and bargain collectively.

ayuntamiento   Municipal council. (See also cabildo, the less commonly used term.)

Barreda, Gabino   (1818–1881) Introduced and modified Auguste Comte's positivism to fit Mexican needs; established the National Preparatory School in 1867.

barrio   Neighborhood or district.

bienes de comunidad   Communal property; assets of a municipality or village.

bracero   Mexican agricultural laborer who worked in the United States during World War II under formal contract and government protection.

cabildo   Municipal council. (See also ayuntamiento, the more frequently used term.)

cacicazgo   Political authority or power, literally chieftainship.

cacique   Political leader; in colonial times, an Indian chief.

camarilla   Political grouping often based around one individual or an extended family; provides a means of achieving political office or power (may be regional or national in composition).

campesino   Peasant; agrarian worker.

Cananea   Site of William Greene's Consolidated Copper Company, where a major violent strike occurred on June 1, 1906; put down in a bloody fashion by the Rurales.

Carranza, Venustiano   (1859–1920) Governor of the state of Coahuila during the presidency of Francisco Madero; rallied resistance to the Huerta regime by becoming self-appointed first Chief of Constitutionalist Army and subsequently president; assassinated in 1920.

caudillo   Political or military chief.

Chicano   Individual of Mexican origin born in the United States. A term used by those who have a somewhat militant focus on issues directly related to their ethnic concerns and who perceive themselves as being very politically involved.

Chilango   Name applied to residents of Mexico City, occasionally with disdain by those outside of Mexico City.

científicos   Prominent national camarilla during the Porfiriato, revolving around José Limantour, Diaz's secretary of the treasury.

Cinco de Mayo   (May 5, 1862) Victory of Mexican defenders of Puebla under command of General Ignacio Zaragoza over French troops at the beginning of the French intervention; now a major national holiday.

cofradía   Parish confraternity dedicated to cult of a saint.

Compañia Nacional de Subsistencias Populares (CONASUPO)   Government agency charged with the sale of subsidized basic commodities in poor and working class areas throughout the republic.

comunidad   Community property, particularly land; a community.

Confederación de Trabajadores de México (CTM)   Union formed by Vicente Lombardo Toledano in 1936 in opposition to the CROM: received support and encouragement from President Lazaro Cárdenas; eventually replaced the CROM.

Confederación Regional Obrera Mexicana (CROM)   Mexico's first national union, founded in 1918 under the direction of Luis Morones. Favored by presidents Alvaro Obregón and Plutarco Elías Calles, it had approximately 1.8 million members in 1928.

Constitution of 1917   Established the political and social orientation of the Mexican Revolution through the 1930s. Seen by many at the time as a radical document, it was more reformist, containing labor reforms and civil guarantees.

Constitutionalist   One who refused to recognize the seizure of presidential power by General Victoriano Huerta in 1913.

corregidor   Local Spanish colonial official with judicial, administrative, and fiscal duties.

criollo   Person born in Mexico of Spanish ancestry.

Cristero Rebellion (July 31, 1926) Pro-clerical revolt and a clerical strike that lasted three years, with massive violence by clerical supporters and federal authorities.

Drug Enforcement Agency (DEA) United States agency charged with suppression of production, distribution, and consumption of narcotics; works in cooperation with Mexican officials within Mexico in pursuit of its objectives.

ejido Land conveyed by the state to be cultivated in common by a designated group.

encomendero Holder of an encomienda.

encomienda Royal grant to collect tribute from specified Indian groups.

federales Members of the national army or other armed unit controlled by the national (federal) government.

Flores Magón, Ricardo (1873–1922) Officially designated intellectual progenitor of the Mexican Revolution. An early opponent of the regime of Porfirio Díaz, who spent most of his life in exile in the United States. An anarchist with a transnational and international view of the need for change, he also served as forerunner of Mexican-American activism.

folk liberalism Popular and semimythical understanding of the spirit and intent of Benito Juárez and the Constitution of 1857 to respect and address the socioeconomic conditions of the lower classes. Developed a psychological sense of entitlement that makes it possible to make demands on the state. Important during the active restructuring of postrevolutionary society after 1911 and remains a factor in the legitimacy of the contemporary Mexican state.

Fomento Agency established at the instigation of Miguel Lerdo de Tejada in 1853. Charged with stimulating economic development, it played a major role in attracting foreign investment and setting economic objectives.

fundo legal Site occupied by the houses of a town or village.

Gadsden Purchase (1853) Mesilla Valley, now southern Arizona and New Mexico, purchased for $10 million by the United States. The last major transfer of territory of the Mexican republic.

gallo, el Individual around which a camarilla has been formed.

hacienda Large landed estate usually devoted to grain production and/or ranching.

Hispanic Term that may include Mexican Americans and others of Latin American origin; implies a greater identification with general Hispanic culture. Somewhat similar to the term Latino, which emphasizes a general Latin American identification.

Huertista Follower of Victoriano Huerta.

indio Indian; native Mexican, sometimes applied to rural people.

jefe político District official.

jornalero Day wage laborer.

Juárez, Benito (1806–1872) Noted liberal president associated with resistance to French intervention, reforms, and the Constitution of 1857.

la migra   Term used by illegal or undocumented Mexican immigrants and workers to refer to the United States Immigration and Naturalization Services (INS), the agency charged with control of entry into the United States.

Land Law of 1883   Authorized land companies to survey public land; in return, companies received one-third of land surveyed and the privilege of purchasing the other two-thirds. Intended to stimulate the subdivision and settlement of unused public land.

League of United Latin American Citizens (LULAC)   Founded in Corpus Christi, Texas, in 1929 to counter anti-Mexican discrimination and to achieve equal rights for U.S. citizens of Mexican descent.

leva   Military forced draft, usually to fill the ranks of the federal army.

Ley Juárez   Drafted by Secretary of Justice Benito Juárez (1855); abolished military and clerical exemptions from civil courts.

Ley Lerdo   Drafted by Secretary of the Treasury Miguel Lerdo de Tejada (1856); prohibited ecclesiastical and civil institutions from owning or administrating real property not used in daily operations.

Limantour, José Yves   (1854–1935) Secretary of the treasury; believer in positivism, credited with establishing Porfirian finances on a stable and respected basis.

Lombardo Toledano, Vincente   Founder of the Confederación de Trabajadores de México (CTM) and its secretary general. A Marxist, but a pragmatist, forced out of office by President Manuel Avila Camacho.

Madero, Francisco I.   (1873–1913) Elected president following the resignation of Porfirio Díaz. A proponent of political reforms who did not believe radical changes were needed to correct social or economic problems.

maquiladora   In-bond assembly plant usually located in the northern states that employs Mexican labor and returns the finished product for sale and distribution to U.S. markets.

Maximato   Period from 1928 to 1936 during which ex-president Plutarco Elías Calles controlled the presidency through a series of puppet presidents until his control was broken by then President Lázaro Cárdenas.

Maximilian (Ferdinand Maximilian Joseph)   Imposed Emperor of Mexico from 1864 until his death by firing squad on June 19, 1867.

mediero   Sharecropper; worker of small marginal plot.

mestizo   Person of mixed European and Indian ancestry.

Mexican Americans   Individuals of Mexican origin, born or naturalized in the United States, who perceive themselves as being reasonably assimilated with both ethnic and general concerns.

milpa   Small plot for maize cultivation.

mordida   A bite; refers to petty extortion, bribe of a minor official, or modest but illegally required payment for services rendered directly to the individual who performs them.

Morones, Luis   Founder of the Confederación Regional Obrera Mexicana (CROM) in 1918; served as secretary of labor during the Calles administration.

Municipio   (municipality) Local political/administrative unit encompassing a number of subordinate settlements.

Municipio Libre   Revolutionary ideal of local control over local governance eliminating undue state and national influence over municipalities.

Nezahualcoyotl Izcalli (Neza)   City established (1946) in a lake bed immediately adjacent to Mexico City by migrating squatters and the marginally employed.

Norteño   Inhabitant of northern Mexico.

North American Free Trade Agreement (NAFTA)   Made in principle (1992) to establish a free trade area covering Mexico, the United States, and Canada; strongly supported by President Carlos Salinas de Gortari.

Obregonismo   Political philosophy of Alvaro Obregón.

Panista   Adherent of the opposition party PAN.

Partido de Acción Nacional (PAN)   Founded in 1939 by Juan Andrea Almazán as a conservative, Catholic party subsequently dominated by industrialist and large commercial agricultural interests. In recent times it has attracted broader support from the middle class.

Partido Liberal Mexicano (PLM)   Founded in St. Louis, Missouri, in 1905 by Ricardo Flores Magón and Enrique Flores Magón to organize political resistance to the regime of Porfirio Díaz.

Partido Revolucionario Democrático (PRD)   Union of small leftist parties under the leadership of Cuauhtémoc Cárdenas, ex-PRI governor and son of Lázaro Cárdenas. Mounted a serious political challenge to the PRI in 1988.

Partido Revolucionario Institucional (PRI)   Established in 1946 as the successor party to the Partido de la Revolucion Mexicano (PRM). A more inclusive party, it incorporated new elements created by prosperity that accompanied World War II. It is the ruling party controlled by the state that assures its electoral dominance through adroit use of patronage and fraud, when necessary. It serves to coordinate regional and national camarillas.

Petróleos Mexicanos (PEMEX)   Created by President Lázaro Cárdenas in 1938 to operate the expropriated oil industry and exercise monopoly control over production and distribution.

Plan of Agua Prieta   (1920) Named after the border city, it announced the revolt of Alvaro Obregón, Adolfo de la Huerta, and Plutarco Elías Calles, all of Sonora, against then President Venustiano Carranza.

Plan of Ayala   (November 1911) Zapatista plan for agrarian reform that called for the immediate return of land to peasants and withdrew recognition of Francisco Madero as leader of the Mexican Revolution.

Plan of Noria   (November 8, 1871) Proclaimed by General Porfirio Díaz with the objective of ending constant reelection of the president as a violation of the spirit of the Constitution of 1857.

Plan of San Diego   Called for an uprising along the border on February 20, 1915, to establish a separate republic consisting of the territory taken from Mexico between 1836 and 1848. It suggested possible reannexation by Mexico. Violence associated with the plan resulted in repression by the Texas rangers and the dispatching of federal troops to the border.

Plan of San Luis Potosí   (October 5, 1910) Issued by Francisco Madero to rally opposition to the regime of Porfirio Díaz; called for support for stricter observance of constitutional practices and effective suffrage and no reelection.

Porfiriato   Period during which Porfirio Díaz served as president of Mexico (1876–1911) with the interregnum of President Manual González (1880–1884).

Porfirista   Follower of Porfirio Díaz.

Priista   Adherent of the PRI.

principal   Village leader.

pueblo   Village or small town.

pulque   Pre-Columbian beverage derived from agave. May be used fermented or fresh. The most common and popular alcoholic drink among the lower classes until the 1940s.

ranchero   Small independent farmer.

Reforma   (1856–1876) Period during which the liberals carried out major reforms, including those incorporated in the Constitution of 1857.

Revolution of Ayutla   Liberal movement that ousted General and President Santa Anna in 1855.

Revolution of Tuxtepec   (March 1876) Mounted by Porfirio Díaz to remove Sebastián Lerdo de Tejada from the presidency; resulted in Díaz's seizure of Mexico City on November 21, 1876, and the beginning of the Porfiriato.

Rio Blanco Strike   (January 7, 1907) Strike at the textile mill that resulted in bloody repression and untold deaths.

Romero, Matías   Advisor to presidents Benito Juárez, Sebastián Lerdo Tejada, and Porfirio Diaz; occupant of several cabinet positions and an extremely effective ambassador to the United States.

Rurales   Police force used to control roads and the countryside as well as to suppress bandit activity and small-scale disorders.

Santa Teresa   (1873–1906) Religious mystic around which a cult formed. Her followers invoked her powers in the Temochic Revolt and in several other violent incidents in Sonora between 1890 and 1906.

sexenio   Six-year presidential term with no reelection during which president seeks to make a particular contribution or mark on the country's historical development.

Soldadera   Female soldier during the Mexican Revolution who provided food and medical attention, helped bury the dead, and often participated in battle.

Solidaridad   Name applied to El Programa Nacional de Solidaridad (Pronasol); program under which the federal government makes funds directly available to local governments to make grassroots improvements decided upon by citizen committees. One of the most popular programs instituted by the Salinas de Gortari administration, which acts to revitalize local PRI support.

Tejano Individuals of border culture, born in Texas.

tienda de raya Company store of a hacienda or mining operation.

tithe A 10 percent tax levied for support of the Church.

Tlatelolco Massacre (October 1, 1968) Bloody end of a rally at the Plaza de las Tres Culturas, when police and army units opened fire on protestors; resulted in an estimated death toll of 300 to 400 and over 2,000 individuals arrested and jailed.

Treaty of Ciudad Juárez (1911) Provided for Porfirio Díaz's resignation and an interim president until elections could be held.

Treaty of Guadalupe Hidalgo Signed February 2, 1848, between Mexico and the United States confirming U.S. title to Texas and ceding vast territories north of the Rio Grande. Mexico received $15 million and exemption from war damage claims by Americans.

Universidad Nacional Autónoma de Mexico (UNAM) Comprehensive national university in Mexico City, complete with professional schools. After 1946, its law school became a cradle of politicians.

Vasconcelos, José Man of letters; secretary of education under President Alvaro Obregón; designer of a plan to incorporate all Mexicans, including Indians, into one race (la raza cósmica); commissioned muralists, including Diego Rivera, José Clemente Orozco, and David Alfaro Siqueiros to interpret Mexican history for the masses in murals on public buildings.

Velásquez, Fidel Installed as secretary-general of the CTM by President Manuel Avila Camacho; began his career as an agrarian organizer for the Zapatistas and remained in office until his death in 1997.

Villista Supporter of Pancho Villa.

War of the Reforma (1858–1861) Major civil war between liberals and conservatives that weakened the nation and increased its vulnerability to foreign pressures.

Zapata, Emiliano (1879–1919) Small landowner, muleteer, and officeholder in the village of Anenecuilco who became a leader of peasants and workers in the states of Morelos and Puebla; played a minor role in the collapse of Porfirio Diaz; subsequently became an important revolutionary until his assassination. The mythical Zapata has become a major figure in the revolutionary mythology of modern Mexico.

Zapatista Supporter of Emiliano Zapata.

Zócalo Popular name for the Plaza de la Constitución, which faces out from the national palace in Mexico City; also a general term for any central plaza.

Bibliography

A DIPLOMATIST (PSEUD). *American Foreign Policy*. New York: Houghton Mifflin Co., 1909.

ABBOT, GORHAM D. *Mexico and the United States, Their Mutual Relations and Common Interests*. New York: G. P. Putnam & Son, 1869.

Above and Beyond: A History of the Medal of Honor from the Civil War to Vietnam. Boston: Boston Pub. Co., 1985.

ACUÑA, RODOLFO F. *Sonoran Strongman: Ignacio Pesqueira and His Times*. Tucson: University of Arizona Press, 1974.

AGUILAR CAMÍN, HÉCTOR. *La frontera nómada: Sonora y la Revolución Mexicana*. México: Siglo Veintiuno Editores, 1977.

———. "The Relevant Tradition: Sonoran Leaders in the Revolution." In D. A. Brading, ed., *Caudillo and Peasant in the Mexican Revolution*. New York: Cambridge University Press, 1980.

ALBA, VICTOR. *The Mexicans: The Making of a Nation*. New York: Pegasus, 1967.

ALBRO, WARD A. *Always a Rebel: Ricardo Flores Magón and the Mexican Revolution*. Fort Worth: Texas Christian University Press, 1992.

ALEXIUS, ROBERT MARTIN. "The Army and Politics in Porfirian Mexico." Ph.D. diss., University of Texas, 1976.

ALLEN, CHERYL. "Una Prensa . . . ¿Libre?: Freedom of the Press in Mexico from 1968 to 1991." Honors Essay, School of Journalism and Mass Communication, University of North Carolina, 1992.

ALVARADO, LOURDES. "Asociación Metodófila Gabino Barreda: Dos ensayos representativos." In *Estudios de historia moderna y contemporánea de México*, pp. 211–45. México: Universidad Nacional Autónoma de México, 1989.

ANDERS, EVAN. *Boss Rule in South Texas*: The Progressive Era. Austin: University of Texas Press, 1982.

ANDERSON, RODNEY D. *Outcasts in Their Own Land: Mexican Industrial Workers, 1906–1911*. Dekalb: Northern Illinois University Press, 1976.

ANDREWS, GREGG. *Shoulder to Shoulder: The American Federation of Labor, the United States and the Mexican Revolution.* Berkeley: University of California Press, 1991.

ANDERSON, DUDLEY. *Agrarian Warlord: Saturnino Cedillo and the Mexican Revolution in San Luis Potosí.* DeKalb: Northern Illinois University Press, 1984.

ANNA, TIMOTHY E. *The Fall of the Royal Government in Mexico City.* Lincoln: University of Nebraska Press, 1978.

———. *The Mexican Empire of Iturbide.* Lincoln: University of Nebraska Press, 1990.

———. "Spain and the Breakdown of the Imperial Ethos: The Problem of Equality." *Hispanic American Historical Review* 62: 2 (May 1982), pp. 254–72.

ANNIS, SHELDON. "Giving Voice to the Poor." *Foreign Policy* 84 (fall 1991).

ARCHER, CHRISTON I. "'La Causa Buena': The Counterinsurgency Army of New Spain and the Ten Years' War." In Jaime E. Rodriguez O., ed., *The Independence of Mexico and the Creation of the New Nation,* pp. 85–108. Los Angeles: UCLA Latin American Center Publications, 1989.

———. "The Young Antonio López de Santa Anna: Veracruz Counterinsurgent and Incipient Caudillo." In Judith Ewell and William Beezley, eds., *The Human Tradition in Latin America: The Nineteenth Century.* Wilmington, Del.: SR Books, 1989.

———, ed. *The Wars of Independence in Spanish America.* Wilmington, Del.: SR Books, forthcoming.

ARCHIVO DE LA Catedral de Santiago, Saltillo, Libro de Gobierno, vol. 5.

ASTON, B. W. "The Public Career of José Yves Limantour." Ph.D. diss., Texas Tech University, 1972.

AVILA, MANUEL. *Tradition and Growth; A Study of Four Mexican Villages.* Chicago: The University of Chicago Press, 1968.

BAILEY, DAVID C. "Obregón: Mexico's Accommodating President." In George Wolfskill and Douglas W. Richmond, eds., *Essays on the Mexican Revolution: Revisionist Views of the Leaders.* Austin: University of Texas Press, 1979.

BAILEY, JOHN J. "Presidency, Bureaucracy, and Administrative Reform in Mexico: The Secretariat of Programming and Budgeting." *Inter-American Economic Affairs* 34 (summer 1980), pp. 27–59.

BALDWIN, DEBORAH J. *Protestants and the Mexican Revolution: Missionaries, Ministers, and Social Change.* Urbana: University of Illinois Press, 1990.

BANCROFT, HUBERT HOWE. *Recursos y desarrollo de México.* San Francisco: Bancroft Co., 1893.

BANJES, ADRIAN A. "Burning Saints, Molding Minds: Iconoclasm, Civic Ritual and the Failed Cultural Revolution." In William H. Beezley, Cheryl E. Martin, and William E. French, eds., *Rituals of Rule, Rituals of Resistance: Public Celebrations and Popular Culture in Mexico.* Wilmington, Del.: SR Books, 1994.

———. *"As If Jesus Walked on Earth:" Cardenismo and the Political Culture of the Mexican Revolution in Sonora, 1929–1940.* Wilmington, Del.: SR Books, 1998.

BANKS, LEO. "The Babe Ruth of Mexico." Eastern Airlines *Review Magazine* (August 1985).

BAQUEIRO FOSTER, GERÓNIMO. *Historia de la música en México.* 3 vols. México: Secretaría de Educación Pública, 1964.

BARBOSA HELDT, ANTONIO. *Cien años en la educación de México.* México: Editorial Pax, 1972.

BARNSTONE, ROBERT. "Border Bonanza." *Texas Monthly* (January 1993).

BARRAGÁN BARRAGÁN, JOSÉ. *Introducción al federalismo*. México: Universidad Nacional Autónoma de México, 1978.

BARTRA, ROGER. *The Cage of Melancholy: Identity and Metamorphosis in the Mexican Culture*. Translated by Christopher J. Hall. New Brunswick, N. J.: Rutgers University Press, 1992.

BASTIAN, JEAN-PIERRE. *Los disidentes: Sociedades protestantes y revolución en México, 1872–1911*. México: Fondo de Cultura Económica, 1989.

BAZANT, JAN. *Alienation of Church Wealth in Mexico: Social and Economic Aspects of Liberal Revolution, 1856–1875*. Cambridge: Cambridge University Press, 1971.

BAZANT, MILADA. "La desamortización de los bienes de la iglesia en Toluca durante la Reforma." In María Teresa Jarquín O., ed., *Temas de historia mexiquense*. Toluca: Ayuntamiento de Toluca, 1988.

———. "Estudiantes mexicanos en el extranjero: El caso de los hermanos Urquidi." *Historia Mexicana* (April–June 1987), pp. 739–58.

BEALS, CARLETON. *Mexico: An Interpretation*. New York: B. W. Huebsch, 1923.

BECKER, MARJORIE. "Torching la Purísima, Dancing at the Altar: The Construction of Revolutionary Hegemony in Michoacán." In Gilbert M. Joseph and Daniel Nugents, eds., *Everyday Forms of State Formation: Revolution and Negotiation of Rule in Modern Mexico* (Durham: Duke University Press, forthcoming).

———. *Setting the Virgin on Fire: Lázaro Cárdenas, Michoacán Peasants, and the Redemption of the Mexican Revolution*. Berkeley: University of California Press, 1995.

BEEZLEY, WILLIAM H. "Governor Carranza and the Mexican Revolution in Coahuila." *The Americas* 33: 1 (July 1976), pp. 50–61.

———. *Judas at the Jockey Club and Other Episodes of Porfirian Mexico*. Lincoln: University of Nebraska Press, 1987.

———. "Madero: The 'Unknown' President and His Political Failure to Organize Rural Mexico." In George Wolfskill and Douglas W. Richmond, eds., *Essays on the Mexican Revolution: Revisionist Views of the Leaders*. Austin: University of Texas Press, 1979.

———. "State Reform during the Provisional Presidency: Chihuahua, 1911." *Hispanic American Historical Review* 40: 3 (August 1970), pp. 524–37.

BEEZLEY, WILLIAM H., CHERYL E. MARTIN, AND WILLIAM E. FRENCH, EDS., *Rituals of Rule, Rituals of Resistance: Public Celebrations and Popular Culture in Mexico*. Wilmington, Del.: SR Books, 1994.

BELL, SAMUEL E., AND JAMES M. SMALLWOOD. *The Zone Libre, 1858–1905: A Problem in American Diplomacy*. El Paso: Texas Western Press, University of Texas at El Paso, 1982.

BENJAMIN, THOMAS. "Laboratories of the New State, 1920–1929." In Thomas Benjamin and Mark Wasserman, eds., *Provinces of the Revolution: Essays on Regional Mexican History, 1910–1929*. Albuquerque: University of New Mexico Press, 1990.

———. *A Rich Land, a Poor People: Politics and Society in Modern Chiapas*. Albuquerque: University of New Mexico Press, 1989.

BENSON, NETTIE LEE. "Territorial Integrity in Mexican Politics, 1821–1833." In Jaime E. Rodriquez O., ed., *The Independence of Mexico and the Creation of the New Nation*, pp. 275–307. Los Angeles: UCLA Latin American Center Publications, 1989.

BERNAL, RAFAEL. *El complot mongol*. Mexico: Joaquin Mortiz, 1975.

BERNINGER, DIETER. "Immigration and Religious Toleration: A Mexican Dilemma, 1821–1860." *The Americas* (April 1976) pp. 37–62.

BERNSTEIN, MARVIN D. *The Mexican Mining Industry, 1890–1950: A Study of the Interaction of Politics, Economics, and Technology*. Albany: State University of New York, 1965.

BERRY, CHARLES R. *The Reform in Oaxaca, 1856–76: A Microhistory of the Liberal Revolution*. Lincoln: University of Nebraska Press, 1981.

BLUM, ANN S. "Children without Parents: Law, Charity, and Social Practice, Mexico City, 1870–1940." Ph.D. diss., University of California, 1997.

BRANNIGAN, WILLIAM. "With Friends Like These, Who Needs Enemies." *Washington Post, National Weekly Edition*, July 23–29, 1990, p. 31.

BRIEGEL, KAYE. "Chicano Student Militancy: The Los Angeles High School Strike of 1968." In Manuel P. Servin, ed., *An Awakened Minority: The Mexican Americans*. 2d ed. Beverly Hills: Glencoe Press, 1974.

BROOKS, DAVID. "We Are All Superbarrio." *Zeta Magazine* (April 1989), pp. 85–91.

BRUSHWOOD, JOHN S. "Innovation in Mexican Fiction and Politics (1010 1034)." *Mexican Studies/Estudios Mexicanos* 5: 1 (winter 1989), pp. 69–88.

BRYAN, ANTHONY T. "Mexican Politics in Transition, 1900–1913: The Role of General Bernardo Reyes." Ph.D. diss., University of Nebraska, 1969.

BUFFINGTON, ROBERT. "Prohibition on the Border: National Government–Border Community Relations." *Pacific Historical Review* (forthcoming).

———. "Revolutionary Reform: The Mexican Revolution and the Discourse in Prison Reform." *Mexican Studies/Estudios Mexicanos* 9: 1 (1993), pp. 71–93.

———. "Forging the Fatherland: Criminality and Citizenship in Modern Mexico." Ph.D. diss., University of Arizona, 1994.

BULNES, FRANCISCO. *Juárez y las revoluciones de Ayutla y de Reforma*. 1st ed. México: Antigua Imprenta de Murguia, 1905.

———. *El verdadero Díaz y la revolución*. México: Editora Nacional, 1920.

BUNKER, STEVEN B. "Making the Good Old Days: Invented Tradition and Civic Ritual in Northern Mexico, 1880–1910." Honors Thesis, University of British Columbia, 1992.

BURNS, REX. *The Alvarez Journal*. New York: Harper & Row, Inc., 1975; reissued by Penguin Books, 1991.

BUTLER, WILLIAM. *Mexico in Transition from the Power of Political Romanism to Civil Religious Liberty*. 3d ed., rev., New York: Hunt & Eaton, 1893.

BUVE, RAYMOND. "Neither Carranza Nor Zapata: The Rise and Fall of a Peasant Movement That Tried to Challenge Both: Tlaxcala, 1910–1919." In Friedrich Katz, ed., *Riot, Rebellion, and Revolution: Rural Social Conflict in Mexico*. Princeton: Princeton University Press, 1988.

CALDERÓN DE LA BARCA, FANNY. *Life in Mexico*. Garden City: Doubleday & Co., 1970.

CALLES, PLUTARCO ELÍAS. *Mexico Before the World*. Translated by Robert H. Murray. New York: Academy Press, 1927.

CALVERT, ROBERT A., AND ARNOLDO DE LEÓN. *The History of Texas*. Arlington Heights, Ill.: Harlan Davidson, Inc., 1990.

CAMARENA OCAMPO, CUAUHTÉMOC. "Las luchas de los trabajadores textiles mexicanos: 1865–1907." Tesis de Licenciatura. Instituto Nacional de Antropología e Historia, 1985.

CAMP, RODERIC A. "Camarillas in Mexican Politics: The Case of the Salinas Cabinet." *Mexican Studies/Estudios Mexicanos* 6: 1 (winter, 1990), pp. 85–104.

———. "La campaña presidencial de 1929 y el liderazgo político en México." *Historia Mexicana* 23: 2 (1977), pp. 231–59.

———. "Education and Political Recruitment in Mexico: The Alemán Generation." *Journal of Interamerican Studies and World Affairs* 18: 3 (August 1976), pp. 295–321.

———. *Generals in the Palacio.* New York: Oxford University Press, 1992.

———. *Mexico's Leaders: Their Education and Recruitment.* Tucson: University of Arizona Press, 1980.

———. *Political Recruitment across Two Centuries: Mexico, 1884–1991.* Austin: University of Texas Press, 1995.

———. *Politics in Mexico: Democratizing Authoritarianism.* New York: Oxford University Press, 1993.

———. "The Time of the Technocrats and Deconstruction of the Revolution," *The Oxford History of Mexico*, edited by Michael C. Meyer and William H. Beezley. New York: Oxford University Press, forthcoming.

CAREY, ELAINE K. "Women and Men on the Threshold of Modernity: A Cultural History of 1968." Ph.D. diss., University of New Mexico, forthcoming.

CARMAGNANI, MARCELLO. "El liberalismo, los impuestos internos y el estado federal mexicano, 1857–1911." *Historia Mexicana* 38: 3 (January–March 1989), pp. 471–96.

CARR, BARRY. *Marxism and Communism in Twentieth Century Mexico.* Lincoln: University of Nebraska Press, 1992.

CARRENO, ALBERTO MARIA, ed. *Archivo del General Porfirio Díaz: Memorias y documentos.* 3 vols. México: Editorial "Elede," 1947–1961.

Caso del americano A. K. Cutting. Nuevas notas cambiadas entre in legación de los Estados Unidos y el Ministerio de Relaciones Exteriores de la República Mexicana. México: Imprenta de Francisco Díaz de León, 1888.

CHAMBERLIN, EUGENE K. "Baja California after Walker: The Zerman Enterprise." *Hispanic American Historical Review* 34: 3 (1954), pp. 175–89.

CHAPMAN, JOHN G. *La construcción del ferrocarril mexicano.* México: Secretaría de Educación Pública, 1975.

CHASSEN-LÓPEZ, FRANCIE R., AND HÉCTOR G. MARTÍNEZ. "Return to the Mixtec Millennium: Agrarian vs. Rancher Revolution on the Costa Chica of Oaxaca, 1911." Paper presented at the Rocky Mountain Council on Latin American Studies, El Paso, Texas, February 1992.

CHÁVEZ, ARMANDO B. *Historia de Ciudad Juárez, Chihuahua.* México: Editorial Pax México, 1991.

CHÁVEZ, JOHN R. *The Lost Land: The Chicano Image of the Southwest.* Albuquerque: University of New Mexico Press, 1984.

CHOWNING, MARGARET. "The Contours of the Post–1810 Depression in Mexico: A Reappraisal from a Regional Perspective." *Latin American Research Review* 27: 2 (1982), pp. 119–50.

CHRISTIAN, GARNA LOY. "Sword and Plowshare: The Symbiotic Development of Fort Bliss and El Paso, Texas, 1849–1918." Ph.D., diss., Texas Tech University, 1977.

CLINE, HOWARD C. *The United States and Mexico.* Cambridge: Harvard University Press, 1953.

COCHRANE, JAMES D. "Mexico's 'New Cientificos': The Díaz Ordaz Cabinet. *Inter-American Economic Affairs* 21: 1 (summer 1967).

COCKCROFT, JAMES D. *Intellectual Precursors of the Mexican Revolution, 1900–1913*. Austin: University of Texas Press, 1968.

COERVER, DONALD M. "Federal–State Relations during the Porfiriato: The Case of Sonora, 1879–1884." *The Americas* 33: 4 (April 1977), pp. 567–84.

———. *The Porfirian Interregnum: The Presidency of Manuel González of Mexico, 1880–1884*. Fort Worth: Texas Christian University Press, 1979.

COLE, RICHARD. "The Mexican Press System: Aspects of Growth, Control and Ownership." *Gazette* 21 (1975), pp. 65–81.

CORBALÁ, MANUEL S. *Rodolfo Elías Calles. Perfiles de un sonorense*. Hermosillo: n.p. 1970.

CORNELIUS, WAYNE. "The Politics and Economics of Reforming the Ejido Sector in Mexico: An Overview and Research Agenda." *LASA Forum* 23: 3 (fall 1992), pp. 3–10.

CORTÉS, CARLOS. "El bandolerismo social chicano." In David Maciel and Patricia Bereno, eds., *Aztlán: Historia del pueblo chicano, 1848–1910*. México: Secretaría de Educación Pública, 1975.

COSÍO VILLEGAS, DANIEL. *American Extremes (Extremos de América)*. Translated by Américo Paredes. Austin: University of Texas Press, 1964.

———. *La Constitución de 1857 y sus críticos*. México: Editorial Hermes, 1973.

———. *Estados Unidos contra Porfirio Díaz*. México: Editorial Hermes, 1956.

———, ed. *Historia moderna de México*. 8 vols. México: Editorial Hermes, 1974.

COSTELOE, MICHAEL P. *Church Wealth in Mexico: A Study of the Juzgado de Capellanías in the Archbishopric of Mexico, 1800–1856*. Cambridge: Cambridge University Press, 1967.

———. *La primera república federal de México, 1824–1835: Un estudio de los partidos políticos en el México independiente*. México: Fondo de Cultura Económica, 1973.

El Cotidiano. Revista de la Realidad Mexicana Actual (July–August 1992).

CRAIG, RICHARD B. *The Bracero Program: Interest Groups and Foreign Policy*. Austin: University of Texas Press, 1971.

CREELMAN, JAMES. *Díaz, Master of Mexico*. New York: D. Appleton and Co., 1911.

CUMBERLAND, CHARLES C. *Mexican Revolution: The Constitutionalist Years*. Austin: University of Texas Press, 1972.

DABBS, JACK A. *The French Army in Mexico, 1861–1867*. The Hague: Mouton, 1962.

DAHL, VICTOR. "Alien Labor on the Gulf Coast of Mexico, 1880–1900." *The Americas* 16: 1 (July 1960), pp. 21–35.

DANTAN, JAVIER GARCIADIEGO. "Movimientos estudiantiles durante la Revolución mexicana." In Jaime E. Rodríguez O., ed., *The Revolutionary Process in Mexico: Essays on Political and Social Change, 1880–1940*, pp. 115–60. Los Angeles: UCLA Latin American Center Publications, 1990.

DAVIS, CHARLES L., AND KENNETH M. COLEMAN. "Structural Determinants of Working-Class Politicization: The Role of Independent Unions in Mexico." *Mexican Studies/Estudios Mexicanos* 5: 1 (winter 1989), pp. 89–125.

Declaración, discursos y cartas del Sr. General de División don Abelardo L. Rodríguez. México, 1961.

DEGER, ROBERT JOHN JR. "Porfirian Foreign Policy and Mexican Nationalism: A Study of Cooperation and Conflict in Mexican–American Relations, 1884–1904." Ph.D. diss., Indiana University, 1979.

DELPAR, HELEN. *The Enormous Vogue of Things Mexican: Cultural Relations be-tween the United States and Mexico, 1920–1935*. Tuscaloosa: University of Alabama, 1993.

Diccionario Porrúa: Historia, Biografía y Geografía de México. México: Editorial Porrúa, 1979.

DINWOODIE, D. H. "Deportation: The Immigration Service and the Chicano Labor Movement in the 1930s." *New Mexico Historical Review* 52: 3 (July 1977), pp. 193–206.

DRAKE, PAUL W. "Mexican Regionalism Reconsidered." *Journal of Inter-American Studies and World Affairs* 12: 3 (July 1970), pp. 401–15.

———. *The Money Doctor in the Andes*. Durham: Duke University Press, 1989.

———. *Money Doctors and Foreign Debts in Latin America*. Wilmington, Del., SR Books, 1993.

DREBEN, SAM, file. Institute of Texan Cultures, University of Texas, San Antonio.

DULLES, JOHN W. F. *Yesterday in Mexico: A Chronicle of the Revolution, 1919–1936*. Austin: University of Texas Press, 1961.

DZIEDZIC, MICHAEL J. "The Essence of Decision in a Hegemonic Regime: The Case of Mexico's Acquisition of a Supersonic Fighter." Ph.D. diss., University of Texas, 1986.

———. "Mexico's Challenges: Problems, Prospects, and Implications." Unpub-lished paper, United States Air Force Academy, April 21, 1989.

EISENHOWER, JOHN S. D. *So Far from God: The U.S. War with Mexico, 1846–1848*. New York: Random House, 1989.

Engineering and Mining Journal, 1890–1911.

ESTRADA, LOUIE. "Mexican Major Leaguers Enter Final Stretch." *Times of the Americas* (September 18, 1991).

ESTRADA, RICHARD MEDINA. "Border Revolution: The Mexican Revolution in the Ciudad Juárez–El Paso Area, 1906–1915." M.A. Thesis, University of Texas at El Paso, 1975.

ESPOSITO, MATTHEW D. "Memorializing Modern Mexico: The State Funerals of the Porfirian Era, 1876–1911." Ph.D. diss., Texas Christian University, 1998.

EVANS, ALBERT S. *Our Sister Republic: A Gala Trip Through Tropical Mexico in 1869–70*. Hartford: Columbian Book Co., 1870.

Excelsior (Mexico City), Jan. 6, 1945; Sept. 8, 1988.

FAGEN, RICHARD R., AND WILLIAM S. TUOHY. *Politics and Privilege in Mexico City*. Stanford: Stanford University Press, 1972.

FALCÓN, ROMANA. "Poderes y razones de las jefaturas políticas: Coahuila en el primer siglo de vida independiente." In Jaime E. Rodríguez O., ed., *The Evolution of the Mexican Political System*. Wilmington, Del.: SR Books, 1992.

———. *Revolución y caciquismo: San Luis Potosí, 1910–1938*. México: El Colegio de México, 1984.

———. "Raíces de la Revolución: Evaristo Madero, el primer eslabón de la ca-dena." In Jaime E. Rodríguez O., ed., *The Revolutionary Process in Mexico: Es-says on Political and Social Change, 1880–1940*, pp. 33–56. Los Angeles: UCLA Latin American Center Publications, 1990.

FEIN, SETH. "Hollywood and United States–Mexico Relations in the Golden Age of Mexican Cinema." Ph.D. diss., University of Texas, 1996.

FELL, JAMES E. JR. *Ores to Metals: The Rocky Mountain Smelting Industry*. Lincoln: University of Nebraska Press, 1979.

FLORES CLAIR, EDUARDO. "Mecanismos de resistencia en Real del Monte y Pachuca." *Historias* (October 1989–March 1990), pp. 39–53.

FRANCO, JEAN. *Plotting Women: Gender and Representation in Mexico.* New York: Columbia University Press, 1988.

FRAZER, ROBERT W. "Matías Romero and the French Intervention in Mexico." Ph.D. diss., University of California, 1941.

FRENCH, WILLIAM E. "A Peaceful and Working People: Manners, Morals, and Class Formation in Northern Mexico." Albuquerque: University of New Mexico Press, 1996.

———. "'Progreso Forzado': Workers and the Inculcation of the Capitalist Work Ethic in the Parral Mining District." In William H. Beezley, Cheryl E. Martin, and William E. French, eds., *Rituals of Rule, Rituals of Resistance: Public Celebration and Popular Culture in Mexico.* Wilmington, Del.: SR Books, 1994.

FRIEDRICH, PAUL. *Agrarian Revolt in a Mexican Village.* Englewood Cliffs: Prentice Hall, 1970.

FUENTES, CARLOS. *The Death of Artemio Cruz.* Translated by Sam Hileman. New York: Noonday Press, 1966.

GAMBOA OJEDA, LETICIA. "Dos aspectos de la clase obrera textil de Atlixco a fines del Porfiriato." *Historias* (October 1989–March 1990).

GARCÍA, MARIO T. *Desert Immigrants: The Mexicans of El Paso, 1880–1920.* New Haven: Yale University Press, 1981.

———. *Mexican Americans: Leadership, Ideology, and Identity, 1930–1960.* New Haven: Yale University Press, 1989.

GARCÍA, RICHARD A. *Rise of the Mexican American Middle Class: San Antonio, 1919–1941.* College Station: Texas A&M University Press, 1991.

GARCÍA DÍAZ, BERNARDO. "La clase obrera textil del Valle de Orizaba, en México: Migraciones y origen." *Siglo XIX* (July–December 1988), pp. 77–108.

GARCÍA Y GRIEGO, MANUEL. "The Importation of Mexican Contract Laborers to the United States, 1942–1964: Antecedents, Operation, and Legacy." In Peter G. Brown and Henry Shue, eds., *The Border That Joins: Mexican Migrants and U.S. Responsibility.* Totowa, N.J.: Rowman and Littlefield, 1983.

GERLACH, ALLEN. "Conditions Along the Border—1915: The Plan de San Diego." *New Mexico Historical Review* 43 (1968), pp. 195–212.

GIL, CARLOS B. *Life in Provincial Mexico: National and Regional History Seen from Mascota, Jalisco, 1867–1972.* Los Angeles: UCLA Latin American Center Publications, 1983.

GILDERHUS, MARK T. R. "Senator Albert B. Fall and 'The Plot against Mexico.'" *New Mexico Historical Review* 48 (October 1973), pp. 299–311.

GILL, MARIO. "Teresa Urrea, la santa de Cabora." *Historia Mexicana* 6: 4 (April–June 1957), pp. 626–44.

GILLETT, JAMES B. *Six Years with the Texas Rangers, 1875–1881.* Lincoln: University of Nebraska Press, 1976.

GILLY, ADOLFO. *La revolución interrumpida; México, 1910–1920: Una guerra campesina por la tierra y el poder.* México: Ediciones El Caballito, 1971.

GINER, REY, MIGUEL ANGEL. *Uruáchic: 250 años de historia.* Chihuahua: Centro Libren La Prensa; 1986.

GOMPERS, SAMUEL. "United States—Mexico—Labor: Their Relations." *American Federationist* (August 1916), pp. 633–51.

GONZALES, NANCIE L. *The Spanish Americans of New Mexico: A Heritage of Pride.* Albuquerque: University of New Mexico Press, 1967.

GONZÁLEZ, NAVARRO, MOISÉS. *Anatomía del poder en México (1848–1853)*. México: El Colegio de México, 1977.

———. *Estadísticas sociales del Porfiriato, 1877–1910*. México: Dirección General de Estadística, 1956.

———. *La pobreza en México*. México: El Colegio de México, 1985.

———. *Sociología e historia en México*. México: El Colegio de México, 1970.

GREEN, GEORGE. "The Pecan Shellers of San Antonio." *The Compass Rose* (Special Collections Division, University of Texas, Arlington) 6: 1 (spring 1992).

GRISWOLD DEL CASTILLO, RICHARD. *The Los Angeles Barrio, 1850–1890: A Social History*. Berkeley: University of California Press, 1979.

GRUNSTEIN, ARTURO. "Railroads and Sovereignty: Policymaking in Porfirian Mexico." Ph.D. diss., UCLA, 1994.

GUEDEA, VIRGINIA. *En busca de un gobierno alterno: Los Guadalupes de México*. México: Universidad Nacional Autónoma de México, 1992.

GUTIÉRREZ, RAMÓN A. *When Jesus Came, the Corn Mothers Went Away: Marriage, Sexuality, and Power in New Mexico, 1500–1846*. Stanford: Stanford University Press, 1991.

HABER, STEPHEN H. *Industry and Underdevelopment: The Industrialization of Mexico, 1890–1940*. Stanford: Stanford University Press, 1989.

HALE, CHARLES A. *Mexican Liberalism in the Age of Mora, 1821–1853*. New Haven: Yale University Press, 1968.

———. *The Transformation of Liberalism in Late Nineteenth-Century Mexico*. Princeton: Princeton University Press, 1989.

HALL, FRANK LOUIS. "El Paso, Texas, and Juárez, Mexico: A Study of a Bi-Ethnic Community, 1846–1881." Ph.D. diss., University of Texas, 1978.

HALL, G. EMLEN, AND DAVID J. WEBER. "Mexican Liberals and the Pueblo Indians, 1821–1829." *New Mexico Historical Review* 59: 1 (1984), pp. 5–32.

HALL, LINDA B., AND DON M. COERVER. *Revolution on the Border: The United States and Mexico, 1910–1920*. Albuquerque: University of New Mexico Press, 1988.

HAMILTON, NANCY. *Ben Dowell: El Paso's First Mayor*. El Paso: Texas Western Press, University of Texas at El Paso, 1976.

HAMMOND, JOHN HAYS. *The Autobiography of John Hammond*. 2 vols. New York: Farrar & Rinehart, 1935.

HAMNETT, BRIAN R. *Roots of Insurgency: Mexican Regions, 1750–1824*. Cambridge: Cambridge University Press, 1986.

———. *Juárez*. London: Longman, 1994.

HAMON, JAMES L., AND STEPHEN R. NIBLO. *Precursores de la revolución agraria en México*. México: Secretaría de Educación Pública, 1975.

HANNA, ALFRED J., AND KATHRYN A. HANNA. *Napoleon III and Mexico*. Chapel Hill: University of North Carolina Press, 1971.

HANSEN, ROGER D. *The Politics of Mexican Development*. Baltimore: Johns Hopkins University Press, 1971.

HARRIS, CHARLES H., III. *A Mexican Family Empire: The Latifundio of the Sánchez Navarro Family, 1765–1867*. Austin: University of Texas Press, 1975.

HARRIS, CHARLES H., III, AND LOUIS R. SADLER. "The Plan of San Diego and the Mexican–United States War Crisis of 1916." *Hispanic American Historical Review* 58: 3 (August 1978), pp. 381–408.

HART, JOHN M., "Agrarian Precursors of the Mexican Revolution: The Development of an Ideology." *The Americas* 29: 2 (1972), pp. 131–50.

———. "Agrarian Reform." In W. Dirk Raat and William H. Beezley, eds., *Twentieth-Century Mexico*. Lincoln: University of Nebraska Press, 1986.

———. *Los anarquistas mexicanos, 1860–1900*. México: Secretaría de Educación Pública, 1974.

———. *Revolutionary Mexico: The Coming and Process of the Mexican Revolution*. Berkeley: University of California Press, 1987.

HAYNES, ALLEN. "Orden y Progreso: The Revolutionary Ideology of Alberto J. Pani." Paper presented at the Sixth Conference of Mexican and U.S. Historians, Chicago, September 1981.

HEATH, HILARIE J. "Los primeros escarceos del imperialismo en México: Las casas comerciales británicas, 1821–1867." *Historias* (April–September 1989), pp. 77–89.

HEATH, SHIRLEY BRICE. *Telling Tongues: Language Policy in Mexico, Colony to Nation*. New York: Teachers College Press, Columbia University, 1972.

HELLMAN, JUDITH ADLER. *Mexico in Crisis*. New York: Holmes & Meier Publishers, Inc., 1978.

HERNÁNDEZ, ALICIA. "Militares y negocios en la revolución mexicana." *Historia Mexicana* 34: 2 (1984), pp. 181–212.

HERRERA, CANALES, INÉS. "Comercio y comerciantes de la costa del Pacífico mexicano a mediados del siglo XIX." *Historias* (April–September 1988), pp. 129–53.

———. *El comercio exterior de México, 1821–1875*. México: El Colegio de México, 1977.

HEYMAN, JOSIAH McC. *Life and Labor on the Border: Working People of Northeastern Sonora, Mexico, 1886–1986*. Tucson: University of Arizona Press, 1991.

HIBINO, BÁRBARA. "Cervecería Cuauhtémoc: A Case Study of Technological and Industrial Development in Mexico." *Mexican Studies / Estudios Mexicanos* 8: 1 (winter 1992), pp. 23–43.

HINDS, HAROLD E. JR. "Kalimán, Mexico's Most Popular Superhero." *Studies in Latin American Popular Culture* 4 (1985), pp. 27–42.

HOFFMAN, ABRAHAM. *Unwanted Mexican Americans in the Great Depression: Repatriation Pressures, 1929–1939*. Tucson: University of Arizona Press, 1974.

HOLLANDER, PAUL. *Political Pilgrims: Travels of Western Intellectuals to the Soviet Union, China, and Cuba, 1928–1978*. New York: Oxford University Press, 1981.

HUERTA JARAMILLO, ANA MA. D. "Insurrecciones campesinas en el estado de Puebla, 1868–1870." In Andrea Sánchez Quintanar and Juan Manuel de la Serna H., eds., *Movimientos populares en la historia de México y América Latina*. México: Universidad Nacional Autónoma de México, 1987, pp. 217–27.

HUMBOLDT, ALEXANDER VON. *Personal Narrative of Travels to the Equinoctial Regions of the New Continent during the Years 1799–1804*. 4 vols. 3d ed. London, 1822.

ILLESCAS, MARÍA DOLORES. "Agitación social y bandidaje en el estado de Morelos durante el siglo XIX." *Estudios* (fall 1988), pp. 59–100.

JACKSON, STEPHEN F. "Killing of Mexican Journalists," and "Journalism in Mexico." *Editor & Publisher*, October 7 and 14, 1989.

JACOBS, IAN. *Ranchero Revolt: The Mexican Revolution in Guerrero*. Austin: University of Texas Press, 1982.

JOHANNSEN, ROBERT W. *A New Era for the United States: Americans and the War with Mexico.* University Lecture Series, University of Illinois. Urbana, 1975.

JOHNSON, DAVID NATHAN. "Exiles and Intrigue: Francisco I. Madero and the Mexican Revolutionary Junta in San Antonio, 1910–1911." M.A. Thesis, Trinity University, 1975.

JOHNSON, DINA. "Hispanic Man Concept Tied to Hispanic Communities." The Eagle (Section for the Hispanic Community), *Fort Worth Star-Telegram*, September 30, 1992.

JONES, GUS T. "The Nazi Failure in Mexico." Hoover Institution Archives, Stanford University.

JONES, OAKAH L. JR. *Santa Anna.* New York: Twayne, 1968.

JOSEPH, GILBERT M. *Revolution from Without: Yucatán, Mexico, and the United States, 1880–1924.* Durham: Duke University Press, 1980.

———. "The United States, Leading Elites, and Rural Revolt in Yucatán, 1836–1915." In Daniel Nugent, ed., *Rural Revolt in Mexico and U.S. Intervention*, pp. 167–97. La Jolla: Center for U.S.—Mexican Studies, University of California, San Diego, 1988.

JOSEPH, GILBERT M., AND ALLEN WELLS. "Yucatán: Elite Politics and Rural Insurgency." In Thomas Benjamin and Mark Wasserman, eds., *Provinces of the Revolution: Essays on Regional Mexican History, 1910–1929*. Albuquerque: University of New Mexico Press, 1990.

JOSEPH, GILBERT M., AND DANIEL NUGENT, EDS., *Everyday Forms of State Formation: Revolution and the Negotiation of Rule in Modern Mexico* (Durham: Duke University Press, 1994).

JOSLIN, DAVID. *A Century of Banking in Latin America.* London: Cassell, 1963.

KANDELL, JONATHAN. *La Capital: The Biography of Mexico City.* New York: Random House, 1988.

KATZ, FRIEDRICH. *The Secret War in Mexico: Europe, the United States and the Mexican Revolution.* Chicago: The University of Chicago Press, 1981.

KEMMERER, EDWIN WALTER. *Modern Currency Reforms: A History and Discussion of Recent Currency Reforms in India, Puerto Rico, Philippine Islands, Straits Settlements and Mexico.* New York: Macmillan Co., 1911.

KENNEDY, PAUL P. *The Middle Beat: A Correspondent's View of Mexico, Guatemala, and El Salvador*, edited by Stanley R. Ross. New York: Teachers College Press, Columbia University, 1971.

KING, ROBIN ANN. "Confrontation and Accommodation: A Multi-Action Approach to Mexican External Debt Policy and Macroeconomic Management." Ph.D. diss., University of Texas, 1991.

———. "Propuesta mexicana de una moratoria de la dueda a nivel continental (1933)." *Historia Mexicana* 38: 3 (January–March 1989), pp. 497–522.

KNAPP, FRANK A. *The Life of Sebastián Lerdo de Tejada, 1823–1889: A Study in Influence and Obscurity.* Austin: University of Texas Press, 1951.

KNIGHT, ALAN. *The Mexican Revolution.* 2 vols. Cambridge: Cambridge University Press, 1986.

———. "Revolutionary Project, Recalcitrant People: Mexico, 1910–1914." In Jaime E. Rodriguez O., ed., *The Revolutionary Process in Mexico: Essays on Political and Social Change, 1880–1940*, pp. 227–64. Los Angeles: UCLA Latin American Center Publications, 1990.

———. "The United States and the Mexican Peasantry, 1880–1940." In Daniel Nugent, ed., *Rural Revolt in Mexico and U.S. Intervention*. La Jolla: Center for U.S.–Mexican Studies, University of California, San Diego, 1988.

KOLONITZ, PAULA (CONDESA). *Un viaje a México en 1864*. México: Secretaría de Educación Pública, 1976.

KRAUSE, ENRIQUE. *Porfirio Díaz: Místico de la autoridad*. México: Fondo de Cultura Económica, 1987.

———. *La reconstrucción económica*. México: El Colegio de México, 1977.

KROEBER, CLIFTON. *Man, Land and Water: Mexico's Farm Lands Irrigation Policies, 1885–1911*. Berkeley: University of California Press, 1983.

KUZIO, BARBARA ALLEN. "President Abelardo Rodríguez (1932–1934): From Maximato to Cardenismo." M.A. thesis, Portland State University, 1997.

LAFRANCE, DAVID G. "Many Causes, Movements, Failures, 1910–1913: The Regional Nature of Maderismo." In Thomas Benjamin and Mark Wasserman, eds., *Provinces of the Revolution: Essays on Regional Mexican History, 1910–1929*. Albuquerque: University of New Mexico Press, 1990.

———. "A Mexican Popular Image of the United States through the Baseball Hero, Fernando Valenzuela." Paper presented at the North American Society for Sport History, May 1984.

———. *The Mexican Revolution in Puebla, 1908–1913: The Maderista Movement and the Failure of Liberal Reform*. Wilmington, Del. SR Books, 1989.

———. "The Myth and the Reality of 'El Negro' Durazo: Mexico City's Most-Wanted Police Chief." *Studies in Latin American Popular Culture* 9 (1990), pp. 237–48.

LANGSTON, EDWARD LONNIE. "The Impact of Prohibition on the Mexican–United States Border: The El Paso–Ciudad Juárez Case." Ph.D. diss., Texas Tech University, 1974.

LANGSTON, WILLIAM S. "Coahuila: Centralization against State Autonomy." In Thomas Benjamin and William McNellie, eds., *Other Mexicos: Essays on Regional Mexican History, 1876–1911*, pp. 55–76. Albuquerque: University of New Mexico Press, 1984.

LARKIN, MARGARET. *Seven Shares in a Gold Mine*. New York: Simon and Schuster, 1959.

LAY, SHAWN. *War, Revolution and the Ku Klux Klan: A Study of Intolerance in a Border City*. El Paso, Texas Western Press, University of Texas at El Paso, 1985.

LEÓN, ARNOLDO DE. *The Tejano Community, 1836–1900*. Albuquerque: University of New Mexico Press, 1982.

LERDO DE TEJADA, MIGUEL. *El comercio exterior de México desde la conquista hasta hoy*. México: R. Rafael, 1853.

LEVENSON, J. C., ERNEST SAMUELS, CHARLES VANDERSEE, AND VIOLA HOPKINS WINNER, EDS., *The Letters of Henry Adams*. 4 vols. Cambridge: Harvard University Press, 1988.

LEVY, DANIEL, AND GABRIEL SZÉKELY. *Mexico: Paradoxes of Stability and Change*. Boulder, Colo.: Westview Press, 1983.

LIDA, DAVID. "Making for Mexico." *Sky Magazine* (July 1992), pp. 81–89.

LIEUWEN, EDWIN. *Mexican Militarism: The Political Rise and Fall of the Revolutionary Army, 1910–1940*. Albuquerque: University of New Mexico Press, 1968.m

LILL, THOMAS R. *National Debt of Mexico: History and Present Status*. New York: Report for the International Committee of Bankers, 1919.

LIMANTOUR, JOSÉ YVES. *Apuntes sobre mi vida pública*. México: Editorial Porrúa, 1965.

LISS, SHELDON. *A Century of Disagreement: The Chamizal Conflict, 1864–1964*. Washington, D.C.: University Press of Washington, D.C., 1965.

LITWICKI, ELLEN M. "From *Patrón to Patria: Fiestas and Mexicano* Identity in Late Nineteenth-Century Tucson." Paper presented at 1992 meeting of the Organization of American Historians.

LLOYD, JANE-DALE. "Ranchos and Rebellion: The Case of Northwestern Chihuahua, 1905–1909." In Daniel Nugent, ed., *Rural Revolt in Mexico and U.S. Intervention*, pp. 299–346. La Jolla: Center for U.S.–Mexican Studies, University of California, San Diego, 1988.

LOMNITZ, LARISSA A. *Networks and Marginality: Life in a Mexican Shantytown.* Translated by Cinna Lomnitz. New York: Academic Press, 1977.

LOMNITZ, LARISSA A., AND MARISOL PÉREZ-LIZAUR. *A Mexican Elite Family, 1820–1980.* Princeton: Princeton University Press, 1987.

LÓPEZ, JAIME. *10 años de guerrillas en México, 1964–1974.* México: Editorial Posada, 1974.

LÓPEZ, CÁMARA, FRANCISCO. *La estructura económica y social de México en la época de la Reforma.* México: Siglo Veintiuno, 1967.

LOREY, DAVID E. *The Rise of the Professions in Twentieth-Century Mexico: University Graduates and Occupational Change since 1929.* Los Angeles: UCLA Latin American Center, 1992.

LOREY, DAVID E., AND AIDA MOSTKOFF-LINARES. "Mexico's 'Lost Decade,' 1980–1990: Evidence on Class Structure and Professional Employment from the 1990 Census." In James W. Wilkie, Carlos Alberto Contreras, and Christof Anders Weber, eds., *Statistical Abstract of Latin America*, vol. 30, part 2. Los Angeles: UCLA Latin American Center Publications, 1993.

———. "Zedillo's Presidency: the Status of Social Development." Presentation, Tulane University, April 12, 1996.

LUDLOW, LEONOR. "La construcción de un banco: El Banco Nacional de México (1881–1884)." In Leonor Ludlow and Carlos Marichal, eds., *Banco y poder en México, 1800–1925*, pp. 299–346. México: Grijalbo, 1985.

LYON, G. F. *Journal of a Residence and Tour in the Republic of Mexico in 1826.* 2 vols. London: J. Murray, 1828.

MACHADO, MANUEL A. *Barbarians of the North: Modern Chihuahua and the Mexican Political System.* Austin: Eakin Press, 1992.

MACIEL, DAVID, AND PATRICIA BERENO, EDS., *Aztlán: Historia del pueblo chicano, 1848–1910.* México: Secretaría de Educación Pública, 1975.

MACLACHLAN, COLIN M. *Anarchism and the Mexican Revolution: The Political Trials of Ricardo Flores Magón in the United States.* Berkeley: University of California Press, 1991.

———. *Spain's Empire in the New World: The Role of Ideas in Institutional and Social Change.* Berkeley: University of California Press, 1988.

MACLACHLAN, COLIN M., AND JAIME E. RODRIGUEZ O., *The Forging of the Cosmic Race: A Reinterpretation of Colonial Mexico.* Expanded edition. Berkeley: University of California Press, 1990.

MCLEOD, JAMES ANGUS. "Public Health, Social Assistance and the Consolidation of the Mexican State, 1888–1940." Ph.D. diss., Tulane University, 1990.

MCWILLIAMS, CAREY. *North from Mexico: The Spanish-Speaking People of the United States.* Philadelphia: J. P. Lippincott, 1949.

MADERO, FRANCISCO I. *La sucesión presidencial en 1910.* Saltillo: Imprenta del Estado de Coahuila, 1958.

MANZANOS, ROSARIO. "Una verdadera 'salinasmanía,' la invasión callejera de objectos con la imagen del expresidente," *Proceso* (December 25, 1995), pp. 50–57.

MARÍN, CHRISTINE. "Go Home, Chicanos: A Study of the Brown Berets in California and Arizona." In Manuel P. Servin, ed., *An Awakened Minority: The Mexican Americans*. Beverly Hills: Glencoe Press, 1974.

MARTÍNEZ, OSCAR J. *Border Boom Town: Ciudad Juárez Since 1848*. Austin: University of Texas Press, 1975.

———. *Troublesome Border*. Tucson: University of Arizona Press, 1988.

MARTÍNEZ, ASSAD, CARLOS. *El laboratorio de la revolucion: El Tabasco garridista*. México: Siglo XXI, 1979.

MASTERSON, DANIEL, AND JOHN BRATZEL. "Unknown Internees: Hemispheric Security and the Latin American Japanese during the Second World War." MS.

MATUTE, ALVARO. *Le carrera del caudillo: Historia de la Revolucion Mexicana, 1917–1920*. México: El Colegio de México, 1980.

MAZÓN, MAURICIO. *Zoot-Suit Riots: The Psychology of Symbolic Annihilation*. Austin: University of Texas Press, 1984.

Memoria de los trabajos emprendidos y llevados a cabo por la Comisión N. del Centenario de la Independencia. México, 1910.

MEYER, JEAN A. *Estado y sociedad con Calles*. México: El Colegio de México, 1977.

———. "Revolution and Reconstruction in the 1920s." In *The Cambridge History of Latin America*, vol. 5. Leslie Bethell, ed. New York: Cambridge University Press, 1986.

MEYER, MICHAEL C. *Huerta: A Political Portrait*. Lincoln: University of Nebraska Press, 1972.

———. "The Mexican–German Conspiracy of 1915." *The Americas* 23: 1 (July 1966), pp. 76–89.

MEYERS, WILLIAM K. *Forge of Progress, Crucible of Revolt: The Origins of the Mexican Revolution in La Comarca Lagunera, 1880–1911*. Albuquerque: University of New Mexico Press, 1994.

MILLER, MICHAEL. "Forging the Nation; Avila Camacho and the Emergence of Modern Mexico." Ph.D. diss., Texas A&M University, 1996.

MILLER, RICHARD U. "American Railroad Unions and the National Railways of Mexico. An Exercise in Nineteenth-Century Proletarian Manifest Destiny." *Labor History*. 15: 2 (spring 1974), pp. 239–60.

MILLS, W. W. *Forty Years at El Paso, 1858–1898*. El Paso: By the Author, 1901.

MONTEJANO, DAVID. *Anglos and Mexicans in the Making of Texas*. Austin: University of Texas Press, 1987.

MORA, PAT. *Borders*. Houston: Arte Público, 1986.

———. *Chants*. Houston: Arte Público, 1984.

MORENO, ROBERTO. *La polémica del Darwinismo en México: Siglo XIX (Testimonios)*. México: Universidad Nacional Autónoma de México, 1984.

MORENO RIVAS, YOLANDA. *Historia de la música popular mexicana*. Mexico: Alianza Editorial Mexicana, 1979.

MORGAN, ANTHONY. "Proletarians, Politicos and Patriarchs: The Use and Abuse of Cultural Customs in the Early Industrialization of Mexico City (1880–1910)." In William H. Beezley, Cheryl E. Martin, and William E. French, eds., *Rituals of Rule, Rituals of Resistance: Public Celebration and Popular Culture in Mexico*. Wilmington, Del. SR Books, 1994.

MORÍN, RAÚL. *Among the Valiant: Mexican-Americans in WW II and Korea*. Los Angeles: Borden Publishing Company, 1966.

MORNER, MAGNUS. *Estado, raza, y cambio social en la Hispanoamérica colonial*. México: Secretaría de Educación Pública, 1974.

————. *Race Mixture in the History of Latin* America. Boston: Little, Brown, 1967.
MORRIS, STEPHEN D. *Corruption and Politics in Contemporary Mexico.* Tuscaloosa: University of Alabama Press, 1991.
MOSES, BERNARD. *The Railway Revolution in Mexico.* San Francisco: The Berkeley Press, 1895.
MOYANO PAHISSA, ANGELA. "Identidad cultural en la frontera entre México y los Estados Unidos." *Estudios de historia moderna y contemporánea de México,* pp. 51–61. México: Universidad Nacional Autónoma de México, 1989.
NEW ORLEANS (LA.) *Picayune,* Aug. 15, 1893; Oct. 16, 1893; Sept. 1–20, 1910.
New York Times, July 28, 1886; Sept. 1–20, 1910; April 11–18, May 4, 1944; July 23, 1986; June 19, 1992.
NIBLO, STEPHEN R. War, *Diplomacy, and Development: The United States and Mexico, 1938–1954.* Wilmington, Del.: SR Books, 1995.
————. *Mexico in the 1940s.* Wilmington, Del.: SR Books, forthcoming.
NORIEGA ELIO, CECILIA. *El Constituyente de 1842.* México: Universidad Nacional Autónoma de México, 1986.
NOVO, SALVADOR. *Cocina mexicana: Historia gastronómica de la Ciudad de México.* México: Editorial Porrúa, 1967.
OCHOA, ENRIQUE C. "Feeding Mexico: The State, The Marketplace, and Social Policy Since 1934." Ph.D. diss., UCLA, 1995.
OFFICER, JAMES E. *Hispanic Arizona, 1536–1856.* Tucson: University of Arizona Press, 1987.
OHMSTEDE, ANTONIO ESCOBAR, AND FRANS J. SCHRYER. "Las sociedades agrarias en el norte de Hidalgo, 1856–1900." *Mexican Studies/Estudios Mexicanos* 8:1 (winter 1992), pp. 1–21.
OLIVERA, ANTONIO, RUTH R., AND LILIANE CRETE. *Life in Mexico Under Santa Anna, 1822–1855.* Norman: University of Oklahoma Press, 1991.
OLLIFF, DONATHON C. *Reforma Mexico and the United States: A Search for Alternatives to Annexation, 1854–1861.* University, Ala.: University of Alabama Press, 1981.
OLSEN, PATRICE ELIZABETH. "Issues of National Identity: Obregón, Calles and Nationalist Architecture, 1920–1930." Ph.D. diss., Pennsylvania State University, forthcoming.
O'MALLEY, ILENE V. *The Myth of the Revolution: Hero Cults and the Institutionalization of the Mexican State, 1920–1940.* New York: Greenwood Press, 1986.
OÑATE, ABDIEL. "Banco y agricultura en México: La crisis de 1907–1908 y la fundacíon del primer banco agrícola." In Leonor Ludlow and Carlos Marichal, eds., *Banco y poder en México, 1800–1925,* pp. 347–73. México: Grijalbo, 1985.
OSTER, PATRICK. *The Mexicans.* New York: William Morrow and Company, Inc., 1989.
OWEN, LOU CRETIA. *Diary.* Tennessee State Library and Archives, Nashville, Tennessee.
PACE, ANNE. "Mexican Refugees in Arizona, 1910–1911." *Arizona and the West* 16: 1 (spring 1974), pp. 5–18.
PANSTERS, WIL. *Politics and Power in Puebla: The Political History of a Mexican State, 1937–1987.* Amsterdam: Center for Latin American Research and Documentation, 1990.
"Paradise Lost." *Time* (November 10, 1975), pp. 88–89.
PAREDES, AMÉRICO. *With His Pistol in His Hand: A Border Ballad and Its Hero.* Austin: University of Texas Press, 1958.

PARLEE, LORENA M. "The Impact of the United States Railroad Unions on Organized Labor and Government Policy in Mexico (1880–1911)." *Hispanic American Historical Review* 64: 3 (August 1984), pp. 443–75.

PASTOR, ROBERT A., AND JORGE G. CASTANEDA. *Limits to Friendship*. New York: A. A. Knopf, 1988.

PERCIVAL, OLIVE. *Mexico City: An Idler's Notebook*. Chicago: Herbert S. Stone Co., 1901.

PÉREZ, ABEL R. *Teodoro A. Dehesa: Gobernante veracruzano*. México: Talleres Stylo, 1960.

PILCHER, JEFFREY M. "'!Viven Tamales!,' The Creation of a Mexican National Cuisine." Ph.D. diss., Texas Christian University, 1993.

PIÑERA RAMÍREZ, DAVID. "La frontera norte: De la independencia a neustros días." *Estudios de historia moderna y contemporánea de México*, pp. 27–50. México: Universidad Nacional Autónoma de México, 1989.

PLENN, J. H. *Mexico Marches*. New York: Bobbs-Merrill, 1939.

PLETCHER, DAVID M. *Rails, Mines, and Progress: Seven American Promoters in Mexico, 1867–1911*. Ithaca: Cornell University Press, 1958.

POINSETT, JOEL R. *Notes on Mexico*. Philadelphia: H. C. Gorey and I. Lee, 1824.

POPE GREGORY XVI. "Breve pontificio sobre diminución de días festivas en la República Mexicana." Rare Book Collection, Latin American Library, Tulane University, New Orleans.

POTASH, ROBERT A. *Mexican Government and Industrial Development in the Early Republic: The Banco de Avio*. Amherst: University of Massachusetts Press, 1983.

PRECIADO MARTIN, PATRICIA. *Songs My Mother Sang to Me: An Oral History of Mexican American Women*. Tucson: University of Arizona Press, 1992.

QUIÑONES, SAM. "Nada Personal," *Fort Worth Star Telegram*, February 14, 1997.

———. "Gus T. Jones and the FBI in Mexico, 1900–1947." Paper presented at the American Historical Association Meeting, San Francisco, December 1989.

———. "Ideas and Society in Don Porfirio's Mexico." *The Americas* 30: 1 (July 1973), pp. 33–51.

———. *El Positivismo durante el Porfiriato*. México: Secretaría de Educación Pública, 1975.

RAAT, WILLIAM D. "The Antipositivist Movement in Prerevolutionary Mexico, 1892–1911." *Journal of Interamerican Studies and World Affairs* 19: 1 (February 1977), pp. 83–98.

RAAT, W. DIRK, AND WILLIAM H. BEEZLEY, EDS. *Twentieth-Century Mexico*. Lincoln: University of Nebraska Press, 1986.

RAMOS, CARMEN. "Mujeres trabajadoras en el Porfiriato." *Historias* (October 1988–March 1989), pp. 113–121.

REAVIS, DICK J. *Conversations with Moctezuma: Ancient Shadows Over Modern Life in Mexico*. New York: William Morrow, 1990.

Recuerdo del Primer Centenario de la Independencia. México: Rondero de Treppiedi, 1910.

REES JONES, RICARDO. El despotismo ilustrado y los intendentes de la Neuva España. México: Universidad Nacional Autónoma de México, 1979.

REYES HEROLES, JESÚS. *El liberalismo mexicano: La integración de las ideas*. 3 vols. México: Universidad Nacional Autónoma de México, 1961.

RICE, JACQUELINE ANN. "The Porfirian Political Elite: Life Patterns of the Delegates to the 1892 Union Liberal Convention." Ph.D. diss., University of California, Los Angeles, 1979.

RICHMOND, DOUGLAS W., ED. *Essays on the Mexican War*. College Station: Texas A&M University Press, 1986.

———. *Venustiano Carranza's Nationalist Struggle, 1893–1920*. Lincoln, 1983.

RIDING, ALAN. *Distant Neighbors: A Portrait of the Mexicans*. New York: Vintage Books, 1986.

RIGUZZI, PAOLA. "México próspero: Las dimensiones de la imagen nacional en el Porfiriato." *Historias* (April–September 1988), pp. 137–57.

RIVERA-GARZA, CRISTINA. "The Masters of the Streets: Bodies, Power and Modernity in Mexico, 1867–1930. Ph.D. diss., University of Houston, 1995.

ROCAFUERTE, VICENTE. *Ensayo sobre la tolerancia religiosa*. México: Imprenta de Rivera, 1831.

ROCHE, DANIEL. *The People of Paris: An Essay in Popular Culture in the Eighteenth Century*. Translated by Marie Evens. Berkeley: University of California Press, 1987.

ROCKWELL, ELSIE. "Rural Schooling and the State in Post-Revolutionary Mexico." In Gilbert M. Joseph and Daniel Nugent, eds., *Everyday Forms of State Formation: Revolution and the Negotiation of Rule in Mexico*. Durham: Duke University Press.

RODDICK, JACQUELINE. *The Dance of the Millions: Latin America and the Debt Crisis*. London: The Latin American Bureau, 1988.

RODMAN, SELDEN. *Mexican Journal: The Conquerors Conquered*. Carbondale and Edwardsville: Southern Illinois University Press, 1965.

RODÓ, JOSÉ ENRIQUE. *Ariel*, with a foreword by James W. Symington and a prologue by Carlos Fuentes. Austin: University of Texas Press, 1988.

RODRIGUEZ O., JAIME E. "The Conflict between Church and State in Early Republican Mexico." *New World: A Journal of Latin American Studies* (1987), pp. 93–112.

———. *Down from Colonialism*. Los Angeles: Chicano Studies Research Center, University of California, 1983.

———. *The Emergence of Spanish America: Vicente Rocafuerte and Spanish Americanism, 1808–1832*. Berkeley: University of California Press, 1975.

———. "Mexico's First Foreign Loans." In Jaime E. Rodríguez O., ed., *The Independence of Mexico and the Creation of the New Nation*, pp. 215–35. Los Angeles: UCLA Latin American Center Publications, 1989.

———. "The Origins of the 1832 Rebellion." In Jaime E. Rodríguez O., ed., *Patterns of Contention in Mexican History*, pp. 145–62. Wilmington, Del.: SR Books, 1992.

———. "From Royal Subject to Republican Citizen: The Role of the Autonomist in the Independence of Mexico." In Jaime E. Rodríguez O., ed., *The Independence of Mexico and the Creation of the New Nation*, pp. 19–43. Los Angeles: UCLA Latin American Center Publications, 1989.

———. "The Struggle for the Nation: The First Centralist-Federalist Conflict in Mexico." *The Americas* 49: 1 (July 1992), pp. 1–22.

ROEHL, CHARLOTTE. "Porfirio Díaz in the Press of the United States." Ph.D. diss., University of Chicago, 1953.

ROHLFES, LAWRENCE JOHN. "Police and Penal Correction in Mexico City, 1876–1911: A Study of Order and Progress in Porfirian Mexico." Ph.D. diss., Tulane University, 1983.

ROMERO, EMILIA. *Corpancho: Un amigo de México*. México: Junta Mexicana de Investigaciones Históricas, 1949.

ROMERO, MATÍAS. *El ferrocarril de Tehuantepec*. México: Secretaría de Fomento, 1894.

————. *Mexico and the United States: A Study of Subjects Affecting Their Political, Commercial and Social Relations Made with a View of Their Promotion*. New York and London: G. P. Putnam's Sons, 1898.

ROSENBERG, EMILY S. "Foundations of United States International Financial Power: Gold Standard Diplomacy, 1900–1905." *Business History Review* 59:2 (summer 1985), pp. 176–89.

ROSS, STANLEY R. *Francisco I. Madero: Apostle of Mexican Democracy*. New York: Columbia University Press, 1955.

RUBENSTEIN, ANNE G. "Comic Books, Censorship, and the Invention of Cultural Imperialism in Mexico, 1936–1976." Ph.D. diss., Rutgers University, 1995.

————. "Naked Ladies, Bad Language, and the Argument Against Comic Books in Mexico." MS.

RUBIO GOLDSMITH, RAQUEL. "Shipwrecked in the Desert: A Short History of the Mexican Sisters of the House of Providence in Douglas, Arizona, 1927–1949." In Vicki L. Ruiz and Susan Tiano, eds., *Women on the U.S.–Mexico Border: Responses to Change*. Boston: Allen and Unwin, 1987.

RUIZ, RAMÓN EDUARDO. *Triumphs and Tragedy: A History of the Mexican People*. New York: W. W. Norton & Co., 1992.

RUIZ, VICKI L. "By the Day or the Week: Mexican Domestic Workers in El Paso." In Vicki L. Ruiz and Susan Tiano, eds., *Women on the U.S.–Mexican Border: Responses to Change*, p. 61–76. Boston: Allen and Unwin, 1987.

SALAMINI, HEATHER FOWLER. *Agrarian Radicalism in Veracruz, 1920–38*. Lincoln: University of Nebraska Press, 1971.

————. "Tamaulipas: Land Reform and the State." In Thomas Benjamin and Mark Wasserman, eds., *Provinces of the Revolution: Essays on Regional Mexican History, 1910–1929*. Albuquerque: University of New Mexico Press, 1990.

SALAMINI, HEATHER FOWLER, AND MARY KAY VAUGHAN, EDS., *Creating Spaces, Shaping Transition: Women of the Mexican Countryside, 1850–1990*. Tucson: University of Arizona Press, 1994.

SALAS, ELIZABETH. "The *Soldaderas*." In Heather Fowler Salamini and Mary Kay Vaughan, eds., *Creating Spaces, Shaping Transition: Women of the Mexican Countryside, 1850–1990*. Tucson: University of Arizona Press.

SALAZAR, ROSENDO, AND JOSÉ G. ESCOBEDO. *Las pugnas de la gleba, 1907–1922*. México: Comisión Nacional Editorial, 1953.

SALVUCCI, RICHARD J. *Textiles and Capitalism in Mexico: An Economic History of the Obrajes, 1539–1840*. Princeton: Princeton University Press, 1987.

SANCHEZ, GEORGE J. *"Go After the Women": Americanization and the Mexican Immigrant Woman, 1915–1929*. Center for Chicano Research, Working Paper Series, 6. Stanford: Stanford University, 1984.

SÁNCHEZ, THOMAS. *The Zoot-Suit Murders: A Novel*. New York: Dutton, 1978.

SANDOS, JAMES A. *Rebellion in the Borderlands: Anarchism and the Plan of San Diego, 1904–1923*. Norman: University of Oklahoma Press, 1992.

SANDS, WILLIAM F. *Our Jungle Diplomacy*. Chapel Hill: University of North Carolina Press, 1944.

SANTONI, PEDRO. "Los federales radicales y la guerra del '47." Ph.D. diss., El Colegio de México, 1987.

SARAGOZA, ALEX M. *The Monterrey Elite and the Mexican State, 1880–1940*. Austin: University of Texas Press, 1988.

SCHELL, WILLIAM JR. "Integral Outsiders: The Role of Mexico City's American Colony in the Making of Porfirian Mexico." Ph.D. diss., University of North Carolina, 1992.

SCHLOMING, GORDON C. "Civil–Military Relations in Mexico, 1910–1940: A Case Study." Ph.D. diss., Columbia University, 1974.

SCHMIDT, ARTHUR PAUL JR. "The Social and Economic Effects of the Railroad in Puebla and Veracruz, Mexico, 1867–1911." Ph.D. diss., Indiana University. 1974.

SCHMIDT, HENRY C. *The Roots of Lo Mexicano: Self and Society in Mexican Thought, 1900–1934.* College Station: Texas A&M University Press, 1978.

SCHMIDT, SAMUEL. "Humor and Politics: Mexican Political Humor." Translated by Gustavo V. Segade. Unpub. Ms.

SCHOLES, WALTER V. *Mexican Politics during the Juárez Regime, 1855–1872.* Columbia: University of Missouri Prss, 1957.

SCHOONOVER, THOMAS D. *Dollars Over Dominion: The Triumph of Liberalism in Mexican–United States Relations, 1861–1867.* Baton Rouge: Louisiana State University Press, 1978.

———. "Mexican Cotton and the American Civil War." *The Americas* 30: 4 (April 1974), pp. 429–47.

SCHULER, FRIEDRICH E. "Cardenismo Revisited: The International Dimensions of the Post–Reform Cárdenas Era, 1937–1940." Ph.D. diss., University of Chicago, 1990.

SEAL, MARK. "Super Barrio." *American Way* (September 1, 1992), pp. 45–48, 82.

SEWARD, JOHN H. "The Veracruz Massacre of 1879." The Americas, 32: 4 (April 1976), pp. 584–96.

SHERIDAN, P. H. *Personal Memoirs.* 2 vols. New York: C. L. Webster, 1888.

SHRAKE, EDWIN R. "Rich Way to Make a Getaway," *Sports Illustrated* (August 31, 1970), pp. 76, 85–87.

SIERRA, JUSTO. *Evolución política del pueblo mexicano.* México: Universidad Nacional Autónoma de México, 1977.

———. *The Political Evolution of the Mexican People.* Austin: University of Texas Press, 1969.

———. *Viajes en Tierra Yankee, en la Europa Latina,* México: Universidad Nacional Autónoma de México, 1948.

SILVA HERZOG, JESÚS. *Una vida en la vida de México.* México: Siglo Veintiuno Editores, 1972.

SINKIN, RICHARD N. *The Mexican Reform, 1855–1876: A Study in Liberal Nation-Building.* Austin: Latin American Institute, University of Texas at Austin, 1979.

SMITH, MICHAEL M. "Social and Political Dynamics of the Kansas City Colonia during the Mexican Revolution: The Role of the Unión Mexicana Benito Juárez and Middle-Class Leadership." In Virginia Guedea and Jaime E. Rodríguez O., eds., *Five Centuries of Mexican History,* vol. 1, pp. 384–401. México: Instituto de Investigaciones Dr. José María Luis Mora; Irvine: University of California Irvine, 1991.

SOTO, MIGUEL. *La conspiración monárquica en México, 1845–1846.* México: Editorial Offset, 1988.

SOUTHWORTH, JOHN R. *El Directorio Oficial de las Minas y Haciendas de México— The Official Directory of Mines and Estates of Mexico: General Description of the Mining Properties of the Republic of Mexico, in Which Is Included a List of*

Haciendas and Ranches in Those States and Territories Where It Is Possible to Obtain Reliable Data. México: J. Southworth, 1910.

SPENSER, DANIELA. "Soconusco: The Formation of a Coffee Economy in Chiapas." In Thomas Benjamin and William McNellie, eds., *Other Mexicos: Essays on Regional Mexican History, 1876–1911*, pp. 123–43. Albuquerque: University of New Mexico Press, 1984.

STAPLES, ANNE. "Policía y buen gobierno: Efforts to Regulate Public Behavior Before the Constitution of 1857." In William H. Beezley, Cheryl E. Martin, and William E. French, eds., Rituals of Rule, *Rituals of Resistance: Public Celebration and Popular Culture in Mexico*. Wilmington, Del.: SR Books, 1994.

STARR, FREDERICK. *Mexico and the United States*. Chicago: Bible House, 1914.

STEVENS, DONALD FITHIAN. *Origins of Instability in Early Republican Mexico*. Durham: Duke University Press, 1991.

STOCKTON, WILLIAM. "Journalism in Mexico Can Turn into a Risky Craft." *New York Times* (July 23, 1986).

STORY, DALE. *The Mexican Ruling Party: Stability and Authority*. New York: Praeger, 1986.

STORY, VICTOR O. "Genesis of Revolution in the Tamaulipas Sierra: Campesinos and Shopkeepers in the Carrera Torres Uprising, 1907–1911." Ph.D. diss., University of North Carolina, 1991.

SUÁREZ, EDUARDO. *Comentarios y recuerdos, 1926–1946*. México: Editorial Porrúa, 1977.

TAIBO, PACO IGNACIO, II. *Calling All Heroes: A Manual for Taking Power*. Translated by John Mitchell and Ruth Mitchell de Aguilar. Kaneohe, Hawaii: Plover Press, 1990.

——. *The Shadow of the Shadow*. Translated by William I. Neuman. New York: Viking Penguin, 1991.

TENENBAUM, BARBARA. "The Making of a Fait Accompli: The Mexican State 1821–1857." In Jaime E. Rodríguez O., ed., *Patterns of Contention in Mexican History*. Wilmington, Del.: SR Books, 1992.

——. *The Politics of Penury: Debts and Taxes in Mexico, 1821–1856*. Albuquerque: University of New Mexico Press, 1986.

——. "Taxation and Tyranny: Public Finance during the Iturbide Regime, 1821–1823." In Jaime E. Rodríguez O., *Patterns of Contention in Mexican History*. Wilmington, Del.: SR Books, 1992.

——. "Streetwise History—The Paseo de la Reforma and the Porfirian State, 1876–1911." In William H. Beezley, Cheryl E. Martin, and William E. French, eds., *Rituals of Rule, Rituals of Resistance: Public Celebrations and Popular Culture in Mexico*. Wilmington, Del.: SR Books, 1994.

TENORIO-TRILLO, MAURICIO. *Mexico at the World's Fairs: Crafting A Modern Nation*. Berkeley: University of California Press, 1996.

TERRAZAS, MARCELA. "Hacia una nueva frontera: Baja California en los proyectos expansionistas norteamericanos, 1846–1865." *Estudios de historia moderna y contemporánea de México*, no. 13 (1990), pp. 105–17.

THOMSON, GUY P. C. "The Ceremonial and Political Role of Village Bands in Mexico, 1846–1968." In William H. Beezley, Cheryl E. Martin, and William E. French, eds., *Rituals of Rule, Rituals of Resistance: Public Celebrations and Popular Culture in Mexico*. Wilmington, Del.: SR Books, 1994.

——. *Puebla de los Angeles: Industry and Society in a Mexican City, 1700–1850*. Boulder, Colo.: Westview Press, 1989.

————WITH DAVID G. LAFRANCE. *Patriotism, Politics and Popular Liberalism in Nineteenth-Century Mexico: Juan Francisco Lucas and the Puebla Sierra.* Wilmington, Del.: SR Books, 1998.

THOMPSON, JERRY D. *Mexican Texans in the Union Army.* El Paso: Texas Western Press, University of Texas at El Paso, 1986.

————. *Warm Weather and Bad Whiskey: The 1886 Laredo Election Riot.* El Paso: Texas Western Press, University of Texas at El Paso, 1991.

Time Magazine, December 26, 1960.

TIMMONS, W. H. *El Paso: A Borderlands History.* El Paso: Texas Western Press, University of Texas at El Paso, 1990.

TOOR, FRANCES. *The Treasury of Mexican Folkways.* New York: Crown Publishers, 1947.

TORRES RAMÍREZ, BLANCA. *Historia de la Revolución Mexicana: México en la Segunda Guerra Mundial.* México: El Colegio de México, 1979.

TREJO, EVELIA. "Consideraciones sobre el factor religioso en la pérdida del territorio de Texas, 1821–1835." *Estudios de Historia Moderna y Contemporánea de México,* no. 13 (1990), pp. 47–60.

TUDOR, W. G. "Flight of Eagles: The Mexican Expeditionary Air Force *Escuadrón* 201 in World War II." Ph.D. diss., Texas Christian University, 1997.

TUTINO, JOHN. "Revolutionary Confrontation, 1913–1917: The Regions, Classes and the New National State." In Thomas Benjamin and Mark Wasserman, eds., *Provinces of the Revolution: Essays on Regional Mexican History, 1910–1929.* Albuquerque: University of New Mexico, 1990.

TYLER, CURTIS R. "Santiago Vidaurri and the Confederacy." *The Americas* 26:1 (1969), pp. 66–76.

ULLOA, BERTA. *La encrucijada de 1915.* México: El Colegio de México, 1979.

————. *La revolución escindida.* México: El Colegio de México, 1979.

UNITED STATES. Senate Committee on Foreign Relations. *Investigation of Mexican Affairs.* Report and Hearings before a Sub-Committee on Foreign Relations, Senator Albert Fall, Presiding, Pursuant to Senate Resolution 106. 66th Cong. 2d Sess. 2 vols. Washington, D.C.: Government Printing Office, 1919–1920.

VANDERWOOD, PAUL J. *Disorder and Progress: Bandits, Police, and Mexican Development.* Revised and enlarged edition. Wilmington, Del.: SR Books, 1992.

————. "Explaining the Mexican Revolution." In Jaime E. Rodríguez O., ed., *The Revolutionary Process in Mexico: Essays on Political and Social Change, 1880–1940,* pp. 97–114. Los Angeles: UCLA Latin American Center Publications, 1990.

————. *Los rurales mexicanos.* México: Fondo de Cultura Económica, 1982.

————. "Santa Teresa: Mexico's Joan of Arc." In Judith Ewell and William H. Beezley, eds., *The Human Tradition in Latin America: The Nineteenth Century,* pp. 215–32. Wilmington, Del.: SR Books, 1987.

VANE, ERIC. "Required Reading," *Inter-American Magazine* 5, no. 8 (August 20, 1945).

VAN YOUNG, ERIC. "Quetzalcóatl, King Ferdinand, and Ignacio Allende Go to the Seashore; or Messianism and Mystical Kingship in Mexico, 1800–1821." In Jaime E. Rodríguez O., ed., *The Independence of Mexico and the Creation of the New Nation,* Los Angeles: UCLA Latin American Center Publication, 1989.

———. "Augustin Marroquín: The Sociopath as Rebel." In Judith Ewell and William H. Beezley, eds., *The Human Tradition in Latin America: The Nineteenth Century*, Wilmington, Del.: SR Books, 1989.

VASCONCELOS, JOSÉ. *A Mexican Ulysses: An Autobiography*. Translated and abridged by W. Rex Crawford. Bloomington: Indiana University Press, 1963.

VAUGHAN, MARY KAY. "Rural Women's Literacy in the Mexican Revolution: The Case of Tecamachalco, Puebla." MS.

———. "Women School Teachers in the Mexican Revolution: The Story of Reyna's Braids." *Journal of Women's History* 2: 1 (spring 1990), pp. 143–68.

VÁSQUEZ DE KNAUTH, JOSEFINA. *Mexicanos y norteamericanos ante la guerra del '47*. México: Secretaría de Educación Pública, 1972.

———. *Nacionalismo y educación en México*. México: El Colegio de México, 1970.

VELEZ-IBAÑEZ, CARLOS G. *Rituals of Marginality: Politics, Process, and Culture in Central Urban Mexico, 1969–1974*. Berkeley: University of California Press, 1983.

VILLEGAS, ABELARDO. *Mexico en el horizonte liberal*. México: Universidad Nacional Autónoma de México, 1981.

VIQUEIRA ALBÁN, JUAN PEDRO. *¿Relajados o reprimidos? Diversiones públicas y vida social en las ciudad de México durante el Siglo de las Luces*. México: Fondo de Cultura Económica, 1987.

VOGT, WOLFGANG. "Influencias extranjeras en el literatura mexicana anterior a la revolución de 1910." *Relaciones* (spring 1990), pp. 89–119.

VOSE, STUART F. "Nationalizing the Revolution." In Thomas Benjamin and Mark Wasserman, eds., *Provinces of the Revolution: Essays on Regional Mexican History, 1910–1929*. Albuquerque: University of New Mexico, 1990.

———. "Porfirian Sonora: Economic Collegiality." Paper presented at the American Historical Association Meeting, 1978.

WAGNER, HENRY RAUP. *Bullion to Books*. Los Angeles: Zamorano Club, 1942.

WALKER, RANDI JONES. *Protestantism in the Sangre de Cristos 1850–1920*. Albuquerque: University of New Mexico Press, 1991.

Wall Street Journal, March 22, 1891; Oct. 15, 1985.

Washington Post, July 23–29, 1990.

WASSERMAN, MARK. *Capitalists, Caciques, and Revolution: The Native Elite and Foreign Enterprise in Chihuahua, México, 1842–1911*. Chapel Hill: University of North Carolina Press, 1984.

———. *Persistent Oligarchs: The Political Economy of Chihuahua, Mexico*. Durham: Duke University Press, 1993.

WASSERSTROM, ROBERTO. *Class and Society in Central Chiapas*. Berkeley: University of California Press, 1983.

WATERS, WENDY. "Calles at the Crossroads of Mexican History: New Roads, Old Directions." Honors Thesis in History, University of British Columbia, 1992.

WATROUS, MARY ANGELINE. "Fiscal Policy and Financial Administration in Mexico, 1890–1940." Ph.D. diss., Washington State University, 1991.

WEBER, DAVID J. *The Mexican Frontier, 1821–1846: The American Southwest under Mexico*. Aubuquerque: University of New Mexico Press, 1982.

———. *Myth and the History of the Hispanic Southwest*. Albuquerque: University of New Mexico Press, 1988.

———. "The Spanish Legacy in North America and the Historical Imagination." *Western Historical Quarterly* 23: 1 (February 1992).

————, ed. *Foreigners in Their Native Land: Historical Roots of the Mexican Americans*. Albuquerque: University of New Mexico Press, 1973.

WEEKS, CHARLES A. *The Juárez Myth in Mexico*. University: University of Albama Press, 1987.

WEISMAN, ALAN. *La Frontera: The United States Border with Mexico*. New York: Harcourt Brace Jovanovich, 1986.

WHITTEN, RONALD E. "Mexican Golf: Turf on the Rocks." *Golf Course Management* (July 1983), pp. 28–32.

WILKIE, JAMES W. *The Mexican Revolution: Federal Expenditure and Social Change Since 1910*. Berkeley: University of California Press, 1967.

————. "The Political Agenda in Opening Mexico's Economy: Salinas Versus the Caciques." *Mexico Policy News* (PROFMEX, San Diego) (spring 1991), pp. 11–13.

WILKIE, JAMES W., AND ALBERT L. MICHAELS, EDS. *Revolution in Mexico: Years of Upheaval, 1910–1940*. New York: Alfred A. Knopf, 1969.

WILKIE, JAMES W., AND PAUL D. WILKINS. "Quantifying the Class Structure of Mexico, 1865–1970." In James W. Wilkie and Stephen Haber, eds., *Statistical Abstract of Latin America*, vol. 21, pp. 577–90. Los Angeles: UCLA Latin American Center Publications.

WILLIAMS, EDWARD J. "The Resurgent North and Contemporary Mexican Regionalism." *Mexican Studies/Estudios Mexicanos* 6: 2 (summer 1990), pp. 299–323.

WILSON, HENRY LANE, AND WILLIAM F. BUCKLEY SR. "The Tragic Ten Days." In W. Dirk Raat and William H. Beezley, eds., *Twentieth-Century Mexico*. Lincoln: University of Nebraska, 1986.

WINTER, NEVIN O. *Mexico and Her People of Today: An Account of the Customs, Characteristics, Amusements, History and Advancement of the Mexicans, and the Development and Resources of Their Country*. Boston: L. C. Page Co., 1907.

WOLFE, BERTRAM D. *The Fabulous Life of Diego Rivera*. New York: Stein and Day, 1969.

————. *Portrait of Mexico*. New York: Covici, Friede, 1937.

WOMACK, JOHN JR., "The Spoils of the Mexican Revolution." *Foreign Affairs* 48, no 4 (July 1970), pp. 677–87.

————. "The Mexican Revolution, 1910–40: Genesis of a Modern State." In Fredrick B. Pike, ed., *Latin American History: Select Problems*. New York: Oxford University Press, 1976.

WOODWARD, RALPH LEE JR. *Central America: A Nation Divided*. New York: Oxford University Press, 1976.

WRIGHT, MARIA ROBINSON. *Mexico: A History of Its Progress and Development in One Hundred Years*, Philadelphia: George Barrie & Sons, 1911.

WYNN, DENNIS J. *The San Patricio Soldiers: Mexico's Foreign Legion*. El Paso: Texas Western Press, University of Texas at El Paso, 1984.

YEAGER, GENE. "Porifirian Commercial Propaganda: Mexico in the World Industry Expositions." *The Americas* 34: 2 (October 1977), pp. 230–43.

YOUNG, DESMOND. *Member for Mexico: A Biography of Weetman Pearson, First Viscount Cowdray*. London: Cassell, 1966.

ZAYAS, ENRÍQUEZ, RAFAEL DE, *Los Estados Unidos Mexicanos: Sus progresos en veinte años de paz, 1877–1897*. New York: H. A. Rost, 1899.

ZEA, LEOPOLDO. *Positivism in Mexico*. Austin: University of Texas Press, 1974.

ZELADE, RICHARD. "Masa Marketing." *Texas Monthly* (May 1989), pp. 132–41.

Index